Frommer's®

4th Edition

Scotland

by Darwin Porter & Danforth Prince

Macmillan • USA

ABOUT THE AUTHORS

Although this is only the 4th edition of this book, **Darwin Porter** has covered Scotland since the beginning of his travel-writing career as author of Frommer's *England & Scotland.* Since 1982 he has been joined in his efforts by **Danforth Prince,** formerly of the Paris bureau of the *New York Times.* Together they have written numerous best-selling Frommer guides—notably to the Caribbean, Germany, France, Italy, and England.

MACMILLAN TRAVEL

A Simon & Schuster Macmillan Company
1633 Broadway
New York, NY 10019

Find us online at **www.frommers.com**.

ISBN 0-02-861669-3
ISSN 1055-5390

Production Editor: Lori Cates
Design by Michele Laseau
Digital Cartography by John Decamillis and Jim Moore
Page creation by Tammy Ahrens, Jerry Cole, Sean Decker, Angel Perez, Terri Sheehan, Karen Teo, and Darci Valentine

SPECIAL SALES

Bulk purchases (10+ copies) of Frommer's and selected Macmillan travel guides are available to corporations, organizations, mail-order catalogs, institutions, and charities at special discounts, and can be customized to suit individual needs. For more information write to Special Sales, Macmillan General Reference, 1633 Broadway, New York, NY 10019.

Manufactured in the United States of America

Travel Discount Coupon

This coupon entitles you to special discounts when you book your trip through the

 **TRAVEL NETWORK®**
RESERVATION SERVICE

Hotels ♦ Airlines ♦ Car Rentals ♦ Cruises
All Your Travel Needs

Here's what you get: *

♦ A discount of $50 USD on a booking of $1,000** or more for two or more people!

♦ A discount of $25 USD on a booking of $500** or more for one person!

♦ Free membership for three years, and 1,000 free miles on enrollment in the unique Travel Network Miles-to-Go® frequent-traveler program. Earn one mile for every dollar spent through the program. Redeem miles for free hotel stays starting at 5,000 miles. Earn free roundtrip airline tickets starting at 25,000 miles.

♦ Personal help in planning your own, customized trip.

♦ Fast, confirmed reservations at any property recommended in this guide, subject to availability.***

♦ Special discounts on bookings in the U.S. and around the world.

♦ Low-cost visa and passport service.

♦ Reduced-rate cruise packages and special car rental programs worldwide.

Visit our website at http://www.travelnetwork.com/Frommer or call us globally at 201-567-8500, ext. 55. In the U.S., call toll-free at 1-888-940-5000, or fax 201-567-1838. In Canada, call at 1-905-707-7222, or fax 905-707-8108. In Asia, call 60-3-7191044, or fax 60-3-7185415.

---

* To qualify for these travel discounts, at least a portion of your trip must include destinations covered in this guide. No more than one coupon discount may be used in any 12-month period, for destinations covered in this guide. Cannot be combined with any other discount or promotion.

**These are U.S. dollars spent on commissionable bookings.

***A $10 USD fee, plus fax and/or phone charges, will be added to the cost of bookings at each hotel not linked to the reservation service. Customers must approve these fees in advance. If only hotels of this kind are booked, the traveler(s) must also purchase roundtrip air tickets from Travel Network for the trip.

Valid until December 31, 1999. Terms and conditions of the Miles-to-Go® program are available on request by calling 201-567-8500, ext 55.

SCO23

Contents

List of Maps

AN INVITATION TO THE READER

In researching this book, we discovered many wonderful places—hotels, restaurants, shops, and more. We're sure you'll find others. Please tell us about them so that we can share the information with your fellow travelers in upcoming editions. If you were disappointed with a recommendation, we'd love to know that, too. Please write to:

Frommer's Scotland, 4th Edition
Macmillan Travel
1633 Broadway
New York, NY 10019

AN ADDITIONAL NOTE

Please be advised that travel information is subject to change at any time—and this is especially true of prices. We therefore suggest that you write or call ahead for confirmation when making your travel plans. The authors, editors, and publisher cannot be held responsible for the experiences of readers while traveling. Your safety is important to us, however, so we encourage you to stay alert and be aware of your surroundings. Keep a close eye on cameras, purses, and wallets, all favorite targets of thieves and pickpockets.

WHAT THE SYMBOLS MEAN
✪ Frommer's Favorites

Our favorite places and experiences—outstanding for quality, value, or both.

The following abbreviations are used for credit cards:

AE	American Express	JCB	Japan Credit Bank
CB	Carte Blanche	MC	MasterCard
DC	Diners Club	V	Visa

FIND FROMMER'S ONLINE

Arthur Frommer's Outspoken Encyclopedia of Travel (www.frommers.com) offers more than 6,000 pages of up-to-the-minute travel information—including the latest bargains and candid, personal articles updated daily by Arthur Frommer himself. No other website offers such comprehensive and timely coverage of the world of travel.

The Best of Scotland

Scotland is a land permeated with legend and romance. Its evocative sites and its ruined castles standing amid heather and bracken speak of a past full of heroism and struggle and events that still ring across the centuries. Scotland's other side is its great outdoors—its awesomely beautiful highlands and lakes, mountains and lochs are a sportsperson's paradise. Scotland's two great cities, historic Edinburgh and restored Victorian Glasgow, are also a magnet for visitors.

Anyone who tries to compile a best of everything in such a diverse country is headed for controversy, but we'll plunge in anyway. Luckily for us, on some of the categories listed below there's some general consensus. Whatever your point of view, the pages that follow are meant as a guide to help you enjoy one of the most spectacular countries of Europe, a place little known to the average European visitor. Here's a point of departure for the voyager; you'll formulate your own judgments as you travel around Scotland.

1 The Best Travel Experiences

Every experience in this list incorporates either the rugged drama of Scotland's great outdoors or authentic encounters with the Scots themselves. Here's a list of our favorites:

- **Horseback Trekking Through the Highlands & Argyll:** Although Scotland's roads are excellent, and views are panoramic even through the windows of a moving car, there's nothing like riding one of the country's sturdy ponies through the Highlands' lichen-covered rocks and heather. Horse and pony owners have always valued the Scottish Highlands for their abundance of grazing lands, and dozens of farms that raise sheep and cows also maintain a complement of horses. One of the country's biggest stables is the **Highland Riding Centre,** Borlum Farm, Drumnadrochit, Highland IV3 6XN (☎ **01456/450220** for information). It's on an 850-acre sheep farm, about 14 miles west of Inverness, on moorlands overlooking the waters of Loch Ness. Follow A82 from Inverness to reach it. Advance reservations are advised. In summer, the stable's approximately 45 horses are all booked throughout their 5-hour working day. Tours depart almost every day of the year, depending on demand, between 9:30am and 5:30pm, and last 60 to 120 minutes. Rides cost £11 to £19 ($18.15 to $31.35), depending on their duration.

For scenic equestrian treks across moors, highlands, and headlands in the Argyll area, **Ardsern Riding Centre** (Appaloosa Holidays), Croabh Haven, Loch Gilphead, Argyll PA31 8QR (☎ 01852/500632 for information), will organize treks of several days' duration. In addition to maintaining around 16 horses and a working cattle and sheep farm between Oban and Loch Gilphead, they have a cottage that can be rented to groups of eight equestrians. The proprietor, Nigel Boase, also has lots of ideas for suitable itineraries for cross-country treks.

* **Sailing off the Coast of Argyll:** Eons ago, glaciers carved the west coast of Scotland into one of the most spectacularly jagged shorelines in Europe. Warmed by the Gulf Stream and dotted with sheltered estuaries and channels, it offers challenging sailing and rugged scenery.

  If you're a qualified sailor, you can rent a vessel from virtually any fisher along the coast for a watery overview of terrain made famous by the Lowland clans. More structured and more certain are the sailing lessons offered by western Scotland's respected sailing school, **Tighnabruaich Sailing School,** Argyll, Strathclyde PA21 2BD (☎ and fax **01700/811396** for information). Established in the 1960s, they've taught thousands of people from all over the world how to sail and offer advanced lessons to yacht lovers already proficient with jibs and spinnakers. It's in the fishing port of Tighnabruaich on the Cowal Peninsula, about a 30-minute drive south of Strachur. The school specializes in sailing dinghies, a shallow-draft seaworthy craft well suited to tricky passages and underwater obstacles. Each has a single mast, a mainsail, and a jib, and in some cases, a spinnaker. Up to three students and an instructor are out on the water, rain or shine, every day between May and September, for 5 to 7 hours a day. A 3-day course costs £76 ($125.40); a 6-day course, £140 ($231). Lodgings are not arranged through the school, but are widely available at guesthouses and inns throughout the hamlet.

* **Cruising Along the Caledonian Canal:** In 1822 a group of enterprising Scots connected three of the Highlands' longest lakes (Loch Ness, Loch Lochy, and Loch Oich) with a canal that links Britain's east and west coasts. Since than, barges have hauled everything from grain to building supplies without having to negotiate the wild storms off Scotland's northernmost tip.

  If you'd like a waterborne view of the countryside tamed centuries ago by the Camerons, the Stewarts, and the MacDonalds, you can rent a cabin cruiser. **Caley Cruises,** Canal Road, Inverness IV3 6NF (☎ **01463/236328** or fax 01463/238323 for information), maintains the largest inventory (45) of 60-horsepower, diesel-powered cruisers in Scotland. All are rented, without skippers, to two to six people at a time, even if their marine experience is relatively limited. Rentals last for 1 week, long enough to negotiate the 60-mile length of the Caledonian Canal in both directions between Inverness and Fort William. (There are about 15 locks en route; tolls are included in the rental fee.) Depending on the craft's size and the season, a week's rental ranges from £400 to £1,700 ($660 to $2,805). Each cruiser contains a galley and comes with lessons on how to operate it as part of the price. The cost of fuel and taxes for a week is £60 ($99), plus another £40 ($66) weekly for a reasonably priced insurance policy. Except for the waters of Loch Ness, which can be rough, the canal is calm enough and doesn't pose the dangers of cruising on the open sea, and is suitable for families with children. Rentals are only between March and October. July and August are the most expensive and crowded months.

* **Nessie-Spotting:** Loch Ness is one of the world's most famous lakes, thanks to tales of its legendary beast, which have circulated for centuries. No one has ever proved the creature's existence, although witnesses include everyone from medieval saints to tourist groups, who have described it as having two humps and

a Tyrannosaurus-size tail. For lack of anything better, scientists have labeled it *Nessiteras rhombopteryx;* locals refer to it simply as "Nessie," and no one can quaff a wee dram on a Highland evening without wondering whether there might indeed be a lonely creature locked beneath the choppy waters of the deepest (and most tempestuous) freshwater loch in Scotland. A sighting, with or without the influence of one of the region's single-malts, might become the highlight of your trip.

- **Checking Out the Local Pub:** You're in a Scottish pub, talking to the publican in front of what looks like an altar to the distillation process of single-malts. Winds blow fitfully outside; a wooden sign creaks audibly above the battered door, and a fire (peat, coal, or logs) might flicker against the blackened bricks of a much-used fireplace. It's the best place in town to quaff a wee dram, or absorb some suds dispensed from ornate taps by the innkeeper. If you head here to ward off the chill of a cold and damp night, you won't be alone. Thousands of pilgrims have trod the pub's floorboards before you. And as the evening wanes and you've established common ground with the locals inside, you might suddenly realize that you're having one of your most authentic experiences in Scotland.
- **Visiting Edinburgh at Festival Time:** Inaugurated to perk up postwar doldrums in 1947, the Edinburgh Festival has become one of the most visible arts festivals in Europe. During 3 weeks in August and September, a phalanx of performers (musicians and actors) descends on the city, infusing it with a kind of manic creative energy. If you're planning to sample the festival's many offerings, make early reservations and give careful attention to acquiring tickets. For information, contact the **Edinburgh International Festival Box Office,** 21 Market St., Edinburgh EH1 1BW (☎ **0131/226-4001** or fax 0131/226-7669 for information). Year-round office hours are Monday through Friday from 9:30am to 5:30pm.
- **A Visit to the Island of Iona:** It's an otherworldly rock, one of the most evocative holy places in Europe, anchored solidly among the Hebrides off the western coast of Scotland. St. Columba (Columcille) established it as a Christian center in 563 and used it as a base for the conversion of Scotland. In the Dark Ages it saved learning and literacy for the emerging European world. There's a ruined Benedictine nunnery and a fully restored cathedral (known as the abbey) where 50 Scottish kings opted to be buried during the early Middle Ages. Hundreds of Celtic crosses once adorned the island; today only three of the original ones remain. The island, now part of the National Trust, is home to the Iona Community, an ecumenical group dedicated to the perpetuation of Christian ideals. Visitors are welcomed into the community for reflection, discussion, and prayer. Reaching the island requires a 10-minute ferryboat ride from the hamlet of Fionnphort, on the island of Mull.
- **Attending a Highland Game:** They're unlike any other sporting event. Emphasis is on clannish traditions rather than athletic dexterity, and the centerpiece is usually the exhibition of brute strength (tossing logs, etc.). Most visitors show up for the kilts, the bagpipe playing, the pomp and circumstance, and the general celebration of all things Scottish. The best known (and most widely televised) of the events is the Braemar Royal Highland Gathering, held near Balmoral Castle the first Saturday in September. Such events crop up with chauvinistic regularity throughout the year, with information about specific dates and times available from any tourist office in the country.
- **Freewheeling in the Highlands:** Only the most stalwart cyclers should consider a two-wheeled excursion in this rugged countryside. But if you're looking for a substitute for the hours you've spent on the StairMaster at your local health club, consider cycling through the Highlands. Drawbacks include changeable weather,

thick fogs, and a relative scarcity of cycle-repair shops. Despite the inconveniences, something about the labor involved makes your experiences—views of clan castles, long and narrow lochs, fjords worthy of the west coast of Norway, and wee drams consumed near the peat-burning fireplaces of croft-style pubs—abundantly worthwhile.

High on the list of cyclers' favorites is the Black Isle, a northerly province known for its flat roads, surprisingly balmy microclimate, and historic buildings. For details on Black Isle and the region that contains it, contact either the **Northern Highlands Tourist Office,** The Square, Dornoch, Sutherland IV25 3SD (☎ **01862/810-490**), or the **North Kessock Tourist Office,** The Picnic Site, Ross-shire IV1 1XB (☎ **01463/731-505**).

- **Exploring the Orkneys:** Archaeologists say that they contain the richest trove of prehistoric monuments in the British Isles—an average of three sites per square mile of the islands' surface. Ornithologists refer to their burgeoning population of birds, claiming that about 16% of all winged animals in the U.K. reside in the Orkneys. Linguists arrive with notepads and tape recorders to document an ancient dialect that still uses Viking terms. These are the Orkneys, an archipelago with some 70 islands that you might not have considered visiting.

Set northwest of the Scottish mainland, closer to Oslo than to faraway London, they're on the same latitude as St. Petersburg to the east, but much more exposed to the raging gales of the North Sea. Sunsets during late spring and the aurora borealis (northern lights) have been called "mystical," and in midsummer the sun remains above the horizon for a full 18 hours per day. In winter the islands are plunged into an equivalent twilight or total darkness. Only 19 of the Orkneys are inhabited; the others seem to float above primordial seas, drenched with rains and the weak sunlight of these northern climes.

2 The Best Golf

Long before golf became one of the most popular sports in the world, Scotland defined its terms, established its legends, and codified its rules. As the sport has enlarged its corps of players, more and more of them make pilgrimages to the cult's shrines, a series of putting greens and fairways whose names are legends in the world of sport. Here's a list of the country's best:

- **Royal Troon Golf Club,** Craigend Road, Troon, Ayrshire KA10 6EP (☎ **01292/ 311555** or fax 01292/318204): Laid out along lines that parallel the Firth of Clyde, it fills a flat lowland terrain whose fairways are almost breathtakingly green despite their foundations on sandy soil. This is Lowland Scotland at its most seductive, a 7,097-yard course (one of the longest in Scotland) with an SSS of 74 and a par of 71. Dignified Georgian and Victorian buildings and the faraway Isle of Arran are visible from fairways, which seem deliberately designed to steer your golf balls into either the sea or the dozens of sand traps that flank either side of your shot. The Old Course is the more famous playing field, reserved only for men. Nonmembers may play only on certain days of the week. A newer addition, the 6,289-yard, par-71 Portland, is open to both men and women, and is by some estimations even more challenging than the Old Course. Established in 1878, the Old Course was granted its Royal Charter by Elizabeth II in 1978. The British Open has been played here off and on since 1923. (See chapter 4, section 1, and chapter 7, section 10.)
- **Turnberry Hotel Golf Courses,** Ayrshire KA26 9LT (☎ **01655/331000** or fax 01655/331706): Established in 1902, this is one of the most sought-after golf

courses in the world. It's not for the weak-hearted—although some of the links are verdant, others are uncomfortably linked with the sands, the tough, salt-resistant grasses, and the powerful winds blasting in from the nearby sea. Come here for the prestige, but prepare yourself for the kind of weather that a lobster fisher in Maine might find daunting. The hotel, a sprawling Edwardian pile set on a panoramic hillside, is appropriately luxurious and provides a level of comfort that's needed after the savagery of the outside elements. The most prestigious of Turnberry's layouts is the Ailsa Course. (Its par is 70, its SSS is 72, and its yardage is 6,976.) Newer, and usually shunted into a role of "also-ran," is the Arran Course. (See chapter 4, section 1, and chapter 7, section 10.)

- **The Old Course, St. Andrews,** % Links Management Committee, Pilmour Cottage, St. Andrews, Fife KY16 9SF (☎ **01334/466666**): Sometime during the late 14th century, a group of bored aristocrats started batting a ball around the nearby meadows. By the time their activities were officially recorded in 1552, the bylaws of the game were well on the way to being part of the lore of Scotland. The Old Course is the world's most legendary temple of golf, one whose difficulty is shaped by nature and the long-ago paths of grazing sheep. Over the centuries, stately buildings have been erected near its start and finish. Aristocrats from virtually everywhere have lent their names and reputations to enhance its glamor, and its nuances have been debated, usually in reverent tones, by golfers in bars and on fairways throughout the rest of the world. Site of some of the most prestigious golf tournaments in the U.K., St. Andrews has a reservations list for tee-off times that sometimes stretches on a year in advance. There are four additional courses (the Jubilee, Eden, Strathtyrum, and the New, which opened during the reign of Queen Victoria) on the site, but none has the medieval cachet of the Old Course. (See chapter 4, section 1, and chapter 9, section 3.)

- **Carnoustie Golf Links,** Links Parade, Carnoustie, Tayside DD7 7JE (☎ **01241/853789** or fax 01241/852720): Site of five British Open tournaments (with another scheduled for 1999), Carnoustie's Championship Course is much more difficult than most players anticipate at first glance. U.S. champions Tom Watson and Gary Player have both referred to it as their favorite, and much of the town of Carnoustie (incorporated as late as 1880) was built because of the stream of world-class golfers who migrated here. Records as early as 1560 refer to "gowff" being played on the surrounding fields, and by the reign of Queen Victoria the course had developed into a factory for training golf instructors and champions who spread word of the game throughout the British Empire. The landscape is rugged and, off the fairways, richly clad in gorse with copses of trees. Skilled golfers call the course stimulating; neophytes refer to it as treacherous, particularly the 16th, 17th, and 18th holes, which are among the most difficult in Scotland.

  In addition to the Championship Course described above, Carnoustie also boasts the Burnside Course and the relatively new Buddon Links Course, which opened in the 1970s. (See chapter 4, section 1, and chapter 10.)

- **Royal Dornoch Golf Club,** Dornoch, Sutherland IV25 3LW (☎ **01862/810219**): It's the most northerly of the world's great golf courses, set in the underpopulated province of Sutherland, only 6° south of the Arctic Circle. Despite its northern isolation, it enjoys a microclimate more akin to the fens around Norfolk, England, than to the Arctic. Nearby hills divert up to 75% of the rain that falls on adjacent districts, and a curious meander of the Gulf Stream as it bypasses northern Scotland keeps the climate balmier than anyone would expect.

  None of this is lost on sports enthusiasts. Golf was played here by monks from St. Andrews as early as 1616. The club itself was founded in 1877, and a royal charter was granted by Edward VII in 1906, when he adopted it as one of his favorite causes. Prince Andrew and the duchess of Sutherland are both members today. Its SSS is 73; its par is 70 for an 18-hole yardage of 6,185. (See chapter 4, section 1, and chapter 11, section 10.)

3 The Best Fishing

For more details about fishing in Scotland, see chapter 4, section 2.

- **The Borders:** As one fisherman put it, "[He] dreamed [he] died and went to fisher's heaven" when he first encountered the possibilities of fishing the Solway Firth, noted for its sea angling. Sea angling is best near the fishing villages of Port William and Portpatrick, within the vicinity of Loch Ryan, and along the shore of the Isle of Whithorn. The elusive salmon is best pursued along the River Tweed, and the lesser-known hill lochans are ideal for trout fishers. Local tourist offices distribute two helpful guides: *A Comprehensive Guide to Scottish Borders Angling* and *Castabout Anglers' Guide to Dumfries and Galloway.* (See chapter 5.)
- **Argyll and the Isles:** This much-visited area in western Scotland is split into two sections by the long peninsula of Kintyre. It's definitely a northern Atlantic ecology filled with open sea and loch and separated by the Firth of Clyde from the islands of the Inner Hebrides. All local tourist offices keep data on fishing, since there are some 50 fishing sites on rivers and lochs that range from game fishing in the open sea to two dozen little fishing villages that are ideal for sea angling. (See chapter 8.)
- **Tayside:** The northeast section of Scotland is filled with major rivers—the Don, Dee, Ythan, and Deverson—plus smaller rivers such as the Ugie, all ideal for salmon fishing. When estuary and loch fishing are considered, this becomes one of the country's best areas for game fishing. Local tourist offices keep abreast of all the details about boat rentals and permit prices, and some country hotels also offer fishing packages. (See chapter 10.)
- **The Great Glen:** From all over the world, fishers flock to the Great Glen with its many lochs and rivers where you can fly-fish for Scottish trout and salmon. Sea angling either from boat or shore is also permitted. The best salmon season is from February through September. Devotees of brown trout find mid-March to early October ideal. Fishers can catch rainbow trout here year-round. (See chapter 11.)
- **Northern Highlands:** There are endless possibilities for fishing here—Sutherland, in fact, is riddled with lochs. Trout fishing is the big lure, and local tourist offices advise about boats and permits. Not only is the fishing great, but your hotel cook will often prepare your catch for you. (See chapter 11, sections 10 and 11.)
- **Orkney Islands:** These far northern islands are one of the major fishing grounds of Britain. At least seven outfitters offer sea angling boat rentals, and fishing equipment can be rented. Local tourist offices keep full details. Loch angling is also a popular pastime in the Orkneys, especially within Loch of Stenness and Loch of Harray. Fishers catch salmon, trout, sea trout, and salmon trout, although porbeagle shark, cod, halibut, bass, hake, skate, and turbot also turn up. (See chapter 13.)

4 The Best Drives

Scotland contains some of Europe's largest tracts of wilderness that have changed very little since the days of the ancient Celts.

- **The Valley of the Tweed:** Its name conjures memories of everything from the textile industry to border raids during the Middle Ages. You won't lack for historic references here: The waters originate in Scotland, define the border with England for part of their length, and are noted for some of the best salmon fishing in Britain. Best of all, the ruins of once-wealthy abbeys dot the landscape like beacons of long-lost power and prestige.

Most travelers begin their excursion in Kelso, then move west through Dryburgh, Selkirk, Melrose, Innerleithen, and Peebles. Although the total distance involves less than 50 miles, with a bit of backtracking en route, the many historic sites call for at least a full day's exploration. (See chapter 5.)

• **The Island of Arran:** Anchored off the southwestern edge of Scotland, Arran combines radically different climates and topographies into a relatively small (10 miles wide by 20 miles long) space. There's a rich trove of prehistoric monuments, a red sandstone pile (Brodick Castle) beloved by medievalists, nostalgic ruins (Lochranza Castle), and sweeping panoramas as far away as Northern Ireland. Its southern tier, warmed by the Gulf Stream, contains a lush and temperate vegetation, while the moors and hills of its northern edge are as wild and craggy as the Highlands. Allow half a day, not including stopover times, for the 56-mile circumnavigation of the island's coastal road. (See chapter 8.)

• **The Lochs and Mountains South of Oban:** It's lonely, but its drama incorporates views of the longest freshwater lake (Loch Awe), one of the longest saltwater fjords (Loch Fyne), some of the most historic buildings (Kilchurn Castle, Carnasserie Castle, and the Kilmartin Church), and one of the most crucial battlefields (the slopes of Ben Cruachan) in Scotland. Locals refer to it as "The Hinterlands near Oban," but luckily, the 87-mile route follows an excellent network of highways that inscribe a large oval along the jagged coastline. Major towns you'll traverse en route include Dalmally, Inveraray, Lochgilphead, and Oban, all of which offer opportunities for refueling, food, and drink. (See chapter 8.)

• **The Trossachs:** Set at the narrowest point of the mainland of Scotland, just to the north of Glasgow, the Trossachs have been famous for their scenery since Queen Victoria decreed them "lovely" in 1869. The value of the region's folk and fairy tales was recognized and recorded as early as 1691. Mystery seems to shroud the waters of Loch Lomond (inspiration for Scotland's most famous song) and Loch Katrine (a source of drinking water, first piped into Glasgow in 1859). According to legend, the region's highest mountain, Ben Venue, is the traditional meeting point for Scotland's goblins.

Ruled for many generations by the MacGregor clan, this is the countryside of Sir Walter Scott's *Rob Roy* and *The Lady of the Lake,* a setting that filled the daydreams and romantic yearnings of Victorian readers. A tour through the region, beginning at Callander and meandering through Aberfoyle, Stronachlacher, and Inversnaid, should take about half a day, unless you opt to extend it with boat rides along Loch Katrine. Expect lots of sightseeing traffic in summer, often from motorcoaches. (See chapter 9.)

• **The Road to the Isles (Highway A830):** It begins in Fort William, western terminus of the Caledonian Canal, and ends at Mallaig—departure point for ferries servicing several offshore islands, including Mull, 46 miles to the northwest. En route, it passes the highest mountains in Britain. Most of the road's appeal derives from the natural beauty that flanks it on either side. One of the Victorian Age's most dramatic engineering triumphs—Neptune's Staircase, a network of eight locks that raise the level of the canal 64 feet in less than 500 yards—can be viewed along the way. Although traffic in summer can be dense, services en route are scarce. Don't embark without a full tank of petrol. (See chapters 11 and 12.)

5 The Best Romantic Getaways

- **Raemoir House,** Banchory (☎ **01330/824884**): This 18th-century mansion is set on a 3,500-acre estate, providing a journey into nostalgia. Tudor four-posters, rich red brocades, and paneled walls, along with museum-calibre antiques, transport you into an elegant past. You sleep well in supreme comfort and enjoy top-quality produce including poached salmon from the River Dee. (See chapter 10.)
- **Carnegie Club at Skibo Castle,** Dornoch (☎ **01862/894600**): Andrew Carnegie called his glorious Highland castle and estate "Heaven on Earth," and so it is. A private residential golf and sporting club, it stands on its own 7,500-acre estate in one of the last great wilderness areas of Europe. Owned by the Carnegie family until the early '80s, it is one of the few places left where you can see how the privileged of a gilded age lived. (See chapter 11.)
- **Inverlochy Castle,** near Fort William (☎ **01397/702177**): It was built in 1863 by Lord Abinger in a style that set into stone the most high-blown hopes of Scottish Romantics. Today, lovers can follow in the footsteps of Queen Victoria (who, although she liked the castle, would probably not approve of their antics) and sojourn amid the frescoed walls of this Scottish baronial hideaway. (See chapter 11.)
- **Rufflets Country House,** St. Andrews (☎ **01334/472594**): Set on 10 acres near Scotland's most prestigious golf course, it has won virtually every hotel award possible to win. Even the gardens have received praise from critics not known for their sense of charity. (See chapter 9.)
- **Dower House,** Muir of Ord (☎ **01463/870090**): Set on 3 isolated acres of mature garden, this small but choice hotel offers attractive lodgings along with a cuisine known throughout Scotland for its discreet but sensual appeal. Although a visit during midsummer is beautiful, its elegant Scottish-country warmth is especially appealing during blustery squalls and gales off-season. (See chapter 11, section 7.)

6 The Best Castles & Palaces

No one understood the value of defensive architecture as did the Scottish clans. Dramatic allure made the castles the setting for some of the Elizabethan Age's best dramas and the Edwardian Age's best murder mysteries.

- **Drumlanrig Castle** (Dumfries): Begun in 1679, it required 12 years to build and so much money that its patron, the third earl and first duke of Queensbury, complained to anyone who'd listen how deeply he resented its existence. Later, it was embroiled in dynastic inheritance scandals worthy of a gothic novel. One of the most prestigious buildings in Scotland, it contains the family antiques and artwork of four illustrious genealogies: the Douglas, Montagu, Scott, and Buccleuch families. (See chapter 5, section 7.)
- **Edinburgh Castle** (Edinburgh): Few other buildings symbolize the grandeur of an independent Scotland as clearly as this one. Begun around A.D. 1000 on a hilltop high above the rest of Edinburgh, it witnessed some of the bloodiest and most treacherous events in Scottish history. They included its doomed defense by Scottish patriot Grange in the name of Mary Queen of Scots in 1573. (See chapter 6, section 5.)
- **Holyroodhouse** (Edinburgh): Throughout the clan battles for independence from England, it served as a pawn between opposing forces, being demolished and rebuilt at the whim of whomever held power at the time. In its changing fortunes, it has housed a strange assortment of monarchs involved in traumatic events—Mary Queen of Scots, Bonnie Prince Charlie, James VII (prior to his ascendancy

to the throne), and French king Charles X (upon his forced abdication after a revolution in 1830). The building's present form dates from the late 1600s, when it was rebuilt in a dignified neo-Palladian style. Today it's one of the official residences of the British monarch. (See chapter 6, section 5.)

- **Culzean Castle** (4 miles west of Maybole): It was built in the late 1700s by Scotland's most celebrated architect, Robert Adam, as a replacement for a dark, dank, and fortified tower that had stood for longer than anyone could remember. Designed for comfort and prestige, it was donated to the National Trust for Scotland just after World War II. Inside, a suite was granted to General Eisenhower for his lifetime use, in gratitude for his role in staving off a foreign invasion of Britain. (See chapter 7, section 10.)

- **Stirling Castle** (Stirling): It's a triumph of Renaissance ornamentation, a startling contrast to the severe bulk of many other Scottish castles. Despite its beauty, after its completion in 1540 it was one of the most impregnable fortresses in the British Isles, thanks partly to its position on a rocky crag. (See chapter 9, section 5.)

- **Scone Palace** (Scone): As early as A.D. 900 Scottish kings were crowned here, on a lump of granite so permeated with ancient magic that the English hauled it off to Westminster Abbey in the 13th century, where it remained until 1995. The building you'll see today was rebuilt in 1802 from ruins that incorporated a structure from 1580 and stones laid during the dim early days of Scottish and Pictish union. (See chapter 10, section 1.)

- **Glamis Castle** (Glamis): Its core was built for defense against rival clans during the 1400s, but over the centuries it evolved into a luxurious dwelling. The seat of the same family since 1372, the castle is said to be haunted by the ghost of one of its former owners, Lady Glamis, who James V had burnt as a witch when she resisted his annexation of her castle. It figured into the ambitions of Macbeth, thane of Glamis, as well. (See chapter 10, section 6.)

- **Braemar** (Grampian): Originally built in 1628 as a hunting lodge by the earl of Mar, it was burned to the ground, then rebuilt by Farquharson of Invercauld, the ancestor of the present owner. Though its history lacks the high operatic drama of many other castles in Scotland, it's often photographed as a symbol of Scottish grandeur and the well-upholstered aristocratic life. (See chapter 10, section 7.)

- **Crathes Castle** (Grampian): Better than any other building, it evokes the severe luxury of a 15th- and 16th-century Scottish laird. Inside, the style focuses on "high heraldry," with frequent references to the persistent Scottish hope of an enduring independence. The gardens contain massive yew hedges originally planted in 1702. (See chapter 10, section 8.)

- **Cawdor Castle** (Cawdor): From its heavily fortified origins in the 1300s, it evolved into the Campbell clan's luxurious seat. According to legend and Shakespearean plot lines, three witches promised this castle to Macbeth to tempt him into the deeds that led to his destruction. (See chapter 11, section 8.)

7 The Best Cathedrals

- **Melrose Abbey** (Melrose, Borders): If it were not for its location in the frequently devastated Borders, Melrose would be one of the most spectacular ecclesiastical complexes in the world. Founded in the 1100s, it acquired vast wealth, and was therefore the target of its covetous enemies—it was burned and rebuilt several times before the Protestant takeover of Scotland. Today it's one of the most beautiful ruins in the world, a site immortalized by the poetry of Robert Burns, who advised future generations to visit it only by moonlight. (See chapter 5, section 3.)

- **Cathedral of St. Kentigern** (Glasgow): In the 7th century St. Mungo built a wooden structure on this site, intending it as his headquarters and his eventual tomb. After it burned, it was rebuilt in the 1300s. It is mainland Scotland's only complete medieval cathedral, with a form based extensively on the pointed arch. In the 1600s the Calvinists stripped it of anything hinting at papist idolatry, although a remarkable set of sculptures survived atop its stone nave screen—said to be unique in Scotland—representing the seven deadly sins. (See chapter 7, section 5.)
- **Dunfermline Abbey** (Fife): During the 1100s, in its role as the Westminster Abbey of Scotland, the abbey became one of the wealthiest organizations in Europe. Three kings of Scotland were born here, and 22 members of the Scottish royal family were buried here. In the early 1800s its ruined premises were partially restored to what you'll see today. Several years later a different kind of benefactor, Andrew Carnegie, was born within the cathedral's shadow. (See chapter 9, section 1.)
- **Dunblane Cathedral** (Dunblane): Partly because the site had been holy since the days of the Celts, David I founded a church here in 1150. Despite later alterations and additions, it's still one of the country's best examples of gothic architecture from the 1200s. (See chapter 9, section 6.)
- **St. Magnus Cathedral** (Orkneys): The most spectacular medieval building in the Orkneys, it features an odd imposition of the Norman gothic style on a territory administered during the time of its construction (the 1100s) by the Norwegians. The bodies of St. Magnus, patron saint of the Orkneys, and his nephew, Earl Rognvald, the church's builder, are both buried inside. (See chapter 13, section 1.)

8 The Best Evocative Ruins

There's no place like Scotland for melancholy reminders of past glories. Architectural testimonies to the shattered hopes and dreams of other times include these poignant ruins.

- **Dryburgh Abbey** (Borders): Set against a meandering curve of the River Tweed, and begun in 1150, these ruins were once home to thousands of monks who transformed the surrounding forests into arable fields and drained many local swamps. The abbey's position astride the much-troubled border with England resulted in its destruction in three different episodes (1322, 1385, and 1544), the last of which included the burning of the nearby village (Dryburgh) as well. Today the red sandstone rocks are dim reminders of a long-ago monastic age. (See chapter 5, section 2.)
- **Linlithgow Palace** (Lothian): It broods over an island in a loch, an unhappy vestige of what was, in the early 1500s, the merriest and most glamorous royal residence during Scotland's golden age of independence. Mary Queen of Scots was born here, but tragedy seemed to permeate the place, as roofs collapsed from lack of maintenance, and early deaths in the royal family hastened an inevitable union of Scotland with England. In 1745, after it was occupied by Bonnie Prince Charlie and his troops, a mysterious fire swept over it. (See chapter 6, section 10.)
- **Kildrummy Castle** (Aberdeen): In 1715, after centuries of playing a decisive role in Scottish history, the castle was demolished by its enemies and dismantled, stone by stone. Thus humbled, it broods as a reminder of former glories. Originally built in the 1200s, it was one of the most important strongholds in northern Scotland, successfully mingling architectural principles of France with those developed in England and Wales. (See chapter 10, section 7.)
- **Elgin Cathedral** (Elgin): It was built during the 1100s, and although many other churches were erected in Scotland at the same time, Elgin was believed to have

been the most beautiful. Burned and rebuilt twice (in 1290 and 1370), it deteriorated after the Reformation, along with many other Catholic churches, to the point that the belfry collapsed in 1711, shattering most of the roof and some of the walls in the process. Although efforts were begun to repair the damage, the place remains an evocative ruin today. (See chapter 10, section 11.)

- **Skara Brae** (Orkney Islands): Last occupied around 2500 B.C., and far humbler than the feudal castles you'll find on the Scottish mainland, this cluster of fortified stone buildings is the best-preserved Neolithic village in northwestern Europe. Buried beneath sand for thousands of years, they were uncovered by a storm as recently as 1850. (See chapter 13, section 1.)

9 The Best Literary Shrines

Scotland has always made a cult of its famous writers, particularly if their literature managed to capture the pathos of the country's soul.

- **Abbotsford** (Borders): Sir Walter Scott has been credited as creator of the most authentic Scottish voice in the history of British literature. The house he enlarged from a simple farmhouse into a "fantasy in stone" contains a collection of objects— some rare, some ordinary—that reflect his almost obsessive passion for Scotland. (See chapter 5, section 3.)
- **Lady Stair's House** (Edinburgh): Built in 1622, and owned by the widow of John Dalyrumple (first earl of Stair), it's a dignified example of a prosperous urban town house. Inside you'll find a trove of literary memorabilia and manuscripts penned by three of Scotland's most widely read authors: Robert Louis Stevenson, Sir Walter Scott, and Robert Burns. (See chapter 6, section 5.)
- **Burns Cottage and Museum** (Alloway): For fans of Robert Burns, the site evokes memories of the national poet's spartan life and the birth of his first son. Even for visitors who have never read Burns's poetry, the low-slung, rustic premises illuminate the thrift and backbreaking labor needed to sustain life in 18th-century Scotland. (See chapter 7, section 10.)
- **Tam o' Shanter Inn** (Ayr): When Robert Burns was alive, he tippled a wee dram or two at what was then a tavern. Today it's a museum of anything and everything related to his life, his poetry, and his patriotic vision. In his poem, the site was the departure point for Tam o' Shanter's eventful ride through a dark, long-ago night. (See chapter 7, section 10.)

10 The Best Museums

- **National Gallery** (Edinburgh): This is a small but choice collection whose presence in Edinburgh is firmly entwined with the city's self-image as cultural capital of Scotland, although Glaswegians dispute that. Highlights include works by Velásquez, Zurbarán, Verrocchio, del Sarto, and Cézanne. (See chapter 6, section 5.)
- **Royal Museum of Scotland** (Edinburgh): In 1985 the collections of two museums established during the Victorian age were united into a coherent whole. Here you'll find everything you'd ever want to know about Scotland, from prehistory through the Industrial Age. (See chapter 6, section 5.)
- **Burrell Collection** (Glasgow): Its contents were accumulated through the exclusive efforts of one collector, Sir William Burrell (1861–1958), an industrialist who devoted the last 50 years of his life to spending his fortune on art. Set in a postmodern building in a suburb of Glasgow, it's one of the most admired

museums in Scotland, with a strong focus on medieval art, 19th-century French paintings, and Chinese ceramics. (See chapter 7, section 5.)

- **Hunterian Art Gallery** (Glasgow): Administered by the University of Glasgow, this museum owns much of the artistic estate of James McNeill Whistler, as well as a re-creation of the home and furnishings of Scotland's most famous designer, Charles Rennie Mackintosh. Other "grand oils" are also on display, including works by Reubens and Rembrandt, as well as one of the country's best collections of 19th-century Scottish paintings. (See chapter 7, section 5.)

- **Glasgow Art Gallery and Museum** (Glasgow): It's the finest municipally funded museum in Britain, a source of pride for Glaswegians everywhere. There's a superb collection of arms and armor, as well as paintings by Whistler and by seemingly everyone else, from Millet to Giorgione, Rembrandt to Salvador Dalí. (See chapter 7, section 5.)

11 The Best Shopping

In times past, Scottish craftspeople labored in isolated crofts crafting items both useful and beautiful. In some cases the modern age has made the processes easier, but there's still an emphatic insistence on quality.

- **Celtic Jewelry:** It's barbaric, it's bulky, and its decorative themes could only have been inspired by ancient mythologies that modern Scots can only interpret intuitively. Modern reproductions of Celtic jewelry are one of Scotland's most creative craft forms. Some of the pieces reflect early Christian themes, including the famous Gaelic cross so often displayed in Presbyterian churches. Others are pure pagan, and sometimes Nordic, rich with symbols that include dragons, intertwined ovals, and geometrics that would gladden the heart of a Celtic lord. You'll find the stuff all over Scotland, displayed proudly as symbols of the national aesthetic.

  Another common theme commemorates the yearnings for a politically independent Scotland (entwined hearts surmounted by a monarch's crown). Clan brooches, ornate kilt pins, and other jewelry are often adorned with the Highland thistle and are sometimes rendered in fine gold, silver, or platinum.

- **Sheepskins:** Some of the rocky districts of Scotland contain more sheep than people. Tanned sheepskins are for sale in hundreds of shops and are usually accompanied by advice from the sales staff on what to do with them once you return home. (*Note:* Black sheepskins are much rarer than white ones.)

- **Sweaters, Tartans, Fabrics:** The industries that dragged 19th-century Scotland into the Industrial Revolution include distilleries and breweries, shipbuilding, and textiles. Textiles are still among the most firmly entrenched. Sweaters come in every design from bulky, rough-textured fisher's pullovers to silk-textured cashmere.

  Some factories pride themselves on duplicating the tartans of every clan in Scotland; others stick to 50 or so of the more popular designs. A meter of fine tartan fabric sells for around £32.75 ($54.05), cheap enough to whet your ambitions as a tailor once you return home.

  For a more authentic shopping experience, buy your garment directly from whomever sewed or knitted it. Ample opportunities to do this will present themselves at isolated crofts and crafts shops throughout the countryside. Another option is the branches of Edinburgh Woolen Mills, which maintain outlets from southern England to the northern tier of Scotland. Adjacent to their factory in Walkerburn in the Scottish borders is an industrial museum that will give you an idea of what working conditions were like in a 19th-century woolen mill when children labored in factories from a very early age. A rich collection of pattern books is also of interest. The Museum of Woollen Textiles, Tweedvale Mills (a division of Edinburgh Woolen Mills), Walkerburn EH43 6AY (☎ **01896/ 870619** for information), is open Monday through Friday from 9am to 5pm.

Less than 6 miles from Walkerburn is the Peter Anderson Company, Nether Mill, Galashiels (☎ **01896/752091** for information), which displays and sells more than 750 types of tartan fabrics, all made on the premises on modernized looms. The factory shop is open Monday through Saturday from 9am to 5pm, and if they don't have a tartan you like (which is doubtful, considering their inventories), you can pop into any of the dozens of other shops in the commercial center of Galashiels, a town that bases its economy on textiles.

- **Liquor:** One of the most famous liquors in the world is named after the country that produced it. Scotch whisky (spelled without the "e") is distilled and aged throughout the country. Use your trip to Scotland as an opportunity to try single-malts you might never have heard of before (Laphroig and MacCallan are two of our personal favorites), and bring a bottle or two home with you after your trip as a souvenir.

12 The Best Hotels

With eminent respect for the warmth and unpublicized appeal of unpretentious, less-heralded inns throughout Scotland, here's a list of the country's best hotels:

- **Knockinaam Lodge,** Portpatrick (☎ **01776/810471**): Memories of Winston Churchill's clandestine meetings with General Eisenhower, a beacon of hope during the darkest days of World War II, pervade the place. Today the late Victorian country house is as well upholstered and wryly sedate as you'd expect from a top-notch hotel with such a pedigree. Adding to its allure is the fact that its restaurant is always included in critics' lists of the best of Scotland. (See chapter 5, section 12.)
- **Howard Hotel,** Edinburgh (☎ **0131/557-3500**): A stroke of good timing and luck allowed its founders to acquire a trio of adjacent Georgian-style town houses in an upscale Edinburgh neighborhood. After millions of pounds' worth of renovations, the resulting hotel is the most alluring in a city filled with worthwhile competitors. A restaurant in one of the cellars serves meals inspired by the traditions and ingredients of Scotland. (See chapter 6, section 3.)
- **Greywalls,** Gullane, East Lothian (☎ **01620/842144**): Although Sir Edward Lutyens designed dozens of opulent Edwardian homes throughout Britain, this is one of the few Lutyens houses that will host you in its role as a hotel. Built in 1901 in what architects praise as perfect harmony with its setting, it features walled-in gardens designed by the doyenne of eccentric turn-of-the-century landscape architects, Gertrude Jekyll. A national treasure and a period piece from the most ostentatious days of the British Empire, it's eccentric but eminently comfortable. (See chapter 6, section 10.)
- **One Devonshire Gardens,** Glasgow (☎ **0141/339-2001**): It's the best-groomed building in a neighborhood filled with similar sandstone-fronted town houses. Ring the bell and a chambermaid, dressed in an Edwardian costume straight out of a scene from a French bedroom farce, answers, curtsies, and ushers you inside. Yes, it's a hotel; even more important, it's a re-creation of a high-bourgeois, very proper Scottish home from the turn of the century, with antique furnishings and discreetly concealed modern comforts. (See chapter 7, section 3.)
- **Aird's Hotel,** Port Appin (☎ **01631/730236**): Its simple, stucco-sheathed exterior resembles any of hundreds of other Scottish waterside buildings. Inside,

however, it's unexpectedly luxurious, with award-winning cuisine, a format endorsed by Relais & Châteaux, and a tradition of hospitality dating back to 1760, when it functioned as an inn serving haggis, tatties, neeps, and whisky to ferryboat passengers. (See chapter 8, section 8.)

- **Auchterarder House,** Auchterarder (☎ **01764/663646**): Scholars refer to its design as a perfect example of the Scots Jacobean Revival as interpreted by builders in the 1830s. Clients refer to it as a supremely comfortable house with well-appointed bedrooms, a worthy dining room, and a polite and hardworking staff. Afternoon tea, plus a sampling of the bar's inventory of single-malts, is part of the experience here. (See chapter 10, section 1.)

- **Kinnaird,** Dunkeld (☎ **01796/482440**): An 18th-century hunting lodge for the duke of Atholl, it dominates an obscenely large estate (9,000 acres) of moor, mountain, and forest. Inside, all the accoutrements of a British country house are arrayed in impeccable, high-Edwardian style. Supremely comfortable interiors contrast dramatically with the tempests of the great outdoors, and its dining room is among the most prestigious and gilt-edged in the country. (See chapter 10, section 4.)

- **Culloden House,** Inverness (☎ **01463/790461**): If you'd like to sleep where Bonnie Prince Charlie did, head for this winning choice, an Adam-style Georgian mansion standing in 40 acres of parkland. Scottish tradition assaults you at every turn—from the grandly proportional lounge to the sound of a bagpiper on the grounds. Several accommodations have spa baths and antique four-posters. Dinner in the Adam Room is an elegant affair—French culinary skills applied to the finest of Scottish produce. (See chapter 11, section 7.)

- **Altanaharrie Inn,** Ullapool (☎ **01854/633230**): Park your car in a private area near the loch, then abandon whatever world you came from as you take the 10-minute ride on a private ferryboat across the fjord. Here a gentrified version of what was originally built as an inn for sheep drovers will immerse you in an otherworldly kind of charm. Naturally, a stay here is accompanied by some of the best cuisine in the district. (See chapter 11, section 11.)

13 The Best Restaurants

Perhaps as a rebellion against Samuel Johnson's complaint that the food in Scotland was horrid, the Scots have labored at perfecting a cuisine that makes good use of the country's abundance of fresh fish and game. Scottish Angus beef is the most prized in Britain, and the abundance of fish caught in coldwater streams and in the surrounding ocean waters is legendary. Even Scottish vegetables seem tastier than their counterparts produced in milder climes, probably because of their struggle against stony soil, cold temperatures, and a short growing season. You can find good food at simple inns throughout the countryside, but here's a list of Scotland's best:

- **La Pompadour,** in the Caledonian Hotel, Edinburgh (☎ **0131/459-9988**): Named after the mistress of Louis XV, this dining room that opened in 1925 was once viewed as the only place in Edinburgh "where you can find a decent meal." It's still serving them—better than ever. Scottish specialties reign supreme at lunch, giving way in the evening to cuisine celebrating the "Auld Alliance" with France. Go for the multicourse "tasting menu." (See chapter 6, section 3.)

- **La Potinière,** Gullane (☎ **01620/843214**): Intimate, with an understated decor best described as "pretty," it brings touches of big-city sophistication to a rural setting. Run by a husband-wife couple who infuse the place with their own personalities, it's one of the best dining rooms in the region. (See chapter 6, section 10.)

- **Rogano,** Glasgow (☎ **0141/248-4055**): Generations of Glaswegians have commended it as a symbol of mercantile Scotland between the world wars. Its decor evokes the dining room of one of the great art deco ocean liners of the 1930s. Uniformed waiters, whose speech patterns recall the language of Robert Burns, handle all comers with charm and deft good manners. (See chapter 7, section 4.)
- **Ubiquitous Chip,** Glasgow (☎ **0141/334-5007**): This former Victorian coach house and stable serves an imaginative and inventive cuisine with a daily changing menu. The Aberdeen Angus steak au poivre is delectable, followed by the heather honey and scotch whisky parfait. The 100 Highland single-malt whiskies will perk up your soul. (See chapter 7, section 4.)
- **Ostlers Close,** Cupar, Fife (☎ **01334/655574**): Chef Jimmy Graham is one of the finest in the St. Andrews area. Golfers with discriminating palates flock to this modestly appointed place, which makes the best use of fish and seafood from the Fife coast. The chef takes such special care with his cuisine that he's even known to pick his own wild mushrooms. Ducks come from a local "free-range" supplier, and everything is accurately cooked and delectable here. (See chapter 9, section 4.)
- **Airds Hotel,** Port Appin (☎ **01631/730236**): Around 1700 its premises were used to feed and house travelers after a ferryboat transit. Today it's considered a citadel of Scottish cuisine, elevating such dishes as Loch Fyne kippers to something with a local cult following. Haunch of venison with rowanberry jam is also notable. (See chapter 8, section 8.)
- **Braeval Old Mill,** Aberfoyle (☎ **01877/382711**): Its setting manages to elevate the rough walls and flagstone floor of an old water mill to a high art form. Food is as elegant and intricate (lobster lasagna, filet of wild Scottish boar with cabbage and juniper berries) as the setting is rustic. (See chapter 9, section 9.)
- **The Georgian Room,** in the Cameron House Hotel, Balloch (☎ **01389/755565**): The setting is lavishly Victorian, the food an award-winning blend of Scottish and French, designed to commemorate the "Auld Alliance." Representative dishes include items you're not likely to find at home—perhaps a terrine of rabbit and hare encased in a sheathing of leeks. (See chapter 9, section 10.)
- **The Cross,** Kingussie (☎ **01540/661166**): A cleverly converted 19th-century tweed mill houses it, and it's a lot more chic than you'd ever have imagined. Menu items are a celebration of Scottish ingredients, prepared with modern international palates in mind. Examples include a West Coast seafood salad laden with ultrafresh monkfish, scallops, prawns, and asparagus. (See chapter 10, section 11.)
- **Inverlochy Castle,** near Fort William (☎ **01397/702177**): Cherubs cavort across frescoed ceilings and chandeliers drip with Venetian crystal in a dining room created in the 1870s as a luxurious hideaway for a Victorian mogul. A Relais & Châteaux, it's likely to welcome titled personages and movie stars for a cuisine that focuses on flavorful and natural interpretations of Scottish delicacies. Examples include Loch Fyne oysters with a watercress cream sauce and loin of Scottish venison with roasted pears. (See chapter 11, section 2.)

14 The Best Pubs

- **Globe Inn** (Dumfries): In the Border Country, this was Robert Burns's favorite "howff," meaning a small, cozy room. Today you can imbibe here as he did in a pub that's been in business since 1610. He liked the place so much that he had a child with the barmaid. A small museum is devoted to Burns. (See chapter 5.)

- **Café Royal Circle Bar** (Edinburgh): It stands out in a city famous for its pubs. This long-enduring favorite has lots of atmosphere and is opulent with the trappings of the Victorian era. It attracts a "sea of drinkers," locals as well as visitors. (See chapter 6.)

- **Deacon Brodie's Tavern** (Edinburgh): The best spot for a wee dram or a pint along Edinburgh's Royal Mile. It perpetuates the memory of Deacon Brodie, good citizen by day, robber by night, the prototype for Dr. Jekyll and Mr. Hyde. It's been around since 1806, and has both a cocktail lounge bar and a large, bustling tavern where things get a bit rough at times.

- **Corn Exchange** (Glasgow): Time was, it took a bit of courage or else a foolish heart to enter a Glasgow pub. Those bad old days are long forgotten at this reliable pub in the center. In the mid-1800s the Corn Exchange was here—hence its name—but today it's a watering hole with good drink and filling, modestly priced bar platters. (See chapter 7.)

- **Rabbie's Bar** (Ayr): Burns didn't confine his drinking to Dumfries—Ayr was also one of his hangouts, and this favorite pub is a nostalgic reminder of another era. There are bits of pithy verse by Burns on the walls, and it has a collection of imported beers that's the best in the area. There's even entertainment several nights a week. (See chapter 7.)

- **Dreel Tavern** (Anstruther): This tavern is a 16th-century wood-and-stone coaching inn that was converted into a pub. Old salts from the harbor along with other locals gather to unwind on windy nights. Try the Orkney Dark Island on hand pump. Anstruther, 46 miles northeast of Edinburgh, is a gem of a Scottish seaside town and former fishing port. (See chapter 9.)

- **Ship Inn** (Elie): Down at the harbor in this little port town, it's one of the best places for a pint along the east coast. The building dates from 1788 and the pub from 1830. In summer you can enjoy your pint outside with a view over the water, but on blustery days in winter the blazing fireplace is the attraction. Stick around for dinner—the menu ranges from pheasant to venison to fresh seafood—not your typical pub grub. (See chapter 9.)

- **Prince of Wales** (Aberdeen): In the heart of the old section, furnished with church pews and antiques, it's got the city's longest bar counter. Oilmen from the North Sea join the regulars to ask for tap beers such as Courage Directors and sample the chef's Guinness pie. You'll find real flavor and an authentic atmosphere; it's a good place to mingle with the locals in a mellow setting. (See chapter 10.)

Getting to Know Scotland 2

A small nation ("'Tis a wee country, aye—but a bonny one"), Scotland is only 275 miles long and some 150 miles wide at its broadest point. No one lives more than 40 miles from salt water. But despite the small size of their country, the Scots have extended their influence around the world. And in this land of bagpipes and clans, you'll find some of the grandest scenery in Europe.

Alexander Graham Bell, the inventor, and explorers Mungo Park and David Livingstone came from Scotland. Scotland gave the world entrepreneur Andrew Carnegie, poet Robert Burns, and novelist Sir Walter Scott. But, curiously, for a long time its most famous resident has been neither man nor woman—it's the Loch Ness monster!

The border is just a line on a map; you'll hardly be aware of crossing out of England into Scotland. But even though the two countries have been joined constitutionally since 1707, Scotland is very different from England, and is very much its own country. You'll discover mountains and glens, lochs and heather-covered moors, skirling bagpipes and twirling kilts, pastel-bathed houses and gray stone cottages, rivers and streams filled with trout and salmon. Eagles soar and deer run free. Lush meadowlands are filled with sheep, and rocky coves and secret harbors wait for the adventurous. You can hear the sound of Gaelic, admire the misty blue hills, and attend a Highland gathering. You'll find quiet contemplation or you can enjoy an activity-filled calendar.

You'll also find one of the biggest welcomes in Europe. But remember one thing: Scotch is a whisky and not the name of the proud people who inhabit the country. They are called Scots, and the adjective is Scottish. Even if you forget and call them Scotch, they'll forgive you. What they won't forgive is calling them English.

1 Regions in Brief

Scotland is the oldest geological formation of Great Britain, divided physically into three regions: the central Lowlands, where three valleys and the estuaries (firths) of the Clyde, Forth, and Tay rivers make up a fertile belt from the Atlantic Ocean to the North Sea; the southern Uplands, smooth, rolling moorland broken with low crags and threaded with rivers and valleys, between the central plain and the English border; and the granite Highlands, with lochs, glens, and mountains, plus the hundreds of islands to the west and north.

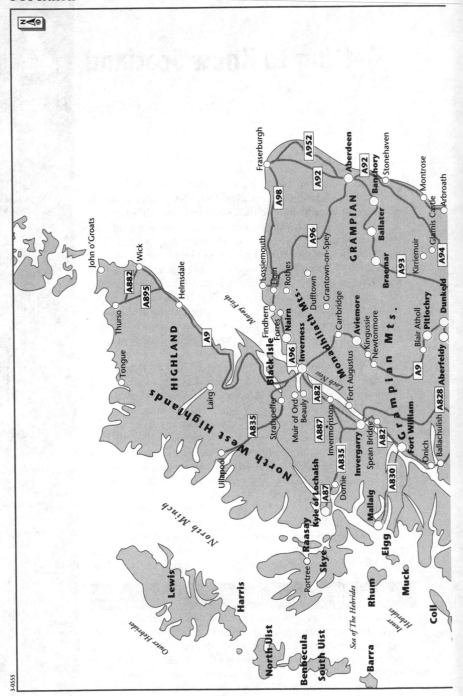

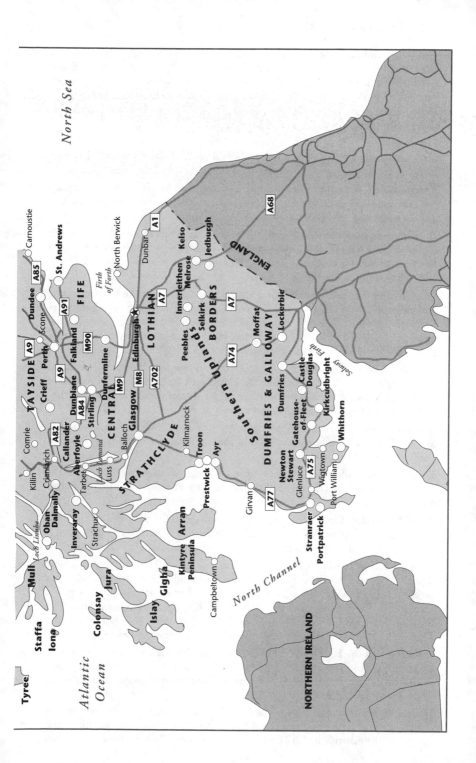

Edinburgh and the Lothian Region   This area includes not only Edinburgh, but West Lothian, most of Midlothian, and East Lothian. The capital of Scotland, Edinburgh, is half medieval and half Georgian. It's at its liveliest at the International Arts Festival every August, but you can visit its castle and walk its "Royal Mile" year-round. Edinburgh is surrounded by major attractions, including the village of Cramond and the ancient town of Linlithgow.

Fife Region   East Neuk and St. Andrews, the golf capital of Scotland, are the major attractions here, but this entire region of eastern Scotland has much to lure you, including Falkland Palace, Culross, Dunfermline Abbey, and the Firth of Forth.

The Borders   Witness to a turbulent history, the border region between England and Scotland is rich in castle ruins and gothic abbeys. Home of the cashmere sweater and the tweed suit, the Borders proved a rich mine for the fiction of Sir Walter Scott.

Aberdeen and the Grampian Region   The old granite-built city of Aberdeen at the mouth of the River Dee is the major center of this history-rich part of northeastern Scotland. Visitors flock here to visit Royal Deeside, former retreat of Queen Victoria, and to follow the Whisky Trail.

Glasgow and the Strathclyde Region   A renaissance has come to the once-grimy and industrial city of Glasgow. The Glasgow Renaissance is real and not just fodder for tourist brochures. The city's Burrell Collection is a major attraction, and once the visitor has explored Scotland's largest city, other sights in the environs are Loch Lomond and the "Burns Country" around Ayr.

Tayside   Carved from the old counties of Perth and Angus, Tayside takes its name from its major river, the Tay, running for 119 miles. One of the loveliest regions of Scotland, it's known for salmon and trout fishing. Major centers include Pitlochry and Dundee. Glamis Castle is one of its ancient monuments.

The Trossachs   This is a collective name given to a wild Highland area lying east and northeast of Loch Lomond. Some of the finest scenery in Scotland is found here—loch, mountain, and moor.

Dumfries and Galloway   This part of southwestern Scotland is often called the "Lowlands." It incorporates much of the former stamping ground of Robert Burns, and includes such centers as Castle Douglas, Moffat, and Dumfries.

Argyll Peninsula   Once an independent kingdom called Dalriada, this area of western Scotland is centered at Oban. Its major attraction is the Argyll Forest Park, covering some 60,000 acres and offering the most panoramic scenery in the country.

Arran, Kintyre & Islay   The western coastline of Scotland—one of the most scenic in Europe—includes the Isle of Arran at the mouth of the Firth of Clyde. This is often called "Scotland in miniature," because it takes in such a sweep of scenery, including lochs, glens, moors, and rocky coasts. Kintyre, the longest peninsula in Scotland, stretches for some 60 miles, and the Isle of Islay, 16 miles west of the Kintyre Peninsula, is the southernmost island of the Inner Hebrides.

Inverness and the Highlands   The capital of the Highlands is Inverness, a royal burgh and seaport lying on both sides of the Ness River. It's the best base for touring the Highlands, a region of natural grandeur and mystical charm, and is the site of the annual Highland Games.

Hebridean Islands   The chain of the Inner Hebridean Islands lies just off the west coast of the mainland. The major center here is the Isle of Skye, a mystical island and subject of the Scottish ballad "Over the Sea to Skye." Other islands carry such humorous names as Eigg and Muck. The Outer Hebrides embrace such islands as Lewis (the most northerly), Harris (known for its tweed), North Uist, Benbecula, and South Uist, among others.

Orkney and Shetland islands   These northern outposts of British civilization are archipelagos consisting of some 200 islands, about 40 of which are inhabited. With a rich Viking heritage, they are far-flung outposts that reward visitors with scenery and antiquities.

2 Scotland Today

Today, throughout the land there's a mood of change in the air. "We call it post-Enlightenment excitement," said one burly Scot. There are lots of reasons for this. For one thing, the Stone of Scone came home, a highly symbolic event—it was finally released by the English, who had held it captive for centuries. And like the Stone, as the economy improves, the Scots are coming home and fewer young people are leaving. In the 19th century, Scotland sent its sons and daughters out around the world to find a better life, and it is estimated that today 20 million Scots—four times the population of Scotland itself—live outside it. Today even the population of the Highlands is the highest it's been in a century.

A lot of this increased optimism is generated by the prospect of Scottish independence. The resounding victory of Labour in the spring elections of 1997 has led to a big payoff for Scotland: its own Parliament. Scotland voted overwhelmingly for the Labour Party. In rapid speed, on September 11, 1997, Scotland voted to establish a legislature of its own for the first time since 1707. The legislature should be up and running by the year 2000, with a $38 billion budget. Nationalists hailed the vote, though some Conservatives denounced it, claiming that it would "lead inevitably to the dissolution of Britain, leaving Scotland impoverished." But Donald Dewar, British Secretary of State for Scotland, declared, "We're a nation that believes in ourselves."

However, even a Parliament of its own may not satisfy the rising tide of Scottish separatism. In the present arrangement, the queen is still the head of state and Blair the chief of government. Scots at sporting events are singing "Flower of Scotland" instead of "God Save the Queen." Riots against supposed English individuals broke out at the first showings of the movie *Braveheart,* that celebration of 13th-century hero and defender of Scottish independence, William Wallace. The movement has such adherents as James Kelman, who won the Booker Prize in 1994 for a novel, *How Late It Was, How Late,* written in dense Glaswegian dialect. Scots are "overlooked and condescended to by London's Anglocentric cultural elite," he says. Polls show that many identify themselves as Scots first, Britons second. Young people, in particular, seem drawn to the idea of independence. But a warning is sounded by Magnus Linklater, former editor of *The Scotsman:* "Scots like putting independence forward as an idea, but when confronted with the reality of it, they retreat."

As Scotland's economy revs up, everything in the country is loosening up—blue laws are giving way, later hours are being kept, nightlife is looking up, and opportunities for enjoying Scotland's great outdoors are being vigorously developed. New ideas are in the air and the recent breakthrough of Scottish science, the cloning of a sheep for the first time, has attracted world attention. Some scientists believe that as a result human engineering is "now really on the horizon," certainly no small achievement.

3 History 101

Dateline

- **6000 B.C.** Earliest known residents of Scotland establish settlements on the Argyll Peninsula.
- **3000 B.C.** Celtic tribes invade, making the use of Gaelic widespread.
- **A.D. 82** Roman armies directed by Agricola push into southern Scotland; Roman victories, however, are short-lived.
- **A.D. 90** Romans abandon hope of conquering Scotland, retreating to England and the relative safety of Hadrian's Wall.
- **500** Newcomers from Ireland, identified as Scots, invade from the west, mingling bloodlines with Norse, Pictish, Celtic, and Teutonic tribes.
- **563** St. Columba establishes a mission on Iona, accelerating the movement already established by earlier ecclesiastics to Christianize Scotland.
- **843** Kenneth MacAlpin unifies the Picts and the Scots.
- **1005–34** Malcolm II unites the four major tribes of Scotland into one roughly cohesive unit.
- **1124–53** David I builds monasteries, consolidates royal power and prestige, and imports clearly defined Norman values.
- **1266** The Hebrides and the coastline of western Scotland are released from Norse control; the Donald clan consolidates power here into a semiautonomous state within Scotland.
- **1272** Edward I of England embarks on an aggressive campaign to conquer both

continues

EARLY HISTORY Scotland was a melting pot in its early history. Standing stones, brochs, cromlechs, cairns, and burial chambers attest to its earliest occupation, but we know little about these first tribes and invaders. By the time the Roman armies decided to attempt an invasion in A.D. 82, the land was occupied by a people the Romans called Picts, or the Painted Ones. Despite spectacular bloodletting, the Romans were unsuccessful, and the building of Hadrian's Wall effectively marked the northern limits of their influence.

By the year A.D. 500 the Picts were again attacked—the name had stuck. This time the invaders, the Dalriad Irish called "Scots," were successful. They established themselves on the Argyll Peninsula and battled and intermarried with the Picts. Britons emigrated from the south and Norsemen from the east, creating new bloodlines and migratory patterns. Druidism, a little-understood mystical form of nature worship, whose most visible monuments are runic etchings and stone circles, flourished at this time. Languages of the era included a diverse array of Celtic and Norse dialects with scatterings of low German and Saxon English.

The power of the Scotians, entrenched in western Scotland, was cemented when a missionary named Columba (later canonized) arrived from Ireland in 563. The rocky Hebridean island of Iona became the base for his Christian mission. Christianity, already introduced by St. Ninian and St. Mungo to Strathclyde and Galloway, became widespread.

THE MIDDLE AGES Scots and Picts were united in 843 under the kingship of an early chieftain named Kenneth MacAlpin. But it was the invasionary pressures from England and Scandinavia and the unifying force of Christianity that molded Scotland into a relatively coherent unit. Under Malcolm II (1005–34), the British and Angles, who occupied the southwest and southeast of the Scottish mainland, merged with the Scots and the Picts. Malcolm's son and heir, Duncan, was killed by Macbeth of Moray, a historic event that fueled the plotlines of one of Shakespeare's most famous plays.

Malcolm III's marriage to an English princess, Margaret, was to further the anglicization of the Scottish Lowlands. A determined woman of strong ideas, she imported English priests into Scotland and carried out a reform of the church that eventually replaced St. Columba's Gaelic form of Christian worship. Her anglicization efforts and her introduction of the English language as a teaching tool laid important groundwork for making Scotland into a potential English kingdom. She led a life of great piety and was canonized as St. Margaret in 1251.

While Europe's feudal system came to full flower, Scotland was preoccupied with the territorial battles of clan allegiances and the attempt to define its borders with England. Cultural assimilation with England was furthered under David I (1081–1153). David made land grants to many Anglo-Norman families, providing Scotland with a feudal aristocracy and bringing in such ancient names as Fraser, Seton, and Lindsay. He also embarked on one of the most lavish building sprees in Scottish history, erecting many abbeys, including Jedburgh, Kelso, Melrose, and Dryburgh. This extravagance, while providing for modern visitors many photogenic medieval monuments, almost bankrupted his treasury.

In 1266, after about a century of Norse control, the foggy and windswept Western Isles were returned to Scotland after the Battle of Largs. Despite nominal allegiance to the Scottish monarch, the inhabitants of this region quickly organized themselves around the Donald (or MacDonald) clan, which for nearly 100 years was one of the most powerful in Scotland and ruled its territory almost as an independent state. Today the honorary title of their patriarch, "Lord of the Isles," is still one of the formal titles employed on state occasions by Britain's Prince of Wales.

In the meantime, real trouble was brewing in the south. Edward I, ambitious Plantagenet king of England (also known as "Longshanks" and later as "The Hammer of the Scots"), yearned to rule over an undivided island nation incorporating England, Scotland, and Wales. Successful at first, he set up John de Balliol as a "vassal king" to do homage to him for Scotland. Many of Scotland's legendary heroes lived and did their deeds during this period: Sir William Wallace (1270–1305), who drove the English out of Perth and Stirling; Sir James Douglas ("The Black Douglas"; 1286–1330), who terrorized the English borders; and Robert the Bruce (1274–1329), who, with skill and courage, finally succeeded in freeing Scotland from England. Crowned Robert I at Scone in 1306 in defiance of the English, Robert the Bruce defeated Edward II of England decisively at the Battle of Bannockburn in 1314, demolishing the English armies. Scotland's independence was formally recognized in the Treaty

Wales and Scotland, but is deflected by Robert the Bruce, among others.

- **1314** Victory of Scots over the English armies at Bannockburn leads to the Treaty of Arbroath (1320), formally recognizing Scotland's independence from England.
- **1468** The Orkney and Shetland islands are given to Scotland as part of the marriage dowry of a Danish princess to a Scottish king.
- **Late 1400s** The "Auld Alliance" with France, a cynical arrangement based mostly on mutual distrust of England, is born.
- **1535** At the urging of Henry VIII of England, Parliament officially severs all ties with the Catholic Church, legally sanctioning the Reformation.
- **1561** Queen Mary returns to Scotland from France.
- **1559–64** John Knox lays out the rough outline of the Scottish Presbyterian church.
- **1568** Mary is defeated and flees to England.
- **1572** Death of John Knox; his work is continued by Andrew Melville.
- **1587** Execution of Mary Queen of Scots.
- **1603** Accession to the throne of England of Mary's son, James VI, as James I unifies the two countries.
- **1689** Parliament strips the uncompromising Catholic James II of his crown and imports the Protestant William and Mary from Holland to replace him.
- **1746** Bonnie Prince Charlie's attempt to reclaim his grandfather's throne ends in defeat at the Battle of Culloden, destroying any hope of a Stuart revival.
- **1750–1850** Rapid industrialization of England

continues

and Scotland; the Clearances strip many crofters of their farms, creating epic bitterness and forcing new patterns of Scottish migrations.

- **1789** The French Revolution; British monarchists tighten their grip on civil unrest in Scotland.
- **Late 19th century** An astonishing success in the sciences propels Scotland into the role of arbiter of industrial know-how around the globe.
- **Mid-20th century** Decline of traditional industries, especially shipbuilding, painfully redefines the nature of Scottish industry.
- **1970** Discovery of North Sea oil deposits brings new vitality to Scotland.
- **1973** Scotland, as part of the United Kingdom, becomes a member of the Common Market.
- **1974** Old counties or shires are reorganized; many regions are renamed.
- **1979** Scots vote on "devolution" (separation from England): 33% vote yes, 31% vote no, and 36% don't vote at all.
- **1981** Largest oil terminal in Europe launched at Sullom Voe, Shetland Islands.
- **1988** Nationalism revives in Scotland under marching cry of "Scotland in Europe."
- **1992** Scots continue to express dissatisfaction with English rule: Polls show one out of two favor independence.
- **1995** Celebration of the 50-year anniversary of the end of World War II.
- **1996** Psychopath guns down 16 kids and a teacher in one of Britain's greatest mass murder sprees.
- **1997** A sheep is cloned for the first time.

continues

of Northampton in 1328, inaugurating a heady but short-lived separation from England.

In 1468 the Orkneys and Shetlands, Norse to the core, were brought into the Scottish web of power as part of the marriage dowry of the Danish princess, Margaret, to the Scottish king, James III. This acquisition represents the last successful expansion of Scottish sovereignty during the period when Scottish power and independence were at their zenith.

It was during these years of bitter battles and turmoil that the Scots entered into an alliance with the French, which was to have far-reaching effects. The line of Stuart (or Stewart) kings, so named because the family had become powerful as stewards of the English king, were generally accepted as the lesser of a series of potential evils. Real power, however, lay with Scotland's great lords, patriarchs of the country's famous clans. Jealous of both their bloodlines and territories, they could rarely agree on anything other than their common distrust of England.

THE REFORMATION The passions of the Reformation burst upon an already turbulent Scottish scene in the person of John Knox, a devoted disciple of the Geneva Protestant John Calvin and a bitter enemy of both the Catholic and Anglican churches. Knox became famous for the screaming insults he heaped upon ardently Catholic Queen Mary and for his complete and absolute lack of a sense of humor. His polemics were famous—in his struggle against Queen Mary, he wrote his *First Blast of the Trumpet Against the Monstrous Regiment of Women.* His was a peculiar mixture of piety, conservatism, strict morality, and intellectual independence that's still a pronounced feature of the Scottish character.

His teachings also helped shape the democratic form of Scottish government and set the Scottish church's austere moral tone for generations to come. He focused on practical considerations as well as religious ones: church administration, funding, and the relationship between church and state. Foremost among the tenets were provisions for a self-governing congregation and pure allegiance to the Word of God as contained in meticulous translations of the Old and New Testaments.

Upon Knox's death in 1562, his work was continued by the Scots-born, Geneva-trained Andrew Melville, who hated ecclesiastical tyranny even more (if that were possible) than Knox himself. Melville reorganized the Scottish universities and introduced an emphasis on classical studies and the study of the Bible in its original Hebrew and Greek. Under his

leadership emerged a clearly defined Scottish Presbyterian church whose elected leaders were responsible
for practical as well as spiritual matters.

Later, the Church of Scotland's almost obsessive
insistence on self-government led to endless con-

■ **Sept. 1997** Scotland votes to establish a legislature of its own for the first time since 1707.

flicts, first with the Scottish, and after unification, with the British monarchs.

MARY QUEEN OF SCOTS   When Mary Stuart, "Queen of Scots" (1542–87), took up her rule, she was a Roman Catholic of French upbringing trying to govern an unruly land to which she was a virtual newcomer. Daughter of James V of Scotland and Mary of Guise of France, she became queen when 6 days old. She was married to the heir to the French throne, and she returned to Scotland only after his death. She set out on two roads that were sure to be anathema to the Scots—to make herself absolute monarch in the French style and to impose Roman Catholicism. The first alienated the lords who held real power in Scotland, and the second made her the enemy of John Knox and the Calvinists. After a series of disastrous political and romantic alliances and endless abortive episodes of often indiscreet intrigue, her life was ended in 1587 in England by the headsman's axe. The order for her execution was issued, reluctantly, by her cousin, Elizabeth I, who considered Mary's presence an incitement both to civil unrest and to the stability of the English throne.

The power of the great lords of Scotland was broken only in 1603, when Mary's son, James VI of Scotland, assumed the throne of England as James I, Elizabeth's heir. James succeeded where his doomed mother had failed. First of the Stuarts to occupy the English throne, his coronation effectively united England and Scotland.

UNION WITH ENGLAND   Despite the hopes for peace that accompanied the union, religion almost immediately became a prime source of discontent. From their base in England the two Stuart kings attempted to promote a Church of Scotland governed by bishops, in opposition to the Presbyterian Church's self-ruling organization. So incensed were the Scots that in 1638 they signed the National Covenant, which not only reasserted the principles of the Reformation but questioned the king's right to make laws, a role the "Covenanters" believed should be filled by Parliament. However, the monarch was still allowed a role in their scheme of things, unlike the position the Puritans took in England. Scotland's subsequent support of Charles I and his son led to Cromwell's invasion of Scotland in 1650, when he defeated the Scots decisively at Dunbar. Religious friction continued, however, after the restoration of Charles II to the English throne.

THE JACOBITES   In 1689 when the English Parliament stripped the Catholic king, James II, of his crown and imported the Protestant monarchs William and Mary from Holland, the exiled ex-king and then his son James Edward (the Old Pretender) became focal points for Scottish unrest. The Jacobites (the name comes from Jacobus, the Latin form of James) attempted unsuccessfully in 1715 to place the Old Pretender on the English throne and restore the Stuart line to power. Though James died in exile, his son Charles Edward (the Young Pretender), better known as "Bonnie Prince Charlie," carried on his father's dream. Known for his charisma, but with an alcohol-induced instability, he was the central figure of the Jacobite uprising of 1745.

Though the revolt was initially promising because of the many Scottish adherents who crossed religious lines to rally to the cause, the Jacobite forces were completely crushed at the Battle of Culloden, near Inverness, by a numerically superior English army led by the duke of Cumberland. Many supporters of the Pretender's cause were killed in battle, some were executed, and others fled to the United States and other safe havens. Fearing a rebirth of similar types of Scottish nationalism, the clan

The Stone of Destiny Comes Home

The Stone of Scone or "Stone of Destiny" has come back home to Scotland. It's been on a "rocky" journey. The stone is physically only a block of sandstone, measuring 26 inches long, 16 inches wide, and weighing 336 pounds. But it's not just a stone. Revered for centuries as a holy relic, it allegedly came from the Middle East. In biblical times Jacob is said to have used the stone as a pillow.

The stone was used at Dunadd, Iona, and Dunstaffnage for enthroning Dalriadic monarchs. Later it was moved to Scone, and in 1292 John Balliol became the last king to be crowned on the stone in Scotland. So powerful was its legend that Edward I took it to England in 1296, believing that possession of the stone gave him sovereignty over Scotland. There it stayed, under the coronation chair in Westminster Abbey. In 1328 the Treaty of Northampton that recognized Scotland's independence returned the stone to Scotland, but the English reneged on the promise and the stone never moved from Westminster Abbey.

On Christmas Day 1950 the stone disappeared—it had been taken from the abbey by a group of Scottish Nationalists. No one knows where it went then, but it was found about 4 months later in Arbroath Abbey and returned to Westminster. A rumor went around that the found stone was actually a replica and that the replica—not the real stone—was carted back to London, but this has never been proven.

In 1996 the Stone of Destiny left Westminster Abbey by Landrover. It crossed from England into Scotland at the Scottish border town of Coldstream, where a small but moving ceremony was held. On November 30 of that year, the stone proceeded with pomp and circumstance up the Royal Mile in Edinburgh to its permanent home beside the Scottish Crown Jewels in Edinburgh Castle, where you can see it today. Andrew, Duke of York, presided over the ceremony. Scots hailed the return of the stone after "700 years in English captivity."

"Thank God it's back where it belongs," said Andrew McGregor, an Edinburgh office worker. Of course, not all Scots are pleased with the return of the stone to Edinburgh. Some denounced it as a "cheap political ploy," especially as the Queen claims she is "lending" it to her Scottish subjects—the idea is that after 7 centuries possession is nine-tenths of the law, and it can be called back to London for a future coronation.

Some Scots want to see the stone returned to Scone from where it was taken. "Edinburgh has no claim whatsoever, legally, morally, or whatever, to the Stone of Scone," said Andrew R. Robinson, administrator of Scone Castle. "It's not called the Stone of Edinburgh, is it?"

system was rigorously suppressed, clans that supported the Jacobite cause lost their lands, and, until 1782, the wearing of Highland dress was illegal.

The Young Pretender himself was smuggled unglamorously out of Scotland, assisted by a resident of the obscure Hebridean island of South Uist, Flora MacDonald. One of the most visible Scottish heroines of her era, she has ever since provided fodder for the Scottish sense of romance. The Bonnie Prince dissipated himself in Paris and Rome, and the hopes of an independent Scotland were buried forever.

ECONOMIC GROWTH & THE INDUSTRIAL REVOLUTION During the 18th century the Scottish economy underwent a radical transformation of growth and diversification. The British government, fearing increased civil unrest, commissioned one of its most capable generals to build a series of roads and bridges throughout the country, presumably to increase military access from London in the event of a revolt, but which actually encouraged business and commerce.

As trade with British overseas colonies, England, and Europe increased, the great ports of Aberdeen, Glasgow, and Leith (near Edinburgh) flourished. The merchants of Glasgow grew rich on a nearly monopolistic tobacco trade with Virginia and the Carolinas, until the outbreak of the American Revolution sent American tobacco elsewhere. Other forms of commerce, however, continued to enrich a battalion of shrewd Scots.

The outbreak of the French Revolution in 1789 engendered so much sympathy in Scotland for the revolutionary cause that a panicked government in London became more autocratic than ever in its attempts to suppress Scottish antimonarchical feelings.

The infamous Clearances (1750–1850) changed forever the demographics of Scotland. Small farmers, or crofters, were expelled from their ancestral lands to make way for sheep-grazing. Increased industrialization, continued civil unrest, migration into urban centers, and a massive wave of emigration out of Scotland into the United States, Canada, Australia, South Africa, and New Zealand all contributed to a changing national demographic and a dispersal of the Scottish ethic throughout the world.

Meanwhile, rapid progress in the arts, science, and education, and the new industrial age meshed neatly with the Scottish genius for thrift, hard work, shrewdness, and conservatism. The 19th century produced vast numbers of prominent Scots who made broad and sweeping contributions to all fields of endeavor. Many of the inventions that altered the history of the developing world were either invented or installed by Scottish genius and industry.

THE 20th CENTURY   Scotland endured bitter privations during the Depression and during the 20th century's two world wars. After World War II, in the 1960s and 1970s, Scotland found that, like the rest of Britain, its aging industrial plants could not compete with more modern commercial competition from abroad.

The most visible decline occurred in the shipbuilding industries. The vast Glasgow shipyards that once produced some of the world's great ocean liners were now bankrupt. The companies that produced automobiles in Scotland were wiped out during the 1930s. Many commercial enterprises once controlled by Scots had been merged into English or multinational conglomerates.

However, all was not bleak on the Scottish horizon. The discovery of North Sea oil by British Petroleum in 1970 boosted the economy considerably and provided jobs for thousands of workers. Oil has continued to play a prominent role in the Scottish economy. In 1981 the largest oil terminal in Europe opened at Sullom Voe in the remote Shetland Islands.

As part of the United Kingdom, Scotland became a member of the European Common Market in 1973, although many Scots opposed entry. In 1974 it underwent a drastic revision of its counties. Many regions were renamed. For example, "Tayside" was carved out of the old counties of Perth and Angus.

In March 1996, a tragedy in Scotland made headlines around the world. In a few short minutes, a heavily armed psychopath, known as "Mr. Creepy," went berserk in a local elementary school in the tiny town of Dunblane. He fatally shot 16 youngsters and their teacher, wounding 12 others. This is the most heart-rending episode of mass murder in the British Isles. Mr. Creepy turned out to be 43-year-old Thomas Hamilton. After the rampage, Hamilton killed himself. As the school's headmaster told the press, "Evil visited us yesterday, and we don't know why."

On the brighter side was a landmark scientific breakthrough in 1997. The Scots have always contributed almost disproportionately to the world's science and technology. Now the land that gave us Sir Alexander Fleming, Nobel Prize winner as discoverer of penicillin, has given us the first cloned sheep. The issue of *Nature* for February 27, 1997, reported the event, the work of scientists in Roslin, Scotland. "Dolly" was the first lamb to be produced by cloning the udder cells of an adult sheep. In the summer of 1997, another major step was taken, and "Polly" was created, a lamb that has a human gene in every cell of its body. The work was hailed as a milestone. Animals with human genes—at least in theory—could be used to produce hormones or other biological products to treat human diseases, or even to produce organs for human transplant.

Scotland's high-tech industries have played an important role in the technological revolution, and today Scotland produces 13% of Europe's personal computers, 45% of Europe's workstations, and 50% of Europe's automatic banking machines. Scotland's time-tested crafts (woolen tweeds and knitwear) are also thriving, the market for scotch whisky has burgeoned, and tourists are visiting Scotland in record numbers.

4 A Portrait of the Scots

LANGUAGE

In Scotland's earliest history, its prevailing tongue was the Celtic language, Gaelic, along with a smattering of Norse dialects. When English was introduced and Scottish English developed, it borrowed heavily not only from Gaelic but from Scandinavian, Dutch, and French. In the 15th and 16th centuries, when Scotland had close ties to France, French was a literary language of precision and grace, and it was the language of Mary Queen of Scots, who spoke no Gaelic at all. After the Scottish court moved to England in 1603, Scottish English was looked on as a rather awkward dialect of English.

As the centuries progressed, Gaelic, the original Celtic tongue and an ancient and complex language, diminished in importance, partly because the British government's deliberate policy was to make English the universal language of all Britain. By the 1980s less than 2% of the Scottish population understood Gaelic in any form. Most of those who still speak it live in the northwestern Highlands and in the Hebridean Islands—especially the Island of Skye, where about 60% of the population still uses the Gaelic language.

Scottish English never developed the linguistic class divisions that still exist so strongly in England between upper-, middle-, and lower-class speech patterns. Throughout most of its English-speaking history, the hardships of Scotland were suffered in common by a society that was well knit and had few barriers between the classes. Social snobbery was relatively unknown and the laird and his man conversed as equals.

At the end of the 20th century the great leveling effects of television and radio have begun to even out some of the more pronounced burrs and lilts of the Scottish tongue. However, the dialect and speech patterns of the Scots are still rich and evocative.

Of course, Scots and English have many similarities. For example, *loch* means lake, *sang* means song, and *tak* means take. You'll hear *dinnae* for don't, *winnae* for won't, *ken* for know, and *aye* for yes. Pro-Scots argue that their language is not a dialect of English but a language in its own right, with Gaelic, French, and old Norse influences thrown in that make it distinct from English. The current controversy over Scots versus standard English is mirrored in the ebonics debate in America.

Today, after years of struggle, Scottish students are rewarded with approval by pro-Scots educators when they say, "Who's all comin tae the jiggin?" ("Who's coming to the dance?"). This increasing pride in the Scottish language is in direct contrast to

---

Tracing Your Ancestral Roots

If you have a name beginning with "Mac" (which simply means "son of") or one of the other Scottish names, you may have descended from a clan, a group of kinsmen claiming a common ancestry. Clans and clan societies have their own museums throughout Scotland, and local tourist offices will have details about where to locate them. In bookstores throughout Scotland, you can purchase clan histories and maps.

In Edinburgh, write to **New Register House,** 3 W. Register St., Edinburgh EH1 3YT (☎ **0131/334-0380**), for a full list of their search fees and the extent of their records before going there yourself. Scottish ancestor hunters come here bitten by the genealogy bug, and facilities get crowded in summer. The house has on record details of every birth, marriage, and death in Scotland since 1855. There are also old parish registers, the earliest dating from 1553, which list baptisms, marriages, and burials, but these older records are far from complete. It also has census returns for every decade from 1841 to 1891 and such data records as the foreign marriages of Scots, adopted children's registers, and war registers.

---

classrooms, say, back in the '50s. At that time, students were under a constant threat of a whack from a tawse (leather strap) if they blurted out a single aye.

In 1997, Scottish educators concluded that as a legitimate language Scottish deserves the same respect as standard English, and for the first time ever, all public schools in the country recognize Scots as a formal part of the curriculum. And writers, remembering the linguistic tradition of Robert Burns, are beginning to turn to Scots again as a literary language.

SCOTTISH TRADITIONAL MUSIC

INSTRUMENTAL MUSIC   When people think of Scottish music, the bagpipe instantly comes to mind. It may come as a surprise to many to learn that the bagpipe originated in the Near East. It may have been introduced into Britain by the conquering Romans, who found Scotland too tough to tame. The great Highland bagpipe survived the defeat at Culloden, at which time it was outlawed, partly because it was prized as a military instrument, the dread sound of the piper often sending terror through enemy ranks. Piping was encouraged in new Highland regiments, and the Scot became feared throughout the world for his prowess as a soldier and for the brave skirl of the pipes.

The *ceol mor* (great music) of the pipes is the *pibroch,* a highly developed theme with variations. The art of pibroch is unique to the Highlands. Lighter types of bagpipe music, called *ceol beag* (small music), are marches, dances, and airs. The great Highland bagpipe has two or more pipes sounded by mouth-blown reeds. Wind is fed to the pipes by arm pressure on a skin bag. It's estimated that it takes about 7 years to learn to play the great Highland bagpipe well. The Lowland or Border bagpipe was bellows-blown, but it lost popularity in the 19th century.

Other traditional musical instruments are the harp and the fiddle. The most ancient of these is the harp, of Irish origin. It lost popularity by the 18th century, when the fiddle, flute, and lute took precedence, and some harp music even passed to the bagpipes. Interest in the harp has revived in this century. The fiddle (derived from the early fedyl) edged out two former competitors, the rebec and the croud (the Welsh crwth), for predominance in the bowed-string category. Today, especially in Strathspey and Shetland, you can hear the fiddle in both solo and concert form.

VOCAL MUSIC   Scottish folk song has been carried all over the world, and today has a lively tradition in America as well as in Scotland. Two traditions exist—the Lowland, where the Scottish version of English is spoken, and the Gaelic music of the Highlands and Hebrides.

The first Lowland songs and ballads were written down in the Skene Manuscript (now in the National Library of Scotland) around 1615, and in about 1650 numerous published editions of Lowland tunes began to appear.

Gaelic songs were not collected until the 19th century, and because the Highland ballads often differed from clan to clan, you may still hear today a version that never has been written down or recorded. The folk traditions of Orkney and Shetland have unfortunately been lost. Ballads were in the ancient Norn language, spoken in Orkney until the late 17th century and in Shetland until the mid-18th, but when it was allowed to die out, the folk songs went with it. The tunes have also almost died out.

A feature of Scottish music is the scotch snap, a form of syncopation consisting of two notes, the second of which is three times as long as the first. The scotch snap apparently originated in the 18th century and is found in some authentic Scottish tunes as well as in the 18th century's pseudo-Scottish melodies.

CHURCH MUSIC   Before the Reformation there was a strong tradition of church music. Most towns of any size had active song schools, mainly under church direction. A major change in church music was brought about by Calvinist reformers who denigrated the organ as a "popish instrument" and destroyed church organs everywhere in the 17th century. This did not, however, interfere with the Gaelic "long psalms" of Celtic Scotland in which each line is intoned musically by the leader with the congregation then singing the line.

HIGHLAND GAMES & GATHERINGS

Highland gatherings or games have their origins in the fairs organized by the tribes or clans for the exchange of goods. At these gatherings there were often trials of strength among the men, and the strongest were selected for the chief's army.

The earliest games were held more than 1,000 years ago. The same tradition is maintained today: throwing hammers, putting rounded stones found in the rivers, tossing tree trunks, running in flat races and up steep hillsides. Playing the bagpipes and performing dances have always been part of the gatherings. The "Heavies," a breed of gigantic men, always draw the most attention with their prowess. Of all the events, the most popular—and the most spectacular—is the tossing of the caber (that is, the throwing of a great tree trunk!).

Queen Victoria, who had a deep love for Scotland, popularized the Highland games, which for many decades had been suppressed after the failure of the 1745 rebellion. In 1848 the queen and her consort, Prince Albert, attended the Braemar Gathering and saw her ghillie, Duncan, win the race up the "hill of Craig Choinnich," as she recorded in her journal.

Impressions

Scotland is renowned as the home of the most ambitious race in the world.

—Frederic Edwin Smith, Rectorial Address, Aberdeen (1928)

It is a peculiar element in Scottish humour, as appreciated by Scotchmen, that the harder it is to see, the better it is esteemed. If it is obvious it is of less account. This rests on the intellectuality of the Scotch; having little else to cultivate, they cultivate the intellect. The export of brains came to be their chief item of commerce.

—Stephen Leacock, *Humour* (1935)

The most famous gathering nowadays is that at Braemar, held in early September of each year and patronized by the royal family. When that "chief of chiefs" takes the salute, Queen Elizabeth is fulfilling a role assumed by a predecessor of hers in the 11th century.

Other major games are held at Ballater (Grampian), Aberdeen, Elgin, and Newtonmore.

CLANS, TARTANS & KILTS

To the outsider, Scotland's deepest traditions appear to be based on the clan system of old with all the familiar paraphernalia of tartans and bagpipes that play such a large part in the country's world image. However, this is a romantic memory, and in any case, a good part of the Scots—the 75% of the population that live in the central Lowland, for example—have little or no connection with the clansmen of earlier times.

The clan tradition of Scotland dates from the tribal units of the country's earliest Celtic history. Power was organized around a series of chieftains, who exacted loyalties from the inhabitants of a particular region in exchange for protection against exterior invasions. The position of chieftain was not hereditary, and land was owned by the clan, not by the chieftain. Clan members had both rights and duties. Rigidly militaristic and paternalistic—the stuff with which Scottish legend is imbued—the clan tradition is still emphasized today, albeit in a much friendlier fashion than when claymores and crossbows threatened a bloody death or dismemberment for alleged slights on a clan's honor.

The word *clan* derives from the ancient Gaelic word *clann,* meaning "children," and the prefix Mac translates as "son of," the same as the prefix "O" in front of an Irish Gaelic name. Therefore, the Clan MacDonald symbolizes "children of Donald."

Chieftains were absolute potentates, with life and death power over members and interlopers, although they were usually viewed as patriarchs actively engaged in the perpetuation of the clan's bloodlines, traditions, and honor. The entourage of a chieftain always included bodyguards, musicians (harpers and pipers), a spokesman (known as a "tatler"), and—perhaps most important to latter-day students of clan traditions—a bard. The bard's role was to sing, to exalt the role of the clan and its heroes, to keep a genealogical record of births and deaths, and to compose or recite epic poems relating to the clan's history.

Most of the clans were organized during two distinctly different eras of Scottish history. One of the country's oldest and largest is Clan Donald, whose original organization occurred during the early mists of the Christianization of Scotland, and whose headquarters has traditionally been Scotland's northwestern coast and its western islands. The fragmentation of Clan Donald into subdivisions (which include the Sleat, the Dunyveg, the Clanranald, and the Keppoch clans) happened after the violent battles of succession over control of the clan in the 1400s. These clan feuds so weakened the once powerful unity of the MacDonalds that a new crop of former vassal tribes in northwestern Scotland declared their independence and established new clans of their own. These included the Mackintoshes, the Macleans, the MacNeils, the Mackinnons, and the MacLeods.

Meanwhile, the giant Celtic earldoms of eastern Scotland disintegrated and Norman influences from the south became more dominant. Clans whose earliest makeup might have been heavily influenced by Norman bloodlines include Clan Frasier (whose name derives from the French *des fraises,* because of the strawberry leaves on the family's coat of arms), de Umfraville, and Rose. Other clans adapted their Celtic names: These include Clan Robertson (Celtic Clan Donnachaidh) and Clan Campbell (Celtic Diarmid).

Garb o' the Gods

Although not every foreign visitor to Scotland is descended from a clan, almost all of them are familiar with plaids and the traditions associated with them. Over the centuries, each clan developed a distinctive pattern to be worn by its members, presumably to better identify its soldiers during the heat of battle. (Although today *tartan* is used interchangeably with *plaid,* the word *tartan* originally referred specifically to a mantle of cloth draped over the back and shoulders.)

Kilts, of course, enjoy an ancient history. "Checkered" tartans are first mentioned in an English inventory of 1471. The clans developed special dyeing and weaving techniques, with colors and patterns that reflected flair and imagination. The craft of dyeing was raised to an art that was a point of pride for the clan. Alder bark, steeped in hot water, produces a black dye; gorse, broom, and knapweed produce different shades of green; cup moss produces purple; dandelion leaves produce magenta; bracken and heather produce yellow; white lichens produce red; and indigo had to be imported for blue.

When Bonnie Prince Charlie launched his abortive rebellion in 1745, he used tartans as a symbol of his army, which threatened the English enemy so much that public display of tartans was banned for a period after his defeat. Tartans came into high fashion in Queen Victoria's day when she and her kilt-wearing German consort, Albert, made all things Scottish popular.

Today there are at least 300 different tartans, each subtly distinct from its neighbor and all available for sale in the shops and markets of Scotland. If you're not fortunate enough to be of Scottish extraction, Queen Victoria long ago authorized two "Lowland" designs as suitable garb for Sassenachs (the English, and more remotely, the Americans).

Few people realize that from 7 to 10 yards of tartan wool cloth goes into the average kilt. Even fewer non-Scots know what is actually worn beneath those voluminous folds strapped over the muscular thighs of a parading Scotsman. For a Highlander, the answer to that question is "nothing," an answer that goes along with such defenders of ancient tradition who hold that only a Steward (MacPherson, etc.) can wear a Stewart (MacPherson, etc.) tartan, and that only a Scotsman looks good in a kilt, and that only a foreigner would stoop to wearing anything under it. Alas, commercialism has reared its head with the introduction of undershorts to match the material making up the swirling folds of bagpipe players' kilts. A story is told of a colonel who heard a rumor that the soldiers of his elite Highland Light Infantry regiment were mollycoddling themselves with undershorts. The next day, his eyebrows bristling, he ordered the entire regiment to undress in front of him. To his horror, half a dozen of his soldiers had disgraced the regiment by putting on "what only an Englishman would wear." He publicly ordered the offending garments removed, and when he gave the order the next day to "drop your kilts," not a soldier in the regiment had on the "trews" (close-cut tartan shorts).

Even in the general decline of standards today, the mark of a man in the Highlands is still whether he can abide drafts up his thighs and the feel of wool cloth against tender flesh.

Simultaneously, in the border region between England and Scotland, families and clans with differing sets of traditions and symbols held a precarious power over one of the most heavily contested regions of Britain, either enduring or instigating raids on their territories from both north and south. But despite the rich traditions of the

Lowland and Border clans, it is the traditions of the Highland clans with their costumes, bagpipes, speech patterns, and grandly tragic struggles that have captured the imagination of the world.

The clans had broken down long before Sir Walter Scott wrote his romantic novels about them and long before Queen Victoria made Scotland socially fashionable. The clans today represent a cultural rather than a political power. The best place to see the remnants of the clan tradition in action is at any traditional Highland gathering, although battalions of bagpipers seem to show up at everything from weddings and funerals to political rallies, parades, and civic events throughout Scotland.

5 A Taste of Scotland

For many years, restaurants in Scotland were known mainly for their modest prices, watery overcooked vegetables, and boiled meats. But the visitor need no longer expect a diet of oats, fried fish, and greasy chips—in the past 20 years there has been a significant improvement in Scottish cookery. There was a time that the Scot going out for dinner would head for the nearest hotel, but independent restaurants are now opening everywhere, often by newly arrived immigrants, along with bistros and wine bars.

More and more restaurants are offering a "Taste of Scotland" menu of traditional dishes prepared with the freshest of local ingredients, a culinary program initiated by the Scottish Tourist Board. Scotland's culinary strength is in its fresh, raw ingredients, ranging from seafood, beef, and game to fresh vegetables and native fruits.

One of Scotland's best-known exports is pedigree **Aberdeen Angus beef.** In fact, the famous "ye olde" roast beef of England often came from Scotland. Scottish **lamb** is known for its tender, tasty meat. A true connoisseur can taste the difference in lamb by its grazing grounds. These range from the coarse pastureland and seaweed of the Shetlands to the heather-clad hills of the mainland.

Game plays an important role in the Scottish diet, from woodcock, red deer, grouse, and capercaillie to the rabbit and hare in the crofter's kitchen. And **fish** in this land of seas, rivers, and lochs is a mainstay, from salmon to the pink-fleshed brown trout, to the modest herring that is transformed into the elegant kipper (the best are the Loch Fyne kippers). Scottish smoked salmon is, of course, a delicacy known worldwide.

One of the joys of traveling around Scotland today is finding a gastronomic shrine in a small town where cookery is practiced to perfection. The best example of this is **La Potinière** at Gullane, where David and Hilary Brown maintain the "Auld Alliance," using French culinary techniques on Scottish ingredients. Another gastronomic surprise comes at the **Peat Inn,** 6 miles southwest of St. Andrews, where David and Patricia Wilson pay homage to the best from field, sky, and stream. They've even encouraged locals to form cottage industries to supply only the best of fresh herbs, vegetables, salads, and game. Sample the deep, rich flavors of their pan-fried venison, kidney, and liver, or their breast of pigeon with wild mushrooms in a truffle sauce. **Braeval** at Aberfoyle is typical of the changing state of Scottish cuisine. Chicken livers with baby leeks was not an unknown dish in the days of yore, but today the dish is likely to appear with pesto dressing, and the roast lamb is likely to be served with couscous from the kitchens of North Africa.

Impressions

Oats—a grain which is generally given to horses, but in Scotland supports the people.
—Samuel Johnson, *A Dictionary of the English Language* (1755)

Silver Darling, a restaurant in Aberdeen, calls itself a barbecued seafood restaurant, cooking the day's catch over charcoal. Oysters are likely to appear with spicy Cajun flavoring, and roasted monkfish might be "awakened" with roasted garlic, cumin, and coriander. Smoked salmon is still on the menu, of course, but chances are that it might be whipped into a Swiss cheese soufflé. Tradition is still respected—filet of red deer marinated in whisky and juniper with a black-currant sauce still gets the vote of the Scottish traditionalist.

There was a time when no serious gourmet would patronize a hotel dining room. Nowadays you can order some of your best cuisine in hotels, notably **Airds Hotel** in Port Appin where that grand delight of Scottish cuisine, Aberdeen Angus beef, is in partnership with roasted shallots, morels, leek confit, and a red-wine sauce.

Finally, the good news is that the word *eclectic* now describes many places in Scotland. Even bang-bang chicken turns up in unlikely dining rooms, fresh salads often are given a Thai kick with lime leaves and chile, and stir-fry and char-grill are standard features. Scots today can eat better than ever in their history. Burns would be shocked at some of the new taste sensations creative chefs are devising. But he would surely feel at home to learn that alcohol—especially whisky—is still a favored ingredient in many dishes and sauces.

Of course, it takes a wise chef to leave well enough alone, and many Scottish cooks know that the simplest dishes have never lost their appeal, especially if that means Lismore oysters or Loch Etive mussels. The Scots have always been good bakers, and many small tearooms still bake their own scones, buttery shortbread, and fruity breads. The heather honey is justly celebrated, and jams make use of Scotland's abundant harvest of soft fruit. Raspberries, for example, are said to be among the finest in the world.

You will most definitely want to try some of Scotland's excellent cheeses. The mild or mature cheddars are the best known. A famous hard cheese, Dunlop, comes from the Orkney Islands as well as Arran and Islay. One of the best-known cheeses from the Highlands is called Caboc, creamy and rich, formed into cork shapes and rolled in pinhead oatmeal. Many varieties of cottage cheese are flavored with herbs, chives, or garlic.

And yes, **haggis** is still Scotland's national dish—it's perhaps more symbolic than gustatory. One wit described this dish as a "castrated bagpipe." Regardless of what you might be told facetiously, haggis is not a bird. Therefore, you should turn down invitations—usually offered in pubs—to go on a midnight haggis hunt. Cooked in a sheep's paunch (nowadays more likely a plastic bag), it's made with bits and pieces of the lung, liver, and heart of sheep mixed with suet and spices, along with onions and oatmeal. It's often accompanied by single-malt whisky.

DINING HOURS   Although closings are getting later in the large cities, Scots tend to eat early. In some places, especially in the more affordable guesthouses and country hotels, dinner is served only between 7 and 8:30pm (no exceptions for latecomers). In major hotels in large cities, you can order dinner until 10:30pm, but rarely later. Some guesthouses or small hotels offer a "high tea" at around 6 or 6:30pm. This meal, found only in Scotland and northern England, consists of tea, bread, butter, jam, and cakes, as well as a cooked dish. Some places also serve a normal dinner later, but we guarantee you won't have room for it if you made the most of your "tea."

SINGLE-MALT OR BLEND?

"It is the only liquor fit for a gentleman to drink in the morning if he can have the good fortune to come by it . . . or after dinner either." Thus wrote Sir Walter Scott of the drink of his country—**scotch whisky.** Of course, if you're here, or for that matter almost anywhere in Britain or Europe, you don't have to identify it as scotch whisky when you order. That's what you'll get if you simply order whisky. In fact, in some parts of Scotland, England, and Wales, they look at you oddly if you order "scotch" as you probably do in the United States.

The true difference in the scotch whiskies you may have become accustomed to seeing on bars or shelves of liquor stores in the United States is whether they are blends or single-malt whiskies. Many connoisseurs prefer single-malts, whose tastes depend on their points of origin: Highlands, Lowlands, Islay, or Campbeltown on Kintyre. These are usually seen as "sipping whiskies," not to be mixed with water (well, maybe soda) and not to be served with ice. Many have come to be used as an after-dinner drink, served in a snifter like cognac.

The blended scotches came into being both because the single-malts were for a long time too harsh for delicate palates and because they were expensive and time-consuming to produce. A shortcut was developed: The clear and almost tasteless alcohol produced in the traditional way could be mixed with such ingredients as American corn, Finnish barley, Glasgow city tap water, and caramel coloring with a certain percentage of malt whiskies that flavored the entire bottle. Whichever you prefer, both the single-malts and the blends must be made within the borders of Scotland and then aged for at least 3 years before they can legally be called scotch whisky.

Two after-dinner drinks are scotch-based liqueurs—**Drambuie** and **Glayva.** The recipe for Drambuie, better known to Americans than Glayva, is supposed to have been given to its first producers, the Mackinnons of Strath on the Isle of Skye, by an impecunious guest, Bonnie Prince Charlie. The name of the drink is derived from the Gaelic *an dram buidheach,* meaning "a dram that satisfies."

The making of Scottish **beer**—the ales drunk by the common folk in earlier days— almost died out when palates became more adapted to scotch whisky and when a malt tax was levied in the 18th century, followed in the 19th century by beer duty. The brewing industry has made a comeback in the last quarter century, and Scottish beer, or "scotch ale," is being produced. Real **ale** is beer made from malted barley, hop flowers, yeast, and water, with a "fining" process (use of an extract from the swim bladders of certain fish) to complete the brewing. Ales are fermented in casks in a series of steps, and a product is now being turned out by Scotland's breweries. Scottish ale, either dark or light, is malty and full of flavor.

Scottish wine? It does exist, although growing grapes in a land of whipping winds and falling rain is not possible. Scots do, however, make wine from silver birch trees and Highland wildflowers. Clans supposedly jealously guarded their wine-making secrets for centuries.

One of the best wines is a crisp and dry brew, Silver Birch, always chilled and best served with wild salmon from Scottish rivers. Queen Victoria drank it because she'd heard that it prevented baldness. Sparkling Silver Birch is a brut bubbly. A country wine, Elderflower, is a medium-sweet white wine often consumed with desserts. Bramble wine (sometimes called Blaeberry) is a "bloody red" made from blackberries. Try it with Scottish venison or an Angus steak. The tayberry, a cross between a blackberry and a raspberry, produces a rather strong medium-dry wine of that name.

Curiosities are citrus wine, traditionally made from oranges and lemons grown in Scottish greenhouses, and "Crabbies," a green ginger wine said to date back to the time of the second Jacobite Rebellion of 1745. The brew is powerful and tart, a spicy elixir.

3 Planning a Trip to Scotland

After deciding where to go, most people have two fundamental questions: What will it cost? and How do I get there? This chapter will answer both these questions and also resolve other important issues such as when to go, what pretrip preparations are needed, where to obtain more information about the destination, and many more.

1 Information & Entry Requirements

VISITOR INFORMATION

To write for information before you go, contact Edinburgh and Scotland Information Centre, Waverley Market, 3 Princes St., Edinburgh EH2 2QP (☎ 0131/557-1700). If you're already in London and are contemplating a trip north, you can visit the Scottish Tourist Board, 19 Cockspur St., London SW1 Y5BL (☎ 0171/930-8661). Tube to Charing Cross or Piccadilly Circus. There are more than 170 tourist information centers in Scotland. All are well signposted in their cities or towns, but some are closed in winter.

IN NORTH AMERICA Before you go, you can obtain information from the **British Tourist Authority** in the United States: 551 Fifth Ave., Suite 701, New York, NY 10176-0799 (☎ 800/462-2748, or 212/986-2200 in New York).

In **Canada,** information is available at 111 Avenue Rd., Suite 450, Toronto, ON M5R 3J8 (☎ 888/847-4885 in Canada, or 416/925-6326 in Toronto). In **Australia,** the tourist authority is at Level 16, Gateway, 1 Macquarie Place, Sydney NSW 200 (☎ 02/9377-4400), and in **New Zealand** at Suite 305, Dilworth Building, Customs and Queen streets, Auckland 1 (☎ 09/303-1446).

The web site address for the British Tourist authority is http://www.visitbritain.com.

ENTRY REQUIREMENTS

DOCUMENTS All U.S. citizens, Canadians, Australians, New Zealanders, and South Africans must have a passport with at least 2 months' remaining validity. No visa is required. The immigration office may also want proof of your intention to return to your point of origin (usually a round-trip ticket) and visible means of support while you're in Britain.

CUSTOMS   For the visitor to **Scotland,** goods fall into two basic categories—those purchased in a non–European Union (EU) country or bought tax-free within the EU, and those purchased and tax paid in the EU. Limits on imports by individuals (17 and older) include 200 cigarettes (or 50 cigars or 250 grams of loose tobacco), 2 liters of still table wine, 1 liter of liquor (more than 22% alcohol content), and 2 fluid ounces of perfume. From EU countries, an individual may import 800 cigarettes, 200 cigars, and 1 kilogram of loose tobacco; 90 liters of wine, 10 liters of alcohol (over 22%), and 110 liters of beer; plus unlimited amounts of perfume.

Once every 30 days, citizens of the **United States** who have been out of the country at least 48 hours or more are allowed to bring back $400 worth of merchandise duty-free. You'll be charged a flat rate of 10% on the next $1,000 worth of purchases. Be sure to keep your receipts handy. You may also mail back duty-free gifts worth up to $100. For more specific guidance, write to the U.S. Customs Service, P.O. Box 7407, Washington, DC 20004 (☎ 202/927-6724), requesting the free pamphlet "Know Before You Go." You can also find information on the department's web site at http://www.customs.ustreas.gov.

For a summary of the **Canadian** rules, write for the booklet "I Declare," issued by Revenue Canada, 2265 St. Laurent Blvd., Ottawa, ON K1G 4KE (☎ 800/461-9999 in Canada, or 613/993-0534). Canada allows its citizens a $300 exemption, and they can bring back duty-free 200 cigarettes, 2.2 pounds of tobacco, 40 imperial ounces of liquor, and 50 cigars. In addition, you are allowed to mail gifts to Canada from abroad valued at Can. $60 a day, provided they aren't alcohol or tobacco (write on the package: UNSOLICITED GIFT, UNDER $60 VALUE). All your valuables should be declared on Form Y-38 before you leave Canada, including serial numbers (for example, expensive foreign cameras). *Note:* The $300 exemption can be used only once a year and only after an absence of 7 days.

The duty-free allowance in **Australia** is A. $400 or, for those under 18, A. $200. Citizens can bring home 250 cigarettes or 250 grams of loose tobacco and 1 liter of alcohol. If you're returning with valuable goods you already own, such as foreign-made cameras, you should file Form B263. Personal property mailed back from Britain should be marked AUSTRALIAN GOODS RETURNED to avoid payment of duty. A helpful brochure, available from Australian consulates or Customs offices, is "Customs Information for All Travellers." For more information, contact Collector of Customs, GPO Box 8, Sydney, NSW 2001, Australia (☎ 02/226-5997).

The duty-free allowance for **New Zealand** is N.Z. $700. Citizens over 17 years of age can bring in 200 cigarettes *or* 250 grams of loose tobacco *or* 50 cigars (or a mixture of all three if their weight does not exceed 250 grams), and 4.5 liters of wine or beer *or* 1.125 liters of liquor. A Certificate of Export listing foreign-made valuables taken out of the country allows you to bring them back without paying duty. Most questions are answered in a free pamphlet, "New Zealand Customs Guide for Travellers," Notice No. 4, available at New Zealand consulates and Customs offices. More information is available by contacting New Zealand Customs, 50 Anzac Ave., P.O. Box 29, Auckland, New Zealand (☎ 09/377-35-20).

2 Money

CURRENCY/CASH   The currency of Britain is the **pound sterling (£),** made up of 100 **pence (p).** Scotland issues its own pound notes, but English and Scottish money is interchangeable. Pence come in 1p, 2p, 5p, 10p, 50p, and £1 coins. Notes are issued in £1, £5, £10, and £50 denominations.

The Pound & the Dollar

At this writing, $1 equals approximately 61 pence (or £1 = U.S. $1.65), and this was the rate of exchange used to calculate the dollar values given in this guide (rounded to the nearest nickel). This rate fluctuates from time to time, and may not be the same when you travel to Scotland, so use the table below only as a general guide.

Note: You read £7.50 as 7 pounds, 50 pence.

U.S.$	UK £	U.S.$	UK £
0.25	0.16	15	9.75
0.50	0.33	20	13.00
0.75	0.49	25	16.25
1.00	0.65	50	32.50
2.00	1.30	75	48.75
3.00	1.95	100	65.00
4.00	2.60	150	97.50
5.00	3.25	200	130.00
6.00	3.90	250	162.50
7.00	4.55	300	195.00
8.00	5.20	350	227.50
9.00	5.85	400	260.00
10.00	6.50	500	325.00

CURRENCY EXCHANGE For the best exchange rate, go to a bank, not to a hotel or shop. Traveler's checks can also be changed at the airport and some travel agencies, such as American Express and Thomas Cook. Note the rates; it can sometimes pay to shop around.

CREDIT & CHARGE CARDS Major credit and charge cards are widely accepted in Scotland, although you should be warned that some of the low-cost establishments, especially outside urban areas, do not accept them. **Visa** is the most widely used card, along with **EuroCard** (the same as **MasterCard**). **American Express** is often accepted, mostly in the middle- and upper-bracket category. **Diners Club** is the least accepted of the "big four." Discover is not used in Europe.

Remember that credit- and charge-card companies base the rate of exchange on the date the charge is posted, not on the date you actually made the transaction.

TRAVELER'S CHECKS Traveler's checks are the most convenient way to carry cash while traveling. Most banks will give you a better exchange rate for traveler's checks than for cash. If you can, purchase them in pound denominations.

A recent survey of various exchange facilities conducted by *Time Out* found American Express (☎ 800/221-7282 in the U.S. or Canada) to have the lowest commission on dollar transactions. Holders of certain types of American Express cards may not be charged commission at all. The company issues checks denominated in U.S. dollars, Canadian dollars, and British pound sterling. For questions or problems that arise outside North America, contact any of the company's many regional representatives.

What Things Cost in Edinburgh	U.S.$
Taxi from the airport to the city center	23.10
Local telephone call	.15
Double room at the Caledonian Hotel (expensive)	334.40
Double room at the 17 Abercromby Place (moderate)	144.00
Double room at the A Haven (inexpensive)	96.00
Continental breakfast in a hotel	9.90
Lunch for one at the Indian Cavalry Club (moderate)	15.00
Lunch for one at Henderson's (inexpensive)	8.00
Dinner for one, without wine, at Pompadour (expensive)	75.00
Dinner for one, without wine, at Cosmo (moderate)	35.00
Dinner for one, without wine, at The Baked Potato Shop (inexpensive)	10.00
Pint of beer	2.95
Coca-Cola	1.65
Cup of coffee	1.65
Roll of ASA 100 color film, 36 exposures	9.50
Admission to Palace of Holyroodhouse	8.80
Movie ticket	7.45
Theater ticket at King's Theatre	8.00–36.00

Citicorp (☎ **800/645-6556** in the U.S. and Canada, or 813/623-1709, collect, from anywhere else in the world) issues checks in U.S. dollars, British pounds, German marks, Japanese yen, and Australian dollars.

Thomas Cook (☎ **800/223-7373** in the U.S., or 609/987-7300, collect, from anywhere else in the world) issues MasterCard traveler's checks denominated in U.S. dollars, British pounds, and other currencies.

Interpayment Services (☎ **800/221-2426** in the U.S. and Canada, or 212/858-8500, collect, from anywhere else in the world) sells Visa checks that are issued by a consortium of member banks and the Thomas Cook organization. Traveler's checks are denominated in U.S. dollars, Canadian dollars, British pounds, and German marks.

Issuers sometimes have agreements with groups to sell checks commission-free. For example, the American Automobile Association (AAA) clubs sell American Express checks in several currencies without commission.

PREPAYING IN BRITISH CURRENCY It's often cheaper and easier to prepay a deposit on a hotel reservation with a check drawn on a British bank. This can be arranged by a large commercial bank or by a currency specialist such as **Ruesch International,** 700 11th St. NW, Washington, DC 20001-4507 (☎ **800/424-2923** or 202/408-1200). To place an order, call them and tell them the type and amount of the sterling-denominated check you need. Ruesch will quote a U.S. dollar equivalent, adding a $3 fee per check as their service charge. After receiving your dollar-denominated personal check for the agreed-upon amount, Ruesch will mail you a sterling-denominated bank draft, drawn on a British bank and payable to the party

What Things Cost in Inverness	U.S.$
Average taxi ride in the city center	5.75
Local telephone call	.15
Double room at the Culloden House (expensive)	338.50
Double room at the Kingsmill (moderate)	206.25
Double room at the Ballifeary (inexpensive)	112.20
Continental breakfast in a hotel	7.45
Lunch for one at Bunchrew House Hotel and Restaurant (moderate)	24.75
Lunch for one at Café 1 (inexpensive)	11.45
Dinner for one, without wine, at the Culloden House (expensive)	57.75
Dinner for one, without wine, at the Riviera (moderate)	35.00
Dinner for one, without wine, at Dickens International Restaurant (inexpensive)	16.50
Pint of beer	2.90
Coca-Cola	1.30
Cup of coffee	1.30
Roll of ASA 100 color film, 36 exposures	5.00
Admission to Culloden Battlefield	2.60
Movie ticket	7.00
Theater ticket to Eden Court Theatre	13.50–41.25

specified. Ruesch also converts checks in foreign currency into U.S. dollars, provides foreign currencies in cash, and sells traveler's checks payable in pounds sterling and other currencies. In addition to its Washington, D.C., office, Ruesch maintains offices in New York, Los Angeles, Chicago, Atlanta, and Boston. It has a London office: Ruesch International Ltd., 18 Savile Row, London W1X 2AD (☎ 0171/734-2300). Any of these offices can supply, through phone or mail orders, the bank draft and traveler's check services mentioned above.

ATMs   You can withdraw sterling from bank cash machines at many locations in Scotland. When using an ATM abroad, the money will be in local currency; the rate of exchange tends to be as good, if not better, than what you would receive at an airport money counter or a hotel. Note that international withdrawal fees will be higher than domestic—ask your bank for specifics. Also, check to see if your PIN code must be reprogrammed for usage in Scotland. Most ATMs outside the United States require a four-digit PIN number.

   To receive a directory of **Cirrus** ATMs, call ☎ 800/424-7787; for **Plus** locations, call ☎ 800/843-7587. You can also access the Visa/PLUS International ATM Locator Guide through the Internet: http://www.visa.com/visa.

MONEYGRAM   If you find yourself out of money, a wire service provided by American Express can help you tap willing friends and family for emergency funds. Through **MoneyGram,** 6200 S. Québec St., P.O. Box 5118, Englewood, CO 80155 (☎ 800/926-9400), money can be sent around the world in less than 10 minutes. Senders should call AMEX to learn the address of the closest outlet that handles

MoneyGrams. Cash, credit card (MasterCard or Visa), or the occasional personal check (with ID) are acceptable forms of payment. AMEX's fee for the service is $10 for the first $300 with a sliding scale for larger sums. The service includes a short telex message. The beneficiary must present a photo ID at the outlet where money is received.

3 When to Go

CLIMATE Weather is of vital concern in Scotland. It can seriously affect your travel plans.

The Lowlands of Scotland usually have a moderate year-round temperature. In spring, the average temperature is 53°F, rising to about 65° average in summer. By the time the crisp autumn has arrived, the temperatures have dropped to spring levels. In winter the average temperature is 43°F. Temperatures in the north of Scotland are lower, especially in winter, and you should dress accordingly. It rains a lot in Scotland, but perhaps not as much as age-old myths would have it: The rainfall in Edinburgh is exactly the same as that in London. September can be the sunniest month.

Edinburgh's Average Daytime Temperature & Days of Rain

	Jan	Feb	Mar	Apr	May	June	July	Aug	Sept	Oct	Nov	Dec
Temp. (°F)	38	38	41	45	50	56	58	58	55	50	42	40
Days of Rain	12	11	11	12	12	10	10	13	11	12	13	13

Glasgow & Central Scotland's Average Daytime Temperature & Days of Rain

	Jan	Feb	Mar	Apr	May	June	July	Aug	Sept	Oct	Nov	Dec
Temp. (°F)	37	37	40	44	51	58	62	59	55	49	41	39
Days of Rain	11	13	14	13	14	15	16	15	12	14	13	13

HOLIDAYS The following holidays are celebrated in Scotland: New Year's (Jan 1–2), Good Friday and Easter Monday, May Day (May 1), spring bank holiday (last Monday in May), summer bank holiday (first Monday in August), Christmas Day (Dec 25), and Boxing Day (Dec 26).

SCOTLAND CALENDAR OF EVENTS

January

- **Burns Night,** in Ayr (near his birthplace), and also at his favorite towns of Dumfries and Edinburgh. Naturally, during the celebrations there are many toasts with scotch and the eating of the haggis, whose arrival is announced by a bagpipe. For more information, call ☎ **01292/288688** in Ayr, **0131/557-5118** in Edinburgh, or **01387/253862** in Dumfries. January 24.
- **Up Helly Aa,** Lerwick, in the Shetland Islands. The most northerly town in Great Britain still clings to tradition by staging an ancient Norse fire festival whose aim is to encourage the return of the sun after the pitch-dark days of winter. Its highlight is the burning of a replica of a Norse longboat. For more information, call ☎ **01595/693434** in Lerwick. Last Tuesday in January.

February

- **Aberdeen Angus Cattle Show,** Perth. Staged early in the north, this show draws the finest cattle raised in Scotland. Sales are lively. For more information, call ☎ **01738/638353** in Perth.

March
- **Whuppity Scourie,** Lanark, in the Strathclyde district. Residents get so tired of winter that they stage this traditional ceremony to chase it away. For more information, call ☎ **01555/661661** in Lanark. March 1.
- **Annual Drama Festival,** Tobermory, on the Isle of Mull. This cultural event draws some of Britain's finest theatrical talent. For more information, call ☎ **01688/302182** in Tobermory. Last week of March.

April
- **Hamilton Flat Races,** Hamilton, near Glasgow, in the Strathclyde district. For more information, call ☎ **0141/204-4400** in Glasgow.
- **Kate Kennedy Procession and Pageant,** St. Andrews, in eastern Scotland. This historic university pageant is staged annually in the university city of St. Andrews. For more information, call ☎ **01334/472021** in St. Andrews.

May
- **Scottish Motorcycle Trials,** Fort William. The trials are run for 6 days at the beginning of the month, drawing aficionados from all over Europe. Phone ☎ **01397/703781** in Fort William for more information. Early May.
- **Ayr Music Festival,** Ayr. This is the major cultural event on the Ayr calendar, attracting an array of classical talent from all over Scotland. Phone ☎ **01292/288688** in Ayr for more information.
- **Pitlochry Theatre Festival,** Pitlochry. Scotland's "theater in the hills" launches its season in mid-May. Call ☎ **01796/472215** in Pitlochry for more information. Mid-May to October.

June
- **Lanimer Day,** Lanark. This week of festivities has a ritual procession around the town's boundaries, the election of a Lanimer Queen and a Cornet King, and a parade with floats, along with Highland dances and bagpipe playing. Call ☎ **01555/661661** for more information. The Thursday between June 6 and 12.
- **Guid Nychtburris,** Dumfries. This age-old festival is an event similar to, but a less impressive festival than, the Selkirk Common Riding (see below). Mid-June.
- ✪ **Selkirk Common Riding.** This is the most elaborate and impressive display of horsemanship in Scotland, celebrating Selkirk's losses in the 1560 Battle of Flodden—only one Selkirk soldier returned alive from the battle to warn the town before dropping dead in the marketplace. Some 400 horses and riders parade through the streets. A young unmarried male of the town is crowned at the sound of the cornet, representing the soldier who sounded the alarm. Call ☎ **01750/20054** in Selkirk for more information. The second Friday following the first Monday in June.
- **Beltane Day,** Peebles. A town "Cornet" rides around to see that the boundaries are safe from the "invading" English, a young girl is elected Festival Queen, and her court is filled with courtiers, swordbearers, guards, and attendants. Children of the town dress in costumes for parade floats through the streets. Call ☎ **01721/720138** in Peebles for more information. The third week in June, beginning the Wednesday before Midsummer Day (June 22).

July
- **Promenade Concerts,** Glasgow. These concerts by the Scottish National Orchestra are given at Kelvin Hall weekly throughout the rest of the summer. Phone ☎ **0141/204-4400** in Glasgow for more information. Early July to August.

- **Folk Festival,** Glasgow. Some of the finest Scottish folk music can be heard here at one of the best—and best-attended—Scottish folk festivals. Phone ☎ **0141/ 204-4400** in Glasgow for more information. Second week of July.

August

- **Lammas Fair,** St. Andrews, in eastern Scotland. This is a medieval market. Phone ☎ **01334/472021** in St. Andrews for more information. Second Monday and Tuesday of August.
- **World Pipe Band Championships,** Glasgow. Phone ☎ **0141/204-4400** in Glasgow for more information. Mid-August.
- **Highland Games and Gatherings,** at various venues throughout the country, including Aberfeldy, Perth, Crieff, Ballater, Oban, and Portree on the Isle of Skye. More details are available from the Edinburgh and Scotland Information Centre (see "Visitor Information" in "Information & Entry Requirements," earlier in this chapter). Throughout August.

September

- **Ben Nevis Mountain Race,** Fort William, in the Highlands. Phone ☎ **01397/ 703781** in Fort William for more information. First Saturday in September.
- ✪ **Highland Games & Gathering in Braemar.** The queen and many members of the royal family often show up for this annual event, with its massed bands, piping and dancing competitions, and performances of great strength by a tribe of gigantic men. Write the tourist office in Braemar, The Mews, Mar Road, Braemar, Aberdeenshire, AB35 5YP, or phone ☎ **013397/41600** about tickets and actual dates. First Saturday in September.

October

- **Highland Autumn Cattle Show,** Oban, in western Scotland. Phone ☎ **01631/ 563122** in Oban for more information. Mid-October.

November

- **Christmas Shopping Festival,** Aberdeen. For those who want to shop early for Christmas. Phone ☎ **01224/632727** in Aberdeen for more information. Third week of November to December.
- **International St. Andrews Day Dinner,** St. Andrews, in eastern Scotland. Only Scottish specialties are served, of course. Phone ☎ **01334/472021** in St. Andrews for more details. November 30.

December

- **Flambeaux Procession,** Comrie, Tayside. A torchlight parade on New Year's Eve. December 31.

EDINBURGH CALENDAR OF EVENTS

March

- **Edinburgh Folk Festival,** at various venues. For more information on this feast of Scottish folk tunes, call ☎ **0131/557-5118.** Late March.

April

- **Exhibitions at the Royal Scottish Academy.** Changing exhibitions of international interest are offered here annually. For more information, call ☎ **0131/ 557-5118.** Mid-April.

June

- **Royal Highland Show,** at the Ingliston Showground on the outskirts of Edinburgh. This show is devoted to agriculture and commerce. Mid-June.

August

○ **Edinburgh Festival.** This, the best-known festival in Scotland, is held for 3 weeks in late summer (more about this in the chapter on Scotland's capital). Called an "arts bonanza," it draws major talent from around the world. More than a thousand shows are presented and a million tickets are sold. Book, jazz, and film festivals are also staged at this time, but nothing tops the Military Tattoo against the backdrop of spotlit Edinburgh Castle. For information about tickets and the various events presented every year, write the Festival Society, 21 Market St., Edinburgh, Scotland EH1 1BW, or phone ☎ **0131/473-2001.** Three weeks in August (dates vary).

November

• **Winter Antiques Fair.** This fair draws dealers and buyers from all over Europe and America. For more information, call ☎ **0131/557-5118.** Third week in November.

4 Health & Insurance

HEALTH

If you suffer from a chronic illness, talk to your doctor before taking the trip. For such conditions as epilepsy, diabetes, or a heart condition, wear a **Medic Alert** emblem on a bracelet or necklace. This not only alerts doctors to your condition but also provides the number of Medic Alert's 24-hour hotline so that a foreign doctor can obtain your medical records. The initial cost is $35; thereafter, there's a $15 annual fee. Contact the Medic Alert Foundation, 2323 Colorado Ave., Turlock, CA 95382 (☎ **800/825-3785**).

Before you leave home, you can obtain a list of doctors in Scotland from the **International Association for Medical Assistance to Travelers (IAMAT),** 417 Center St., Lewiston, NY 14092 (☎ **716/754-4883**); or 40 Regal Rd., Guelph, ON N1K 1B5 (☎ **519/836-0102**).

It's a good idea to bring along enough prescribed medications to sustain you during your stay. Take along copies of your prescriptions written in the generic—not brand-name—form.

INSURANCE

HEALTH   Before leaving home, check to see if your health coverage extends to Europe. If it doesn't or if the coverage is inadequate, consider purchasing short-term travel insurance that will cover medical emergencies. Remember that Medicare covers U.S. citizens while traveling outside the United States in Mexico and Canada only. *Note:* U.S. visitors who become ill while in Britain are only eligible for free *emergency* care. For other treatment, including postemergency care, you will be asked to pay.

LOSS & THEFT   Check your homeowner's or renter's insurance for coverage for off-premises theft. If you need more coverage, consider a short-term policy.

TRIP CANCELLATION   If you're traveling as part of a tour or are taking a charter or any other flight that has cancellation penalties, or if you've prepaid your vacation expenses, you may also want to purchase insurance that covers you if you have to cancel for any reason. However, your credit- or charge-card company may provide cancellation coverage if you have used your card to pay for your trip.

AUTOMOBILE   If you're going to rent a car while in Scotland, check to see whether your automobile insurance, automobile club, or credit/charge card covers personal accident insurance (PAI), the collision-damage waiver (CDW), or other insurance options. You may be able to avoid added charges by the car-rental companies if you're already covered.

TRAVEL CLUBS   If you belong to a travel club, inquire about the insurance coverage or options to which your membership entitles you.

Documentation   Note that to submit any claim, you must always have thorough documentation—including all receipts, police reports, medical records, and the like.

INSURANCE COMPANIES   The following insurance companies, among others, offer policies of particular interest to travelers:

Access America, 6600 W. Broad St., Richmond, VA 23230 (☎ **800/284-8300**), offers a comprehensive travel insurance and assistance package, including medical expenses, on-the-spot hospital payments, medical transportation, baggage insurance, trip cancellation/interruption insurance, and collision-damage insurance for a car rental. Their 24-hour hotline connects you to multilingual coordinators who can offer advice and help on medical, legal, and travel problems. Varying coverage levels are available.

Healthcare Abroad (MEDEX), c/o Wallach and Co., 107 W. Federal St. (P.O. Box 480), Middleburg, VA 20118-0480 (☎ **800/237-6615** or 540/687-3166), offers coverage for between 10 and 120 days at $4 per day; this policy includes accident and sickness coverage to the tune of $250,000. Medical evacuation is also included, along with a $25,000 accidental death and dismemberment compensation. Provisions for trip cancellation can also be written into this policy at a nominal cost.

Travelex, P.O. Box 9408, Garden City, NJ 11530-9408 (☎ **800/228-9792**), offers a comprehensive coverage plan that costs $49 for a 3-week period. The plan includes trip delay, itinerary changes, delay or loss of baggage, accident and medical coverage, emergency medical evacuation, and a travel assistance hotline for anything that may come up during your trip. Trip cancellation protection is not part of the plan, but may be added for an additional $6 per $100 of coverage.

Travel Insured International, Travel Insurance Division, P.O. Box 280568, East Hartford, CT 06128-0568 (☎ **800/243-3174**), offers travel accident and illness coverage starting at $10 for 6 to 10 days; $500 worth of coverage for lost, damaged, or delayed baggage costs $20 for 6 to 10 days; and trip cancellation costs $5.50 for each $100 worth of coverage. The insurance is underwritten by The Travelers.

Travel Guard International, 1145 Clark St., Stevens Point, WI 54481 (☎ **800/826-1300**), offers a comprehensive policy starting as low as $40 that covers basically everything: emergency assistance, accidental death, trip cancellation and interruption, medical coverage abroad, lost luggage, bankruptcy and financial default, and a 24-hour worldwide emergency hotline.

5 Tips for Travelers with Special Needs

FOR PEOPLE WITH DISABILITIES   Many agencies can provide advance-planning information. Knowing in advance which hotels, restaurants, and attractions are wheelchair accessible can save you a lot of frustration. There are some companies that offer tours specifically designed for such travelers. Contact the **Travel Information Service,** Moss Rehab Hospital, 1200 W. Tabor Rd., Philadelphia, PA 19141 (☎ 215/456-9603 or 215/456-9602 for TTY), for names and addresses of accessible hotels, restaurants, and attractions, often based on firsthand reports of travelers who've been there.

You can also obtain a copy of **"Air Transportation of Handicapped Persons,"** published by the U.S. Department of Transportation. It's free if you write to Free Advisory Circular No. 12032, Distribution Unit, U.S. Department of Transportation, Publications Division, M-4332, Washington, DC 20590.

You may also want to consider joining a tour of visitors with disabilities. Names and addresses of such tour operators can be obtained by contacting the **Society for the Advancement of Travel for the Handicapped,** 347 Fifth Ave., Suite 610, New York, NY 10016 (☎ 212/447-7284; fax 212/725-8253). Yearly membership dues are $45 for adults or $30 for senior citizens and students. This fee includes quarterly issues of *Open World* magazine, which features articles of interest to travelers with disabilities.

FEDCAP Rehabilitation Services (formerly known as the Federation of the Handicapped), 211 W. 14th St., New York, NY 10011 (☎ 212/727-4200; fax 212/721-4374), operates summer tours to Europe and elsewhere for its members.

For those with visual impairments, the best information source is the **American Foundation for the Blind,** 11 Penn Plaza, Suite 300, New York, NY 10001 (☎ 800/232-5463).

The **Information Center for Individuals with Disabilities,** Fort Point Place, 27–43 Wormwood St., Boston, MA 02210 (☎ 617/727-5540; fax 617/345-5318), is another good source. It has lists of travel agents who specialize in tours for people with disabilities.

Flying Wheels Travel, 143 West Bridge (P.O. Box 382), Owatonna, MN 55060 (☎ 800/525-6790), offers various escorted tours and cruises internationally. It's one of the best organizations serving the needs of those who use wheelchairs and walkers.

Mobility International USA, P.O. Box 10767, Eugene, OR 97440 (☎ 541/343-1284 voice and TDD; fax 541/343-6812), answers questions on various destinations and also offers discounts on videos, publications, and programs it sponsors.

In the U.K. The **Royal Association for Disability and Rehabilitation (RADAR)** publishes two annual holiday guides for those with disabilities: "European Holidays and Travel Abroad" and "Long Haul Holidays and Travel"; both are £5. RADAR (whose patroness is Elizabeth, the Queen Mother) also provides a number of holiday fact sheets on such subjects as sports and outdoor holidays, insurance, financial arrangements for persons with disabilities, and accommodations with nursing-care units for groups or for the elderly. Each of these fact sheets is available for 75p. Fact sheets or the above-mentioned holiday guides can be mailed outside the U.K. for a nominal mailing fee. You can also call the information desk (☎ 0171/250-3222) with questions.

Another good resource is the **Holiday Care Service,** Imperial Building, 2nd Floor, Victoria Road, Horley, Surrey RH6 7PZ (☎ 01293/774535 or fax 01293/784647), a national charity that advises on accessible accommodations for the elderly and persons with disabilities. Annual membership costs £25. Once you're a member, you can receive a newsletter and access to a free reservations network for hotels throughout Britain and—to a lesser degree—Europe.

The **Air Transport Users' Council,** 5th Floor, Kingsway House, 103 Kingsway, London WC2B 6QX (☎ 0171/242-3882), publishes a free pamphlet called "Flight Plan," which is full of good information for those with or without impairments.

FOR SENIORS Be sure to ask for senior-citizen discounts at attractions, and have your identification ready as proof. Educational programs specially designed for seniors, as well as cruises and tours, are available.

SAGA International Holidays, 222 Berkeley St., Boston, MA 02116 (☎ 800/ 343-0273), runs all-inclusive tours and cruises for seniors 50 years or older.

In the United States, the best organization to join is the **American Association of Retired Persons (AARP),** 601 E St. NW, Washington, DC 20049 (☎ 202/ 434-AARP). Members are offered discounts on car rentals and hotels.

Information is also available from the **National Council of Senior Citizens,** 8403 Colesville Rd., Suite 1200, Silver Springs, MD 20910 (☎ 301/578-8800). A nonprofit organization, the council charges $12 annually per person/couple, for which you receive a magazine six times a year and membership benefits. Discounts on hotel and auto rentals are provided, as well as a discount pharmacy program and accidental death insurance.

Elderhostel, 75 Federal St., Boston, MA 02110-1941 (☎ 617/426-8056), offers senior citizens an array of university-based summer educational programs throughout the world, including England and Scotland. Most courses last around 3 weeks and are remarkable values, considering that airfare, accommodations in student dormitories or modest inns, all meals, and tuition are included. Courses include field trips, involve no homework, are ungraded, and emphasize the liberal arts. Participants must be over 55. Meals consist of solid, no-frills fare typical of educational institutions worldwide. The program provides a safe and congenial environment for single "golden girls," who make up some 64% of the enrollment.

Mature Outlook, P.O. Box 9390, Des Moines, IA 50306-9519 (☎ 800/ 336-6330; fax 847/286-5024), is a travel organization for people over 50 years of age. Members are offered discounts at ITC-member hotels and receive a bimonthly magazine. The annual membership of $14.95 to $19.95 entitles members to discounts and in some cases free coupons for discounted merchandise from Sears Roebuck & Co. Savings are also offered on selected auto rentals and restaurants.

For a free copy of **"101 Tips for the Mature Traveler,"** contact Grand Circle Travel, 347 Congress St., Suite 3A, Boston, MA 02210 (☎ 800/221-2610 or 617/ 350-7500; fax 617/350-6206). This travel agency also offers escorted tours and cruises for seniors.

FOR SINGLE TRAVELERS Unfortunately for the millions of single Americans, the travel industry is geared to duos. Singles often wind up paying the penalty. It pays to travel with someone and split accommodations costs. There are, of course, dynamic and action-packed tours and vacations designed for the unattached, as well as companies that will match you with a compatible traveling partner.

Travel Companion Exchange, P.O. Box P-833, Amityville, NY 11701 (☎ 516/ 454-0880), matches single travelers with like-minded companions. It's headed by Jens Jurgen, who charges $99 for an 8-month listing in his well-publicized records. People seeking travel companions fill out forms stating their preferences and needs and receive a minilisting of potential travel partners. Companions of the same or opposite sex can be requested. A bimonthly newsletter averaging 49 large pages also gives numerous money-saving travel tips of special interest to solo travelers. A sample copy is available for $6. For an application and more information, contact Jens Jurgen at the address above.

Cosmos, with offices at 5301 S. Federal Circle, Littleton, CO 80123 (☎ 800/ 851-0728; fax 303/347-0665), offers a "guaranteed-share plan"—that is, it agrees to locate a single traveler of the same gender for you to cut down on the hefty price tags charged as single supplements.

FOR FAMILIES Advance planning is the key to a successful overseas family vacation.

Farmhouse Holidays

One unusual way to learn to understand the agricultural roots of Scotland is to overnight on a Scottish farm. **Scottish Farmhouse Holidays,** Drumtenant, Ladybank, Fife KY15 7UG (☎ **01337/830451;** fax 01337/831301), will find you an appropriate croft. The company was established in 1982 by Scots-born Jane Buchanan, who describes herself as a farmer's daughter, a farmer's wife, a businesswoman steeped in both agriculture and tourism, and a former exchange student with 4H programs in Michigan and Utah. The company was established in 1982 by Scots-born Jane Buchanan.

Only family-managed working farms are selected for the program, most within easy driving distance of at least a handful of historic sites. Many (but not all) of the farmhouses are at least a century old, and many have been in the same family for several generations. Rates for bed and breakfast in bathless rooms are £15 to £16 ($24.75 to $26.40), whereas rates for dinner, bed, and breakfast run £20 to £26 ($33 to $42.90), depending on the establishment. Rooms with private bath (toilet and tub or shower) are available for a supplement of £7 ($11.55) per person. Occupants of single rooms usually pay a supplement of £7 ($11.55) as well. If you're interested, the most reliable way to make a booking is to call the number given above. A free brochure is available.

On airlines, a special menu for children must be requested at least 24 hours in advance. If baby food is required, you must bring your own and ask a flight attendant to warm it to the right temperature.

Make advance arrangements for cribs, bottle warmers, and car seats if you're driving anywhere (in Scotland, small children aren't allowed to ride in the front seat).

Many hotels will be able to find you a baby-sitter. For accommodations, meals, and attractions, be sure to read the "Family Friendly" features in this guide.

Family Travel Times is published four times a year by TWYCH, Travel With Your Children, and includes a weekly call-in service for subscribers. Subscriptions cost $40 a year and can be ordered by writing to TWYCH, 40 Fifth Ave., New York, NY 10011 (☎ 212/477-5524; fax 212/477-5173). TWYCH also publishes several books that are helpful to parents who want to travel with their children. An information packet describing TWYCH's publications, including a recent sample issue, is available by sending $2 to the above address. You can also contact the **Family Travel Forum,** 891 Amsterdam Ave., New York, NY 10025 (☎ **212/666-6124**), for a newsletter and information about traveling with children.

FOR STUDENTS   The **International Student Identity Card (ISIC)** is good for discounts on travel fares and attractions. Youth hostels provide an inexpensive network of accommodations while trekking through the country.

Council Travel, a subsidiary of the Council on International Educational Exchange, with headquarters at 205 E. 42nd St., New York, NY 10017 (☎ **800/ 2-COUNCIL** or 212/822-2700), is America's largest student, youth, and budget travel group, with more than 60 offices worldwide. International Student Identity Cards (ISIC) are available to all bona-fide students from any Council Travel office for $19 and entitle the holder to generous travel and other discounts.

Discounted international and domestic air tickets are available with special prices for student and youth travelers. Eurotrain rail passes, YHA passes, weekend packages, overland safaris, and hostel/hotel accommodations are all bookable from Council Travel.

The **International Youth Hostel Federation (IYHF)** was designed to provide bare-bones overnight accommodations for serious budget-conscious travelers. For information, contact Hosteling International American Youth Hostels (HI-AYH), 733 15th St. NW, Suite 840, Washington, DC 20005 (☎ **202/783-6161**). Membership costs $25 annually; those under 18 pay $10, and those 55 and over pay $15.

FOR GAY MEN & LESBIANS   Bars, clubs, restaurants, and hotels catering to gays are confined almost exclusively to Edinburgh, Glasgow, and Inverness. Call the **Edinburgh Gay and Lesbian Switchboard** (☎ **0131/556-4049**) for information about local events.

Scotland is not much of a gay scene. Gay-bashing happens, especially in the grimy industrial sections of Glasgow, where neo-Nazi skinheads hang out. Though a crime, it's rarely punished. Open displays of affection between same-sex couples usually invite scorn in rural Scotland, although there is none of the fanatical homophobia that's so prevalent among the lunatic fringe in the United States.

Ironically, for men the legal age for consensual homosexual activity is 18; however, for straights and lesbians it's only 16. You figure that one!

Publications   The best general guide for gay men traveling abroad is *Spartacus International* ($32.95). More focused on the British Isles is the first edition of *Spartacus: Britain and Ireland* ($24.95), which is useful to both gay men and lesbians. Lesbians might also find Ferrari Guides' *Women's Travel in Your Pocket* ($14) to be informative, as well as *Women Going Places: A Woman's Guide to International Travel* ($14), which has a well-researched section on Scotland by an experienced traveler. These books and others are available from **Giovanni's Room,** 1145 Pine St., Philadelphia, PA 19107 (☎ **215/923-2960;** fax 215/923-0813).

Our World, 1104 N. Nova Rd., Suite 251, Daytona Beach, FL 32117 (☎ **904/441-5367** or fax 904/441-5604), is a magazine devoted to gay and lesbian travel worldwide. It costs $35 for 10 issues. *Out & About,* 8 W. 19th St., Suite 401, New York, NY 10011 (☎ **800/929-2268** or fax 800/929-2215), has been hailed for its "straight" reporting about gay travel. It profiles the best gay or gay-friendly hotels, gyms, clubs, and other places. It costs $49 a year for 10 issues. It's aimed at the more upscale gay traveler and has been praised by everybody from *Travel & Leisure* to the *New York Times.*

Organizations   The **International Gay and Lesbian Travel Association (IGLTA),** 4331 N. Federal Hwy., Suite 304, Fort Lauderdale, FL 33308 (☎ **954/776-2626;** fax 954/776-3303), is an international network of travel-industry businesses and professionals who encourage gay/lesbian travel worldwide. With around 1,600 members, it offers quarterly newsletters, marketing mailings, and a membership directory that's updated four times a year. Membership often includes gay or lesbian businesses, but is open to individuals as well for $150 yearly, plus a $100 administration fee for new members. Members are kept informed of gay or gay-friendly hoteliers, tour operators, airline and cruise-line representatives, and also ancillary businesses such as the contacts at travel guide publishers and gay-related travel clubs.

Travel Agencies   **Our Family Abroad,** 40 W. 57th St., Suite 430, New York, NY 10019 (☎ **800/999-5500** or 212/459-1800), operates escorted tours that include about a dozen itineraries through Europe. Tour guides are gay-friendly and gay comfortable.

In California, a leading gay-friendly option for travel arrangements is **Above and Beyond,** 330 Townsend St., Suite 107, San Francisco, CA 94107 (☎ **800/397-2681** or 415/284-1666; fax 415/284-1660).

Also in California, **Skylink Women's Travel,** 3577 Moorland Ave., Santa Rosa, CA 95407 (☎ **800/225-5759** or 707/585-8355), runs about eight international trips for lesbians yearly.

6 Getting There

BY PLANE

While the facts and figures below are as accurate as research can make them, the fast-moving economics of the airline industry, particularly since deregulation, make them all very tentative. Always check for the very latest flight and fare information.

The best strategy before buying your ticket involves shopping around and remaining as flexible about flight dates as possible. Keep calling the airlines or your travel agent because often, as the departure date nears, airlines will discount seats if a flight is not fully booked.

Other general rules to keep in mind are that fares are usually lower during the week (Monday through Thursday noon) and that there are also seasonal fare differences (peak, shoulder, and basic). Transatlantic peak season is summer, basic season is winter, and shoulder season is in between. Travel during Christmas and Easter weeks is usually more expensive than in the weeks just before or after those holidays.

In any season, airlines offer regular first-class, business, and economy seating. Most airlines also offer discounted fares, such as the Advance Purchase Excursion (APEX), which carry some restrictions (some severe). These usually include the need for an early purchase, a minimum stay abroad, and cancellation or alteration penalties.

THE MAJOR AIRLINES

British Airways (☎ **800/AIRWAYS;** web site: http://www.British-Airways.com), the national carrier of Britain, operates the greatest number of flights into all parts of the country, including Scotland. Beneficiary of a 1991 expenditure of $17 million (part of which was spent to upgrade the ground facilities most used by North American travelers), the airline is the only non–U.S. carrier with its own terminal at New York's JFK.

Six nonstop flights per week go directly from New York to Scotland's busiest airport, Abbotsinch, outside Glasgow, a 90-minute car or bus ride from Edinburgh. Glasgow-bound flights depart every day except Wednesday at 7:25pm from JFK and arrive at 7:10am the following morning. BA serves at least 20 North American cities with nonstop flights at least once a day into London's most convenient airport, Heathrow. From Heathrow, BA offers 22 nonstop flights daily to both Edinburgh and Abbotsinch, Glasgow. Some Scotland-bound passengers opt for flights into Manchester, a city in the Midlands of England that's closer to the Highlands and islands of Scotland than London. BA offers frequent flights into Manchester, many nonstop, from various parts of the United States.

British Airways telephone representatives in North America can give price and schedule information, and make reservations for flights, hotels, car rentals, and tours in the U.K. Cost-conscious options include a 7-day, 14-day, and 21-day round-trip APEX that must be reserved and paid for 7, 14, and 21 days in advance, respectively.

American Airlines (☎ **800/624-6262;** web site: http://www.americanair.com) is the U.S. carrier with the most routes into London. From May 15 to October 31, American offers a daily nonstop flight to Glasgow from Chicago; the rest of the year you'll make at least one transfer. In addition, the airline has six daily nonstops from New York's JFK to London's Heathrow Airport and one flight a day from Chicago's O'Hare Airport to Manchester, England. Depending on the season, there's also one

CyberDeals for Net Surfers

It's possible to get some great deals on airfare, hotels, and car rentals via the Internet. The web sites highlighted below are worth checking out, especially since all services are free (but don't forget that time is money when you're on-line).

Microsoft Expedia (www.expedia.com)   The best part of this multipurpose travel site is the "Fare Tracker": You fill out a form on the screen indicating that you're interested in cheap flights and they'll e-mail you the best airfare deals. The site's "Travel Agent" will steer you to bargains on hotels and car rentals, and you can book everything, including flights, right on-line. This site is even useful once you're booked: Before you go, log on to Expedia for oodles of up-to-date travel information, including weather reports and foreign-exchange rates.

Preview Travel (www.reservations.com and www.vacations.com)   Another useful travel site, "Reservations.com" has a "Best Fare Finder," which will search the Apollo computer reservations system for the three lowest fares for any route on any days of the year. Just fill out the form on the screen with times, dates, and destinations, and within minutes Preview will show you the best deals. If you find an airfare you like, you can book your ticket right on-line—you can even reserve hotels and car rentals on this site. If you're in the preplanning stage, head to Preview's "Vacations.com" site, where you can check out the latest package deals for Hawaii and other destinations around the world by clicking on "Hot Deals."

Travelocity (www.travelocity.com)   This is one of the best travel sites out there. In addition to its "Personal Fare Watcher," which notifies you via e-mail of the lowest airfares for up to five different destinations, Travelocity will track the three lowest fares for any routes on any dates in minutes. You can book a flight right then and there, and if you need a rental car or hotel, Travelocity will find you the best deal via the SABRE computer reservations system (a huge database used by travel agents worldwide). Click on "Last Minute Deals" for the latest travel bargains.

Trip.Com (www.thetrip.com)   This site is really geared toward the business traveler, but vacationers-to-be can also use Trip.Com's valuable fare-finding engine, which will e-mail you every week with the best city-to-city airfare deals on your selected route or routes.

Discount Tickets (www.discount-tickets.com)   Operated by the ETN (European Travel Network), this site offers discounts on airfares, accommodations, car rentals, and tours on flights between the United States and other countries.

Epicurious Travel (travel.epicurious.com)   This is another good travel site.

—Jeanette Foster

daily flight from JFK to Manchester. American also offers at least one daily nonstop to London from Chicago, Dallas/Fort Worth, Los Angeles, Boston, and Miami.

United Airlines (☎ 800/241-6522; web site: http://www.ual.com) offers daily nonstop service to Glasgow from Dulles Airport in Washington, D.C. It also flies to London's Heathrow from New York's JFK, San Francisco, Washington, D.C., Los Angeles, and New Jersey's Newark Airport.

Northwest Airlines (☎ 800/225-2525; web site: http://www.nwa.com) operates nonstop flights between Boston and Glasgow daily in summer, somewhat less frequently in winter. It also offers daily nonstop flights from Minneapolis to Gatwick and from Boston to Gatwick. Thanks to Northwest's partnership with the national airline of Holland, KLM, Northwest also offers easy connections through Amsterdam to Britain and most of the other countries of Europe.

Several airlines offer flights to London where easy connections may be made for flights into Scotland. **Delta** (☎ **800/241-4141;** web site: http://www.delta.air.com) has daily nonstop flights to London's Gatwick Airport from its headquarters in Atlanta, as well as flights from Cincinnati. **TWA** (☎ **800/221-2000;** web site: www.twa.com) offers daily nonstop service to Gatwick Airport from St. Louis, Baltimore, and Philadelphia. **Virgin Atlantic Airways** (☎ **800/862-8621;** web site: http://www.fly.vifgin.com/atlantic/) offers services, amenities, and, in many cases, prices comparable to those of most of the world's major carriers. The airline flies to London's Gatwick from Boston, Orlando, and Miami, and to London's Heathrow from Los Angeles, Newark, and New York's JFK. Depending on point of origin, flights leave four to seven times a week.

For travelers departing from Canada, **Air Canada** (☎ **800/776-3000;** web site: http://www.aircanada.ca) flies to London's Heathrow from both Toronto and Montréal's Mirabel airport nonstop daily, and has three to seven flights a week, depending on the season, between Toronto and Manchester. The airline also offers nonstop service from Calgary to London five times a week during the summer; this service drops to once a week during the off season. Air Canada does not offer nonstop service from Edmonton. However, you can take a direct flight that stops in Calgary but does not require you to change planes. This service is also offered 5 days a week during the summer. Daily nonstops to London also depart from Vancouver from June to September; that number falls to two per week during the winter months. An add-on to Glasgow or Edinburgh can be arranged when the initial flight is booked.

BEST VALUE FARES

APEX   Generally, your cheapest option on a regular airline is to book an APEX fare, hopefully taking advantage of any price war being waged over the Atlantic at the time of your booking. By planning your trip carefully and defining your dates of travel several weeks, if not months, in advance, you might save yourself hundreds of dollars. For example, a round-trip ticket from New York to Glasgow on British Airways purchased 21 days in advance for travel during the high season (defined by BA as mid-June to September 30) will cost you $740. If you were instead to purchase the same ticket 90 days in advance, the price would fall to around $600. In addition, the earlier you buy your tickets, the more lenient the restrictions on trip duration; with a 90-day advance purchase, your trip can last from 5 to 45 days. In contrast, the 21-day advance-purchase ticket has a minimum-stay requirement of 1 week and a maximum-stay requirement of 1 month. Also remember that traveling on a weekend—Friday through Sunday—will cost you more. You may also be required by some airlines to pay a surcharge for airport services—usually around $25. Of course, prices are always subject to change; if you're lucky, last-minute sales promotions may drop your cost even lower.

For purposes of contrast only, it's useful to note that the "straight economy fare" between New York and Glasgow at press time was quoted at $1,220 round-trip, the only restriction being that your return flight departure date and airport remain the same. For complete freedom from any restrictions at all, the fare was quoted at $2,364; the extra convenience is probably not worth the added cost.

SPECIAL PROMOTIONAL FARES   British Airways, and every other major air-line, is always introducing promotional fares designed to make travel to Britain more affordable than ever. These fares usually carry restrictions such as a stay abroad of between 6 and 30 days, and unavailability of travel during certain peak holiday periods.

The Late Saver Fare is another possible option. It offers deeply discounted tickets that become available only 48 hours prior to a Britain-bound flight from any of British Airways' North American departure points.

These fares are cited only to give you an idea of what is likely to be available. Even though they may be discontinued, rest assured that others will quickly come along to take their place.

DISCOUNTS   Senior citizens (anyone older than 60) are sometimes granted discounts of 10% on selected published fares whose details vary with the season and market conditions. Senior citizens, in some cases, qualify for less stringent restrictions on APEX cancellation policies.

BA also offers youth fares to ages 12 to 24 for round-trip transatlantic tickets whose return can be scheduled for up to a full year from the date of departure. Reservations for youth fares can be accepted only 72 hours or less prior to departure. Youth fares, when available, also apply to one-way tickets.

Note that both senior citizen's fares and youth fares might be undercut at any time by more attractive offers to the general public that are part of recurring sales promotions. As always, it's best to communicate with a reservations agent for the whole story about the many available options.

OTHER GOOD-VALUE CHOICES

BUCKET SHOPS   In the 1960s, mainstream airlines in Britain gave this insulting name to resellers of unsold tickets consigned to them by major transatlantic carriers; it might be more polite to refer to them as "consolidators." They act as clearinghouses for blocks of tickets usually discounted 20% to 35% below the full fare. Terms of payment can vary—anything between last-minute and 45 days prior to departure. Tickets can be purchased through regular travel agents, who mark up the ticket 8% to 10% or more, thereby greatly reducing your discount.

A survey of flyers who use consolidators voiced only one major complaint: Use of such a ticket doesn't qualify you for an advance seat assignment, and you are therefore likely to be assigned a "poor seat" at the last minute. The survey revealed that most passengers estimated their savings at around $200 per ticket; nearly a third reported savings of up to $300 off the regular price. But—and here's the hitch—many who booked consolidator tickets reported no savings at all because the airline had matched the consolidator fare by announcing a promotional fare. The situation is a bit tricky and calls for some careful investigation on your part.

Bucket shops abound from coast to coast. Look also for their ads in your local newspaper's travel section—they're usually very small and a single column in width. Since dealing with unknown bucket shops might be a little risky, it's wise to call the Better Business Bureau in your area to see if complaints have been filed against the company from which you plan to purchase a ticket. Here are some recommendations:

TFI Tours International, 34 W. 32nd St., 12th Floor, New York, NY 10001 (☎ **800/745-8000,** or 212/736-1140 outside New York State). This tour company offers services to 177 cities worldwide.

Sunline Express Holidays, Inc., 273 Meserole Ave., Brooklyn, NY 11222 (☎ **800/786-5463** or 718/383-9000) is another discount specialist.

Travel Management International, 1129 E. Wayzata Blvd., Wayzata, MN 55391 (☎ **800/245-3672**), offers a wide variety of discount fares, including youth fares. Often, its contract fares are lower than those offered by some rebators (see below).

CHARTER FLIGHTS Strictly speaking, a charter flight is an aircraft reserved months in advance for a one-time-only transit to some predetermined point. Before paying for a charter, check the restrictions on your ticket or contract. You may be asked to purchase a tour package and pay far in advance. You'll pay a stiff penalty or forfeit the ticket entirely if you cancel. Charters are sometimes canceled when the plane doesn't fill up. In some cases, the charter-ticket seller will offer you an insurance policy for legitimate cancellation (hospital confinement or death in the family, for example). There is no way to predict whether a proposed flight will cost less on a charter or from a bucket shop. You have to investigate at the time of your trip.

One of the biggest charter operators is **Travac,** 989 Sixth Ave., New York, NY 10018 (☎ **800/TRAV-800** or 212/563-3303). The **Council on International Educational Exchange (Council Travel),** 205 E. 42nd St., New York, NY 10017 (☎ **800/2-COUNCIL** or 212/822-2900), arranges charter seats on regularly scheduled aircraft.

REBATORS To confuse the situation even more, rebators also compete in the low airfare market. These outfits pass along to the passenger part of their commission, although many of them assess a fee for their services. Most rebators offer discounts that range from 10% to 25% (but this could vary from place to place), plus a $25 handling charge. They're not the same as travel agents, although they sometimes offer similar services, including discounted land arrangements and car rentals.

Specializing in clients in the Midwest, **Travel Avenue,** 10 S. Riverside Plaza, Suite 1404, Chicago, IL 60606 (☎ **800/333-3335** or 312/876-6866), is one of the oldest agencies of its kind. It offers up-front cash rebates on every airline ticket over $300 it sells. In a style similar to a discount brokerage firm, they pride themselves on *not* offering travel counseling. Instead, they sell airline tickets to independent travelers who have already worked out their travel plans. Also available are tours and cruise fares, plus hotel reservations, usually at prices lower than if you had prereserved them on your own.

Another major rebator is the **Smart Traveller,** 3111 SW 27th Ave., Miami, FL 33133 (☎ **800/448-3338** or 305/448-3338; fax 305/443-3544). This agency also offers discounts on packaged tours.

GOING AS A COURIER This cost-cutting technique may not be for everybody. You travel as a passenger and courier, and for this service you'll secure a greatly discounted airfare, or in certain very rare instances, even a free ticket. Most courier services operate from Los Angeles or New York, but some operate out of other cities, such as Chicago or Miami. Courier services are often listed in the *Yellow Pages* or in advertisements in travel sections or newspapers.

You're allowed one piece of carry-on luggage only; your baggage allowance is used by the courier firm to transport its cargo. You don't actually handle the merchandise you're "transporting" to Europe—you just carry a manifest to present to Customs. Upon arrival, an employee of the courier service will reclaim the company's cargo. A friend may be able to arrange a flight as a courier on a consecutive day.

Try **Now Voyager,** 74 Varick St., Suite 307, New York, NY 10013 (☎ **212/431-1616** from 10am to 6pm daily). Now Voyager works with several daily flights to London, one of which allows couriers a stay of up to 30 days and transport of a modest amount of personal luggage. Also try **Halbart Express,** 147–05 176th St., Jamaica, NY 11434 (☎ **718/656-8189;** open daily 10am to 3pm).

For an annual membership of $45, the **International Association of Air Travel Couriers,** P.O. Box 1349, Lake Worth, FL 33460 (☎ **561/582-8320;** fax 561/582-1581), will send you six issues of its newsletter, *Shoestring Traveler,* and six issues of *Air Courier Bulletin,* a directory of air courier bargains around the world. Other advantages of membership are that photo identification cards are issued, and the organization acts as a troubleshooter if a courier runs into difficulties. The fee also includes a 24-hour fax-on-demand service, listing last-minute courier flights available. This flight information is updated daily.

TRAVEL CLUBS Another possibility for low-cost air travel is the travel club, which supplies an unsold inventory of tickets offering discounts in the usual range of 20% to 60%.

After you pay an annual fee, you're given a "hotline" number to call to find out what discounts are available. Many of these discounts become available several days in advance of actual departure, sometimes as long as a week and sometimes as much as a month—it all depends. Of course, you're limited to what's available, so you have to be fairly flexible.

Some of the best of these clubs include the following:

Moment's Notice, 7301 New Utrecht Ave., Brooklyn, NY 11204 (☎ **718/234-6295**), charges $25 per year for membership, which allows spur-of-the-moment participation in dozens of tours. Each is geared for impulse purchases and last-minute getaways, and each offers air and land packages that sometimes represent substantial savings over what you'd have paid through more conventional channels. Although membership is required for participation in the tours, anyone can call the company's hotline (see above) to learn what options are available. Most of the company's best-valued tours depart from New Jersey's Newark Airport.

Traveler's Advantage, 3033 S. Parker Rd., Suite 900, Aurora, CO 80014 (☎ **800/548-1116**), offers a 3-month trial period for $1; the annual membership fee is $49. Benefits include a hotel card, which gets you 50% off the regularly published room rate at more than 3,000 hotels, members-only vacation packages at discounted rates, and a 5% cash bonus on all purchases made through the service with a copy of your itinerary and any receipts.

BY TRAIN

From England, two main rail lines link London to Scotland. The most popular route is from King's Cross Station in London to Edinburgh, going by way of Newcastle and Durham. Trains cross from England into Scotland at Berwick-upon-Tweed. This line is the fastest way of reaching the Scottish capital other than flying. Fifteen trains a day leave London for Edinburgh from 8am to 6pm. Night service is more limited, and sleepers must be reserved. Three of these trains go on to Aberdeen.

If you're going on to the western Highlands and islands, Edinburgh makes a good gateway, with better train connections to those areas than Glasgow.

If you're going via the west coast, trains leave Euston Station in London for Glasgow, by way of Rugby, Crewe, Preston, and Carlisle, with nearly a train per hour during the day. Most of these trains take about 5 hours to reach Glasgow. You can also take the *Highland Chieftain,* going direct to Stirling and Aviemore, terminating in Inverness, the capital of the Highlands. There's overnight sleeper service from Euston Station to Glasgow, Perth, Stirling, Aviemore, Fort William, and Inverness. It's possible to book a family compartment.

Scotland is also served by other trains from England, including regular service from such cities as Birmingham, Liverpool, Manchester, Southampton, and Bristol. If you're in Penzance (Cornwall), you can reach either Glasgow or Edinburgh directly by train without having to return to London.

BY BUS (COACH)

Long-distance buses, called "coaches" in Britain, are the least expensive means of reaching Scotland from England. Some 20 coach companies run services, mainly from London to either Edinburgh or Glasgow. The major operators are National Express, Scottish Omnibuses, Western SMT, Stagecoach, and Eastern Scottish. It takes 8 to 8^1/$_2$ hours to reach either Edinburgh or Glasgow from London.

It's estimated that coach fares are about one-third of the rail charges for comparable trips into Scotland. Most coaches depart from Victoria Coach Station in London. If you're visiting from June to August, it's wise to make seat reservations at least 3 days in advance (4 or 5 days in advance if possible). For timetables, available from London to Edinburgh, telephone National Express coaches at ☎ **0990/808080** in London. Travel centers and travel agents also have details. Most travel agents in London sell coach seats and can make reservations for you.

BY CAR

If you're driving north to Scotland from England, it's fastest to take the M1 motorway north from London. You can reach M1 by driving to the ring road from any point in the British capital. Southeast of Leeds you'll need to connect with A1 (not a motorway), which you take north to Scotch Corner. Here M1 resumes, ending south of Newcastle-upon-Tyne. From here you can take A696, which becomes A68, for its final run north into Edinburgh.

If you're in the west of England, you can go north along M5, which begins at Exeter (Devon). Eventually this will merge with M6. Continue north on M6 until you reach a point north of Carlisle. From Carlisle you cross into Scotland near Gretna Green. Continue north along A74 via Moffat. Highway A74 will eventually connect with a motorway, M74, which heads toward Glasgow. If your goal is Edinburgh, not Glasgow, various roads will take you east to the Scottish capital, including a motorway (M8) that goes part of the way, as do A702, A70, and A71 (all these routes are well signposted).

BY SHIP

Cunard Line, 555 Fifth Ave., New York, NY 10017 (☎ **800/5-CUNARD** or 212/880-7500), boasts as its flagship the *Queen Elizabeth 2,* quite accurately billed as "the most advanced ship of the age." It's the only five-star-plus luxury ocean liner providing regular transatlantic service—18 sailings a year between April and December—docking at such cities as New York, Baltimore, and Fort Lauderdale before sailing to the European ports of Cherbourg, France, and Southampton, England.

Fares are extremely complicated, based on cabin standard and location and the season of sailing. During the supervalue season (April 12 to May 13 and December 9 to 15), the fares for a 6-day crossing range from $1,300 to $9,200. During peak season (June 2 to October 1), fares for a 6-day crossing range from $2,400 to $12,125. These prices are per person, based on double occupancy. All passengers pay a $185 port tax, regardless of the class of cabin. Many different packages are promoted, most of which add on relatively low airfare from your home city to the port of departure, plus a return to your home city from London on British Airways.

From Southampton, you can make rail connections north to Scotland.

PACKAGE TOURS

GENERAL TOURS   Europe's largest tour operator is Britain's national airline, **British Airways** (☎ **800/AIRWAYS** for details).

BA has a full spectrum of what they call "designer holidays," constructed for radically differing kinds of clients. Offerings include carefully structured, tightly scheduled motorcoach tours for clients who feel they need the greatest amount of channeling and guidance. Equally popular are tours designed for independent souls needing no more than discounted vouchers for a car rental and prereserved rooms at specific types of hotels. Depending on your tastes and your pocketbook, BA can arrange vouchers for discounted accommodations in everything from simple inns to the finest baronial mansions of Scotland and can also provide you with a cost-conscious rented car so that you can drive yourself over the mountains and through the glens without interference from guides and fellow travelers.

Tours can be as straightforward as a 1-day jaunt from London to Scotland for a round of golf (with a return to London in time for cocktails), or a 3- or 5-day escorted tour through the gardens and manor houses of Royal Deeside. Also available are 1- and 2-week motorcoach tours of the Highlands and islands, with perhaps a detour to visit a local exhibition of Highland Games.

RAILWAY TOURS   Ever since Scots-born James Watt invented the steam engine, much of the lore of Scotland has involved the entrepreneurial and engineering challenges sparked by the construction and maintenance of its railway lines. Today historians and nostalgia buffs appreciate the complicated network of steel that crisscrosses Scotland's dramatic terrain.

Abercrombie & Kent, 1520 Kensington Rd., Oak Brook, IL 60521 (☎ **800/ 323-7308;** fax 630/954-2944), offers what have been called the most glamorous railway tours in Europe. On a solidly elegant train known as the *Royal Scotsman,* the experience has been compared to a movable version of a five-star hotel with an equivalent restaurant, an amply stocked bar car, an expert group of well-informed lecturers and guides, and an accompanying van for transfer to sights.

Abercrombie & Kent is the only U.S. sales agent for this train, and bases much of its European reputation upon it. Known for its carriage-trade adventure tours to such places as China, Antarctica, Vietnam, and the Great Rift Valley of Africa, Abercrombie is a respected tour operator whose equivalent rail tours in France and Switzerland are cited by many organizations as being especially appropriate for disabled, elderly, or infirm passengers.

The train incorporates only eight passenger cars (each built in the old-fashioned tradition of 1940s style and comfort), one of the most sophisticated restaurants in Scotland, and a big-windowed bar and observation car with a veranda trailing along at the back. Accommodations are snug but elegant, with wood paneling, private bathrooms, conventional (not bunk-style) beds, climate control, full-length wardrobes, and many of the accessories you'd find on an elegant private yacht.

Tours usually begin and end at Edinburgh's Waverley Station, include a guide and an animated university-class lecturer, and completely eliminate the hassles and inconveniences of baggage transfers through the entire 6-day tour. Itineraries include overnight stopovers at quiet railway sidings along the way and a wide array of landscapes such as the regions around Glasgow, Fort William, Mallaig, Perth or Pitlochry, Inverness and the historic battlefield of Culloden Moor, Keith and the Hebridean island of Skye, Aberdeen, and Dundee and Royal Deeside. Included in the cost are motorcoach excursions and tours of castles, manor houses, gardens, and historic sites of Scotland, many of which are not open to the general public.

The all-inclusive price for the 7-day/6-night tour is $5,500 per person.

WALKING TOURS   Abercrombie and Kent (see above) also offers a leisurely walking tour of Scotland that combines stays in small country inns with short cruises, bus rides, and hikes through some of the best scenery of the country. A group of no more than 20 participants begins the tour in Glasgow, then heads out on a weeklong adventure that includes trips to such places of interest as the Isle of Eriska and Lochs Fyne and Melfort. You don't have to be in great shape to enjoy this unique way of touring Scotland; however, the company does advise that participants be at a moderate level of fitness. Don't expect whirlwind tours of museums and monuments in the big cities; instead, these trips are geared toward those who want their time in Scotland to be a true European experience; small towns are visited, meals are traditional, and tour guides know the best routes and most interesting stories about each place you visit. The "Walking in Scotland" tour costs $2,990 per person, double occupancy. This price includes all meals, transportation, and hotel costs; it does not include, however, airfare to and from Scotland.

SEA CRUISES No area of Scotland is ever far from a loch, an estuary, or the wide-open sea, a fact that has greatly affected the country's history. One of the best ways to visit its far-flung islands is by ship, a means of transport offering a luxury and convenience difficult to duplicate any other way.

One company especially geared for this kind of travel is **Hebridean Island Cruises,** Acorn Park, Skipton, North Yorkshire BD23 2UE (☎ **800/659-2648** in the U.S. and Canada, or 01756/701338). Established in 1989, and the only cruise operators to sail solely in British waters, the company operates a single ship, the *Hebridean Princess,* a shallow-draft, much-refitted and -retooled remake (in 1990) of an older vessel. Equipped with 29 staterooms and a crew of 38, it can carry up to 50 passengers in cozy circumstances to some of the most remote and inaccessible regions of Scotland. The ship is equipped with beach landing craft especially useful during explorations of the fragile ecosystems and bird life of the more remote islands.

The company offers 10 different itineraries that focus either on nature and ecology or on the castles, gardens, and archaeology of Scotland. Tours usually depart from the port of Oban, and cruise through the Inner and Outer Hebrides and the Orkneys, stopping in places such as Saint Kilda's, the most remote and westerly of the islands, known for its bird life and tundra. Tours are offered only between March and October. For a 14-day cruise at the start of the season, a midrange room is £1,200 ($1,980) per person, double occupancy; during high season, that price rises to £4,300 ($7,095). First-class rooms start at £1,800 ($2,970) and rise to £5,400 ($8,910) in high season. All meals and shore excursions are included in the price, but liquor tabs at the well-stocked bar, wine at dinner, and gratuities are extra.

Another, better-known company, offering more luxurious tours through the islands and lochs of Scotland, is **Cunard** (☎ **800/5-CUNARD**), whose top-of-the-line yacht *Royal Viking Sun* offers some of the most upscale accommodations in Cunard's 13-vessel inventory. The company's Castles and Highlands cruise sails in late May from Rouen, France. The 2-week sailing includes stops in both Ireland and Scotland and ends in Copenhagen. Per-person prices, double occupancy, including airfare, begin at $6,320; the most deluxe accommodations go for $15,030. Early bookings will usually result in a discount, sometimes up to 20% off the quoted price. In addition to the cost of the cruise, travelers pay a $195 port tax.

7 Getting Around

BY PLANE

British Airways Europe Airpass allows travel in a continuous loop to between 3 and 12 cities on BA's European and domestic routes. Passengers must end their journey at the same point they began. If such a ticket is booked (say, London to Manchester to Glasgow to Aberdeen to the Shetland Islands, with an eventual return to London), each segment of the itinerary will cost about 40% to 50% less than if it had been booked individually. The pass is available for travel to about a dozen of the most visited cities and regions of Britain with discounted add-ons available to most of BA's destinations in Europe as well. It must be booked and paid for at least 7 days before departure from the United States, and all sectors of the itinerary must be booked simultaneously. Some changes are permitted in flight dates (but not in the cities visited) after the ticket is issued. Check with BA for full details and restrictions.

BY TRAIN

The cost of rail travel here can be quite low, particularly if U.S. travelers take advantage of certain cost-saving travel plans, some of which can only be purchased in North America before leaving for Scotland. You should be warned that *your Eurailpass is not valid on trains in Great Britain.*

Trains are generally punctual in Scotland, carrying you across the country, or at least to ferry terminals if you're exploring the islands. A comprehensive timetable costing 40p (65¢) is available at all stations. Free timetables covering only certain regions are also available at various stations. For £16 ($26.40) a young person's rail card (valid for ages 16 to 25) is sold at major stations. Two photos are needed to be granted one. It's estimated that the coach card reduces all fares by one-third for 1 year.

If you plan to travel a great deal on the European railroads, it's worth securing a copy of the *Thomas Cook European Timetable of European Passenger Railroads.* It's available exclusively in North America from **Forsyth Travel Library,** P.O. Box 2975, Shawnee Mission, KS 66201 (☎ **800/FORSYTH**), at a cost of $27.95 plus $4.50 priority airmail postage in the United States or plus $2 (U.S.) for shipments to Canada.

For information on rail travel in Scotland, call or write **ScotRail,** Caledonian Chambers, 87 Union St., Glasgow G1 3TA, Scotland (☎ **0141/332-9811**).

BRITRAIL PASS   This pass permits unlimited rail travel in England, Scotland, and Wales on all British Rail routes (it's not valid on ships between the U.K. and the Continent, the Channel Islands, or Ireland). An 8-day first-class pass costs $355; a standard pass, $249; a 15-day pass costs $549 and $379, respectively; a 22-day pass costs $700 and $485; and a 1-month pass, $815 and $565. Kids 5 to 15 are charged half fare, and children under 5 travel free.

Youth passes (for ages 16 to 25), all standard, are $199 for 8 days, $305 for 15 days, $389 for 22 days, and $450 for 1 month. If you choose to go first class, you pay full adult fare.

Senior citizens (60 plus) qualify for 8-day rates of $305; $469 for 15 days; $595 for 22 days; and $695 for 1 month. All BritRail senior citizen rates are for first-class travel.

Note: Prices for BritRail passes are higher for Canadian travelers because of the different conversion rate for Canadian dollars.

BritRail passes cannot be obtained in Britain, but should be secured before leaving North America either through a travel agent or by writing or visiting **BritRail Travel International,** 1500 Broadway, Suite 100, New York, NY 10036 (☎ **888/ BRITRAIL** or 212/575-2667; fax 212/575-2542).

BRITRAIL FLEXIPASS   The Flexipass lets you travel anywhere on British Rail, but limits travel to 4, 8, or 15 days within a 30-day period. The 4-day Flexipass costs $305 in first class and $209 in economy; seniors pay $259 for a first-class pass, students (ages 16 to 25) pay $169 for a standard pass. The 8-day pass costs $439 in first class, $305 in economy, $305 for seniors, and $245 for students. The Flexipass for 15 days of travel in 1 month goes for $659 in first class and $469 in economy; seniors pay $560. Students are charged $365 for a 15-day pass, but can spread their travel over a 2-month period.

The Flexipass must also be purchased from either your travel agent or from BritRail Travel International in North America (see addresses above).

TRAVELPASS FOR SCOTLAND   If you plan to tour throughout the U.K., one of the previously described BritRail passes might be appropriate for your needs. If you plan to focus intensively on Scotland, however, a BritRail pass might not be adequate. Recognizing the inadequacy of BritRail passes for intensive tours of Scotland, the Scottish Tourist Authorities developed the **Freedom of Scotland Travelpass.** Designed for the serious Scottish enthusiast, it offers unlimited transportation on trains and most ferryboats throughout Scotland, with discounts for bus travel. It includes access to obscure bus routes to almost forgotten hamlets, and free rides on ferries operated by Caledonian MacBrayne and discounted fares with P&O Scottish Lines. Their ferries connect to the Western Islands, the islands of the Clyde, and the historic Orkney Islands.

The Travelpass covers all the Scottish rail network and is usable from Carlisle on the western border of England and Scotland and from Berwick-upon-Tweed on the eastern Scottish border. In addition, if you have to fly into London and want to go straight to Scotland from there, a reduced rate is available for a round-trip ticket between London and Edinburgh or Glasgow for Travelpass holders.

The Freedom of Scotland Travelpass is available for 8 days for $165, 15 days for $235, and 22 days for $280. When you validate the pass at the beginning of your first journey, you'll receive a complete packet of rail, bus, and ferry schedules. For more information, contact **Scots-American Travel Advisors,** 26 Rugen Dr., Harrington Park, NJ 07640 (☎ **800/247-7268** or 201/768-5505). Information is also available from the Manager of Public Affairs, British Rail–Scottish Region, **ScotRail,** Caledonian Chambers, 87 Union St., Glasgow G1 3TA, Scotland (☎ **0141/332-9811**).

BY BUS

No doubt about it, the cheapest means of transport from London for the budget traveler to Scotland is the bus or coach. It's also the least expensive means of travel within Scotland.

All major towns have a **local bus service.** Every tourist information center throughout the country will provide details about half-day or full-day bus excursions to scenic highlights. If you want to explore a particular area, you can often avail yourself of an economical bus pass. If you're planning to travel extensively in Scotland, see the Freedom of Scotland Travelpass, already described in "By Train," above.

Many adventurous travelers like to explore the country on one of the **postal buses,** which carry not only mail but a limited number of passengers to rural areas. Ask at any local post office for details. A general timetable is available at the head post office in Edinburgh.

The **Scottish CityLink Coaches** are a good bet. They link the major cities (Glasgow and Edinburgh) with the two most popular tourist centers, Inverness and Aviemore. Travel is fast and prices are low. For example, it takes only 3 hours to reach Aviemore from Edinburgh. Inverness is just 3$^{1}/_{2}$ hours from Edinburgh. There's also a direct Scottish CityLink overnight coach making the run from London to Aviemore and Inverness at reasonable fares.

Coaches offer many other popular runs, including links between Glasgow and Fort William, Inverness and Ullapool, and Glasgow and Oban. For more detailed information, get in touch with **Highland Bus and Coach,** Farralane Park, Inverness (☎ **01463/233371**); or **Scottish CityLink,** Buchanan Street Bus Station, Glasgow (☎ **0141/332-9191**).

BY CAR

Scotland has many excellent roads, often "dual carriageways" (divided highways), as well as fast trunk roads, linking the Lowlands to the Highlands. In more remote areas, especially the islands of western Scotland, single-lane roads exist. Here, caution in driving is most important. Passing places are provided.

However, many of the roads are unfenced, and livestock can be a serious problem when you're driving, either day or night. Drive slowly when you're passing through areas filled with sheep.

CAR RENTALS   In brief, it's best to shop around, compare prices, and have a clear idea of your automotive needs before you reserve a car. All companies give the best rates to clients who reserve at least 2 business days in advance and who agree to return the car to its point of origin, and some require that drivers be at least 23 (in some cases, 21) years of age. It's also an advantage to keep the car for at least a week, as opposed to 3 or 4 days. Be warned that all car rentals in the U.K. are slapped with a 17.5% government tax known as VAT.

To rent a car in Scotland, your passport and your own driver's license must be presented along with your deposit. No special British or international license is needed.

Partly because of the huge number of visitors to the U.K., the car-rental market is among the most competitive in Europe. Several recent arrivals on the car-rental scene promise lower rates.

Of the big three, **Budget** (☎ **800/472-3325**) offers some of the cheapest cars, including a small but peppy Ford Fiesta (Aspire), barely big enough to fit two people with their luggage inside. With unlimited mileage, it rents for around £85 ($140.25) per week, plus 17.5% tax, plus a well-spent £8 ($13.20) per day for collision-damage insurance. Be fully warned, however, that even with the purchase of this insurance, you'll still be liable for up to £150 ($247.50) in costs in the event of an accident (see "Car Insurance," below).

Hertz (☎ **800/654-3001**) offers a similar car for £150 ($247.50) per week, including unlimited mileage and the 17.5% tax. For around £80 ($132) more, the company will add a collision-damage waiver and theft protection insurance. The collision-damage waiver covers all but the first £150 ($247.50) worth of damage. It is also worth noting that frequent flyers on British Airways may be eligible for discounts on Hertz rentals if they make their reservations through the airlines.

Budget, Hertz, and their major competitor, **Avis** (☎ **800/321-3652**), also offer a wide range of midsize cars, including the very popular Ford Sierra.

Cautious and thrifty renters have increasingly taken notice of **EuroDollar Rent-a-Car** (☎ **800/800-6000**) and **Alamo** (☎ **800/522-9696**), whose rates in Britain, including Scotland, tend to be competitive with their better-known colleagues. In some instances, EuroDollar rents a pint-size Vauxhall Nova for rates similar to those charged by Budget (see above), but requires an advance payment about a week ahead.

Also worthwhile—and sometimes even cheaper—are the services of a car-rental reservations network based in Florida. **I.T.S. of Broward County,** 3332 NE 33rd St., Fort Lauderdale, FL 33308 (☎ **800/521-0643**, 800/227-8990, or 800/248-4350), represents two of Britain's largest car-rental companies, Kenning and Town & Country. I.T.S. usually offers prices ranging up to 40% lower than those available at most car-rental kiosks. Prepayment is not required, although a printed confirmation will be faxed or mailed to anyone who reserves a car in advance. Cars can be arranged for pickup at any of the major airports of the U.K. (including Glasgow, Aberdeen, and Edinburgh), include unlimited mileage, and carry the possibility of buying optional collision insurance priced around £8 ($13.20) per day.

At press time, a week's rental of a Rover Mini or Fiat 500 costs £80 ($132) with unlimited mileage and tax. Be warned, however, that pickups at certain off-the-beaten-path places might require a phone call upon your arrival before an I.T.S. representative arrives to carry you to what might be an out-of-the-way (and sometimes unlikely) location. If you can maintain your sense of humor, you might save enough money on the car rental to make the inconvenience worthwhile.

CAR INSURANCE   With the rise in inflation and a staggering increase in the cost of car repairs, insurance premiums are on the rise worldwide, many benefits have been decreased, and it's more important than ever to purchase additional insurance to avoid financial liability in the event of an accident.

In other words, it pays to ask questions—lots of them—before renting a car. You can purchase a collision-damage waiver at each of the major car-rental companies for around £8 ($13.20) a day. Without it, you might be responsible for up to the full cost of the eventual repairs of the vehicle. Considering the unfamiliar practice of driving on the left, different road rules, and roads that tend to be narrow and sometimes congested, we consider purchase of an optional collision-damage waiver almost essential.

Check to see if you are covered by the credit or charge card you use, thus avoiding the added cost of coverage if possible. This can make a big difference in your bottom-line costs.

GASOLINE   There are plenty of gas ("petrol") stations in the environs of Glasgow and Edinburgh. However, in remote areas they're often few and far between, and many are closed on Sunday. If you're planning a lot of Sunday driving in remote parts, always make sure that your tank is full on Saturday.

Note that gasoline costs more in Britain than you're used to paying in North America, and to encourage energy saving the government has imposed a new 25% tax on gas. The price of a liter of gas is typically 64p ($1), including taxes.

DRIVING RULES & REQUIREMENTS   In Scotland you drive on the left and pass on the right. Road signs are clear and the international symbols are unmistakable.

To drive a car in Scotland, U.S. visitors need a passport and driver's license (no special British license is needed). The wise driver will secure a copy of the *British Highway Code,* available from almost any stationers or news agent.

A word of warning: Pedestrian crossings are marked by striped lines (zebra striping) on the road and flashing orange curbside lights. Drivers must stop and yield the right of way if a pedestrian has stepped into the zebra zone to cross the street. Wearing seat belts is mandatory in the British Isles.

ROAD MAPS   The best road map, especially if you're trying to locate some obscure village in Scotland or Wales, is *The Ordnance Survey Motor Atlas of Great Britain,* revised annually and published by Temple Press. It's available at most bookstores in Scotland. If you're in London and plan to head north to Scotland, go to W. & G. Foyle Ltd., 113 and 119 Charing Cross Rd., London, WC2 HOEB (☎ 0171/439-8501).

Other excellent maps include *Michelin's Map of Scotland* (no. 401) and *Michelin's Map of Great Britain* (no. 986). Before you leave North America, you can purchase these maps at BritRail's British Travel Shop, 551 Fifth Ave., 7th Floor, New York, NY 10176 (☎ **212/490-6688;** fax 212/490-0219).

BREAKDOWNS   Membership in one of the two major auto clubs can be helpful: the **Automobile Association (AA)** at Norfolk House, Priestly Road, Basingstoke, Hampshire RG24 9NY (☎ **01256/20123**), or the **Royal Automobile Club (RAC),** P.O. Box 700, Bristol, Somerset BS99 1RB (☎ **01454/208000**). You can secure membership in one of these clubs through the car-rental agent. There are roadside emergency telephone boxes about every mile along the motorways. If you don't see one, walk down the road for a bit to the blue-and-white marker with an arrow that points to the nearest box. The 24-hour number to call for AA is ☎ **0800/887766;** for RAC it's ☎ **0800/828282.** In addition, you can call a police traffic unit that will contact either of the auto clubs on your behalf.

HITCHHIKING   *Frommer's Scotland* does not recommend hitchhiking, which is legal except on motorways. However, if you decide to do it anyway, know that getting into a car with a stranger anywhere in the world can be extremely dangerous, especially for solo travelers. Always exercise caution. The cleaner and tidier you look, the better your chances for getting a ride. Have a sign with your destination written on it to hold up for drivers to see. Again, consider the great risk involved before you get into somebody's car. Women alone should never contemplate hitchhiking, although men as well are at danger.

BY FERRY

You can use a variety of special excursion fares to reach Scotland's islands. They're available from Caledonian MacBrayne for the Clyde and the Western Isles or from P&O Scottish Ferries, serving the Orkneys and Shetlands. Caledonian MacBrayne, operating 30 ferries in all, sails to 23 Hebridean and all Clyde islands. The fares, times of departure, and even accommodation suggestions are in a special book, *Ferry Guide to 23 Scottish Islands,* published by Caledonian MacBrayne. There are reasonably priced fares for vehicles and passengers through a "Go As You Please" plan, a kind of island hopscotch program offering a choice of 24 preplanned routes. Tickets are valid for 1 month and can be used in either direction for one trip on each leg of the tour. You choose your own route, and can skip from island to island at your own pace. You're given savings on the cost of individual tickets. Cyclists can take their bikes aboard free.

Full details are available from **Caledonian MacBrayne,** The Ferry Terminal, Gourock PA19 1QP (☎ **01475/650100**). The brochure hotline number is ☎ **01475/650288.**

P&O Scottish Ferries operates the services to the Orkney and Shetland Islands. Information is available from P&O Scottish Ferries, P.O. Box 5, Jamieson's Quay, Aberdeen AB11 5NP (☎ **01224/572615**).

SUGGESTED ITINERARIES

Edinburgh & the Lowlands in 7 Days

Day 1   From England, enter Scotland through the southeast known as "the Borders." At Newcastle-upon-Tyne (England), take A696 in the direction of Otterburn. It becomes A68 and will lead you right into Jedburgh and then via A6091 into Melrose, the heart of the Border Country with its ancient abbeys. From Melrose, take A6091 west in the direction of Galashiels. The road runs into A7 north. At Galashiels, turn west onto A72 in the direction of Peebles for an overnight stopover.

Day 2   You'll wake up at Peebles in the Tweed Valley, with its associations with novelist Sir Walter Scott, whose home can be visited at nearby Abbotsford. From Peebles it's a short drive along a secondary road, A703, and then the main A702 leading into Edinburgh, which many critics consider one of the most beautiful cities of Europe.

Days 3–5   Explore the attractions of Edinburgh's Old and New Towns and walk along the Royal Mile after visiting Edinburgh Castle.

Day 6   Cross the Forth Bridge, taking the southern coastal road along the firth, and head east to the ancient Kingdom of Fife. Follow the coastal road to visit the fishing villages of East Neuk, eventually reaching the capital of golf, St. Andrews, at a point 49 miles from Edinburgh. Spend the night in St. Andrews.

You can take A91 west to return to Edinburgh. In the vicinity of Loch Leven and its historic castle, this becomes an express highway, returning to Edinburgh across the Forth Bridge.

The Trossachs, the Road to the Isles & Nessie in 9 Days

Day 1   From Edinburgh, head for the Trossachs, one of the most beautiful areas of Scotland. A84 goes west in that direction, but eventually you must cut onto A821, a little northwest of Callander. The Trossachs have been called "Scotland in miniature," and include Loch Katrine and the famous Loch Lomond. Sometimes this is called "Rob Roy Country" or "Lady of the Lake Country" because Sir Walter Scott used the area as a setting for his novels. You can either stay overnight at a country hotel somewhere in the Trossachs or continue west to Loch Lomond.

Day 2   The next day, leave the Trossachs or Loch Lomond. Go along the western shore of Loch Lomond, connecting with A83, which will take you to Inveraray, a small holiday resort, seat of the dukes of Argyll at Inveraray Castle. Spend the night here.

Day 3   From Inveraray, you can head north along A819 to Dalmally, which lies along A85. Continue east from Dalmally until you reach the junction with A82. Here you can head north, going through Glencoe, site of the famous 1692 massacre. If you stay on A82, you'll reach Fort William for the night.

Day 4   After a night in Fort William, continue north along A82 until you reach the junction at Invergarry. Here you can turn west along A87, taking you on the "road to the isles." At Kyle of Lochalsh, frequent ferries sail back and forth to Skye, the most visited of Scottish islands. Since you'll spend a good part of the day getting here, allow Day 5 for exploring the island.

Day 5   Spend the day exploring the island.

Days 6–7   Head back to Invergarry and continue north to Inverness, a distance of 41 miles. A82 will take you along the western bank of Loch Ness, where you can try to spot the monster rearing its head from the water as you drive along. You'll arrive in the late afternoon in Inverness, capital of the Highlands, where you can stay overnight. While still based at Inverness, spend Day 7 exploring the Culloden Battlefield and other attractions in the environs.

Days 8–9   Head south again to Glasgow and spend your last day exploring that city. Don't miss the Burrell Collection.

On the Trail of Robert Burns in 3 Days

Day 1   In one very busy day in the county town and royal burgh of Dumfries, in the Scottish Lowlands, you can see sights famously associated with the national poet of Scotland. He died at Burns House, on Burns Street, which is now a museum of memorabilia. On the banks of the River Nith you can visit a converted 18th-century water mill that has been turned into the Robert Burns Centre with various exhibitions, some audiovisual, connected with the bard.

Later you can go to the Burns Mausoleum, the family tomb in St. Michael's Churchyard. The Dumfries Museum and Camera Obscura, at the intersection of Church Street and Rotchell Road, also has many Burns relics. Finally, to cap your day and to visit a much needed refueling stop, have a pint at the Globe Inn, where Burns drank with his friends. His favorite chair is still there—but you can't sit in it.

Day 2   From Dumfries, continue northwest along A76, which becomes A70 as it winds west into Ayr, a good center for touring Burns Country. Around Ayr you can see the 13th-century Auld Brig o' Ayr, the poet's "poor narrow footpath of a street," and can also visit a Burns museum, now housed in the Tam o' Shanter Inn on Ayr High Street (this was an alehouse in Rabbie's day). The Auld Kirk of Ayr dates from 1654, and in it Burns was baptized. For your refueling, visit the local pub, Rabbie's Bar, on Burns Statue Square. Stay overnight in Ayr.

Day 3   While still based in Ayr, true fans of the Scottish bard will continue their exploration of Burns Country for another day. In Tarbolton village, 7$^1/_2$ miles northeast of Ayr, stands the Bachelors' Club on Sandgate, a 17th-century house where in 1780 Burns and his friends founded a literary and debating society.

In the afternoon you can go to Alloway, 2 miles south of Ayr, where Burns was born on January 25, 1759, in a gardener's cottage. There a 200-year-old inn, the Burns Monument Hotel, looks out onto the Doon River and the bridge, Brig o' Doon, immortalized in "Tam o' Shanter." You can also visit the Burns Monument and Gardens, the Burns Cottage and Museum, and the Land o' Burns Centre.

FAST FACTS: Scotland

American Express   American Express offices are at 139 Princes St. in Edinburgh (☎ **0131/225-7881**) and at 115 Hope St. in Glasgow (☎ **0141/221-4366**).

Business Hours   Most banks are open Monday through Thursday from 9:30am to 12:30pm and 1:30 to 3:30pm; Friday hours are often 9:30am to 1:30pm. Basic **bar and pub hours** are Monday through Saturday from 11am to 11pm, but this can vary widely; Sunday hours are usually 12:30 to 2:30pm and 6:30 to 11pm, but some pubs are closed Sunday. **Office hours** are Monday through Friday from 9am to 5pm; the lunch break lasts an hour, but most places stay open all day. **Post offices** and sub–post offices are centrally situated and are open Monday through Friday from 9am to 5pm and Saturday from 9am to noon. **Stores** are generally open Monday through Saturday from 9am to 5:30 or 6pm. Most stores close early on Tuesday or Wednesday afternoon.

Camera/Film   All types of film are available, especially in Glasgow, Inverness, and Edinburgh. Processing takes about 24 hours, and many places will do it almost while you wait. There are few restrictions on the use of your camera, except when notices are posted, as in churches, theaters, and certain museums. If in doubt, ask.

Crime   See "Safety," below.

Currency   See "Money," earlier in this chapter.

Customs   See "Customs" in "Information & Entry Requirements," earlier in this chapter.

Dentists   You can find one listed in the yellow pages of the telephone book or you can ask at your hotel. Appointments are usually necessary, but if you're in pain a dentist will generally fit you in.

Doctors   Hotels have their own list of local practitioners. If not, dial "0" (zero) and ask the operator for the local police, who will give you the name, address, and phone number of a doctor in your area. Emergency treatment is free, but if you're admitted to a hospital, referred to an outpatient clinic, or treated for an already existing condition, you'll be required to pay. You'll also pay if you visit a doctor in his or her office or if the doctor makes a "house call" to your hotel.

Documents   See "Information & Entry Requirements," earlier in this chapter.

Drug Laws   Britain is becoming increasingly severe in enforcing drug laws. Persons arrested for possession of even tiny quantities of marijuana have been deported, forced to pay stiff fines, or sentenced to jail for 2 to 7 years. Possession of "white powder" drugs such as heroin or cocaine carries even more stringent penalties.

Drugstores   In Britain they're called "chemist" shops. Every police station in the country has a list of emergency chemists; dial "0" (zero) and ask the operator for the local police. Emergency drugs are normally available at most hospitals, but you'll be examined to see that the drugs you request are really necessary.

Electricity   The electricity is 240 volts AC (50 Hz). Some international hotels are specially wired to allow North Americans to plug in their appliances, but you'll usually need a transformer plus an adapter for your electric razor, hair dryer, or soft-contact-lens sterilizer. Ask at the electrical department of a large hardware store for the transformer size you'll need.

Embassies & Consulates   All embassies are in London, the capital of the U.K. The consulate of the **United States** is in Edinburgh at 3 Regent Terrace (☎ 0131/ 556-8315), open Monday through Friday from 1 to 4pm. The **Australian Consulate** is at 23 Mitchell St., in Edinburgh (☎ 0131/467-8333), open Monday through Friday from 9:30am to 3:30pm.

Some nationals have to use London to conduct their business: Australian High Commission is at the Strand, London WC2B 4LI (☎ 0171/379-4334), and is open Monday through Friday from 9:30am to 3:30pm. Citizens of **Canada** should go to the Canadian High Commission, MacDonald House, 1 Grosvenor Sq., W1 (☎ 0171/258-6600), open Monday through Friday from 8am to 5:30pm; citizens of **New Zealand** should go to the New Zealand High Commission at New Zealand House, 80 Haymarket at Pall Mall, London SW1Y 4TQ (☎ 0171/930-8422), open Monday through Friday from 8am to 5pm. Citizens of the **Republic of Ireland** should deal with their embassy in London at 17 Grosvenor Place, London SW1X 7HR (☎ 0171/235-2171).

Emergencies   For police, fire, or ambulance, dial ☎ **999.** Give your name, address, and phone number, and state the nature of the emergency. Misuse of the 999 service will result in a heavy fine (cardiac arrest, yes; dented fender, no).

Holidays   See "When to Go," earlier in this chapter.

Legal Aid   Your consulate, embassy, or high commission (see above) will give you advice if you run into trouble. They can advise you of your rights and even provide a list of attorneys (for which you'll have to pay if services are used), but they cannot interfere on your behalf in the legal process of Great Britain. For questions about American citizens who are arrested abroad, including ways of getting money to them, telephone the Citizens Emergency Center of the Office of Special Consulate Services in Washington, D.C. (☎ 202/647-5225). Other nationals can go to their nearest consulate or embassy.

Liquor Laws   The legal drinking age is 18. Children under 16 aren't allowed in pubs, except in certain rooms, and then only when accompanied by a parent or guardian. Don't drink and drive—penalties are stiff. Basically, you can get a drink from 11am to 11pm, but this can vary widely, depending on the discretion of the local tavern owner. Not all pubs are open on Sunday; those that are generally stay open from noon to 3pm and 7 to 10:30 or 11pm. Restaurants are also allowed to serve liquor during these hours, but only to people who are dining on the premises. The law allows 30 minutes for "drinking-up time." A meal, incidentally, is defined as "substantial refreshment." And you have to eat and drink sitting down. In hotels, liquor may be served from 11am to 11pm to both residents and nonresidents; after 11pm, according to the law, only residents may be served.

Lost Property   Report the loss to the police first, and they will advise you where to apply for its return. Taxi drivers are required to hand lost property to the nearest police station. For lost passports, credit/charge cards, or money, report the loss and circumstances immediately to the nearest police station. For lost passports, you should then contact your consulate, embassy, or high commission (see "Embassies & Consulates," above). For lost credit/charge cards or traveler's checks, report immediately to the issuing bank or company.

Luggage Storage   You may want to make excursions throughout Scotland taking only your essentials along. It's possible to store suitcases at most railway stations, but you must be prepared to allow luggage to be searched for security reasons, and be warned: If you object, you could be viewed with suspicion.

Mail   Have your mail addressed "Poste Restante" at any of the big towns, or give your hotel address. When claiming personal mail, always carry identification. To send an airmail letter to North America costs 41p (70¢) and postcards require a 35p (60¢) stamp. British mailboxes are painted red and carry a royal coat-of-arms as a signature. A letter generally takes about 7 to 10 days to arrive in North America. All post offices will accept parcels for mailing provided they're properly and securely wrapped.

Newspapers & Magazines   Each major Scottish city publishes its own newspaper. All newsstands carry the major London papers as well. In summer, you can generally pick up a copy of the *International Herald Tribune,* published in Paris, along with the European editions of *USA Today, Time,* and *Newsweek* to bring you up to date on world affairs.

Pets   It's illegal to bring pets into Britain from any other country, except with veterinary documents, and even then they're subject to a quarantine of 6 months. Hotels have their own rules, but generally don't allow dogs in restaurants or public rooms, and often not in the bedrooms either.

Police   The best source of help and advice in emergencies is the police (for non-life-threatening situations, dial "0" zero and ask for the police, or ☎ 999 for emergencies). If the local police can't assist, they'll have the address of a person who can. Losses, thefts, and other crimes should be reported immediately to the police.

Radio/TV   There are 24-hour radio channels operating throughout the United Kingdom. TV starts around 6am with breakfast TV and educational programs. Lighter entertainment begins around 4 or 5pm, after the children's programs, and continues until around midnight. There are now four television channels—two commercial and two BBC without commercials.

Rest Rooms   These are usually found at signs saying PUBLIC TOILETS. They're clean, often have an attendant, and may be used with confidence. Hotels can be used, but they discourage nonresidents. Garages (filling stations) don't always have facilities for the use of customers. There's no need to tip, except to a hotel attendant.

Safety   Although crime is not a serious problem for the average visitor to Scotland, many areas in and around Glasgow are dangerous, with dozens of muggings reported weekly. Caution should always be taken. Never leave your car unlocked and always protect your valuables.

Smoking   It's banned at an increasing number of places, and many bed-and-breakfast houses accept only nonsmokers as guests. Trains have "smokers," and in most buses smoking is allowed in a specially designated section. Some restaurants restrict smoking, as do certain theaters and other public places.

Taxes   There is no local sales tax. However, Great Britain imposes a standard value-added tax (called VAT, for short) of 17.5%. Hotel rates and meals in restaurants are taxed 17.5%; the extra VAT charge will show up on your bill unless otherwise stated. This can be refunded if you shop at stores that participate in the Retail Export Scheme (signs are posted in the window). When you make a purchase, show your passport and request a Retail Export Scheme form (Form VAT 407) and a stamped, preaddressed envelope. Show the VAT form and your sales receipt to British Customs when you leave the country—they may also ask to see the merchandise. After Customs has stamped it, mail the form back to the shop in the envelope provided *before you leave the country.* Your VAT refund will be mailed to you.

Here are three organizing tips to help you through the Customs procedures: Keep your VAT forms with your passport; pack your purchases in a carry-on bag so that you'll have them handy; and allow yourself enough time at your departure point to find a mailbox.

Several readers have reported a scam regarding VAT refunds. The refund forms must be obtained from the retailer on the spot (don't leave the store without one). Some merchants allegedly tell customers that they can get a refund form at the airport on their way out of the country. This is not true. The form must be completed by the retailer on the spot, or else there is no refund coming later.

In October 1994 Britain imposed a departure tax: £10 ($16.50) for passengers flying worldwide, including the United States, and £5 ($8.25) for flights within Britain and the European Union.

As part of an energy-saving scheme, the British government has also added a special 25% tax on gasoline ("petrol").

Telephone, Telex & Fax   Consult "Directory Enquiries" ("Information") to aid you; dial 192, give the operator the town where you want the number, the subscriber's name, and then the address.

If you're calling from a **pay phone,** the machine will accept all British coins except 1p. A local call costs 10p (15¢). Phone books contain detailed instructions about how to make a call in the British Isles. You can also dial the operator for assistance. There are special phone booths used only by phone-card holders. The phone cards are sold at post offices and at the tourist board in denominations of £2, £4, £10, and £20. You put your card into the phone box and make your call. The card is valid until all its units have been used.

Telexes are mostly restricted to business premises and hotels. If your hotel has a **Telex,** they will send it for you. You may need to arrange the receipt of an expected message in advance. British Telecom sends **telegrams and telemessages.** Depending on your location in Scotland, you dial either 190 or 100 on your phone and ask for the telegram-telemessage service. Telemessages are used for sending messages within the U.K. An overseas telegram is used to reach non-British destinations. If your message is more than 50 words, consider a Mailgram; you must know the postal code, however. Each of the three will usually be delivered the following day, unless a bank holiday intervenes.

Time   Britain is based on Greenwich mean time (GMT), 5 hours ahead of the U.S. East Coast, with British summer time (BST, or GMT plus 1 hour) used roughly from April to October. When it's noon in Edinburgh or Glasgow, it's 7am in New York, 6am in Chicago, 5am in Denver, and 4am in Los Angeles.

Tipping   For cab drivers, add about 10% to 15% to the fare as shown on the meter. However, if the driver personally unloads or loads your luggage, add 25p (40¢) per bag.

Hotel porters get 75p ($1.25) per bag even if you have only one small suitcase. Hall porters are tipped only for special services. Maids receive £1 ($1.65) per day. In top-ranking hotels the concierge will often submit a separate bill, showing charges for newspapers and the like; if he or she has been particularly helpful, tip extra.

Hotels often add a service charge of 10% to 15% to bills. In smaller B&Bs, the tip is not likely to be included. Therefore, tip for special services, such as the waiter who serves you breakfast. If several people have served you in a B&B, many guests ask that 10% to 15% be added to the bill and divided among the staff.

In both restaurants and nightclubs, a 15% service charge is added to the bill. To that, add another 3% to 5%, depending on the quality of the service. Waiters in deluxe restaurants and nightclubs are accustomed to the extra 5%, which means you'll end up tipping 20%. If that seems excessive, you must remember that the initial service charge reflected in the fixed price is distributed among all the help. Sommeliers (wine stewards) get about £1 ($1.65) per bottle of wine served. Tipping in pubs is not common, although in cocktail bars the waiter or barmaid usually gets about 75p ($1.25) per round of drinks.

Barbers and hairdressers expect 10% to 15%. Tour guides expect £2 ($3.30), although it's not mandatory. Petrol station attendants are rarely tipped. Theater ushers also don't expect tips, but won't turn one down either.

Tourist Offices   See "Information & Entry Requirements," earlier in this chapter, and also specific cities and towns in the chapters that follow.

Water   Tap water is considered safe to drink throughout Scotland.

Weather   Robert Louis Stevenson said it all: "The weather is raw and boisterous in the winter, shifty and ungenial in summer, and downright meteorological purgatory in spring." If you're planning a motor trip for the day, always check the weather forecasts in the local newspapers or listen to the early-morning radio and TV broadcasts.

Yellow Pages   Throughout Scotland, local phone books contain yellow pages at the back of the book. If you can't find what you're looking for, you may not be looking under the proper English equivalent. For example, instead of drugstore, try "Chemist" or "Pharmacist."

4 The Active Vacation Planner

Except for a handful of urbanized pockets, you might think Scotland was created specifically for the breeding of birds and wildlife and the enjoyment of outdoor activities. The cool air, soft temperatures, and frequent rains are usually healthful and invigorating. Unless you're a serious party person, you'll want to join the country's early-to-bed, early-to-rise motif where sports participants rise with the roosters.

Don't think that the impact of your desire to ramble through the heather on Scottish hills has been ignored by government bureaucrats: Surveys have determined that along with shipbuilding, tourism, and textiles, sports is one of the country's major industries, employing more than 58,000 people and generating some £1 billion in profits and wages annually. In fact, government strategists view Scotland's wilderness areas as billion-dollar possibilities for an increase in income and national prestige. Their plan was laid out in a thousand-page statement, *Sport 2000,* a widely publicized and applauded national strategy for the development of sports in Scotland up to the end of the century. The organization entrusted with the program's development is the **Scottish Sports Council,** Caledonian House, South Gyle, Edinburgh EH12 9DQ (☎ **0131/ 317-7200;** fax 0131/317-7202).

Its priorities involve promotional campaigns, raising the standards of sports coaching at schools throughout Scotland, breaking down the class divisions sometimes associated with sports such as golf and shooting, and fundraising for the construction of new sports facilities.

If you're headed to Scotland to golf, fish, trek, hill climb, canoe, sail, or whatever, you can write for information and guidance. Depending on your area of interest, they'll supply names of playing fields, prices, and facilities. They'll also send you copies of a newsletter, *Arena,* an information-filled bulletin packed with advice about sporting programs and facilities. And if you are a potential investor, they'll try to steer you toward the country's growing sports-related infrastructure. For information about this organization's programs, contact the address above.

1 Golf

What's the quickest way to provoke wrath in a Scottish pub? Bring up the fact that several nations, including France, the Netherlands, and Ireland, have claimed the invention of golf as part of their national patrimony. Evidence cited involves stick-and-ball games played since the Renaissance, including *jeu de mail* in France, *kolven* in Holland, and *hurly* in Ireland. But the true origins of *gowff* (the 17th-century term) began on the sandy soil of seafront terrain in Scotland.

Don't think that the sport was always well received. Monks around St. Andrews were not applauded when they diverted themselves from a schedule of felling trees and praying to play gowff, and both James I and James II rather churlishly issued edicts prohibiting its practice. Despite that, however, by the mid-1700s the game was firmly entrenched in Scotland and viewed as a bucolic oddity by Englishmen chasing after the hounds in the milder climes to the south.

A description of the game was recorded in the early 1500s, and Mary Queen of Scots was reputed to have played golf. A colorful brochure on golf claims, "Its origins are lost in the mists of antiquity." The St. Andrews Club (now the Royal and Ancient Golf Club) set down the first charter of rules in 1754, and was formally recognized as the world's supreme authority for the rules of golf in 1919. This role it more or less gracefully shares today with the United States Golf Association. The first Open Championship was held at Prestwick during the reign of Queen Victoria (1860), establishing a long tradition of contests that would eventually generate hundreds of millions of dollars worldwide.

Golf is usually played on courses with 18 holes over a total length of between 5,000 and 7,500 yards. Each hole represents a test of skill: using as few strokes as possible to hit the ball into the hole. Hazards (streams, rocky areas, patches of long grass, copses of trees, sand or water traps) are deliberately positioned along the course to confuse—and sometimes enrage—players.

Demographic experts cite golf as one of the world's perfect sports. It can be played by participants of all ages, and variations in the layout of courses compensate for widely different climates and terrains. It's healthful for the cardiovascular system, but rarely involves the bodily injuries of contact sports. The sport's handicapping system enables a comparative neophyte to compete against a highly skilled player and still maintain an element of competition.

Despite the sport's association with aristocratic families and patrician incomes, Scotland maintains more than 440 golf courses, many of them municipal courses open to everyone. Some are both royal and ancient, such as St. Andrews; others are modern and hip. An example of a much-discussed, well-received newcomer is the Loch Lomond course in the Trossachs, established as a private club in 1993. Although they lie as far north as Sutherland, only 6° south of the Arctic Circle, most courses are in the country's "Central Belt," an area stretching from Stirling down to Edinburgh and Glasgow.

A beginner doesn't need to lug a complete set of golf clubs across the Atlantic. Many courses rent full or half sets of clubs. If you're female, or if you plan on playing golf with someone who is, be aware that some courses are restricted to men, and either ban women completely or limit women to designated days of the week. Despite this tradition-bound holdover from another era, women's golf thrives in Scotland, with about 33,000 members in the Scottish Ladies' Golfing Association. The Ladies' British Open Amateur Championship was first held in 1893 (the U.S. equivalent was first held in 1895). For information about tournaments or the procurement of women golf partners, contact Mrs. L. H. Park, Secretary, **Scottish Ladies' Golfing Association,** which shares offices with the **Scottish Golf Union,** an organization established in 1920 to "foster and maintain a high standard of amateur golf in Scotland, and to administer, organize, and act as the governing body for amateur (i.e., not professional) golf in Scotland." For information from either group, contact

Mrs. Park or Ian Hume, Esq., Secretary, Scottish National Golf Centre, Drumoig, Leuchars, St. Andrews, Fife KY16 0DW, Scotland (☎ **01382/549500;** fax 01382/549510).

Don't think that a neophyte unfamiliar with the rules of the game will be allowed to use any of the country's legendary golf courses without a mastery of the rudiments. Many courses will want evidence of your familiarity with the game before you're allowed on the links. Depending on the setting and the season, this could include a letter citing your ability and experience from your club back home, or visual proof that you've mastered a basically sound swing and an understanding of golf-related etiquette.

Any golf enthusiast who anticipates a long sojourn in Scotland should consider joining a local golf club. Membership makes procurement of tee-off times easier, and attending or competing in a local club's tournaments can be both fun and sociable. But if you anticipate only a brief fling in Scotland, a letter from a golf club in your home country can open a lot of doors otherwise closed to the general public.

Access to many private clubs can be dicey, particularly those with so much tradition that waiting lists for tee-off times can stretch on for up to a year in advance. You can always stay in a hotel (Gleneagles or Turnberry) that has its own course, thereby guaranteeing the availability of tee-off times.

What should you expect from your first visit to a Scottish golf course? Abandon forever any hope of balmy tropical weather, azure skies, and lush fairways burgeoning in the sun. Don't anticipate the sprinklers that flood many warm-weather courses in other countries. The rains and fogs of Scotland produce an altogether different kind of golf-related aesthetic, one buffeted by coastal winds, sometimes torn by gales and storms, and in some places, accented only with tough, salt-tolerant grasses and stunted, wind-blown trees and shrubs such as gorse and heather.

Knowing a term or two in advance might help in picking your golf course. The Scots make a strong distinction between their two types of courses: links courses and upland courses. **Links courses** nestle into the sandy terrain of coastal regions, and although years of cultivation have rendered their fairways and putting greens emerald colored, there's a vague sense that eons ago the terrain was submerged beneath the water. Links courses are among the famous names in Scotland, and include Royal Troon, Turnberry, Prestwick, North Berwick, and Glasgow Gailes. Examples of **upland courses,** among many others, include Gleneagles, Loch Lomond, and Pitlochry.

GOLF TOURS

Many visitors consider golf and whisky Scotland's most outstanding attractions. But while the whisky was usually readily available in the past, access for nonmembers to the country's maze of golf courses was not. All that changed in 1988, however, with the establishment of a New York–based company, **Golf International,** 275 Madison Ave., New York, NY 10016 (☎ **800/833-1389** or 212/986-9176). The company maintains a branch office in St. Andrew's, the ivy-clad *sanctum sanctorum* of the golfing world, and caters to golfers from moderate to advanced abilities. Against hitherto impossible odds, the company will guarantee their clients' starting times at 40 or so of the most sought-after golf courses of Scotland, including St. Andrews as well as Carnoustie, Royal Troon, Prestwick, and Gullane.

Potential clients, in self-organized groups of 2 to 12, proffer a "wish list" of the courses they'd like to play. Starting times are prearranged—sometimes rigidly—with an ease that an individual traveler or even a conventional travel agent would find impossible. Packages can be arranged for anywhere from 7 to 14 days (the average package is about 7 days) and can include as much or as little golf, at as many different courses, as a client might want. Weekly prices, with hotels, breakfasts, car rentals, greens fees, and the services of a greeter and helpmate at the airport upon arrival, range from $1,750 to $7,000 per person. Discounted airfares to Scotland can also be arranged. For more information, talk to one of Golf International's sales agents at the toll-free number listed above.

Other companies specializing in golf tours include: **Adventures in Golf,** 11 Northeastern Blvd., Suite 360, Nashua, NH 03062 (☎ **603/882-8367**); **Celtic Golf Tours,** 124 Sunset Blvd., P.O. Box 417, Cape May, NJ 08204 (☎ **609/884-8090**); **Classic Golf & Leisure,** 75706 McLachlin Circle, Palm Desert, CA 92211 (☎ **760/ 772-2560**); **ITC Golf Tours,** 4134 Atlantic Ave., Suite 205, Long Beach, CA 90807 (☎ **800/257-4981** or 562/595-6905); and **Pery Golf,** 8302 Dunwoody Place, Suite 305, Atlanta, GA 30350 (☎ **800/344-5257** or 770/641-9696).

THE CLASSIC COURSES

For more details about these fabled golf courses, refer to "The Best Golf," in chapter 1.

The **Carnoustie Golf Links,** Links Parade, Carnoustie, Tayside (☎ **01241/ 853789;** fax 01241/852720), has a par of 72. This 6,941-yard championship course requires the use of a caddy, costing £25 ($41.25) for 18 holes. As with most championship courses, electric golf carts are not allowed, but you can rent a trolley for £2.50 ($4.15) per round. Greens fees are £52 ($85.80), and club rental, available at Simpson's Golf Shop, 6 Links Parade (☎ **01241/854477**), or David Low's, 7 Links Ave. (☎ **01241/853439**), costs £8 ($13.20) per round.

The **Old Course, St. Andrews,** Golf Place, St. Andrews, Fife (☎ **01334/ 466666**), is a 6,566-yard 18-hole course. Golf was first played here around A.D. 1400, and it is billed as "the Home of Golf." Greens fees are £70 ($115.50) and a caddy will cost £22 ($36.30) plus tip. Golf clubs rent for £15 ($24.75) per round. There are no electric carts allowed, and you can only rent a trolley on afternoons between May and September for £3 ($4.95). The course is a par 72.

The **Royal Dornoch Golf Club,** Dornoch, Sutherland (☎ **01862/810219**), 40 miles north of Inverness, offers an 18-hole course with a par of 70. At this 6,185-yard course the greens fees are £40 ($66) per round Monday through Friday and £50 ($82.50) per round on Saturday and Sunday, with a 3-day ticket, available for consecutive weekdays only, costing £100 ($165). Golf club and trolley rentals are £10 to £15 ($16.50 to $24.75) and £2 ($3.30) per round, respectively. No caddy service is available.

The **Royal Troon Golf Club,** Craigend Road, Troon, Ayrshire (☎ **01292/ 311555;** fax 01292/318204), has one of the largest courses in Scotland with 7,097 yards of playing area. The par is 71. The greens fee—£100 ($165) for a day—includes a buffet lunch and two 18-hole sets. For one round of play, a trolley rents for £3 ($4.95), a caddy costs £25 ($41.25), and club rental is £20 ($33) per round or £70 ($115.50) per day.

The **Turnberry Hotel Golf Courses,** Ayrshire (☎ **01655/331000;** fax 01655/ 331706), gives priority at its 6,971-yard par-70 course to residents of the hotel. The greens fee of £75 ($123.75) for guests and £105 ($173.25) for nonguests includes 18 holes on the Ailsa course and an additional 18-hole round on the less-desirable Arran course. For a round of golf, clubs rent for £40 ($66) and caddy service costs £25 ($41.25) plus tip. If you are not staying here, telephone in the morning to check on any unclaimed tee-off times—but it's not likely that there'll be one.

OTHER LEADING GOLF COURSES

Although not as famous as the clubs above, Scotland abounds in golf courses. Some of our favorite tee-off spots include the following.

Scotland's Best Golf Courses

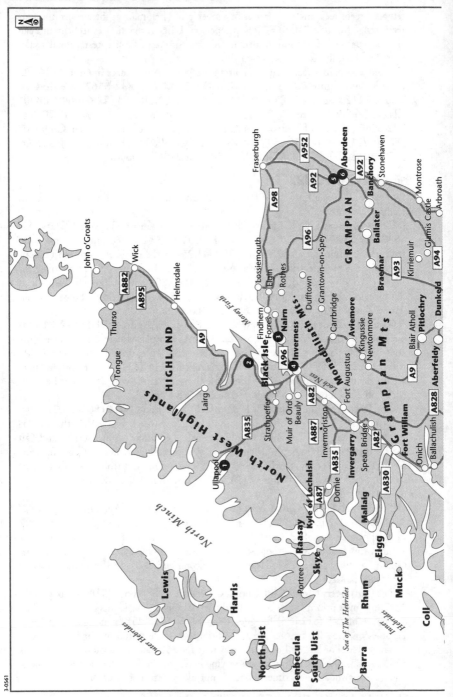

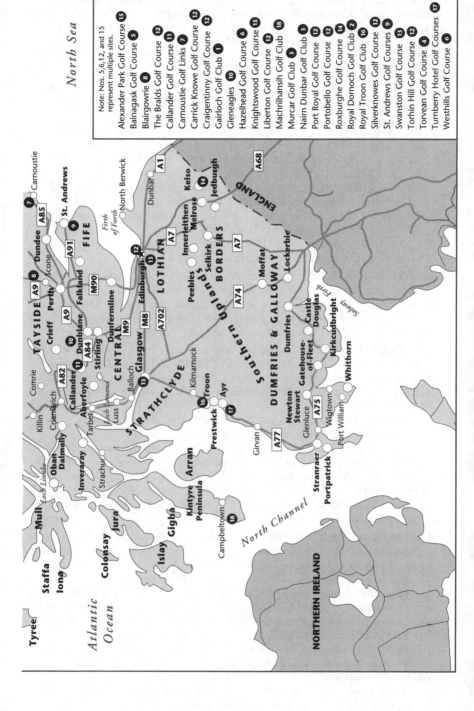

Note: Nos. 5,6,12, and 15 represent multiple sites.

Alexander Park Golf Course **15**
Balnagask Golf Course **5**
Blairgowrie **8**
The Bralds Golf Course **12**
Callander Golf Course **11**
Carnoustie Golf Links **7**
Carrick Knowe Golf Course **12**
Craigentinny Golf Course **12**
Gairloch Golf Club **1**
Gleneagles **10**
Hazelhead Golf Course **6**
Knightswood Golf Course **15**
Liberton Golf Course **12**
Machrihanish Golf Club **18**
Murcar Golf Club **5**
Nairn Dunbar Golf Club **3**
Port Royal Golf Course **12**
Portobello Golf Course **12**
Roxburghe Golf Course **14**
Royal Dornoch Golf Club **2**
Royal Troon Golf Club **16**
Silverknowes Golf Courses **12**
St. Andrews Golf Courses **9**
Swanston Golf Course **13**
Torhin Hill Golf Course **12**
Torvean Golf Course **4**
Turnberry Hotel Golf Courses **17**
Westhills Golf Course **6**

NORTHERN HIGHLANDS The leading course here is the Royal Dornoch Golf Club (see above). One of the few courses on the western coast is the **Gairloch Golf Club,** Gairloch Ross-shire (☎ 01445/712407). It's a 9-hole course with 1,942 yards of playing area and a par of 62. The greens fees are £14 ($23.10) per day and £49 ($80.85) per week. No caddy service is offered, and a trolley costs £2 ($3.30). Golf clubs rent for £5 ($8.25).

AROUND THE GREAT GLEN Two courses ideal for visitors are the **Torvean Golf Course,** Glen Q Road, Inverness (☎ 01463/711434), and the **Nairn Dunbar Golf Club,** Loch Loy Road, Nairn (☎ 01667/452741).

The 5,451-yard Torvean offers an 18-hole par-68 course with greens fees of £10.10 ($16.65) Monday through Thursday and £11.60 ($19.15) Friday through Sunday. Caddy service is not available, but you can rent a trolley for £1.90 ($3.15). Club rental costs £5 ($8.25) per round.

The 18-hole Nairn course consists of 6,700 yards of playing area with a par of 72. Caddy service must be reserved in advance, costing £15 to £30 ($24.75 to $49.50). A pull trolley costs £2 ($3.30) per round, and the more expensive electric one goes for £4 ($6.60) per round. Greens fees break down as follows: Monday through Friday, £23 ($37.95) per round, £30 ($49.50) per day; Saturday and Sunday, £28 ($46.20) per round, £35 ($57.75) per day; and £150 ($247.50) weekly.

ARGYLL & THE ISLES The **Machrilhansih Golf Club,** Machrilhansih, by Campbeltown (☎ 01586/810213), welcomes visitors to its 6,228-yard par-70 course. Monday through Friday and Sunday the greens fees are £23 ($37.95) per round or £32 ($52.80) per day. On Saturday, day rates are offered at £38 ($62.70). Bring your own clubs because rentals are not available. Trolleys cost £2 ($3.30).

CENTRAL HIGHLANDS A good choice for a round or two is the **Blairgowrie,** Golf Course Road, Rosemont, Blairgowrie (☎ 01250/872622). The 18-hole course includes 6,229 yards of playing area with a par of 72. The greens fees are £35 ($57.75) for one round and £48 ($79.20) for two. On Saturday and Sunday, the rate is a flat £40 ($66) per round. The pro shop charges £2.50 ($4.15) for a trolley, £18 ($29.70) for an electric cart, and £12 ($19.80) for rental of clubs per round. The caddy costs £15 ($24.75) plus tip for each round.

Another suitable choice is the **Callander Golf Course,** Aveland Road, Callander (☎ 01877/330090). At this 5,125-yard par-66 course, greens fees are £18 ($29.70) per round, £26 ($42.90) per day, Monday through Friday, and £26 ($42.90) per round or £31 ($51.15) per day on Saturday and Sunday. The trolley charge is included in the golf club rental, costing £8 ($13.20) for 18 holes; otherwise, you pay £1.50 ($2.45). No caddy service is available.

ABERDEEN & THE NORTHEAST Several courses throughout this region are for members only, but there are some acceptable courses that tourists can use, including the **Westhills Golf Course,** West Hill Heights, West Hill Skene, Aberdeen (☎ and fax 01224/740159). Seven miles west of Aberdeen, this par-69 course features 5,921 yards of playing area. West Hills does not offer caddy service, but you can rent a trolley for £2 ($3.30). The charge for club rental is £12 ($19.80) for 18 holes Monday through Friday and £18 ($29.70) on weekends. Greens fees are £12 ($19.80) Monday through Friday and £18 ($29.70) on Saturday and Sunday.

Other 18-hole options that are adequate, but rather basic, include: **Balnagask,** St. Fitticks Road, Aberdeen (☎ 01224/876407), a par-70, 5,986-yard course; and the **Murcar Golf Club,** Bridge of Don, Aberdeen (☎ 01224/704354), a par-71, 6,241-yard course. Neither Mucar nor Balnagask has caddies or rentals of golf clubs and trolleys. Greens fees are £7.65 ($12.60) at Balnagask; and at Murcar, £28 ($46.20) per round and £38 ($62.70) per day, Monday through Friday, and on the weekend a day rate only of £43 ($70.95)—although it's nearly impossible to get a weekend slot. **Hazlehead Golf Course,** Aberdeen (☎ 01224/321830), is two 9-hole courses, a 2,559-yard course and a 2,917-yard course, and charges a greens fee of £3.85 ($6.35) for 9 holes or £7.65 ($12.60) to play both courses. Clubs and a trolley can be rented at a rate of £7 ($11.55) per 9 holes, but no caddy service is offered.

FIFE & ANGUS   On Golf Place on the north border of **St. Andrews,** the St. Andrews Club features some of the best 18-hole courses in this region, including The Old Course (see above); the **Eden Course** (☎ 01334/474296), a 6,112-yard par 70; the **Jubilee Course** (☎ 01334/473938), a 6,805-yard par 71; the **New Course** (☎ 01334/473938), a 6,604-yard par 72; and the **Strathyrum Course** (☎ 01334/474296), a 5,094-yard par 67. At each of these courses, golf club rentals are £11.50 ($18.95) per round and £15 ($24.75) per day; £2 ($3.30) for trolleys; and £21 ($34.65) plus tip per round for caddies. The greens fees are £16 to £20 ($26.40 to $33) for Eden, £20 to £25 ($33 to $41.25) for Jubilee, £24 to £30 ($39.60 to $49.50) for New, and £13 to £15 ($21.45 to $24.75) for Strathyrum.

GLASGOW   Several courses are near Glasgow, but there's a limited number of courses inside the city. Two 9-hole courses suitable for play are **Alexander Park,** Alexandra Parade (☎ 0141/556-1294), and **Knightswood,** Lincoln Avenue (☎ 0141/959-6358). Neither course offers caddy service or rentals of clubs and trolleys. Both Alexander, a 2,281-yard, par-31 course, and Knightswood, a 2,793-yard, par-34 course, charge greens fees of £3.15 ($5.20) per round.

EDINBURGH   A number of courses are featured here with a varied range of services, although caddies seem to be a scarce resource—none of the following courses has caddy service.

The **Silverknowes Golf Course,** Silverknowes Parkway (☎ 0131/336-3843), is a 6,202-yard course with a par of 74. The greens fee is £7.95 ($13.10) for 18 holes, with club and trolley rentals costing £7 to £10 ($11.55 to $16.50) and £1.75 ($2.90), respectively.

Three miles east of Edinburgh, **Craigentinny,** Craigentinny Gold, Fillyside Road (☎ 0131/554-7501), features 5,413 yards of playing area and a par of 67. Clubs rent for £6.25 ($10.30) per round, but trolleys are not offered. The greens fee is £7.95 ($13.10) for 18 holes.

The **Liberton Golf Course,** Kingston Grange, 297 Gilmerton Rd. (☎ 0131/664-8580), a 5,306-yard, par 67, requires 2 days' notice if you want to rent golf clubs, the price of which is included in the greens fees of £17 ($28.05) Monday through Friday and £30 ($49.50) Saturday and Sunday for 18 holes. No trolley rentals are offered.

The Braids, Braid House Golf Course, Approach Road (☎ 0131/447-6666), located within city limits, is 3 miles south of Edinburgh city center. The greens fee at this 5,731-yard, par-70 course is £7.85 ($12.95). Clubs rent for £7.10 ($11.70) and trolleys go for £1.75 ($2.90) per 18 holes of play.

Nine miles southwest of Edinburgh, the **Swanston Golf Course,** Swanston Road (☎ 0131/445-2239), is an 18-hole, 4,825-yard, par-66 course. Clubs go for £7.50 ($12.40) per round and trolleys for £2.50 ($4.15) per round. Greens fees are £15 ($24.75) per round Monday through Friday and £20 ($33) Saturday and Sunday. The per-day rates are £20 ($33) Monday through Friday and £25 ($41.25) Saturday and Sunday.

The **Portobello,** Stanley Street (☎ 0131/669-4361), is a 9-hole course with a par of 64. The greens fee at this 2,410-yard course is £3.95 ($6.50) per round. A deposit of £10 ($16.50) is required for golf club rental, costing £6.95 ($11.45). Trolleys go for £1.75 ($2.90).

The **Carrick Knowe,** Glen Devon Park (☎ 0131/337-1096), is one of Scotland's larger courses, featuring 6,229 yards of playing area. Currently, it is being redesigned, so only a 3,000-yard 9-hole is playable at present. The revamped 18-hole course is scheduled to reopen in its entirety during July 1998. Five miles west of Edinburgh, this par-71 course offers club rentals at £7 ($11.55) per round and trolleys at £1.75 ($2.90). The greens fee is £7.90 ($13.05) for 18 holes of golf.

The **Torphin Hill Golf Course,** Torphin Road (☎ 0131/441-1100), is a 4,648-yard, 18-hole, par-66 course, offering no caddy services, club rentals, or trolleys. The greens fee is £10 ($16.50) per round weekdays, £15 ($24.75) per round weekends.

THE BORDERS   A new championship golf course opened in 1997 near Kelso, 43 miles from Edinburgh. **Roxburghe Golf Course** (☎ 01573/450331), is an 18-hole course set in 250 acres of grounds owned by the Duke and Duchess of Roxburghe. This 7,111-yard course was designed by Dave Thomas, one of Britain's leading golf course architects. Open to nonmembers, it is the only championship golf course in the Borders. Greens fees cost £20 ($33) for 18 holes of play, or £30 ($49.50) for a full day's play Monday through Friday, rising to £29 ($47.85) for 18 holes on weekends or £41 ($67.65) for a full day.

2 Fishing

Anglers consider Scotland a paradise, citing its fast-flowing rivers, the availability of Atlantic **salmon** ("the king of all gamefish"), and some of the most beautiful scenery in Europe, along with the marvelous hospitality extended by its innkeepers. Permits for fishing (often arranged by your hotel) can be expensive. For one of the grand beats on the River Tay, a week's permit could run into hundreds of pounds. However, there are many lesser-known rivers where a club ticket costs only pounds a day.

The Tweed and the Tay are just two of the famous Scottish salmon rivers. In Perthshire, the Tay is the broadest and longest river in the country. The Dee, with all its royal associations, is the famous salmon-fishing river of Aberdeenshire. The royal family fishes this river. The queen herself has been seen casting from these banks. Other anglers prefer to fish the Spey, staying at one of the inns along the Malt Whisky Trail. Certain well-heeled fishers travel every year to Scotland to fish in the lochs and rivers of the Outer Hebrides.

In general the season for salmon fishing in Scotland runs from the latter part of February until sometime in late October. But these dates vary from region to region.

TYPES OF FISHING   Here's a breakdown of terms you're likely to hear even before you cast your first line into the country's glittering waters.

Coarse Fishing   Its bounty includes all species of freshwater fish except salmon and trout. Especially prized trophies, known for putting up a spirited Scottish fight, include carp, tench, pike, bream, roach, and perch. Because few lochs actually freeze during the winter, the sport can be practiced throughout the year. For access to like-minded participants, contact local tourist boards.

Game Fishing   Salmon and trout (brown, rainbow, or sea) are the most desired of the game fish, and the ones that have inspired the image of a fly fisher whipping a lure and line in serpentine arcs above a loch. Game fishers usually immerse themselves in bulky rubber waders up to their waists in streams and freshwater lochs. Angling for these kinds of highly desirable fish is subject to seasonal controls, and sometimes requires the acquisition of a permit. For specific information about game fishing in

Scotland, contact the **Salmon and Trout Association (Scottish Branch),** 10 Great Stuart St., Edinburgh EH3 7TN (☎ and fax **0131/225-2417**).

Sea Fishing   The Scots designate types of fishing with their own idiosyncratic terms. The most commonplace and least complicated involves fishing from a beach, a rocky shoreline, or a pier. "Inshore fishing" involves dropping a line into ocean waters within 3 miles of any Scottish coastline; "deep-sea fishing" is off a boat more than 3 miles offshore in a style made popular by cigar-chomping tycoons and Hemingway clones. Offshore waters have produced several species of shark, including porbeagle, thresher, mako, and blue shark. For information about what to expect from deep off-shore waters, contact the **Scottish Tourist Board,** 23 Ravelston Terrace, Edinburgh EH14 3TP (☎ **0131/332-2433**).

FISHING CLUBS   Acquisition of permits and easy availability of information about worthwhile places to fish seem easier if you join one of the more than 380 fishing clubs headquartered in Scotland. (The oldest angling club in the world, the Ellem Fishing Club, was founded in Scotland in 1829.) Each of their activities is supervised by the **Scottish Anglers' National Association,** an organization that firmly believes that newcomers should learn at the side of the more experienced. Courses and re-unions are offered in the fine art of fishing in or around Scotland. For information, contact the Scottish Tourist Board (see above).

3 Other Sports Vacations

Because of the publicity generated by Scottish golf and fishing, a first-timer might think that was all there was. Not so! Scotland is an outdoors country, and the Scots are a people in tune with nature. Here are the major sporting activities:

BICYCLING

Embedded in many visitors' memories is the sight of a tweed-clad Scot, with a tam o' shanter and perhaps a pipe, two-wheeling his way across the moorlands, perhaps to a pub warmed by a peat-burning fireplace. Although many cyclists consider their two-wheeled conveyance a simple way to get from point A to point B without the pollution and expense of a car, others view bicycling as a leisure activity that requires only a modest investment, and can provide aerobic exercise while avoiding unnecessary stress to ligaments and joints.

Naturally, the scenery and relative scarcity of population in Scotland provide heavenly opportunities for getting around by bike. The first source of information for cyclists is the **Scottish Cyclists' Union,** an organization that provides an annual handbook and a regular newsletter for members. They're also one of the most potent lobbying groups in Scotland for the inauguration and preservation of cyclists' byways. They distribute maps showing worthwhile bike routes and support the publication of technical material of interest to cyclists. For information, contact Jim Riach, Executive Office, Scottish Cyclists' Union, The Velodrome, Meadowbrook Stadium, London Road, Edinburgh EH7 6AD (☎ **0131/652-0187;** fax 0131/661-0474).

Although based in England, the **Cyclist's Tourist Club,** Cotterell House, 69 Meadrow, Godalming, Surrey GU7 3HS (☎ **01483/417217;** fax 01483/426994), offers information on cycling holidays in Scotland. Membership costs £25 ($41.25) a year for adults, £12.50 ($20.65) for those 17 and under. A family with three or more members can obtain a membership for £42 ($69.30).

Bicycles are forbidden on most highways, trunk roads, and on what the British call "dual carriageways" (divided highways). In town or in the country, the bike is a great way to get around.

Here's a lexicon of **bicycling terms** you'll need to know before maintaining your end of a cycling-related dialogue in a Scottish pub: "Cycle touring" is a term for riding through scenic Scottish countryside between two fixed points on the Scottish map. "BMX" refers to Bicycle Motor Cross, a sporting subdivision where special cycles with rough-surface tires and heavy-duty chains battle their way in relays across natural or man-made obstacle courses. This is not to be confused with "Cyclo-Cross," a competitive and sometimes messy cross-country event that includes negotiating hazards and carrying or running with the bike over rough or muddy terrain.

Mountain bikes are souped-up versions of pedal bikes, with oversized gear ratios, enlarged tires with bulky treads, and frames especially strengthened for negotiating rough-paved, steeply inclined roads. They're often the means of conveyance in competitive races whose courses lead over rocky terrains of heath, mooreland, and bog.

Road racing is held on open roads, can involve timed events over short or long distances, and can last for an afternoon (in which case they're sometimes known as time trials, especially if the course is a circular track) or over a span of several days.

Regardless of which of the above-mentioned events appeals to you (as spectator, participant, or organizer), you should know that the Scottish Cyclists' Union promotes more than 300 cycling events a year throughout Scotland. The organization will give advice about where to rent or buy a cycle; they also offer legal advice, without charge, to members involved in cycle-related upsets, and advice about easily available medical insurance for members.

It's possible to take your bicycle without restrictions on car and passenger ferries in Scotland. There is almost no case where it's necessary to make arrangements in advance. However, the transport of your bike is likely to cost £6 to £10 ($9.90 to $16.50), plus the cost of your own passage.

May, June, and September are the best months for cycling in spite of often bad weather. Many of the narrow and scenic roads are likely to be very overcrowded with cars in July and August.

BICYCLE TOURS

Try one of the following tour operators: **Bespoke Highland Tours,** The Bothy, Camusdarach, Inverness PH39 4NT (☎ 01687/450272), offers a number of tours for all fitness levels throughout the countryside and the isles. Another operator that offers a wide array of bike treks, including off-road mountain tours, is **Scottish Border Trails,** Drummore, Venlaw High Road, Peebles EH45 87RL (☎ 01721/720336; fax 01721/723004).

BICYCLE RENTALS

Leading bike-rental shops offer a wide range of bicycles from three-speeds to mountain bikes.

EDINBURGH   You are required to pay a deposit of £50 to £100 ($82.50 to $165), depending on the bike, at **Central Cycle Hire,** 13 Lochrin Place (☎ 0131/228-6333; fax 0131/228-3686). Rates range from £8 to £15 ($13.20 to $24.75). Open Monday through Saturday from 10am to 5:30pm and Sunday from 10am to noon and 5 to 7pm.

Sandy Gilchrist Cycles, 1 Cadzow Place (☎ 0131/652-1760), offers day rentals at £15 ($24.75) and half days at £10 ($16.50). A £100 ($165) deposit is required. Open Friday through Wednesday from 9am to 5:30pm and Thursday from 9am to 7:30pm.

Second Hand Bike Shop, 25–27 Iona St. (☎ 0131/553-1130), rents bikes for £7.50 ($12.40) per day, requiring a £50 ($82.50) deposit. Open Tuesday through Saturday from 9am to 5:30pm.

THE BORDERS & THE SOUTHWEST **Ace Cycles,** 11 Church St., Castle Douglas (☎ and fax **01556/504542**), rents bikes for £10 ($16.50) a day and £50 ($82.50) a week. The shop requires a £50 ($82.50) deposit. Open Monday through Saturday from 9am to 5pm.

Glentress Bicycle Trekking Centre, Glentress, Peebles (☎ **01721/722934;** fax 01721/723004), requires a deposit of £50 ($82.50). Daily rates range from £10 to £18 ($16.50 to $29.70) and rentals must be arranged in advance. Open daily from 9:30am to 5pm.

At the **Hawick Cycle Centre,** 45 N. Bridge St., Hawick (☎ **01450/373352**), you'll pay £10 ($16.50) per day and £50 ($82.50) per week. The shop requires a £50 ($82.50) deposit. Open Monday and Wednesday through Friday from 9am to 8pm, Tuesday from 9am to 5pm, and Sunday from noon to 4pm.

Nithsdale Cycle Centre, 46 Broons Rd., Dumfries (☎ **01387/254870**), requires a £15 ($24.75) deposit and charges £7 ($11.55) daily, £35 ($57.75) weekly. Open Tuesday through Saturday from 10am to 5pm.

FIFE & ANGUS You'll pay a deposit of £10 to £40 ($16.50 to $66) at **East Neuk Outdoors,** Cellardyke Park (☎ **01333/311929**). Rental rates are £12 ($19.80) daily and £36 ($59.40) weekly. Open daily from 10am to 5pm.

ABERDEEN & THE NORTHEAST **Alpine Bikes,** 66–70 Holburn St., Aberdeen (☎ **01224/211455;** fax 01224/211388), requires only a credit- or charge-card number as a deposit. Rates are £12 ($19.80) daily or £25 ($41.25) for the weekend. Open Sunday from 11am to 4pm, Monday through Wednesday and Friday from 9am to 6pm, and Thursday from 9am to 8pm.

You pay £12 ($19.80) for a day rental and £59 ($97.35) weekly at **Outdoor Gear,** 88 Fonthill Rd., Aberdeen (☎ **01224/573952**). A deposit of £50 ($82.50) is required along with some form of ID. Open Monday through Friday from 9am to 5:30pm and Saturday from 9am to 2pm.

ARGYLL & THE ISLES At **Mr. Bilsland,** The Gift Shop, Brodick, Isle of Arran (☎ **01770/302272**), you pay a £10 ($16.50) deposit. Rental rates include a helmet and are £4 to £8.50 ($6.60 to $14) daily, £16 to £30 ($26.40 to $49.50) weekly. Open daily from 9am to 6pm.

On Yer Bike, Salen (☎ **01680/300501**), does not require a deposit and charges £5 ($8.25) for daily rentals and £9 ($14.85) for weekly rentals. This business is run out of a home, so you must call in advance and make the arrangements to pick up a bike.

Spinning Wheels, The Trossachs, Corrie (☎ **01770/810640**), only requires proof of identity for a deposit. The shop charges £4.50 to £8 ($7.45 to $13.20) daily rental and £22 to £35 ($36.30 to $57.75) weekly. You must call in advance to make arrangements to pick up a bicycle.

AROUND THE GREAT GLEN **Wilderness Cycles,** The Green, Drumnadrochit (☎ **01456/450223**), only requires proof of identity for a deposit. A half-day rental costs £7 ($11.55), £12 ($19.80) daily, and £45 ($74.25) weekly. Open daily from 9am to 6pm.

Inverdruie Mountain Bikes, Rothiemurchus Visitor Centre, Cairngorms Road, Inverdruie (☎ **01479/810787**), charges £8 ($13.20) for a half day and £14 ($23.10) for a full day, and requires a form of ID for a deposit. Open April through October, daily from 9am to 5pm; the same hours are kept, weather permitting, the rest of the year.

At **OffBeat Bikes,** Fort William (☎ **01397/704008**), the daily rate is £12.50 ($20.65); it's £8.50 ($14) for a half day and £60 ($99) for a week. You only need your ID for the deposit. Open daily from 9:30am to 5pm.

Speyside Sports, Main Street, Aviemore (☎ **01479/810656**), rents bikes at £6 ($9.90) for a half day, £10 ($16.50) daily, £38 ($62.70) for 6 days, and £40 ($66) for 7 days. ID will suffice for a deposit. Open daily from 9am to 5:30pm.

Sporthaus, Main Street, Aviemore (☎ **01479/810655**), charges £12 ($19.80) daily, £47.50 ($78.40) for 5 days, and £55 to £60 ($90.75 to $99) weekly, requiring ID for deposit. Open daily from 9am to 7pm.

NORTHERN HIGHLANDS The **Alex Dan Cycle Centre,** 67 Kenneth St., Stornoway (☎ **01851/704025**), requires no deposit and charges £7.50 ($12.40) daily, £25 ($41.25) weekly. Open Monday through Saturday from 9am to 6pm.

Barra Cycle Hire, Brendan Road, Castlebay (☎ **01871/810284**), charges £8 ($13.20) daily and £35 ($57.75) weekly. No deposit is required. Open Monday through Saturday from 10am to 1pm.

You'll pay £8.50 ($14) for a daily rental and £50 ($82.50) weekly at the **Bike Shop,** 35 High St., Thurso (☎ **01847/896124**). The deposit is £15 ($24.75). Open Monday through Saturday from 9am to 5:30pm.

Broadford Bicycle Hire, Fairwinds, Egol Road, Broadford (☎ **01471/822270**), requires a £5 ($8.25) deposit for 1 day and £10 ($16.50) for 2 days or longer. Rates are £7 ($11.55) daily and £36 ($59.40) weekly. Open Monday through Saturday from 9am to 7pm.

At the **Ferry Filling Station,** Ardvasar, Skye (☎ **01471/844249**), a deposit of £10 ($16.50) is required. Rentals range from £3 to £6 ($4.95 to $9.90) daily and £18 to £36 ($29.70 to $59.40) weekly. Open daily 9am to 6pm.

Island Cycles, The Green, Portee (☎ **01478/613121**), charges £7.50 to £12.50 ($12.40 to $20.65) for daily rentals and £30 to £48 ($49.50 to $79.20) weekly. A £10 ($16.50) deposit is required. Open Monday through Saturday from 10am to 5pm.

ID is required as deposit at **Duncaan Hostel,** The Pier, Clanachan (☎ **01599/ 534795**). The shop charges £10 ($16.50) per day. Open daily from 9am to 9pm.

ORKNEY & SHETLAND **Baby Linen Shop,** 52 Dundas St., Stromness, Orkney (☎ **01856/850255**), rents bikes for £5 to £10 ($8.25 to $16.50) a day and £27 to £39 ($44.55 to $64.35) a week. No deposit is required. Open daily in summer from 8:30am to 10pm.

Pattersons Cycle Hire, Kirkwall, Orkney (☎ **01856/873097**), doesn't charge a deposit and has rates of £7 ($11.55) daily, with 1 free day if you rent for a week. Open Monday through Friday from 9am to 6pm and Saturday from 9:30am to 5pm.

CENTRAL HIGHLANDS At **Loch Tay Mountain Bike,** Pedlars, Main Street, Killin (☎ **01567/820652**), rentals are as follows: £9 ($14.85) for a half day, £13 ($21.45) per day, £55 ($90.75) for 5 days, and £60 ($99) for a week.

You pay £10 ($16.50) daily and £50 ($82.50) weekly with only your ID for a deposit at **Lochside Mountain Bike Hire,** Lochside Guest House, Arrochar (☎ **01301/702467**). Open daily from 8am to 5pm.

Your ID is all you need for a deposit at **Trossachs' Cycle Hire,** Trossachs Holiday Park, Aberfoyle (☎ **01877/382614**). The daily rental is £10 ($16.50), with weekly rates of £50 ($82.50). Open daily from 9am to 7pm.

Wheels, Invertiossachs Rd., Callander (☎ **01877/331-100**), charges £10 ($16.50) daily, £30 ($49.50) for 4 days, and £50 ($82.50) for a week. They also provide bikers with sleeping rooms for £10 ($16.50) per night.

BIRD WATCHING

The passion of the British for bird watching has factored into British humor since the days when Margaret Rutherford, clad in tweeds and sensible shoes, took to the fields of Scotland in her famous movies. The moors and Highlands of Scotland, partly because of their low population density, attract millions of birds. For reasons not fully understood by ornithologists, the Orkneys shelter numbers of birds that are by some accounts absolutely staggering. Bird-watchers cite the Orkneys as even richer in native species than the more isolated Shetlands, with species such as the hen harrier, the short-eared owl, and the red-throated diver (a form of Arctic loon) not frequently seen in the Shetlands.

Any general tour of the Orkneys will bring you into contact with thousands of birds, as well as Neolithic burial sites, cromlechs, dolmens, and other items with intriguing backgrounds and histories. A worthy local tour operator is **Wild About,** 5 Clouston Corner, Stenness, Orkney KW17 3LD (☎ **01856/851011**). Minivans will help in spotting birds whose breeding and mating habits will be one of the many other factors discussed on the tours. Depending on the destination, the per-person cost ranges from £8.50 to £16 ($14 to $26.40) for tours that last between 4½ and 5 hours.

If you're deeply devoted to bird watching, however, only a more intensive, on-site exposure to the landscape will bring you the ornithological overview you're looking for. A bird-watching specialist, established in the mid-1980s, is **Orkney Island Wildlife,** Shapinsay 12, Orkney KW17 2DY (☎ **01856/711373**). Every year between May and November, they choreograph 5-day bird-watching tours that include full board, housing, and exposure to the fields, moors, and wetlands of Shapinsay and Orkney. Tours are conducted from a rustic croft that was upgraded and enlarged into a streamlined modern format in 1990. Your hosts are Paul and Louise Hollinrake, both qualified wardens at the Mill Dam Wetlands Reserve, and accredited by the Royal Society for the Protection of Birds. Tours depart every morning around 9am (allowing participants to either sleep late or embark on sunrise expeditions of their own). Lunches are picniclike box-lunch affairs where the makings of sandwiches and other items are laid out in the morning on a long table, allowing birders to compile their own packed feast. Touring is by minivan or by inflatable boat, allowing close-up inspection of offshore skerries (small islets without vegetation) and sea caves. No more than six participants are allowed in any tour. All-inclusive prices are from £499 to £599 ($823.35 to $988.35) per person for the 5-day/5-night experience, with no supplement required for participation by single travelers.

During the winter and early spring the entire Solway shoreline, Loch Ryan, Wigtown Bay, and Auchencairn Bay areas are excellent locations for observing wintering wildfowl and waders. Inland, too, Dumfries and Galloway have a rich and varied range of birdlife, including British barn owls, kestrels, tawnies, and merlins. Bird-watching fact sheets are available at tourist offices in Dumfries and Galloway.

CANOEING

Originating among the native tribespeople of North America (the canoe) and the Eskimos/Inuits living around or above the Arctic Circle (the kayak) as a means of transport and a hunting aid, today the canoe and the kayak are seen more as a recreational water sport. In 1866 a Scot named John MacGregor got the North American sport off to a rousing Scottish start by organizing the first canoe club, an organization that was later designated as the Royal Canoe Club.

The Scots make a distinction between kayak canoeing, which involves sitting down using a double-bladed paddle, and Canadian-style canoeing, which is practiced kneeling down using a single-bladed paddle.

Recently developed canoe- and kayak-related sports are hybrids, developed in California. They include canoe polo (played in an indoor pool), sea kayaking (pay attention to never straying too far from the edge of the shore), straight-line sprint racing on flat water, and racing against other contenders down white-water rapids.

Several canoe clubs offer instruction and advice about where and how best to pursue your hobby. Supervising their activities is the **Scottish Canoe Association (SCA),** Caledonia House, South Gyle, Edinburgh EH12 9DH (☎ **0131/317-7314**). It coordinates all competitive canoeing events in Scotland, including slaloms, polo games, and white-water races. Details about where and how, as well as the application of proficiency tests and coaching awards, can be obtained through the SCA. It also offers a handbook and a range of other publications, and promotional material of interest to canoers, including its own magazine, *Scottish Paddler.* (Equivalent magazines published in England include *Canoe Focus,* a guide published by the British Canoe Union. Either can be bought at newsstands throughout the U.K.)

EXERCISE & MOVEMENT

Like most urbanites, Scottish city dwellers must limit their physical activities most of the time to supervised exercise and/or aerobics classes. If you find yourself hankering for a good sweaty exercise session in the company of like-minded enthusiasts, here are some key contacts that can provide information, addresses, and schedules:

The **Women's League of Health and Beauty** is a pioneer in movement classes for women, with special emphasis on posture, movement to music, use of weighted clubs and balls, and classes designed for bodies of all ages, including the elderly, teenagers, and people with disabilities. For information, contact Mrs. Fiona Gillanders, Secretary, Ashgrove, 23 Carrick Rd., Ayr KA27 2RD (☎ **01292/262299**).

Margaret Morris Movement Classes offer a carefully rehearsed program of physical-fitness routines and exercises. At their most advanced they incorporate aspects of modern and classical dance, with emphasis on the aesthetics and creative expression in movement. For information about the location of classes in Scotland, you can write (not call) Margaret Morris Movement, Suite 3–4, 39 Hope St., Glasgow G2 6AE.

Yoga's tenets are as timeless as Asian philosophy. It combines aspects of the purely meditational with the physically active, and involves physical postures that were carefully defined and prescribed thousands of years ago. Precise, controlled, and in some cases infuriatingly difficult for neophytes, it's excellent for the development of strength, suppleness, and overall stress reduction and relaxation. For information about where instruction can be obtained in Scotland, contact Mrs. Angela Porter, Manager, **Fitness Scotland,** Caledonia House, South Gyle, Edinburgh EH12 9DQ (☎ **0131/317-7200**).

HEALTH & FITNESS FACILITIES

A wide range of health and fitness facilities is offered at a number of hotels in Scotland, together with sporting amenities, such as golf, riding, and fishing at some places. Included in the hotels' offerings are saunas, solariums, gymnasiums, whirlpools, steam cabinets, massage facilities, slimming and beauty treatments, jogging tracks, squash and tennis courts, and indoor or outdoor heated swimming pools.

Health farms and hydros are also available, with a selection of therapies and treatments, such as Swedish, gyratory, and underwater massages, deep-cleansing facials, hair removal by waxing, manicure, and pedicure.

Local tourist offices keep a list of centers offering such diversions. Also refer to separate listings under Edinburgh, Glasgow, and Aberdeen.

HORSEBACK RIDING

Horseback riding and trekking through the panoramic countryside of Scotland—from the Lowlands to the Highlands, and through all the in-between lands, can be enjoyed by most everyone, from novices to experienced riders in the United States.

ARGYLL & THE ISLES   You'll find a wide array of options at **Castle Riding Centre,** Brenfield Estate, Ardrishaig, Argyll (☎ **01546/603274**). Alternatives include hourly rides at £12 ($19.80) for 1 hour, £20 ($33) for 2, up to weeklong holidays, including accommodations and meals, ranging in price from £580 to £1,100 ($957 to $1,815). Daily rides begin at 9:30am; the last one leaves at 4pm, though later rides can be arranged.

The **Lettershuna Riding Centre,** Appin, Argyll (☎ **01631/730227;** fax 01631/730209), charges from £12 ($19.80) per hour for a ride. Rides last 1 to 2 hours, with the services of a leader, starting daily at 10:30am with the final ride offered at 4:30pm. English-style riding lessons in the arena are also given by a fully qualified staff. The center lies on the main Oban–Inverness bus route, with a stop only 200 yards from the stables.

At the **Rothesay Riding Centre,** Canada Hill, Rothesay, Isle of Bute (☎ **01700/504971**), you must reserve 24 hours in advance. The center offers a range of rides from pony trekking by the hour to 4-week riding tours. One-hour rides go for £8 ($13.20), and 2-hour rides cost £14 ($23.10). Open daily from 10am to 4pm.

THE BORDERS & THE SOUTHWEST   You'll find a full range of courses offered at the **Barend Properties Riding School and Trekking Centre,** Sandyhills, Dalbeattie, Kirkcudbrightshire (☎ **01387/780663**). Lessons are the main emphasis here, but there are some trekking options available, including a picnic ride for £24 ($39.60).

MOUNTAINEERING

As defined by the Scots, mountain climbing can range from fair-weather treks over heather-clad hilltops, a more complicated form of rambling, to demanding climbs up rock faces in wintry conditions of snow and ice. At its most comprehensive, it includes scrambling and climbing over cliffs, rocky outcroppings, and crags in all parts of the country, in all conditions of weather and temperature.

The Southern Uplands, the offshore islands, and the Highlands of Scotland contain Britain's best mountaineering sites. We advise, regardless of your abilities, that you treat the landscape with respect. The weather can turn foul during any season with almost no advance notice and create dangerous conditions.

If you're climbing rock faces, you should be familiar with basic techniques and the use of such specialized equipment as carabiners, crampons, ice axes, and ropes. Don't even consider climbing without proper instruction and equipment. Scottish authorities cite the most common mishap for climbers as the "slip and stumble," caused by a misplacement of a climber's feet on loose, eroded rock, and a subsequent fall.

Ben Nevis is the highest (but by no means the most remote) peak in Scotland. Despite its loftiness at 4,406 feet, it has attracted some daredevils who have driven cars and motorcycles to points near its top; one eccentric even arranged the transport of a dining table with formal dinner service and a grand piano.

In the Gaelic dialect a "munro" is any peak rising 3,000 feet or more above sea level, and Scotland is full of them. An eccentric hobby for British climbers is "munro-bagging," or collecting munros (that is, scaling their summits) and making notations of their characteristics.

As a means of improving your familiarity with rock-climbing skills, consider joining a club or signing on for a mountaineering course at a climbing center maintained by the Scottish Sports Council. Also contact the **Mountaineering Council of Scotland,** at Perth (☎ **01738/638227**). Membership allows overnight stays at the club's climbing huts on the island of Skye (in Glen Brittle), in the Cairngorms (at Glen Feshie), and near the high-altitude mountain pass at Glencoe. True aficionados of rock climbing looking to obtain certification might contact the **Scottish Mountain Leader Training Board** at Glenmore, Aviemore, Inverness-shire PH22 1QU (☎ **01479/861-248**).

PONY TREKKING

This form of sport, taking you across moors and dales, is, in the words of one enthusiast, "reason enough to come to Scotland." Pony trekking originated—or so it is believed—as a job for Highland ponies that weren't otherwise engaged in toting dead deer off the hills during deer-stalking season. Most treks last from 2½ hours up to a full day. Centers have ponies that are suitable for most age groups.

ARGYLL & THE ISLES   Make arrangements for your trek at least a day in advance at **Ballivicar Pony Trekking,** Ballivicar Farm, Port Ellen, Islay (☎ **01496/302251**). You'll pay £8 ($13.20) per hour, with rides conducted from 11am to 2pm.

The **Cairnhouse Riding Centre,** Blackwaterfoot, Arran (☎ **01770/860466**), offers treks for beginners at £9 ($14.85) per hour, whereas experienced riders may opt for a more strenuous ride and hike for £18 ($29.70) for 2 hours. Open Monday through Friday from 10am to 4pm.

The **Cloyburn Trekking Centre,** Brodick, Arran (☎ **01770/302800**), offers a variety of options including a children's program and riding lessons on Saturday. Treks cost £8 ($13.20) per hour beginning daily at 10am, with the last ride at 3pm.

THE HEBRIDES   Uig Pony Trekking, Skye (☎ **01470/542205**), offers 1-hour rides at £8.50 ($14) and 2-hour treks at £13.50 ($22.30). Rides are daily from 10am to noon, 2 to 3pm, and 3:30 to 4:30pm.

NORTHERN ISLES   Riding centers are scarce here, but a choice location on Shetland is **Broothom Ponies,** Braeside, Dunrossness (☎ **01950/4605560**). You have to call at least 24 hours in advance to make arrangements. Riding costs £9 ($14.85) an hour. Open daily from 8am to 8pm.

THE SOUTHWEST   The **Pony Trekking Centre,** Brighouse Bay Holiday Park, Borgue, Kirkcudbright (☎ **01557/870267**), caters mainly to beginners and tourists. A 1-hour ride costs £9.50 ($15.65). Open daily from 8:30am to 6pm.

RAMBLING

Despite its poetic implications, the Scots define rambling as walking for pleasure, and because the hills and vales of Scotland are ripe with possibilities for communions with nature, it's the most universally practiced sport in the country. It's also the cheapest sport and is available to everyone of all ages. If you find yourself in a Scottish inn, gauge your abilities, make careful mental notes of your whereabouts, and set out. If the countryside is particularly wild, avoid straying from the predesignated path. Stout shoes and a raincoat are important, and if you intend to go into truly wild countryside, a map, a compass, and a rucksack filled with emergency food and clothing are almost indispensable. Worthy destinations for long-distance hikes (walks of more than 20 miles) include the Southern Upland Way and the West Highland Way, for which maps and guidebooks are available through any of the addresses listed below.

One organization that can put you in touch with like-minded people includes the **Ramblers' Association (Scotland),** Crusader House, Haig Business Park, Markinch, Fife KY7 6AQ (☎ **01592/611177**).

Some of the most memorable walks in Scotland are along Loch Lomond and the Trossachs. From tourist information centers and at various bookstores in Scotland, you can purchase a copy of *Walk Loch Lomond and the Trossachs* to guide you on your way.

To book a rambling tour before you go to Scotland, contact **English Lakeland Ramblers** at 18 Stuyvesant Oval, Suite 1A, New York, NY 10009 (☎ 212/ 505-1020).

SAILING & WATER SPORTS

Wherever you travel in Scotland, you're never far away from the water. Windsurfing, canoeing, waterskiing and jet skiing, and sailing are just some of the sports available at a number of sailing centers and holiday parks in Scotland.

ARGYLL & THE ISLES   **Linnhe Marine Watersports Centre,** Lettershuna, Appin, Argyll (☎ **01631/730227**), offers rentals of skis, wet suits, and a range of boats, including ones powered by sail, motor, and oar. Boats range in price from £12 ($19.80) for 1 hour to £40 ($66) for 6 hours, with skis costing £15 ($24.75) for half an hour. Open daily from 9am to 6pm.

THE BORDERS & THE SOUTHWEST   Boat rentals range from £12 to £40 ($19.80 to $66) with a half-day minimum requirement at the **Galloway Sailing Centre,** Loch Ken, Castle Douglas (☎ **01644/420626**). Open daily from 10am to 5pm.

CENTRAL HIGHLANDS   At the **Loch Tay Boating Centre,** Pier Road, Kenmore (☎ **01887/830291**), you can choose from a wide selection of sailing vessels, including Canadian canoes and cabin cruisers. Prices range from £5 ($8.25) per hour for a rowboat to £130 ($214.50) for 2 days on a cabin cruiser. Open daily from 9am to sundown.

You'll pay £10 to £45 ($16.50 to $74.25) at the **Lochearnhead Water Sports Centre,** Loch Earn (☎ **01567/830330**). Choices include dinghies for £15 ($24.75) an hour, £25 ($41.25) per half day, and £45 ($74.25) per full day; Canadian canoes for £7.50 ($12.40) an hour, £15 ($24.75) per half day, and £20 ($33) per full day; and kayaks for £4 ($6.60) an hour.

NORTHERN HIGHLANDS   At the **Raasay Outdoor Centre,** Raasay House, Isle of Raasay, Wester Ross (☎ **01478/660266**), you can choose from a multitude of sailing vessels and courses, including windsurfing and canoeing. The center charges by the person from £17 ($28.05) for half-day rentals to £30 ($49.50) for a full day, with price breaks depending on the number of people. Open daily from 9am to 6pm.

SKIING

It isn't naturally associated with Britain, and it isn't available in England at all. Frankly, it's a contrived sport in Scotland, with a nascent infrastructure that might develop into something bigger, depending on its acceptance by the British public, before the year 2000. Don't think for a minute that it will come anywhere near the skiing in Switzerland, eastern France, Austria, or Norway, but for an offbeat experience in a growing industry, you might devote a day or two to skiing in Scotland.

To compensate for reliable snowfalls, the Scots have been remarkably ingenious at creating ersatz solutions for cost-conscious winter holidays. Natural snowfall is enhanced with artificial snow spewed onto hillsides or "artificial slope" skiing.

The principal areas for skiing include the Cairngorms by Aviemore (see chapter 11). Other centers are at Glenshee, south of Braemar (the season here is likely to be very short). There's also a 54-yard-long plastic ski slope at Alford (☎ **019755/63024** for details), which is open year-round. Skiing is also possible at Glencoe, Aonach Mor, and the Lecht, the latter lying at a low altitude and suitable only for beginners.

If you're intent on skiing in Scotland, here's a list of contacts you might find useful: The **Association of Ski Schools in Great Britain,** Glenmore, Aviemore, Invernessshire PH22 1QU (☎ **01479/821-279**); the **British Association of Ski Instructors,**

Glenmore, Aviemore, Inverness-shire PH22 1QU (☎ **01479/861-717**); and/or the **Scottish National Ski Council,** Caledonia House, South Gyle, Edinburgh EH12 9DQ (☎ **0131/317-7280**).

SPORTS LEARNING CENTERS

NATIONAL CENTRES   The Scottish government maintains three different schools for the promotion and enjoyment of outdoor activities such as golfing, hiking, hill climbing, kayaking, and canoeing.

The **Scottish National Sports Centre,** Glenmore Lodge, Aviemore, Inverness-shire PH22 1QU (☎ **01479/861256;** fax 01479/861212), maintained by the Scottish government and in existence for 50 years, is one of the premier hill- and rock-climbing schools in the U.K. Courses are also offered in canoeing and kayaking. Facilities include an indoor climbing wall, a heated canoe "rolling pool," a fitness training room, a lecture hall for presentation of new climbing techniques, and a highly trained staff adept at leading rock- and hill-climbing tours through the wilderness areas of Scotland. An on-site lodge charges £26 ($42.90) per day, double occupancy, for basic overnight accommodations with full board. Courses last for 5 to 6 days and cost between £280 and £400 ($462 and $660). The staff-to-student ratio in the rock-climbing courses is one instructor for each pair of students, which ensures the safety of all participants. Some courses are specifically geared toward the elderly.

At the **Scottish National Sports Centre,** Inverclyde, Burnside Road, Largs, Ayrshire KA30 8RW (☎ **01475/674666;** fax 01475/674720), most of the facilities are reserved for the training of national sports teams, and therefore closed to members of the general public. One area of expertise, however, that draws a large and enthusiastic crowd is Inverclyde's assortment of golfing tutorials, each lasting 2 to 4 days, which are offered every year between March and September. Courses include high-tech tutorials assisted by videotapes of drives and putting strokes, and include lectures on the selection of golf clubs and golf-related fitness exercises. A 2-day course runs £160 ($264) with room and board or £130 ($214.50) for classes only. A 4-day tutorial costs £318 ($524.70) with room and board or £252 ($415.80) for instruction only.

The **Scottish National Sports Centre,** Cumbrae, Largs, Ayrshire KA30 8RW (☎ **01475/530-757;** fax 01475/674720), known as one of the premier canoe and kayaking schools in Scotland, specializes in teaching sailing, canoeing, and kayaking techniques to newcomers and experienced boaters alike. It benefits from a location on the island of Great Cumbrae, a mile from the mainland hamlet of Largs and 30 miles from Glasgow, northeast of the Isle of Arran. It sits beside a channel in the heart of the southern Hebrides, astride some of the best sailing channels in western Scotland. Weekend classes are available in canoeing, kayaking, or sailing a dinghy, and cost £110 ($181.50) per person for room and board. Anyone older than 14 who has reasonable swimming abilities is eligible for these courses.

LOCAL SPORTS CENTERS

FIFE & ANGUS   The **Arbroath Sports Centre,** Keptie Road, Arbroath (☎ 01241/872999), features a wide range of activities, including karate, aerobics, and gymnastics. Open Monday through Friday from 9am to 10pm and Saturday and Sunday from 9am to 9pm.

At the **Cupar Sports Centre,** Main Street, Cupar (☎ **01334/654793**), you'll find a steam bath, rooms for weightlifting and aerobics, sunbeds, a swimming pool, and a squash court. Open Monday through Friday from 10am to 10pm and Saturday and Sunday from 10am to 5pm.

The facilities at the **Dundee Olympia Leisure Centre,** Earl Grey Place (☎ 01382/203888), include exercise equipment, a sauna, a diving pool, and four swimming pools, as well as a restaurant. Open Monday through Friday from 9am to 9pm and Saturday and Sunday from 10am to 5pm.

You'll find three squash courts, a sauna, and sunbeds at the **Montrose Sports Centre,** Marine Avenue, Montrose (☎ 01674/676211). The activities include basketball, soccer, table tennis, and aerobics, along with a children's program. Open Monday through Friday from 9am to 10pm and Saturday and Sunday from 9am to 9pm.

The **Saltire Centre,** 58 Montrose Rd., Abroath (☎ 01241/431060), offers badminton, tennis, basketball, soccer, aerobics, martial arts, and a children's program. The facilities also include a steam room, sauna, and health club. Open Monday through Friday from 9am to 10:30pm and Saturday and Sunday from 9am to 8:30pm.

5 The Borders & the Southwest

Romantic castle ruins and skeletons of gothic abbeys in the ballad-rich Borders stand as reminders of the battles that once raged between England and the proud Scots. For a long time the so-called Border Country was a no-man's land of plunder and destruction.

Southeastern Scotland is the land of Sir Walter Scott, master of romantic adventure, who topped the best-seller list in the early 19th century. The remains of the four great abbeys built in the mid-12th century are here—Dryburgh (where Scott is buried), Melrose, Jedburgh, and Kelso. And the Borders are also the home of the cashmere sweater and the tweed suit. Ask at the local tourist office for a "Borders Woollen Trail" brochure, which will tell you where you can visit woolen mills and museums, see and follow the process of weaving from start to finish, and visit at the mill shops.

Southwestern Scotland, part of the famous Lowlands, is often overlooked by motorists rushing north from the Lake District of England. But this is a land of unspoiled countryside, fishing harbors, color-washed houses, and romantic ruins, a fine country for touring. Most places to stay here are of the small Scottish provincial variety, which usually means a warm welcome from a smiling staff and good traditional Scottish cookery using local produce.

GETTING THERE Trains from London's King's Cross Station to Waverley Station in Edinburgh enter Scotland at Berwick-upon-Tweed. From Berwick, a network of local buses runs between the villages and towns. Three rail lines pass through the region from London's Euston Station (call ☎ **01713/879400** in London for schedules) en route to Glasgow. Dumfries is the best center if you're traveling by rail, or Stranraer on the west coast. For rail information and schedules, call National Rail Inquiries at ☎ **0345/484950.** Bus travel isn't recommended for reaching the region, but once you're there you'll find it a reliable means of transport for getting around. Many smaller towns have no rail connections.

The nearest airport to Dumfries and Galloway is Glasgow Airport, about 75 miles north of Dumfries.

A DRIVING TOUR OF THE BORDERS & THE SOUTHWEST

The principal express highway through the area is the Carlisle–Glasgow route, A74, cutting north and south.

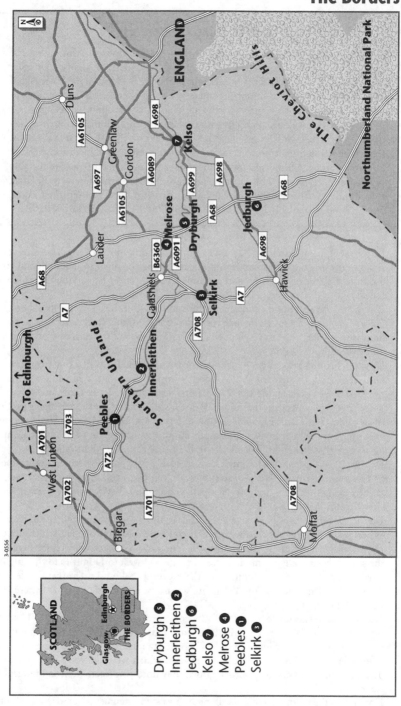

3-0556

Dryburgh **5**
Innerleithen **2**
Jedburgh **6**
Kelso **7**
Melrose **4**
Peebles **1**
Selkirk **3**

A Walk Along the Borders

You can walk in the footsteps of St. Cuthbert, a 7th-century saint, along the Scotland–England border. The 62^1/$_2$-mile walk stretches from Melrose, 40 miles south of Edinburgh, across the border into northeast England to the Holy Island of Lindisfarne on the Northumberland coast. St. Cuthbert started his ministry in Melrose in about A.D. 650 and was later appointed prior at Lindisfarne. The walk passes many places linked to his legend, prehistoric relics, Roman ruins, and historic castles. The high point of the walk is at Wideopen Hill, 1,430 feet above sea level. Permission from landowners along the route has been obtained, and the walk is clearly marked. A leaflet is available suggesting distances that can be comfortably covered in a day, along with recommendations for overnight stopovers. Contact Roger Smith, Walking Development Officer, Scottish Border Enterprise Center, Bridge Street, Galashiels TB1 ISW (☎ **01896/758991;** fax 01896/758625).

Day 1   Begin in Jedburgh, 325 miles north of London or 48 miles southeast of Edinburgh. If you've driven up from England, spend the night in Jedburgh and visit the ruined abbey of Jedburgh and explore Mary Queen of Scots House on Queen Street.

Day 2   From Jedburgh, continue northeast on A698 to Kelso, to see its abbey and Floors Castle, the home of the present duke of Roxburghe. In the environs at Gordon, you can visit the historic home of Mellerstain, seat of the earls of Haddington. Stay overnight in Kelso.

Day 3   From Kelso, drive west on A699 toward St. Boswells, but stop first at Dryburgh Abbey where Sir Walter Scott is buried. The gothic ruins here are surrounded by yew trees and cedars of Lebanon. Near Dryburgh, see the famous "Scott's View" over the Tweed to the Eildon Hills; from Dryburgh go north along B6356 (it's signposted). Continue via St. Boswells along A6091 to Melrose. Here you can visit the ruins of Melrose Abbey and pay an interesting visit to Abbotsford, former home of Sir Walter Scott (reached along B6360). Spend the night in Melrose.

Day 4   Pass through Innerleithen by taking A72 west from Melrose. Stop to look at Traquair House, on A72, 16 miles west of Melrose. From here you can travel to Peebles along B7062 for a visit to Neidpath Castle and Dawyck Botanic Garden. Stay overnight in Peebles.

Day 5   From Peebles, head west along A721, cutting south at the signpost to Biggar. When you reach the junction with A701, continue south for Moffat, which lies 60 miles south of Edinburgh. Continue south along A74 via Lockerbie, remembered as the site of the tragic Pan American crash, and A709 west to Dumfries for the night.

Day 6   Explore around Dumfries in the morning, taking in Threave Castle and Threave Garden. Then get on A75 going southwest into Castle Douglas, where you can stay the night.

Day 7   From Castle Douglas, take A75 southwest to the junction with A711 leading to Kirkcudbright. See the town and enjoy lunch here. Then get on A755 going west until you reach the junction of B727, pointing northwest to Gatehouse-of-Fleet. After a brief visit, follow the signposts to A75, which will take you south and west across a scenic road opening onto Wigtown Bay until you reach Newton Stewart for the night.

Day 8   In the morning, continue along A75 west to Stranraer for an overnight stopover, visiting Glenluce Abbey along the way. If you arrive in Stranraer early enough in the day, pay a late-afternoon visit to Portpatrick (follow A77) on the coast. You can either find overnight accommodations here or return to Stranraer for the night.

1 Jedburgh

48 miles SE of Edinburgh, 57 miles N of Newcastle-upon-Tyne

The little town of Jedburgh, divided by the River Jed, developed around Jedburgh Abbey on a Roman road called Dere Street. Today the market town gives little hint of the turbulence of its early history, as a royal burgh in the beleaguered border area.

ESSENTIALS
GETTING THERE

BY TRAIN   There is no direct rail link to Jedburgh. The nearest rail station is at Berwick-upon-Tweed (☎ **0345/484950** for rail information, tickets, or schedules). However, we recommend taking a train to Newcastle-upon-Tyne (England) and from there taking a bus to Jedburgh.

BY BUS   Call the **Tourist Information Office** at ☎ **01835/863435** for bus schedules. There are daily buses from Edinburgh; a bus leaving Edinburgh at 8:50am will arrive at Jedburgh at 10:55am. Call ☎ **0990/808080** for information and schedules.

BY CAR   At Corbridge (England), continue north into Scotland along A68, using Jedburgh as your gateway town into the Borders.

VISITOR INFORMATION

The **tourist office** is at Murray's Green (☎ **01835/863435**). The **Visitors Centre,** near the police station, shows a film of the history of the area.

SEEING THE SIGHTS

Jedburgh Abbey. Abbey Place. ☎ **01835/863925.** Admission £2.80 ($4.60) adults, £1.80 ($2.95) seniors, £1 ($1.65) children. Apr–Sept, Mon–Sat 9:30am–6pm or dusk, Sun 2–6:30pm; Oct–Mar, Mon–Sat 9:30am–4:30pm, Sun 2–4:30pm.

This famous ruined abbey, founded by David I in 1138, is one of the finest in Scotland. Inside is a small museum containing fragments of medieval works.

Mary Queen of Scots House. Queen St. ☎ **01835/863331.** Admission £2 ($3.30) adults, £1 ($1.65) children. Mar–Oct, daily 10am–5pm. Closed Nov–Feb.

Here she spent 6 weeks in 1566 and almost died after a tiring ride, returning from a visit to her beloved Bothwell at Hermitage Castle. She later wrote, "Would that I had died at Jedworth." The house, in the center off High Street, contains articles dealing with her life, paintings, and engravings. Ancient pear trees still stand on the grounds, a reminder of the days when Jedburgh was famous for its fruit. "Jethard pears" were hawked in the streets of London.

Castle Gaol. Castlegate. ☎ **01835/863254.** Admission £1.25 ($2.05) adults, 75p ($1.25) children, seniors, and students. Easter–Sept, Mon–Sat 10am–5pm, Sun 1–5pm. Closed Oct–Easter.

This museum stands on the site of Jedburgh Castle. When the jail was opened in 1825 it was considered a "modern reform jail." Now it serves the community as a museum of social history.

WHERE TO STAY

Ferniehirst Mill Lodge. Hwy. A68, Jedburgh, The Borders TD8 6PQ. ☎ **01835/863279.** Fax 01835/863279. 9 rms. TEL. £23 ($37.95) per person. Rates include breakfast. Dinner £13 ($21.45) extra. MC, V. Free parking. Take A68 2¹/₂ miles south of Jedburgh.

Built in 1980, this modern, chalet-inspired guesthouse is in a quiet neighborhood away from the center of town. Its pine-paneled rooms are functional but comfortable. It attracts people (including hunters and fishers) seeking quiet and rural charm. Horseback riding (experienced riders only, please) costs about £10 ($16.50) per hour. Riding packages are available, but only for equestrians willing to stay for a full week.

Glenfriar's Hotel. The Friars, Jedburgh, The Borders TD8 6BN. ☎ and fax **01835/862000.** 6 rms. TV. £64 ($105.60) double. Rates include breakfast. MC, V.

This small private hotel, run by Ms. Jenny Bywater, is in a Georgian house on a quiet corner next to St. John's Church. It features antique wooden furnishings, including four-poster beds in two of the rooms, and all accommodations have well-groomed private baths. Since Ms. Bywater cooks, cleans, and books accommodations single-handed, she never accepts more than 10 guests at any given time.

The Spinney. Langley, Jedburgh, The Borders TD8 6PB. ☎ **01835/863525.** 2 doubles, 2 chalets. £20 ($33) per person. Rates include breakfast. No credit cards.

This B&B, run by Mr. and Mrs. Fry, is located 2 miles south of Jedburgh on A68. The complex includes a main house plus a modernized cottage with two double bedrooms with private baths plus pinewood chalets with a bath, sitting room, and kitchen. The latter are rented as self-catering units. Leather and wood furnishings are found throughout the well-maintained guest rooms, to which the Scottish Tourist Board recently bestowed a deluxe rating.

WHERE TO DINE

Carters' Restaurant. Abbey Place. ☎ **01835/863414.** Main courses £5.75–£11 ($9.50–$18.15); bar lunches from £1.65 ($2.70). AE, MC, V. Restaurant: daily noon–2:30pm and 6–9pm. Pub: Mon–Sat 11am–11pm, Sun 11am–10:30pm. SCOTTISH/CONTINENTAL.

This pub, with a downstairs dining room built of old abbey stones, is the favorite gathering place for locals. The owners, Mr. and Mrs. Hume, serve wholesome and hearty food and drink. Their simple but tasty menu includes such dishes as steaks, scampi, chicken Cordon Bleu, pork or lamb chops, and fresh vegetables in season. The pub also serves eight regional beers on tap.

2 Kelso

44 miles SE of Edinburgh, 68 miles NW of Newcastle-upon-Tyne, 12 miles E of Melrose

Another typical historic border town, Kelso lies at the point where the Teviot meets the Tweed. Sir Walter Scott called it "the most beautiful, if not the most romantic, village in Scotland." A settlement that grew up around a river ford developed into a town around Kelso Abbey. In 1614, when Robert Ker became the first earl of Roxburghe, the town became a "burgh of barony."

Kelso today is a flourishing market town, the center of an agricultural district boasting farming and stock raising, and one of the best centers for touring the Borders.

ESSENTIALS
GETTING THERE

BY TRAIN   The nearest rail connection is Berwick-upon-Tweed, from which you can take a bus to Kelso. For information and schedules, call ☎ **0345/484950.**

BY BUS   From Edinburgh, board the bus to Galashiels, with connecting service to Kelso. Phone ☎ **0990/808080** for schedules and more information.

BY CAR   If you're driving from Jedburgh (see above), follow A698 northeast to Kelso.

VISITOR INFORMATION

The summer-only **Kelso Tourist Office** is at Town House, The Square (☎ **01573/ 223464**), open April through October.

SEEING THE SIGHTS

Kelso Abbey. Free admission. Apr–Sept, Mon–Sat 9:30am–7pm, Sun 2–7pm; Oct–Mar, Mon–Sat 9:30am–4pm, Sun 2–4pm.

Once a great ecclesiastical center, Kelso Abbey has lain in ruins since late in the 16th century when it suffered its last and most devastating attack by the English, who ripped off its roofs, burned it, and declared it officially defunct. The lands and remaining buildings were given to the earl of Roxburghe. The oldest (1128) and probably the largest of the Border abbeys, it was once one of the richest, collecting revenues and rents from granges, fisheries, mills, and manor houses throughout the region. In 1919 the abbey was given to the nation.

✪ **Floors Castle.** Hwy. A697, just north of Kelso. ☎ **01573/223333.** Admission £4.50 ($7.45) adults, £3.75 ($6.20) seniors, £2.50 ($4.15) age 8 or older, free for age 7 and under. Apr–Sept, daily 10:30am–4:30pm; Oct, Wed and Sun 10:30am–4:30pm. Closed Nov–Mar. Follow the signs north from Kelso center.

The home of the dukes of Roxburghe was designed in 1721 by William Adam and remodeled in the mid-19th century by William Playfair. Part of the castle, which is open to the public, contains superb French and English furniture, porcelain, tapestries, and paintings by Gainsborough, Reynolds, and Canaletto. There are a licensed restaurant, coffee shop, and gift shop as well as a walled garden and garden center. The castle was a major location for the Tarzan film, *Greystoke*.

Mellerstain. Gordon. ☎ **01573/410225.** Admission £4.50 ($7.45) adults, £2 ($3.30) children. May–Sept, Sun–Fri 12:30–5pm. Closed Oct–Apr. From Edinburgh, follow A68 to Earlston, then follow the signs to Mellerstain for another 5 miles; from Kelso, head northwest along A6089 until you see the signposted turn to the left.

The seat of the earls of Haddington, Mellerstain is one of Scotland's famous Adam mansions. It lies near Bordon, 9 miles northeast of Melrose and 7 miles northwest of Kelso. Mellerstain is associated with Lady Grisell Baillie, a Scottish heroine whose courage in hiding her father and facing down the English saved her father's life. Lord Haddington is her descendant. William Adam built two wings on the house in 1725, and the main building was designed by his more famous son, Robert, some 40 years later. You can see the interior, with its decorations and ceilings, and the impressive library as well as paintings and antique furniture. The garden terrace has a panoramic view, south to the lake, with the Cheviot Hills in the distance. Afternoon tea is served, and souvenir gifts are on sale.

WHERE TO STAY & DINE

Ednam House Hotel. Bridge St., Kelso, The Borders TD5 7HT. ☎ **01573/224168.** Fax 01573/226319. 32 rms. TV TEL. £69–£97 ($113.85–$160.05) double. Rates include breakfast. MC, V.

Ednam House Hotel, on the fringe of Kelso, is a conversion of a Georgian house, often referred to as "that lovely place beside the river." The building dates from 1761 and is a fine example of Georgian architecture. The atmosphere is pleasant, and there's an unusual collection of antiques in the oldest section. Period furnishings are found throughout the house. The most expensive accommodations, called "Prince William rooms," are on the third floor and offer a view of the river; less expensive and scenic are comfortable accommodations on the first and second floors. For those wanting to chance it with the highly unreliable Scottish sun, there's a terrace.

A fixed-price dinner is available at a cost of £19.50 ($32.15) per person. The daily menu includes dishes such as braised guinea fowl, rabbit, and lamb cutlets.

✪ **Sunlaw's House Hotel.** Hwy. A698, Helton, Kelso, Roxburghshire TD5 8JZ. ☎ **01573/450331.** Fax 01573/450611. 22 rms, 2 suites. TV TEL. £145 ($239.25) double, £185 ($305.25) double with four-poster bed; £230 ($379.50) suite. Rates include breakfast. AE, DC, MC, V. Take A698 3 miles southwest of Kelso.

The manorial walls of this late 19th-century castle rise on 200 acres of woodland, lawns, and gardens. It was built as the family home of the Roxburghes, who valued its location on the trout-filled Teviot River. In 1982 it was converted into a country hotel. The old stable block contains 6 bedrooms; another 16 rooms are in the main house. Amid a subdued but elegant decor, the hotel has four log-burning fireplaces even in summer.

Many guests come for shooting and fishing; others to observe wildlife, especially the deer. Golf can be arranged on an 18-hole course that opened in 1997. A glassed-in conservatory offers clusters of wicker chairs for enjoying drinks or tea when the weather is fine; a tennis court and croquet lawn are on the grounds.

A SIDE TRIP TO DRYBURGH

Dryburgh Abbey. Hwy. A68, Dryburgh, Roxburghshire. ☎ **01835/822381.** Admission £2.30 ($3.80) adults, £1.70 ($2.80) seniors, £1 ($1.65) ages 5–15, free for age 4 and under. Apr–Sept, Mon–Sat 9:30am–6:30pm, Sun 2–6:30pm; Oct–Mar, Mon–Sat 9:30am–4pm, Sun 2–4:30pm. Drive south from Dryburgh along B6356 (it's signposted); from Edinburgh take A68 to St. Boswells and turn onto B6404 and then left again onto B6356.

These gothic ruins are surrounded by gnarled yew trees and cedars of Lebanon, said to have been planted there by knights returning from the Crusades. Sir Walter Scott is buried here. Near Dryburgh is "Scott's View," over the Tweed to his beloved Eildon Hills, the most beautiful view in the region.

The adjoining town is St. Boswells, an old village on the Selkirk–Kelso road.

WHERE TO STAY & DINE

Dryburgh Abbey Hotel. Hwy. B6404, outside St. Boswells, The Borders TD6 0RQ. ☎ **01835/822261.** Fax 01835/823945. 24 rms, 2 suites. £115 ($189.75) double; £155 ($255.75) suite for two. Rates include full Scottish breakfast. MC, V.

Next to the abbey ruins, this hotel was originally built in 1845 as the home of Lady Grisell Baillie and remained in her family until 1929. The house is said to be haunted by "the gray lady," who had an ill-fated affair with a monk that led to his execution and her suicide by drowning. New owners in 1991 launched a restoration of the deteriorated property. When it reopened, the hotel was the first in the Borders to be awarded five crowns by the Scottish Tourist Board.

Bedrooms include both deluxe rooms with half-tester or four-poster beds and standard abbey- or river-view rooms. The **Tweed Restaurant** offers some of the finest dining in the area. It serves a Sunday lunch from 12:15 to 2:15pm and dinner nightly from 7:30 to 9:15. A two-course table d'hôte menu costs £17.50 ($28.90), with a three-course meal running £22.50 ($37.15). There's also a cocktail bar and lounge and a swimming pool. Some 14 golf courses are within an easy drive. Arrangements can be made for salmon and trout fishing. Services include room service, laundry, and baby-sitting.

3 Melrose

37 miles SE of Edinburgh, 70 miles NW of Newcastle-upon-Tyne

Melrose enjoys many associations with Sir Walter Scott. As was common in the Middle Ages, the town developed around the abbey, in the shadow of the Eildon

Hills. In summer the attractive little town, a center for exploring the border area, is congested with visitors.

ESSENTIALS
GETTING THERE

BY TRAIN   The nearest rail connection is Berwick-upon-Tweed, to which Melrose is linked by bus; call the Tourist Information Office in Berwick-upon-Tweed at ☎ **01289/330733** for bus schedules and ☎ **0345/484950** for train schedules.

BY BUS   From Edinburgh, board the bus to Galashiels, with connecting service to Melrose. Phone ☎ **0990/808080** for more information and schedules.

BY CAR   From Edinburgh, Melrose can be reached by going southeast along A7 and following the signs to Galashiels. From Kelso, take A699 west to St. Boswells and at the junction with A6091 head northwest.

VISITOR INFORMATION

A summer-only **tourist office** is open at Abbey House, Abbey Street (☎ **01896/ 822555**).

SEEING THE SIGHTS

✪ **Melrose Abbey.** Abbey St. ☎ **01896/822562.** Admission £2.80 ($4.60) adults, £1.80 ($2.95) seniors, £1 ($1.65) children. Apr–Sept, Mon–Sat 9:30am–6pm, Sun 2–6pm; Oct–Mar, Mon–Sat 9:30am–4pm, Sun 2–4pm.

These lichen-covered ruins, among the most beautiful in Europe, are all that's left of the ecclesiastical community established by Cistercian monks in 1136. The pure gothic lines of the complex were made famous by Sir Walter Scott, who was instrumental in getting the decayed remains repaired and restored in the early 19th century. The heart of Robert the Bruce is supposed to be interred in the abbey, although the location is unknown. Look for the beautiful carvings and the tombs of other famous Scotsmen buried in the chancel. In Scott's narrative poem, *The Lay of the Last Minstrel,* the abbey's east window received rhapsodic treatment, and in *The Abbott* and *The Monastery,* Melrose appears as "Kennaquhair."

SIR WALTER SCOTT'S HOUSE

✪ **Abbotsford.** Hwy. B6360, Melrose. ☎ **01896/752043.** Admission £3.40 ($5.60) adults, £1.70 ($2.80) children. Apr–Oct, Mon–Sat 10am–5pm, Sun 2–5pm. Closed Nov–Mar. Head just off A7, south of the junction with A72, onto B6360, some 2 1/2 miles southeast of Galashiels.

This was the home that Sir Walter Scott built and lived in from 1812 until he died. Designed in the Scots baronial style, and considered, after his literary works, Scott's most enduring monument, it contains many relics, including artifacts and mementos that the famous author collected from the battlefield at Waterloo. Other exhibits include his clothes and his death mask. Especially interesting is his study, with his writing desk and chair. In 1935 two secret drawers were found in the desk. One of them contained 57 letters, part of the correspondence between Sir Walter and his wife-to-be. Scott purchased Cartley Hall farmhouse on the banks of the Tweed in 1812. In 1822 he had the old house entirely demolished to be replaced by the building you see today. Some of the relics he collected include Montrose's sword and Rob Roy's gun. There are also 9,000 rare volumes in his library. Visitors today can see his study, library, drawing room, entrance hall, and armories, even the dining room overlooking the Tweed where he died on September 21, 1832. There are also extensive gardens and grounds to visit, and visitors can view the private chapel, added after Scott's death.

Sir Walter Scott: Master of Romance

Today it's hard to imagine the fame and popularity this poet and novelist enjoyed in his heyday as best-selling author of his time. However, the brutal appraisal of one critic is certainly exaggerated: He wrote that Scott's novels have "virtually been assigned to the dust bin of literary history."

Sir Walter Scott (1771–1832) was a master storyteller. He premiered a new genre, the romantic adventure in a panoramic setting. He created lively characters and realistic pictures of Scottish life and customs in such works as *The Heart of Midlothian, Rob Roy,* and *Waverly.* Today he is best known as the prolific father of the historical novel, a genre that began with *Ivanhoe* and its romantic Jewish heroine, Rebecca (played by Elizabeth Taylor in the popular film), followed by *Kenilworth, The Pirate,* and many others. He was also a popular poet.

Born into an old Border family at Edinburgh on August 15, 1771, Scott became permanently lame after an attack of fever in infancy. All his life he was troubled by ill health, and later by finances. He spent his latter years writing to clear his enormous debts. Through his poetry and novels, Scott made both his country and its scenery fashionable with the English. He even persuaded George IV to wear that once-outlawed tartan during the king's visit to Scotland. Although Scott became the most prominent literary figure in Edinburgh, his heart lay in the Border Country. It was here he chose to live and here he built his house in a style that became known as "Scottish baronial," reflecting the nostalgia for medieval days that his novels had popularized. Starting with a modest farmhouse, he enlarged Abbotsford into a mansion and fulfilled his ambition to become a laird. In the crash of 1826, he offered the estate to his creditors, who turned it down. Still heavily in debt and suffering from the effect of several strokes, in 1831 Scott set out on a cruise through the Mediterranean, but he returned to Abbotsford the following year to die. He was buried at Dryburgh Abbey, sited in a loop of the Tweed 2 miles from the panoramic view of the river and the Eildon Hills he so admired. It's reported that the horses pulling the author's hearse stopped at this spot out of habit, so accustomed were they to Scott's pausing to take in the vista.

Scott's name is also linked to the Trossachs, which he used as a setting for both his poem, *The Lady of the Lake,* and his tale of Rob Roy MacGregor, the 18th-century outlaw.

In Edinburgh, the gothic-inspired Scott Monument is one of the most famous statues in Scotland, but it was actually Glasgow that beat every other place in honoring Scott—Glasgow erected the first statue of Scott in George Square in 1837.

WHERE TO STAY & DINE

Burt's Hotel. Market Square, Melrose, The Borders TD6 9PN. ☎ **01896/822285.** Fax 01896/822870. 20 rms. TV TEL. £82 ($135.30) double. Rates include breakfast. AE, DC, MC, V. Free parking.

In the center of town, within walking distance of the abbey, this family-run inn offers a taste of small-town Scotland. It was built in 1722 in a traditional three-story town-house design, and its located between the main square and a garden. The decor is modern, with a light, airy, and restful feeling. All guest rooms have radios, hair dryers, tea- or coffeemaking equipment, and a private bath (tub or shower).

There's an attractive bar with Windsor chairs and a coal-burning fireplace. Tasty bar lunches and suppers begin at £6.95 ($11.45). You can take a table d'hôte lunch in the hotel restaurant, overlooking the garden, for £17.50 ($28.90) and a table d'hôte dinner for £24.75 ($40.85). You can also order à la carte. If you want to dine at the hotel, a reservation is needed.

A SIDE TRIP TO LAUDER

One of the most imposing country houses of Scotland is ✪ **Thirlestane Castle** (☎ **01578/722430**), about half a mile from Lauder, overlooking Leader Water. The castle has been in the ownership of the Lauderdale family since 1218. A T-shaped building, the castle has a keep from around the end of the 16th century. The structure was much altered after Queen Victoria took the throne to begin her long reign. The interior rooms are known for their ornamental plaster ceilings, the finest in the country from the Restoration period. In the old nurseries is a Historic Toy Collection, and "Border Country Life" exhibitions have been installed, depicting life in the Borders from prehistoric times to the present.

The castle is on A68 at Lauder in Berwickshire, 10 miles north of Melrose along A68, and 28 miles south of Edinburgh on A68. The family home and grounds are open from 2 to 4:30pm, when the last ticket is sold. May, June, and September open days are Sunday, Monday, Wednesday, and Thursday; July and August, Sunday through Friday. It closes from October until Easter, although it's open for about a week over the Easter holiday. Admission to the complex and its exhibitions costs £4 ($6.60) for adults, £3 ($4.95) for children, or £10 ($16.50) for a family ticket (two adults plus children).

4 Selkirk

40 miles SE of Edinburgh, 73 miles SE of Glasgow

In the heart of Sir Walter Scott country, this royal burgh and county town can make an ideal center for exploring some of the historic homes in the Borders. It's noted for its tweed industry, and some mills can be visited on day trips. Check with the tourist office (see below) at the time of your visit as visits are subject to change. Selkirk was the birthplace of the African explorer Mungo Park. Both explorer and novelist are honored with statues.

ESSENTIALS

GETTING THERE

BY TRAIN   Take the train to Berwick-upon-Tweed, the nearest rail connection. Proceed the rest of the way by bus; call the Tourist Information Office in Berwick-upon-Tweed at ☎ **01289/330733** for bus schedules or ☎ **0345/484950** for rail information.

BY BUS   Buses running between Newcastle-upon-Tyne and Edinburgh make stops at Selkirk. Most visitors arrive by train from Edinburgh (☎ **0990/808080** for ticket information and data about departures).

BY CAR   From Edinburgh, head southeast along A7 to Galashiels, then cut southwest along B6360. From Melrose, take B6360 southwest to Selkirk.

VISITOR INFORMATION

A summer-only **tourist office** is at Halliwell's House (☎ **01750/720054**).

SEEING THE SIGHTS

Bowhill. Hwy. A708 west of Selkirk. ☎ **01750/22204.** Admission to house £4 ($6.60) adults, £3.50 ($5.75) seniors, £1 ($1.65) children. July, daily 1–4:30pm. Closed Aug–June. Admission to Country Park £1 ($1.65). Park: May–Aug, daily 1–4:30pm. Closed Sept–Apr. Take the A708 Moffat road 3 miles west of Selkirk.

This 18th- and 19th-century Border home of the Scotts, the dukes of Buccleuch, contains a rare art collection, French furniture, porcelain, silverware, and mementos of Sir Walter Scott, Queen Victoria, and the duke of Monmouth. It also has paintings by Canaletto, Claude, Raeburn, Gainsborough, and Reynolds. In the Country Park, there's an Adventure Woodland play area, a Victorian kitchen, an audiovisual presentation, a gift shop, and a tearoom/restaurant. Sotheby's "Works of Art" courses are offered here.

Scottish Museum of Woollen Textiles. Walker Burn, Peebles-shire EH43 6AS. ☎ **01896/ 870619.** Free Admission. May–Oct, Mon–Sat 9am–5:30pm, Sun 11am–5pm; Nov–Apr, Mon– Sat 10am–5pm, Sun noon–4pm. Beside A72, 15 miles south of Selkirk and 8 miles north of Galashiels.

This unusual museum is privately funded by Tweedvale Mills. The oldest textile mill in the Borders, with a pedigree dating back to the 18th century, it's a sprawling stone-sided building that contains a coffee shop, a museum, and a shop specializing in woolen goods. Look for exhibitions of old looms, spinning wheels, and illustrations of what life was like for mill workers during the late 18th- and 19th-century Industrial Revolution. Texts and captions explain the role of various organic materials (nettles, bark, onion leaves, and urine) in the dyeing process. In the adjacent shop, look for tartan kilts and women's skirts, jackets for men and women, sweaters, Celtic-inspired gift items, and woolen goods gathered from manufacturers throughout Scotland.

WHERE TO STAY & DINE

Heatherlie House Hotel. Heatherlie Park, Selkirk, The Borders TD7 5AL. ☎ **01750/21200.** Fax 01750/20005. 7 rms (6 with shower). TV TEL. £55 ($90.75) double. Rates include breakfast. MC, V. Closed Jan 1 and Dec 25–26.

An imposing stone-and-slate Victorian mansion with steep gables and Victorian turrets, this hotel is set in 2 acres of wooded lands and mature gardens, west from the center along the Green, and a short walk from the town of Selkirk and local woolen mills. The bedrooms are spotlessly maintained and furnished with reproductions of older pieces. The lone single has no bath.

A coal-burning fireplace adds warmth to the lounge, where reasonably priced bar meals are available daily from noon to 9:30pm, and the high-ceilinged dining room is open for dinners in the evening from 5:30 to 9pm. A table d'hôte dinner costs £12 ($19.80). Golf, fishing, and shooting packages can be arranged. About a half-dozen golf courses are within a reasonable drive.

A SIDE TRIP TO INNERLEITHEN

Innerleithen is a modest little mill town east of Peebles on B709. The unmarred beauty of the River Tweed valley, as seen from the town's surrounding hillsides, remains constant. Ballantyne cashmeres are manufactured here.

✪ **Traquair House.** Hwy. A72, 16 miles west of Melrose. ☎ **01896/830323.** Admission £4.50 ($7.45) adults, £4 ($6.60) seniors, £2.25 ($3.70) students and children, £12 ($19.80) for a family of four. Easter–June and Sept, daily 12:30–5:30pm; July–Aug, daily 10:30am–5:30pm; Oct, Fri–Sun 2–5pm. Closed Nov–Apr.

This place is perhaps the oldest-inhabited and most romantic house in Scotland. Dating back to the 10th century, it's rich in associations with Mary Queen of Scots and, later on, with the Jacobite risings. One of the most poignant exhibits is an ornately carved oak cradle in the King's Room—in this cradle Mary rocked her infant son, who was to become King James VI of Scotland and James I of England. Other treasures include glass, embroideries, silver, manuscripts, and paintings. Of particular interest is a brew house equipped as it was two centuries ago and still used regularly. The great house is lived in by the Stuarts of Traquair. There are craft work-shops to be seen on the grounds, as well as a maze and woodland walks.

WHERE TO STAY & DINE

Traquair Arms Hotel. Innerleithen, The Borders EH44 6PD. ☎ **01896/830229.** Fax 01896/830260. 10 rms. TV. £64 ($105.60) double. Rates include breakfast. AE, DC, MC, V.

This small border-town hostelry was built as a three-story coaching inn around 1780 and has later Victorian additions. Open fires in the bar lounge and fresh flowers in the dining room create a pleasant ambience. The hotel's cozy bedrooms have tea/coffeemaking facilities and views over the valley. The hotel was a finalist in the "Best Pub Food in Britain" contest in 1993, and the cuisine still reflects those high standards. Dinner costs £14.50 to £18 ($23.90 to $29.70). Vegetarian and special diets can be arranged. All dishes are freshly prepared on the premises by chefs Hugh Anderson and Sara Currie. It's within a 5-minute walk of the River Tweed, and salmon and trout fishing can be arranged for guests.

5 Peebles

23 miles S of Edinburgh, 53 miles SE of Glasgow, 20 miles W of Melrose

This royal burgh and county town is a market center in the valley of the Tweed. Scottish kings used to come here when they hunted in Ettrick Forest. The town is noted for its large woolen mills.

Peebles is also known as a "writer's town." It was home to Sir John Buchan (Baron Tweedsmuir, 1875–1940), a Scottish author who later was appointed governor-general of Canada. He is remembered chiefly for the adventure story *Prester John,* and was also the author of *The Thirty-Nine Steps,* the first of a highly successful series of secret-service thrillers and later a Hitchcock film. Robert Louis Stevenson also lived for a time in Peebles, and drew upon the surrounding countryside in his novel *Kidnapped,* published in 1886.

ESSENTIALS

GETTING THERE

BY TRAIN   Trains arrive in Berwick-upon-Tweed, where bus connections can be made to Peebles. Call ☎ **0345/484950** for rail information and schedules.

BY BUS   Buses between Newcastle-upon-Tyne and Edinburgh also service Peebles. Phone ☎ **0990/808080** for information about tickets and schedules.

BY CAR   Take A703 south from Edinburgh.

VISITOR INFORMATION

The **Peebles Tourist Information Centre** is at Chamber Institute, 23 High St. (☎ **01721/20138**), open only from April to November.

SEEING THE SIGHTS

Neidpath Castle. Tweeddale, on A72, 1 mile west of Peebles. ☎ **01721/720333.** Admission £2.50 ($4.15) adults, £2 ($3.30) seniors, £1 ($1.65) children. Easter–Sept, Mon–Sat 11am–5pm, Sun 1–5pm. Closed Oct–Easter.

This is an early 14th-century L-shaped tower house on the north bank of the Tweed. A rock-cut well and a pit prison are inside the 11-foot-thick walls. The castle was besieged by Cromwellian forces in 1650, and soon after the Civil War it was upgraded for 17th-century living. However, by late in the 18th century it had been abandoned by its owner and occupied by tenants. Artifacts found in the castle and a tartan display can be seen.

Kailzie Gardens. Kailzie on B7062, 2¹/₂ miles southeast of Peebles. ☎ **01721/720007.** Admission £2 ($3.30) adults, 50p (85¢) children. Gardens only £1 ($1.65). Easter–Oct, daily 11am–5:30pm. Closed Nov–Easter.

The 17 acres of formal walled gardens, dating from 1812, include a rose garden, woodland, and burnside walks. Restored during the last 20 years, it provides a stunning array of plants from early spring to late autumn, and has a collection of waterfowl and owls. There's also an art gallery, a shop, and a restaurant.

Dawyck Botanic Garden. Hwy. B712, 8 miles southwest of Peebles. ☎ **01721/760254.** Admission £2 ($3.30) adults, £1.50 ($2.45) seniors and students, 50p (85¢) children, £4.50 ($7.45) family ticket. Mar 15–Oct 22, daily 10am–6pm. Local bus marked BIGGAR.

This botanic garden, run by the Royal Botanic Garden in Edinburgh, has a large variety of conifers, some exceeding 100 feet in height, as well as many species of flowering shrubs. There's also a fine display of early spring bulbs, plus woodwalks rich in wildlife interest.

SHOPPING

Knitwear, crafted from yarn culled from local sheep, is what to look for here as you walk along High Street. **Woolgathering,** 1 Bridge House Terrace (☎ **01721/720388**), has knitwear, tartans, and all kinds of sweaters. Two sprawling branches of **Castle Warehouse,** 7–13 Old Town (☎ **01721/723636**) and 29–31 Northgate (☎ **01721/720814**), sell gift items with a Scottish flavor, and clothing, including traditional Scottish garb and all the clothing you might need for a fishing trip to an obscure loch. Sporting goods stores with lots of durable clothing and footwear for trekking through the fens and heather of Scotland are **Caledonian Countrywear, Ltd.,** 74 High St. (☎ **01721/723055**), and **Out & About,** 2 Elcho St. Brae (☎ **01721/723590**). For Border handcrafts such as pinewood furniture and handcrafted stoneware and porcelain, go to **Peebles Craft Centre,** 9 Newby Court (☎ **01721/722875**), or the **Couchee Righ,** 26 Northgate (☎ **01721/721890**). The town's most visible purveyor of fishing gear is **Tweeddale Tackle,** 1 Bridgegate (☎ **01721/720979**).

WHERE TO STAY

✪ **Cringletie House Hotel.** Eddleston, Peebles, The Borders EH45 8PL. ☎ **01721/730233.** Fax 01721/730244. 13 rms. TV TEL. £100–£120 ($165–$198) double. Rates include breakfast. MC, V. Closed early Jan–Mar 10.

This imposing country hotel, with towers and turrets, stands on 28 acres of private grounds on A703, 2¹/₂ miles north of Peebles. Built of red sandstone in the design of a small French château, the hotel rents spacious bedrooms. The public rooms are rich in the character and style befitting an 1861 Victorian mansion. There is an elevator as well. The elegant restaurant has a limited but well-selected choice of dishes and attentive service. In season, the vegetables come fresh from the on-site garden. A special dish is a delectable smoked haddock mousse. A Sunday luncheon costs £16 ($26.40), and a four-course dinner, served from 7:30 to 8:30pm, goes for £25.50 ($42.05). Lunch is à la carte Monday to Saturday, costing £5.50 ($9.05) and up. You should be punctual because of the short serving hours (the food is freshly cooked), and you'll need a reservation.

The Tontine. 39 High St., Peebles, Peebles-shire EH45 8AJ. ☎ **01721/720892.** Fax 01721/729732. 35 rms. TV TEL. £70 ($115.50) double. Rates include breakfast. Children 14 and under stay free in parents' room. AE, DC, MC, V. Free parking.

The Tontine was originally constructed in 1807 as a private club by a group of hunters, who sold shares in its ownership to their friends. The actual construction of the building was executed by French prisoners-of-war during the Napoleonic era; later enlargements were made by the Edwardians. Flower boxes adorn its stone lintels and a stone lion guards the fountain in its forecourt. Inside is a cozy and rustic bar, the Tweeddale Shoot Bar. The Adam-style dining room is one of the architectural gems of Peebles, containing tall fan-topped windows and a minstrel's gallery. The modestly furnished, no-frills bedrooms are in an angular modern wing built in back of its 19th-century core. Units are equipped with radios and coffeemakers. The most expensive rooms have views of the river.

WHERE TO DINE

Horse Shoe Inn. Eddleston. ☎ **0721/730225.** Reservations recommended Sat. Main courses £5–£15 ($8.25–$24.75). AE, DC, MC, V. Easter–Oct, Wed–Sun noon–3pm and 6–10pm; Nov–Easter, Wed–Sat noon–3pm and 6–9pm, Sun noon–10pm. SCOTTISH.

In the center of the village of Eddleston, 4^1/$_2$ miles north of Peebles, this country-comfortable place is one of the best in the region for top-quality beef and steaks. Appetizers include everything from the chef's own pâté with oat cakes to smoked Shetland salmon with brown bread. House favorites include steak-and-stout pie, Meldon game pie, and vegetable moussaka. The main focus is the food and drink served in the bar, site of most lunches and dinners. On Friday and Saturday nights and on Sunday at lunch, the bar is supplemented with a more formal dining room.

PEEBLES AFTER DARK

The town has many options for drinking and dining, and some of the most appealing are in the hotels on the town's edge that may have seemed rather monumental and staid at first glance. The **Park Hotel,** Innerleithen Road (☎ 01721/720451), and its nearby neighbor, the **Hotel Hydro,** Innerleithen Road (☎ 01721/720602), contain pubs and cocktail lounges. For an earthier and less formal venue, we highly recommend dropping into Peebles' oldest pub, on the ground floor of the **Cross Keys Hotel,** 94 Northgate (☎ 01721/724222). Here, amid an ambience of 300-year-old smoke-stained panels, a blazing fireplace, and an evocatively crooked bar, you can question the staff members about the resident ghost. Like the Loch Ness monster, she's taken on an almost mythic identity since her last sighting, but the rumor goes that she's the spirit of Sir Walter Scott's former landlady, Marian Ritchie. Here, no one will be shy about telling you their theory, especially if you buy them a drink.

6 Moffat

61 miles S of Edinburgh, 22 miles NE of Dumfries, 60 miles SE of Glasgow

An Annandale town, Moffat thrives as a center of a sheep-farming area, symbolized by a statue of a ram on the wide High Street. It has been a holiday resort since the mid-17th century because of the curative properties of its water. It was here that Robert Burns composed the drinking song "O Willie Brew'd a Peck o' Maut." Today people visit this town on the banks of the Annan River for its good fishing and golf.

North of Moffat is panoramic hill scenery. Five miles northwest is a huge, sheer-sided 500-foot-deep hollow in the hills called the **Devil's Beef Tub,** where border cattle thieves, called reivers, once hid cattle lifted in their raids.

Northeast along Moffat Water, past White Coomb, which stands 2,696 feet high, is the **Grey Mare's Tail,** a 200-foot hanging waterfall formed by the Tail Burn dropping from Loch Skene; it's under the National Trust for Scotland.

ESSENTIALS

GETTING THERE

BY TRAIN The nearest railway station is in Lockerbie, 15 miles south of Moffat. Access to Lockerbie sometimes requires a change of train in Dumfries, so passengers from Edinburgh or Glasgow often transfer to a bus at Dumfries. Phone ☎ **0345/ 484950** for train schedules and information.

BY BUS National Express runs buses from Dumfries to Moffat four or five times a day, stopping on the town's High Street after a 30-minute ride. The same company runs buses from Lockerbie to Moffat four times a day. Call ☎ **0990/808080** for more information.

BY CAR From Dumfries, head northeast along A701; from Edinburgh, head south along A701.

VISITOR INFORMATION

A summer-only **tourist information center** is at Churchgate (☎ **01683/220620**).

SHOPPING

Most of the town's merchandisers line both sides of High Street. An especially noteworthy shop is **Ram Antiques,** 19 Ram St. (☎ **01683/220405**), where the decorative accessories of many generations of local residents are on display and for sale. Within a 2-minute walk from High Street, the town's largest purveyor of woolen goods, **Moffat Woolens,** Lady Nowe (☎ **01683/220134**), has kilts, sweaters, and the kind of overcoats that can stand up to the fiercest Scottish weather.

WHERE TO STAY & DINE

Auchen Castle Hotel. Beattock, Dumfries and Galloway DG10 9SH. ☎ **01683/300407.** Fax 01683/300667. 24 rms. TV TEL. £78–£86 ($128.70–$141.90) double; £60 ($99) double in Cedar Lodge. Rates include breakfast. MC, V. Take A74 2 miles north of Moffat.

About a mile north of the village of Beattock, the area's most luxurious accommodations are at the Auchen Castle Hotel, a Victorian mock-castle. It's really a charming country house built in 1849 on the site of Auchen Castle, with terraced gardens, a trout-filled loch, and vistas from its windows. Of the hotel's 24 often-spacious rooms, 14 are in the main house (known as the castle); the remaining 10 are in the Cedar Lodge, a less desirable annex built in the late 1970s. The lofty dining room overlooks ornamental grounds that flower in late spring. Simple dishes such as Scottish roast beef are appetizingly prepared, served by an efficient staff. Lunch (bar lunches only) is daily from noon to 2pm and dinner from 7 to 9pm; a dinner costs £17.25 ($28.45) for three courses.

Beechwood House Hotel. Harthope Place, Moffat, Dumfries and Galloway DG10 9RS. ☎ **01683/220210.** Fax 01683/220889. 7 rms. TV TEL. £108 ($178.20) double. Rates include half board. AE, MC, V. Free parking.

Beechwood House Hotel was originally the 19th-century headquarters of Miss Thompson's Private Adventure Boarding Establishment and School for Young Ladies. Today it's a charming country hotel and restaurant. It lies behind a dark facade of chiseled stone at the end of a narrow rural lane at the north end of town between the local church and school. A "tea lawn," smooth as a putting green, is the site for outdoor refreshments on sunny days. Each bedroom has a certain amount of homespun charm, and many have been recently renovated. If you just want to stop in for a meal (and you'll be welcome if you phone in advance), lunch is daily from noon to 1:30pm; dinner, from 7:30 to 9pm. A fixed-price dinner costs £23 ($37.95). The menu is limited but often filled with surprises; for example, a recent meal that began with smoked rabbit and wild boar sausages went on to include braised quail with green and black grapes, and concluded with a chilled orange soufflé mousse.

Moffat House Hotel. High St., Moffat, Dumfries and Galloway DG10 9HL. ☎ **01683/ 220039.** Fax 01683/221288. 20 rms. TV TEL. £65–£84 ($107.25–$138.60) double. Rates include breakfast. DC, MC, V. Free parking.

Moffat House Hotel is one of the town's most architecturally noteworthy buildings—it was constructed in 1751 by John Adam. It sits in a garden in the center of town behind a facade of red and black stone, a pair of symmetrical wings stretching out on either side. Ancient trees shelter its rear. The modernized bedrooms are comfortable and functional. The hotel offers some of the best food in town, especially at night when the chef prepares an international menu. Bar suppers are served Monday through Thursday from 6 to 9pm and Friday through Sunday from 5 to 9:30pm. However, dinner in the regular restaurant, beginning at £16 ($26.40), is served from 7 to 9pm only, and is likely to feature haunch of venison, mallard duck in cherry sauce, and fresh salmon.

WHERE TO DINE
Well View. Ballplay Rd., Moffat DG10 9JU. ☎ **01683/220184.** Fax 01683/220088. Reservations recommended. Fixed-price 3-course lunch £13 ($21.45); fixed-price 6-course dinner £26 ($42.90). AE, MC, V. Mon–Sat 12:30–1:15pm; daily 7–8:30pm. Closed 2 weeks Jan–Feb. BRITISH/CONTINENTAL.

Set three-quarters of a mile east of Moffat's center, beside the A708 to Selkirk, this restaurant serves some of the best food in the region. Behind a stone facade, the setting is mid-Victorian with Laura Ashley country-cottage charm. Views from the dining room overlook the town of Moffat, which sprawls out below the house, and a kitchen garden that produces many of the herbs and vegetables used in the food. Set-price menus vary almost every day of the week, depending on the season and the inspiration of Janet and John Schuckardt (who run the establishment's kitchen and dining room, respectively). Recent examples include roasted breast of Perthshire pigeon with red-wine sauce; fillet of sea bass on a bed of Provençal ratatouille dressed with olive oil; roasted saddle of venison with a gin and juniper sauce; and filet of Aberdeen Angus beef with whole-grain mustard sauce. Dessert might be a medley of red summer fruits served in a phyllo basket with homemade ice cream.

Upstairs are five bedrooms and one junior suite, each with TV but no telephone, outfitted with a combination of modern furniture and reproduction antiques, Laura Ashley fabrics and accessories, teamaking facilities, hair dryers, and clock radios. Depending on the season, doubles cost from £60 to £72 ($99 to $118.80); the suite from £66 to £78 ($108.90 to $128.70).

7 Dumfries

80 miles SW of Edinburgh, 79 miles SE of Glasgow, 34 miles NW of Carlisle

A county town and royal burgh, this Scottish Lowland center enjoys associations with Robert Burns and James Barrie. In a sense it rivals Ayr as a mecca for Burns admirers. He lived in Dumfries from 1791 until his death in 1796. Here he wrote some of his best-known songs, including "Auld Lang Syne" and "Ye Banks and Braes of Bonnie Doon." A statue of Burns stands on High Street. Barrie was a pupil at the Academy, and he later wrote that he got the idea for Peter Pan from his games in the nearby garden.

At the Whitesands, four bridges span the Nith. The earliest of these was built by Devorgilla Balliol, widow of John Balliol. Their son, John Balliol, was made Scotland's "vassal king," by Edward I of England, the "Hammer of the Scots," who established himself as Scotland's overlord. The bridge originally had nine arches, but now has six and is still in constant use as a footbridge.

The wide esplanade was once the scene of horse and hiring fairs and now is a fine place to park your car and explore the town.

ESSENTIALS
GETTING THERE

BY TRAIN   Seven trains per day make the run from Glasgow's Central Station, taking 1³/₄ hours. A ticket costs £15 ($24.75) for one-way transit, but only £18 ($29.70) for a round-trip. For 24-hour information about departures, call ☎ **0345/484950.**

BY BUS   Western Scottish Buses depart from Glasgow (from both Buchanan Street Station and Anderston Station); a one-way fare from either station is £6.30 ($10.40). Buses also run to Dumfries from Edinburgh's St. Andrew's Square, a one-way ticket costing £5.20 ($8.60). For complete bus information into Dumfries, call ☎ **0990/ 808080.**

BY CAR   From Edinburgh, take A701 to Moffat, then continue southwest to Dumfries. From Glasgow, take M74, which becomes A74 before it approaches Moffat. At Moffat, continue southwest along A701.

VISITOR INFORMATION

The tourist information office is at 64 Whitesands (☎ **01387/253862**).

EXPLORING THE AREA

In St. Michael's Churchyard, a burial place for at least 900 years, stands the **Burns Mausoleum.** The poet is buried here along with his wife, Jean Armour, as well as five of their children. Burns died in 1796, but his remains weren't moved to the tomb until 1815.

The 18th-century **St. Michael's Church,** on St. Michael's Street, is the original parish church of Dumfries. Its foundation is of great antiquity—the site was sacred before the advent of Christianity, and a Christian church has stood here for more than 1,300 years. The earliest written records date from 1165–1214. The church and the churchyard are interesting to visit because of all their connections with Scottish history, continuing through World War II. The Burns family pew can still be seen inside.

The **Mid Steeple** on High Street was built in 1707 as municipal buildings, a courthouse, and a prison. The old Scots "ell" measure of 37 inches is carved on the front of the building, and a table of distances includes the mileage to Huntingdon, England, which in the 18th century was the destination for Scottish cattle driven south for the markets of London.

Dumfries Museum. Church St. ☎ **01387/253374.** Museum: Free. Camera Obscura: £1.20 ($2) adults, 60p ($1) children and seniors. Museum: Apr–Sept, Mon–Sat 10am–1pm and 2–5pm, Sun 2–5pm; Oct–Mar, Tues–Sat 10am–1pm and 2–5pm. Camera Obscura: Apr–Sept, Mon–Sat 10am–1pm and 2–5pm, Sun 2–5pm; closed Oct–Mar. Cross the river at St. Michael's Bridge Rd. and turn right onto Church St.

The largest museum in southwestern Scotland, the Dumfries Museum is in a converted 18th-century windmill on top of Corbelly Hill. The Camera Obscura, on the upper floor of the museum, provides panoramic views of the town and surrounding countryside.

Burns House. Burns St. ☎ **01387/255297.** Free admission. Apr–Sept, Mon–Sat 10am–5pm, Sun 2–5pm; Oct–Mar, Tues–Sat 10am–1pm and 2–5pm.

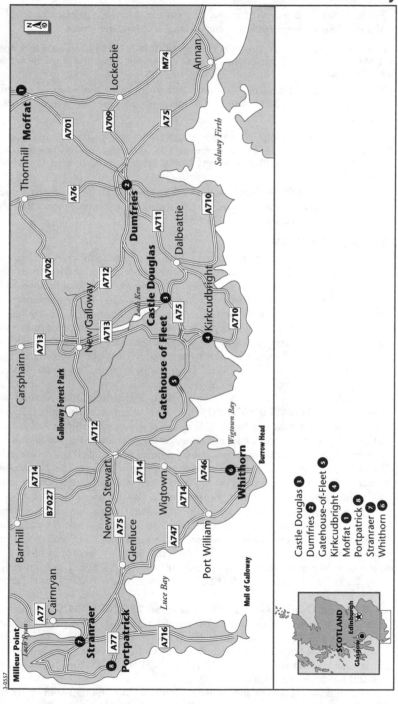

Castle Douglas ③
Dumfries ②
Gatehouse-of-Fleet ⑤
Kirkcudbright ④
Moffat ①
Portpatrick ⑧
Stranraer ⑦
Whithorn ⑥

Scotland's national poet died in this house off St. Michael's Street. The simple, unpretentious stone structure contains personal relics and mementos.

Old Bridge House. Mill Rd. at Devorgilla's Bridge. ☎ **01387/256904.** Free admission. Apr–Sept, Mon–Sat 10am–5pm, Sun 2–5pm. Closed Oct–Mar. From Whitesands, cross the river at Devorgilla's Bridge.

This building dates from 1660, and has been restored and furnished in a style typical of the period between 1850 and 1900. Devorgilla's Bridge itself was constructed in the 16th century.

Robert Burns Centre. Mill Rd. ☎ **01387/264808.** Exhibition: Free. Audiovisual theater: £1.20 ($2) adults, 60p ($1) children, seniors, and students. Apr–Sept, Mon–Sat 10am–8pm, Sun 2–5pm; Oct–Mar, Tues–Sat 10am–1pm and 2–5pm. From Whitesands, cross the river at Devorgilla's Bridge.

On the banks of the River Nith you'll find this converted 18th-century water mill. Facilities include an exhibition on the poet, a cafe, and an audiovisual theater showing films about Burns and the town of Dumfries.

MORE SIGHTS NEARBY

From Dumfries, you can set out on treks in all directions. South on A710 leads to the village of New Abbey, dominated by the red sandstone ruins of **Sweetheart Abbey,** founded in 1273 by Devorgilla Balliol. When her husband, John Balliol the Elder, died, she became one of the richest women in Europe—most of Galloway, as well as estates and castles in England and in Normandy, belonged to her. Devorgilla founded Balliol College, Oxford, in her husband's memory. She kept his embalmed heart in a silver-and-ivory casket by her side for 21 years until her death in 1289 at the age of 80, when she and her casket were buried in front of the abbey altar. The abbey gained the name of "Dulce Cor," Latin for "sweet heart," a term that has become a part of the English language.

Directly south from New Abbey on A710 to Southerness are the **Arbigland Gardens** at Kirkbean (☎ 01387/880283), 15 miles southwest of Dumfries. The gardens were once the private estate of William Craik, who employed John Paul Jones's father as a gardener. John Paul Jones, "father" of the American navy, was born here, in a two-room cottage that has been carefully restored to its mid–18th-century style. In an adjacent room the museum has created the great cabin of the *Bonhomme Richard,* Jones's flagship during his 1779 campaign in British waters. There is an audiovisual presentation of Jones's victory over the Royal Navy.

The present mansion on site was built by William Craik, a linguist, merchant, architect, and smuggler. By coincidence, Craik's son, Dr. James Craik, also emigrated to America, and became George Washington's personal physician. You can visit the woodland with its water gardens where John Paul Jones once worked as a boy. The site is open May to September only, Tuesday through Sunday from 2 to 6pm, charging £2 ($3.30) for adults, £1.50 ($2.45) for seniors, and 50p (85¢) for children. There's a tearoom.

North from Dumfries via A76 is **Ellisland Farm** (☎ 01387/740426), where from 1788 to 1791 Robert Burns made his last attempt at farming. The present occupants of the house will show you through the Burns Room. At this farm Burns wrote "Tam o' Shanter." The farm is open March through October, Tuesday through Saturday from 10am to 1pm and 2 to 5pm. Admission is £1.50 ($2.45) for adults and 75p ($1.25) for children and seniors.

The main target is **Drumlanrig Castle,** Thornhill (☎ 01848/330248 or 01848/ 331555), the seat of the dukes of Buccleuch and Queensberry, 3 miles north of Thornhill, off A76 and 16 miles southwest of A74 at Elvanfoot. This pink castle, built between 1679 and 1689, contains some outstanding paintings, including a famous Rembrandt, a Leonardo da Vinci, and a Holbein, and relics related to Bonnie Prince Charlie. The castle stands in a parkland ringed by wild hills, and there's even an "Adventure Woodland Playground." The gardens are gradually being restored to their 1720 magnificence. There's a working crafts center in the old stable yard. Meals are served in the old kitchen, hung with gleaming copper. The castle and park are open May through August only, Monday through Saturday from 11am to 5pm and Sunday from 1 to 5pm; the castle is closed Thursday, although the park remains open. Admission is £5 ($8.25) for adults, £4 ($6.60) for seniors, £2 ($3.30) for children, and £12 ($19.80) for a family ticket.

An interesting excursion from Dumfries is to **Lockerbie,** 13 miles to the east along A709. A Border market town, Lockerbie lies in the valley of Annandale, offering much fishing and golf. It was the scene of a battle in 1593 that ended one of the last great Border family feuds. The Johnstones routed the Maxwells, killing Lord Maxwell and 700 of his men. Many of the victims had their ears cut off with a cleaver—a method of mutilation that became known in Scotland as the "Lockerbie Nick."

But most of the world today knows Lockerbie for a different reason. It was here on December 21, 1988, that Pan Am Flight 103 from London went down, killing all passengers on board and also some of the local residents. In the "Garden of Remembrance" in the Dryfesdale Cemetery, 1 mile west of Lockerbie on the Dumfries Road (Route A709), is a memorial to the victims. Yet another memorial to the victims is in a small chapel on the grounds of Tundergarth Parish Church on Route B7068 several miles east of Lockerbie where a major section of the Pan Am jet came down. The small chapel contains two memorial books, one with the name and home of each victim on a separate page, the second with a picture, biography, and special remarks about each victim of the terrorist disaster.

SHOPPING

Most of the town's merchants maintain premises along High Street, whose turn-of-the century facades evoke the novels of Charles Dickens, and a nearby thoroughfare, Queensberry Street. **Alternatives,** 73 Queensberry St. (☎ **01387/257467**), is an attractive new-age shop stocking herbal remedies, artfully abstract wind chimes, and gift items, especially jewelry inspired by Celtic designs. The town's most interesting antiques shop is **The Antiquarian,** 71 Queensberry St. (☎ **01387/267351**), where everything from easy-to-transport estate jewelry and silver to monumental furniture worthy of a palace is available for inspection and sale. If you're interested in acquiring men's or women's kilts in any of dozens of tartan patterns, as well as sweaters, overcoats, hats, and socks, always at realistic prices, head for the town's largest purveyor of Scottish woolens, **Edinburgh Woolen Mill,** 8 Church Place (☎ **01387/267351**).

WHERE TO STAY

Cairndale Hotel and Leisure Club. 132–136 English St., Dumfries, Dumfries and Galloway DG1 2DF. ☎ **800/INTER-50** in the U.S., or 01387/254111. Fax 01387/250555. 76 rms, 3 suites. TV TEL. £99.50–£109.50 ($164.15–$180.65) double; from £119.50 ($197.15) suite. Rates include breakfast. AE, DC, MC, V. Free parking.

A four-story stone-fronted building dating from around 1900, the Cairndale Hotel is a fine and substantial choice. In its bedrooms, special care has been paid to modern amenities. All contain hair dryers and hot-beverage facilities. Executive rooms and suites have queen-size beds, minibars, trouser presses, and whirlpool baths, and the public lounges are handsome.

You have a choice of three bars, and guests quickly decide which one they'll make their "local." Dinner, served from 7 to 9:30pm, is generally quite good, including roast sirloin of Galloway beef, West Coast scallops, mealed herring with Arran sauce, or perhaps Ecclefechan flan with Drambuie cream. A three-course table d'hôte lunch goes for £9.50 ($15.65) and a four-course dinner costs £17.50 ($28.90). In addition, the Continental Cafe Bar overlooks the hotel's heated indoor swimming pool, and the Forum offers light snacks and refreshments daily. Sawney Bean's Bar and Grill serves tasty bar snacks, lunches, and dinners as well. Regular entertainment from May to October includes a dinner dance on Saturday and a popular Cairndale ceilidh and "Taste of Burns Country" dinner every Sunday night with a piper, accordionist, drummer, soloist, and Highland dancer. The hotel is owned and managed by the Wallace family. A leisure center includes a swimming pool, sauna, steam room, spa bath, solarium, and gym.

Station Hotel. 49 Lovers Walk, Dumfries, Dumfries and Galloway DG1 1LT. ☎ **01387/ 254316.** Fax 01387/250388. 32 rms. TV TEL. £70–£90 ($115.50–$148.50) double. Rates include breakfast. AE, DC, MC, V. Free parking.

Station Hotel is among the most traditional in Dumfries, a few steps from the gingerbread-fringed train station. It was built in 1896 of hewn sandstone, in a design of heavy timbers, polished paneling, and soaring ceilings. The modernized but still somewhat dowdy bedrooms are accessible via long corridors of old-fashioned design. Each contains a teamaker, comfortable bed, and electric trouser press. The welcome and dinner menu at the Dining Room and Somewhere Else Bistro are purely Scottish. Before dinner, drinks can be enjoyed in the lounge bar, followed by dinner in a high-ceilinged room framed on one side with bay windows overlooking century-old trees and the station.

WHERE TO DINE

Bruno's. 3 Balmoral Rd. ☎ **01387/255757.** Reservations required Sat–Sun. Main courses £4.95–£14.50 ($8.15–$23.90); 3-course fixed-price dinner £16 ($26.40); supper pasta menu £6.50 ($10.75). MC, V. Wed–Mon 6–10pm. ITALIAN.

It may seem ironic to recommend an Italian restaurant in the heart of Rabbie Burns territory, in the town center across from the Balmoral Hotel, but Bruno's serves some of the best food in town. It's most unassuming, but that's part of its charm. The chef's repertoire is familiar—first-rate minestrone, homemade pastas, veal with ham, and spicy chicken—but it's done with a certain flair. The fillet of pork is particularly tender, and the tomato sauce well spiced and blended. Bruno's serves only dinner and a special three-course menu is very popular with customers.

BURNS'S FAVORITE "HOWFF"

♻ **Globe Inn.** 56 High St. ☎ **01387/252335.** Main courses £3.20–£4.70 ($5.30–$7.75). No credit cards. Mon–Fri 10am–11pm, Sat 10am–midnight, Sun 12:30–11pm. SCOTTISH.

This was a favorite haunt of Burns, who used an old Scottish expression, *howff*— meaning a small, cozy room—to describe his local. He not only imbibed here but had a child with the barmaid, Anna Park. The pub, in business since 1610, is reached down a narrow flagstone passageway off High Street opposite the Marks & Spencer department store. You can go here for lunch, drinks, or to play a nightly game of dominoes. A little museum is devoted to Burns, and on window panes upstairs you can see verses he scratched with a diamond. The menu includes such items as kipper pâté, haggis, mealed herring, and Globe steak pie, rather like the food Burns himself might have preferred. Food is served only Monday through Saturday at lunchtime, from noon to 3pm. No food is served at night or on Sunday. Taps include Belhaven, Tennet's Lager, McEwen's 60 and 80 Shilling, Galloway Ale, Stela Lager, and Black Throne Cider.

DUMFRIES AFTER DARK

The town's most important and most frequently showcased pub is the previously recommended **Globe Inn,** 56 High St. (☎ **01387/252335**), site where Robert Burns tipped many a dram during his evenings in Dumfries. A smaller, equally historic pub loaded with local color is **The Hole in the Wall,** 156 High St. (☎ **01387/252770**), where live music is usually provided by an accordionist. If you want to go dancing, head for either of the town's two discos, **Chancer's Nightclub,** 25 Munches St. (☎ **01387/263170**); and **The Junction,** 36 High St. (☎ **01387/267262**). Be warned that the clientele and musical venue at these two clubs changes abruptly, depending on the theme for the night. A phone call in advance is usually helpful so that you'll know whether to expect soca, reggae, and punk rock, or 1970s retro disco, when some of the clientele, at least, will be in their 40s, dancing nostalgically to the music of their heyday.

8 Castle Douglas

16 miles SW of Dumfries, 98 miles SW of Edinburgh, 49 miles SE of Ayr

An old cattle- and sheep-market town, Castle Douglas, at the northern tip of Carlingwark Loch, makes a good touring center for Galloway. On one of the islets in the loch is an ancient lake dwelling known as a "crannog."

ESSENTIALS
GETTING THERE

BY TRAIN   The nearest railway station is in Dumfries. Call ☎ **0345/484950** for schedules and information.

BY BUS   There are Great Western Bus Co. buses from Dumfries to Castle Douglas every hour throughout the day and early evening; travel time is about 30 minutes. Call ☎ **0990/808080** for more information.

BY CAR   From Dumfries, head southwest along A75.

VISITOR INFORMATION

A summer-only **tourist information center** is at the Markethill Car Park (☎ **01556/502611**).

SEEING THE SIGHTS

Unique in this country, **Orchardton Tower,** off A711, 5¹/₂ miles southeast of Castle Douglas, is an example of a round tower house. It was constructed around 1450 by John Cairns, and if you ask the custodian who lives at the cottage nearby, you can see inside. This is the only round tower in Scotland (they were usually built in Ireland). Later on, the site was purchased by a member of the Maxwell family. The adventures of one family member, Sir Robert Maxwell of Orchardton, a fervent Jacobite captured in the Battle of Culloden, figured in Sir Walter Scott's novel *Guy Mannering.* Admission is free.

   Mote of Urr, off B794, 5 miles northeast of Castle Douglas, is a circular mound enclosed by a deep trench. Students of history will know that this is an example of the motte-and-bailey type of defense popular in Norman days.

Threave Castle. 1¹/₂ miles west of Castle Douglas on an islet in the River Dee. Free admission. Apr–Sept, Mon–Sat 9:30am–6:30pm, Sun 2–6:30pm. Closed Oct–Mar.

The district's favorite excursion is to Threave Castle, the ruined 14th-century stronghold of the Black Douglases. The seven-story tower was built between 1639 and 1690 by Archibald the Grim, lord of Galloway. In 1455 Threave Castle was the last Douglas stronghold to surrender to James II, who employed some of the most advanced armaments of his day (including a cannon similar to "Mons Meg," the massive cannon now displayed in Edinburgh Castle) in its subjection. Over the doorway projects the "gallows knob" from which the Douglases hanged their enemies. The castle was captured by the Covenanters in 1640 and dismantled.

Owned by a public group known as Historic Scotland, the site must be reached by a half-mile walk through farmlands, and then by small boat across the Dee. A ferry charge of £1.50 ($2.45) for adults and 75p ($1.25) for children is the only alternative to that long walk. Last sailing to the castle is at 6pm. For information, get in touch with Historic Scotland, Longmore House, Salisbury Place, Edinburgh (☎ **01316/688800**).

Threave Garden. Off Hwy. A75. ☎ **01556/502575.** Admission £3.70 ($6.10) adults, £2.50 ($4.15) children and seniors. Garden: daily 9:30am–sunset. Visitor Center: Apr–Oct, daily 9:30am–5:30pm. Take A75 half a mile west of Castle Douglas.

A mile southeast of the castle, the gardens are built around Threave House, a Scottish baronial mansion constructed during the Victorian era. It's run by the National Trust for Scotland, which uses the complex as a school for gardening and a wildfowl refuge. The garden is at its best in April when the daffodils bloom, and in June when rhododendrons and the rock garden are in flower. There's a visitor center and a restaurant.

WHERE TO STAY & DINE

Douglas Arms. King St., Castle Douglas, Dumfries and Galloway DG7 1DB. ☎ **01556/502231.** Fax 01556/504000. 24 rms. TV TEL. £65 ($107.25) double. Rates include breakfast. MC, V.

Douglas Arms is a 17th-century coaching inn, but it has been turned into a modernized hotel, right in the commercial center of town. Behind a rather stark, two-story facade, the public rooms are bright and cheerful, giving you a toasty feeling on a cold night. By the end of 1998, all the bedrooms will have been refurbished; private baths were recently added to all accommodations. Dinner is served from 5 to 9pm, and of course, trout and salmon are featured, along with good beef and lamb. Try the mixed wild mushrooms sautéed in garlic and flambéed in whisky, followed by the roast sirloin of Galloway beef in a loose grain mustard sauce. An à la carte dinner begins at £13 ($21.45).

King's Arms. St. Andrew's St., Castle Douglas, Dumfries and Galloway DG7 1EL. ☎ **01556/502626.** Fax 01556/502097. 10 rms (9 with bath). £40 ($66) double without bath, £52 ($85.80) double with bath. Rates include breakfast. DC, MC, V. Free parking.

Open all year, this longtime inn provides reasonably priced accommodations ranging from single rooms to a family room. The bedrooms are newly redecorated, and nine are equipped with TVs and phones. A sun patio for tea or coffee, perhaps a "sundowner" of malt whisky, is also provided. Guests can enjoy bar snacks during the day and fixed-price or à la carte menus in the dining room at night, where meals are served from 6 to 8:45pm. The cuisine is British with a Scottish emphasis; the range is extensive, featuring local produce and including Solway salmon and succulent Galloway beef. Prices range from £3.50 ($5.75) for bar snacks to £7.50 ($12.40) and up for dinner. There's also a reasonably priced selection of wines available in the three bars. The helpful staff will direct you to various activities in the area, including a nine-hole golf course within a 45-minute drive.

9 Kirkcudbright

108 miles SW of Edinburgh, 28 miles SW of Dumfries, 50 miles E of Stranraer, 10 miles SW of Castle Douglas

Stewartry's most ancient burgh, Kirkcudbright (pronounced "Kir-*coo*-bree") lies at the head of Kirkcudbright Bay on the Dee estuary. Many of this intriguing old town's color-washed houses belong to artists. There's a lively group of weavers, potters, and painters who live and work in the 18th-century streets and lanes.

ESSENTIALS
GETTING THERE

BY TRAIN   Go to Dumfries (see above), then proceed by train the rest of the way. Call ☎ **0345/484950** for schedules and information.

BY BUS   Kirkcudbright lies on the same bus route that serves Castle Douglas from Dumfries, with departures during the day about once per hour. For bus information call ☎ **0990/808080.**

BY CAR   From Castle Douglas (see above), continue along A75 southwest until you come to the junction with A711, which takes you into Kirkcudbright.

VISITOR INFORMATION

A **tourist information office** is at Harbour Square (☎ **01557/330494**), open only from Easter to October.

SEEING THE SIGHTS

In the old town **graveyard** are memorials to Covenanters and to Billy Marshall, the tinker (gypsy) king, who died in 1792 at the age of 120, reportedly having fathered four children after the age of 100.

McLellan's Castle, off High Street (☎ **01557/331856**), built in 1582 for the town's provost, Sir Thomas McLellan, dominates the center of town. This castellated mansion has been a ruin since 1752. It's open April through September, Monday through Saturday from 9:30am to 6pm and Sunday from 2 to 6pm; October and November, Saturday through Wednesday from 9:30am to 4pm. Admission is £1 ($1.65) for adults and 50p (85¢) for children.

The **Tolbooth,** a large building from 1629 on High Street, has functioned during its life as a prison, the town hall, and a courthouse. In front of it is a Mercat Cross of 1610. The Tolbooth contains a memorial to John Paul Jones (1747–92), the gardener's son from Kirkbean who became a slave trader, a privateer, and in due course, the father of the American navy. For a time before his emigration he was imprisoned for murder in the Tolbooth. In 1993 the queen inaugurated the building as an art gallery, the **Tolbooth Art Centre,** High Street (☎ **01557/330437**). It contains paintings by famous local artists. Inside, you'll find works by Jessie M. King, Lena Alexander, Robert Sivell, and S. J. Peploe. It is open April through October daily from 1 to 5:30pm. Adult admission is £2.30 ($3.80); seniors, students, and children pay £1.50 ($2.45).

Included in the admission fee at the Tolbooth, you can view the art exhibitions regularly sponsored at **Broughton House,** High Street (☎ **01557/330437**), an 18th-century mansion that once belonged to artist E. A. Hornel. The house contains a large reference library with a Burns collection, along with pictures by Hornel and other artists, plus antiques and other works of art. You can stroll through its beautiful garden. It keeps the same hours as the Tolbooth Art Centre.

In addition, the **Stewartry Museum**, St. Mary Street (☎ **01557/331643**), contains a fascinating collection of antiquities, depicting the history and culture of Galloway. It's open in May, June, and September, Monday through Saturday from 11am to 5pm; in June and September it is also open Sunday from 2 to 5pm. In July and August, hours are Monday through Saturday from 10am to 6pm and Sunday from 2 to 5pm; October through April, Monday through Saturday from 11am to 4pm. Admission is £1.50 ($2.45) for adults and 75p ($1.25) for children, seniors, and students.

WHERE TO STAY

Selkirk Arms. Old High St., Kirkcudbright, The Borders DG6 4JG. ☎ **01557/330402.** Fax 01557/331639. 15 rms. TV TEL. £80 ($132) double. Rates include breakfast. AE, DC, MC, V. Free parking.

Selkirk Arms, where Robert Burns stayed when he composed the celebrated "Selkirk Grace," was built in the 1770s in a stone-fronted Georgian design with a slate roof. The bedrooms were refurbished in 1995, and all have tea/coffeemakers and standard, not-very-imaginative but hotel-style furniture and a view of the gardens. The restaurant and bistro offers a wide range of fresh local produce; bar lunches and suppers are also available. The lounge bar features an array of malt whiskies. The hotel has ample parking and a spacious garden in the rear. The neighborhood evokes memories of John Paul Jones.

WHERE TO DINE

Auld Alliance Restaurant. 5 Castle St. ☎ **01557/330569.** Reservations recommended. Main courses £8.50–£15 ($14–$24.75). No credit cards. Daily 6:30–9pm (last booking). Closed Halloween–Easter. SCOTTISH/FRENCH.

One of the most appealing restaurants in the region is this family-owned and -operated establishment, in an interconnected pair of 1880s buildings constructed with stones from the ruins of Kirkcudbright Castle, a minute's walk from the town's harborfront. The restaurant is the domain of Alistair Crawford, who prepares a savory cuisine served by his wife, Anne, and their sons, Andrew and Alistair, Jr. Many of the floors throughout the place are covered with tartan-patterned carpeting. The restaurant's cooks are almost obsessed with the freshness of the fish they serve, and salmon (likely to have been caught several hours before preparation in the Kirkcudbright estuary and its tributary, the River Dee) has all its legendary freshness and flavor.

A special house dish is "queenies," or queen-size scallops, from deeper waters than the great scallop. They may be yellow, orange, pink, red, purple, or brown in color. Other choices include a pâté of chicken livers flavored with wild Scottish garlic, and a dessert crêpe layered with fresh Scottish raspberries and freshly made ice cream, drizzled in butterscotch sauce, and dusted with cinnamon.

10 Gatehouse-of-Fleet

113 miles SW of Edinburgh, 33 miles SW of Dumfries, 42 miles E of Stranraer

This sleepy former cotton town on the Water of Fleet was the Kippletringan in Sir Walter Scott's *Guy Mannering*. Burns composed "Scots Wha' Hae wi' Wallace Bled" on the moors nearby and wrote it down in the Murray Arms Hotel here.

The town's name probably dates from 1642 when the English government opened the first military road through Galloway to assist the passage of troops to Ireland.

In 1661 Richard Murray of Cally was authorized by Parliament to widen the bridge and to erect beside it an inn that was to serve as a tollhouse, with the innkeeper responsible for the maintenance of a 12-mile stretch of road. This is believed to have been the original house on the "gait," or road, which later became known as the "gait house of Fleet," and by 1790 it was being written in its present form and spelling. This ancient "gait house" is now part of the Murray Arms Hotel, used as a coffee room, and is the oldest building still in existence in the town.

ESSENTIALS

GETTING THERE

BY TRAIN   Go first to Dumfries (see above), then continue the rest of the way by train. Call ☎ **0345/484950** for information and schedules.

BY BUS   Four buses a day arrive in Gatehouse-of-Fleet from Dumfries. The trip, although short, takes 90 minutes because the bus stops frequently along the way. For information about schedules, call ☎ **0990/808080.**

BY CAR   From Castle Douglas (see above), continue west along A75.

VISITOR INFORMATION

A summer-only **tourist information center** operates from the Town Car Park (☎ **01557/814212**).

EXPLORING THE AREA

West of Gatehouse, on the road to Creetown, is the well-preserved 15th-century **tower of the McCullochs,** with its sinister "murder hole" over the entrance passage. Through this trap door, boiling pitch was poured onto attackers.

   Cardoness Castle (☎ **01557/814427**) was originally the seat of the McCulloch family, one of whom, Sir Godfrey McCulloch, was the last person in Scotland to be executed by the "Maiden," the Scots version of the guillotine, at Edinburgh in 1697. The location is off A75, a mile southwest of Gatehouse-of-Fleet. It's open from early April to the end of September, Monday through Saturday from 9:30am to 6:30pm and Sunday from 2 to 6:30pm; October and November, Monday through Saturday from 9:30am to 4:30pm and Sunday from 2 to 4:30pm; the remainder of the year, only on Saturday from 9:30am to 4:30pm and Sunday from 2 to 4:30pm. The last ticket is sold 30 minutes before closing. Admission costs £1.50 ($2.45) for adults, 75p ($1.25) for children.

WHERE TO STAY & DINE

Cally Palace Hotel. Along Hwy. A75, Gatehouse-of-Fleet, Dumfries and Galloway DG7 2DL. ☎ **01557/814341.** Fax 01557/814522. 55 rms. TV TEL. £60–£71 ($99–$117.15) double. Rates include breakfast. MC, V. Free parking.

Cally Palace Hotel is a large mansion, built in 1763 in 150 acres of gardens, loch, and wooded parkland, 1¹/₂ miles south by A75. Especially popular with more mature travelers, it's an oasis of peace and quiet—most comfortable and more suited for spending a few days in Galloway than for a fleeting overnight stop. The public lounges are overscale with some fine period pieces. Amenities and activities include a bar, an indoor leisure centre, a sauna, table tennis, pool, and croquet. Tennis, game fishing, and loch boating are available. There's a 5,802-yard, par-70, 18-hole golf course on the site, with greens fees costing £22 ($36.30). Some of the bedrooms have balconies opening onto the grounds. The guest rooms come in widely varying styles and sizes, some in a modern annex, others in the historic main building; all have hot-beverage facilities. A dinner-dance is held on Saturday night. Every night you can order a four-course table d'hôte dinner for £21.50 ($35.50) from 6:15 to 9:30pm.

Murray Arms. Ann St., Gatehouse-of-Fleet, Dumfries and Galloway DG7 2HY. ☎ **01557/ 814207.** Fax 01557/814370. 13 rms. TV TEL. £85 ($140.25) double. Rates include breakfast. AE, DC, MC, V. Free parking.

The Murray Arms is a long, low, white-painted building that functioned as a posting inn in 1760. Its coffeehouse (which sometimes converts into a small-scale art gallery) is even older, with traditions dating back to 1642. This is where Burns wrote down his stirring song, "Scots Wha' Hae wi' Wallace Bled," an occasion still commemorated by the Burns Room with its Leitch pictures. The inn has been considerably updated and modernized now that it's back in the Cally family—and that's as it should be, since it was James Murray of Cally who made the Murray Arms into a coaching inn so long ago. The bedrooms overlook either the garden or the main street of town.

You can stop in for a complete dinner in the inn's attractive restaurant opening onto the garden. From 7:30 to 9pm daily, you can order an à la carte meal for between £15 and £18 ($24.75 and $29.70). Specialties include Galloway beef and fresh Solway Firth salmon. There are three bars, and the Lunky Hole Restaurant is open daily from noon to 9:45pm and serves a wide variety of hot and cold food.

11 Stranraer

132 miles SW of Edinburgh, 75 miles W of Dumfries

The largest town in Wigtownshire, Stranraer is the terminal of the 35-mile ferry crossing from Larne, Northern Ireland. An early chapel, built by a member of the Adair family near the 16th-century Castle of St. John in the heart of town, gave the settlement its original name of Chapel, later changed to Chapel of Stranrawer and then shortened to Stranraer. The name is supposed to have referred to the row or "raw" of original houses on the "strand" or burn, now largely buried beneath the streets. The Castle of St. John became the town jail and in the late 17th century held Covenanters during the campaigns of religious persecution.

ESSENTIALS
GETTING THERE

BY TRAIN   Monday through Saturday four trains per day run from Glasgow to Stranraer, and seven trains on Sunday. The one-way fare is £18.50 ($30.55). Call ☎ **0345/484950,** 24 hours a day, for information about schedules.

BY BUS   Bus no. 502 departs Newton Stewart for Stranraer seven times per day (trip time: 30 min.). Call ☎ **0990/808080** for schedules.

BY CAR   From Dumfries (see above), continue west along A75.

BY FERRY   Sealink Ferries go between Stranraer and Belfast in Northern Ireland. Seven daily ferries depart Monday through Saturday, and five on Sunday. Trip time is 2 hours, 20 minutes. The one-way fare for travelers without cars is £18–£20 ($29.70–$33) for adults and £10–£14 ($16.50–$23.10) for children. A driver with a car pays £146–£220 ($240.90–$363) each way, and a driver with a car and up to four passengers pays £115 ($181.70). Weather conditions can interfere with ferry departures; call ☎ **01776/702262** in Stranraer for schedule information.

VISITOR INFORMATION

A summer-only **tourist information center** is at Burns House, Harbour St. (☎ **01776/702595**).

In case you want to see the world.

At American Express, we're here to make your journey a smooth one. So we have over 1,700 travel service locations in over 120 countries ready to help. What else would you expect from the world's largest travel agency?

do more

Travel

In case you want to be welcomed there.

We're here to see that you're always welcomed at establishments everywhere. That's why millions of people carry the American Express® Card – for peace of mind, confidence, and security, around the world or just around the corner.

do more

Cards

In case you're running low.

We're here to help with more than 118,000 Express Cash locations around the world. In order to enroll, just call American Express before you start your vacation.

do more

Express Cash

And just in case.

We're here with American Express® Travelers Cheques and Cheques *for Two*.® They're the safest way to carry money on your vacation and the surest way to get a refund, practically anywhere, anytime.

Another way we help you...

do more

Travelers
Cheques

EXPLORING THE AREA

Four miles east of Stranraer on A75 are the **Castle Kennedy Gardens** (☎ **01776/ 702024**). In the grounds are the White and Black lochs and the ruins of Castle Kennedy, a late 19th-century Scots baronial mansion built during the reign of James IV, but burned down in 1716. The gardens contain one of the finest pinetums in Scotland. In the right season you can wander among blossoming rhododendrons, azaleas, and magnolias. The castle is not open to the public. The gardens are open from Easter to September only, daily from 10am to 5pm. Admission is £2 ($3.30) for adults, £1.50 ($2.45) for seniors, and £1 ($1.65) for children.

SHOPPING   Despite its small size, the town has a great number of shops. Most are clustered along Charlotte, George, and Castle streets. **Rogers Sports,** Charlotte Street (☎ **01776/703996**), can provide all kinds of gear for fair and foul weather, and any equipment you might need for a sports holiday on the moors or golf links. One of the most endearing china shops in the Borders, the **China Shop,** Charlotte Street (☎ **01776/702697**), carries most of the grand names of British porcelain and crystal, as well as cunning figurines of the animals that trek across the nearby hills.

If woolens, tartans, and knitwear appeal to you, a drive 7 miles north of Stranraer will bring you to **McGills,** Loch Ryan Bank, Kirkcolm (☎ **01776/853270**). They sell woolen sweaters and other goods from such manufacturers as Pringles. An art gallery known throughout the region for its evocative landscapes by local artists is the **Waterloo Gallery,** Harbour Street (☎ **01776/702888**). A bit farther afield, in the village of Ardwell, 7 miles south of Stranraer, the **Clachenmore Art Gallery** (☎ **01776/860200**) incorporates a coffee shop, a gift shop, and a winning collection of sculptures and paintings by British and Scottish artists into one highly appealing whole. For women, two choice personalized and tasteful clothing shops are **Whispers,** George Street (☎ **01776/706591**), and **Nowadays,** George Street (☎ **01776/703938**).

WHERE TO STAY

✪ **Corsewall Lighthouse Hotel.** Kirkcolm, Stranraer, Dumfries and Galloway DG9 0QG. ☎ **01776/853220.** Fax 01776/854231. 6 rms, 2 suites. TV TEL. £50–£85 ($82.50–$140.25) double; £85 ($140.25) suite. Rates are per person, double occupancy, and include dinner and breakfast. AE, DC, MC, V. From Stranraer, take A77 for 12 miles north, following signs to Kirkcolm and Corsewall Point.

After centuries of shipwrecks on the treacherous shoals and shallow bottoms off this coastal area of the Irish Sea, a lighthouse was erected in 1815. In modern times, it was electrified and computerized, and is still beaming warning signals from an isolated point a mile from the nearest farmhouse, and surrounded by verdant fields and forests. But don't set your hopes on being able to climb the 125 steps leading up to the top of the lighthouse. However, if your visit coincides with the twice-per-month visit of maintenance personnel you can indeed—if circumstances allow it—climb to the top.

Late in 1994, the solid stone walls, barns, and outbuildings of the lighthouse keeper's home were transformed into a well-managed inn. Charming and convivial, the format you'll see today was the creation of Scots–Canadian emigrés Jim and Mary Neilson, who welcome guests into an upscale, undeniably luxurious setting. Bedrooms are individually decorated; those facing the Irish sea are outfitted in tones of blue and white; those fronting the surrounding fields in tones of green, yellow, and gold. Five-course set-price dinners, costing £22 ($36.30) per person, are served every night from 7 to 9:15pm. Most ingredients (fresh produce, beef, lamb, salmon, trout, and venison) are local—undeniably fresh and prepared with skill and finesse. There's a pub on the premises open to the public, and passersby are welcome to drop in for drinks and meals. Simple lunches, consisting of platters priced from £4.50 to £6.50 ($7.45 to $10.75) each, are served daily from noon to 2:30pm.

Craignelder Hotel. Cairn Ryan Rd., Stranraer, Dumfries and Galloway DG9 8HA. ☎ **01776/ 703281.** Fax 01776/705456. 13 rms. TV TEL. £50 ($82.50) double. Rates include breakfast. MC, V. Free parking.

This comfortably weatherproof hotel was built before World War I near the wharves that service the ferryboat to Ireland. Cream colored and angular, the hotel has been severely modernized several times during its lifetime, most recently in 1991. The bedrooms have hot-beverage facilities and contemporary furniture. On the premises are two bars, a restaurant, and a clientele that seems to be constantly waiting for a ferryboat to carry them home to Ireland. A fixed-price dinner, served between 5 and 8pm, costs £10.50 ($17.35).

✪ **Kildrochet House.** By Stranraer, Stranraer, Dumfries and Galloway DG9 9BB. ☎ and fax **01776/820216.** 3 rms. £48 ($79.20) double. Rates include breakfast. DC, MC, V. Drive 3¹/₂ miles south of Stranraer, following A716.

Calming, bucolic, and charming, the stone walls of this house were designed and built in 1720 by William Adam, the father of the famous architect, Robert Adam, who would later bring Palladian symmetry to many of the grandest buildings in Britain. The place was originally conceived as a dower house for the mother of the lord of the manor. Built of stucco-covered stone and painted white, it's prefaced with a stately row of beech trees that flank either side of the driveway. Bedrooms evoke the inner recesses of a private home, and are outfitted with dignified furniture and many personalized accessories (no phones or TVs). Each has a view over the 3¹/₂ acres of gardens and fields that surround the place. Liz and Peter Witworth are the congenial owners and will prepare an evening meal—served in the family dining room surrounded by family portraits—for any client who gives advance notice. The establishment's name translates from the Gaelic as "Over the Bridge."

✪ **North West Castle Hotel.** Royal Crescent, Stranraer, Dumfries and Galloway DG9 8EH. ☎ **01776/704413.** Fax 01776/702646. 68 rms, 4 suites, 1 penthouse. TV TEL. £70 ($115.50) double; £90 ($148.50) suite; £100 ($165) penthouse. Rates include breakfast. MC, V. Free parking. Walk north from the ferryboat terminal for 3 minutes.

This is the largest and most prominent hotel in Stranraer. Its oldest part was built in 1820 by Capt. Sir John Ross, R.N., the Arctic explorer. The hotel owners will give you a brochure that relates the exploits and disappointments of this local hero. The original building has been altered and expanded with a modern flat-roofed addition that contains most of the comfortably modern bedrooms. The lounges are cozy and the dining room is impressive. Fresh local ingredients are used in the in-house restaurant, where continental food with Scottish overtones is served. A five-course table d'hôte, available daily from 7 to 9:30pm, costs £21 ($34.65). The bars in the hotel's cellar are well stocked, but we prefer the Ross Lounge with its views of the harbor. Further amenities include a garden, sauna, solarium, curling rink (from October to April), games room, indoor swimming pool, and dancing to a live band most Saturday nights in winter.

WHERE TO DINE

L'Apéritif Restaurant. London Rd. ☎ **01776/702991.** Reservations recommended. Main courses £5.50–£12 ($9.05–$19.80); pizzas £4–£6 ($6.60–$9.90). MC, V. Mon–Sat noon–2pm and 5:30–9pm. ITALIAN/INTERNATIONAL.

Here you find some of the best and most reasonably priced food at the port. Directly east of town, it's operated by Italians who have thrived here for more than 30 years. One of the two lounges contains a pub popular with local residents. Homemade soups, fresh salads, pastas, and hot dishes are offered at lunch. In the evening you have the choice of continental meals upstairs from an à la carte menu. They also serve pizza.

STRANRAER AFTER DARK

The town has a good representative of historic and/or popular pubs that might help while away a foggy evening. Small and hospitable but not particularly historic is the **Bridge Pub,** Bridge Street (☎ 01776/704839). **The Grapes,** Bridge Street (☎ 01776/703386), has a retro design of vintage 1940s–1950s decor and has been virtually untouched since it was modernized shortly after World War II. Also worth your tippling and attention is the pub on the ground floor of the **Royal Hotel,** Hanover Street (☎ 01776/702426), where on Wednesday night you can enjoy live Scottish folk music. If you want to see how London's punk rock has mutated on its northward pilgrimage, head for the town's most viable disco, **The Venue,** Hanover Street (☎ 01776/889880). Be warned that you might not really appreciate this place unless you're under 35 and familiar with the tastes of Generation X.

12 Portpatrick

141 miles SW of Edinburgh, 8 miles SW of Stranraer, 80 miles W of Dumfries

Until 1849 steamers sailed the 21 miles from Donaghdee in Northern Ireland to Portpatrick, which became a "Gretna Green" for the Irish who wanted to marry quickly. Couples would land on Saturday, have the banns called on Sunday, and marry on Monday. When the harbor silted up, Portpatrick was replaced by Stranraer as a port. Commanding a clifftop to the south are the ruins of **Dunskey Castle,** a grim keep built in 1510.

ESSENTIALS

GETTING THERE

BY TRAIN   Go to Stranraer (see above) by train, then take a bus to Portpatrick. For train schedules and information, call ☎ 0345/484950.

BY BUS   Bus no. 64 from Stranraer makes frequent runs throughout the day to Portpatrick. For bus schedules and information, call ☎ 0990/808080.

BY CAR   From Stranraer, take A77 southwest.

VISITOR INFORMATION

The nearest tourist information office is in Stranraer (see above).

EXPLORING THE AREA

Some 10 miles south of Portpatrick is the little hamlet of Port Logan. In the vicinity is Logan House (not open to the public), the seat of the McDougall family, which claimed they could trace their ancestry so far back that they were as "old as the sun itself." This family laid out the gardens at Logan.

   Logan Botanic Garden (☎ 01776/860231), an annex of the Royal Botanic Garden, Edinburgh, contains a wide range of plants from the warm temperate regions of the world. Cordylines, palms, tree ferns, and flowering shrubs grow well in the mild climate of southwestern Scotland. The garden is open from March 15 through October only, daily from 10am to 6pm. Admission is £2 ($3.30) for adults,

£1.50 ($2.45) for seniors, and 50p (85¢) for children. There's a pleasant refreshment room at the entrance. The site is 14 miles south of Stranraer off B7065.

The ancient church site of **Kirkmadrine** lies in the parish of Stoneykirk, south of Portpatrick. The site now has a modern church, but there's an old graveyard with inscribed stones and crosses from the early 5th or 6th century, including three of the earliest Christian monuments in Britain, showing the Chi-Rho symbol.

SHOPPING This old-timey fishing port has become something of a magnet for individual artisans who produce charming, and sometimes eccentric, handcrafts. Examples of handcrafted plant pots, slip-cast and glazed figurines, Spanish recycled glass, and Indian coffee tables can be found at the port's largest gift shop, **Lighthouse Pottery,** South Pier (☎ 01776/810284). The **Green Gillie Crafts Shop,** High Street (no phone), specializes in woolen jerseys and mittens, throw rugs, and calfskins. At the **Copper Wheel,** High Street (call the local garage at ☎ 01776/810543 and ask for Ron Farquer), a highly skilled local artisan grinds heraldic or free-form designs into wine glasses, beer mugs, and other objects. You can either bring your own object or buy one from him. Fly fishers appreciate his renderings of trout or salmon on a line.

WHERE TO STAY & DINE

Crown Hotel. North Crescent, Portpatrick, Dumfries and Galloway DG9 8FX. ☎ 01776/810261. Reservations recommended. Main courses £7.95–£23 ($13.10–$37.95). MC, V. Daily noon–2:30pm and 6–10pm. SEAFOOD/INTERNATIONAL.

One of the region's most popular restaurants occupies the ground floor of a century-old stone-sided, white-painted hotel. You might enjoy a drink or two in the pub before heading into the dining room, which opens onto a wide-angled view of the ocean. Menu items are firmly rooted in the town's seafaring traditions, and although meat is available, the restaurant's greatest allure lies in its wide selection of scampi, monkfish, scallops in wine sauce, mullet, cod, and fillets of plaice, salmon, or sole. Some platters, especially one priced at £23 ($37.95), are enormous and can be shared by two diners. The establishment maintains 12 uncomplicated but very clean bedrooms upstairs, each with private bath, TV, and telephone. With a hearty Scottish breakfast included, doubles rent for £72 ($118.80) each.

Fernhill Hotel. Heugh Rd., Portpatrick, Dumfries and Galloway DG9 8TD. ☎ 01776/810220. Fax 01776/810596. 20 rms. TV TEL. £75–£95 ($123.75–$156.75) double. Rates include breakfast. AE, DC, MC, V. Free parking. On the approach to Portpatrick, turn right at the War Memorial.

A widely acclaimed accommodation, this gray stone 1872 building stands on its own grounds above the village, looking down at the harbor. It's a 5-minute walk from the first tee of the clifftop Dunskey Golf Course. Renovated in 1990, the color-coordinated bedrooms are decorated with flair. The most desirable accommodations are six executive rooms opening onto the sea; three have patio doors leading to private balconies. The windows are double glazed, and amenities often include teamakers, trouser presses, and hair dryers. The cocktail bar with its lounge and the Victorian conservatory have a panoramic view over the town and sea. The excellent cuisine, using Scottish produce whenever available, is one of the reasons for staying here. Meals available daily from 6 to 9:30pm begin at £15 ($24.75) à la carte, with a four-course table d'hôte costing £21 ($34.65).

✪ **Knockinaam Lodge Hotel.** Along Hwy. A77, Portpatrick, Dumfries and Galloway DG9 9AD. ☎ 01776/810471. Fax 01776/810435. 10 rms. TV TEL. £160–£250 ($264–$412.50) double. Rates include half board. AE, DC, MC, V. Free parking.

Instead of going to the larger town, Stranraer, you might prefer to stay at the Knockinaam Lodge Hotel, 3¹/₄ miles southeast off A77, built as a Victorian holiday house in 1869, enlarged in 1901, and discreetly renovated in 1995. It stands on a little terraced bay right at the foot of a deep and thickly wooded glen, surrounded on three sides by cliffs, looking out to sea and the distant Irish coast. In the heat of World War II, Sir Winston Churchill chose the lodge for a secret meeting with General Eisenhower. The prime minister enjoyed a long hot bath (in a tub that's still here) while smoking a cigar. Knockinaam is run in the best country-house tradition by the resident owners. There's a garden with lawns running down to a private sandy beach.

Dining/Entertainment: The lodge serves the best food in the area. All ingredients used in the kitchen are fresh. You can dine in the restaurant, overlooking the sea as it breaks over the rocks at the end of the garden. A specialty is tender Galloway beef, lobsters, scallops, and other local dishes, accompanied by home-grown vegetables. Both à la carte and table d'hôte meals are cooked to order. Service is polite and efficient, and the inventory of wines is among the largest and most comprehensive in the region. Lunch, daily from noon to 2pm, is offered for £25 ($41.25); a fixed-price dinner, from 7:30 to 9:30pm, costs £35 ($57.75).

Services: Laundry, baby-sitting.

Facilities: Sea fishing, helipad, croquet.

6 Edinburgh

Edinburgh has been called one of the fairest cities in Europe, "the Athens of the North," and it's the gateway to central Scotland. You can use it as a base for excursions to the Trossachs (Scotland's Lake District), the silver waters of Loch Lomond, and the Kingdom of Fife on the opposite shore of the Firth of Forth.

Edinburgh is filled with historical and literary association—John Knox, Mary Queen of Scots, Robert Louis Stevenson, Sir Arthur Conan Doyle (creator of Sherlock Holmes), Alexander Graham Bell, Sir Walter Scott, and Bonnie Prince Charlie are all part of its past.

The city has become famous as the scene of the ever-growing international Edinburgh Festival, with its action-packed list of cultural events. But remember that the treasures of this ancient seat of Scottish royalty are available all year—in fact, when the festival-hoppers have gone home, the pace is more relaxed, prices are lower, and the people themselves, under less pressure as hosts, return to their traditional hospitable nature.

1 Orientation

ARRIVING

BY PLANE Edinburgh is about an hour's flying time from London, 393 miles to the south. **Edinburgh Airport** (☎ 0131/333-1000 for flight information) lies 6 miles west of the center, receiving flights from within the British Isles and the rest of Europe. A double-decker Airlink bus makes the trip between the airport and the city center every 20 minutes, letting you off near Waverley Bridge, between Old Town and New Town; the one-way fare is £3.20 ($5.30). A taxi into the city will cost £12 ($19.80) or more, depending on traffic conditions.

BY TRAIN InterCity trains link London with Edinburgh and are fast and efficient, providing both restaurant and bar service as well as air-conditioning. Trains from London's King's Cross Station arrive in Edinburgh at **Waverley Station,** at the east end of Princes Street (☎ 0131/556-2451, or 0345/484950 in London, for rail information). Trains depart London every hour or so, taking 4 to 5½ hours. An overnight sleeper—reservations are required—also runs between London and Edinburgh. Taxis and buses are found right outside the station in Edinburgh.

BY BUS   The least expensive way to go from London to Edinburgh is by bus, but it's a long (8 hours) journey. Nevertheless, it'll get you there for only about £20 ($33) one-way or £25 ($41.25) round-trip. Scottish CityLink coaches depart from London's Victoria Coach Station, delivering you to Edinburgh's **St. Andrew's Square Bus Station,** St. Andrew Square (☎ **0990/808080** in Edinburgh for more data).

BY CAR   Edinburgh lies 46 miles east of Glasgow and 105 miles north of Newcastle-upon-Tyne in England. There is no express motorway linking London and Edinburgh. The M1 motorway from London takes you part of the way north, but you'll have to come into Edinburgh along secondary roads: A68 or A7 from the southeast, A1 from the east, or A702 from the north. Highway A71 or A8 comes in from the west, A8 connecting with M8 just west of Edinburgh; A90 comes down from the north over the Forth Road Bridge.

VISITOR INFORMATION

The **Edinburgh & Scotland Information Centre,** Waverley Shopping Centre, 3 Princes St. (☎ **0131/557-1700**), can give you sightseeing information and also can help with finding lodgings (see "Accommodations," later in this chapter, for more details). The center sells bus tours, theater tickets, and souvenirs of Edinburgh. There's also an **information and accommodation desk** at Edinburgh airport (☎ **0131/333-2167**), open according to the frequency of incoming flights. The center is open in July and August, Monday through Saturday from 9am to 8pm and Sunday from 10am to 8pm. In May, June, and September, hours are Monday through Saturday from 9am to 7pm and Sunday from 10am to 7pm. October through April, hours are Monday through Saturday from 9am to 6pm and Sunday from 10am to 6pm.

CITY LAYOUT

Edinburgh is divided into an Old Town and a New Town. Chances are, you'll find lodgings in New Town and visit Old Town only for dining, drinking, shopping, or sightseeing.

New Town, with its world-famous **Princes Street,** came about in the 18th century in the "Golden Age" of Edinburgh. Everybody from Robert Burns to James Boswell visited in that era. The first building went up in New Town in 1767, and by the end of the century classical squares, streets, and town houses had been added. Princes Street runs straight for about a mile; it's known for its shopping and also for its beauty, as it opens onto the Princes Street Gardens with panoramic views of Old Town.

North of Princes Street, and running parallel to it, is the second great street of New Town, **George Street.** It begins at Charlotte Square and runs east to St. Andrew Square. Directly north of George Street is another impressive thoroughfare, **Queen Street,** opening onto Queen Street Gardens on its north side. You also hear a lot about **Rose Street,** directly north of Princes Street. It has more pubs per square block than any other place in Scotland, and is also filled with shops and restaurants.

Everyone, seemingly, has heard of the **Royal Mile,** which is the main thoroughfare of **Old Town,** beginning at Edinburgh Castle and running all the way to the Palace of Holyroodhouse. A famous street to the south of the castle (you have to descend to it) is **Grassmarket,** where once convicted criminals were hung on the dreaded gallows that stood there.

Discovering Edinburgh's many hidden lanes and branching out to some of its interesting satellite communities is one of the pleasures of coming here.

FINDING AN ADDRESS   Street numbering can be confusing. Edinburgh's streets often follow no pattern whatsoever, and both names and house numbers seem to have been perpetrated by a group of xenophobes with an equal grudge against postal carriers and strangers.

Edinburgh is checkered with innumerable squares, terraces, "circuses," "wynds," and "closes," which jut into or cross or overlap or interrupt whatever street you're trying to follow, usually without the slightest warning.

House numbers run in odds, evens, clockwise, or counterclockwise as the wind blows. That is, when they exist at all—and frequently they don't. Many establishments don't use street numbers. (This is even truer when you leave Edinburgh and go to a provincial town.) Even though a road might run for a mile, some buildings on the street will be numbered; others will say only "King's Road" or whatever, giving no number, although the neighbor next door uses a number. This is just one aspect that makes traveling around Scotland a bit maddening. Of course, you can always ask for a location to be pinpointed, and locals are generally glad to assist a bewildered foreigner.

Get a detailed map of Edinburgh before setting out. If you're seeking an address, try to get the name of the nearest cross street ("near the corner of," etc.).

NEIGHBORHOODS IN BRIEF

Old Town   This is where Edinburgh began. Its "backbone" is the Royal Mile, a medieval thoroughfare stretching for about a mile from Edinburgh Castle running downhill to the Palace of Holyroodhouse. It's composed of four connected streets, including Castlehill nearest the castle, Lawnmarket, and High Street. Canongate, the fourth section of the Royal Mile, was once a separate burgh. This is "perhaps the largest, longest, and finest street for buildings and number of inhabitants in the world," or so wrote English author Daniel Defoe.

New Town   Lying below Old Town, New Town burst into full bloom between 1766 and 1840, one of the largest Georgian developments in the world. It takes in most of the northern half of the heart of the city, covering some 790 acres. With about 25,000 citizens living within its boundaries, it's known as the largest "conservation area" in all of Britain. It's made up of a network of squares, streets, terraces, and "circuses," which reach from Haymarket in the west to Abbeyhill toward the east. New Town also goes from Canonmills on the northern perimeter down to Princes Street, its main artery, along the southern tier.

Marchmont   About a mile south of High Street, the suburb of Marchmont borders a public park, the Meadows. It was constructed between 1869 and 1914 as a massive building program of new housing for people who could no longer afford to live in New Town.

Bruntsfield   This suburb lies to the west on the other side of Bruntsfield Links. Now a residential district of moderate-income families, it was the ground on which James IV once gathered the Scottish army that he marched to its defeat at Flodden in 1513. Plague victims were once brought here for burial; now suburban gardens have grown over those graves. Many low-cost B&Bs are found in this area.

Churchill   Churchill is known as "holy corner" because of the wide array of Scottish churches inside its borders at the junctions of Colinton Road, Chamberlain Road, and Bruntsfield Road. These churches are primarily for local worshippers and are not

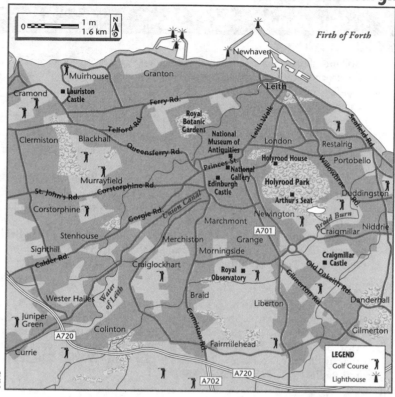

of artistic interest. Many famous Scots have lived in this district, including Jane Welsh Carlyle. George Meikle Kemp, the architect who created the Scott Monument on Princes Street, was a resident.

Leith   The Port of Leith lies only a few miles north of Princes Street and is the city's major harbor, opening onto the Firth of Forth. It's currently going through a gentrification process, and many visitors come here to patronize its restaurants and pubs, which specialize in seafood. The Port of Leith isn't what it used to be in terms of maritime might—its glory days existed back when stevedores unloaded cargoes by hand. Leith was once a bitter rival of Edinburgh, but now, as one local resident put it, "We're just another bloody part of Auld Reekie."

Newhaven   The adjacent fishing village to Leith, Newhaven was once known as "Our Lady's Port of Grace." Founded in the 1400s, this former little fishing harbor with its bustling fishmarket was greatly altered in the 1960s. Many of its "bow-tows" (a nickname for closely knit, clannish residents) were uprooted, like the Leithers, in a major gentrification program. Many of the old houses of the fisherfolk have been restored, and the fishwife no longer goes from door to door hawking fish from her basket (known as a creel). She'd gut and fillet the fish right on your doorstep if you asked her. Newhaven's harbor is now mostly filled with pleasure craft instead of fishing boats.

2 Getting Around

BY BUS

This will probably be your chief method of transport in the Scottish capital. The fare you pay depends on the distance you ride. The minimum fare is 50p (85¢) for three stages or less, and the maximum fare is £2 ($3.30) for 44 or more stages. (A stage is not a stop; it's a distance of about half a mile with a number of stops.) Children 5 to 15 are charged 40p (65¢) to 80p ($1.30), and children 4 and under ride free.

DISCOUNT PASSES The **Edinburgh Freedom Ticket** allows 1 day of unlimited travel on city buses at a cost of £2 ($3.30) for adults and £1.40 ($2.30) for children.

For daily commuters or for die-hard Scottish enthusiasts, a **RideCard** season ticket allows unlimited travel on all buses at £9 ($14.20) for adults for 1 week and £27 ($44.55) for 4 weeks. Travel must begin on Sunday. Prices for children are £5.50 ($9.05) for 1 week, £15.50 ($25.60) for 4 weeks.

These tickets and further information may be obtained at the **Waverley Bridge Transport Office,** Waverley Bridge in Edinburgh (☎ 0131/554-4494), or the **Lothian Region Transport Office,** 14 Queen St. (☎ 0131/555-6363).

BY TAXI

Cabs can be hailed or picked up at a taxi stand. Meters begin at £1.20 ($2). Taxi ranks are found at Hanover Street, North St. Andrew Street, Waverley Station, Haymarket Station, and Lauriston Place. Fares are displayed in the front of the taxi, and charges are posted, including extra charges for night drivers or destinations outside the city limits. You can also call a taxi: Try **City Cabs** (☎ 0131/228-1211) or **Central Radio Taxis** (☎ 0131/229-2468).

BY CAR

Car rentals are relatively expensive, and driving in Edinburgh is a tricky business, even for native motorists. It's a warren of one-way streets, with parking spots at a premium. However, a car is convenient for touring in the countryside. Most companies will accept your U.S. or Canadian driver's license, provided you have held it for more than a year and are over 21.

RENTALS Many companies grant discounts to clients who reserve in advance before leaving home (see "Car Rentals," under "Getting Around," in chapter 3, for toll-free numbers and a preview of rates).

Most of the major car-rental companies such as Avis and Hertz maintain offices at the Edinburgh airport should you want to rent a car on the spot. Call **Avis** (☎ 0131/333-1866), **Hertz** (☎ 0131/333-1019), or **Eurodollar** (☎ 0131/333-2588). Rates at Avis begin at £64.50 ($106.45) per day or £195.20 ($322.10) per week; at Hertz, £40.50 ($66.85) per day or £205.60 ($339.25) per week; and at Eurodollar, £52 ($85.80) per day or £235 ($387.75) per week. The prices above include unlimited mileage.

PARKING It's expensive and difficult to find. Metered parking is available. You'll need the right change and you'll also have to watch out for traffic wardens who issue tickets. Some zones are marked PERMIT HOLDERS ONLY. Don't park here unless you have a permit as a local resident—your vehicle will be towed if you do. A yellow line along the curb indicates "No Parking."

Major **parking lots** (car parks) are found at Castle Terrace, a large multistory car park convenient for Edinburgh Castle and the west end of Princes Street; at Lothian

Road, a surface car park near the west end of Princes Street; at St. John Hill, a surface car park convenient for the Royal Mile, the west end of Princes Street, and Waverley Station; and at St. James Centre (entrance from York Place), a multistory car park close to the east end of Princes Street.

BY BICYCLE

You can rent bikes by the day or by the week from a number of outfits. Nevertheless, bicycling is not a good idea for most visitors because the city is constructed on a series of high ridges and terraces.

You may, however, want to rent a bike for exploring the flatter countryside. Try **Central Cycle Hire,** 13 Lochrin Place (☎ 0131/228-6333), off Home Street in Tollcross, near the Cameo Cinema. Depending on the type of bike, charges range from £10 to £15 ($16.50 to $24.75) per day. A deposit of £50 to £100 ($82.50 to $165) is imposed. The shop is open Monday through Saturday from 10am to 5:30pm, and June to August also on Sunday from 10am to noon and 5 to 7pm.

ON FOOT

Because of its narrow lanes, "wynds," and closes, Old Town can only be explored in any depth on foot. Edinburgh is fairly convenient for the visitor who likes to walk, as most of the attractions are along the Royal Mile, along Princes Street, or on one of the major streets of New Town. Remember, cars drive on the left. Always look both ways before stepping off a curb.

FAST FACTS: Edinburgh

American Express   The office in Edinburgh is at 139 Princes St. (☎ 0131/225-7881), five blocks from Waverley Station, open Monday through Friday from 9am to 5:30pm and Saturday from 9am to 4pm.

Baby-sitters   Two of the most reliable services are Peter Pan Nannies U.K., 35 Dinmont Dr. (☎ 0131/557-5311), and Care Connections, 45 Barclay Place (☎ 0131/228-1382).

Business Hours   In Edinburgh, **banks** are usually open Monday through Thursday from 9:30am to 12:30pm and 1:30 to 3:30pm, and Friday from 9:30am to 1:30pm. **Shops** are generally open Monday through Saturday from 10am to 5:30 or 6pm; on Thursday stores are open until 8pm. **Offices,** in the main, are open Monday through Friday from 9am to 5pm.

Crime   See "Safety," below.

Currency Exchange   There's a bureau de change of the Clydesdale Bank at 5 Waverley Bridge and at Waverley Market.

Dentist   For a dental emergency, go to the Edinburgh Dental Institute, 1 Lauriston Place (☎ 0131/536-4900), open Monday through Friday from 9am to 3pm.

Doctor   In a medical emergency, you can seek help from the Edinburgh Royal Infirmary, 1 Lauriston Place (☎ 0131/536-1000). Medical attention is available 24 hours.

Drugstores   There are no 24-hour drugstores (called "chemists" or "pharmacies") in Edinburgh. The major drugstore is Boots, 48 Shandwick Place (☎ 0131/225-6757), open Monday through Saturday from 8am to 9pm and Sunday from 10am to 5pm.

Embassies & Consulates   See "Fast Facts: Scotland," in chapter 3.

Emergencies   Call ☎ **999** in an emergency to summon the police, an ambulance, or firefighters.

Eyeglasses   Your best bet is Boots Opticians, 101–103 Princes St. (☎ **0131/ 225-6397**), open Monday through Saturday from 9am to 6pm (on Thursday until 7:30pm).

Hospital   The most convenient is the Edinburgh Royal Infirmary, 1 Lauriston Place (☎ **0131/536-1000**).

Hotlines   For a rape crisis center, call ☎ **0131/556-9437.**

Laundry/Dry Cleaning   If you're looking for a launderette, go to Bruntsfield Launderette, 108 Bruntsfield Place (☎ **0131/229-2669**), open Monday through Friday from 9am to 5pm and Saturday from 8:30am to 4pm. For your dry-cleaning needs, check out Johnson's Cleaners, 23 Frederick St. (☎ **0131/ 225-8095**), open Monday through Friday from 8am to 5pm and Saturday from 8am to 4pm.

Libraries   The largest library is Edinburgh's Central Library, at George IV Bridge (☎ **0131/225-5584**). Its Edinburgh Room contains information, both historical and current, on all aspects of the city, including the lives of such famous Scots as Stevenson and Sir Walter Scott. It's open Monday through Friday from 9am to 9pm.

Lost Property   If you've lost property (or had it stolen), go to Police Headquarters on Fettes Avenue (☎ **0131/311-3131**).

Luggage/Storage/Lockers   You can store luggage at Waverley Station, at Waverley Bridge (☎ **0131/556-2451**), open daily from 6:10am to 11pm.

Newspapers/Magazines   Published since 1817, *The Scotsman* is a quality daily newspaper. Along with national and international news, it's strong on the arts. Among magazines, the field is not outstanding, except for the *Edinburgh Review,* published quarterly by the University Press, mainly a cultural journal.

Photography   All your photographic needs can be met at Edinburgh Cameras, 55 Lothian Rd. (☎ **0131/229-4416**), open Monday through Saturday from 9am to 5:30pm.

Police   See "Emergencies," above.

Post Office   The Edinburgh Branch Post Office, St. James's Centre, is open Monday through Friday from 9am to 5:30pm and Saturday from 9am to 6pm. For postal information and customer service, call ☎ **0131/550-8232.**

Radio   The national network is BBC Radio Scotland (FM 92.4–94.7; AM/MW 810kHz/370m), dominated by news and talk shows. The local commercial station is Radio Forth (FM 97.3; AM/MW 1548kHz).

Religious Services   If you're Catholic, you can attend mass at St. Mary's Metropolitan Cathedral, Broughton Street (☎ **0131/556-1798**). The Scottish Episcopal church is represented at St. Mary's Cathedral, Palmerston Place (☎ **0131/225-6293**). Baptists can worship at Bristo Church, Buckingham Terrace (☎ **0131/332-3682**), and the Hebrew congregation meets at the Synagogue at 4 Salisbury Rd. (☎ **0131/667-3144**). There's also a Methodist church, Central Halls, at Tollcross (☎ **0131/229-7937**). Of course, there are many Church of Scotland (Presbyterian) churches.

Rest Rooms These are found at rail stations, terminals, restaurants, hotels, pubs, and department stores. Don't hesitate to use the system of public toilets, often marked WC, found at various strategic corners and squares throughout the city. They're perfectly safe and clean, but likely to be closed late in the evening.

Safety Edinburgh is generally safer than Glasgow, and is in fact one of the safest capitals of Europe for a visitor to stroll about—either day or night. But that doesn't mean that crimes, especially muggings, don't occur. They do, largely because of Edinburgh's shockingly large drug problem.

Shoe Repairs A chain operation, Mister Minit, 22 Frederick St. (☎ 0131/ 226-6741), only a few blocks from the east end of Princes Street, is open Monday through Saturday from 8:30am to 5:30pm.

Taxes A 17.5% value-added tax (known as VAT) is added to all goods and services in Edinburgh, as elsewhere in Britain. There are no special city taxes.

Television BBC Scotland and Scottish Television (STV) are Glasgow-based television stations that reach Edinburgh with their daily roundup of news, features, comedy, and drama, plus documentaries.

Transit Information Contact the Waverley Bridge Transport Office, Waverley Bridge (☎ 0131/554-4494), or the Lothian Region Transport Office, 14 Queen St. (☎ 0131/220-4111).

Weather For weather forecasts and road conditions, call ☎ 0891/600284. This number also provides data about weather information for Lothian, the Borders, Tayside and Fife, Glasgow and western Scotland, the Grampian region, and the Highlands.

3 Accommodations

Edinburgh offers a full range of accommodations throughout the year. However, during the 3-week period of the Edinburgh Festival, the establishments fill up with international visitors, so it's prudent to reserve in advance.

The **Edinburgh & Scotland Information Centre,** Waverley Shopping Centre, 3 Princes St. (☎ 0131/557-1700), compiles a well-investigated and lengthy list of small hotels, guesthouses, and private homes that provide bed-and-breakfast for as little as £13 ($21.45) per person. A £3 ($4.95) booking fee and a 10% deposit are charged. You can write in advance, but allow about 4 weeks' notice, especially during the summer and during the festival weeks. The center is open in July and August, Monday through Saturday from 9am to 8pm and Sunday from 11am to 8pm; May through June and September, Monday through Saturday from 9am to 7pm and Sunday from 11am to 7pm; April and October, Monday through Saturday from 9am to 6pm and Sunday from 11am to 6pm; and November through March, Monday through Saturday from 9am to 6pm.

There's also an **information and accommodation desk** at Edinburgh airport, open according to the frequency of incoming flights.

IN THE CENTER
VERY EXPENSIVE

✪ **Balmoral Hotel.** Princes St., Edinburgh, Lothian EH2 2EQ. ☎ 800/225-5843 in the U.S. or 0131/556-2414. Fax 0131/557-8740. 164 rms, 22 suites. A/C MINIBAR TV TEL. £165–£195 ($272.25–$321.75) double; from £210 ($346.50) suite. AE, DC, MC, V. Parking £10 ($16.50). Bus: 4, 15, or 44.

Edinburgh Accommodations

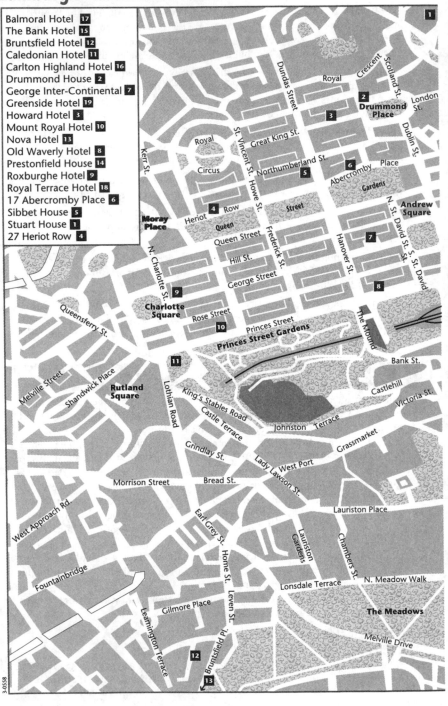

Balmoral Hotel **17**
The Bank Hotel **15**
Bruntsfield Hotel **12**
Caledonian Hotel **11**
Carlton Highland Hotel **16**
Drummond House **2**
George Inter-Continental **7**
Greenside Hotel **19**
Howard Hotel **3**
Mount Royal Hotel **10**
Nova Hotel **13**
Old Waverly Hotel **8**
Prestonfield House **14**
Roxburghe Hotel **9**
Royal Terrace Hotel **18**
17 Abercromby Place **6**
Sibbet House **5**
Stuart House **1**
27 Heriot Row **4**

3-0558

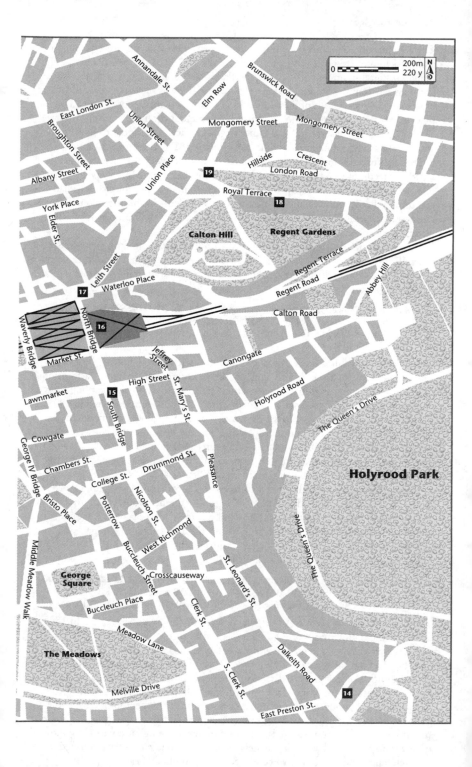

This legendary establishment was originally opened in 1902 as the largest, grandest, and most impressive hotel in the north of Britain. In 1991 it reopened after a $35 million restoration under a new name, the Balmoral. Located almost directly above the Waverley Railway Station, it features a soaring clock tower that many residents of Edinburgh consider one of the landmarks of their city. Kilted doormen and a bagpiper supply the Scottish presence. Furnished with reproduction pieces, the bedrooms are distinguished, conservative, and rather large—a graceful reminder of Edwardian sprawl with a contemporary twist. The hotel is managed by the Forte chain.

Dining/Entertainment: The hotel's most elegant eatery, No. 1 Princes Street, is separately recommended (see "Dining," later in this chapter). More convivial is an informal brasserie, Hadrian's, open every day from 7am to 11pm for platters, salads, and drinks. Tea is served in the high-ceilinged Palm Court in the afternoon. There are several bar areas; foremost among these is N.B.'s, a Scottish pub with an entrance directly on Princes Street.

Services: Concierge, 24-hour room service, laundry, valet, baby-sitting, hairdresser.

Facilities: A large and well-equipped health club with Jacuzzi, sauna, exercise equipment, and pool; direct access to the city's largest railway station; upscale shops selling cashmere, crystal, and flowers.

Caledonian Hotel. Princes St., Edinburgh, Lothian EH1 2AB. ☎ **0131/459-9988.** Fax 0131/ 225-6632. 246 rms, 23 suites. MINIBAR TV TEL. £209–£299 ($344.85–$493.35) double; from £325 ($536.25) suite. Children 15 and under stay free in parents' room. AE, DC, MC, V. Parking £5 ($8.25). Bus: 4, 15, or 44.

"The Caley" is Edinburgh's most visible hotel, with commanding views over Edinburgh Castle and the Princes Street gardens. Dumfriesshire stone—a form of deep red sandstone—used in its construction appears in only three other buildings in town, a fact of which the hotel is justifiably proud. Completely renovated in 1991, the hotel remains one of the city's landmarks. The pastel-colored public rooms are reminiscent of an age of Edwardian splendor, and the bedrooms are conservatively but individually styled with reproduction furniture, and often exceptionally spacious. The rooms on the fifth floor are the smallest. Many of its expensive bedrooms are not that different from those in the city's leading first-class hotels.

Dining/Entertainment: The hotel contains two bars: a traditional pub, Henry J. Bean's, and Carriages Bar, adjacent to Carriages Restaurant. More formal meals are served in La Pompadour Restaurant (see "Dining," later in this chapter). A traditional British tea is featured in late afternoon in the hotel's high-ceilinged lounge.

Services: 24-hour room service, baby-sitting, laundry, valet.

Facilities: Garden, Scottish shop, health club.

George Inter-Continental. 19–21 George St., Edinburgh, Lothian EH2 2PB. ☎ **800/327-0200** in the U.S., or 0131/225-1251. Fax 0131/226-5644. 195 rms, 10 suites. MINIBAR TV TEL. £165– £190 ($272.25–$313.50) double; from £385 ($635.25) suite. AE, DC, MC, V. Bus: 4, 15, or 44.

The George began its life with an original design in 1755 by Robert Adam. In 1845 it housed the trading room of the Caledonian Insurance Company, and in 1881 it was massively enlarged and graced with a new facade. In 1972 a new wing was added, and the place has thrived ever since as one of the town's leading hotels. It lies only yards from St. Andrew Square, the city's financial center. A member of the Inter-Continental Hotel group, the George is only a few short blocks from Princes Street, in the midst of boutiques and bus, rail, and air terminals. All bedrooms have undergone frequent refurbishments, and offer radios and hot-beverage facilities. Some rooms have minibars (not stocked). The best rooms, opening onto views, are those on the fourth floor and above in the new wing. The public rooms have retained the style, elegance, and old-fashioned comfort of a country house.

Dining/Entertainment: The Carvers Table, in the oldest part of the hotel, with some of Robert Adam's original design still intact, has fed hungry diners for almost a century on prime Scottish beef, lamb, and pork. Le Chambertin, the hotel's exclusive French restaurant, is the establishment's gourmet choice. The Gathering of the Clans Bar is decorated with artifacts of the whisky industry and clan mementos.

Services: 24-hour room service, baby-sitting, laundry/valet.

Facilities: Public lounge linking reception with the new wing.

✪ **Howard Hotel.** 32–36 Great King St., Edinburgh, Lothian EH3 6QH. ☎ **800/323-5463** or 0131/557-3500. Fax 0131/557-6515. 13 rms, 2 suites. TV TEL. £195 ($321.75) double; £275 ($453.75) suite. AE, DC, MC, V. Rates include breakfast. Bus: 13, 23, 27, or C5.

Three Georgian terrace houses (circa 1770–1825) have been combined into one of the finest resting places in Edinburgh. The decor is a combination of traditional and modern, with antiques and reproductions. The spacious, well-equipped bedrooms have hot-beverage equipment and radios, among other amenities, such as elaborate baths with freestanding tubs. The bedroom decor is inspired by Georgian style.

Dining/Entertainment: An elegant restaurant in the basement, known as No. 36, specializes in smoked Scottish salmon and pan-fried Scottish sirloin. Lunches are à la carte and rather light. In the basement is a cocktail lounge, and drinks are also served in the lounge.

Services: 24-hour room service, baby-sitting, laundry, valet.

Facilities: Club-style lounges. Visits to a fitness center outside the hotel can be arranged.

✪ **Sheraton Grand Hotel.** 1 Festival Square, Edinburgh, Lothian EH3 9SR. ☎ **800/ 325-3535** in the U.S. and Canada, or 0131/229-9131. Fax 0131/228-4510. 244 rms, 17 suites. A/C MINIBAR TV TEL. £180–£260 ($297–$429) double; from £280 ($462) suite. Children 16 and under stay free in parents' room. AE, DC, MC, V. Free parking. Bus: 4, 15, or 44.

Town leaders still praise this development of a former railway siding into a six-story postmodern structure that houses a glamorous hotel and office complex, a short walk from Princes Street. The hotel is elegantly appointed, with soaring public rooms. The designers drew upon local loyalties by choosing carpeting in appropriate tones of thistle and mauve. With a central location and a well-chosen staff, this is the most appealing modern hotel in the capital.

The spacious, well-upholstered rooms offer double-glazed windows and easy contact with a team of concierges. Prices are reasonable, considering the quality of the hotel. More glamorous, more expensive suites are also available. Preferred are the castle-view rooms on the top three floors.

Dining/Entertainment: A plushly modern cocktail bar is a favorite rendezvous for local residents. The main restaurant, with views over the fountain on Festival Square, presents well-prepared main courses and a lavish Sunday buffet. In 1993 the hotel opened two other restaurants: The Terrace, with views of the castle, a brasserie-style restaurant where chefs prepare specialties in front of you; and the Grill Room, small and intimate, and providing the best of Scottish produce.

Services: 24-hour room service, baby-sitting, laundry/valet.

Facilities: A leisure center offers a swimming pool (too small for lap swimming), whirlpool, sauna, and fully equipped gym.

EXPENSIVE

Carlton Highland Hotel. 19 North Bridge, Edinburgh, Lothian EH1 1SD. ☎ **0131/ 556-7277.** Fax 0131/5562691. 197 rms, 4 suites. MINIBAR TV TEL. £160 ($264) double; from £260 ($429) suite. Rates include breakfast. Children 14 and under stay free in parents' room. AE, DC, MC, V. Bus: 4, 15, or 44

A century ago, the Carlton Highland Hotel building was one of Edinburgh's leading department stores, with 4 of its 10 stories extending deep below the surface of the sidewalk. In 1984 this baronial pile got a new lease on life when it was converted into a plush hotel. Its Victorian turrets, Flemish-style gables, and severe gray stonework rise imposingly from a street corner on the Royal Mile, a few paces from Waverley Station. The interior was converted into a bright and airy modern space—each bedroom has a kind of Scandinavian simplicity, most with unbaronial matching tartan draperies and spreads. Amenities include coffeemakers, hair dryers, and trouser presses; baths tend to be quite small.

Dining/Entertainment: A pianist entertains in the lounge, and the hotel also has a nightclub, Minus One, with disco action on Friday and Saturday. Bands play for dancing on other nights. The hotel's restaurant, Quills, is designed like a private 19th-century library and offers an international and Scottish regional menu. A buffet is offered at the Eureka.

Services: Concierge, 24-hour room service, baby-sitting, laundry/valet, hairdresser.

Facilities: Exercise room with a swimming pool, solarium, whirlpool, sauna, two squash courts, and an aerobics studio.

✪ Channings Hotel. South Learmonth Gardens, Edinburgh, Lothian EH4 1EZ. ☎ **0131/ 315-2226.** Fax 0131/332-9631. 48 rms. TV TEL. £125–£170 ($206.25–$280.50) double. Rates include breakfast. Children 14 and under stay free in parents' room. AE, DC, MC, V.

Seven blocks north of Dean Village, in a tranquil residential area, this leading townhouse hotel has only one competitor, the Howard (see above). Five Edwardian terrace houses were combined to create a privately owned hotel. Although it's a 5-minute drive from the city center, it maintains the atmosphere of a Scottish country house, with oak paneling, ornate fireplaces, molded ceilings, and antiques. The bedrooms are outfitted in a modern style. The front rooms get the view, but the accommodations in back are quieter. Standard rooms are a bit cheaper but much smaller. The most desirable units are labeled "Executive," and these often have bay windows with wingback chairs. Most of the rooms have full bath facilities; a few offer a shower instead of a tub, and all have trouser presses and hair dryers. The decor is tranquil, with subdued colors. Those facing north open onto views of the Fife.

In the downstairs bar and brasserie, a Scottish/French cuisine is served, with a table d'hôte offered at dinner for only £17 ($28.05). The lunch fixed-price menus at £7.50 ($12.40) and £9.50 ($15.65), one of the bargains of this upscale neighborhood, draw in the locals. The cuisine is British modern, making use of fresh ingredients. The adjoining bar with a fireplace is cozy on a winter's night, but in summer perhaps you'd prefer to escape from the basement and go elsewhere. Only street parking is available, and often there are no spaces.

Mount Royal Hotel. 53 Princes St., Edinburgh, Lothian EH2 2DG. ☎ **0131/225-7161.** Fax 0131/220-4671. 156 rms. TV TEL. £129 ($212.85) double; £149 ($245.85) triple or family room. AE, DC, MC, V. Bus: 2, 4, 15, 21, or 44.

Mount Royal Hotel is right in the middle of the famed thoroughfare, complete with its major shops. A modern world emerges as you climb the spiral staircase or take an elevator to the second floor, with its reception rooms and lounges and floor-to-ceiling windows opening onto views of Old Town and the castle. In reality, the Mount Royal is a remake of an old hotel from the 1860s, providing streamlined bedrooms with a view. The emphasis is utilitarian, not on frills, although the comfort is genuine. This is a tour group favorite.

Dining/Entertainment: The main dining room serves reasonably priced lunches and dinners, offering both a carving table and à la carte menus. The lounge on the second floor, with floor-to-ceiling windows and views over the Scott Memorial and Princes Street, provides a wide range of savory and sweet snacks and beverages throughout the day.

Services: Room service, laundry/valet.

Old Waverley Hotel. 43 Princes St., Edinburgh, Lothian EH2 2BY. ☎ **0131/556-4648.** Fax 031/557-6316. 66 rms. TV TEL. £144 ($237.60) double. AE, DC, MC, V. Parking £4 ($6.60) for 8 hours. Bus: 4, 15, or 44.

Opposite Waverley Station, Old Waverley goes back to 1848, a seven-floor structure originally built to celebrate the then-newfangled railroads. About half the rooms are being refurbished, and more renovations will continue (but not during the busy summer tourist season). The lounges on the second floor have been given that contemporary look. Some of the rooms look onto Princes Street and, at night, the floodlit castle. Rooms have satellite TVs, trouser presses, hair dryers, and direct-dial phones.

The hotel has a good restaurant serving à la carte and table d'hôte meals. The restaurant is a carvery-style affair, charges depending on how many courses you take. Room service (24 hours) is available.

✪**Prestonfield House.** Priestfield Rd., Edinburgh, Lothian EH16 5UT. ☎ **0131/668-3346.** Fax 0131/668-3976. 29 rms, 2 suites. A/C TV TEL. £135–£165 ($222.75–$272.25) double; £285 ($470.25) suite. Rates include breakfast. AE, DC, MC, V. Bus: 21 or 33.

Rising in Jacobean splendor above 14 acres of forest, field, and garden, this three-story establishment is more celebrated as a restaurant than as a hotel (see "Dining," later in this chapter). Some visitors, however, appreciate its historic calm, its sense of decorum, its venerable 1689 architecture, and the peacocks and Highland cattle that strut or stroll decoratively across the grounds. It was designed by Sir William Bruce, who also designed Holyrood Palace. The accommodations are dignified and elegant, decorated in a Scottish country-house theme. Each accommodation opens onto a view of Arthur's Seat, a golf course, and the recently restored gardens. In 1997 the five rooms in the main house were supplemented by a three-story white-sided annex that can't be seen from the front. Architecturally, the style matches the main building, and rooms here are more modern and up to date, with lots of sunlight thanks to the large windows. However, traditionalists still prefer the more antique-laden rooms of the main house. Antiques are used throughout the premises.

Dining/Entertainment: The hotel has one of the city's finest dining rooms (see below), plus two bars.

Services: Baby-sitting, laundry/dry cleaning.

Facilities: Private rooms for meetings, receptions, but nothing else for the individual client except the parklike gardens.

Roxburghe Hotel. 38 Charlotte Square, Edinburgh, Lothian EH2 4HG. ☎ **0131/225-3921.** Fax 0131/220-2518. 75 rms, 1 suite. A/C TV TEL. £135 ($222.75) double; £165 ($272.25) suite. Rates include breakfast. Children 13 and under stay free in parents' room. AE, DC, MC, V. Parking £5 ($8.25). Bus: 3, 21, 26, 31, or 85.

The four-story Roxburghe Hotel is a stately Adam town house of dove-gray stone on a tree-filled square. It's a short walk from Princes Street, at a corner of noisy George Street. The atmosphere is traditional, reflected in the drawing room with its ornate ceiling and woodwork, antique furnishings, and tall arched windows opening toward the park. All the bedrooms, reached by elevator, have clock radios, trouser presses, and tea- and coffeemakers, plus sewing kits, shower caps, and foam baths, as well as baskets of fruit. The units, renovated in 1993, are handsomely traditional with Adam-style paneling. Some rooms are small and very modestly furnished.

Dining/Entertainment: A place to congregate for drinks is the Consort Bar, with its festive decor. A dining room that serves good meals gives diners a view of the square. The Melrose Room Buttery serves light refreshments.

Services: Concierge, 24-hour room service, dry cleaning/laundry, valet parking.

Facilities: Residents' lounge; large health club nearby.

Royal Terrace Hotel. 18 Royal Terrace, Edinburgh, Lothian EH7 5AQ. ☎ **0131/557-3222.** Fax 0131/557-5334. 93 rms, 4 suites. TV TEL. £155 ($255.75) double; from £195 ($321.75) suite. Children 13 and under stay free in parents' room. AE, DC, MC, V. Parking on street 50p (85¢) per hour Mon–Sat 8:30am–5:30pm; free other times. Bus: 4, 15, or 44.

Royal Terrace Hotel has been called "the country-house hotel in the city." Offering luxurious double bedrooms, it was formed from six four-story interconnected Georgian town houses on an elegant crescent, about a 10-minute stroll from Waverley Station. The rooms have a host of amenities, including hair dryers, in-house movies, and marble bathrooms, some with whirlpool baths. They're reached by an elevator that likes to take its time. Try to get a room in the back opening onto gardens. The bedrooms vary greatly in style. Recent restorations, while providing the most up-to-date comfort, have retained much of the period styling, including oil paintings, antiques, open Adam fireplaces, and Viennese crystal chandeliers; some have four-poster beds.

Dining/Entertainment: Both international and Scottish dishes are served in the Peacock Restaurant, preceded by a before-dinner drink in the well-stocked Peacock Bar, which has more than 21 brands of the finest malt whiskies.

Services: Room service, baby-sitting, laundry/valet, beauty salon. (Several readers have cited a chilly reception staff; to confuse matters, other readers have praised the *esprit de corps* of the staff.)

Facilities: Leisure Club with indoor pool, Jacuzzi, sauna, massage room, steam room, and solarium.

MODERATE

Bank Hotel. Royal Mile at 1–3 South Bridge St., Edinburgh EH1 1LL. ☎ **0131/556-9043.** Fax 0131/558-1362. 9 rms (8 with bath). TV TEL. £80–£100 ($132–$165) double with bath. Rates include breakfast. AE, MC, V. Bus: 100.

Clean and unpretentious, this simple hotel offers better value and more dignity than many of its competitors in this congested and highly commercialized neighborhood beside the Royal Mile. Until around 1990, it was a severely dignified, solidly stone-built branch of the Royal Bank of Scotland, a past still evident today in its bulky, no-nonsense design. Today, a restaurant (which demands more time and attention from its staff than the bedrooms upstairs) occupies its ground floor. Upstairs, high ceilings and simple furnishings provide comfort and respite. It's central to almost everything in town. Only one room is without a private bathroom, a cramped single, selling for £40 ($66), with breakfast included.

In the restaurant, you can order lunch (daily from noon to 6pm) and dinner (daily from 6 to 10:30pm) near a marble bar inserted into an echoing area that used to be the bank's showcase. Stuffed baguettes, priced at £2.95 ($4.85) each, and steaming bowls of soup, at £2.25 ($3.70) each, are served at lunch, making way for a slightly more elaborate menu after 6pm. Main dishes, priced from £4.95 to £6.25 ($8.15 to $10.30) at lunch, and from £5.95 to £9.25 ($9.80 to $15.25) at dinner, include vegetarian lasagna, North Sea John Dory with red peppers, red mullet in wine sauce, and platters of lamb and venison.

Drummond House. 17 Drummond Place, Edinburgh EH3 6PE. ☎ and fax **0131/557-9189.** 4 rms. £90 ($148.50) double. Rates include breakfast. MC, V. Bus: 13.

Its small size, its historic early 19th-century premises, and its desirable location at the edge of a gated park in the center of New Town make this B&B run by Josephine and Alan Dougall more desirable than the usual run-of-the-mill place. As such, its quartet of individually decorated, antique-filled bedrooms are usually booked several weeks in advance, often with repeat visitors from Europe. Frankly, there isn't much here that will remind you of a hotel at all. There are no phones or TVs in the rooms, and clients breakfast communally at a large mahogany table in the ground-floor dining room. Bedrooms are named after their predominant color and accessorized with unusually elaborate window coverings. Access to the rear garden, as well as three of the six floors of this solid row house, are reserved only for the Dougalls. You can compensate, however, by borrowing the key to the gated park (Drummond Place Gardens) across the street, and admire the flower beds and pansies planted and cared for by local residents. Smoking isn't allowed within the house, and no meals are served other than breakfast.

17 Abercromby Place. 17 Abercromby Place, Edinburgh, Lothian EH3 6LB. ☎ **0131/ 557-8036.** Fax 0131/558-3453. 6 rms. TV TEL. £90 ($148.50) double. Rates include breakfast. MC, V.

Eirlys Lloyd gained a reputation in Edinburgh when she ran the highly recommended 28 Northumberland Street nearby. She has since moved into what some guests consider an even better B&B address not far away, and just a 5-minute walk north of Princes Street. Although built by a less well-known architect, the five-story gray stone terrace house was the home in the 1820s of William Playfair, who designed many of Edinburgh's most visible landmarks, including the Royal Scottish Academy and Surgeon Hall on the campus of the Royal College of Surgeons. Two of the rooms in what was once a mews house today are connected to the main house. Evening meals can be arranged for £25 ($41.25) per person, although faced with the choice of nearby restaurants, that isn't a popular option.

Sibbet House. 26 Northumberland St., Edinburgh, Lothian EH3 6LS. ☎ **0131/556-1078.** Fax 0131/557-9445. 3 rms, 1 suite. TV TEL. £90–£100 ($148.50–$165) double; £110 ($181.50) suite. Rates include breakfast. MC, V. Bus: 13, 23, or 27.

Set on a residential terrace a 10-minute walk from Princes Street, this sandstone-fronted, three-story Georgian house is the cheerful domain of James Sibbet and his French-born wife, Aurora, who do everything they can to distinguish their family home from "just another hotel." If asked, James (proud of his Lowland Scottish origins) will play the bagpipes. There's a drawing room/salon where, if requested, drinks are served, and an ambience that never wavers from the homelike. The bedrooms are furnished in part with antiques (one has a four-poster bed). The neighborhood offers several restaurants serving evening meals.

✪ **27 Heriot Row.** 27 Heriot Row, Edinburgh, Lothian EH3 6EN. ☎ **0131/2205-9474.** Fax 0131/220-1699. 3 rms. TV TEL. £80–£90 ($132–$148.50) double. Rates include breakfast. MC, V.

At least part of the allure of this 18th-century Georgian row house is its magazine-illustration decor. Andrea and Gene Targett-Adams are the likable owners, who have won several awards from the Scottish Tourist Board. You'll find high ceilings, elaborate cove moldings, and many elegant touches that make this a truly desirable B&B. Guests enjoy use of a private sitting room on the second floor. Only breakfast is served. Be warned in advance that this establishment, like others of its smaller competitors in the neighborhood, sometimes shuts down operations if advance reservations don't justify staying open.

⚅ Family-Friendly Hotels

Thrums Private Hotel *(see p. 140)* This hotel takes its name from J. M. Barrie's fictional name for his hometown of Kirriemuir. Barrie is known to children as the author of *Peter Pan.* Kids are made especially welcome here and are housed in family rooms with their parents.

Teviotdale House *(see p. 140)* Some enthusiastic visitors rate this place the best B&B in Edinburgh. Three rooms are large enough for families with up to four members. Great value.

Nova Hotel *(see p. 140)* This hotel features five spacious family rooms, each designed for total comfort. It's in a quiet, secluded cul-de-sac.

INEXPENSIVE

A Haven. 180 Ferry Rd., Edinburgh, Midlothian EH6 4NS. ☎ **0131/554-6559.** Fax 0131/ 554-5252. 12 rms. TV TEL. £60–£85 ($99–$140.25) double. Rates include breakfast. AE, MC, V. Bus: 1, 6, 7, 11, 14, 25, C3, 17, 14A, or 25A.

This is a semidetached gray stone four-story Victorian house, built in 1862, within a 15-minute walk or a 5-minute bus ride north of the rail station. The rooms are substantially furnished with traditional pieces; all have been refurbished. Some rooms in back overlook the Firth of Forth, and those in the front open onto views of Arthur's Seat. Moira and Ronnie Murdock extend a Scottish welcome in this family-type place and often help guests with sightseeing tips. They have a licensed bar, but the only meal served is breakfast. Located in an Edinburgh district of character, the establishment has many antiques and skylights.

Greenside Hotel. 9 Royal Terrace, Edinburgh, Midlothian EH7 5AB. ☎ and fax **0131/ 557-0022.** 14 rms. £55–£80 ($90.75–$132) double. Rates include breakfast. AE, DC, MC, V. Bus: 4, 15, or 44.

A four-floor Georgian house originally built in 1786, the Greenside is furnished with a number of antique pieces to give it the right spirit. There are singles, doubles, twins, and three family rooms, all centrally heated and all with private bath. The rooms, refurbished in 1995, have views of a private garden or the Firth of Forth. There's a color TV set in the lounge, where coffee and tea are available all day. Guests like the full breakfast included in the rates. Evening dinners can also be arranged, a four-course Scottish dinner going for £12.50 ($20.65). Drinks are served in the bar.

✪ 7 Danube Street. 7 Danube St., Edinburgh HH4 1NN. ☎ **0131/332-2755.** Fax 0131/ 343-3648. 3 rms. £65–£80 ($107.25–$132) double. Rates include breakfast. MC, V. Bus: 28.

This B&B is in a quiet, stylish residential neighborhood, within a 15-minute walk north of the commercial center. It's the 1825 home of Fiona Mitchell-Rose and her husband, Colin. Designed by noteworthy architect James Milne, it was once the home of the late Scottish painter Horatio McCallach. Public areas and bedrooms are awash with artfully draped flowered fabrics that reflect Fiona's experience as a decorator in London. The most desirable bedroom has a four-poster bed and direct access to the garden. The establishment is proud of its charmingly decorated, cellar-level bedrooms, clustered into a shared area with a private entrance independent from the rest of the house. You are likely to meet your hosts and other guests in the formal (upstairs) dining room in the morning, where the lavish breakfast is inspired by Scotland's old-fashioned agrarian tradition: Look for ample portions of Scottish herring and kippers, venison sausages, omelets made from free-range eggs, homemade scones, and raspberry, strawberry, and Tayberry jams and marmalades put up by Fiona herself.

Stuart House. 12 East Claremont St., Edinburgh EH7 4JP. ☎ **0131/557-9030.** Fax 0131/557-0563. 8 rms (6 with bath) TV TEL. £40 ($66) double with bath. AE, MC, V. Closed 1 week in September and 1 week at Christmas. Bus: 19.

Set at the western end of Claremont Street, in one of the many dozens of nearly identical row houses, this is a charming, well-managed B&B run by the Anglo-Scottish team of June and Alex Watson. Convenient to the commercial center, it offers modernized, high-ceilinged bedrooms that retain many of their original 1830 cove moldings. Each has teamaking facilities. All doubles contain baths; two singles at £35 ($57.75) do not. No meals are served other than breakfast, although the Watsons are helpful in pointing out the comparable merits of a half-dozen restaurants close by. A garden in back offers respite from the urban congestion.

WEST OF THE CENTER
MODERATE

Jarvis Ellersly Country House Hotel. 4 Ellersly Rd., Edinburgh, Lothian EH12 6HZ. ☎ **0131/337-6888.** Fax 0131/313-2543. 57 rms, 1 suite. TV TEL. £129 ($212.85) double; £132 ($217.80) suite. AE, DC, MC, V. Take A8 2$^1/_2$ miles west of the city center.

Standing in walled gardens, this three-story Edwardian country house has been said to offer the "privacy of a home." It's in a dignified west-end residential section near the Murrayfield rugby grounds, about a 5-minute ride from the center, and is one of Edinburgh's best moderately priced hotels. The well-equipped bedrooms are in either the main house or a less desirable annex. The rooms vary in size. After a refurbishment program, the hotel is better than ever, and service is first class. The hotel possesses a well-stocked wine cellar and offers good-tasting Scottish and French meals, with dinner going for £23 ($36.35). Room service and laundry/valet are offered. A fitness center is nearby.

INEXPENSIVE

Dunstane House Hotel. 4 West Coates, Edinburgh, Lothian EH12 5JQ. ☎ **0131/337-5320.** Fax 0131/337-6169. 15 rms (all with shower). TV. £50–£72 ($82.50–$118.80) double. AE, MC, V. Bus: 26, 31, or 69.

This stone-sided 1850 house sits behind a pleasant garden, a 10-minute walk from Princes Street. The owner maintains the place in well-scrubbed condition, with respectful awareness of the building's architectural importance. All the bedrooms have been completely redecorated, each equipped with a radio, tea- or coffeemaking equipment, a hair dryer, and shaver points. Antiques or reproductions are used throughout the hotel, whose various areas are connected via a labyrinth of narrow staircases.

SOUTH OF THE CENTER
MODERATE

Bruntsfield Hotel. 69–74 Bruntsfield Place, Edinburgh, Lothian EH10 4HH. ☎ **800/528-1234** in the U.S. and Canada, or 0131/229-1393. Fax 0131/229-5634. 50 rms, 1 suite. TV TEL. £115 ($189.75) double; £130 ($214.50) suite. AE, DC, MC, V. Bus: 11, 15, 16, 17, or 23.

Bruntsfield's neogothic facade overlooks an expanse of city park south of the city center, opposite Bruntsfield Links. Like the other 19th-century buildings lining this residential street, this four-story hotel is built of evenly spaced rows of honey-colored stones. Inside, all is neat and stylish, with a formal milieu of French-inspired armchairs and pastel shades of peach and blue. Just across the street are the trees and putting greens of what may be the world's oldest golf course, the Bruntsfield Links.

The bedrooms are comfortably renovated, each with a radio, trouser press, hair dryer, tea- and coffeemaker, and in-house movies. Some have been recently refurbished. There's an attractive restaurant on the premises, the Potting Shed, along with a pub. The hotel is frequented mainly by commercial clients during the week, giving way to couples and families on weekends.

Nova Hotel. 5 Bruntsfield Crescent, Edinburgh, Lothian EH10 4EZ. ☎ **0131/447-6437.** Fax 0131/452-8126. 12 rms. TV TEL. £60–£100 ($99–$165) double; £80–£130 ($132–$214.50) family room for up to 3. MC, V. Bus: 42 or 46.

Nova Hotel, a two-floor 1875 Victorian, is on a quiet cul-de-sac near the city center, with a view over Bruntsfield Links in front and the Pentland Hills to the back, within walking distance of the Royal Mile and Princes Street. Visitors are welcomed to its large, well-appointed bedrooms, all with hair dryers, trouser presses, hot-beverage facilities, and full central heating. On the ground floor, guests enjoy the cocktail bar, and the public bar also provides an inviting atmosphere.

Thrums Private Hotel. 14–15 Minto St., Edinburgh, Midlothian EH9 1RQ. ☎ **0131/667-5545.** Fax 0131/667-8707. 15 rms (14 with bath). TV TEL. £70 ($115.50) double with bath; £75–£100 ($123.75–$165) family room with bath. Rates include breakfast. MC, V. Bus: 3, 7, 8, 31, or 37.

The Thrums, a two-story 1820 Georgian building, takes the fictional name that J. M. Barrie gave his hometown of Kirriemuir. This choice hotel's well-decorated and furnished bedrooms, in two buildings, all have radios, tea/coffeemakers, electric blankets, and hair dryers. A lone single doesn't have a bath. Family rooms are also offered, and a peaceful garden is at guests' disposal. A small bar is available to residents. The hotel operates an à la carte restaurant for lunches and dinners, where a three-course meal costs £9 to £15 ($14.85 to $24.75). Good fresh produce is used in the preparation of all meals, and a children's menu is available.

INEXPENSIVE

✪ **Teviotdale House.** Grange Loan, Edinburgh, Lothian EH9 2ER. ☎ **0131/667-4376.** Fax 0131/667-4376. 7 rms. TV TEL. £56–£74 ($92.40–$122.10) double. AE, MC, V. Bus: 42.

Some visitors rate this three-story 1848 house as the finest B&B accommodation in Edinburgh. Jane E. Coville's attention to detail has earned her an enviable reputation. Each of the individually decorated bedrooms has hot and cold running water, a hair dryer, and a restful bed. The house is completely no-smoking and is furnished with antiques. The home-cooked breakfast may be the highlight of your day's dining and can include smoked salmon, kippers, and home-baked bread and scones. The house lies about 10 minutes from Princes Street, Waverley Station, and Edinburgh Castle, on a main bus route leading to the heart of the city.

LEITH

The satellite neighborhood of Leith was once a run-down district, but now, for about a decade, it has been attracting counterculture residents that you might associate with New York City's East Village and Tribeca.

MODERATE

The Malmaison. 1 Tower Place, Leith, Edinburgh EH6 7DB. ☎ **0131/555-6868.** Fax 0131/555-6999. 16 rms, 6 suites. TV TEL. £90 ($148.50) double; £125 ($206.25) suite. AE, DC, MC, V. Bus: 16.

This is the most interesting hotel within Edinburgh's dockyard district. It's positioned a few steps from Leith Water, within sight of dozens of cargo ships and the industrial paraphernalia of harborfront life. The building is capped with a stately stone clock tower, a folly that only the late 19th century could have provided. The premises were converted in the 1990s from an 1883 seaman's mission and dormitory. Four floors interconnected with an elevator. Its owners have created a hip, unpretentious hotel whose postmodern decors are airy, stylish, and minimalist. Color schemes vary according to floor; the purple and beige floor has been favored by the members of rock bands who have stayed here during concert tours. Each room has a CD player and teamaking facilities, and in many cases, views over the water. Don't expect conventional hotel facilities—there is no baggage-carrying service, and amenities and facilities are sparse. On the premises, however, is the Malmaison Brasserie (separately recommended in "Dining") and the Malmaison Vegetarian Cafe & Bar that's favored by lots of locals. Open daily from 10am to 1am, it serves drinks and all-vegetarian salads, soups, and stuffed baguettes that almost never exceed £3.95 ($6.50) per platter. In warm weather, tables are set up on the pavement outside, overlooking the activities in the harbor.

CASTLE & COUNTRY-HOUSE HOTELS

To fulfill your fantasy, you might want to spend your first night in Scotland in a real castle or a baronial country house surrounded by gardens and spacious grounds.

AT BONNYRIGG

Dalhousie Castle. Bonnyrigg, Edinburgh, Lothian EH19 3JB. ☎ **01875/820153.** Fax 01875/821936. 28 rms, 1 suite. TV TEL. £110–£145 ($181.50–$239.25) double; £175 ($288.75) suite. AE, DC, MC, V. Take the A7 Carlisle–Edinburgh road 8 miles southeast of Edinburgh; it's just outside the village of Bonnyrigg.

Dalhousie Castle dates back to 1450, and over its long history it has entertained such illustrious guests as Edward I, Henry IV, Oliver Cromwell, Sir Walter Scott, and Queen Victoria. Today it's the family seat of the Ramsays of Dalhousie, who have converted it into a luxurious hotel that retains its finest architectural features. A turreted and fortified house with ramparted terraces and battlements, it has such delights as a dungeon restaurant, which offers many local Scottish dishes. The rooms all have plenty of space for sitting and relaxing, although each varies greatly from its neighbor in size and decor. The suite has a four-poster bed. The castle overlooks the banks of South Esk, where the red sandstone to build it was quarried. The hotel can arrange salmon and trout fishing, horseback riding, and shooting.

AT NORTH MIDDLETON

Borthwick Castle. North Middleton, Gorebridge, Midlothian EH23 4QY. ☎ **01875/820514.** Fax 01875/821702. 10 rms. TEL. £110–£190 ($181.50–$313.50) double. Rates include breakfast. AE, DC, MC, V. Take the A7 motorway about 12 miles south of Edinburgh; the castle is three-quarters of a mile south of the hamlet of North Middleton.

Set in a pastoral valley, this castle is the ancestral home of Lord Borthwick. The noble twin-towered keep, built in 1430, is the finest example of its kind in Britain today. It was here that the ill-fated Mary Queen of Scots sought refuge with her third husband, Bothwell, in 1567. In 1650 the castle was besieged by the armies of Oliver Cromwell, and the damage inflicted by their cannon fire can still be seen. Inside, the building's centerpiece is the Great Hall, which boasts a minstrels' gallery, a hooded fireplace, a 40-foot vaulted ceiling in the gothic style, a collection of medieval armor, and an alcove bar with a reassuringly complete collection of single-malt whiskies. A four-course fixed-price dinner is available at £28.50 ($47.05) per person.

All bedchambers are centrally heated. The most expensive long ago sheltered the historic figures mentioned above. Four contain four-poster beds, and each has a scattering of antiques and chintz fabrics. Borthwick Castle is known for the excellence of its cuisine, its personal service, its authentic medieval ambience, and the re-creation of the gracious lifestyle of an earlier era. Candlelit meals are served in the Great Hall where the cuisine has been described as "modern British with a strong bias for Scotland's natural larder."

4 Dining

IN THE CENTER: NEW TOWN
EXPENSIVE
✪ **The Atrium.** 10 Cambridge St. (beneath Saltire Court). ☎ **0131/228-8882.** Reservations recommended. Main courses £7.50–£9.50 ($12.40–$15.65) at lunch, £11.50–£18.50 ($18.95–$30.55) at dinner. AE, MC, V. Mon–Fri noon–2:30pm and 6–10:30pm, Sat 6–10:30pm. Closed 1 week at Christmas. MODERN MEDITERRANEAN.

This is the most frequently analyzed, frequently discussed, and frequently emulated restaurant in Edinburgh. It opened in 1993 in the atrium of an office building that local architectural critics have awarded stars. The modern decor has been called "moonscape," as guests dine in the glazed courtyard of an office complex. Tables are put together from railroad ties, and chairs are slipcovered in natural canvas. Junkyard sculpture forms part of the decor. Design teams worked hard to create a "deliberately moody" environment for no more than 60 diners, where flickering oil lamps and dark colors create an environment that has been called a mixture between an Argentinian hacienda and upmarket Beverly Hills.

Menu items change with the inspiration of chef Glyn Stevens and his manager, James Sankey, but might include such main courses as grilled salmon with a medley of mushrooms and caviar, or loin of lamb with spinach and dried tomatoes, the lamb flavored with saffron. Or else try duck samosa sassy with ginger and nutmeg. Desserts are marvelously tempting, including a recent blackcurrant torte garnished with red berries.

✪ **La Pompadour Restaurant.** In the Caledonian Hotel, Princes St. ☎ **0131/459-9988.** Reservations required. Jacket required. Main courses £19–£24 ($31.35–$39.60). AE, DC, MC, V. Tues–Sun 7:30–10:30pm. Bus: 4, 15, or 44. SCOTTISH/FRENCH.

La Pompadour Restaurant, on the mezzanine floor of the famous hotel, is one of Edinburgh's best, serving fine Scottish and French cuisine—a celebration of the Auld Alliance since 1925. The restaurant has been refurbished in a sort of Louis XV decor—after all, the restaurant bears the name of his mistress. The chef blends cuisine moderne with traditional menus in this intimate, luxurious place. A daily menu reflects the best available from the markets that day, and Scottish salmon, venison, and other game are often included in a meal. The menu also features fresh produce from both local and French markets—items such as goose liver with wild mushrooms, fillet of lamb with spinach and rosemary, and charlotte of marinated salmon filled with seafood. There is a no-smoking area. The wine list is lethal in price and bottles from the New World are strangely absent.

✪ **L'Auberge.** 56 St. Mary's St. ☎ **0131/556-5888.** Reservations required. Main courses £13–£25 ($21.45–$41.25); fixed-price meals £13 ($21.45) at lunch, £23–£26 ($37.95–$42.90) at dinner. AE, DC, MC, V. Daily 12:15–2pm and 7–9:30pm (until 10:30pm in summer). Bus: 1, 6, 34, or 35. FRENCH.

L'Auberge, just off the Royal Mile, between Cowgate and Canongate, is ranked among the top three or four restaurants in Edinburgh. It's known for using the finest of Scottish ingredients in its classic French cuisine, which is backed up by a carefully chosen wine list. Service is the most polished in the Scottish capital. Game and fish are specialties, and each dish—whether from the moors, loch, or sea—is individually prepared. Some of the main dishes taste as if you've been transported to the Périgord region of France. The menu changes frequently but has been known to offer confit of duck in a Madeira wine sauce with mushrooms, Scottish salmon in a Provençal vinaigrette sauce, and saddle of hare.

✪ **Martins.** 70 Rose St., North Lane. ☎ 0131/225-3106. Reservations required. Main courses £17–£19 ($28.05–$31.35); 2-course lunch £12.95 ($21.35). AE, DC, MC, V. Tues–Fri noon–2pm; Tues–Sat 7–10pm. Closed Dec 24–Jan 23, 1 week in May/June and 1 week Sept/Oct. Bus: 2, 4, 15, 21, or 44. INTERNATIONAL.

The owners, Gay and Martin Irons, and their trio of top chefs are deeply committed to wild and organically grown foods at this leading restaurant. Although the setting, off Edinburgh's pub street and down an unpromising alley is unlikely, the restaurant's celadon-green rooms are now an Edinburgh landmark. The menu changes daily to take advantage of the freshest of ingredients. Martin's father provides herbs for the restaurant from his own garden. The best of the country's venison, fish (especially salmon), and West Coast shellfish appear regularly on the menu, appetizingly roasted, baked, poached, or served in a casserole. Sautéed wild mushrooms is a particular favorite, followed by breast of guinea fowl with a burgundy jus. You might try, for example, phyllo parcels filled with langoustines and earthy leeks, each sparked by a basil dressing. A tuna steak might be chargrilled with shiitake mushrooms and served with an avocado and tomato compote. Special care is taken with the cheeses—many are unpasteurized farmhouse delights, including a pressed goat cheese from the Orkneys. You can also opt for one of the absolutely delectable fruit tarts, or an intriguing basil, lime, and elderflower sorbet. No children under 8 are allowed.

✪ **No. 1 Princes Street.** In the Balmoral Hotel, 1 Princes St. ☎ 0131/556-2414. Reservations recommended. Main courses £15–£23 ($24.75–$37.95); fixed-price lunch £17.50 ($28.90) for two courses, £19.25 ($31.75) for 3 courses; fixed-price 5-course dinner £35 ($57.75). AE, DC, MC, V. Daily noon–2:30pm and 7–10:30pm. SCOTTISH/CONTINENTAL.

This is the premier restaurant in the Balmoral Hotel, an intimate, crimson-colored enclave one floor below the reception area. The walls are studded with Scottish memorabilia in patterns just informal enough to be sporting and just formal enough to be very, very elegant. You'll sit in comfortably upholstered armchairs as the staff pampers you with attentive service. This is very much the grand-style hotel dining room, and it offers good food if you don't mind paying such high tabs. From the North Sea comes turbot flavored with rosemary. Angus beef is used in abundance, or perhaps the poached River Tay salmon will interest you. For dessert you can have a symphony of five different chocolates. There's a separate vegetarian menu and a wide-ranging wine list with celestial tariffs.

MODERATE

Alp Horn Restaurant. 167 Rose St. ☎ 0131/225-4787. Reservations recommended. Main courses £6.50–£11.25 ($10.75–$18.55); 2-course lunch £5.75 ($9.50); 3-course supper menu £9.95 ($16.40). AE, DC, MC, V. Mon–Sat noon–2pm and 6:30–10pm. Bus: 31 or 33. SWISS/SCOTTISH.

Alp Horn Restaurant, just off Charlotte Square in an antique stone building, provides a meal that's like a step into Switzerland—checked gingham curtains, potted plants, and simple wooden tables and chairs in Swiss chalet style. As you'd expect, the menu offers air-dried meats (Grisons style), several fondues, venison in season, and a version of rösti, the famous potato dish of Switzerland. Fresh Scottish fish is also served. All this might be capped off with a slice of apfelstrudel, which is made on the premises. Nonsmokers get a room to themselves.

Edinburgh Dining

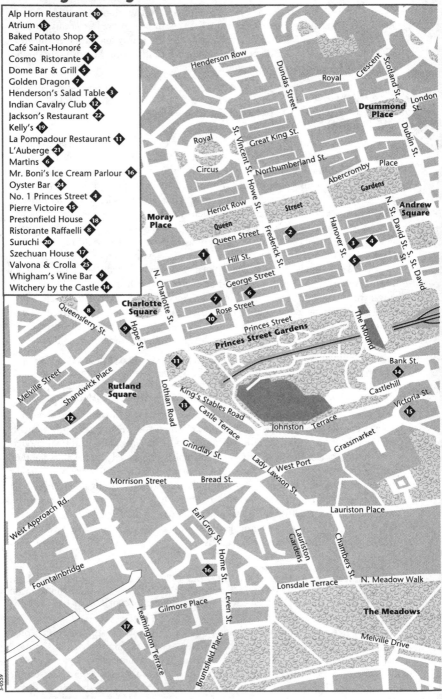

Alp Horn Restaurant **10**
Atrium **13**
Baked Potato Shop **23**
Café Saint-Honoré **2**
Cosmo Ristorante **1**
Dome Bar & Grill **5**
Golden Dragon **7**
Henderson's Salad Table **3**
Indian Cavalry Club **12**
Jackson's Restaurant **22**
Kelly's **19**
La Pompadour Restaurant **11**
L'Auberge **21**
Martins **6**
Mr. Boni's Ice Cream Parlour **16**
Oyster Bar **24**
No. 1 Princes Street **4**
Pierre Victoire **15**
Prestonfield House **18**
Ristorante Raffaelli **8**
Suruchi **20**
Szechuan House **17**
Valvona & Crolla **25**
Whigham's Wine Bar **9**
Witchery by the Castle **14**

3-0559

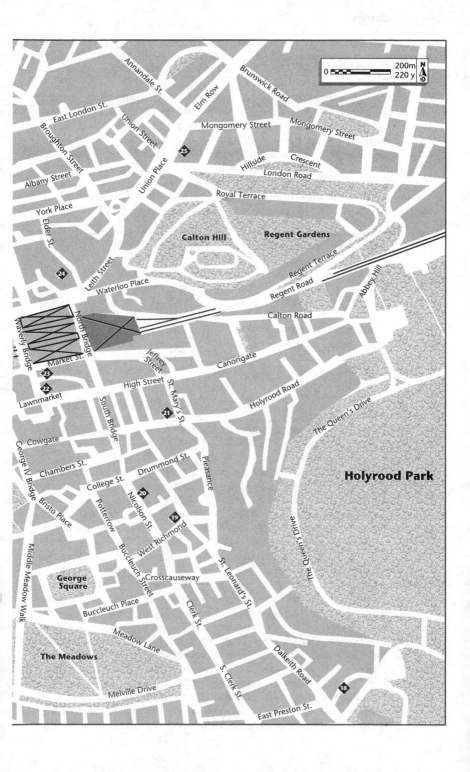

Café Saint-Honoré. 34 NW Thistle Street Lane. ☎ **0131/226-2211.** Reservations recommended. Main courses £7.70–£11.50 ($12.70–$18.95) at lunch, £15–£17 ($24.75–$28.05) at dinner. AE, DC, MC, V. Mon–Fri noon–2:15pm; Mon–Sat 7–10pm. Bus: 12. FRENCH/SCOTTISH.

This French-inspired bistro is set behind a blue-and-gold storefront, a short walk north of Frederick Street. The menu is completely revised every day, based on whatever's fresh in the market and whatever the chefs feel inspired to cook. An up-beat and usually enthusiastic staff serves a combination Scottish and French cuisine that includes venison with juniper berries and wild mushrooms, local pheasant in wine and garlic sauce, and lamb kidneys with broad beans inspired by the cuisine of the region around Toulouse. Fish is usually very fresh. Dinners are candlelit and intimate, and formal; lunches are popular with workers at many of the nearby offices, and consequently, brisk, high-energy, and breezy, and also less expensive.

Cosmo Ristorante. 58A N. Castle St. ☎ **0131/226-6743.** Reservations required. Main courses £13–£20 ($21.45–$33). AE, MC, V. Mon–Fri 12:30–2:15pm; Mon–Sat 7–10:30pm. Bus: 31 or 33. ITALIAN.

In business since 1969, Cosmo Ristorante is one of the most heavily patronized Italian restaurants in the Scottish capital. Courtesy, efficiency, and good cookery are featured here. In season, you can ask for mussels as an appetizer, and the soups and pastas are always reliable. Remember that the cost as well as the size of your pasta portion is doubled if you order it as a main course. Saltimbocca (veal with ham) is a specialty, and the kitchen is known for its light-handed Italian-inspired preparations of fish. The cassata siciliana is well made and not unbearably sweet. This is not the greatest Italian dining in the U.K., but dishes seem to have survived reasonably well this far north of the Mediterranean.

Dome Bar & Grill. 14 George St. ☎ **0131/624-8624.** Main courses £6.50–£13.50 ($10.75–$22.30) at lunch, £8.50–£15.50 ($14–$25.60) at dinner; fixed-price dinner menu £25 ($41.25). AE, DC, MC, V. Restaurant: Sun–Thurs noon–9:30pm, Fri–Sat noon–10:30pm. Bar: Sun–Thurs noon–11:30pm, Fri–Sat noon–1am. Bus: 3, 21, 26, 31, or 85. SCOTTISH/ BRITISH/CONTINENTAL.

Located in a fully restored Georgian building with an elaborate domed ceiling, this is part of The Dome entertainment complex. The building was originally designed in 1775 by James Craig, planner of Edinburgh's New Town, to house the Physician's Hall of the College of Physicians. When it went over budget, the college halted construction, and 70 years later, in 1843, sold the site. Architect David Rhind demolished the building to its foundation and rebuilt it, adhering to Craig's vision of the frontage, but replacing Craig's original Greek inspiration with Greco-Roman keystones and arches and Corinthian porticos. Throughout the building are elaborate columns, pedimental sculpture, and marble mosaic floors. The menu is an ambitious and creative combination of dishes with starters such as insalata caprese; duck liver pâté with Cumberland sauce and oat cakes; Japanese breaded prawns with a chile and mint dip; chargrilled polenta served with fresh asparagus, Parmesan cheese, and sun-dried tomatoes; and lobster, mango, and basil salad with a mango coulis. Main courses may include tagliatelle with smoked trout, crème fraîche, and chives; calf's liver with creamed potatoes, savoy cabbage, and caramelized onions; sea bass stuffed with basil, mint, dill, and black olives served on dauphinois potatoes with teriyaki sauce; and a phyllo basket filled with baby vegetables coated with a Tuscan tomato and basil sauce. For lighter fare, there is a wide selection of equally creative baguettes and canapés. The fixed-price menu includes an appetizer, main course, dessert, coffee, and mints.

Oyster Bar. 17 W. Register St. ☎ **0131/556-4124.** Reservations recommended year-round, but essential during the festival. Main courses £14.80–£29.50 ($24.40–$48.70). MC, V. Mon–Sat noon–2pm and 7–10:15pm, Sun 7:30–10:15pm. Bus: 42 or 44. SEAFOOD/GAME.

Its physical plant is one of the most dramatic in Edinburgh, thanks to its richly ornate Victorian bar and its soaring windows inset with stained-glass depictions of 19th-century Scotsmen in full Highland dress. An intimate and quiet corner in the large and busy Café Royal dining emporium, it specializes in seafood and game. You might like the salmon with mussels, shrimp with Camembert and white wine, or oak-smoked haddock poached in cream and topped with spinach.

Ristorante Raffaelli. 10 Randolph Place. ☎ **0131/225-6060.** Reservations recommended. Main courses £10–£15 ($16.50–$24.75). AE, DC, MC, V. Mon–Fri 12:15–9:30pm; Sat 6:15–10:30pm. Bus: 3, 34, or 35. ITALIAN.

This well-managed, long-established Italian restaurant is a staple on Edinburgh's dining scene. Even if you happen to pop in as early as 4pm, no one will object to serving you a full meal. Ingredients are always fresh and might include a Tuscan version of osso bucco, grilled T-bone of veal, or grilled sea bass with olive oil and balsamic vinegar. Two endlessly popular pastas are tagliatelle with porcini mushrooms and spinach-stuffed agnollotti with butter and cheese. Popular with business diners, especially at lunchtime, the place is within a single dining room that's lined with landscape paintings showing the geography of Italy at its most romantic advantage.

INEXPENSIVE

Far Pavilions. 10 Craigleith Rd., Comely Bank. ☎ **0131/332-3362.** Reservations recommended. Lunch main courses £6.50–£15 ($10.75–$24.75), lunch buffet £6.95 ($11.45); dinner main courses £7.50–£15 ($12.40–$24.75). AE, DC, MC, V. Mon–Fri noon–2:30pm; Mon–Sat 5:30–11:30pm. Bus: 21. INDIAN.

Since it was established in 1987 by a father-son team from the Chaudhry family, this Indian restaurant has fine-tuned its cuisine and service. You might appreciate a drink in the cocktail bar near the entrance before confronting a long menu, peppered with dishes from the Portuguese colony of Goa and the north Indian province of Punjab. Highly recommended is the house specialty, Murgi Massalam, concocted from tandoori chicken that falls off the bone thanks to slow cooking in a garlic-based butter sauce. Menu items include curry dishes influenced by British tastes as well as authentic dishes, together with the garnishes and side dishes that form a worthy Indian meal. Many dishes are vegetarian based, redolent with herbs and in some cases mild yogurt bases.

✪ **Henderson's Salad Table.** 94 Hanover St. ☎ **0131/225-2131.** Main courses £3.75–£4.10 ($6.20–$6.75). AE, MC, V. Mon–Sat 8am–10:30pm. Bus: 23 or 27. VEGETARIAN.

This is a Shangri-La for health-food lovers, as well as those who want an array of nutritious salads. It's self-service, and you can pick and choose eggs, carrots, grapes, nuts, yogurt, cheese, potatoes, cabbage, watercress—you name it. Hot dishes, such as peppers stuffed with rice and pimiento, can be ordered. A new twist on the national dish of Scotland is vegetarian haggis. Among the homemade desserts, you may choose a fresh-fruit salad or a cake with double-whipped cream and chocolate sauce. Henderson's is furnished with pinewood tables (often shared) and chairs. The wine cellar provides a choice of 30 wines, most of which may be ordered by the glass. Live music, ranging from classical to jazz to folk, is played every evening. The adjoining Bistro Bar serves meals with table service from 11am to 5pm daily.

Indian Cavalry Club. 3 Atholl Place. ☎ **0131/228-3282.** Reservations required. Main courses £6–£10 ($9.90–$16.50); 5-course table d'hôte dinner £16 ($26.40); 2-course buffet lunch £6.95 ($11.45). AE, DC, MC, V. Daily noon–2pm and 5:30–11:30pm. Bus: 3, 21, 23, or 26. INDIAN.

This place is near the top of the list of Edinburgh's many Indian dining rooms and is nothing like your average Edinburgh curry place. The elegant atmosphere evokes the British heyday in India, when Queen Victoria was known as "Empress of India." Along with the classic and tandoori Indian food items, many dishes are based on recipes from Nepal or Burma. Vegetarians flock here, and much of the cuisine is steamed. The restaurant has many areas, including the ground-floor Officers' Mess and the marquee-style Club Tent downstairs.

Suruchi. 14A Nicholson St. ☎ **0131/556-6583.** Reservations recommended. Main courses £5–£7 ($8.25–$11.55); fixed-price lunch £4.95 ($8.15); fixed-price dinner £9.95 ($16.40). MC, V. Daily noon–2pm and 5:30–11:30pm. Bus: 3, 21, or 33. INDIAN.

One of the city's most interesting Indian restaurants occupies a gray stone early 19th-century storefront immediately opposite Edinburgh's Festival Hall. Two peach-colored dining rooms are showcases for furniture, artwork, table linens, embroideries, and artifacts that come exclusively from India. Notice the elaborate blue wall tiles and the rows of miniature paintings from the owner's hometown of Jaipur, in Rajastan. The set-price menu, which is fresh-made and changes daily, is always an interesting option. At regular intervals, a culinary "festival" will feature the artwork, music, and cuisine of a different region of India. There's light jazz presented during the luncheon hour every Wednesday, Friday, and Saturday, and a year-round menu that divides its cuisine regionally in a way that helps you understand the country's complexity and subtleties. Menu items include grilled kebabs and vegetarian, lamb, seafood, or chicken tikka massalams, slow-cooked with herbs and spices in an earthenware casserole. One of these is an unusual version of fresh Scottish trout. No British colonial recipes are found here—the dishes are all authentic Indian cuisine.

Szechuan House. 12–14 Leamington Terrace. ☎ **0131/229-4655.** Main courses £6.25–£10 ($10.30–$16.50). AE, MC, V. Tues–Sun 5:30pm–midnight. Bus: 9, 10, or 27. SZECHUAN.

You don't come here for elegant trappings, but you get zesty, chile-hot platters of poultry and fish, especially chicken, duck, and prawns. You might begin with either "bang-bang" chicken or fish-head soup, and follow with diced chicken with chile or fried squid family style. Vegetarians can also dine happily. The cookery is classic and authentic, since the chef, Chao Gang Liu, comes from Szechuan province and has brought his bag of spices with him to tempt the haggis-and-neeps crowd, who might—just, might—have once (rather fearfully) added a half teaspoon of curry to mutton stew.

Valvona & Crolla. 19 Elm Row. ☎ **0131/556-6066.** Breakfast £3.95 ($6.50); pizzas, pastas, or platters £4.75–£6.50 ($7.85–$10.75). AE, DC, MC, V. Cafe with limited food service Mon–Sat 8:30am–5pm; full lunch service Mon–Sat noon–2pm. Bus: 7, 10, 11, 12, or 14. INTERNATIONAL.

In 1872 a recent arrival from Italy opened this restaurant, and it's still going strong. It shares space with a delicatessen and food emporium where exotic coffees, Parma ham, Italian cheeses, and breads, as well as takeaway sandwiches and casseroles, are sold. A satellite room, a few steps down from the main shopping area, contains a cafe and luncheon restaurant where food is very fresh and prices refreshingly low. Here, you can order three kinds of breakfasts (continental, Scottish, or vegetarian) for a fixed price of £3.95 ($6.50); or platters of pasta, mixed sausages, and cold cuts; crostini, risottos, and omelets. Also available for sale is an inventory of books and gift items. Don't expect leisurely dining, as the place caters to a daytime crowd of office

> ### 👪 Family-Friendly Restaurants
>
> **Mr. Boni's Ice Cream Parlour**   Every kid comes away loving Mr. Boni, who makes the best homemade ice cream in Edinburgh, plus sandwiches, jumbo hot dogs, and beef burgers with french fries. Mr. Boni's is located at 4 Lochrin Bridge (☎ **0131/229-5319**).
>
> **Henderson's Salad Table** *(see p. 147)*   The leading vegetarian restaurant of Edinburgh has an array of nutritious salads, followed by some of the most delectable homemade desserts in the city.
>
> **Witchery by the Castle** *(see p. 150)*   Kids delight in being taken to this Royal Mile restaurant that claims to be the "oldest and most haunted" restaurant in Old Town. The homemade desserts are sumptuous too.

workers and overscheduled shoppers who, in words they might use, "dash" in for midday sustenance, appreciating the informality of the venue and the freshness and low prices of the food.

Whigham's Wine Cellars. 13 Hope St. ☎ **0131/225-8674.** Reservations recommended. Main courses £5.25–£9.95 ($8.65–$16.40). V. Mon–Fri noon–10pm, Sat noon–9pm. Bus: 2, 4, or 34. SEAFOOD.

Whigham's Wine Cellars lies in a basement in the heart of Edinburgh's financial center and serves only seafood. Before the premises became a fashionable wine-cellar restaurant, wine was actually bottled here. Whigham's has been in business since the mid-18th century, and it used to ship wines to the American colonies. Walk across its mellowed, old stone floors until you find an intimate alcove. A range of continental wines is offered. Each day, you can make your selection from an assortment of appetizers and *plats du jour*. Look for the chalkboard specials. Their smoked fish (not just salmon) is exceptional. Marine fresh oysters come from Loch Fyne, and smoked venison occasionally appears on the menu.

IN THE CENTER: OLD TOWN
MODERATE

Jackson's Restaurant. 209 High St., Royal Mile. ☎ **0131/225-1793.** Reservations recommended. Main courses £13.95–£17 ($23–$28.05). AE, MC, V. Daily noon–2pm and 6:30–10:30pm, Sat–Sun 6–11pm. Bus: 35. SCOTTISH/FRENCH.

Serving a cuisine described as "Scottish with a French flair," this bustling and popular restaurant is in the austere but cozy stone cellar of a 300-year-old building. Your apéritif might be one of almost 40 kinds of Highland malts or a glass of Scottish wine, before you select from a "Taste of Scotland" menu featuring local ingredients. The charming staff will help you translate such items as "beasties of the glen" (haggis with a whisky cream sauce), noisettes of venison served in a blackberry, red currant, and port wine sauce, or "kilted salmon" pan-fried in a green ginger and whisky sauce. The menu items sound so cute you might think it's a tourist trap, but it isn't.

Pierre Victoire. 10 Victoria St. ☎ **0131/225-1721.** Reservations recommended. Main courses £5.80–£8.90 ($9.55–$14.70); fixed-price lunch £5.90 ($9.75). MC, V. Daily noon–4pm and 5:30–11:30pm. Bus: 1, 34, or 35. FRENCH.

This was the model for a series of franchise copies, all named Pierre Victoire, that have sprouted up in recent years in Edinburgh. It's an ideal, if chaotic, stopover if you're antique shopping and climbing Victoria Street. It's also one of the most popular evening gathering places—it keeps long hours. Wine specials "direct from France" are posted on the chalkboard. In a bistro setting with crowded tables, you can order grilled mussels in garlic with Pernod butter, salmon with ginger, or roast pheasant with Cassis. Pierre le Vicky, the owner and chef de cuisine, is well known locally, so advance reservations are needed. Vegetarians are also welcome.

Witchery by the Castle. Castlehill, Royal Mile. ☎ **0131/225-5613.** Reservations recommended. Main courses £14–£21.50 ($23.10–$35.50); fixed-price 2-course lunch £12.95 ($21.35); fixed-price dinner £21.95 ($36.20). AE, DC, MC, V. Daily 6–11:30pm. Bus: 1, 34, or 35. SCOTTISH.

This place bills itself as the "oldest and most haunted" restaurant in town. The building has been linked with witchcraft since the period between 1470 and 1722 when more than 1,000 people were burned alive on Castlehill. One of the victims is alleged to haunt the Witchery. She is known as Old Mother Long Nose, once a practitioner of herbal medicine, and a model of her sits by the entrance. James Thomson, the owner, uses his creative flair as a chef to make the restaurant a member of the "Taste of Scotland" program for unfussy Scottish food and hospitality. Menus change seasonally and might include Skye prawns or Tay salmon. Angus steak is a specialty, as is heather-fed lamb. Vegetarian dishes are also offered, including a walnut-and-carrot ravioli, and desserts are homemade, but skip the bread-and-butter pudding with crème anglaise: too heavy. Some 600 wines and 40 malt whiskies are available. A theatre-supper menu is available for £9.95 ($16.40) from 5:30 to 6:30pm and from 10:30 to 11:30pm.

INEXPENSIVE

Baked Potato Shop. 56 Cockburn St. ☎ **0131/225-7572.** Reservations not accepted. Food items 50p–£2.80 (85¢–$4.60). No credit cards. Daily 9am–9pm (until 10pm in summer). Bus: 5. VEGETARIAN/WHOLE FOOD.

The least expensive restaurant in a very glamorous neighborhood, it attracts mobs of office workers every day. Place your order at the countertop and it will be served in ecology-conscious recycled cardboard containers by the T-shirt and apron-clad staff. Only free-range eggs, whole foods, and vegetarian cheeses are used. Food items include more than 20 different kinds of salads, large and flaky baked potatoes (dug from the soil of nearby East Lothian) stuffed with your choice of half a dozen hot fillings, India-inspired curried dumplings known as bhajias, and such other dishes as mushroom risotto, chili, and cauliflower in cheese sauce. New Age nostalgia buffs can even sample the establishment's version of vegetarian haggis. There's a small table, seating no more than six diners, but there's lots of seating outdoors in the vicinity of the Royal Mile.

SOUTH OF THE CENTER
MODERATE

✪ **Kelly's.** 46 W. Richmond St. ☎ **0131/668-3847.** Reservations recommended. Fixed-price 3-course dinner £25 ($41.25); lunch £11.50–£18 ($18.95–$29.70). AE, DC, MC, V. Wed–Sat noon–2pm and 7–9:30pm. Closed Oct. Bus: 11, 12, or 14. MODERN BRITISH/MODERN FRENCH.

Catering to a discriminating crowd of barristers, artists, financiers, and employees of the nearby university, this stylish restaurant, housed in a former bakery, sports a decor reminiscent of a sophisticated restaurant in California. A 20-minute walk south of the center in a residential neighborhood, the place offers an intimate setting lined with flowers, bleached-pine furniture, watercolors, and unusual ceramics. Meals are prepared by Stephen and Anne Frost, who manage the dining room as well as the art gallery (Kelly's) next door. Focusing on fresh ingredients, the menu includes such dishes as galantine of duck with Cumberland sauce, roast breast of duck with garlic, and a platter containing a loin of lamb. Dessert might be a simple but succulent lemon tart with crème anglaise.

LEITH

In the northern regions of Edinburgh, the old port town of Leith opens onto the Firth of Forth. Once it was a city in its own right until it (and its harbor facilities) were slowly absorbed into Edinburgh. After decades of decay, it's become an arty neighborhood with a collection of restaurants, wine bars, and pubs.

EXPENSIVE

Vintner's Room. The Vaults, 87 Giles St., Leith. ☎ **0131/554-6767.** Reservations recommended. Main courses £7–£10 ($11.55–$16.50) at lunch, £14–£18 ($23.10–$29.70) at dinner. AE, MC, V. Mon–Sat noon–2:30pm and 7–10:30pm. Closed 2 weeks at Christmas. Bus: 7 or 10. FRENCH/SCOTTISH.

Many Edinburghers consider a trek out to Leith to the Vintner's Room well worth the effort. The stone-fronted building was built around 1650 as a warehouse for the barrels of bordeaux (claret) and port that came in from Europe's mainland. Near the entrance, beneath a venerable ceiling of oaken beams, a wine bar serves drinks and food platters beside a large stone fireplace. Most diners, however, head for the small but elegant dining room, lit with flickering candles. Here, in a room decorated with elaborate Italianate plasterwork, wine auctions took place 300 years ago. Owners Tim and Sue Cummings, who manage the kitchens and front rooms, respectively, prepare a robust cuisine that might include seafood salad with mango mayonnaise, a terrine of smoked salmon and rabbit, loin of pork with mustard sauce, and fillet of turbot with essence of crabmeat, all finished off with a two-chocolate mousse served with a bitter-chocolate sauce. The British would call the wine list "sound"—it's appropriately elaborate.

MODERATE

Denzler's 121. 121 Constitution St., Leith. ☎ **0131/554-3268.** Reservations recommended. Main courses £7–£12 ($11.55–$19.80); fixed-price lunch £7.95 ($13.10); fixed-price dinner £17.95 ($29.60). AE, DC, MC, V. Tues–Fri noon–2pm and 6:30–10pm, Sat 6:30–10pm. Bus: 16. SCOTTISH/SWISS.

Just beyond Leith Walk, this restaurant took over the former North of Scotland Bank building. Today many consider it Leith's finest dining choice, although the restaurant would be considered rather ordinary in Zurich. Nothing could be more typically Swiss than Bundnerpattli, an appetizer of wafer-thin slices of air-dried Swiss beef and ham from the Grisons. The most typical main course is émincée de veau zurichoise, slices of veal with mushrooms in a cream sauce served with spätzli. Of course, it wouldn't be a Swiss restaurant without fondue, or without a collection of Swiss wines that include Swiss Fendant and Dole, as well as those from such faraway places as Chile and Argentina.

Malmaison Brasserie. In the Malmaison Hotel, 1 Tower Place, in Leith. ☎ **0131/555-6868.** Reservations recommended for dinner. Fixed-price lunches £8.95–£9.95 ($14.75–$16.40); fixed-price dinners £8.95–£13.95 ($14.75–$23). Daily noon–2:30pm and 6–10:30pm. Bus: 16. FRENCH/SCOTTISH.

Set on the street level of the previously recommended hotel, this is an airy, unpretentious French-inspired brasserie that's charming enough to merit a trip out from Edinburgh. The setting is simple, with lots of polished brass. A French bistro-inspired menu is served that includes fried steak with pommes frites, sea bass with vinaigrette sauce, fillets of cod with Parma ham and basil-flavored mashed potatoes, and ham hock terrine with chicory and whole-grain mustard sauce. Everyone's favorite dessert here is crème brûlée. Regrettably, the restaurant doesn't have a view of the harbor but faces a side street, although few of the regular clients really seem to care.

PRESTONFIELD
EXPENSIVE

Prestonfield House. Priestfield Rd., Edinburgh, Lothian. EH16 5UT. ☎ **0131/668-3346.** Reservations required. Jacket and tie required. Main courses £13.20–£17.95 ($21.80–$29.60); table d'hôte £17 ($28.05) at lunch, £26 ($42.90) at dinner. AE, DC, MC, V. Daily 12:30–2pm and 7–9:30pm. Bus: 21 or 33. BRITISH.

Hidden away amid 23 acres of privately owned parkland and gardens 3 miles south of Edinburgh's center, this is one of the most elegant restaurants in town, a venue for birthday and other celebrations for local residents. Some kind of manor house has stood on the site since 1355, although the graceful Dutch-style rooflines of the Jacobean building you'll see today date from 1687. Highland cattle and peacocks add to the ornamentation of the grounds. Inside is an enviable collection of antiques. Curiously enough, although the restaurant has the same fine quality as always, it seems to have fallen out of fashion with the guidebooks, which seem to have dropped it in pursuit of something trendier. Menu items include grilled smoked salmon served with braised leeks and gazpacho sauce, marinated smoked pigeon with an avocado-and-raspberry salad, baked fillet of lamb in phyllo pastry with tomatoes and wild mushrooms, and venison-and-oyster pie with spring vegetables.

5 Attractions

THE TOP ATTRACTIONS
The Royal Mile

The Royal Mile stretches from Edinburgh Castle all the way to the Palace of Holyroodhouse. Walking along, you'll see some of the most interesting old structures in Edinburgh, with their turrets, gables, and towering chimneys. Take bus no. 1, 6, 23, 27, 30, 34, or 36 to reach it.

An outstanding feature of the **High Kirk of St. Giles** on High Street (☎ 0131/ 225-9442), its Thistle Chapel, was designed by Sir Robert Lorimer, housing beautiful stalls and notable heraldic stained-glass windows. The church is open Monday through Saturday from 9am to 5pm and Sunday, from 1 to 5pm. Of course, you're welcome to join in the cathedral's services on Sunday, conducted at various times from 7am to 9pm. A group of cathedral guides is available at all times to conduct guided tours. John Knox, the leader of the Reformation in Scotland, was minister of St. Giles from 1560 to 1572. Admission is free, but a £1 ($1.65) donation is suggested.

The **Writers' Museum** is situated in Lady Stair's House off Lawnmarket (☎ 0131/ 529-4901). It was built in 1622, and it takes its name from a former owner, Elizabeth, the dowager countess of Stair. Today it's a treasure house of portraits, relics, and manuscripts relating to three of Scotland's greatest men of letters—Robert Burns (1759–1796), Sir Walter Scott (1771–1832), and Robert Louis Stevenson (1850–1894). The Burns collection includes his writing desk, rare manuscripts, portraits, and many other items relating to the poet. Also on display are some of Sir Walter Scott's possessions, including his pipe, chess set, and original manuscripts. The museum also holds one of the most significant Stevenson collections anywhere, including personal belongings, paintings, photographs, and early editions. It's open Monday through Saturday from 10am to 5pm. Admission is free.

? Did You Know?

- Monuments to native son Sir Walter Scott abound in Edinburgh, but he wrote surprisingly little about the city of his birth.
- In 1842 the city had 200 brothels; the best were on Rose Street. Business peaked at the annual reunion of the General Assembly of the Church of Scotland.
- Burke and Hare were the original "body-snatchers," robbing fresh graves to sell bodies to surgeons for anatomical dissection.
- Lincoln Monument, built in 1893, honors the Scottish-American soldiers who died in America's Civil War.
- William Brodie, the original Dr. Jekyll and Mr. Hyde, ended his days dancing at the end of a hangman's rope suspended from an improved gallows he himself had designed and built.
- A Scottish mixture of rhubarb, ginger, and magnesia was until quite recently the world's most frequently prescribed medication.
- In the 18th century, Scotch was drunk as freely as spring water, in contrast to its upmarket image today.
- Edinburgh has the dubious distinction of being the AIDS capital of Europe.

The **Museum of Childhood,** 42 High St. (☎ 0131/529-4142), stands just opposite John Knox's House, the first museum in the world devoted solely to the history of childhood. Contents of its four floors range from antique toys to games to exhibits on health, education, and costumes. Because of the youthful clientele it naturally attracts, it ranks as the "noisiest museum in the world." It's open June to September, Monday through Saturday from 10am to 5pm, and also from 2 to 5pm on Sunday during the Edinburgh Festival. Admission is free.

Farther down the street at 43–45 High St. is the **John Knox House** (☎ 0131/556-9579), with a history going back to the late 15th century. Even if you're not interested in the reformer who founded the Scottish Presbyterian church, you may want to visit his house, as it is characteristic of the "lands" that used to flank the Royal Mile. All of them are gone now, except Knox's house, with its timbered gallery. Inside, you'll see the tempera ceiling in the Oak Room, along with exhibitions of Knox memorabilia. The house may be visited Monday through Saturday from 10am to 4:30pm for £1.75 ($2.90) for adults, £1.25 ($2.05) for children.

Continue along Canongate toward the Palace of Holyroodhouse. At 163 Canongate stands one of the handsomest buildings along the Royal Mile. **Canongate Tolbooth** was constructed in 1591 and was once the courthouse, prison, and center of municipal affairs for the burgh of Canongate.

Across the street at 142 Canongate is **Huntly House** (☎ 0131/529-4143), an example of a restored 16th-century mansion. Now it's Edinburgh's principal museum of local history. You can stroll through period rooms and reconstructions Monday through Saturday from 10am to 5pm, and during the festival also on Sunday from 2 to 5pm. Admission is free.

At 354 Castlehill, Royal Mile, the **Scotch Whisky Heritage Center** (☎ 0131/220-0441) is privately funded by a conglomeration of Scotland's biggest whisky distillers. It highlights the economic effect of whisky on both Scotland and the world and illuminates the centuries-old traditions associated with whisky-making, showing the exact science and art form of distilling. There's a 7-minute audiovisual show, and

Edinburgh Attractions

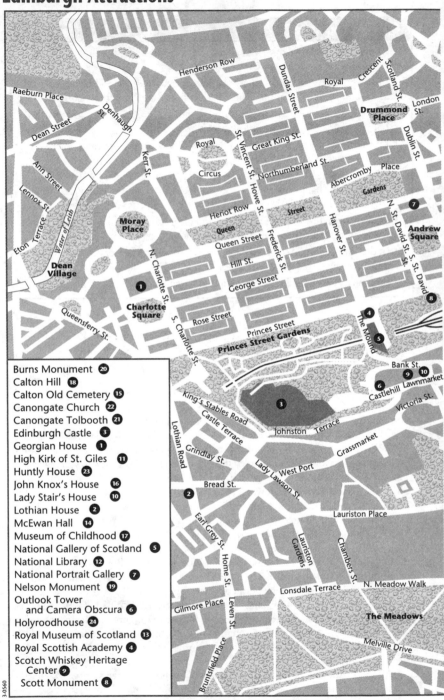

Burns Monument **20**
Calton Hill **18**
Calton Old Cemetery **15**
Canongate Church **22**
Canongate Tolbooth **21**
Edinburgh Castle **3**
Georgian House **1**
High Kirk of St. Giles **11**
Huntly House **23**
John Knox's House **16**
Lady Stair's House **10**
Lothian House **2**
McEwan Hall **14**
Museum of Childhood **17**
National Gallery of Scotland **5**
National Library **12**
National Portrait Gallery **7**
Nelson Monument **19**
Outlook Tower
  and Camera Obscura **6**
Holyroodhouse **24**
Royal Museum of Scotland **13**
Royal Scottish Academy **4**
Scotch Whiskey Heritage
  Center **9**
Scott Monument **8**

3-0560

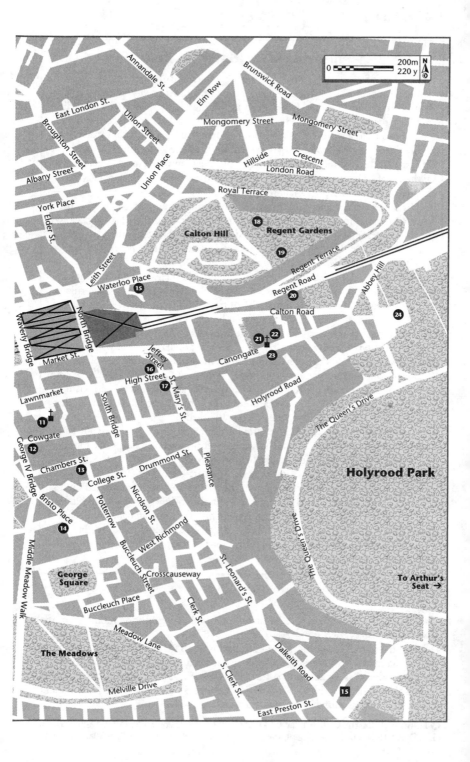

The Father of Dr. Jekyll & Mr. Hyde

Robert Louis Stevenson (1850–1894) was a complex and often mysterious character. Some saw him as Dr. Jekyll, a poet of intellect and sensitivity, others as a "debauched rake" very like Mr. Hyde. Born in Edinburgh, he spent much of his life restlessly roaming the world. He's been both hailed as Scotland's greatest writer and dismissed as a writer of "tall tales for children with limited brain capacity."

Stevenson was the son of Robert Stevenson, the famed Scottish civil engineer. He was a sickly child and, not surprisingly, a big disappointment to his father. When at the age of 22 he announced that he was an agnostic, his father declared, "My son has rendered my whole life a failure."

His father's stingy allowance drove the promising author to abandon his parents' respectable upper-class neighborhood and live cheaply among Scotland's lowliest dock areas and bordellos. Determined to roam ("I shall be a nomad . . ."), he traveled to France. His journey there resulted in early works: *An Inland Voyage* (1878) and *Travels with a Donkey in the Cévennes* (1879).

In 1876, he met a married American, Fanny Osborne, who would eventually become his wife. She found him "an enticing enigma." Journeying to California to see a stricken Fanny, Stevenson himself contracted tuberculosis. By Christmas of 1879, Fanny had divorced her husband and she wed Stevenson the following May. Fanny proved a poor critic of his work. She didn't like *The Sea-Cook* (1881), which became *Treasure Island,* a book that has never lost popularity. That was followed by *Kidnapped* (1886), which Stevenson set in the moorland and wilderness of western Scotland. But his most famous work was *The Strange Case of Dr. Jekyll and Mr. Hyde* (1886; pronounced "Jee-kill" according to the author). Fanny's criticism of the first version of this book caused Stevenson to burn it, although he later felt that his first version was better than the one he published.

Eventually Stevenson and Fanny settled in Samoa, where he purchased 300 acres of land, hoping to find a climate that would suit his damaged lungs. He found a place where he was happy at last. The Samoans loved Stevenson—they called him Tusitala, the Teller of Tales—but they did not care for Fanny. The Samoan servants labeled her the "Witch Woman of the Mountain." Here he worked on his masterpieces, *The Ebb-Tide* (1894) and his unfinished *Weir of Hermiston* (published posthumously in 1886), and translated one of his tales into Samoan. But his happiness did not last long. On December 3, 1894, he suddenly collapsed. He was only 43. In his memory, the Samoans dug a road up Mount Vaea so that he could be buried on the mountain he loved.

---

an electric car ride moves past 13 theatrical sets showing historic moments in the whisky industry. For a supplement of £10 ($16.50), you can sample two whiskies during the tour. A tour with tutored tasting costs £18 ($29.70) per person, entitling you to sample five whiskies and take away a miniature bottle to enjoy later. Otherwise, admission is £4.20 ($6.95) for adults, £3 ($4.95) for senior citizens, £2.50 ($4.15) for students with ID, £2 ($3.30) for ages 5 to 17, free for children 4 and under. Open year-round from 10am to 5pm.

✪ **Edinburgh Castle.** Castlehill. ☎ **0131/225-1012.** Admission £5.50 ($9.05) adults, £1.50 ($2.45) age 15 and under. Apr–Sept, daily 9:30am–5:15pm; Oct–Mar, daily 9:30am–4:15pm. Bus: 1 or 6.

It's believed that the ancient city grew up on the seat of the dead volcano, Castle Rock. Early history is vague, although it is known that in the 11th century Malcolm III (Canmore) and his Saxon queen, later venerated as St. Margaret, founded a castle on this spot. The only fragment left of their original castle—in fact the oldest structure in Edinburgh—is St. Margaret's Chapel, built in the Norman style, the oblong structure dating principally from the 12th century.

Inside the castle you can visit the State Apartments, particularly Queen Mary's Bedroom, where Mary Queen of Scots gave birth to James VI of Scotland (later James I of England). Scottish Parliaments used to convene in the Great Hall. The highlight is the Crown Chamber, which houses the Honours of Scotland (Scottish Crown Jewels), used at the coronation of James VI, along with the scepter and the sword of state of Scotland. The French Prisons were put to use in the 18th century, and these great storerooms housed hundreds of Napoleonic soldiers during the early 19th century. Many of them made wall carvings that you can see today.

✪ **Palace of Holyroodhouse.** Canongate, at the eastern end of the Royal Mile. ☎ 0131/556-1096. Admission £5.50 ($9.05) adults, £3.70 ($6.10) seniors, £2.60 ($4.30) age 15 and under; £15 ($24.75) family pass (up to 2 adults and 2 children). Mon–Sat 9:30am–5:15pm, Sun 10:30am–4:40pm. Closed the last 2 weeks in May and 3 weeks in late June and early July (dates vary). Bus: 1 or 6.

This palace was built by James IV early in the 16th century, adjacent to an Augustinian abbey that David I had established in the 12th century. The nave of the abbey church, now in ruins, remains today, but only the north tower of James's palace is left. Most of what you see today was built by Charles II after Scotland and England were united in the 17th century.

The old wing was the scene of Holyroodhouse's most dramatic incident. Mary Queen of Scots's Italian secretary, David Rizzio, was stabbed 56 times in front of her eyes by her husband, Lord Darnley, and his accomplices. A plaque marks the spot where he died on March 9, 1566. One of the more curious exhibits here is a piece of needlework done by Mary, depicting a cat-and-mouse scene—her cousin, Elizabeth I, is the cat!

The palace suffered long periods of neglect, although it basked in glory at the ball thrown by Bonnie Prince Charlie in the mid-18th century.

The present queen and Prince Philip live at Holyroodhouse whenever they visit Edinburgh. When they're not in residence, the palace is open to visitors.

Scott Monument. In the East Princes St. Gardens. ☎ 0131/529-4068. Admission £2 ($3.30). Apr–Sept, Mon–Sat 9am–6pm; Oct–Mar, Mon–Sat 9am–3pm. Bus: 1 or 6.

The gothic-inspired Scott Monument is the most famous landmark of Edinburgh, completed in the mid-19th century. Sir Walter Scott's heroes are carved as small figures in the monument, and you can climb to the top. The monument is slated to reopen in the spring of 1999, following extensive repairs.

✪ **National Gallery of Scotland.** 2 The Mound. ☎ 0131/556-8921. Free admission. Mon–Sat 10am–5pm, Sun 2–5pm (during the festival, Mon–Sat 10am–6pm, Sun 11am–6pm). Bus: 3, 21, or 26.

This museum is located in the center of Princes Street Gardens. The gallery is small as national galleries go, but the collection was chosen with great care and has been expanded considerably by bequests, gifts, and loans. Recent major acquisitions include Giulio Romano's *Vièrge à la Légende.* Other important Italian paintings are Verrocchio's *Ruskin Madonna,* Andrea del Sarto's *Portrait of a Man,* Domenichino's *Adoration of the Shepherds,* and Tiepolo's *Finding of Moses.* There are paintings by El Greco and Velázquez.

> ### ⭐ Frommer's Favorite Edinburgh Experiences
>
> **Contemplating Edinburgh from Arthur's Seat.** At 823 feet—reached by a climb up Holyrood Park—you'll see the Highlands in miniature. The view from here has been called "magical." Scots congregate here to await the solstice.
>
> **Visiting Dean Village.** About 100 feet below the level of the rest of the city, Dean Village is an 800-year-old grain-milling town on the Water of Leith. Go here to soak up local color—never better in summer than the view from its woodland walk along the river. Exotic denizens of nearby Stockbridge village amuse with their zany makeup and dress.
>
> **Shopping Along Princes Street.** This is the main street of Edinburgh—for locals, the equivalent of New York's Fifth Avenue. Flower-filled gardens stretch along the street's whole south side. When not admiring the flowers, you can window-shop and make selections from the country's finest merchandise—everything from kilts to Scottish crystal.
>
> **Having a Pint in an Edinburgh Pub.** The city is famous for its pubs. Sampling a pint of McEwan's real ale or Tennent's lager is a chance to soak up the special atmosphere of Edinburgh, following an age-old tradition set by Robert Louis Stevenson and Arthur Conan Doyle and their friends when they were students at the University of Edinburgh in the 1870s.

The duke of Sutherland has lent the museum two Raphaels, Titian's two Diana canvases and the Venus rising from the sea, and a work of the great 17th-century Frenchman Nicolas Poussin, *The Seven Sacraments.* On loan from the queen is an early Netherlandish masterpiece historically linked to Edinburgh, Hugo van der Goes's *Trinity Altarpiece.*

Notable also are Rubens's *The Feast of Herod* and *The Reconciliation of Jacob and Esau* and Rembrandt's *Woman in Bed,* as well as superb landscapes by Cuyp and Ruisdael. One of the gallery's most prized acquisitions, *Interior of St. Bavo's Church, Haarlem,* by Pieter Saenredam, his largest and arguably finest painting, was bought in 1982.

The most valuable gift to the gallery since its foundation, the Maitland Collection, includes one of Cézanne's *Mont St-Victoire* series, as well as works by Degas, van Gogh, Renoir, Gauguin, and Seurat, among others. A rare early Monet, *Shipping Scene—Night Effects,* was bought in 1980. In the same year, for the first time in living memory, a stunning landscape, *Niagara Falls, from the American Side,* by the 19th-century American painter Frederic Church, went on show. You can also see excellent examples of English painting, and naturally, the work of Scottish painters is prominent. In the new wing, opened in 1978, Henry Raeburn is at his best in the whimsical *The Rev. Robert Walker Skating on Duddingston Loch.*

MORE ATTRACTIONS

Camera Obscura. Castlehill. ☎ **0131/226-3709.** Admission £2.50 ($4.15) adults Sept–June, £3.75 ($6.20) July–Aug; £2.25 ($3.70) senior citizens Sept–June, £2.40 ($3.95) July–Aug; £2.80 ($4.60) students Sept–June, £3 ($4.95) July–Aug; £1.80 ($2.95) children Sept–June, £1.90 ($3.15) July–Aug. Apr–Oct, daily 9:30am–6pm; Nov–Mar, daily 10am–5pm. Bus: 1 or 6.

It's at the top of the Outlook Tower and offers a panoramic view of the surrounding city. Trained guides point out the landmarks and talk about Edinburgh's fascinating history. In addition, there are several entertaining exhibitions, all with an optical theme, and a well-stocked shop selling books, crafts, and compact discs.

Georgian House. 7 Charlotte Square. ☎ **0131/226-3318.** Admission £4.20 ($6.95) adults, £2.80 ($4.60) children, students, and seniors. Apr–Oct, Mon–Sat 10am–4:30pm, Sun 2–4:30pm. Closed Nov–Mar.

Architecturally, the most interesting district of New Town is the north side of Charlotte Square, designed by Robert Adam. Together with his brother James, he developed a symmetrical but airy architectural style with an elegant reworking of Greek and Roman classical motifs. Their influence was widespread, both in Britain and in the United States, especially in the American South. Georgian House has been refurbished and opened to the public by Scotland's National Trust. The furniture in this Adam house is mainly Hepplewhite, Chippendale, and Sheraton, all dating from the 18th century. In a ground-floor bedroom is a sturdy old four-poster with an original 18th-century canopy. The dining-room table is set for a dinner on fine Wedgwood china, and the kitchen is stocked with gleaming copper pots and pans.

Royal Observatory Visitor Centre. Blackford Hill. ☎ **0131/668-8405.** Admission £2.50 ($4.15) adults; £1.50 ($2.45) ages 5–16, students, and seniors; free for children 4 and under. Mon–Sat 10am–5pm, Sun noon–5pm. Bus: 41 or 42.

Exhibits feature images of astronomical objects, Scotland's largest telescope, and a display of antique instruments. There's also a panoramic view of the city from the balcony. An exhibit, *The Universe,* uses photographs, videos, computers, and models to take you on a cosmic whirlwind tour from the beginning of time to the farthest depths of space in a couple of hours. The astronomy shop is well stocked. The location is in a public park on the south side of Edinburgh.

MUSEUMS

National Museum of Scotland (NMS). Chambers St. ☎ **0131/225-7534.** Admission £3 ($4.95); supplement for some temporary exhibitions. Mon–Sat 10am–5pm, Sun noon–5pm. Walk south from Waverley Station for 10 min. to reach Chambers St. or take bus no. 1 or 6.

After being housed (rather awkwardly) in several different locations during the 1990s, these two long-established museums were united into a single headquarters early in 1998. Formerly the Royal Scottish Museum and the National Museum of Antiquities, their newest incarnation, the National Museum of Scotland, occupies an 1861 building near the Royal Mile that has been radically upgraded and enlarged with a postmodern wing. Displays include Scotland's most impressive collection of decorative arts, ethnography, natural history, geology, archaeology, technology, and science.

۞ Scottish National Gallery of Modern Art. Belford Rd. ☎ **0131/624-6200.** Free admission, except for some temporary exhibitions. Mon–Sat 10am–5pm, Sun 2–5pm. Bus: 13 stops right by the gallery, but is infrequent; nos. 18, 20, and 41 pass along Queensferry Rd., a 5-minute walk up Queensferry Terrace and Belford Rd. from the gallery.

In 1984, Scotland's national collection of 20th-century art moved into a gallery converted from a former school building. The building, dated 1828, is set in 12 acres of grounds just a 15-minute walk from the west end of Princes Street. The collection is international in scope and quality in spite of its modest size.

Major sculptures sited outside the building include pieces by Henry Moore and Barbara Hepworth. Inside, the collection ranges from a fauve Derain and cubist Braque and Picasso to recent works by Paolozzi. There's a strong representation of English and Scottish art, as well as artists from Europe and America, notably Matisse, Miró, Kirchner, Kokoschka, Ernst, Ben Nicholson, Nevelson, Balthus, Lichtenstein, Kitaj, Hockney, and many others. Prints and drawings can be studied in the Print Room. The licensed cafe sells light refreshments and salads.

Scottish National Portrait Gallery. 1 Queen St. ☎ **0131/624-6200.** Free admission, except for some temporary exhibitions. Mon–Sat 10am–5pm, Sun 2–5pm. Bus: 18, 20, or 41.

Housed in a red stone Victorian gothic building by Rowand Anderson, this portrait gallery gives you a chance to see what the famous people of Scottish history looked like. The portraits, several by Ramsay and Raeburn, include everybody from Mary Queen of Scots to Flora Macdonald to Sean Connery.

MONUMENTS

Calton Hill is often credited with giving Edinburgh a look somewhat like that of Athens. It's a hill of monuments, and when some of them were created they were called "instant ruins" by critics of the day. The landmark lies off Regent Road in the eastern sector of Edinburgh. Rising 350 feet, the hill is visited not only by those wishing to see its monuments but also by those wanting to enjoy panoramic views of the Firth of Forth and the city spread beneath it. The Parthenon was reproduced in part on this location in 1824. The intention of the builders was to honor the brave Scottish dead killed in the Napoleonic wars. However, the city fathers ran out of money and the monument—often referred to as "Scotland's shame"—was never finished.

The **Nelson Monument** (☎ **0131/556-2716**), containing relics of the hero of Trafalgar, dates from 1815 and rises more than 100 feet above the hill. A time ball at the top falls at 1pm Monday through Saturday. The monument is open April to September, Monday from 1 to 6pm and Tuesday through Saturday from 10am to 6pm; October to March, Monday through Saturday from 10am to 3pm. Admission is £2 ($3.30). Take bus no. 26, 85, or 86.

For Americans, however, the curiosity here is the **Lincoln Monument,** which Edinburghers erected in 1893. It was dedicated to the thousands of American soldiers of Scottish descent who lost their lives in America's Civil War.

Below Waterloo Place, on the flatter slope of Calton Hill, visitors can walk through the **Calton Old Cemetery,** dating from the 1700s. Many famous Scots were buried here, often with elaborate tombs honoring their memory—notably the Robert Adam–designed tomb for philosopher David Hume.

GARDENS

Gardeners and nature lovers will be attracted to the **Royal Botanic Garden,** Inverleith Row (☎ **0131/552-7171**). Main areas of interest are Exhibition Hall, Alpine House, the Demonstration Garden, annual and herbaceous borders (summer only), the copse, the Woodland Garden, Wild Garden, Arboretum, Peat Garden, Rock Garden, Heath Garden, and the Pond. Admission is by voluntary donation, and it's open May through August, daily from 10am to 8pm; March through April and September through October, daily from 10am to 6pm; November through February, daily from 10am to 4pm.

DEAN VILLAGE

The village is one of the most photographed sights in the city. Set in a valley about 100 feet below the level of the rest of Edinburgh, it is full of nostalgic charm. A few minutes from the West End, it's located at the end of Bell's Brae, off Queensferry Street, on the Water of Leith. The settlement dates from the 12th century, and the fame of Dean Village grew as a result of its being a grain-milling center. You can enjoy a celebrated view by looking downstream under the high arches of Dean Bridge, designed by Telford in 1833. It's customary to walk along the water in the direction of St. Bernard's Well.

ESPECIALLY FOR KIDS

Other than Old Town with its castles and palaces, two attractions always thrill children—the **Museum of Childhood** (see "The Royal Mile" in "The Top Attractions," above), and the zoo.

Edinburgh Zoo. 134 Corstorphine Rd. ☎ **0131/334-9171.** Admission £6 ($9.90) adults, £3.80 ($6.25) seniors, £4.40 ($7.25) students, £3.20 ($5.30) children, £16.50 ($27.20) family ticket (2 adults and 2 children). Apr–Sept, daily 9am–6pm; Oct–Mar, Mon–Sat 9am–4:30pm, Sun 9:30am–4:30pm. Parking £1.30 ($2.15). Bus: 2, 26, 69, 85, or 86 from Princes St.

Just 10 minutes from Edinburgh's city center, the zoo is Scotland's largest animal collection, set in 80 acres of scenic hillside parkland offering unrivaled views from the Pentlands to the Firth of Forth.

The zoo contains more than 1,500 animals, including many endangered species—snow leopards, white rhinos, pygmy hippos, and many more. Famous for its penguins, the zoo has the largest colony in Europe, with four different species, plus the world's largest penguin enclosure. A penguin parade is held daily at 2pm from April to September only.

ORGANIZED TOURS

If you want a quick introduction to the principal attractions in and around Edinburgh, then consider one or more of the tours offered by **Lothian Region Transport,** 14 Queen St. (☎ **0131/554-4494**). You won't find a cheaper way to hit the highlights, and later you can go back on your own if you want a deeper experience. The coaches (buses) leave from Waverley Bridge, near the Scott Monument. The tours start in April and run through late October. A curtailed winter program is also offered.

You can see most of the major sights of Edinburgh, including the Royal Mile, Holyrood Castle, Princes Street, and Edinburgh Castle, by double-deck motorcoach for £5.50 ($9.05) for adults and £1.50 ($2.45) for children. This ticket is valid all day on any LRT Edinburgh Classic Tour bus, which allows passengers to get on and off at any of the 15 stops along its routes. Buses start from the Waverley Railway Station every day beginning at 9:10am, departing every 15 minutes in summer and about every 30 minutes in winter, then embark on a touristic circuit of Edinburgh which—if you remain on the bus without ever getting off—will take about 2 hours. Guided commentary is offered along the way. Most participants find it easy to pick up the thread of their visit as their tour progresses, despite the frequency of their exits and entrances into one or another of the vehicles.

LRT also operates half-day and full-day motorcoach excursions throughout the various regions of Scotland. White-sided buses identified by their black trim depart from the Waverley Station for "Highland Splendour Tours" to such places as Loch Lomond, Loch Katrine, and the Trossachs, St. Andrews, the Isle of Arran, and selected sights in Braemar and Deeside. Their prices, depending on the distance they travel from Edinburgh and their duration, range from £8.50 to £23 ($14 to $37.95) per person, and, in some cases, include lunch. Itineraries vary with the day of the week.

Tickets for any of these tours can be bought at LRT offices at Waverley Bridge, or at 27 Hanover St., or at the tourist information center in Waverley Market. Advance reservations are a good idea for the half-day and full-day tours. For more information, call ☎ **0131/555-6363,** 24 hours a day.

WALKING TOUR
Historic Edinburgh

Start: Edinburgh Castle.
Finish: Princes Street Gardens.
Time: 3 hours.
Best Time: Any sunny day.
Worst Times: Morning and early evening rush hours.

Begin by walking up to:

1. **Edinburgh Castle,** where you can visit, among other attractions, St. Margaret's Chapel and see Mons Meg, a 15th-century artillery piece. The castle well is 110 feet deep and has been in use since 1313 at least.

   The Royal Mile (generic name of four different streets) starts from the Castle Esplanade at Castlehill. Walk along Castlehill. The house at the top of Castle Wynd is known as the Cannonball House because of the ball embedded in the gable on its west side. At the Church of Tolbooth St. John's, services are celebrated in Gaelic.

   The street now becomes Lawnmarket, once the center for linen sellers. Farther on, stop at:

2. **Gladstone's Land,** 447B Lawnmarket (☎ **0131/226-5856**), an example of a 17th-century tenement building. The six-story building was completed in 1620. On the ground floor, a reconstructed shop booth displays replicas of goods of the period, and an upstairs apartment of four rooms is furnished as it might have been in the 17th century. It's open April to October only, Monday through Saturday from 10am to 4:30pm and Sunday from 2 to 4:30pm. The admission charge is £2.80 ($4.60) for adults, £1.90 ($3.15) for children and seniors.

   Next you come to **Brodie's Close,** the 18th-century home of the notorious Deacon Brodie, a respectable councilor by day and a thief by night. He was hanged in 1788. The mechanism used for the "drop" had previously been improved by Brodie himself—for use on others! He was the inspiration for Robert Louis Stevenson's *The Strange Case of Dr. Jekyll and Mr. Hyde,* although Stevenson set his story in foggy London town, not in Edinburgh.

   Lawnmarket ends at the intersection of Bank Street and George IV Bridge, and you can see the brass strips on the road in the southeast corner of the busy junction marking the site of the scaffold where public hangings were continued until 1864.

   ☕ **TAKE A BREAK** The most famous pub along the Royal Mile is **Deacon Brodie's Tavern,** 435 Lawnmarket (☎ **0131/225-6531**), named for the Edinburgher who inspired the character of Dr. Jekyll/Mr. Hyde (see above). Snacks such as cottage pie and scotch eggs are served, or you can drop in only for a drink.

   The Royal Mile continues, as High Street, with:

3. **Parliament Square,** on the right. In the square is Parliament House, built in 1632, along with Parliament Hall, a fine gothic hall with an open timber roof. The building is now the Courts of Justice, and it is sometimes possible to attend sessions by using Door 11.

   Farther on is the:

4. **John Knox House,** 43–45 High St., associated with James Mossman, goldsmith to Mary Queen of Scots, as well as John Knox, Scotland's religious reformer. Linked with the John Knox House, the Netherbow Theatre and Cafe marks the

Walking Tour — Edinburgh

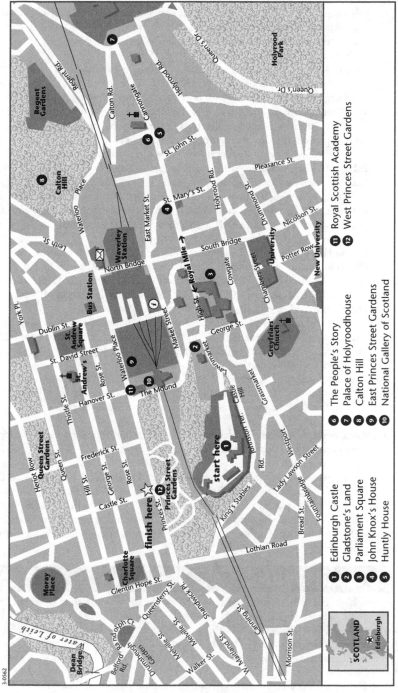

1. Edinburgh Castle
2. Gladstone's Land
3. Parliament Square
4. John Knox's House
5. Huntly House
6. The People's Story
7. Palace of Holyroodhouse
8. Calton Hill
9. East Princes Street Gardens
10. National Gallery of Scotland
11. Royal Scottish Academy
12. West Princes Street Gardens

Church   Post Office ☒   Information ⓘ

halfway point of the Royal Mile. Almost opposite is the Museum of Childhood, really intended more for adults than for children. Still farther on is Chessells Court, once an excise office (robbing it was Deacon Brodie's last crime).

Next comes the City Museum in:

5. **Huntly House,** 142 Canongate, a restored 16th-century mansion that was the home of the first marquess of Huntly in 1636. You can visit its displays of Edinburgh silver and glass, Scottish pottery, and other relics. Opposite is:

6. **The People's Story,** 163 Canongate, Tolbooth, a museum in the Canongate Tolbooth, with an exhibition illustrating the story of the ordinary people of Edinburgh from the late 18th century to the present day.

Continue walking up the Royal Mile until you reach the:

7. **Palace of Holyroodhouse,** at the end, the former abode of Mary Queen of Scots but today used by Queen Elizabeth whenever she's in Edinburgh.

After a visit, walk back up Canongate and High Street along the Royal Mile to Canongate Church, then take Tolbooth Wynd to the footpath leading to Regent Road and Princes Street. When you reach Regent Road, turn left and continue along Waterloo Place with:

8. **Calton Hill** on the right. On top of the hill are the Nelson Monument, the City Observatory, and the unfinished "Parthenon," intended to be a memorial to the dead of the Napoleonic wars. On this street is the General Post Office and the Philatelic Bureau, and, opposite, the Register House, where most of Scotland's historic and legal records since the 13th century are stored.

Walk by the Waverley Railway Station to the left, and then you'll be in the:

9. **East Princes Street Gardens,** with the Scott Monument, a 200-foot spire forming a canopy over the statue of Sir Walter Scott and his dog.

Next on the left is the:

10. **National Gallery of Scotland,** 2 The Mound, called "the most enjoyable small gallery in Europe." It has any number of masterpieces, ranging from Raphael to Turner, as well as the world's finest collection of Scottish masterpieces. Also on the Mound is the:

11. **Royal Scottish Academy,** widely acknowledged as the venue for some of the foremost exhibitions of contemporary art in Scotland.

Next you reach:

12. **West Princes Street Gardens** and the famous Floral Clock, believed to be the oldest in the world, built in 1903. A cuckoo announces each quarter hour and the flowers often portray some current local event. Also in the gardens is the American War Memorial, erected by Americans of Scottish descent and the Churches of St. John and St. Cuthbert, the former having a brass-rubbing center in its church hall.

6 Special Events

The highlight of Edinburgh's year—some would say the only time when the real Edinburgh emerges—comes in the last weeks of August during the **Edinburgh International Festival.** Since 1947 the festival has attracted artists and companies of the highest international standard in all fields of the arts, including music, opera, dance, theater, exhibition, poetry, and prose, and "Auld Reekie" takes on a cosmopolitan air.

During the period of the festival, one of the most exciting spectacles is the **Military Tattoo** on the floodlit esplanade in front of Edinburgh Castle, high on its rock above the city. Vast audiences watch the precision marching of Scottish regiments and military units from all parts of the world, and of course the stirring skirl of the bag-pipes and the swirl of the kilt. First performed in 1950, the Tattoo today features not only the British Army's Scottish regiments but performers from some 30 countries, including bands, dancers, drill teams, gymnasts, flag wavers, and motorcyclists, even such animals as camels, elephants, and police dogs as well as horses. The music range is from ethnic to pop, from military to jazz. Ticket prices range from £20 to £33 ($33 to $54.45) and mail-order bookings are available from the Edinburgh Military Tat-too, Tattoo Office, 32 Market St., Edinburgh EH1 1QB (☎ **0131/225-4783**).

Less predictable in quality but greater in quantity is the **Edinburgh Festival Fringe,** an opportunity for anybody—professional or nonprofessional, an individual, a group of friends, or a whole company of performers—to put on a show wherever they can find an empty stage or street corner. Late-night reviews, outrageous and irreverent contemporary drama, university theater presentations, maybe even a full-length opera—Edinburgh gives them all free rein. As if that weren't enough, Edinburgh has a **Film Festival,** a **Jazz Festival,** a **Television Festival,** and a nonannual **Book Festival** at the same time.

Ticket prices vary from £5 ($8.25) up to about £50 ($81) a seat. Information can be obtained at **Edinburgh International Festival,** 21 Market St., Edinburgh EH1 1BW (☎ **0131/473-2000;** fax 0131/473-2003), open Monday through Friday from 9:30am to 5:30pm.

Other sources of information include **Edinburgh Festival Fringe,** 180 High St., Edinburgh EH1 1BW (☎ **0131/226-5257**); **Edinburgh Book Festival,** 25A S.W. Thistle Street Lane, Edinburgh EH2 1EW (☎ **0131/228-5444**); **Edinburgh Film Festival,** 88 Lothian Rd., Edinburgh EH3 9BZ (☎ **0131/228-4051**); and **Edinburgh Military Tattoo,** 32 Market St., Edinburgh EHL 1QB (☎ **0131/ 225-4783**).

7 Sports & Outdoor Pursuits

SPECTATOR SPORTS

HORSE RACING   Place your bets at the **Musselburgh Racecourse,** Musselburgh Park (☎ **0131/665-2859**), which lies about 4 miles east of Edinburgh. In summer the races are on a flat circular track, whereas in winter the more elaborate "National Hunt" format challenges horses and riders to a series of jumps and obstacle courses of great technical difficulty. Admission is £6 ($9.90) to the grand stand or £12 ($19.80) to the club stand.

RUGBY   One of the more physical of British sports is played at **Murrayfield Sta-dium,** Murrayfield (☎ **0131/346-5000**), home of the National Rugby Team of Scotland, about a mile west of Edinburgh center. Attracting a loyal entourage, the sport is played between September and April, usually on Saturday. Some of the most passionate matches are those among teams from the five-nation bloc comprising Scot-land, Wales, England, Ireland, and France. These matches are presented only between January and March, when most sports enthusiasts in Scotland seem to talk about very little else. Entrance to the stadium, depending on the seat and the game, ranges in price from £23 to £30 ($37.95 to $49.50).

SOCCER   You might quickly get swept up in the zeal of Edinburghers for their local soccer (referred to as "football") clubs. Both teams, when not battling with one another, challenge other teams from throughout Europe. The home of the Edinburgh Hearts (more formally known as the Heart of Midlothian Football Club) is at **Tynecastle Park,** Gorgie Road (☎ **0131/337-7004**); the home of the Hibs (short for the Hibernians) is at **Easter Road Park,** Easter Road (☎ **0131/661-2159**). The traditional playing times are Saturday afternoons, when games are likely to be televised in pubs throughout Scotland.

ACTIVITIES

GOLF One public golf course that welcomes nonresidents is the **Port Royal Golf Course,** Ingliston (☎ **0131/333-4377**). This course features only driving ranges and putting greens. The driving range charge is £2 ($3.30) for 45 to 50 golf balls and £3.80 ($6.25) for 90 to 100 golf balls. The putting green charges are £1 ($1.65) or £2 ($3.30) if you want to work your way through nine different putting greens. It is especially busy on weekends, so an advance phone call and a scheduled arrival for a weekday are usually the best insurance for an agreed-upon starting time. For data on other courses in and around Edinburgh (the Lothian region), refer to "Golf" in chapter 4.

ICE SKATING The **Murrayfield Ice Rink,** Riversdale Crescent (☎ **0131/ 337-6933**), offers a rink, along with skate rentals, in wintertime. Phone in advance to avoid arriving during practice by the local ice hockey teams. Hours are Monday through Friday from 2:30 to 4:30pm when admission is £1.80 ($2.95). Other hours are Monday, Tuesday, and Thursday from 7 to 9pm, Wednesday from 7:30 to 10pm, and Saturday and Sunday from 2:30 to 4:30pm when admission is £2.50 ($4.15). On Friday and Saturday from 7:30 to 10:30pm the admission goes up to £4 ($6.60). Skate rental is always 70p ($1.15). If you want to try disco dancing with a new twist, come on Friday or Saturday evening when roller disco is in full swing.

SAILING Visit the Firth of Forth firsthand by renting a sailboat. For information, contact the **Port Edgar Sailing Centre,** Port Edgar, South Queensferry (☎ **0131/ 331-3330**). Located about 9 miles west of the city center, between Easter and mid-October it offers instruction in small-craft sailing, canoeing, and powerboating, as well as half-day rentals. The rate for a dinghy, suitable for four adults, is £21 ($34.65) for 2 hours. The center is open daily from 10am to noon and 2 to 4pm, and also Monday through Thursday from 7 to 9pm.

SKIING Even the highest peaks of Scotland aren't cold enough to permit year-round skiing, so if you yearn to practice your slalom during your stay in Edinburgh, you'll have to improvise. One possible solution is the **Midlothian Ski Centre,** Hillend Park, Biggar Road (☎ **0131/445-4433**), the largest "dry ski" center in Europe. Located 5 miles south of Edinburgh, it has three different slopes with uplift facilities. One of the slopes is around 400 meters, allowing dry-ski enthusiasts to careen down one of the highest hills this side of St. Moritz. It can be reached via bus no. 4 from Princes Street. A chairlift ride, costing £1 ($1.65) for adults and children, leads to a lofty perch where a panoramic view unfolds. Before you begin your return journey on the chair, you can see the whole of the city of Edinburgh and across the River Forth to the Hills of Life. The center is open year-round and floodlit during the winter. Opening hours, April to August, are Monday through Friday from 9:30am to 9pm, Saturday and Sunday from 9:30am to 7pm; September to March, Monday through Saturday from 9:30am to 9pm, Sunday from 9:30am to 7pm.

SQUASH The **Craiglockhart Sports Centre,** 177 Colinton Rd. (☎ **0131/ 444-1969**), offers several squash courts, and you can rent equipment if you need it. Court costs are £6.45 ($10.65) for 45 minutes, with free rackets provided if you need them. Open Saturday through Thursday from 9am to 11pm, and Friday from 10am to 11pm. Somewhat more expensive are the squash courts at **Marco's Leisure Centre,** 51 Grove St. (☎ **0131/228-2141**). Nonmembers can't reserve courts, but if you show up to use the gym here and a court becomes available, you'll probably be allowed to use it. Forty minutes of court time costs £6 ($9.90) before 5pm and £7 ($11.55) thereafter. Racket rental is £1 ($1.65). Open daily from 9am to 11pm. Rackets in both facilities leave a lot to be desired; if you're serious, bring your own.

SWIMMING   There are several small Victorian-era swimming pools scattered around Edinburgh, but the undisputed leader of them all is the modern Olympic-size **Royal Commonwealth Pool,** 21 Dalkeith Rd. (☎ 0131/667-7211). In a low-slung concrete building on the outskirts of town, it opened in 1970 in time for the world-famous Commonwealth Games, which were hosted that year in Edinburgh. Access to the pool costs £2.25 ($3.70) all day, £1.25 ($2.05) in the afternoon. Access to the (sexually segregated) saunas costs £5.95 ($9.80). Take bus no. 3, 7, 21, or 33. It's open Monday through Friday from 9am to 9:30pm and Saturday and Sunday from 8am to 7pm. Call before you go to avoid arriving during specially scheduled tournaments.

TENNIS   Several tennis courts are within an easy commute of the center. These include the **Craiglockhart Sports Centre,** 177 Colinton Rd. (☎ 0131/444-1969). Advance reservations are necessary, and of course your plans will quickly go awry if it starts to rain. (You'll also find badminton courts and a gym.) Indoor courts cost £13.50 ($22.30) per hour and are available Monday through Thursday from 9am to 9:30pm, Friday from 10am to 9:30pm, and Saturday and Sunday from 9am to 9pm. The outdoor courts don't feature electric lighting, so closing hours adhere to seasonal lighting. These courts cost £5.65 ($9.30) per hour and are available Saturday through Wednesday from 9am until dark, Friday from 10am until dark. More convenient and sometimes more crowded are a handful of concrete-surfaced **public tennis courts** behind George Square, on the north side of the public park known as the Meadows.

8 Shopping

The best buys are in tartans and woolens, along with bone china and Scottish crystal. New Town's Princes Street is the main shopping artery. George Street and Old Town's Royal Mile are also major shopping arteries.

BOOKS

James Thin. 57 George St. ☎ 0131/225-4495.

This has been the leading bookseller in Edinburgh since 1848. Tastes and reading customs have changed over those many decades, but James Thin keeps abreast of the times. The store has all sorts of titles about Edinburgh life. There's a quiet tearoom upstairs.

Waterstones. 128 Princes St. ☎ 0131/226-2666.

This bookstore is giving the legendary James Thin serious competition. It has a wide range of stock in nearly all fields of publishing. There's a branch store at 83 George St. (☎ 0131/225-3436), and another at 13–14 Princes Street (☎ 0131/556-3034).

BRASS RUBBINGS

Scottish Stone and Brass Rubbing Centre. Trinity Apse, Chalmers Close, near the Royal Mile. ☎ 0131/556-4364.

For beautiful wall hangings, you can make your own brass rubbings or buy them ready-made. You can visit the center's collection of replicas molded from ancient Pictish stones, rare Scottish brasses, and medieval church brasses. No experience is needed to make a rubbing—the center will show you how and supply materials.

CLOTHING

Bill Baber. 66 Grassmarket. ☎ 0131/225-3249.

Set near the Royal Mile, this highly creative design team occupies a four-story building. On three of the floors between 10 and 15 craftspeople work to create the artfully modernized adaptations of traditional Scottish patterns designed by Bill and Helen Baber. Be warned in advance that virtually everything here sells for from £65 ($107.25) and up, with the noteworthy exception of whatever's on a "Sale Rack" near the entrance. Garments are not considered "fashion" in the sense that they'll go out of style in the future—expect durable and traditional Scottish jacquard-patterned knits "spiced up" with strands of Caribbean-inspired turquoise or aqua; rugged-looking blazers, jackets, and sweaters suitable for treks or bike rides through the moors; and tailored jackets that a woman might feel comfortable wearing to a glamorous cocktail party. In business since 1977, the site inventories garments for men and women but not for children.

Millshop. 134C Princes St. ☎ 0131/225-2319.

One of about 30 such shops through the United Kingdom, it sells knitwear, skirts, giftware, and travel rugs. You can purchase some good Scottish woolens here. Note, however, that most of the merchandise is made in Britain.

CRYSTAL

Edinburgh Crystal. Eastfield, Penicuik. ☎ 01968/675128. Bus: 62, 64, 65, 81, or 87.

The Edinburgh crystal factory lies about 10 miles south of Edinburgh, just off A701 to Peebles, devoted entirely to handmade crystal glassware. Tours of the factory to watch glassmakers at work are available Monday through Friday from 9am to 3:30pm. From April through September, weekend tours are also given between 11am and 2:30pm. The Visitor Centre is the starting point for the tour and is the location of the factory shop where the world's largest collection of Edinburgh crystal is on view and on sale. Here, too, are the inexpensively priced factory seconds. The Centre also has a woolen mill and a coffee shop specializing in home baking. Open Monday through Saturday from 9am to 5pm and Sunday from 11am to 5pm.

DEPARTMENT STORES

Debenham's. 109–112 Princes St. ☎ 0131/225-1320.

This, along with Jenners (see below), competes for the honor of the best department store in Edinburgh. Its modernized Victorian shell stocks a wide array of Scottish and international merchandise in a marble-covered department-store format.

Jenners. 48 Princes St. ☎ 0131/225-2442.

Everyone in Edinburgh has probably been to Jenners at least once. Its neogothic facade, opposite the Sir Walter Scott Monument, couldn't be more prominent. Its array of Scottish and international merchandise qualifies it as one of the best-stocked department stores in town.

DOLLS

Doll Hospital (Geraldine's of Edinburgh). 35A Dundas St. ☎ 0131/556-4295.

A purveyor of innocence and nostalgia on a grand scale, this is the only shop of its kind in Edinburgh. Entirely lined with glass-fronted display cases, it operates as a basement showroom for Edinburgh's only doll factory, with more than 100 richly costumed dolls on exhibit. Each of the heirloom-quality dolls requires about 10 full days' labor to create, and reflects what connoisseurs consider the climax of the dollmaker's art, the Victorian and Edwardian ages. Each has a hand-painted porcelain head and sometimes elaborate coiffure made from modacrylic fibers. Dolls range in price from £50 to £600 ($82.50 to $990). Also available are all-mohair, fully jointed teddy bears that would make a memorable souvenir for your favorite child.

Haggis Macsween of Edinburgh. 118 Brunsfield Place. ☎ **0131/229-9141.**

This outfit is a long-established Scottish family business that specializes in the production of traditional haggis, the national dish of Scotland. Lamb, beef, oatmeal, onion, and a special blend of seasonings and spices are cooked together to make this product, which was immortalized by Robert Burns. Macsween haggis is already cooked and simply requires reheating in the oven.

JEWELRY
Alistir Tait. 116A Rose St. ☎ **0131/225-4105.**

This is one of the most charming jewelry stores in Edinburgh, with a reputation for selling Scottish minerals, such as agates mined within the country's borders, jewelry fashioned from Scottish gold, and garnets, sapphires, and freshwater free-form pearls. There's also a mishmash of estate jewelry in every conceivable style, as well as modern pieces. If you didn't realize that Scotland was so rich in gemstones, think again— and ask to see the artful depictions of *Luckenbooths*. Fashioned as pendants, usually in the form of two entwined hearts capped with a royal crest, they're associated with the loves and tragedies of Mary Queen of Scots, and often accessorized with a baroque pearl. These come in subtle hues of petal, orange, brown, and most desirable and rare of all, purple. Prices for Luckenbooths range from £28 to £250 ($46.20 to $412.50) and can be purchased here tax-free if a passport is presented at the time of purchase.

Hamilton & Inches. 87 George St. ☎ **0131/225-4898.**

Since 1866, this intensely prestigious jeweler has sold gold and silver jewelry, porcelain and silver, and gift items from dignified premises that are a fine example of late-Georgian design. You'll find everything you could want for an upscale wedding present for a favored relative or business associate, all sorts of jewelry, including some valuable pieces from Scottish estate sales, and two memorable kinds of silver dishes. These include impressively weighty "Armada plates" copied from items found in the wrecks of the Spanish Armada during the era of Elizabeth I and endearingly folkloric "quaichs." These originated in the West Highlands as whisky measures crafted from wood or horn and were later gentrified into something like silver porringers or chafing dishes, each with a pair of "lugs" (ears) fashioned into Celtic or thistle patterns. Many visitors find that, engraved, they make memorable and evocative baby gifts. Also unusual is an exclusive pattern of Hungarian-based Herend china, emblazoned prominently with a Scottish thistle.

Robert Anthony. 108B Rose St. ☎ **0131/226-4550.**

One of Edinburgh's best jewelry stores, it sells new, antique, and second-hand jewelry, as well as gold chains, diamonds, and fine gemstones. Of enduring popularity, however, are the gold bangles and pendants available immediately in 9-karat gold. (If you prefer 18-karat gold, it can be crafted for you in about a week.) Gold replicas of Scottish pipers and/or dancers, thistles, and Edinburgh Castle and its famous cannon, Mons Meg, make good souvenirs.

KNITWEAR
Shetland Connection. 491 Lawnmarket. ☎ **0131/225-3525.**

The owner of this shop, Moira-Ann Leask, promotes Shetland Island knitwear, and her shop is packed with sweaters, hats, and gloves in colorful Fair Island designs.

She also offers hand-knitted mohair, Aran, and Icelandic sweaters. Her oldest knitter is 89 years old. Items range from fine-ply cobweb shawls to chunky ski sweaters handcrafted by skilled knitters in top-quality wool. A large range of Celtic jewelry and gifts makes this shop a top-priority visit.

LINENS

Linens Fine. 22 Howe St. ☎ 0131/225-6998.

The danger associated with popping into this upscale shop is that you might make a much larger investment than you intended when you see the fine-textured bedsheets and pillowcases. Most feature Irish and British cotton (not linen), mostly in white and cream. *Note:* An upscale British brand name here is Wendy Woods, Ltd. There's also a collection of ornate brass, iron, and wooden beds, many of them extraordinarily beautiful, on which the sheets are displayed. They can be ordered in several different sizes and shipped anywhere. Beds begin at £500 ($825) and stretch all the way up to £3,500 ($5,775) for something really unusual.

MALLS

Waverley Market Shopping Centre. Next to Waverley Station, Princes St. ☎ 0131/557-3759.

There's something for everyone here, all under one roof in the center of Edinburgh. You can browse through some 80 shops on three levels selling fashions, accessories, gifts, books, jewelry, beauty products, and a wide selection of Scottish arts and crafts. A Food Court has tempting snacks, and top-quality produce is for sale in the Food Hall. Unique handmade items can be purchased in the craft center.

MUSIC

Virgin Megastore. 125 Princes St. ☎ 0131/220-2230.

One of the biggest selections of records, CDs, videos, and tapes in Scotland is found here. The shop has a special strength in traditional and Scottish music. The staff is knowledgeable and charming, and also eager to imbue their love of Scottish music to interested visitors.

TARTANS & KILTS

Clan Tartan Centre. 70–74 Bangor Rd., Leith. ☎ 0131/553-5100.

This is one of the leading specialists in Edinburgh, regardless of which clan you claim as your own. If you want help in identifying a particular tartan, the staff at this shop will assist you.

Geoffrey (Tailor) Highland Crafts. 57–59 High St. ☎ 0131/557-0256.

On two floors of a prestigious-looking shop in the heart of Edinburgh, this is the most famous and marketing-oriented kiltmaker in the Scottish capital. Clients who have come seeking an authentically Scottish appearance have included Sean Connery, Charlton Heston, Dr. Ruth Westheimer, many members of Scotland's rugby teams, and Mel Gibson, who favors the tartan design Hunting Buchanan, and who wore his outfit when he received an award from the Scottish government after his filming of *Braveheart.* Expect a delay of between 4 and 6 weeks before your costume can be completed. The company sets up sales outlets at Scottish reunions and Highland Games around the world (there are at least 21 of these in the U.S. alone every year) and maintains a toll-free phone line (☎ 800/566-1467) and an after-hours clerk for anyone who calls from the U.S. or Canada and wants to be outfitted. Expect to pay from £275 ($453.75) for a kilt and around £600 ($990) for a complete Highland outfit. The company stocks 300 of Scotland's best-known tartan patterns.

James Pringle Woolen Mill. 70–74 Bangor Rd., Leith. ☎ **0131/553-5161.**

Whether you have a clan to your name or would like to borrow one, this is the place to go. The mill produces a large variety of top-quality wool items, including a range of Scottish knitwear—cashmere sweaters, tartan and tweed ties, travel rugs, tweed hats, and tam o' shanters. In addition, the mill has the only Clan Tartan Centre in Scotland, where more than 2,500 sets and trade designs are accessible through their research facilities. A free audiovisual presentation shows the history and development of the tartan. You can visit free, as well as taking advantage of free taxi service to the mill from anywhere in Edinburgh (ask at your hotel).

John Morrison Ltd. 461 Lawnmarket. ☎ **0131/225-8149.**

If you can't take delivery of your Highland dress, this shop will mail your order throughout the world. Women can order an authentic hand-tailored kilt or a semikilt or a kilt skirt. The store also provides evening sashes and stoles to match, and specializes in kilts for men, a heavy handwoven worsted in your favorite tartan. To go with it, there are doublets and jackets. That's followed up with accessories—a jabot and cuffs along with kilt hose and a tie.

Tartan Gift Shops. 54 High St. ☎ **0131/558-3187.**

If you've ever suspected that you might be Scottish, this establishment has a chart indicating the place of origin (in Scotland) of your family name. You'll then be faced with a bewildering array of hunt and dress tartans for your personal use. The high-quality wool is sold by the yard as well as in the form of kilts for both men and women. There's also a line of lambswool and cashmere sweaters, and all the accessories to round out your perfect image as a Scot. The shop lies in a stone-fronted building close to John Knox's house.

9 Edinburgh After Dark

The Edinburgh Festival brings numerous cultural offerings to the city, but year-round there are plenty of choices, whether you prefer theater, opera, ballet, or other nighttime diversions. The waterfront district, featuring many jazz clubs and restaurants, is especially lively in the summer, and students flock to the pubs and clubs around Grassmarket. Discos are found off of High and Princes Streets, and in the city's numerous pubs you can often hear traditional Scottish folk music for the price of a pint. While Edinburgh lacks the live music scene that is such a big part of Glasgow, it still has a lot to offer. For a thorough list of entertainment options during your stay, pick up a copy of *The List,* a biweekly entertainment paper available at the Tourist Information Office for £1.90 ($3.15).

THE PERFORMING ARTS
CLASSICAL MUSIC, OPERA & DANCE

✪ **Edinburgh Festival Theatre.** 13–29 Nicolson St. ☎ **0131/662-1112** for administration, 0131/473-2000 for tickets during non-Festival times, 0131/225-5756 for tickets during the Edinburgh Festival. Tickets £5–£45 ($8.25–$74.25). Bus: 3, 21, or 33.

This is the showcase of Edinburgh theaters, opened in 1994. Set on the eastern edge of Edinburgh, near the old campus of the University of Edinburgh, it has since been called "Britain's *de facto* Dance House" because of its sprung floor, its enormous stage (the largest in Britain), and its suitability for opera presentations of all kinds. Costs were kept down (it cost a relatively modest $38 million) by partially adapting the old Empire Theater that had stood on the site since 1928. The consequence is a new entity that has a postmodern facade of concrete and sweeping glass walls, a lobby area dramatically bathed in uplighting and downlighting, and a performance area of 1,900 seats still outfitted in a plush rose-and-cream combination of art deco and neoclassical swirls.

The theater's most visible role is as a venue for the Edinburgh Festival, although its administrators work hard to maintain some of the excitement of the festival throughout the entire year. Ironically, since the theater's inauguration, it has become the venue for many dance and theater premieres before they open in London, partly because of the superb technical facilities, partly as a testing ground before exposing the show to the tough London audiences.

King's Theatre. 2 Leven St. ☎ **0131/557-2590.** Tickets £5–£22.50 ($8.25–$37.15).

Edinburgh's second most important theater presents a wide repertoire of classical entertainment, including ballet and opera. West End productions from London are also presented at this 1,340-seat Victorian theater.

Playhouse Theatre. 18–22 Greenside Place. ☎ **0131/557-2590.** Tickets £8–£30 ($13.20–$49.50).

The largest theater in Edinburgh, this 3,100-seat playhouse was originally built in 1929 at the height of the vaudeville age. Inspired by London's Palladium, it retains the gold-and-scarlet trappings of its construction and a hint of the greasepaint of long-ago stars. Home of both the **Scottish Ballet** and the **Scottish Opera,** its most popular performances are presented every Saturday. The establishment also presents rock concerts, operettas, musical comedies, experimental theater, and a wide array of musical acts from North America and Europe. In summer it's a performance venue for the Edinburgh Festival. The box office, which has its own access to Greenside Place, is open Monday through Saturday from 10am to 6pm.

Queen's Hall. Clerk St. ☎ **0131/668-2019.** Tickets £5–£20 ($8.25–$33).

The Queen's Hall is home to the **Scottish Chamber Orchestra** and a major venue for the Edinburgh International Festival. It also plays host to a full range of concerts, from classical to rock music, including a Friday-night jazz club. The box office and restaurant are open daily from 10am to 5pm.

Usher Hall. Lothian Rd., near Princes St. ☎ **0131/228-8616.** Tickets £10–£18 ($16.50–$29.70).

Originally built in 1914 with a design inspired by the Royal Albert Hall in London, this is the home of the **Royal Scottish Orchestra,** which performs here on Friday night between October and April. Lesser musical ensembles are scheduled throughout the week. Gilbert and Sullivan operettas by Edinburgh's **D'Oyly Carte** company are also presented here. In summer the theater is used by the Edinburgh Festival. The box office is open Monday through Saturday from 10am to 5pm.

THEATER

Edinburgh has a lively theater scene. The major theater in town is the King's Theatre (see above), which also presents ballet and opera. The **Netherbow Arts Centre,** 43 High St. (☎ **0131/556-9579**), has been called "informal," but productions are often experimental and intriguing—new Scottish theater at its best. Ask about lunchtime performances as well, if you're not too busy sightseeing during the day. Tickets range from £3 to £5 ($4.95 to $8.25), with box office hours Monday through Saturday from 10am to 5pm.

The highly respected resident company of the **Royal Lyceum Theatre,** Grindlay Street (☎ **0131/229-9697**), has a repertoire that ranges from Shakespeare to new Scottish playwrights. The theater is a restored Victorian building dating from 1883, with a restaurant, four bars, and facilities for the disabled. The box office is open Monday through Saturday from 10am to 7pm, and tickets cost £5 to £12.50 ($8.25 to $20.65) on Tuesday through Thursday, rising to £5 to £14 ($8.25 to $23.10) on Friday and Saturday.

Traverse Theatre, Cambridge Street (☎ **0131/228-1404**), is one of the few theaters in Britain funded solely to present new plays by British writers and first translations into English of international works. In a modern location, it now offers two theaters under one roof: Traverse 1, with a seating capacity of 250, and Traverse 2, with a smaller capacity of 100. On the premises is a bar and cafe, open at 10:30am daily, serving theater patrons throughout the day. Tickets cost £6 to £10 ($9.90 to $16.50). The box office is open Monday through Saturday from 10am to 6pm.

THE CLUB & MUSIC SCENE
DANCE CLUBS & ROCK

The Cavendish. 3 West Tollcross. ☎ **0131/228-3252.** Cover £5 ($8.25) Fri–Sat.

This is not necessarily where you go to hear the next Oasis or Blur, but who knows? A rock-and-roll legend might be born here every Friday or Saturday night when the doors open at 10pm and a cover is imposed. There is a dress code—that is, no tennis shoes or jeans. The bar is open Thursday through Saturday from 10pm to 3am.

Century 2000. 31 Lothian Rd. ☎ **0131/229-7670.** Cover £7 ($11.55) Fri–Sat and after midnight on Wed, Thurs, and Sun.

This is the largest night club in Edinburgh, very popular with an under-25 crowd. It's open Wednesday through Sunday from 11pm to 3am. Special events are sometimes planned, but not with regularity. There are also three bars around the dance floor and one above it.

Club Mercado. 25–27 Market St. ☎ **0131/226-4224.** Cover £3–£10 ($4.95–$16.50).

This popular hard dance club attracts an 18-to-35 age clientele. Once the headquarters of the Scottish version of British Rail, it hangs suspended over the railway tracks behind the city's main station. On Friday the action alternates between Kerplunk, a brass and drum dance club, and mixed dance styles from 5pm to 3am. Admission is free. On Saturday, the popular Alternaclub swings into action between 11pm and 4am, bringing out a cultural cross-section of Edinburgh, with a cover ranging from £8 to £10 ($13.20 to $16.50). Also popular is a techno party on Sunday from 11pm to 3am when the cover is lowered to £3 ($4.95) to £4 ($6.60).

The Subway. 69 The Cowgate, off Grassmarket. ☎ **0131/225-6766.** Cover £2 ($3.30) on Fri.

The best time to visit this joint is on Friday night when it imports a live rock band, almost always a local or regional act, and charges a cover. The bar is open Monday through Thursday from 5pm to 3am, and Friday through Sunday from 7pm to 3am. On Monday through Thursday, patrons are entertained by karaoke, from 7 to 10:30pm, or else they do the entertaining themselves.

The Venue. 15 Calton Rd. ☎ **0131/557-3073.**

Behind the main Post Office and Waverley Station is the city's principal venue for live music. Some of the biggest bands in the U.K. perform here, and when they are not appearing the entertainment is by Scottish wannabees. Posters and flyers throughout the town let you know what's on at any given time. This large hall is not open unless there's a concert, and admission fees and times are dictated on a per-show basis. You must call first for acts, dates, cover, and starting times.

Whynot. 14 George St. ☎ **0131/624-8633.**

In the basement of the Dome Bar & Grill (see above), this club is a hot new entertainment complex that opened in 1997 in the former Bank of Scotland building across from the George Inter-Continental Hotel. It has low ceilings with curtains hanging like veils above the dance floor and lots of seating coves tucked away for privacy. The club holds 690 people and on weekends it fills to overflowing. The club swings open Thursday through Sunday from 10pm to 3am. On Thursday night, there's a £3 ($4.95) cover for dancing to the music of the '60s, '70s, and '80s. Friday night re-creates the disco era, with a £5 ($8.25) cover before 11pm and a £7.50 ($12.40) cover thereafter. Saturday features the best in contemporary dance music, with a £7.50 ($12.40) cover imposed all night. On Sunday, a local radio station hosts a party when a cover of £5 ($8.25) is imposed.

FOLK MUSIC & CEILIDHS

Ceilidhs are often spontaneous. Many clubs and pubs in Edinburgh have live folk music, but the strolling players tend to be somewhat erratic or irregular in their appearances. It's best to read notices in pubs and talk to the tourist office to see where the ceilidh will be on the night of your visit.

In addition to pubs that sometimes feature folk music, the Edinburgh Folk Club offers performances on stage at the **Pleasance Cabaret Bar,** 60 The Pleasance (☎ **0131/652-1471**), every Wednesday at 8pm. The cover charge is £4 ($6.60) for adults and £3 ($4.95) for seniors and students (free for children 15 and under).

Some hotels regularly feature traditional Scottish music evenings. You might check with the **Carlton Highland Hotel** on North Bridge (☎ **0131/556-7277**). A dinner and show here costs £34.50 ($56.95) per person, including a full meal of traditional Scottish dishes, unlimited wine, and the musical performance. Dinner service is nightly from 7 to 9pm, and the concerts run from 9 to 10:30pm. Tickets for the performance only cost £11 ($18.15). Also call the **George Hotel** on George Street (☎ **0131/225-1251**) to see if any program is featured at the time of your visit. Performances, when they are staged, start at 7pm in the Adams Room, where a ticket for the event sells for £36.50 ($60.20), including a full meal plus the show. **Jamie's Scottish Evening** is presented at the King James Hotel on Leith Street (☎ **0131/556-0111**) Tuesday through Sunday at 7pm, costing £6 ($9.90).

Malt Shovel. 11–15 Cockburn St. ☎ **0131/225-6843.** No cover.

Every night, it dispenses lots of real ales and single-malt whiskies to a neighborhood clientele, but every Tuesday its live bands draw in a bigger-than-average crowd. Live jazz and traditional Scottish music are featured. The club is open Sunday through Thursday from 11am to 12:30am and Friday and Saturday from 11am to 1am. Live music is presented only on Tuesday from 9 to 11:15pm. A pint of ale runs £1.90 ($3.15).

PUBS & BARS
Black Bull. 12 Grassmarket. ☎ **0131/225-6636.**

Because it's located on a shop-lined street below the Royal Mile, the Black Bull is often overlooked by visitors. You can take a shortcut on foot from Edinburgh Castle by descending a steep flight of stone steps or window-shop along the streets. The pub is decorated like a scarlet version of a Victorian railway car, with an ascending series of platforms leading up to the carved bar. Of course, the head of a black bull

---

A Wee Dram

It requires a bit of an effort to reach it (take bus no. 10A, 16, or 17 from Princes Street to Leith), but for fans of malt whisky, the **Scotch Malt Whisky Society** has been called "The Top of the Whisky Pyramid" by distillery industry magazines in Britain. It's on the second floor of a 16th-century warehouse at 87 Giles St., Leith (☎ **0131/554-3451**), originally designed to store bordeaux and port wines from France and Portugal. Don't even think of ordering a fancy cocktail or mixed drink— you won't find anything other than single-malt whiskies, served neat, usually in a dram (unless you want yours watered down with branch water) and selected from a staggering choice of whiskies from more than 100 distilleries throughout Scotland.

Beware of the potency of these firewaters: Whereas most brands of conventionally distilled single-malts contain a mere 40% alcohol, the alcoholic content of the Scotch Malt Whisky Society's specially purchased stocks rarely dips below 51%, and usually hovers around a head-spinning 60%. Some brands taste gamey, some are peaty, some are fruity, and some are floral. Regardless of what you select, you'll find yourself elbow-to-elbow with fellow drinkers for whom single-malts are indeed the water of life. Treat the place as you would a chi-chi wine bar, but with a lot more wallop and authenticity. Soups and sandwiches are offered Monday through Saturday from noon to 2pm, and a restaurant (the Vintner's Room, which is not associated with the organization in any way, but which is separately recommended in "Dining," earlier in this chapter) is on the building's street level.

When is the place at its most rollicking and hearty? Thursday through Saturday after around 6pm. Mercifully, on those nights shutdown and meltdown is early enough (11pm) to allow everyone to totter off home before any real damage is done. It's open Monday through Wednesday from 10am to 5pm and Thursday through Saturday from 10am to 11pm.

---

is a focal point. The place jumps at night to the recorded music of whatever group is hot at the time. Open Monday through Wednesday from 11am to midnight, Thursday through Saturday from 11am to 1am, and Sunday from 12:30pm to 11pm. A popular menu features a hearty breakfast served all day for only £1.49 ($2.45), with mixed grills ranging from £1.99 to £2.99 ($3.30 to $4.95).

✪ **Café Royal Circle Bar.** 17 W. Register St. ☎ **0131/556-1884.**

Edinburgh's most famous pub is a long-enduring favorite. One part is now occupied by the Oyster Bar of the Café Royal, but life in the Circle Bar continues at its usual pace. The opulent trappings of the Victorian era are still to be seen. Go up to the serving counter, which stands like an island in a sea of drinkers, and place your order. Hours are 11am to 11pm on Monday through Wednesday, 11am to midnight on Thursday, 11am to 1am on Friday and Saturday, and 12:30pm to 11pm on Sunday.

✪ **Deacon Brodie's Tavern.** 435 Lawnmarket. ☎ **0131/225-6531.**

Established in 1806, this is the neighborhood pub along the Royal Mile. It perpetuates the memory of Deacon Brodie, good citizen by day, robber by night. The tavern and wine cellars contain a cocktail and lounge bar. It offers a traditional pub setting and lots of atmosphere, making it popular with visitors and locals alike. The tavern is open Sunday through Thursday from 10am to midnight, and Friday and Saturday from 10am to 1am. Light meals begin at £5 ($8.25).

Frazier's. 14 George St. ☎ 0131/624-8626.

This is a real ale bar located in the Dome entertainment complex (see above). One of Edinburgh's most popular watering holes, it features Deuchar's I.P.A., Courage Directors, Murray's Summer Ale, McEwen's 80 Shilling, Caledonian 70 Shilling and 80 Shilling, and an ever-changing guest tap. If you want a stronger drink, they also stock 75 malt whiskies ranging from £1.40 to £10 ($2.30 to $16.50) per shot. In the life of this edition, the bar will open the Cigar Cocktail Bar, hoping to capture the feel of a New York club, with an array of cigars and cocktails. It's open Monday through Saturday from noon to midnight and Sunday from noon to 6pm.

Guildford Arms. 1–5 W. Register St. ☎ 0131/556-4312.

Guildford Arms got a facelift back to the "mauve era" of the 1890s, although a pub has stood on this spot for 200 years. This Victorian Italianesque corner pub, still harboring its old-time memories, has seven arched windows with etched glass, plus an ornate ceiling. It's large, bustling, and at times a bit rough—but it's got plenty of character. Upstairs is a fish-and-chips emporium run by the same company, where a platter of greasy goodies from the sea begins at £4.50 ($7.45). Place your order at the upstairs bar. At festival time, folk is presented here nightly. It's open Monday through Wednesday from 11am to 11pm, Thursday through Saturday from 11am to midnight, and Sunday from 12:30am to 11pm.

Kenilworth. 152–154 Rose St. ☎ 0131/226-4385.

This intriguing bar was named after the novel by Sir Walter Scott. Originally built as a private home, it was sold to a brewery in 1904, when it was lavishly decorated and turned into a popular pub in the Edwardian style. In 1981, its owners initiated a piece-by-piece renovation of each detail of the elaborately crafted interior. The blue-and-white wall tiles, coupled with the rows of stained-glass windows, a massive wooden bar, and a coal-burning fireplace, make an alluring setting that attracts members of the performing arts. Basic malt whiskies start at £1.30 ($2.15) per shot. The bar is open Monday through Wednesday from 10am to 11pm, Thursday from 10am to midnight, and Friday and Saturday from 9am to 12:45am.

GAY BARS & CLUBS

C.C. Bloom's. 23–24 Greenside Place. ☎ 0131/556-4349.

This is one of the most popular gay stops in Edinburgh. The upstairs bar offers drinks and camaraderie from a mixed gay crowd. On Thursday and Sunday at 11pm there's karaoke. Sunday afternoons heat up with a male stripper. The downstairs club offers dancing to a wide range of music. But there's never a cover charge here. The bar is open Monday through Friday from 6pm to 3am, and Saturday and Sunday from 11pm to 3am. Next door is **Cafe Kudos,** 22 Greenside Place (☎ 0131/556-4349), which draws a mixed gay crowd daily from noon to 1am.

New Town Bar. 26B Dublin St. ☎ 0131/538-7775.

At the corner of Queen Street in the heart of Edinburgh's business district, this is a bar favored by the region's gay men. In the street-level pub, everyday chaps gather for a pint of lager (£1.95/$3.20) and a platter of bar grub (£2.50/$4.15). It's open daily from noon to 2am. For something a bit less conventional, and if it's late at night, head downstairs to the basement. Here the Cruise Bar emulates the gay sleaze pits of cities such as New York and Los Angeles, encouraging patrons to wear their own interpretations of combat gear, leather, or uniforms inspired by Tom of Finland. Depending on the crowd, the scene can be intense or amusing. It's open Wednesday through Sunday from 10pm to 2am.

Route 66. 6 Baxter's Place. ☎ **0131/556-5991.**

This bar also hosts a mixed crowd but attracts more women than do most gay bars in Edinburgh. It describes itself as a friendly and unpretentious "neighborhood bar" where you're likely to run into your favorite gay uncle or aunt and share a bit of family gossip, and then meet either the love of your life or a decent building contractor. Drinks are served Monday through Saturday from 3:30pm to 1am. It's mainly a place to drink, although there's an occasional drag night.

10 Side Trips from Edinburgh

LINLITHGOW

In this royal burgh, a county town in West Lothian, 18 miles west of Edinburgh, Mary Queen of Scots was born. The roofless Linlithgow Palace, site of her birth in 1542, can still be viewed here today, even if it's but a shell of its former self. Buses and trains arrive daily from Edinburgh. The ride takes only 20 to 25 minutes.

SEEING THE SIGHTS

✪ **Linlithgow Palace.** South shore of Linlithgow Loch, Linlithgow. ☎ **01506/842896.** Admission £2.50 ($4.15) adults, £1.60 ($2.65) seniors, £1 ($1.65) children. Mon–Sat 9:30am–6pm, Sun 10am–6pm.

Birthplace of Mary Queen of Scots, this was once a favorite residence of Scottish kings. The queen's suite was in the north quarter, but was rebuilt for the homecoming of James VI (James I of Great Britain) in 1620. In one of the many tragic events associated with the concept of Scottish sovereignty, the palace burned to the ground in 1746, along with many of the hopes and dreams of Scottish independence. The Great Hall is on the first floor, and a small display shows some of the more interesting architectural relics. The ruined palace is half a mile from Linlithgow Station.

St. Michael's Parish Church. Adjacent to Linlithgow Palace. ☎ **01506/842188.** Free admission. Daily 10am–4:30pm.

South of the palace stands the medieval kirk of St. Michael the Archangel, site of worship of many a Scottish monarch since its consecration in 1242. Despite being ravaged by the disciples of John Knox and transformed into a stable by Cromwell, it's one of Scotland's best examples of a parish church.

✪ **Hopetoun House.** Two miles from the Forth Road Bridge near South Queensferry, off A904. ☎ **0131/331-2451.** Admission £4.50 ($7.45) adults, £4 ($6.60) seniors, £2.50 ($4.15) children; family ticket (for up to 6) £14.50 ($23.90). Easter weekend and May–Sept, daily 10am–5:30pm. Closed Oct–Apr.

Set in the midst of beautifully landscaped grounds laid out along the lines of Versailles, Hopetoun House lies near the Forth Road Bridge at South Queensferry, 10 miles from Edinburgh. This is Scotland's greatest Adam mansion and a fine example of 18th-century architecture. It's the seat of the marquess of Linlithgow, whose grandfather and father were respectively the governor-general of Australia and the viceroy of India. You can wander through splendid reception rooms filled with 18th-century furniture, paintings, statuary, and other works of art. From a rooftop viewing platform you look out over a panoramic view of the Firth of Forth. Or you can take the nature trail, explore the deer parks, investigate the Stables Museum, or stroll through the formal gardens, all on the grounds. Near the Ballroom Suite, refreshments are available.

DINING

✪ **Champany Inn.** Champany Corner. Linlithgow, East Lothian E449 7LU. ☎ **01506/ 834532.** Reservations required. Main courses £14.50–£30 ($23.90–$49.50); fixed-price lunch £15.75 ($26). AE, DC, MC, V. Mon–Fri 12:30–2pm and 7–10pm. Closed Jan 1–2 and Dec 25. Take A904 2 miles northeast of Linlithgow to the junction with A803. SCOTTISH.

In this converted farmhouse, you'll find the best steaks in Britain. The owner, Clive Davidson, is an expert on beef, and he insists that his steaks be 1¼ inches thick, and his meat is hung for at least 4 weeks, which adds greatly to its flavor. He also prepares an assortment of oysters, salmon, and lobsters that are kept in a pool on the premises. Next door to the main dining room is a chophouse that has less expensive cuts. You can choose your own cut and watch it being grilled. There's also a raw bar. Meals in the chophouse begin at £7.50 ($12.40).

The inn recently opened 16 handsomely furnished bedrooms, each with TV, minibar, and phone, costing £135 ($222.75) for a double.

NORTH BERWICK

This royal burgh, created in the 14th century, was once an important Scottish port. In East Lothian, 24 miles east from Edinburgh, it is today a holiday resort popular with the Scots and an increasing number of foreigners. Visitors are drawn to its golf courses, beach sands, and harbor life on the Firth of Forth. You can climb the rocky shoreline or enjoy the heated outdoor swimming pool in July and August.

North Berwick lies on a direct rail line from Edinburgh (trip time: 30 min.). There is also bus service to North Berwick from Edinburgh, taking 1¼ hours.

SEEING THE SIGHTS

At the **Information Centre,** Quality Street (☎ **01620/892197**), you can pick up data on how to take boat trips to the offshore islands, including **Bass Rock,** a breeding ground inhabited by about 10,000 gannets. The volcanic island is 1 mile in circumference. It's possible to see the rock from the harbor. The viewing is even better at **Berwick Law,** a volcanic lookout point.

Some 2 miles east of North Berwick, and 25 miles east of Edinburgh on A198, stand the ruins of the 14th-century diked and rose-colored **Tantallon Castle** (☎ **01620/892727**). This was the ancient stronghold of the Douglases from its construction in the 14th century until its defeat by Cromwell's forces in 1650. Overlooking the Firth of Forth, the castle ruins still are formidable, with a square five-story central tower and a dovecote, plus the shell of its east tower, a D-shaped structure with a wall from the central tower. Tantallon Castle can be visited April to September, Monday through Saturday from 9:30am to 6:30pm and Sunday from 2 to 6:30pm; October to March, Monday through Wednesday and Saturday from 9:30am to 4pm, Thursday from 9:30am to 4:30pm, and Sunday from 2 to 4:30pm. Admission is £2.30 ($3.80) for adults, £1.50 ($2.45) for seniors, and £1 ($1.65) for children.

ACCOMMODATION & DINING

If you're a golfer, you may want to stay in this hotel, near the West Links Course. The location is only a 30-minute drive from Edinburgh Castle and makes an ideal base for golfing or touring.

The Marine. 18 Cromwell Rd., North Berwick, East Lothian EH39 4LZ. ☎ **800/225-5843** in the U.S., or 01620/892406. Fax 01620/894480. 83 rms, 5 suites. TV TEL. £85–£110 ($140.25– $181.50) double; from £140 ($231) suite. AE, DC, MC, V.

This is a fine, turreted Victorian Hotel, commanding panoramic views across the West Links Course, some of whose putting greens come close to the hotel's foundations. The Marine is a home away from home for Nicklaus, Trevino, Player, and most of the

U.S. Ryder Cup Team during the Open, and lies in an area with almost 20 golf courses nearby. Inside, there's the aura of an elegant country house. The hotel has recently undergone refurbishment, and all the bedrooms have private baths, color TVs, tea- and coffeemaking equipment, and trouser presses. The bar is lined with antique golfing photos. Additional facilities include saunas, squash, snooker, putting, tennis, gardens, children's playgrounds, and an outdoor heated pool (open May to September).

The cuisine is international, with many Scottish specialties. Dinners start at £19.95 ($32.90) for a table d'hôte. Even if you're not a resident of the hotel, the Marine serves the best food in town.

GULLANE

Lying 19 miles east of Edinburgh in East Lothian, Gullane, with a population of around 2,000 people, is really a pocket of posh. Not only does it have one of the great country hotels of Scotland but it's also home to a small restaurant that some food critics have suggested is "the best in Scotland."

ACCOMMODATION

✪ **Greywalls Hotel.** Muirfield, Duncur Rd., Gullane, East Lothian EH31 2EG. ☎ **01620/ 842241.** Fax 01620/842-241. 22 rms. TV TEL. £165–£190 ($272.25–$313.50) double. Rates include Scottish breakfast. AE, DC, MC, V. Closed Oct 15–Apr 15. Follow the signs from A198 about 5 miles from North Berwick.

This Edwardian country house was designed as a private home by the most renowned architect of his day, Sir Edwin Lutyens. It was visited from time to time by Edward VII, who admired the views across the Firth of Forth and south to the Lammermuir Hills. The gardens were laid out by Gertrude Jekyll, who often worked with architect Lutyens in supplying a complete Edwardian home package. Today Greywalls is the property of Giles and Ros Weaver, who have combined the atmosphere of a home with the amenities of a country-house hotel. In the paneled library guests relax on comfortable sofas before a blazing log fire (in cool weather). The garden room is done in bamboo furnishings. There's also a small bar. The bedrooms vary in size: Some smaller ones are simply decorated, and others, more spacious, are furnished with period pieces. Many of the clients here are gardening enthusiasts who come to pay homage to a quintessentially Edwardian combination of turn-of-the-century architecture with superb landscape design.

Dining/Entertainment: The food served in the elegant dining room reflects culinary expertise. Light French-style dishes are made almost as appealing to the eye as to the palate. Specialties include fresh seafood. Other tasty main courses might be venison, breast of pheasant, smoked duck, or local beef. A five-course table d'hôte dinner is served for £35 ($57.75). Men are required to wear jackets and ties in the dining room, which is open daily from 12:30 to 2pm and 7:30 to 9:30pm.

Services: 24-hour room service, laundry, baby-sitting.

Facilities: Hard tennis court, croquet lawn, 10 golf courses within 5 miles.

DINING

✪ **La Potinière.** Main St., Gullane. ☎ **01620/843214.** Reservations required. Fixed-price 4-course lunch £20 ($33); fixed-price 5-course dinner £30 ($49.50). No credit cards. Sun–Tues and Thurs at 1pm; dinner Fri–Sat at 8pm. Closed June 1–8 and Oct. CONTINENTAL/SCOTTISH.

La Potinière is a small and pretty restaurant beautifully run by David and Hilary Brown. The excellent food produced by Hilary, using local ingredients so far as possible, is complemented by a fine choice of wines from the cellar supervised by David. The first course is usually a light and subtly flavored soup, followed by a fish dish or by one of Hilary's creations. The main courses are all done with flair. Although main courses change daily, typical dishes we have enjoyed include red pepper and orange soup, crisp-skinned salmon with virgin olive oil, and breast of corn-fed chicken on a bed of savoy cabbage with bacon and garlic and a sweet-and-sour sauce. Cheese and dessert wind up the meal. A special dinner is served on Friday and Saturday only, starting promptly at 8pm; reservations for this five-course gourmet's delight should be made well in advance. No smoking is permitted in the dining room. Many guests come here from Greywalls (see above). From Greywalls, guests drive or walk a mile west heading toward the village of Gullane; the restaurant lies in the heart of Gullane on its Main Street.

DIRLETON

Another popular day trip from Edinburgh is to this little town that vies for the title of "prettiest village in Scotland." The town plan, drafted in the early 16th century, is essentially unchanged today. Dirleton has two greens shaped like triangles, with a pub opposite Dirleton Castle, placed at right angles to a group of cottages. Dirleton is a preservation village and as such is subject to careful control of any development. It's on the Edinburgh–North Berwick road (A198). North Berwick (see above) is 5 miles to the east and Edinburgh is 19 miles to the west.

SEEING THE SIGHTS

Dirleton Castle. Dirleton, East Lothian. ☎ **01620/850330.** Admission £2.30 ($3.80) adults, £1.50 ($2.45) seniors, £1 ($1.65) children. Apr–Sept, Mon–Sat 9:30am–6pm, Sun 10am–6pm; Oct–Mar, Mon–Sat 9:30am–4pm, Sun 2–4pm.

A rose-tinted 13th-century castle with surrounding gardens, once the seat of the wealthy Anglo-Norman de Vaux family, Dirleton Castle looks like a fairy-tale fortification, with its towers, arched entries, and an oak ramp similar to the drawbridge that used to protect it. The prison, bakehouse, and storehouses are carved from bedrock. Ruins of the Great Hall and kitchen can be seen, as well as what's left of the lord's chamber where the de Vaux family lived. You can view windows and window seats, a wall with a toilet and drains, and other household features. The 16th-century main gate has a hole through which boiling tar or water could be poured to discourage unwanted visitors.

The castle's country garden and a bowling green are still in use, with masses of flowering plants rioting in the gardens and bowlers sometimes seen on the green. A 17th-century dovecote with 1,100 nests stands at the east end of the garden. A small gate at the west end leads onto one of the village greens.

ACCOMMODATION & DINING

Open Arms. Dirleton, East Lothian EH39 5BG. ☎ **01620/850241.** Fax 01620/850570. 7 rms. TV TEL. £110–£120 ($181.50–$198) double. Rates include Scottish breakfast. MC, V. Free parking.

The Open Arms will receive you in keeping with the promise of its name. This old stone hostelry has been transformed into a handsome hotel and restaurant, serving the finest food in the area. Off A198 overlooking the castle ruins, the hotel is owned by Mr. and Mrs. Hill, who have built up a local reputation for serving Scottish dishes, using local produce, plus regional venison, beef, lamb, and freshly caught salmon. The whiskies used in the sauces are of the region too. The people who serve are informed and skillful. Dinners begin at £25 ($41.25). Lunch is served daily from 12:30 to 2:15pm and dinner nightly from 7 to 10pm.

The Open Arms will also receive you as an overnight guest. However, it's small, only seven bedrooms, each with private bath, color TV, phone, and—joy of joys— room service, available at no extra cost. Log fires crackle and blaze, and it must surely be a golfer's paradise, as it's surrounded by nine courses.

Glasgow 7

Glasgow is only 40 miles west of Edinburgh, but forms an amazing contrast. Scotland's largest city, its commercial capital, and Britain's third-largest city, it's home to half of Scotland's population. Glasgow has long been famous for shipbuilding, ironworks, and steelworks. It's the birthplace of the *Queen Mary,* the *Queen Elizabeth,* and other fabled liners that once crossed the Atlantic. But Glasgow is no longer the smoking industrial city, blighted by the Gorbals and some of the worst slums in Europe. Urban development and the decision to locate the Scottish Exhibition and Conference Center here have brought about a great change. Industrial grime is being sandblasted away, overcrowding in the city center has been reduced, and more open space and less traffic congestion mean cleaner air.

The Victorian splendor of the city has reemerged. John Betjeman and other critics have hailed Glasgow as "the greatest surviving example of a Victorian city." The planners of the 19th century thought on a grand scale when they designed the terraces and villas west and south of the center.

Glasgow's origins are very ancient, making Edinburgh, for all its wealth of history, seem comparatively young. The village that grew up beside a ford 20 miles from the mouth of the River Clyde as a medieval ecclesiastical center began its commercial prosperity in the 17th century. As it grew, the city engulfed the smaller medieval towns of Ardrie, Renfrew, Rutherglen, and Paisley.

Glasgow is part of Strathclyde, a powerful and populous district whose origins go back to the Middle Ages. The name is ancient—Irish chroniclers wrote of the kingdom of Stratha Cluatha some 1,500 years ago. Strathclyde was known to the Romans, who called its people Damnonii. The old capital, Dumbarton, on its high rock, provided a natural fortress in the days when local people had to defend themselves against enemy tribes.

The fortunes of Strathclyde changed dramatically in the 18th century when the Clyde estuary became the gateway to the New World. Glasgow merchants grew rich on tobacco and then on cotton. It was the fastest-growing region in Britain in the days of the Industrial Revolution, and Glasgow was known as "the Second City of the Empire." Until 1996 Strathclyde functioned as a governmental entity that included Glasgow, but it is now broken down into several new divisions: the City of Glasgow; Inverclyde, which includes the important industrial center of Greenock; and several others. Greenock in 1736 was the birthplace of James Watt, inventor of the steam engine.

Glasgow is a good center for exploring the heart of the Burns Country, Culzean Castle, and the resorts along the Ayrshire coast, an hour away by frequent train service (see "Side Trips from Glasgow," below). From Glasgow you can also tour Loch Lomond, Loch Katrine, and the Trossachs. On Glasgow's doorstep is the scenic estuary of the Firth of Clyde, down which you can cruise on a paddle-steamer. The Firth of Clyde, with its long sea lochs—**Gareloch, Loch Long, Loch Goil,** and **Holy Loch**—is one of the most scenic waterways in the world. This was once a holiday region, but Holy Loch now has its Polaris base, and British atomic subs are stationed in these waters.

Gourock, 3 miles west of Greenock, is a resort and yachting center. On the cliff side of Gourock is **"Granny Kempock,"** a 6-foot-high stone of gray schist that was probably significant in prehistoric times and in past centuries was used by fishers for rites to ensure fair weather. Couples planning marriage used to circle Granny to get her blessing and to ensure fertility in their marriage. From Gourock, car ferries take travelers to **Dunoon** on the Cowal Peninsula. You can also visit **Rothesay** and the **Isle of Bute,** where the Glaswegians themselves go for fun in the sun.

In what was once an industrial wasteland between Hamilton and Motherwell, the Strathclyde Regional Council has created the 1,600-acre **Strathclyde Regional Park,** with a 2-mile loch, the site of many water sports including competition sailing. There's also a bird sanctuary and a nature reserve, along with the Hamilton Mausoleum.

1 Orientation

ARRIVING

BY PLANE　The **Glasgow Airport** is at Abbotsinch (☎ **0141/887-1111**), 10 miles west of the city via the M8 motorway. You can use the regular Glasgow CityLink bus service to get to the city center. From bus stop no. 2, take bus no. 900 or 901 to reach the Buchanan Street Bus Station in the center of Glasgow. The ride takes about 20 minutes and costs £2 ($3.30). A taxi to the city center costs about £12 ($19.80). You can also go from the airport to Edinburgh by bus, the trip taking 1³/₄ hours and costing £6 ($9.90) per ticket.

British Airways runs almost hourly shuttle service from London's Heathrow Airport to Glasgow on Monday through Friday. The first flight departs London at 7:15am; the last one leaves at 8:15pm; service is reduced on weekends, depending on volume. For flight schedules and fares, call British Airways in London at ☎ **0181/897-4000.**

British Airways planes from Boston and New York now fly direct to Glasgow Airport (see "Getting There," in chapter 3).

BY TRAIN　Headquarters for British Rail is at the **Central Station** and **Queen Street Station.** For National Rail Inquiries, phone ☎ **0345/484950.** For sleeper reservations by credit or charge card, contact Virgin West Coast at ☎ **0345/991995.** The Queen Street Station serves the north and east of Scotland. Trains arrive from Edinburgh every 30 minutes during the day; a one-way ticket between the two cities costs £6.50 ($10.75). You'll also be able to travel to such Highland destinations as Inverness and Fort William from this station. Central Station serves southern Scotland, England, and Wales. Trains arrive from London's Euston and King's Cross Stations (call ☎ **0345/484950** in London for schedules) frequently throughout the day (trip time is approximately 5¹/₂ hours). The first train departs Euston at 6:25am

Ahead of His Time: Charles Rennie Mackintosh

Although a legendary figure today, and viewed as a "tragic genius," Charles Rennie Mackintosh (1868–1928) was largely forgotten in Scotland at the time of his death. He is a perfect example of the old saw, that the prophet is accorded little honor in his own country. An architect/designer/decorator, his approach, poised between art nouveau and Bauhaus, influenced his colleagues from Frank Lloyd Wright in Chicago to Josef Hoffmann in Vienna. His ideas, however, were too revolutionary in Glasgow's Victorian age with its pompous eclecticism and overstuffed and overupholstered fussiness.

Born on June 7, 1868, the son of a Scottish police superintendent, he began his career as a draftsman for the architectural firm of Honeyman & Keppie in 1889. In the 1880s Glasgow was viewed as the British Empire's "second city," and the city exploded—hundreds of new homes, public buildings, railway stations, and factories were needed. The situation would seem to offer the perfect opportunity for a rising young architect. In 1896 his design for a new headquarters of the Glasgow School of Art won a prestigious competition. Ironically, he won because his design was the cheapest to build. He had drunk deeply from the creative cauldron of artistic development that swept Europe during the final days of the belle époque, and his theories insisted that "decoration should not be constructed; but rather, construction should be decorated." The forms of nature, especially the forms of plants, were used in his interiors, which had a simplicity and harmony that was utterly new. Instant applause came from the Vienna secessionists and the arts-and-crafts movement in such faraway places as England and America, but Glasgow was not so pleased. Today Mackintosh's building is recognized as one of the city's greatest architectural design treasures.

Unfortunately, Mackintosh was neither a tactful nor diplomatic person, and he developed a reputation as a meticulous planner of rigid ideas who refused to compromise in any way with builders or their crews. Later failures to win either commissions or architectural awards led to local ridicule of his avant-garde ideas, a break with his partners, and an eventual move out of Glasgow. He declared Glasgow "a Philistine city." Recent research has shown that he was actually exiled from his native Scotland in 1914 because of his Austrian and German artistic connections. In London he continued to have difficulties, and his career there never got off the ground.

By 1923 Mackintosh, with his wife, English architect Margaret MacDonald, gave up the struggle and moved to the south of France. There he devoted himself to watercolor paintings of botanical specimens and landscapes. They returned to London in 1927, where the architect died a year later.

Most of the acclaim that made Mackintosh the most famous designer ever to emerge from Scotland came from Europe, England, and the United States. In 1902 Hermann Muthesius, a leading German architect and critic of his day, wrote, "In any enumeration of the creative geniuses of modern architecture, Charles Rennie Mackintosh must be counted among the first."

Vienna may not have appreciated Mozart in his day, but it does now. So does Glasgow belatedly revere Mackintosh. Mackintosh boosterism reigns supreme, and his designs are a commodity hawked right along with the tartans.

and the last train runs out of Euston at 11:45pm. Try to avoid Sunday travel, however; frequency of trains is considerably reduced and the trip takes 7 hours or longer because there are more stopovers en route.

BY BUS   The **Buchanan Street Bus Station** is 2 blocks north of Queen Street Station on North Hanover Street (☎ **0141/332-7133**). National Express runs daily coaches from London's Victoria Coach Station to Buchanan frequently throughout the day. Buses from London take $7^1/_2$ to $8^1/_2$ hours to reach Glasgow, depending on the number of stops en route. Scottish CityLink also has frequent bus service to and from Edinburgh, a one-way ticket costing only £4.50 ($7.45). Contact National Express Inquiries at ☎ **0990/808080** for more information.

BY CAR   From England in the south, Glasgow is reached by M74, a continuation of M8 that goes right into the city, making an S-curve. Call your hotel and find out what exit you should take. The M8, another express motorway, links Glasgow and Edinburgh.

Other major routes into the city are A77 northeast from Prestwick and Ayr, and A8 from the west (this becomes M8 around the port of Glasgow). Highway A82 comes in from the northwest (the Highlands) on the north bank of the Clyde, and A80 also goes into the city (this route is the southwestern section of M80 and M9 from Stirling).

Glasgow, as mentioned, lies 40 miles west of Edinburgh, 221 miles north of Manchester, and 388 miles north of London.

VISITOR INFORMATION

The **Greater Glasgow and Clyde Valley Tourist Board,** 11 George Square (☎ 0141/204-4400), is the most helpful office in the country. From October through May it is open Monday through Saturday from 9am to 6pm; June, Monday through Saturday from 9am to 7pm and Sunday from 10am to 6pm; July and August, Monday through Saturday from 9am to 8pm, Sunday from 10am to 6pm; September, Monday through Saturday from 9am to 7pm and Sunday from 10am to 6pm.

CITY LAYOUT

Monumental Glasgow—that is, the "Victorian City" and "Merchant City," along with the Central Station—lies on the north bank of the **River Clyde,** which runs through the metropolis. The ancient center of Glasgow has as its core the great St. Kentigern's Cathedral, a perfect example of pre-Reformation gothic architecture that, in part, dates back to the 12th century. Behind it lies the Necropolis, burial ground of many Victorians. Across the square is Provand's Lordship, the oldest house in the city built in 1471. Down **High Street** can be found the Tolbooth Steeple (1626) at Glasgow Cross, while nearer the River Clyde is **Glasgow Green,** Britain's first public park (1662).

From Ingram Street, South Frederick Street will take you to **George Square,** with its many statues, including one dedicated to Sir Walter Scott. This is the center of modern Glasgow.

Merchant City, a compact area of imposing buildings, is the location of the National Trust for Scotland's shop and visitor center at Hutcheson's Hall. The broad pedestrian thoroughfares of Buchanan Street, Argyle Street, and Sauchiehall Street are the heart of the shopping district.

Glasgow's **West End** is just a short taxi journey from the city center, easily accessible from any part of the city and close to the M8 motorway (inner ring road) and the Clydeside Expressway. An extensive network of local bus routes serves the West End. The Glasgow Underground operates a circular service; by boarding at any

Greater Glasgow

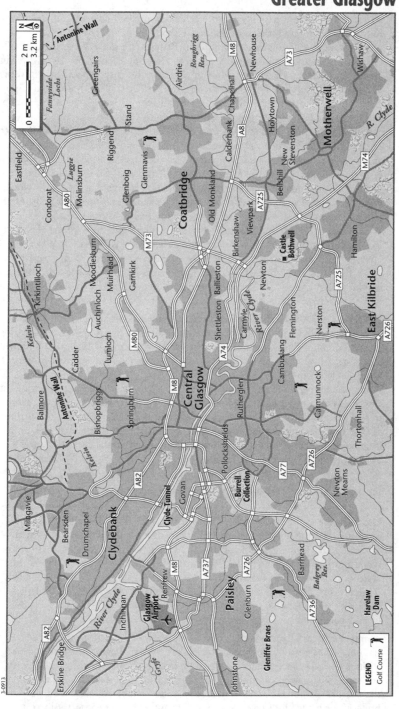

station on the system passengers can reach the four stations serving the district—Kelvinbridge, Hillhead (the most central), Kelvin Hall, and Partick.

The West End is the finest example in Britain of a great Victorian city. The terraces of the Park Conservation Area rise to afford excellent views. Across Kelvingrove Park is the Art Gallery and Museum. Nearby, the tower of Glasgow University dominates Gilmorehill. Beyond is the Hunterian Art Gallery, home to a famous collection of Whistlers. Just a few strides away is Byres Road, a street of bars, shops, and restaurants. To the north is the Botanic Gardens.

A little more than 3 miles southwest of the city center lies the **Pollok Country Park** and Pollok Estate. An extensive network of bus routes passes close by the park area, which is also served by two suburban rail stations. An electric bus service is in operation from the Country Park gates on Pollokshaws Road to Pollok House and the Burrell Collection Gallery. The Burrell Collection is housed in the heavily wooded Pollok Country Park, Scotland's top tourist attraction and the focal point of any visit to the South Side. Nearby is the 18th-century Pollok House.

Extensive parklands and greenery characterize the southern environs of the city. In addition to the Pollok Country Park and Estate, there is Haggs Castle Golf Club, home of the Glasgow Open, and **Bellahouston Park,** scene of the historic papal visit in 1983. En route to the Burrell Collection, you cross by the 148-acre **Queens Park,** honoring Mary Queen of Scots, where panoramic views of the city are possible from the hilltop. Near **Maxwell Park** is the Haggs Castle Museum in a 400-year-old building.

FINDING AN ADDRESS   Street numbering is often confusing. Glasgow was built in various sections and districts over the years, and massive sections have been torn down—some for slum clearance, others to make way for new highways. Following a consistent street plan can be tough, as squares or terraces can suddenly interrupt a route you're tracing.

House numbers can run in odds or evens, clockwise or counterclockwise, and sometimes Glaswegians don't even use numbers at all. Therefore don't be surprised to see "Blackfriars Street" given as an address without a number. Get a detailed map of Glasgow before setting out. Always find the nearest cross street, then look for your location from there. If it's a hotel or restaurant, the sign for the establishment is likely to be more prominent than the number anyway.

NEIGHBORHOODS IN BRIEF

Old Glasgow   This is where St. Mungo arrived in 543 and built his little church in what is now the northeastern part of the city. At the top of High Street stands St. Kentigern's Cathedral. One of Britain's largest Victorian cemeteries is in this section; after leaving the cathedral, turn left and then left once more. The Necropolis is entered by crossing over the Bridge of Sighs. Old Glasgow's major terminus is High Street Station near the former site of the University of Glasgow. Its largest "green lung" is Glasgow Green, opening onto the River Clyde, a public park since 1662.

Along the River Clyde   Glasgow is no longer as dependent on the Clyde as it was once when it was said: "The Clyde made Glasgow; Glasgow made the Clyde." Visitors take the Clyde Walkway stretching from King Albert Bridge, at the western end of Glasgow Green, for 2 miles downstream to Stobcross, now the site of the Scottish Exhibition and Conference Centre. The river is crossed by several bridges, one named for Queen Victoria and another for her consort, Albert.

The Merchant City   Leaving High Street, Glasgow spread west in the 18th century, largely because of profits made from sugar, cotton, and tobacco in trade with the Americas. This area extends from Trongate and Argyle Street in the south to George Street in the north. Its major terminus is Queen Street Station and its major shopping venue is Argyle Arcade. It's also the site of City Hall and Strathclyde University.

Glasgow Center   Continuing its western progression, the city center of Glasgow is now dominated by the Central Station on Hope Street. This is the major shopping district of Glasgow, including such venues as the Princes Square Shopping Mall. The Stock Exchange is also in this section, as is the Anderston Bus Station (near the Central Station).

West End   Lying beyond Charing Cross in the west end is the University of Glasgow and several of the city's major galleries and museums, some of which are in Kelvingrove Park.

2 Getting Around

BY PUBLIC TRANSPORTATION

BY BUS   Glasgow is serviced by two principal bus companies, the Kelvin Central (with blue-and-yellow buses) and the Strathclyde Transport (in stark orange). Some of Kelvin Central's buses are of the old London variety—painted red. Service is frequent throughout the day, but after 11pm night service is greatly curtailed. The major bus station is the **Buchanan Street Bus Station,** North Hanover Street (call ☎ **0141/226-4826** for schedule information), 2 blocks north of Queen Station. Fares are 65p ($1.05), but you must have the exact change.

BY UNDERGROUND   Called "Clockwork Orange" by Glaswegians, a 15-stop subway services the city. The nickname comes from the vivid orange of its trains. Most Underground trains operate from these stops every 5 minutes, with longer intervals between trains on Sunday and at night. Service is Monday through Saturday from 6:30am to 10pm and Sunday from 11am to 6pm. The fare is 65p ($1.05). However, you can go to the **Travel Centre** at St. Enoch Square (☎ **0141/226-4826**), 2 blocks from the Central Station, any time Monday through Saturday from 6:30am to 10:30pm. Here you can purchase an **Underground pass,** valid for unlimited travel on the system for 1 day for £2 ($3.30); a weekly pass sells for £5.40 ($8.90).

BY TAXI

Taxis are the same excellent ones found in Edinburgh or London. They can be hailed on the street, or for service, phone **TOA Taxis** (☎ **0141/332-7070**). Fares are displayed on a meter next to the driver. When a taxi is available on the street, a TAXI sign on the roof is lit a bright yellow. Most taxi trips within the city cost £2.50 to £3.50 ($4.15 to $5.75), with an extra 10p (15¢) assessed for each additional passenger. A 50p (85¢) surcharge is imposed from midnight to 6am. Tip at least 10% of the fare shown on the meter.

BY CAR

Driving around Glasgow is a tricky business, even for native motorists. It's a warren of one-way streets, and parking spots are at a premium. You're better off with public transportation.

AUTO CLUBS   Call the **Automobile Association** (☎ **0141/848-8782** or 0141/ 848-8622), or the **Royal Automobile Club** (☎ **0141/248-4444**) for information about RAC services within Glasgow.

CAR RENTALS   It's best to arrange a car rental before you leave home (see "Getting There" in chapter 3). However, if you want to rent a car locally, most companies will accept your American or Canadian driver's license if you're over 21 and have held the permit for more than a year. **Avis Rent-a-Car** is at 161 North St. (☎ **0141/ 221-2827**), **Budget Rent-a-Car** is at 101 Waterloo St. (☎ **0141/226-4141**), and **Europcar** is at 38 Anderson Quay (☎ **0141/423-5661**). Local rates at Avis begin at £37 ($61.05) a day, at Budget at £49 ($80.85) a day, and at Europcar at £35 ($57.75) a day.

PARKING   It's expensive and difficult to find. Metered parking is available, but you'll need the right change—20p (35¢) coins, which entitles you to only 12 minutes of parking. You must also watch out for zealous traffic wardens who issue tickets. Some zones are marked PERMIT HOLDERS ONLY—your vehicle will be towed if you have no permit. A yellow line along the curb indicates "No Parking."

Multistory car parks (parking lots), open 24 hours a day, are found at Anderston Cross and Cambridge, George, Mitchell, Oswald, and Waterloo streets.

BY BICYCLE

Bicycling is quite possible in much of Glasgow, particularly the flatter areas of the city. You can also use a bike for exploring the surrounding countryside. For what the Scots call "cycle hire," go to the **Bicycle Chain,** with two branches on the periphery of Glasgow. At the center at 1417 Dumbarton Rd., Scottstoun (☎ **0141/ 958-1055**), cycles and mountain bikes are rented and tour suggestions are freely shared. Charges begin at £10 ($16.50) per day and go up, with a deposit usually beginning at £50 ($82.50).

ON FOOT

This is the best way to explore Glasgow. You can easily get around to the major attractions in the center by foot. The center of Glasgow is laid out on a grid system, which makes map reading relatively easy. However, many of the major attractions, such as the Burrell Collection, are in the environs, and for those you'll need to rely on public transportation. Remember when you cross streets that cars drive on the left.

FAST FACTS: Glasgow

American Express   The office in Glasgow is at 115 Hope St. (☎ **0141/ 226-3077**), open Monday through Friday from 8:30am to 5:30pm and Saturday from 9am to noon.

Baby-sitters   Make arrangements through your hotel as far in advance as possible.

Business Hours   Most **offices** are open Monday through Friday from 9am to either 5 or 5:30pm. Most **banks** are open Monday through Wednesday and Friday from 9:30am to 4:45pm and Thursday from 9:30am to 5:30pm. **Shops** are generally open Monday through Saturday from 10am to either 5:30 or 6pm. Some stores, usually smaller ones, close for lunch from 1 to 2pm. On Thursday, stores remain open until 7pm.

Crime   See "Safety," below.

Currency Exchange   The tourist office (see above) will exchange most major foreign currencies, as will the American Express office (see above). City-center banks operate *bureau de change,* and nearly all banks will cash traveler's checks if you have the proper identification. Thomas Cook at the Glasgow Airport (☎ **0141/ 840-2299**) operates a bureau de change service daily from 5am to 11pm in summer; off-season, Monday through Saturday from 8am to 8pm and Sunday from 8am to 6pm. It also operates a larger branch at 15 Gordon St. (☎ **0141/221-6614**), open Monday through Friday from 9am to 5:30pm.

Dentist   Overseas visitors who develop emergency dental problems can go to the Accident and Emergency Department of Glasgow Dental Hospital & School NHS Trust, 378 Sauchiehall St. (☎ **0141/211-9600**). Its hours are Monday through Friday from 9:15am to 3:15pm and Sunday and public holidays from 10:30am to noon.

Doctor   The major hospital is the Royal Infirmary, 82–84 Castle St. (☎ **0141/ 211-4000**).

Drugstores   The best is Boots, 200 Sauchiehall St. (☎ **0141/332-1925**), open Monday through Wednesday from 8:30am to 6pm, Thursday from 8:30am to 7pm, and Friday and Saturday from 8:30am to 6pm.

Embassies & Consulates   See "Fast Facts: Scotland," in chapter 3.

Emergencies   Call ☎ **999** in an emergency to summon the police, an ambulance, or firefighters.

Eyeglasses   Dolland & Aitchison, originally established in 1837, can usually replace contact lenses or broken eyeglasses in about an hour. There's a branch at 7 Union St. (☎ **0141/204-4394**), open Monday through Saturday from 9am to 5:30pm. There's also a resident optometrist at the 200 Sauchiehall St. branch of Boots Chemists (☎ **0141/332-1925**).

Hairdressers/Barbers   The best place to go in all of Glasgow is Taylor Ferguson, 106 Bath St. (☎ **0141/332-0397**), award-winning stylists. It's open Monday through Wednesday from 9am to 6pm, Thursday and Friday from 9am to 7:15pm, and Saturday from 9am to 5pm. Always call for an appointment.

Hospitals   See "Doctor," above.

Hotlines   The police emergency number, ☎ **999,** is the major "hotline" in Glasgow. Women in crisis may want to call Women's Aid (☎ **0141/553-2022**). Gay men can call the Gay Switchboard (☎ **0141/221-8372**) daily from 7 to 10pm, and there's also a Lesbian Line (☎ **0141/552-3355**), open Monday only from 7 to 10pm. Call the Rape Crisis Centre at ☎ **0141/331-1990.**

Laundry/Dry Cleaning   Try the Park Laundrette at 14 Park Rd. (☎ **0141/ 337-1285**), open Monday through Friday from 8:30am to 7:30pm and Saturday and Sunday from 9am to 6:30pm.

Library   The Mitchell Library in Glasgow—the city's largest and best stocked—is on North Street at Kent Road (☎ **0141/287-2999**). One of the largest libraries in Europe, it's a massive 19th-century pile dedicated to the academic pursuit of all kinds of research. Newspapers and books, as well as miles of microfilm, are available. It's open Monday through Thursday from 9am to 8pm and Friday and Saturday from 9am to 5pm.

Lost Property   The Lost Property Department is at 173 Pitt St. (☎ **0141/ 204-2626**).

Luggage Storage/Lockers   There are two Left Luggage Offices in Glasgow, including the main one at the Central Station (☎ 0141/332-9811), open Monday through Friday from 6:30am to 11pm and Saturday and Sunday from 7:30am to 11pm. The other office is at the Queen Street Station (same phone), open Monday through Saturday from 7am to 10pm and Sunday from 10am to 6pm.

Newspapers/Magazines   Published since 1783, the *Glasgow Herald* is the major newspaper with national, international, and financial news, sports, and cultural listings. *Scottish Field* and *Scots Magazine* are monthly publications, dealing with many topics of interest to visitors to Scotland.

Photographic Needs   Boots Chemists are at 200 Sauchiehall St. (☎0141/332-1925) or at Saint Enoch Centre, Argyle Street at St. Enoch Square (☎ 0141/248-7387).

Police   In an emergency, call ☎ 999. For other inquiries, contact police headquarters at ☎ 0141/532-2000.

Post Office   The main branch is at 47 St. Vincent's St. (☎ 0141/204-3689). If you want your mail sent general delivery, mark it "Poste Restante" and send it to this branch, using the postal code of G2 1AA. It's open Monday through Friday from 8:30am to 5:45pm and Saturday from 9am to 5pm.

Radio   BBC Radio Scotland (FM 92.5–94.6, AM/MW 810kHz/370m) is a national network featuring both the latest news and lots of talk shows. The local station, emphasizing local events, is Radio Clyde (FM 102.5, AM/MW 1152kHz/261m).

Religious Services   Most churches conduct services at 11am on Sunday. Church of Scotland services are at Glasgow Cathedral, Castle Street (☎0141/552-6891), and St. George's Tron Church, 165 Buchanan St. (☎ 0141/221-2141), which also has a 7pm service. Other services are at St. Andrews Roman Catholic Cathedral, 90 Dunlop St. (☎ 0141/221-3096); Patrick Methodist Church, 524 Dumbarton Rd. (☎ 0141/339-1499); and Adelaides Place Baptist Church, 209 Bath St. (☎ 0141/248-4970). Jewish services on Saturday are at New Synagogue, Ayr Road, Newton Mearns (☎ 0141/639-1838).

Rest Rooms   These are found at rail stations, bus stations, air terminals, restaurants, hotels, pubs, and department stores. Glasgow also has a system of public toilets, often marked WC. Don't hesitate to use them, but they are likely to be closed late in the evening.

Safety   Glasgow is the most dangerous city in Scotland, but relatively safe when compared to cities of its size in the United States. Muggings do occur, and often they are related to Glasgow's rather large drug problem. The famed "razor gangs" of Calton, Bridgeton, and the Gorbals are no longer around to earn the city a reputation for violence, but you still should keep alert.

Television   BBC Scotland and Scottish Television (STV) are the two major stations based at Glasgow. Throughout the day they offer programs of Scottish news and features, although most programs are the same as those carried over the national BBC networks.

Transit Information   For 24-hour passenger inquiries regarding rail travel in Scotland, call ☎ 0345/484950. The Buchanan Street Bus Station is reached at ☎ 0141/332-7133. For flight schedules at Glasgow Airport in Abbotsinch, call ☎ 0141/887-1111, or ☎ 0345/222111, the number for British Airways in London.

Weather   Call the Glasgow Weather Centre at ☎ 01891/500421.

3 Accommodations

Because of Glasgow's growing popularity as a tourist destination, it often experiences a shortage of beds in summer, especially in late July and August. Therefore it's best to make reservations for that time at least 2 months in advance. Glasgow's hotel rates are generally higher than those in Edinburgh. See individual hotel tariffs for discount weekend bargains.

CENTRAL GLASGOW

VERY EXPENSIVE

Glasgow Hilton International. 1 William St., Glasgow G3 8HT. ☎ **800/445-8667** in the U.S. and Canada, or 0141/204-5555. Fax 0141/204-5004. 315 rms, 4 suites. A/C MINIBAR TV TEL. £163–£196 ($268.95–$323.40) double; from £295 ($486.75) suite. Weekend discounts available, depending on bookings. AE, DC, MC, V. Free parking. Bus: 62.

Opened late in 1992, this is the only five-star hotel in Glasgow. It's housed in the tallest building (20 floors) in all of Scotland. It rises in dignified modernity in the heart of the West End's business district, near the northern end of Argyll Street and near exit 18 (Charing Cross) of the M8 motorway. The bedrooms, plush and conservative, are popular both with upscale vacationers and business travelers, and offer fine views over the city as far as the legendary dockyards of the Clyde. The three uppermost are the executive floors, which have a complimentary bar and the enhanced facilities of a semiprivate club room. Throughout the hotel, the uniformed staff, youthful and well trained, are alert and helpful.

Dining/Entertainment: The hotel's most upscale restaurant, Cameron's, is separately recommended (see "Dining," later in this chapter). Almost as appealing is Minskey's, inspired by a New York deli, offering all-day dining every day of the week. No one ever goes thirsty at the Hilton: Two bars pour two-fisted libations. The Scotch Bar has more than 200 kinds of single-malts and blends. Raffles, named for the legendary hotel in Singapore, celebrates the role of Scotland during the building of the British Empire and serves the best gin martini in town.

Services: 24-hour room service, laundry, baby-sitting, a "know-everything" concierge.

Facilities: The Leisure Club, one of the best-equipped health clubs in Glasgow, with an indoor swimming pool, Jacuzzis, and saunas. There are also two gift shops, and a hairdresser for men and women.

EXPENSIVE

Copthorne Hotel. George Square, Glasgow GD2 1DS. ☎ **0141/332-6711.** Fax 0141/332-4264. 136 rms, 5 suites. TV TEL. Mon–Thurs, £118 ($194.70) double; £145 ($239.25) suite. Fri–Sun, £80 ($132) double; £95 ($156.75) suite. Rates include breakfast Fri–Sun. AE, DC, MC, V. Parking £6 ($9.90). Underground: Buchanan St.

Copthorne Hotel is a landmark hostelry near the Queen Street Station, where trains depart for the north of Scotland. A five-story hotel, it dates from 1810, when it was the North British Hotel. A new extension was added in 1974. It's down on the totem pole from the Hilton and the Marriott. When the high-ceilinged public rooms of the hotel were renovated, the designers searched out antiques and glistening marble panels. Each of the bedrooms offers in-house movies, plush carpeting, and an upgraded decor. The worst rooms, called "classics," are in the rear with no views. "Connoisseurs" are larger-size executive rooms. The best rooms, called "Antique," are at the front of the building facing St. George Square, and have four-poster or elaborate sleigh beds.

Glasgow Accommodations

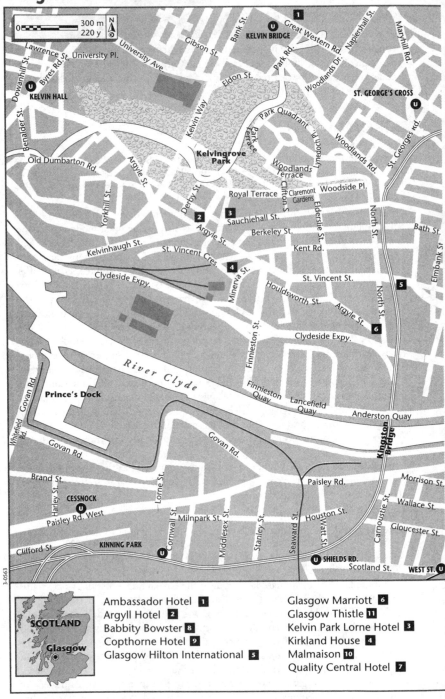

Ambassador Hotel **1**	Glasgow Marriott **6**
Argyll Hotel **2**	Glasgow Thistle **11**
Babbity Bowster **8**	Kelvin Park Lorne Hotel **3**
Copthorne Hotel **9**	Kirkland House **4**
Glasgow Hilton International **5**	Malmaison **10**
	Quality Central Hotel **7**

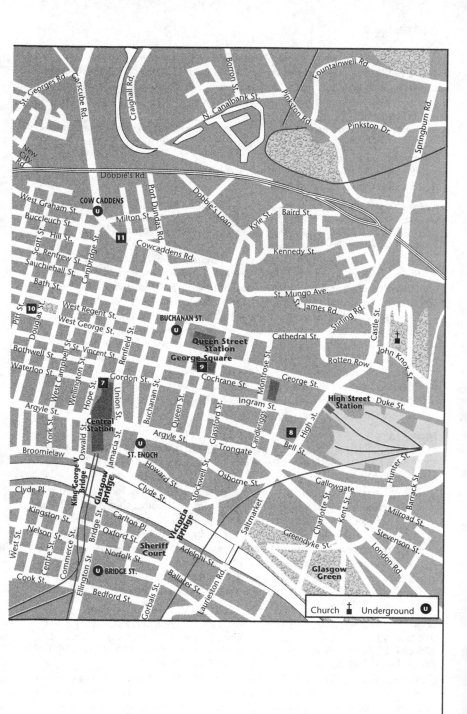

The hotel's role in history was played when Winston Churchill met in Room 21 with FDR's envoy, Harry Hopkins, in 1941, a pivotal meeting that is credited with securing Hopkins's support for the Lend-Lease Bill, a commitment that eventually helped usher the United States into active participation in the European theater of World War II.

Dining/Entertainment: The more formal dining room is called Windows on the Square, whereas La Mirage Café and Bar is one of the most alluring spots in Glasgow for a drink or a light meal.

Services: 24-hour room service, laundry/valet, baby-sitting.

Facilities: Business center; gym nearby.

Glasgow Marriott. 500 Argyle St., Glasgow G3 8RR. ☎ **800/228-9290** in the U.S. and Canada, or 0141/226-5577. Fax 0141/221-7676. 298 rms, 6 suites. TV TEL. £85–£110 ($140.25–$181.50) single or double; £150 ($247.50) suite. AE, DC, MC, V. Free parking. Underground: St. Enoch.

A 13-story building, originally a Holiday Inn, this hotel challenges the Glasgow Hilton as the top commercial choice in town. Although we prefer the Hilton, the Marriott's soaring profile at the Anderston exit of the M8 adds a vivid accent to the Glasgow City skyline. Its bedrooms have all modern amenities and free in-house movies. After work, local residents unwind in the popular bars, where open fireplaces compete with a garden of potted plants for visual supremacy.

Dining/Entertainment: Two restaurants offer you a wide choice of dining to suit any occasion. These include the Café Rendezvous, serving international and British food; and the Terrace, with informal à la carte service.

Services: 24-hour room service, laundry service, baby-sitting, courtesy coach.

Facilities: Squash courts, spacious well-equipped gym, health and beauty salon, hairdresser, whirlpool, sauna, large indoor pool.

MODERATE

✪ Malmaison. 278 W. George St., Glasgow G2 4LL. ☎ **0141/221-6400.** Fax 0141/572-1002. 65 rms, 8 suites. MINIBAR TV TEL. £90 ($148.50) double; £120–£165 ($198–$272.25) suite. AE, DC, MC, V. Bus 11.

One of Glasgow's most unusual hotels opened in 1994 in a historically important building that was built in the late 1700s as a Greek Orthodox church. In 1997, an annex with additional bedrooms was added, designed to preserve the architectural character of the church's exterior. Inside, few of the original details remain. This hotel prides itself on relatively reasonable room rates, thanks to reduced services and amenities. Bedrooms are smallish, but comfortable and clean, with the minimalist postmodern decors you might expect in a cutting-edge hotel in London. There's a small gymnasium on the premises, as well as a brasserie and cafe, both separately recommended below.

Quality Central Hotel. 99 Gordon St., Glasgow G1 3SF. ☎ **0141/221-9680.** Fax 0141/226-3948. 221 rms, 1 suite. TV TEL. Mon–Thurs, £80–£96 ($132–$158.40) double. Fri–Sun, £76–£80 ($125–$132) double. Suite £100 ($165). Rates include Scottish breakfast Fri–Sun. AE, DC, MC, V. Parking £7.75 ($12.80). Underground: Central Station.

When it officially opened in 1883, the Central Hotel was the grandest Glasgow had seen. Near the rail station, it was the landmark of the city's most famous street. Now revamped and restored to at least a glimmer of its former glory, it offers standardized rooms at affordable prices. Today the place may be too old-fashioned and creaky for some tastes, but traditionalists like it. The guest rooms, with an uninspired decor, are priced according to size and plumbing.

The massive baronial wooden staircase leading from the lobby to the upper floors was painstakingly stripped and refinished as part of the continuing restoration of this historic building. Sandblasting the facade revealed elaborate Victorian cornices and pilasters. The hotel's finest hour might have been the transmission, shortly after World War II, of the first TV broadcast on a private line extending from London to a bedroom on the fourth floor.

Dining/Entertainment: The bar with its old panels has a good selection of Highland malts, and the Entresol Restaurant serves freshly prepared Scottish food.

Facilities: Leisure center with swimming pool, Jacuzzi, spa, sauna, and two gyms.

INEXPENSIVE

Babbity Bowster. 16–18 Blackfriars St., Glasgow G1 1PE. ☎ **0141/552-5055.** Fax 0141/552-7774. 6 rms. £65 ($107.25) double. Rates include Scottish breakfast. AE, MC, V. Free parking. Underground: Buchanan St.

In the heart of Glasgow in an area known as Merchant City, this small but delightful three-story hotel doubles as an art gallery. Named for an ancient Scottish fertility dance, the hotel is in a Robert Adam building. The work of Glaswegian artists is displayed in the upstairs restaurant (most are for sale). The restaurant has a reputation for good food, and attracts students and faculty from Strathclyde University up the road. The menu changes daily. Traditional Scottish ales, Murphy's stout from Cork, and whisky are served, and musical events are also presented in the cafe-bar on some Sunday evenings. In summer there's an outdoor barbecue area.

Kirkland House. 42 St. Vincent Crescent, Glasgow G3 8NG. ☎ and fax **0141/248-3458.** 5 rms. TV. £60 ($99) double. No credit cards. Free parking. Underground: Exhibition Centre.

Situated on a quiet street, the two-story hotel offers pleasant rooms, each with hot- and cold-water basin and tea/coffeemaker. This hotel is about a 10-minute walk from the art museum, university, and Scottish Exhibition Centre. Kirkland is an early Victorian crescent house from 1832 and is maintained to a high standard. A mixture of antiques and reproductions is used in the bedrooms. The hotel is centrally heated, and you get a warm welcome from owners Carole and Ewing Divers. Ewing is a keen admirer of American swing band music and has a collection of 78-rpm gramophone records, old photographs, and pictures on display. Guests are welcome to listen to recordings of Harry James, Benny Goodman, and many others of the Great Swing Era. A health club is across the road.

THE WEST END
VERY EXPENSIVE

✪ **Devonshire Hotel.** 5 Devonshire Gardens, Glasgow G12 0UX. ☎ **0141/339-7878.** Fax 0141/339-3980. 12 rms, 2 suites. TV TEL. £150 ($247.50) double; £175 ($288.75) suite. Children 9 and under stay free in parents' room. AE, DC, MC, V. Underground: Hillhead.

Opened in 1989, this is one of the best-recommended and most charming small hotels in Glasgow. An imposing Victorian terrace house behind a blond sandstone facade, it was originally built in the late 1800s. Its successful mingling of perfect manners with a laissez-faire attitude attracted Michael Jackson, Whitney Houston, and Canadian rock 'n' roll star Bryan Adams. Rumors have been heard about the presence on the top floor of a benign ghost, although that doesn't bother the cheerfully efficient Scottish staff. Bedrooms usually have antique furnishings and carefully restored detailing. A restaurant on the premises (advance reservations recommended) serves lunches in a setting similar to an upscale pub, and dinners are formal sit-down affairs with lots of conservative Scottish panache. Lunch platters cost about £14 ($23.10); dinner runs to around £30 ($49.50).

🙂 Family-Friendly Hotels

Glasgow Thistle   In the heart of the city at 36 Cambridge St., Glasgow G2 3HN
(☎ **0141/332-3311;** fax 0141/332-4050), this nine-story hotel offers roomy bedrooms suitable for tucking in children. There are 220 rooms and 80 doubles, with
both doubles and suites beginning at £100 ($165). Kids like the self-service carvery-
style lunch, one of the best dining values in Glasgow, at £15 ($24.75) per person.

Glasgow Marriott *(see p. 194)*   Large and bustling in the city center, this hotel
has a children's playroom, gym, and a coffee shop that serves meals kids like from
11am to 10:30pm for around £5–£7 ($8.25–$11.55) at lunchtime and £15.25
($25.15) at dinnertime.

✪ **One Devonshire Gardens.** 1–3 Devonshire Gardens, Glasgow G12 0UX. ☎ **0141/
339-2001.** Fax 0141/337-1663. 27 rms, 2 suites. TV TEL. £140–£195 ($231–$321.75) double;
from £200 ($330) suite. AE, DC, MC, V. Free parking. Underground: Hillhead.

In 1880 this dignified edifice was built as an upper-crust private home, but by the
early 1980s it had degenerated into a seedy rooming house. In 1986 a professional
designer bought it and embarked on a major restoration, making it more elegant even
than it was in its heyday, and attracting the likes of Elizabeth Taylor and Luciano
Pavarotti. Behind its sandstone facade have been added such Georgian touches as cove
moldings patterned into laurel and urn motifs, along with floral-patterned chintz
against a backdrop of deep-blue walls. At the sound of the doorbell, a pair of cham-
bermaids clad in Edwardian costume with frilly aprons and dust bonnets appear to
welcome you. Each of the eight upstairs bedrooms, individually designed, is impeccably furnished in the best of period taste and offers a double bed and lots of luxurious accessories. The success of the first venture led to the acquisition of nos. 2 and
3, bringing the room count to 27. The newer rooms have the same facilities and are
priced the same. The location is in the Hyndland district, just west of the center, in
a neighborhood of stone Victorian houses.

   Dining/Entertainment: See "Dining," later in this chapter.
   Services: 24-hour room service, laundry service/valet.
   Facilities: Patio garden.

EXPENSIVE

Stakis Grosvenor Hotel. 1–10 Grosvenor Terrace, Great Western Rd., Glasgow G12 0TA.
☎ **0141/339-8811.** Fax 0141/334-0710. 96 rms, 3 suites. TV TEL. Mon–Thurs, £102
($168.30) double; Fri–Sun, £76 ($125.40) double. Suite £164–£170 ($270.60–$280.50).
AE, DC, MC, V. Rates include Scottish breakfast Fri–Sun. Free parking. Underground: Hillhead.

The most interesting thing about this hotel is the way a team of award-winning
engineers saved its early 20th-century neoclassical facade, using a revolutionary technique of impregnating the decaying sandstone with a combination of fiberglass and
concrete. The Greek-owned Stakis company almost completely gutted the interior,
reconstructing it in a casino-style sweep of crystal chandeliers and brassy accents.
Today the hotel offers fairly standardized and routine rooms that fill up mainly with
commercial travelers during the week and out-of-towners on the weekend. The bedrooms have such amenities as trouser presses, satellite TVs, and coffeemakers.

   Dining/Entertainment: The hotel has a piano bar in its only restaurant, the West
End, where well-prepared à la carte lunches and dinners cost around £15 ($24.75).
One floor above the lobby level is an upstairs sitting room with bar service.
   Services: 24-hour room service, laundry/valet, baby-sitting.
   Facilities: Ample parking area; large health club nearby.

MODERATE

Kelvin Park Lorne Hotel. 923 Sauchiehall St., Glasgow G3 7TE. ☎ **0141/314-9955.**
Fax 0141/337-1659. 99 rms, 20 suites. TV TEL. £74 ($122.10) single or double; £104 ($171.60)
suite. AE, DC, MC, V. Underground: Kelvin Hall.

Set in the heart of the residential West End, this is a comfortable and discreet hotel
whose public rooms are in the style of the famous turn-of-the-century Scottish
designer Charles Rennie Mackintosh. Though the hotel was built 40 years ago,
after his death, its bar (Newbery's, honoring Frances Newbery, Mackintosh's men-
tor) and restaurant (Seasons Brasserie and Art Gallery) are both designed according
to Mackintosh's theories. The hotel consists of an older building (early 19th century,
rising four floors) and a later five-story structure, combined to form one hotel. The
bedrooms were renovated in 1995, resulting in a kind of neutrally contemporary
comfort.

Dining/Entertainment: Season's offers a fixed-price menu at £4.95 ($8.15) at
lunchtime and £12.95 to £18.95 ($21.35 to $31.25) in the evening. Typical dishes
include duckling in orange sauce, salmon braised in Madeira wine, a selection of vegetarian dishes, and herb-flavored lamb.

Services: 24-hour room service, laundry, baby-sitting.

Wickets Hotel. 52–54 Fortrose St., Glasgow G11 5LP. ☎ **0141/334-9334.** Fax 0141/
334-9334. 10 rms. TV TEL. £64.95 ($107.15) double; £80–£91 ($132–$150.15) family room.
AE, DC, MC, V. Free parking. Underground: Partick.

Better known for its dining and drinking facilities than for its handful of comfortable bedrooms, this two-story hotel dating from the 1890s is an undiscovered gem
in Glasgow's West End, opposite one of the city's largest cricket grounds (the West
of Scotland Cricket Club). Each room has a brightly cheerful decor and such amenities as coffeemakers, trouser presses, and hair dryers.

The Conservatory Restaurant is the glamor spot of the hotel, offering both regional
and continental fare amid old photographs of local cricket teams. Fixed-price meals
are served throughout the day and evening and cost £9.95 to £14.95 ($16.40 to
$24.65). You can also order à la carte. Adjacent to the restaurant is an open-air beer
garden—one of the few in Glasgow. A few steps away, Randall's wine bar sells wine
by the glass in an art deco setting filled with Erté fashion prints. The bar food is
excellent.

INEXPENSIVE

Ambassador Hotel. 7 Kelvin Dr., Glasgow G20 8QJ. ☎ **0141/946-1018.** Fax 0141/
945-5377. 16 rms. TV TEL. £52 ($85.80) double; £62 ($102.30) family room. AE, MC, V.
Rates include Scottish breakfast. Free parking. Underground: Hillhead.

Across from the BBC Studios and the Botanic Garden, this small privately run
hotel in a three-story circa-1900 Victorian town house is one of the better B&Bs in
Glasgow. Singles and doubles are rented along with some family rooms, furnished
with modern pieces. Amenities include trouser presses, hair dryers, tea/coffeemakers,
radio alarms, and central heating. The hotel is well situated for exploring the West
End. Several art galleries and many good local restaurants or brasseries are nearby.
Dinner is served nightly from 6:30 to 8:30pm.

Argyll Hotel. 969–973 Sauchiehall St., Glasgow G3 7TQ. ☎ **0141/337-3313.** Fax 0141/
337-3283. 38 rms. TV TEL. £64 ($105.60) double. AE, MC, V. Rates include Scottish breakfast.
Free parking. Underground: St. George's Cross. Bus: 9, 16, 42, 57, 62, or 64.

This hotel is small but special, a privately owned Georgian building near many
major points of interest, including Glasgow University, the Museum and Art
Gallery, the Kelvin Hall International Sports Arena, and the Scottish Exhibition

Centre. The hotel overlooks Kelvingrove Park. Although completely modernized, it shows a healthy respect for tradition. The bedrooms are comfortable and convenient, each with such amenities as tea/coffeemakers, hair dryers, and digital radios. Room service is available, as are dry cleaning and laundry. On the premises, Scoffs Restaurant serves three meals a day, and a special feature is its garden dining. Both international and Scottish specialties are offered.

Kirklee Hotel. 11 Kensington Gate, Glasgow G12 9LG. ☎ **0141/334-5555.** Fax 0141/ 339-3828. 9 rms. TV TEL. £64 ($105.60) double. AE, DC, MC, V. Rates include Scottish breakfast. Parking on nearby streets. Underground: Hillhead.

In 1903 a shipping magnate built this three-story redbrick Victorian as a home for his family. Today it's graced with a rose-packed front garden that has won several awards from the Glasgow Garden Club. Behind the richly ornate stained-glass door you'll find sedately comfortable bedrooms, each of which contains a tea/coffeemaker, trouser press, and hair dryer. Mr. and Mrs. Peter Steven opted long ago to eliminate their dining room, so breakfast is served in the bedrooms. The establishment is near the university, the Botanic Gardens, and the city's major art galleries.

NEARBY PLACES TO STAY

Gleddoch House Hotel. Langbank, Renfrewshire PA14 6YE. ☎ **01475/540711.** Fax 01475/ 540201. 38 rms, 4 suites. TV TEL. £140 ($231) double; £170 ($280.50) suite. AE, DC, MC, V. Rates include Scottish breakfast. Children 11 and under stay free in parents' room. Free parking. Drive west along A8/M8 from Glasgow and the Erskine Bridge toward Greenock and Gourock; turn left at the sign for Langbank on B789, going left again under the railway bridge and then steeply up the hill to the hotel entrance on the right, about 15 miles west of Glasgow.

This deluxe hotel is set on large grounds that include farmlands, riding stables, an 18-hole par-74 golf course, and gardens. The rooms are named for birds—Golden Eagle, Mallard, Osprey—and have good baths, plus radios, hair dryers, trouser presses, and hot-beverage facilities. The paneled hallway is bright with a roaring fire and there's a cozy bar. The residents' sitting room is upstairs. The original antiques are still in place throughout the house.

Breakfast is a leisurely, help-yourself affair. At lunch, you can order smoked trout and salmon mousse, clear Highland game broth, and perhaps a traditional warm pudding. A fixed-price lunch costs £15 ($24.75) and up. In the evening, you can dine from an à la carte menu, although we recommend the four-course fixed-price dinner for £32.50 ($53.65), which changes daily. Many guests prefer to have lunch in the Golf Club House. There's a sauna, as well as horseback riding.

Services: 24-hour room service, dry cleaning/laundry, baby-sitting, secretarial services.

Facilities: 18-hole golf course, sports shop, sauna, squash, snooker, riding, fishing.

4 Dining

The days are long gone when a meal out in Glasgow meant mutton pie and chips. Some of the best of Scottish food is offered, and there are a rising number of foreign restaurants.

Many restaurants close on Sunday, and most are shut by 2:30pm, reopening again for dinner around 6pm.

CENTRAL GLASGOW

EXPENSIVE

✪ **The Buttery.** 652 Argyle St. ☎ **0141/221-8188.** Reservations recommended. Main courses £13–£15 ($21.45–$24.75); table d'hôte lunch £14.85 ($24.50); bar platters at the Oyster Bar £4–£6 ($6.60–$9.90). AE, DC, MC, V. Mon–Fri noon–2:30pm; Mon–Sat 7–11pm. Underground: St. Enoch. SCOTTISH/FRENCH.

This is the perfect hunter's restaurant, with oak panels, racks of wine bottles, and an air of baronial splendor. The bar in the anteroom used to be the pulpit of a church. The waitresses wear high-necked costumes of which Queen Victoria would have approved. Menu items include smoked trout, rare roast beef, terrine of Scottish seafood, and several preparations of venison—two of these include roebuck in a Madeira sauce with skirlie (a traditional Scottish combination of oats, bacon, and onions fried in bacon fat), and fillet of venison with apples, pears, and brown lentils in a nutmeg sauce. Increasingly, the cooking is less heavy than in years past. The only criticisms we've heard are from long-time habitués who find some of the new taste sensations a bit overwhelming—as exemplified by the likes of fig-vinegar sorbet and white sausage with morels on a bed of zucchini and kale with a raisin marmalade.

The Buttery's less formal restaurant, The Belfry, is in the cellar, and is recommended below.

✪ **Cameron's.** In the Glasgow Hilton International, 1 William St. ☎ **0141/204-5555.** Reservations recommended. Main courses £12–£25 ($19.80–$41.25); table d'hôte menus £20.50–£29.50 ($33.80–$48.70) at lunch, £29.50 ($48.70) at dinner. AE, DC, MC, V. Daily noon–2:30pm and 7–10:15pm. Bus: 62 or 64. MODERN BRITISH.

This is the most glamorous restaurant in Glasgow's most visible hotel. Its four sections are outfitted like baronial hunting lodges in the wilds of Highland Scotland. Amid scarlet walls and the accessories of an upscale Edwardian-era "sporting life," you can enjoy the chef's conservative menu, which holds few surprises, but is a celebration of market-fresh ingredients deftly prepared. Small slip-ups sometimes mar the effect of a dish or two, but we've been dining here since its opening and have always come away pleased. Your best bet is to "stay Scottish" when ordering—Isle of Arran salmon cured with whisky, confit of Highland duck, Firth of Lorne sea scallops—and that's only the list of appetizers. For a main course, try roast fillet of Ayrshire pork or rack of Scottish lamb with a whisky-steeped oatmeal and Arran mustard crust, or a medley of Highland game with forest mushrooms. Since its opening in 1992, Glasgow's most prominent music, sports, and political stars have enjoyed this restaurant.

✪ **Rogano.** 11 Exchange Place. ☎ **0141/248-4055.** Reservations recommended but not required. Main courses £10–£27.50 ($16.50–$45.40); fixed-price lunch £16.50 ($27.20). AE, DC, MC, V. Restaurant: Mon–Sat noon–2:30pm and 7–10:30pm, Sun noon–2:30pm and 6–10pm. Cafe: Mon–Thurs noon–11pm, Fri–Sat noon–midnight, Sun noon–10pm. Underground: Buchanan St. SCOTTISH/INTERNATIONAL.

Rogano has one of the most perfectly preserved art deco interiors in Scotland and a menu that features seafood. Its decor dates from 1935, when Messrs. Rogers and Anderson combined their talents and names to create an ambience that has hosted virtually every star of the British film industry since the invention of the talkies. It may be the oldest surviving restaurant in Glasgow. The bartender has been employed for decades. You can enjoy dinner in an ambience of lapis lazuli clocks, etched mirrors, spinning ceiling fans, cozy semicircular banquettes, and potted palms. The array of menu items, changing every 2 months, emphasizes seafood, such as halibut in champagne-and-oyster sauce. There are at least six varieties of temptingly rich desserts, although the scotch whisky parfait with Earl Grey tea sauce might not be for every diner. Most customers are pleased with the food, but rarely happy when the bill is presented. A less expensive menu is offered downstairs in the Cafe Rogano, where meals begin at £12 ($19.80).

MODERATE

The Belfry. 652 Argyle St. ☎ **0141/221-0630.** Reservations recommended. Main courses £6–£9 ($9.90–$14.85). AE, DC, MC, V. Mon–Sat 6–11pm. Underground: St. Enoch. SCOTTISH/FRENCH.

Glasgow Dining

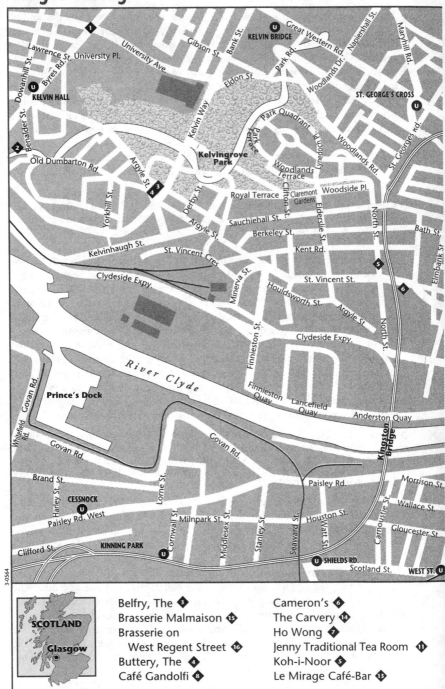

Belfry, The ③
Brasserie Malmaison ⑮
Brasserie on
   West Regent Street ⑯
Buttery, The ④
Café Gandolfi ⑧

Cameron's ⑥
The Carvery ⑭
Ho Wong ⑦
Jenny Traditional Tea Room ⑪
Koh-i-Noor ⑤
Le Mirage Café-Bar ⑬

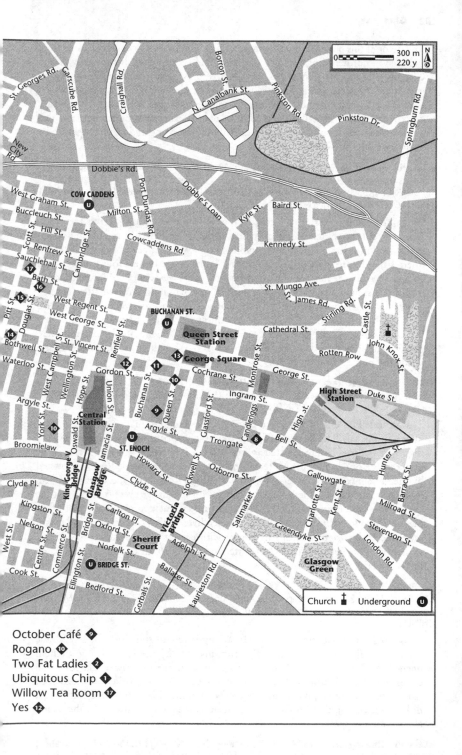

October Café ❾
Rogano ❿
Two Fat Ladies ❷
Ubiquitous Chip ❶
Willow Tea Room ⓱
Yes ⓬

The decor of this place, on the basement level of The Buttery (see above), came from a church in northern England: pews, pulpits, and stained glass. It's the only pub in Glasgow that affords a contemplation of Christ in Majesty while its patrons enjoy a pint of ale. The cramped and partially exposed kitchen produces daily specials such as poached salmon in lemon mayonnaise, smoked mackerel pâté, and chicken-and-broccoli pie. One critic called the food here "old hat," and to some extent that's true, but it does make clever use of fresh Scottish produce. Meals can be accompanied by a vintage from the wine list.

Brasserie Malmaison. In the Hotel Malmaison, 278 W. George St. ☎ **0141/221-6400.** Reservations recommended for dinner Thurs–Sun. Main courses £7.50–£16.95 ($12.40–$27.95). AE, DC, MC, V. Daily noon–2:30pm and 6–10:30pm. Limited menu available daily 2:30–6pm. Bus: 11. SCOTTISH/CONTINENTAL.

In the hotel converted from a Greek Orthodox Church (see above), this restaurant is set beneath the church's original ceiling vaults. It serves well-prepared and imaginative food in a dark and masculine-looking decor with a large bar and wooden banquettes that afford a lot of privacy. Menu items arrive in generous portions and include French-style rumpsteak with garlic butter and *pommes frites,* salmon fish cakes with fresh spinach, chargrilled liver served with balsamic-flavored fried onions, chargrilled chicken with a roasted red pepper salsa, and roasted fillets of codfish garnished with Parma ham. In complete contrast, the greenhouse-inspired, rather feminine-looking Café Mal was opened in 1997 with a menu of salads, sandwiches, pizzas, light platters, and drinks. The cafe keeps the same hours as the brasserie, and salads and platters range from £2.95 to £7 ($4.85 to $11.55).

Brasserie on West Regent Street. 176 W. Regent St. ☎ **0141/248-3801.** Reservations not necessary. Fixed-price menus £12.95–£15.95 ($21.35–$26.30). AE, DC, MC, V. Mon–Sat noon–11pm. Bus: 57. BRITISH/CONTINENTAL.

This upscale brasserie is in a white-painted stone building that was once a private house. Inside, you'll find a pair of dining rooms whose paneling, tartan patterns, and dignified wallpaper were selected to emulate an Edwardian-era men's club. The polite service rituals from the white-aproned staff evoke the upscale Rogano's, owned by the same investors. The set-price menus change frequently, and even the sauces on some of the staple dishes, such as roasted venison, change every 6 weeks. (At the time of our visit, it was succulently done up with caramelized onions.) Other offerings are likely to include such dishes as chicken livers with a Madeira-flavored cream sauce, Scottish oysters, filet of Angus beef with pepper sauce, suprême of Scottish salmon with peppercorn-laced vinaigrette, and vegetarian dishes that change based on whatever's fresh at the time.

Ho Wong Restaurant. 82 York St. ☎ **0141/221-3550.** Reservations required. Main courses £12–£18 ($19.80–$29.70); fixed-price 3-course lunch £8.50 ($14). AE, DC, MC, V. Mon–Sat noon–2pm and 5:30pm–midnight, Sun 6pm–midnight. Underground: Central Station. CHINESE.

Two blocks from Central Station, Ho Wong is one of the city's finest Chinese restaurants. Jimmy Ho and David Wong, inspired by the Hong Kong kitchen, opened this "remote outpost" of their East Asian cuisine in faraway Glasgow. You can pause for a drink in the front, perusing the menu before being shown to your table in the rear. Service is obliging. As a novelty, some dishes are labeled "bird's nest dishes"; others, "sizzling" dishes. There are at least eight duck dishes on the menu, along with four types of fresh lobster.

Mitchells Charing Cross. 157 North St., Charing Cross. ☎ **0141/204-4312.** Reservations recommended. Main courses £5–£6 ($8.25–$9.90) at lunch, £10–£12 ($16.50–$19.80) at dinner; fixed-price pretheater suppers, 5–7pm only, £8.95–£10.95 ($14.75–$18.05). AE, DC, MC, V. Mon–Sat noon–2:30pm and 5–10pm. Bus: 23 or 57. MODERN SCOTTISH.

Named after its position near Glasgow's largest library (the Mitchell Library), this attractively decorated upscale bistro is proud of its role as a purveyor of Scottish cuisine moderne. Within a large room lined with verdant plants and sophisticated paintings, usually by Glaswegian artists, you can order dishes that are sure to bring a smile to the face of any Scottish nationalist. Examples include a "rendezvous of exotic West Coast seafood" that includes red snapper, grouper, salmon, and smoked haddock netted off the Hebridean coast and drenched in a mussel stock sauce; scallops of Scottish venison with a celeriac purée and port wine glaze; cold poached salmon with a chive-flavored mayonnaise; and a defiantly nationalistic version of haggis served with fresh tatties and neeps. The restaurant maintains an almost equivalent branch, with almost the same prices, hours, and menus, at **Mitchells West End,** 31–35 Ashton Lane, near Byres Road and the Hill Head tube station (☎ **0141/339-2220**). Even if you happen to miss mealtime here, consider dropping in for a drink at its basement-level bar. Exotic cocktails aren't really the thing to order—more appropriate are two-fisted pints of beer, or anything from a selection of the country's whiskies.

October Café. The Rooftop, Princes Square. ☎ **0141/221-0303.** Reservations recommended. Main courses £5–£7 ($8.25–$11.55). AE, MC, V. Mon–Wed and Fri–Sat noon–5:30pm, Thurs noon–7:30pm, Sun noon–5pm. Underground: St. Enoch. INTERNATIONAL.

At the top of the Princes Square shopping district, this bar and restaurant offers a widely diversified cuisine that reflects culinary influences worldwide. Try an array of dishes—everything from Perthshire game terrine with beetroot-and-tarragon dressing to mussels with white wine, flavored with herbs and garlic. Chicken might be stuffed with cream cheese and broccoli, or you might order teriyaki beef with wasabi. For dessert, try either crème brûlée or chocolate terrine with an espresso sauce. If you prefer, you can also order from the cafe menu, including such dishes as smoked haddock Florentine, or a phyllo basket of salmon and prawns with a light white-wine-and-dill sauce. Most plates in the cafe cost £3.75 to £5.25 ($6.20 to $8.65).

Two Fat Ladies. 88 Dumbarton Rd. ☎ **0141/339-1944.** Reservations recommended. Fixed-price lunch £8.95 ($14.75); fixed-price pretheater supper, 6–7pm only, £9.75 ($16.10); fixed-price dinners £19.50–£23.50 ($32.15–$38.80). MC, V. Fri–Sat noon–2pm; Tues–Sat 6–10pm. Bus: 16, 42, or 57. MODERN BRITISH.

This ranks high on the list of everybody's favorite restaurant, especially if they have a sense of humor for the irreverent, the unexpected, and the colorful. The "Two Fat Ladies" are its street number, 88—a nickname used for the number 88 in Scotland's ubiquitous church-sponsored bingo games. But in honor of the name, owner and chef Calum Matheson displays an impossible-to-miss painting of two voluptuous Venus wannabes, in a style akin to Botero's, near the entrance. Decor is custard-colored, minimalist, and sometimes described as "postpunk." The food? Despite the establishment's limited hours (lunch is served only 2 days a week), it's sought out for such specialties as pan-fried squid salad with a coriander-flavored yogurt sauce, grilled fillet of chicken salad with apple chutney, chargrilled king scallops with a tomato-flavored basil sauce, and pan-fried sea bass with red-pepper chile pesto. Dessert is never better than when it's in the form of a Pavlova (a form of chewy meringue) with summer berries and Drambuie sauce.

Yes. 22 West Nile St. ☎ **0141/221-8044.** Reservations recommended for cellar-level restaurant, not necessary in street-level brasserie. Restaurant: fixed-price lunches £12.95–£15.95 ($21.35–$26.30); fixed-price dinners £19.95–£24.50 ($32.90–$40.40). Brasserie: lunch platters £4.95–£7.95 ($8.15–$13.10); fixed-price dinners £8.95–£10.95 ($14.75–$18.05). AE, DC, MC, V. Mon–Sat noon–2:30pm and 7–11pm. Bus: 66. MODERN EUROPEAN.

Set in a dignified building in one of Glasgow's most congested neighborhoods, this is a two-tiered restaurant with one of Glasgow's most sophisticated dining venues in the cellar, and a less expensive and less complicated cuisine in the street-level brasserie. Platters, sandwiches, and salads are the choices at lunch in the brasserie, and evenings feature straightforward food such as oriental chargrilled chicken with stir-fried vegetables, chile, and ginger. The cellar-level area is a lot more charming, much like an avant-garde restaurant in New York, but with an all-Scottish staff outfitted in long white aprons, white shirts, and neckties. High sun-flooded windows illuminate a striking purple and red decor and an oversized collection of modern Scottish paintings. A pianist performs evenings from Wednesday through Saturday. Lunch menus change weekly; the more elaborate dinner menus change with the seasons. Expect such carefully contrived dishes as gateau of haggis, prepared in several imaginative ways, but garnished with whisky sauce and the traditional neeps and tatties. There's also vodka-cured salmon with caviar and baby baked potatoes with sour cream. Also expect a platter of grilled West Coast seafood with chile garlic and lime-butter sauce; roast pepper duckling with corn cakes and a rhubarb, ginger, and apple reduction; or baked codfish with a stuffed herb crust, strips of smoked salmon, and vegetable sauce.

INEXPENSIVE

Cafe Gandolfi. 64 Albion St. ☎ **0141/552-6813.** Reservations recommended on weekends. Main courses £7–£10 ($11.55–$16.50). MC, V. Mon–Sat 9am–11:30pm, Sun noon–11:30pm. Underground: St. Enoch. SCOTTISH/FRENCH.

Many students at the university will take you here, telling you that this popular cafe in Merchant City is their favorite "caff." You may sometimes have to wait for a table in this bustling atmosphere. The remake of a Victorian pub, it has rustic wooden floors, wood benches, and stools. At lunch you should look for chalkboard specials. Vegetarians will find solace here; otherwise, if you don't fill up on soups and salads, try smoked venison with gratin dauphinois or smoked pheasant with an onion tartlet. Dress is, of course, casual.

The Carvery. In the Forte Posthouse Hotel, Bothwell St. ☎ **0141/248-2656.** Reservations required. Buffet £17 ($28.05). AE, DC, MC, V. Mon–Sat 6–10pm, Sun noon–3pm and 6:30–10pm. Underground: Central Station. BRITISH.

The price of a meal at the Carvery is low considering what you get. In an ambience of brick-lined walls and pinpoint lighting, you can select from one of Glasgow's most amply stocked buffets, spread on an altarlike centerpiece and laden with dishes hot and cold. It's augmented with carved roasts and joints produced by uniformed chefs. The cookery is of the type that has delighted Brits for years—aimed at filling you up more than causing sensations in the taste buds.

THE WEST END

EXPENSIVE

✪ **One Devonshire Gardens.** 1 Devonshire Gardens. ☎ **0141/339-2001.** Reservations required. Fixed-price 3-course lunch £25 ($41.25); fixed-price 4-course dinner £40 ($66). AE, DC, MC, V. Sun–Fri noon–2pm and daily 7–10pm. Underground: Partick. BRITISH.

The high-ceilinged restaurant of One Devonshire Gardens, recommended as a hotel (see "Accommodations," earlier in this chapter), is one of Glasgow's most charming and unusual dining rooms. Drinks are served in the elegantly decorated drawing room, and you dine amid flowery Victorian-inspired wallpaper, with servers dressed in frilly aprons and muslin mob caps. A fixed-price menu at both sessions offers ample choice, and quality ingredients are handled with care and finesse in the kitchen. Perhaps you'll begin with a curried-parsnip soup, then follow with terrine of brill and trout, going on to rack of Borders lamb. None of this is startlingly innovative, but all dishes are competently prepared.

MODERATE

✪ Puppet Theatre. 11 Ruthven Lane. ☎ **0141/339-8444.** Fixed-price lunch £12.95 ($21.35) for 2 courses, £14.50 ($23.90) for 3 courses; fixed-price dinner £21.95 ($36.20) for 2 courses, £24.95 ($41.15) for 3 courses. AE, MC, V. Tues–Fri and Sun noon–2:30pm and 7–10:45pm, Sat 7–10:45pm. Tube: Hillhead. SCOTTISH/MEDITERRANEAN.

Set in a partially residential neighborhood about 1 1/2 miles west of Glasgow's financial district, this restaurant occupies what was an isolated farmhouse in 1870. In 1994 a pair of new owners added a glass-sided conservatory to the back and divided the rest of the interior into a glossy and urban-stylish trio of dining rooms. If you're looking for a quiet dialogue, opt for one of the cool and urbane inner rooms. If you want to be part of an animated public, request a table in the conservatory. Regardless of your choice, menu items are among the best prepared and most stylish in Glasgow. A starter might be cream of mussel and onion soup. Main courses, accompanied by vegetables, range from filet of Aberdeen Angus to prime seafood fresh from the market. One specialty is pan-roasted guinea fowl and wood pigeon. The desserts are sumptuous, ranging from iced mango-and-raspberry parfait to poached figs filled with strawberry ice cream.

✪ Ubiquitous Chip. 12 Ashton Lane, off Byres Rd. ☎ **0141/334-5007.** Reservations recommended. Fixed-price lunch £18.60 ($30.70) for 2 courses, £23.60 ($38.95) for 3 courses; fixed-price dinner £26.60 ($43.90) for 2 courses, £31.60 ($52.15) for 3 courses. Bar meals £8 ($13.20) at lunch, £10–£15 ($16.50–$24.75) at dinner. Restaurant: Mon–Sat noon–2:30pm and 5:30–11pm, Sun 5:30–11pm. Bar: daily noon–11pm. Underground: Hillhead. SCOTTISH.

This well-known traditional restaurant is inside the roughly textured stone walls of what once were stables for the nearby elegant houses. A glass-covered courtyard has masses of climbing vines that entwine themselves along the rafters. Upstairs is a pub, where informal platters are served simultaneously with pints of lager and drams of whisky. Bar meals here are cheaper than those in the restaurant and might include such dishes as chicken, leek, and white-wine casserole or finnan haddies with bacon.

Despite the implications of this establishment's name, its menu does not include fish-and-chips. The cookery is bistro style. Specialties fuel the brain as well as the stomach, and might include Scotch silverside beef with a rich gravy and root vegetable, Ayrshire ham with butter beans, fillet of lemon sole baked with lemon butter, and chicken piri-piri (hot peppers). Baked Scotch salmon is likely to be marinated in honey, ginger, and tamari. Begin perhaps with a feuillette of wild mushrooms with cream and tarragon, finishing with a matured Mull of Kintyre truckle cheddar with apple. The chef also makes a Scotch whisky and heather honey parfait.

INEXPENSIVE

Koh-i-Noor. 235 North St., Charing Cross. ☎ **0141/221-1555.** Reservations recommended. Main courses £10–£12 ($16.50–$19.80); fixed-price 3-course business lunch £3.75 ($6.20); fixed-price 4-course business lunch £5.95 ($9.80); Sun buffet £7.95 ($13.10); Mon–Sat buffet £9.95 ($16.40). AE, DC, MC, V. Sun–Thurs noon–midnight, Fri–Sat noon–1am. Underground: St. Georges. INDIAN.

This is one of the city's leading Indian restaurants and the most reasonable in price. The family that runs this large, spacious place comes from the Punjab, and naturally such Punjabi specialties as paratha and bhuna lamb are recommended. The Sunday Indian buffet is a Glasgow event and one of the great food values of the city; the Indian buffet weekdays is another treat. You can also order a three- or four-course business lunch.

ⓐ Family-Friendly Restaurants

Willow Tea Room *(see p. 206)*   Time was, when it was a big treat for a Glaswegian child to be taken here for delectable pastries and ice-cream dishes, and it still is.

Le Mirage Café Bar   A good luncheon stopover, in the center of Glasgow in the Copthorne Hotel (see "Accommodations"), this is a kid pleaser, with its tasty chili, lasagna, and well-stuffed sandwiches.

Cafe Gandolfi *(see p. 204)*   At this popular Scottish venue, kids always find something to order, perhaps a soup-and-salad lunch, followed by one of the homemade ice creams, the best in the city. A 10-year-old Chicago boy, eating at the table next to ours, endorsed the daily special: cheese gougère stuffed with mushrooms and ham.

A NEARBY PLACE TO DINE

✪ Fifty-Five B.C. 128 Drymen Rd., Bearsden. ☎ **0141/942-7272.** Reservations recommended for restaurant, not necessary for the bar. Main courses £7.95–£13.50 ($13.10–$22.30); bar platters £3.95–£4.50 ($6.50–$7.45). AE, MC, V. Restaurant: Mon–Tues noon–11pm, Wed–Sat noon–midnight. Bar: daily noon–3pm and 5–6:30pm. From Glasgow's center, take the Clydesdale Expressway to Anniesland and from there follow the signs to Bearsden. SCOTTISH/MODERN FRENCH.

Named in honor of the year the ancient Romans invaded Britain (a date that is, at least in theory, memorized by schoolchildren throughout the country), this restaurant is boisterous, convivial, and fun. In the suburb of Bearsden, about a 15-minute drive north of Glasgow's center, it offers a large and usually crowded bar area near the entrance, and a quieter and much smaller restaurant in back. Meals in the bar might include a sandwich or soup of the day, or a combination of the two, lasagna, chili, or any of several different salads. Preferred drinks include pints of lager, or frothy drinks like piña coladas or margaritas you might expect in the Caribbean. The restaurant in back offers more elaborate fare, including breast of duck on a bed of pineapple and pink peppercorns, marinated chicken served with Japanese spices on a bed of stir-fried vegetables, or fillet of pigeon in a thyme-and-honey sauce. Despite the allure of this establishment's food, many of its clients come just for the sense of companionship and the crowd.

TEAROOMS

Jenny Traditional Tea Room. 18 Royal Exchange Square. ☎ **0141/204-4988.** Main courses £2–£4.25 ($3.30–$7); afternoon tea £5.85 ($9.65). AE, DC, MC, V. Mon–Wed 8am–6pm, Thurs–Sat 8am–11pm, Sun 11am–5:45pm. Underground: Queen Street Station. SCOTTISH.

A re-creation of a Victorian tea room, "The Jenny" is an ideal place for a pick-me-up at any time during the day. Many arrive for breakfast, although the place is at its most popular for the set afternoon tea. Waitresses in floral print dresses add to the charm. If you're visiting for lunch, try dishes that probably delighted your great-grandmother, including one of the meat pies (steak and mushroom, or turkey and corn). The place is also licensed to serve drinks, and there's seating outside in fair weather for up to 60 patrons.

Willow Tea Room. 217 Sauchiehall St. ☎ **0141/332-0521.** Reservations recommended. Main courses £3.10–£5.50 ($5.10–$9.05); afternoon tea with pastry £7.25 ($11.95). No credit cards. Daily 9:30am–4:30pm. Underground: Cowcaddens. INTERNATIONAL.

One of the best places for tea, light lunches, and snacks, this famed place is on the major shopping artery of the city. All the sensation when it opened in 1904 for its design by Charles Rennie Mackintosh, the Willow Tea Room has been restored to its original condition. On the ground floor is a well-known jeweler, M. M. Henderson Ltd. The "room de luxe" is found in the heart of the architecturally interesting old building, and it's elegantly furnished with tables and chairs made to the Mackintosh design. It's fashionable to drop in here for afternoon tea any time of day. You can also order such standard, often lackluster dishes as homemade soup, chili, and lasagna.

5 Attractions

If time is limited, plan your visit carefully and arm yourself with a good map. Many points of interest, such as the Burrell Collection, are outside the city center. If you're dependent on public transportation, you'll need to figure in travel time between sights. The tourist office is most helpful in advising you. Those with limited time can always opt for an organized tour.

THE TOP ATTRACTIONS

✪ **Glasgow Art Gallery and Museum.** Kelvingrove. ☎ **0141/287-2699.** Free admission. Mon–Sat 10am–5pm, Sun 11am–5pm. Underground: Kelvin Hall.

The headquarters of Glasgow Museums and Art Galleries, this is the finest municipal gallery in Britain. The art gallery contains a superb collection of Dutch and Italian old masters, including Giorgione and Rembrandt, and French 19th-century paintings by Millet, Derain, and others. Salvador Dalí's *Christ of St. John of the Cross* is on display. Scottish painting is well represented, from the 17th century to the present day.

One of the gallery's major paintings is Whistler's *Arrangement in Grey and Black no. 2: Portrait of Thomas Carlyle,* the first Whistler to be hung in a British gallery. The artist took great pride in his Scottish background. The James McNeill Whistler collection, given to Glasgow by the artist's nephew, includes the contents of his studio.

The museum has an outstanding collection of European arms and armor, displays from the ethnography collections, as well as a large section devoted to natural history, with major new exhibits on the natural history of Scotland. There are also small, regularly changing displays from the decorative art collections, plus furniture and other decorative art items by Charles Rennie Mackintosh and his contemporaries. Teas and light lunches are available in the museum.

✪ **Burrell Collection.** Pollok Country Park, 2060 Pollokshaws Rd. ☎ **0141/649-7151.** Free admission. Mon and Wed–Sat 10am–5pm, Sun 11am–5pm. Closed Jan 1 and Dec 25. Bus: 45, 48, or 57.

This collection is housed in a building opened in 1983 to display the mind-boggling treasures left to Glasgow by Sir William Burrell, a wealthy shipowner who had a lifelong passion for art collecting. A vast aggregation of furniture, textiles, ceramics,

Impressions

[Glasgow is] a place which I shall ever hold in contempt as being filled with a set of unmannerly, low-bred, narrow-minded wretches; the place itself, however, is really pretty, and were the present inhabitants taken out and drowned in the ocean, and others with generous souls put in their stead, it would be an honour to Scotland.

—David Boswell, in a letter to James Boswell (1767)

Glasgow Attractions

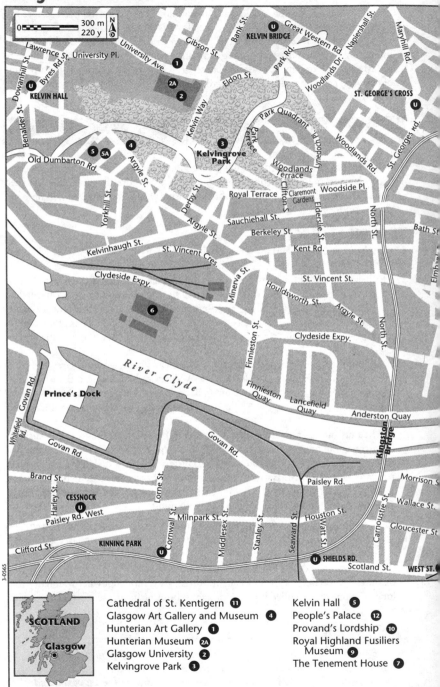

SCOTLAND
Glasgow

Cathedral of St. Kentigern ⓫
Glasgow Art Gallery and Museum ➍
Hunterian Art Gallery ➊
Hunterian Museum ➋Ⓐ
Glasgow University ➋
Kelvingrove Park ➌

Kelvin Hall ➎
People's Palace ⓬
Provand's Lordship ➓
Royal Highland Fusiliers
  Museum ➒
The Tenement House ➐

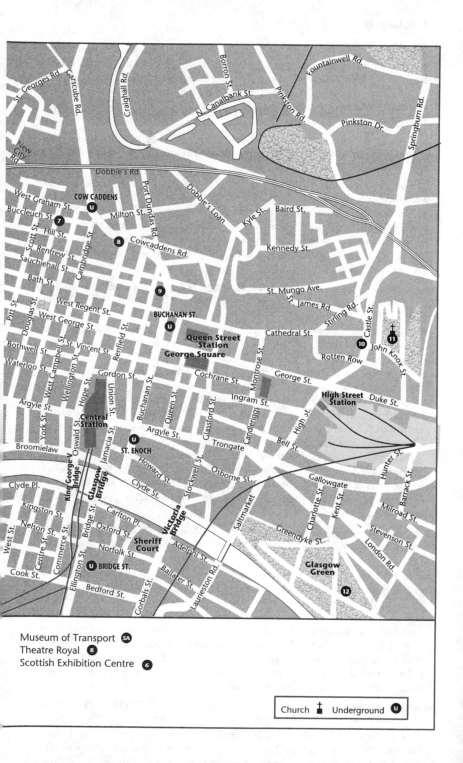

Museum of Transport ⑤A
Theatre Royal ⑧
Scottish Exhibition Centre ⑥

Church ✝   Underground Ⓤ

stained glass, silver, art objects, and pictures—especially 19th-century French art—can be seen in the dining room, hall, and drawing room reconstructed from Sir William's home, Hutton Castle at Berwick-upon-Tweed. Ancient artifacts, Asian art, and European decorative arts and paintings are featured. There's a restaurant, and you can roam through the surrounding park, which is 3 miles south of Glasgow Bridge.

Pollok House. Pollok Country Park, 2060 Pollokshaws Rd. ☎ **0141/649-7151.** Free admission. May–Sept, Mon and Wed–Sat 10am–5pm, Sun 11am–5pm. Closed Oct–Apr. Bus: 57 or 57A.

The ancestral home of the Maxwells, Pollok House was built around 1750, with additions from 1890 to 1908 designed by Robert Rowand Anderson. The house and its 360 acres of parkland were given to the city of Glasgow in 1966. Today a branch of the Glasgow Museums and Art Galleries, it contains one of the finest collections of Spanish paintings in Britain, with works by El Greco, Goya, and Murillo, among others. There are displays of silver, ceramics, and glass from the Maxwell family's and the city's collections.

People's Palace. Glasgow Green. ☎ **0141/554-0223.** Free admission. Mon–Sat 10am–5pm, Sun 11am–5pm; Apr–Sept, also Thurs 5–9pm. Closed Jan 1 and Dec 25. Bus: 14, 14A, 18, 18A, 18B, 20, or 62.

A branch of the Glasgow Museums and Art Galleries, the People's Palace provides a visual record of the rise of Glasgow. The palace was built originally as a cultural center for the people of the East End of Glasgow, between 1895 and 1897. Exhibitions trace the foundation of the city in 1175–78. Personal relics of Mary Queen of Scots represent her reign. The bulk of the collections are from Victorian 19th-century Glasgow, including posters, programs, and props from the music-hall era. Items relating to trades and industries, such as the Glasgow potteries and stained-glass studios, trade unions, newspapers, and similar matters are also featured. Paintings of Glasgow by John Knox and others may be seen, plus portraits of Glaswegians, even St. Mungo. There's a tearoom in the Winter Gardens.

The palace is situated in Glasgow Green, the oldest public park in the city. Seek out, in particular, Nelson's monument, the first of its kind in Britain; the Saracen Fountain, opposite the palace; and Templeton's Carpet Factory, modeled on the Doge's Palace in Venice.

✪ Hunterian Art Gallery. University of Glasgow, Hillhead St. ☎ **0141/330-5431.** Free admission. Mon–Sat 9:30am–5pm (Mackintosh House closed 12:30–1:30pm). Underground: Hillhead.

This art gallery owns the artistic estate of James McNeill Whistler, with some 60 paintings on display. It's also known for its Charles Rennie Mackintosh collection, including the architect's home on three levels, with his own furniture and decorated in the original style. The main gallery exhibits 17th- and 18th-century paintings (Rembrandt to Rubens) and 19th- and 20th-century Scottish painters (McTaggart, Scottish Colourists, Gillies, Philipson, and others). Temporary exhibitions, selected from the largest collection of artists' prints in Scotland, are presented in the print gallery, which also houses a permanent display of print-making techniques. Contemporary sculpture is displayed in an outdoor courtyard.

Hunterian Museum. University of Glasgow, Gilmorehill Building. ☎ **0141/339-8855**, ext. 4221. Free admission. Mon–Sat 9:30am–5pm. Closed public holidays. Underground: Hillhead.

This is Glasgow's oldest museum, having opened its doors in 1807; it's in the main Glasgow University buildings 2 miles west of the heart of the city. The museum is named after William Hunter, its early benefactor, who donated his private collections to get the museum going. The museum is wide-ranging, from dinosaur fossils to coins. There are relics of the Roman occupation and plunder by the Vikings. The story of Captain Cook's voyages is pieced together in ethnographic material from the South Seas. The museum has a bookstall, a coffeehouse in 18th-century style, and temporary exhibitions.

Museum of Transport. Kelvin Hall, 1 Bunhouse Rd. ☎ **0141/287-2720.** Free admission. Mon and Wed–Sat 10am–5pm, Sun 11am–5pm. Closed Jan 1 and Dec 25. Underground: Kelvin Hall.

This museum contains a fascinating collection of all forms of transportation and related technology. Displays include a simulated Glasgow street of 1938 with period shop fronts and appropriate vehicles and a reconstruction of one of the Glasgow Underground stations. An authentic motor-car showroom has a display of mass-produced automobiles. Superb and varied ship models in the Clyde Room reflect the significance of Glasgow and the River Clyde as one of the world's foremost areas of shipbuilding and engineering. There's a self-service cafeteria.

Tenement House. 145 Buccleuch St. ☎ **0141/333-0183.** Admission £2.80 ($4.60) adults, £1.90 ($3.15) seniors, students, and children. Mar–Oct, daily 2–5pm. Closed Nov–Feb. Underground: Cowcaddens.

This house has been called a "Glasgow flat that time passed by." Until her death, Agnes Toward was an inveterate hoarder of domestic trivia. She lived in an 1892 building on Garnethill, not far from the main shopping street, Sauchiehall Street. For 54 years she lived in this flat and stuffed it with the artifacts of her era, everything from a porcelain "jawbox" sink to such household aids as Monkey Brand soap. After her death the property came into the care of the National Trust for Scotland as a virtual museum of a vanished era.

MORE ATTRACTIONS

The center of Glasgow is **George Square,** dominated by the City Chambers that Queen Victoria opened in 1888. Of the statues in the square, the most imposing is that of Sir Walter Scott, on an 80-foot column. Naturally, you'll find Victoria along with her beloved Albert, plus Robert Burns. The **Banqueting Hall,** lavishly decorated, is open to the public on most weekdays.

The ✪ **Cathedral of St. Kentigern,** Cathedral Street (☎ **0141/552-8198** or 0141/427-2757), originally consecrated in 1136, burned down in 1192. It was rebuilt soon after, and the Laigh Kirk (Lower Church), whose vaulted crypt is said to be the finest in Europe, remains to this day. Visit the tomb of St. Mungo in the crypt, where a light always burns. The edifice is mainland Scotland's only complete medieval cathedral, dating from the 12th and 13th centuries. It was once a place of pilgrimage, but 16th-century zeal purged it of all "monuments of idolatry."

Highlights of the interior include the nave from the 1400s, built later than the choir, with a stone screen, unique in Scotland, showing the seven deadly sins. Both the choir and the lower church are in the First Pointed style, dating from the mid-1200s. The church, even though a bit austere, is filled with intricate details left by long-ago craftspeople—note the tinctured bosses of the ambulatory vaulting in the back of the main altar.

The lower church, reached via a set of steps north of the pulpit, is where gothic reigns supreme, with an array of pointed arches and piers. Seek out, in particular, the Chapel of the Virgin, with its intricate net vaulting and bosses carved with fine detailing. The Blacader Aisle projecting from the south transept was the latest addition to the church, a two-story extension, of which only the lower part was completed in the late gothic style.

⭐ Frommer's Favorite Glasgow Experiences

Touring the Burrell Collection. The pièce de résistance of Glasgow (some say of Scotland), this gallery is the city's major attraction. See what good taste and an unlimited pocketbook can acquire in a lifetime.

Following Walkways and Cycle Paths. Greater Glasgow has an array of trails and cycle paths cutting through areas of historic interest and scenic beauty, including the Paisley/Irvine Cycle and Walkway, 17 miles of unused railway line converted to a trail. Tourist leaflets outline these trails.

Riding the World's Last Seagoing Paddle Steamer. From spring until early fall, the Waverley makes day trips to scenic spots on the Firth of Clyde, past docks that once supplied more than half the tonnage of oceangoing ships. (Call ☎ 0141/ 221-8152 for more details.)

Shopping Paddy's Market. This daily market by the railway arches on Shipbank Lane gives you the real flavor of the almost-vanished Glaswegian style of street vending.

To approach the cathedral, go to the eastern end of Cathedral Street, in back of the Queen Street Station (the nearest Underground stop). It's open April to September, Monday through Saturday from 9:30am to 6pm and Sunday from 2 to 4pm; October to March, Monday through Saturday from 9:30am to 4pm and Sunday from 2 to 4pm. Sunday services are held at 11am and 6:30pm. Admission is free.

For the best view of the cathedral, cross the Bridge of Sighs into the **Necropolis,** the graveyard containing almost every type of architecture in the world. Built on a rocky hill and dominated by a statue of John Knox, the graveyard was opened in 1832, and, typical of the mixing of all groups in this tolerant cosmopolitan city, the first person to be buried here was a Jew.

Glasgow's **Botanic Garden,** Great Western Road (☎ 0141/334-2422), covers 40 acres—an extensive collection of tropical plants and herb gardens. The garden is acclaimed especially for the collection of orchids and begonias. It's open all year, daily from 7am to dusk. Admission is free. Underground: Hillhead.

NEARBY ATTRACTIONS IN PAISLEY

The largest town in the district, Paisley, 7 miles west of Glasgow, became a famous name in the weaving trade in the days of the Industrial Revolution. The Paisley shawl was born here. Actually, the inspiration for the pattern came from India, but no matter—it's forever associated with this industrial town.

⭐ **Paisley Abbey.** Abbey Close. ☎ 0141/889-7654. Free admission. Mon–Sat 10am–3:30pm; Sun services year-round at 11am, Sept–June also at 6:30pm, July–Aug also at 12:15pm. Take the Paisley-bound train from Glasgow's Central Station.

This is one of the great attractions of Strathclyde. The church grew out of a Cluniac abbey founded in 1163. Nearly demolished in 1307 on orders of Edward I of England, it was subsequently reconstructed. In the mid-16th century a tower fell in, causing great damage to the transept and choir. New work began around the turn of this century, and by 1928 Paisley Abbey was restored, including a superb stone-vaulted roof. A chapel is dedicated to the monk, Saint Mirin, who founded the town. You can also see an 11-foot-high Celtic cross from the 10th century.

Paisley Museum and Art Galleries. High St. ☎ 0141/889-3151. Free admission. Mon–Sat 10am–5pm. Take the Paisley-bound train from Glasgow's Central Station.

This museum is visited mainly because of its famous collection of Paisley shawls. This teardrop pattern dominated the world of fashion for some 70-odd years, and today the shawls are extremely valuable as collector's items. The museum has collected these colorful textiles since 1905 and now has more than 700 examples. The museum also has a collection relating to the history of Strathclyde, along with some fine art and natural history displays.

ESPECIALLY FOR KIDS

Many of the attractions already mentioned appeal to kids. Children like the **People's Palace,** the dinosaur fossils at the **Hunterian Museum,** and the **Museum of Transport.**

Linn Park, on Clarkston Road, is 212 acres of pine and woodland, with many scenic walks along the river. Here you'll find a nature trail, pony rides for children, an old snuff mill, and a children's zoo. The park is open all year, daily from 8am to dusk. **Gleniffer Braes Country Park,** Glenfield Road, in Paisley, covers 1,300 acres of woodland and moorland and has picnic areas and an adventure playground.

House of Art Lovers. Bellahouston Park, Dumbreck Rd. ☎ **0141/353-4770.** Free admission. Sat–Sun 10am–5pm. Bus: 9A, 39, 54, 59, or 36. Underground: Ibrox.

This house for art lovers, which opened in 1996, is based on an unrealized competition entry of Charles Rennie Mackintosh's in 1901. The impressive building with its elegant interiors was brought to life by contemporary artists and craftspeople. The house is based on Mackintosh's early design, although the drawings were not complete. Architects Graeme Robertson and John Cane expanded the originals and reinterpreted missing details.

The recession of 1992 caused the work to be suspended, but it was revived in 1994 with private and public gifts. The final construction tab came to £3 million. The tour begins in the main hall and leads through the dining room with its elegant geso panels, on to the music room, which shows Mackintosh designs at their most inspirational. Finally, one can visit the oval boardroom before entering an audiovisual display. Visitors can also enjoy the art cafe, design shop, and a striking parkland setting adjacent to Victorian walled gardens.

It's a 5-minute ride from the center of Glasgow. On weekdays you can call the art lovers' hotline at ☎ **0141/353-4449** to find out if there are any extra open hours during the week.

Museum of Education. 225 Scotland St. ☎ **0141/429-1202.** Free admission. Mon–Sat 10am–5pm, Sun 2–5pm. Underground: Shiels Rd.

This branch of the Glasgow Museums and Art Galleries explores changing lifestyles in Glasgow for the past 4 centuries. There is an activities workshop where children can take part in sessions that include weaving, archery, butter-making, and sampler sewing.

ORGANIZED TOURS

The *Waverley* is the last of the seagoing paddle steamers in the world, and from spring until early fall (depending on weather conditions), the Paddle Steamer Preservation Society conducts 1-day trips from Anderston Quay in Glasgow to historic and scenic places beyond the Firth of Clyde. As you go along, you can take in what was once vast shipyards, turning out more than half the earth's tonnage of oceangoing liners. You're allowed to bring your own sandwiches for a picnic aboard or you can enjoy lunch in the Waverley Restaurant. Boat tours cost £7.95 to £23 ($13.10 to $37.95). For more information, call **Waverley Excursions,** Waverley Terminal, Anderston Quay, Broomielaw (☎ **0141/221-8152**).

The best Glasgow tours are run by **Scotguide Tours,** operated from the Strath-clyde Buses Travel Centre at St. Enoch Square (☎ **0141/226-4826**). From March 27 until October 11, there are four departures daily between 9:30am and 4pm. The price is £6 ($9.90) for adults and £4 ($6.60) for children.

WALKING TOUR
Historic Glasgow

Start: Cathedral Square.
Finish: Glasgow Green.
Time: 2 hours.
Best Time: Any sunny day.
Worst Times: Rush hours Monday through Saturday.

Begin the tour in Cathedral Square, where, in A.D. 543 St. Mungo arrived in "Glasgu" (meaning "the beloved green place"). Here, out of timber and wattle, he built his first house of worship, opening onto the banks of Molendinar Burn.

Today, in its place, is the:

1. **Cathedral of St. Kentigern,** Cathedral Square, dating from the 12th century. It has been called "a splendid example of pre-Reformation gothic architecture."
   After viewing the cathedral, turn left upon leaving it, then take another left to go into the:

2. **Necropolis,** reached by crossing the Bridge of Sighs. This is one of the greatest Victorian cemeteries in the world and has been compared to Père Lachaise in Paris. An example of every type of architecture, from Egyptian vaults to tombs designed by Charles Rennie Mackintosh, can be viewed here. A monumental Doric column holding an effigy of John Knox towers over the cemetery.
   Cut back across Cathedral Square and Castle Street to reach:

3. **Provand's Lordship,** at Castle Street and McLeod Street, dating from 1471, making it the oldest house in Glasgow. It's said that in 1567 Mary Queen of Scots stayed here.
   On leaving Provand's Lordship, cut right and go down Castle Street, which leads to:

4. **High Street,** which, along with Castle Street, is one of the oldest thoroughfares in Scotland. In the 6th century it was called "King's Highway," although it could hardly have been more than a pathway then.
   At the intersection of Duke Street, note the plaque marking the:

5. **Site of the old University of Glasgow,** which was moved here from Rotterdam in 1470. It flourished until its move to Gilmorehill in 1870, the height of the Victorian era. Part of the area is now used by the University of Strathclyde.
   Continue down High Street to Glasgow Cross, dominated by the steeple of the:

6. **Tolbooth,** a seven-story stone "traffic cop" placed at the intersection of five streets. The tower was constructed in 1636 and rises 126 feet. Originally, visitors to the city had to pay a toll here—hence, the name. The gaol (jail) in Sir Walter Scott's *Rob Roy* once stood here.
   Directly south of the Tolbooth stands the:

7. **Mercat Cross,** which in 1929 replaced the original that had stood here until 1659. It marks the site of Glasgow's first market from the Middle Ages. It was also a place where the condemned were sent to be hanged.

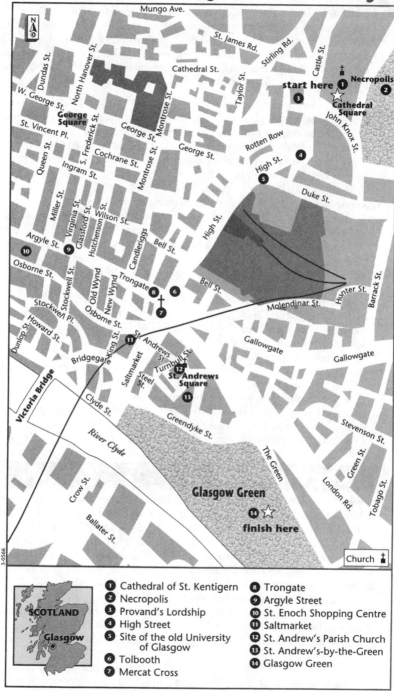

Mungo Ave.

St. James Rd.

Stirling Rd.

Castle St.

Cathedral St.

Taylor St.

start here ① Necropolis ②

Cathedral Square

③

John Knox St.

Dundas St.

North Hanover St.

W. George St.

George Square

George St.

Montrose St.

George St.

George St.

Rotten Row

High St.

④

⑤

Duke St.

St. Vincent Pl.

Queen St.

S. Frederick St.

Cochrane St.

Ingram St.

Miller St.

Virginia St.

Glassford St.

Wilson St.

Hutchenson

Candleriggs

Bell St.

High St.

Argyle St.

⑨

⑩

Osborne St.

Stockwell St.

Old Wynd

New Wynd

Osborne St.

Trongate

⑧ ⑥

⑦

Bell St.

Molendinar St.

Hunter St.

Barrack St.

Stockwell Pl.

Howard St.

Dunlop St.

King St.

Bridgegate

Saltmarket

⑪ St. Andrews St.

Turnbull St.

⑫

St. Andrews Square

⑬

Gallowgate

Gallowgate

Steel St.

Clyde St.

Greendyke St.

Stevenson St.

Victoria Bridge

River Clyde

Crow St.

Ballater St.

Glasgow Green

⑭

finish here

The Green

London Rd.

Green St.

Tobago St.

Church ✝

3-0566

SCOTLAND

Glasgow

① Cathedral of St. Kentigern
② Necropolis
③ Provand's Lordship
④ High Street
⑤ Site of the old University of Glasgow
⑥ Tolbooth
⑦ Mercat Cross
⑧ Trongate
⑨ Argyle Street
⑩ St. Enoch Shopping Centre
⑪ Saltmarket
⑫ St. Andrew's Parish Church
⑬ St. Andrew's-by-the-Green
⑭ Glasgow Green

☕ **TAKE A BREAK** On the southeast corner of Glasgow Cross, the **Tolbooth Bar** introduced the *hauf an' hauf*—a half measure of a single-malt scotch whisky which is then "chased down" by a half pint of draft lager. If you'd like to be authentically Glaswegian about this, take the glass and turn it upside down over the mug of lager. Tap the glass firmly on its bottom into the beer. That way, a true imbiber knows that "ne'er a drap is lost."

At Glasgow Cross, turn west onto:

 8. Trongate, dominated by Tron Steeple, a four-tiered steeple that is what remains from a church constructed in the late 1500s, a building destroyed by members of the Hell Fire Club who were attempting to show that they were immune to the fires of hell. The fire got out of hand and burned the church. A new church was built in 1793 by John Adam.

Trongate leads into:

 9. Argyle Street, one of the city's major shopping thoroughfares.

Along Argyle Street, take a left onto Maxwell Street, which will lead to the:

10. St. Enoch Shopping Centre, one of the major venues for shopping in Glasgow. After leaving the center, head east again along Osborne Street until you reach the:

11. Saltmarket, where, it is said, there once stood 200 whorehouses and 150 illicit stills (called *shebeens* by the Scots).

At St. Andrews Street, continue east to St. Andrew's Square, site of:

12. St. Andrew's Parish Church, dating from 1739 and reminding many visitors of the more famous St. Martin–in–the–Fields in London. From the south side of the square, approached by about a 110-yard walk, you come to:

13. St. Andrew's–by–the–Green, opening onto Greendyke Street, the fourth-oldest building in Glasgow and a splendid example of Georgian architecture from the 1750s. This was the first Episcopalian church in Scotland.

At Greendyke Street, you're on the threshold of:

14. Glasgow Green, bordering the River Clyde. This is Britain's oldest public park, dating from 1662. Sheep grazed here until the end of Queen Victoria's reign. Everything from political rallies to pop concerts are staged on the green today.

6 Special & Free Events

Mayfest is a 3-week event launched on May Day, with an excellent cultural program of local and international music concerts and theatrical performances. For more details, get in touch with Mayfest, 18 Albion St., in Glasgow (☎ **0141/552-8000**).

After an absence of 120 years, the **Glasgow Fair** (held during most of the month of July—actual dates vary) returned in 1990. The fair is likely to contain everything, including carnivals, tea dances, European circuses, Victorian rides, even a country-and-western stampede. For information, call ☎ **0141/305-7348.**

The **Glasgow International Jazz Festival** opens in the last days of June and usually runs through the first week of July. This festival has attracted some big names in the past, including the late Miles Davis and also Dizzy Gillespie. Tickets are available from the Ticket Centre, Candleriggs (☎ **0141/227-5511**), although some free events are always announced.

The **Carmunnock Highland Games** are held at Carmunnock village and at the Hughenden playing field, Anniesland Road, Glasgow. Throwing events test strength and technique, and piping and dancing competitions add to the festivities. The games are usually held the second week in June. Consult the tourist office at ☎ **0141/ 848-4440** for more details.

7 Sports & Outdoor Pursuits

BICYCLING   The tourist office for Glasgow (see above) provides maps with detailed bicycle paths in the city. Many are scenic routes. Bicycle rentals are available from **West End Cycles,** 16 Chancellor St. (☎ **0141/357-1344**), charging £10 ($16.50) per day and requiring a deposit of £50 ($82.50). You can also rent bikes from the **Bicycle Chain,** 1417 Dumbarton Rd. (☎ **0141/958-1055**), which charges £10 ($16.50) a day, plus a deposit of £50 ($82.50).

GOLF   See "Golf" for Glasgow in chapter 4.

HEALTH & FITNESS CLUBS   Glasgow boasts some 40 such clubs, mainly those offering both a swimming pool and a gym. The best ones are at the **Glasgow Hilton International,** 1 William St. (☎ **0141/204-5555**), which has a fully equipped gym with a treadmill stair, plus a sauna, steam room, Jacuzzi, and large swimming pool. The charge is £10 ($16.50) for nonguests to use the facilities. Hours are daily from 6:30am to 9:30pm. The **Glasgow Marriott,** 500 Argyle St. (☎ **0141/226-5577**), features a swimming pool, Jacuzzi, squash court, and a fully equipped gymnasium. The charge is £12 ($19.80) for nonguests between the hours of 6:30am and 10pm Monday through Friday and from 7am to 10pm on weekends.

JOGGING   The tourist office (see above) will provide a list of the many parks and gardens in the city with jogging trails. Some of these parks also offer bowling greens and tennis courts.

SPORTS COMPLEXES   The **Kelvin Hall International Sports Arena** is on Argyle Street (☎ **0141/357-2525**), near the River Kelvin (Underground: Kelvin Hall). It offers volleyball and basketball courts, as well as an indoor track. Visitors can come here and use the weight room daily from 9am to 9:30pm for £2.50 ($3.95). This is also the major venue in Scotland for national and international sports competitions. Look in the newspapers or check with the tourist office for any events that might be planned at the time of your visit.

The **Crownpoint Sports Complex,** 183 Crownpoint Rd. (☎ **0141/554-8274**), is another major venue for national and international tournaments. This outdoor sports complex has two artificial turf parks, an athletics park, and a track. Nonmembers can use the complex Monday through Friday from 3 to 10pm and on weekends from 10am to 5pm. Use of the track costs £1.65 ($2.70), and the weight room goes for £2.25 ($3.70).

The city's newest center, which opened in the spring of 1993, is the **Scotstoun Leisure Centre,** James Drive, Scotstoun (☎ **0141/959-4000**), about 2 miles from the city center. It's open Monday through Friday from 9am to 10pm and Saturday and Sunday from 9am to 6pm.

WATER SPORTS & ICE SKATING   The **Lagoon Leisure Centre,** Mill Street, Paisley (☎ **0141/889-4000**), offers indoor facilities with a free-form leisure pool with a wave machine, fountains, and flume. Sauna suites with sunbeds are also offered, along with Jacuzzis and a Finnish steam room. The ice rink boasts an international ice pad with six curling lanes, and is home to the Paisley Pirates ice hockey team. The center also offers bar and catering facilities. The center is open Monday through Friday from 10am to 10pm and Saturday and Sunday from 9:30am to 5pm.

Public swimming is available Monday through Friday from 10am to 10pm and from 9:30am to 5pm on the weekends. Ice skating is available Monday through Friday from 9:30am to noon, and Monday, Wednesday, and Thursday from 1:30 to 4pm; Tuesday from 12:30 to 3pm; Tuesday, Wednesday, and Thursday from 7:30 to 9:30pm; Friday from 2:45 to 5pm and 7:30 to 10pm; Saturday and Sunday from

10:45am to 12:45pm, 2:30 to 4:30pm, and 8 to 10pm. Admission to the ice rink costs £1.75 to £2.25 ($2.90 to $3.70) for adults and £1.25 to £1.75 ($2.05 to $2.90) for children. Skate rental is 80p ($1.30). You can go swimming for £2.20 ($3.65) for adults and £1.25 ($2.05) for children, or use the sauna for £3 to £4.50 ($4.95 to $7.45).

8 Shopping

Take along your passport when you go shopping in case you make a purchase that entitles you to a VAT (value-added tax) refund.

THE SHOPPING SCENE   One of the principal shopping districts is **Sauchiehall Street,** Glasgow's fashion center, containing many shops and department stores where you'll often find quite good bargains, particularly in woolen goods. The major shopping area, about three blocks long, has been made into a pedestrian mall. **Argyle Street,** which runs by the Central Station, is another major shopping artery.

All dedicated world shoppers know of **Buchanan Street,** a premier pedestrian mall. This is the location of the famed Fraser's Department Store (see below). From Buchanan Street you can also enter **Princes Square,** an excellent shopping complex with many specialty stores, restaurants, and cafes.

The Barras, the weekend market of Glasgow, takes place about a quarter of a mile east of Glasgow Cross. It's held all year on Saturday and Sunday from 9am to 5pm. This century-old market has some 800 traders selling their wares in stalls and shops. You cannot only browse for that special treasure but can become a part of Glasgow life and be amused by the buskers.

The **Argyll Arcade** stands at 30 Buchanan St. Even if the year of its construction (1827) were not set in mosaic tiles above the entrance, you'd still know that this is an old collection of shops beneath a curved glass ceiling. The arcade contains what is possibly the largest single concentration of retail jewelers, both antique and modern, in Europe, surpassing even Amsterdam. The fame of the arcade has traveled far beyond Glasgow. It's considered lucky to purchase a wedding ring here.

The exorbitant rents charged here even exceed those charged along London's fashionable Bond Street. Since the arcade is officially classified as a historic building, a portion of its rental income goes toward maintaining it in mint condition. The arcade maintains an impressive security system to protect the area's shops and multi-million-pound inventories.

Antiques lovers will want to browse through **Victorian Village,** 57 W. Regent St. (☎ 0141/332-0808), a warren of tiny shops in a slightly claustrophobic cluster. Much of the merchandise isn't particularly noteworthy, but there are many exceptional pieces. Several of the owners stock reasonably priced 19th-century articles; others sell old jewelry and clothing, a helter-skelter of artifacts.

Paddy's Market, by the railway arches on Shipbank Lane, operates daily if you'd like to see an old-fashioned slice of Glaswegian street vending.

In the heart of Glasgow is the city's latest and most innovative shopping complex, **St. Enoch Shopping Centre.** Open year-round, it's climatically controlled. You can shop under the biggest glass roof in Europe. The center lies to the east of Central Station on St. Enoch Square.

ART GALLERIES

Compass Gallery. 178 W. Regent St. ☎ 0141/221-6370.

Here, art objects begin at around £40 ($66) each, and tend to be the product of younger, less-well-known artists, often students from the local universities. Although the Compass Gallery is larger, a bit older, and somewhat less prestigious than the Cyril Gerber, both galleries occupy what the staffs refer to as "semibasements."

Cyril Gerber Fine Art. 148 W. Regent St. ☎ 0141/221-3095.

One of Glasgow's most respected art galleries veers away from the avant garde, specializing instead in British paintings, sculptures, and ceramics crafted between around 1880 and today and Scottish landscapes and cityscapes. Cyril Gerber is a respected local art authority with lots of contacts in art circles throughout Britain. Objects begin at around £100 ($165).

BOOKSTORES

John Smith & Son. 57 St. Vincent St. ☎ 0141/221-7472.

This is a thoroughly Scottish bookshop, called "part of Scotland's cultural history."

DEPARTMENT STORE

Fraser's Department Store. Buchanan St. ☎ 0141/221-3880.

This is Glasgow's version of Harrods. A soaring Victorian-era glass arcade rises four stories, and inside you'll find everything ranging from clothing to oriental rugs, from crystal to handmade local artifacts of all kinds.

GIFTS & DESIGN

Catherine Shaw. 24 Gordon St. ☎ 0141/204-4762.

Named after the long-deceased matriarch of the family that runs the place today, this is a small-scale and somewhat cramped gift shop that has cups, mugs, postcards, and gift items based on the designs of Charles Rennie Mackintosh. There's also some highly evocative Celtic mugs called *quaichs* (welcoming cups or whisky measures, depending on who you talk to), and tankards in both pewter and silver. A great place for small-scale, easy-to-pack, high-quality, and somewhat offbeat gifts. Look for a second branch at 32 Argyll Arcade (entrances to the arcade are on both Argyll and Buchanan streets; ☎ 0141/221-9038).

Mackintosh Shop. In the foyer of the Glasgow School of Art, 167 Renfrew St. ☎ 0141/353-4526.

This one-room gift shop prides itself on an inventory of books, cards, stationery, coffee and beer mugs, glassware, and sterling-and-enamel jewelry that's more carefully tuned to the original designs of Scottish design luminary Charles Rennie Mackintosh than any other outlet in Glasgow. Although they don't sell furniture, they're ready and willing to refer you to a small-scale craftsman of whose work they approve. **Bruce Hamilton, Furnituremaker,** 4 Woodcroft Ave., Broomhill (☎ 01505/322550), has been involved in the restoration of many Rennie Mackintosh interiors and has produced a worthy group of chairs, sideboards, and wardrobes authentic to Mackintosh's original designs. Expect to pay around £250 ($412.50), not including upholstery fabric, for a copy of the designer's best-known chair (the Mackintosh–Ingram chair), and delays of at least a month before your furniture is shipped to wherever you specify.

National Trust for Scotland Shop. Hutcheson's Hall, 158 Ingram St. ☎ 0141/552-8391.

No one will object if you buy a year's membership to Britain's National Trust, available for adults at this shop for £25 ($41.25) for adults or for £17 ($28.05) for persons over 60. Most visitors, however, drop in for gifts—maps, calendars, postcards, pictures, dish towels, bathroom accessories, and kitchenware. Some of the crockery is fashioned Mackintosh-design styles. The historically important building that contains this place, incidentally, was originally built in 1641 as a hospital for elderly men and orphans.

HABERDASHERY

✪ Hector Russell. 110 Buchanan St. ☎ **0141/221-0217.**

There's possibly no more prestigious store in Scotland than this elegant haberdashery. The welcome of the experienced sales staff is genuinely warm-hearted. Crystal and gift items are sold on street level, but the real heart and soul of the establishment is on the lower level where you'll find impeccably crafted and reasonably priced tweed jackets, tartan-patterned accessories, waistcoats, and sweaters of top-quality wool for men and women. Men's kilts contain as much as 8 yards of material. Women's and children's hand-stitched kilts are also available. The establishment was founded in 1881 and is the oldest established kilt maker in Scotland.

LUGGAGE

Bag and Baggage. 11 Royal Exchange Square. ☎ **0141/221-8005.**

If the other purchases you couldn't resist place you in the market for a new suitcase, this store has a wide selection of reasonably priced but high-quality merchandise. Most of the valises and briefcases were designed for women.

MUSIC

Virgin Retail Music. 28–32 Union St. ☎ **0141/221-0103.**

The staff here is both knowledgeable and charming, eager to pass on their love of Scottish music to interested newcomers. This outlet offers the biggest and best selections of records and tapes in the city with special strengths and insights in both traditional and contemporary Scottish music.

PORCELAIN & CRYSTAL

Stockwell China Bazaar. 67–77 Glassford St. ☎ **0141/552-5781.**

This is Glasgow's largest purveyor of porcelain, with four floors bulging with Royal Doulton, Wedgwood, Noritake, and Royal Worcester; plus crystal stemware by many different manufacturers. Anything you buy can be insured and shipped to whatever address you specify. Many of the clients you're likely to meet here are Glaswegian brides-to-be picking out table settings.

9 Glasgow After Dark

Glasgow, not Edinburgh, is the cultural center of Scotland, and the city is alive with performances. Request a copy of *Culture City* or *What's On* at the tourist office. Both these monthly publications are free and usually contain complete listings of what's happening in Scotland's largest city.

At most newsstands, you can also purchase a copy of *The List,* which is published every other week and sells for £1.80 ($2.95). It details arts and other events for Edinburgh as well as Glasgow.

You can purchase tickets to most cultural events at the **Ticket Centre,** City Hall, Candleriggs (☎ **0141/227-5511** or 0141/305-7500). The box office there sells tickets to at least a dozen theaters in the city. You can buy tickets in person Monday through Saturday from 9:30am to 6:30pm and Sunday from noon to 5pm. Phone reservations are accepted from 9am to 9pm Monday through Saturday and from noon to 5pm on Sunday.

THE PERFORMING ARTS
OPERA & CLASSICAL MUSIC

In the winter season, the **Royal Scottish National Orchestra** offers Saturday-evening concerts at the **Glasgow Royal Concert Hall**, 2 Sauchiehall St. (☎ 0141/332-6633). The **BBC Scottish Symphony Orchestra** presents Friday-evening concerts at the BBC Broadcasting House, Queen Margaret Drive, or at City Halls, Albion Street. In the summer months, the Scottish National Orchestra has a short Promenade season (dates and venues are announced in the papers and information is also available at the tourist office). Tickets to all concerts are available at the Ticket Centre (see above).

✪ **Theatre Royal.** Hope St. and Cowcaddens Rd. ☎ 0141/332-9000. Ballet tickets £5–£36 ($8.25–$59.40); opera tickets £3.50–£45 ($5.75–$74.25).

This is the home of the **Scottish Opera,** which has attracted attention on the world scene, as well as of the **Scottish Ballet.** The theater also hosts visiting companies from around the world. The building, designed by C. J. Phipps, first opened in 1895. It was completely refurbished for the Scottish Opera, reopening in 1975. It offers 1,547 comfortable seats, including spacious bars and buffets on all four levels. It has been called "the most beautiful opera theatre in the kingdom" by the *Daily Telegraph,* which noted its splendid Victorian Italian Renaissance plasterwork and glittering chandeliers. But it's not the decor that attracts operagoers—rather, the ambitious repertoire. On performance days, the box office is open Monday through Saturday from 10am to 7:30pm; on nonperformance days, Monday through Saturday from 10am to 6pm. The Scottish Opera also performs at the Robin Anderson Auditorium on West Princes Street.

THEATER

Although hardly competition for London, the theater scene in Glasgow is certainly the equal of Edinburgh. Young Scottish playwrights often make their debuts here, and you're likely to see anything from Steinbeck's *The Grapes of Wrath* to Wilde's *Salome* to *Romeo and Juliet* done in Edwardian dress.

The prime symbol of Glasgow's verve remains the **Citizen's Theatre,** Gorbals and Ballater streets (☎ 0141/429-0022), founded after World War II by James Bridie, a famous Glaswegian whose plays are still produced on occasion there. It's home to a repertory company. Tickets range from £2 to £8 ($3.30 to $13.20). The box office is open Monday through Saturday from 10am to 9pm.

The **Glasgow Arts Centre,** 12 Washington St. (☎ 0141/221-4526), directed by George Cherrie, always seems to be doing something interesting, including children's productions. Activities range from theatrical performances to folk concerts. It's open Monday through Saturday from 9:30am to 5pm and 6:30 to 10pm; in summer, it's closed in the evening. Tickets, costing £10 to £16 ($16.50 to $26.40), can be reserved over the phone.

King's Theatre, 297 Bath St. (☎ 0141/248-5153), has a wide range of productions, including straight plays, musicals, and comedies. During the winter season it's noted for its pantomime presentations. Tickets range from £6 to £25 ($9.90 to $41.25). The box office is open Monday through Saturday from 10am to 6pm.

Mitchell Theatre, 6 Granville St. (☎ 0141/287-5511), has earned a reputation for small-scale entertainment, ranging from dark drama to dance, as well as conferences and seminars. A modern little theater, it adjoins the well-known Mitchell Library. The theater box office is open Monday through Saturday from 9am to 5pm and 7:30 to 10:30pm. Ticket prices vary with each production.

Pavilion Theatre, 121 Renfield St. (☎ 0141/332-1846), is still alive and well, specializing in modern versions of vaudeville which, as they will assure you around here, isn't dead. The Pavilion sells its own tickets, which are not available at City Centre. Tickets range from £8 to £15 ($13.20 to $24.75). The box office is open Monday through Saturday from 10am to 8pm.

Tron Theatre, 63 Trongate (☎ 0141/552-4267), occupies one of the three oldest buildings in Glasgow, the former Tron Church. The old structure, with its famous Adam dome and checkered history, has been transformed into a small theater that presents the best of contemporary drama, dance, and music events.

The Tron also has a beautifully restored Victorian cafe/bar serving traditional home-cooked meals, including vegetarian dishes and a fine selection of beer and wine. The box office is open on Monday from 10am to 5pm, Tuesday through Saturday from 10am to curtain time, and Sunday from 5pm to curtain time. Tickets range from £3 to £8 ($4.95 to $13.20) for adults and £3 to £4 ($4.95 to $6.60) for children.

THE CLUB & BAR SCENE
DANCE CLUBS & LIVE MUSIC
Barrowland. Gallowgate. ☎ 0141/552-4601.

This stripped-down hall seats 2,000 and only opens on nights that shows are booked, usually from 7 to 11pm, although some performances run until 2am. July and August are the quiet months, as most entertainment is geared toward a student audience that is on vacation at that time. Cover charges vary, depending on the act, but are generally £8 to £20 ($13.20 to $33), the latter charge for such U.K.–popular bands as White Zombie or The Breeders.

Fury Murrys. 96 Maxwell St. ☎ 0141/221-6511. Cover £2 to £5 ($3.30 to $8.25).

At least 95% of its clientele are students looking for nothing more complicated than a good, sometimes rowdy, time. It's in a cellar, a 2-minute walk from the very central St. Enoch Shopping Centre. The disco music is upbeat but not ultratrendy. There's one very busy bar, a single dance floor, and ample opportunities to meet the best and brightest in Scotland's university system. Jeans and T-shirts are the right garb for the place. It's open Thursday through Sunday from 10:30pm to 3:30am. Thursday features live bands and other nights are strictly for dancing. Other nights are reserved for private parties.

The Garage. 490 Sauchiehall St. ☎ 0141/332-1120. Cover £3 ($4.95) Mon–Thurs and Sun, £4 ($6.60) Fri, £5 ($8.25) Sat.

This former warehouse is popular with students, who test the limits of its 800-person capacity on weekends. In the downstairs area, surrounded by rough stone walls, you get the impression you're in a castle. The music is a mix of Britpop and indie. Most regulars, however, gravitate to the huge main dance floor, where lots of shiny metal fixtures stand out in contrast to the stone walls. Deejays spin an eclectic mix of music ranging from Abba to Prodigy. There are three bars downstairs and one upstairs.

Grand Ole Opry. 2–4 Govan Rd., Paisley Toll Rd. ☎ 0141/429-5396. Cover £2–£5 ($3.30–$8.25).

In a sprawling sandstone building, once a movie theater, 1¹⁄₂ miles south of Glasgow's center, it's the largest club in Europe devoted exclusively to country-western music. It might be something of a cultural shock to North Americans who assume (incorrectly) that country-western is a uniquely new-world phenomenon. There's a bar and dancing arena on both levels and a "chuck wagon" eatery serving steaks and other such fare on the upper level. Live music is always performed from a large stage at the front, which is visible from everywhere in the club. Performers are usually from the U.K., although a handful of visiting artists from the States turn up. It's open Friday through Sunday and occasionally on Thursday (if demand warrants it) from 6:30pm to midnight. A three-course fixed-price steak dinner in the restaurant goes for £10 ($16.50).

King Tut's Wah-Wah Hut. 272 St. Vincent St. ☎ **0141/221-5279.** Cover £3.50–£12 ($5.75–$19.80).

This sweaty, crowded rock-and-roll bar, in business for nearly a decade, is a good place to check out the Glasgow music and arts crowd, as well as bands ranging from local to the occasional international act. Successful Scottish acts My Bloody Valentine and Teenage Fan Club got their start here. The club is open Monday through Friday from noon to midnight, Saturday from 1pm to midnight, and Sunday from 6pm to midnight.

Nice 'n' Sleazy. 421 Sauchiehall St. ☎ **0141/333-9637.**

This club books live acts Thursday through Sunday when the cover charge is normally £2 ($3.30) to £3 ($4.95). It can get more expensive, though, as bands like the Cranberries, Alice Donut, and Helmet play here as well. Holding some 200 patrons, it provides a rare opportunity to catch internationally popular bands that have the capacity to sell out vast arenas in other parts of the world. Upstairs, on Sunday and Monday nights, deejays spin an eclectic mix of music for dancing, but most people come for the bands. Open daily 11:30am to midnight.

Renfrew Ferry. 55 Clyde Place. ☎ **0141/227-5511.** Cover £5.50 ($9.05).

This club is an old car ferry that once provided service on the River Clyde. Now it hosts a Friday night ceilidh with traditional Scottish music and dancing from 9pm to 1am. Other musical acts are booked infrequently throughout the year. The club has the capacity to hold 450 people, and there are several bars scattered about the vessel.

The 13th Note. 80 Glassford St. ☎ **0141/553-1638.**

This club has moved away from jazz in the past couple of years and now books mainly rock and punk bands on Tuesday, Wednesday, and Thursday nights. On Friday, Saturday, and Sunday, deejays mix a jazz-funk concoction for dancing. It's a comfortably trashy candlelit club with no cover for entertainment. Open daily noon to midnight.

Victoria's Nightclub. 98 Sauchiehall St. ☎ **0141/332-1444.** Cover £5 ($8.25) Wed and Sun, £4 ($6.60) Thurs, £7 ($11.55) Fri–Sat. Closed Mon–Tues.

Victoria's prides itself on being the only nightclub in all of Scotland with cabaret performances. On two floors of high-tech design in the heart of town, it contains a restaurant, two dance floors, several bar areas (one of which features a live pianist), and a stage on which singers, comedians, and cabaret artists amuse and titillate the audience between 9pm and 3am. Dress is "smart casual," and the crowd tends to be older than age 30, affluent, and sophisticated.

Dinner, costing £12 to £16 ($19.80 to $26.40) per person, without wine, is served Wednesday through Saturday from 7:30pm to 3am. Cabaret starts at 9pm.

FAVORITE PUBS
Bon Accord. 153 North St. ☎ **0141/248-4427.**

Bon Accord's amiably battered paneling with nicks and dents offers proof of this establishment's enduring popularity. The bar has a bristling array of hand-pumps, a dozen devoted to real British ales, the rest to beers and stouts from Germany, Ireland, and Holland. The pub is likely to satisfy your taste in malt whisky as well. The place is clean and tidy, a safe haven in a big city. Bar snacks cost around £3.50 ($5.75) each. It's open daily from 11am to midnight.

Cask of Still. 154 Hope St. ☎ **0141/333-0980.**

This is the best place for sampling malt whisky. A selection of more than 250 single-malt whiskies, at a variety of different strengths, can be tasted (perhaps not on the same night). You can also order malt whiskies at a variety of maturities—that is, years spent in casks. Many prefer the malt whisky that has been aged in a sherry cask. On one shelf is displayed a Dalmore and a Springbank whisky, each bottled more than half a century ago. They're to be looked at—never sampled. You can also enjoy good bar food at lunch, including cold meat salads or sandwiches. Light meals cost £2.75 ($4.55) and up. The "Still" is open Monday through Saturday from 11am to midnight and Sunday from 6 to 11pm.

✪ **Corn Exchange.** 88 Gordon St. ☎ **0141/248-5380.**

Located opposite the Central Station, this was the Corn Exchange in the mid-19th century, but now it is one of the most popular pubs of Glasgow. Amid dark paneling and high ceilings, guests can enjoy a pint of lager or other beer. The pub is open Monday from 11am to 11pm, Tuesday through Saturday from 11am to midnight, and Sunday from 12:30pm to midnight. Food is served daily from noon to 9pm, with a bar platter beginning at £3.85 ($6.35).

L'Attaché. 27 Waterloo St. ☎ **0141/221-3210.**

One of several traditional Scottish pubs in its neighborhood, L'Attaché is outfitted with stone floors and rows of decorative barrels that evoke an aura of yesteryear. There's a self-service counter for food—steak pie, lasagna, and salads for £5 ($8.25)—and an impressive array of ales and single-malts. There is a disco on Thursday, Friday, and Saturday nights and a live jazz band on Saturday afternoon. The pub is open Monday through Thursday from 7:30am to 11pm, Friday and Saturday from 7:30am to midnight, and Sunday from noon to 5pm.

Gay Bars & Clubs

There is no strongly visible lesbian bar or night club scene in Glasgow. Many lesbians who attend bars frequent those that cater mainly to males.

Austin's. 183A Hope St. ☎ **0141/332-2707.**

This basement bar has a vamped-up cocktail lounge look, a proper setting for the popular drag shows held here on Tuesday through Sunday nights. A mixed crowd gathers to cheer on their favorite performers. There is never a cover charge, and nightly drink specials are offered during happy hour from 7 to 9pm. The bar is open daily from noon to midnight, with mixed drinks costing from £1.70 ($2.80).

Bennet's. 90 Glassford St. ☎ **0141/552-5761.** Cover £2–£6 ($3.30–$9.90).

While this place attracts most of the gay and lesbian nightlife activity of Glasgow, on certain nights of the week (especially Tuesday) it's known as the most fun and crowded straight disco in all of Scotland. One floor above street level in a building a short walk from the Central Station and George Square, its clientele includes men and women ages 17 to 60. The music plays on and on, interrupted only by the occasional drag show. Performers are usually imported from London or the States; shows last about 45 minutes and begin after 1am on Wednesday and Saturday nights. The club is open Tuesday through Sunday from 11pm to 3:30am.

Café Delmonica's. 68 Virginia St. ☎ **0141/552-4803.**

Don't let the old wooden pub interior fool you; this is a popular gay bar that keeps a busy weekly schedule, with karaoke on Sunday, drag shows on Wednesday and Thursday, and deejays spinning dance tunes on Friday and Saturday. Some drag shows are orderly performances, whereas others are rowdy competitions where any-thing goes. Mixed drinks start at £1.85 ($3.05), and the cafe is open daily from noon to midnight.

Court Bar. 69 Hutcheson St. ☎ **0141/552-2463.**

This is a small cozy pub, a popular meeting place for a mixed gay clientele to come together for drinks and talk. It's a good starting point for a gay evening on the town. Hours are daily from noon to midnight.

Squares Lounge. 106 W. Campbell St. ☎ **0141/221-9184.**

This is a small gay drinking lounge during the week, but it heats up on weekends when deejays play to dancers on the small, tightly packed floor. There's no cover and hours are daily from noon to midnight. Mixed drinks start at £1.35 ($2.25).

Waterloo Bar. 306 Argyle St. near Central Station. ☎ **0141/221-7359.**

The friendly bartenders here are a good source of information about what's happen-ing in the gay scene at any given time. A popular gay bar, Waterloo gets most crowded during happy hour, which is held nightly during the unusual hours of 9pm to midnight when you can make your drink a double for just £2.05 ($3.40). Like most Glasgow pubs, it is open daily from noon to midnight.

10 Side Trips from Glasgow

As Sir Walter Scott dominates the Borders, so is the presence of Robert Burns felt in the country around Ayr and Prestwick. There's also a string of famous seaside resorts stretching from Girvan to Largs. Some of the greatest golf courses in Britain, including Turnberry, are found here; and Prestwick, of course, is the site of one of Scotland's airports.

Glasgow makes a good gateway to Burns Country, as it has excellent bus and rail connections to Ayr, which is your best bet for exploring the area. Motorists should take A77 southwest from Glasgow to Ayr. Prestwick and Troon link directly north of Ayr along the coastal road.

AYR

Ayr is the most popular resort on Scotland's west coast, lying 81 miles southwest of Edinburgh, 35 miles southwest of Glasgow, and 5 miles south of Prestwick. A busy market town, it offers 2¹/₂ miles of beach. This royal burgh is also noted for the manufacture of fabrics and carpets, so you may want to allow time to browse through its shops. With its steamer cruises, fishing, golf, and racing, it faces the Isle of Arran and the Firth of Clyde.

For centuries Ayr has been associated with horse racing, and it now has the top racecourse in Scotland. One of the main streets of the town is named Racecourse Road for a stretch near the town center.

Ayr was the birthplace of road builder John L. MacAdam, whose name was immortalized in the road surfacing called "macadam."

Trains from Glasgow's Central Station (call ☎ **0345/484-950,** 24 hours a day, for passenger inquiries) service Ayr. From Glasgow, Stagecoach Express buses arrive in Ayr in just 1 hour and 25 minutes. For departure information, phone

Impressions

And, wow! Tam saw an unco sight!
Warlocks and witches in a dance:
Nae Cotillion, brent new frae France,
But hornpipes, jigs, strathspeys, and reels,
Put life and mettle in their heels.

—Robert Burns, "Tam o' Shanter"

☎ **0990/808080.** The **Ayr Tourist Information Centre** is at Burns House, Burns Statue Square (☎ **01292/288688**).

Seeing the Sights

Ayr is full of Burns associations. The 13th-century **Auld Brig o' Ayr,** the poet's "poor narrow footpath of a street / Where two wheelbarrows tremble when they meet" was renovated in 1910.

The **Auld Kirk of Ayr** dates from 1654 when it replaced the 12th-century Church of St. John. Burns was baptized in the kirk. **Wallace Tower,** on High Street, is another attraction, rising some 112 feet. Constructed in 1828, it has a statue of William Wallace.

Another architectural curiosity is **Loudoun Hall,** Boat Vennal, off Cross in the heart of town. A wealthy merchant had this town house constructed in the late 1400s. It's one of the oldest examples of "burgh architecture" left in the country. It's open from mid-July to the end of August only, Monday through Saturday from 11am to 6pm.

On the outskirts of the town, the **Maclaurin Gallery and Rozelle House,** on Monument Road in Rozelle Park (☎ **01292/443708**), are installed in what had been stables and quarters for servants attached to a manor house. A Henry Moore bronze sculpture and a major collection of contemporary art are on display, as well as changing exhibitions of sculpture, paintings, and crafts. There's a nature trail through woodland. The location is about 1¹/₂ miles south of Ayr off the road to the Burns Cottage at Alloway. Open year-round, it can be visited Monday through Saturday from 10am to 5pm; from April to October it's also open on Sunday from 2 to 5pm. No admission is charged.

Nearby Attractions

In Tarbolton village, 7¹/₂ miles northeast of Ayr off A758, is the **Bachelors' Club,** 7 Sandgate (☎ **01292/541940**), a 17th-century house where in 1780 Burns and his friends founded a literary and debating society; it's now a property of the National Trust for Scotland. In 1779 Burns attended dancing lessons there, against the wishes of his father. There also, in 1781, he was initiated as a Freemason in Lodge St. David. Eleven months later he became a member of Lodge St. James, which continues today in the village. The Bachelors' Club is open for visitors from April to the end of October only, daily from 11:30am to 5pm. The custodian, Yule Lithgow, will arrange to show it at other times if you phone him at ☎ **01290/550503.** Admission is £1.80 ($2.95) for adults, £1.20 ($2) for seniors and children. Tarbolton is 6 miles from Prestwick Airport.

Accommodations

Caledonian Hotel. Dalblair Rd., Ayr, Ayrshire KA7 1UG. ☎ **01292/269331.** Fax 01292/610722. 110 rms, 4 suites. TV TEL. £105 ($173.25) double; £160 ($264) suite. AE, DC, MC, V. Free parking.

The six-floor 1970s modern Caledonian Hotel is centrally situated, just a few hundred yards from Ayr's seashore and 500 yards from the rail station. It offers refurbished but unimaginative bedrooms with radios, hair dryers, and tea- and coffeemakers. Many of the rooms have views of the sea. Hudson's Bar and Grill is a lively place to meet and eat. There's a selection of freshly roasted joints on the captain's table. The hotel also boasts a fully equipped leisure complex and is located near several championship golf courses. Services range from laundry and dry cleaning to 24-hour room service.

✪ **Fairfield House.** 12 Fairfield Rd., Ayr, Ayrshire KA7 2AR. ☎ **01292/267461.** Fax 01292/261456. 25 rms, 8 suites. TV TEL. £130 ($214.50) double; £180 ($297) suite. AE, DC, MC, V. Rates include Scottish breakfast. Free parking.

On the seafront near Low Green, this two-story 1912 Edwardian town house built for a Glaswegian tea merchant has been restored to its original elegance and converted into the best hotel in Ayr. The staff is especially attentive and helpful, and can direct you to nearby golfing possibilities. The noted designer of classic British interiors, Lady Henrietta Spencer-Churchill, created the public rooms and bedrooms in a British country-house style. The guest bedrooms are large, comfortable, and luxurious, and often decorated with chintz. They contain such amenities as radios, trouser presses, and hair dryers, and most of the bathrooms have a bidet.

Dining/Entertainment: The food at Fairfield has been called an "oasis in a culinary desert." In the Conservatory, the best of Scottish produce—from Highland lamb to Spey salmon—goes into the food. Meals are served from noon to 2:30pm and 7 to 9:30pm, with main courses ranging from £15 to £20 ($24.75 to $33). The French Fleur de Lys serves dinner from 7 to 9:30pm, with meals ranging from £24 to £30 ($39.60 to $49.50).

Facilities: Leisure club, with a swimming pool, spa bath, sauna/steam room, solarium, and gym.

Services: Room service, laundry/valet.

Pickwick Hotel. 19 Racecourse Rd., Ayr, Ayrshire KA7 2TD. ☎ **01292/260111.** Fax 01292/285348. 15 rms. TV TEL. £59.50 ($98.20) double. AE, MC, V. Rates include Scottish breakfast. Free parking.

It may seem odd to have a hotel commemorating a character in a Charles Dickens novel in a town noted for its memories of Rabbie Burns. But this three-story, late-Victorian hotel, set on its own grounds directly east of the Esplanade, does just that. The Pickwick is really a large-size house, renting fairly routine but clean private bedrooms. Each unit bears a Dickensian title. All rooms have radios, trouser presses, and hot-beverage facilities. In the paneled Pickwick Club, you can soak up the Dickensian atmosphere. The food is simple but fresh. Baby-listening devices are installed, dry cleaning and laundry are available, and room service is 24 hours.

Quality Station Hotel. Burns Statue Square, Ayr, Ayrshire KA7 3AT. ☎ **01292/263268.** Fax 01292/262293. 73 rms, 1 suite. TV TEL. £77.50 ($127.90) double; £87 ($143.55) suite. AE, DC, MC, V. Free parking.

The three-story Station Hotel has been an Ayr landmark since its original Victorian construction in 1888. Connected to the town's railway station, it sits behind a red sandstone exterior, and although it isn't the most modern hotel in town, many visitors consider its high ceilings, elaborate detailing, and old-world charm more than enough reason to check in. The bedrooms are routine, many quite spacious, sometimes with minibars. There's an evening restaurant one floor above the lobby level, where table d'hôte dinners cost £14.50 ($23.90), and a piano bar on the ground floor where bar lunches cost around £5 ($8.25). Most of the clients are families and couples, who fill the rooms along with regular business clients. There's a health club in the hotel, with a gym, solarium, sauna, and Jacuzzi.

DINING

Fouter's Bistro. 2A Academy St. ☎ **01292/261291.** Reservations recommended. Main courses £5–£6 ($8.25–$9.90) at lunch, £9–£12.50 ($14.85–$20.65) at dinner; fixed-price lobster lunch (in season only) £12.50 ($20.65). AE, DC, MC, V. Tues–Sun noon–2pm and 6:30–10:30pm. MODERN BRITISH.

Set in the historic heart of Ayr, this restaurant occupies the solidly built cellar of what was originally an 18th-century bank. It retains the original sandstone floor and a vaulted ceiling covered in terra-cotta tiles. Despite its fortified look, all traces of the room's original severity are overcome by the warm hospitality of its owners, Fran and Laurie Black. The restaurant's name derives from Scottish argot: *foutering about* is a charming way of saying "bumbling about" (although this place is anything but bumbling).

The smooth demeanor and seamless service focus on such modern British dishes as venison with rowanberry sauce, local Gresshingham duck with black-cherry sauce, and seafood that includes whatever's fresh on the day of your arrival, served with a tarragon-flavored cream sauce.

Tudor Restaurant. 8 Beresford Terrace. ☎ **01292/261404.** Main courses from £10 ($16.50); fixed-price meal £4.70 ($7.75) for 2 courses, £5.20 ($8.60) for 3 courses; high tea £5–£8.50 ($8.25–$14). MC, V. July–Aug, Mon–Sat 9am–9pm (last order), Sun 4–8pm (last order); Sept–June, Mon–Sat 9am–8pm. SCOTTISH/INTERNATIONAL.

This busy and best-recommended family-oriented restaurant has a real Tudor look with its dark half-timbering. Most popular here are the fixed-price lunch, and the cost-conscious high tea served from 3:15pm to closing. Food items are well prepared and copious, and include such rib-sticking specialties as a version of chicken Maryland (breaded and fried breast of chicken with bacon, tomatoes, peaches, and pineapple fritters). The restaurant, in a turn-of-the-century building, is a 20-yard walk south of Burns Statue Square.

AYR AFTER DARK

✪ **Rabbie's Bar.** Burns Statue Square. ☎ **01292/262112.**

This famous pub, in a way, mixes Scottish poetry with electronic music. The exposed stone of the walls is highlighted with the pithy verses of one of its earlier clients, Robert Burns, who used to drop in for a pint of ale and conversation with his friends. A portrait of Rabbie is painted directly onto the wall. However, don't come here expecting poetry readings in a quiet corner. The crowd, while not particularly literary, is talkative and fun, and they enjoy live music several nights a week. There's a large selection of imported beers, a busy stand-up bar, long rows of crowded banquettes and copper-topped tables, and an extra-large TV screen showing videos of whatever musical group is hot in the English-speaking world. Bar snacks average 55p (90¢). Open Monday through Saturday from 11am to 12:30am and Sunday from noon to midnight.

ALLOWAY

Some 2 miles south of Ayr is where Scotland's national poet was born on January 25, 1759, in the gardener's cottage—the "auld clay biggin"—that his father, William Burns, built in 1757.

Robert Burns: National Poet & Penniless Genius

Robert Burns (1759–96), or "Rabbie," is the national poet of Scotland, who carried the Scottish vernacular to its highest point in his satiric, earthy, and bawdy romantic poems and songs.

Born in Alloway in Ayrshire on a wind-tossed night, Burns was the son of an impoverished gardener, who encouraged him to read and seek an education. Burns became an unsuccessful farmer and later an exciseman, but the world knows him as the "heaven-taught ploughman," author of the narrative masterpiece, "Tam o' Shanter," and the humanitarian "A Man's a Man for A' That."

Rabbie was a great womanizer ("Once heartily in love, never out of it"), and he fathered at least 15 children, 9 of whom were legitimate. In his short time on earth, he wrote approximately 370 poems and songs, only to die at the age of 37, wracked with rheumatic fever and harassed by his debtors for the sum of £5. His pregnant wife, Jean, had to beg a shilling from the poet's brother to feed her children on the day of his funeral.

Every year on his birthday, January 25, the poet is honored all over the world—from Edinburgh to San Francisco, from Bombay to Tokyo—at male-dominated Bachelors' Clubs, like the one founded by Burns and his friends. Even Shakespeare doesn't get this kind of attention. At these Burns suppers, guests who are entitled wear the kilt; non-Scottish admirers of the poet dress formally. After a dram of whisky is drunk as a welcome, the first course, or *Het Hail*, is carried in; it's invariably cock-a-leekie soup, made with chicken and leeks. Next comes *Caller Fish Frae Loch and Sea*, usually fresh salmon. But for the main course, there can be no deviation in the menu: It must be the "Great Chieftain o' the Puddin' Race," the dreaded haggis. The chef comes in bearing the haggis on a large platter, preceded by a kilted piper playing "Scotland the Brave." Of course, everyone drinks a whisky to the "health of the haggis." After all, a small nip is known as *usquabaugh* or "water of life."

The chairman of the club—again, after a quaff of whisky—takes out a Scottish dirk and recites Burns's "Address to a Haggis" before he plunges the blade into the beast. Out gushes the meat, entrails, or whatever the chef decided to stuff into the sheep's stomach. This seasoned minced meat, oatmeal, and onions is enjoyed by all the "bachelors."

The sad truth is that although haggis is consumed at all birthday celebrations for Burns, the poor poet missed out on it himself. He considered haggis "one of the most delicious meals on earth." But rarely could he afford the dish, settling instead for tatties (mashed potatoes) or neeps (turnips).

SEEING THE SIGHTS

The **Auld Brig Over the Ayr,** mentioned in "Tam o' Shanter," still spans the river, and **Alloway Auld Kirk,** also mentioned in the poem, stands roofless and "haunted" not far away. The poet's father is buried in the graveyard of the kirk.

Burns Monument and Gardens. Alloway. ☎ **01292/441215.** Admission included in the entrance fee to Burns Cottage and Museum (see below). Apr–Oct, Mon–Sat 9am–6pm; Nov–Mar, Mon–Sat 10am–4pm. Drive 2 miles south of Ayr on B7024.

The monument is a Grecian-style building erected in 1823, containing relics, books, and manuscripts associated with Robert Burns, dating back to the 1820s.

Burns Cottage and Museum. Alloway. ☎ **01292/441215.** Admission £2.50 ($4.15) adults, £1.25 ($2.05) children and seniors, £6 ($9.90) family ticket (2 adults and 3 children). Apr–Oct, daily 9am–6pm; Nov–Mar, Mon–Sat 10am–4pm. Drive 2 miles south of Ayr on B7024.

More than 80,000 people visit this place annually. It still contains some of its original furniture, including the bed in which the poet was born. Chairs displayed here were said to have been used by Tam o' Shanter and Souter Johnnie. Beside the cottage in which the poet lived is a museum.

Tam o' Shanter Experience. Murdoch's Lane. ☎ **01292/443700.** Admission £2.50 ($4.15) adults, £1.25 ($2.05) children and seniors. Daily 9am–6pm. Drive 2 miles south of Ayr on B7024.

Here you can watch a multiscreen film on Burns's life, his friends, and his poetry. Information is available from the personnel, and there's a well-stocked gift shop plus a tearoom. The Russians are particularly fond of Burns and his poetry, and many come annually to visit the cottage and pore over his original manuscripts.

ACCOMMODATIONS & DINING

Belleisle House Hotel. Belleisle Park, Doonfoot Rd., Alloway, Ayr, Ayrshire KA7 4DU. ☎ **01292/442331.** Fax 01292/445325. 16 rms, 1 suite. TV TEL. £75 ($123.75) double; £80 ($132) bridal suite. AE, MC, V. Rates include Scottish breakfast. Free parking.

This imposing three-story country house was built in 1755. Set beside A719, in the suburb of Alloway about 2 miles south of Ayr, it stands in a public park noted for its two golf courses. Today functioning as a country-house hotel, it has a stone exterior and interior paneling with ornate carvings that depict some scenes from Robert Burns's "Tam o' Shanter." Blazing fireplaces add to the traditional Scottish country-house ambience. The hotel has two dining rooms: one inspired by the music room of Marie Antoinette at Versailles, the other by her bedroom. The Scottish cooking is excellent, with table d'hôte lunches priced at £9.50 ($15.65) and dinners at £17 ($28.05). Open all year, the establishment extends a special welcome to children and has a play area set aside for them.

Brig o' Doon Hotel. Alloway, Ayr, Ayrshire KA7 4PQ. ☎ **01292/313343.** 5 rms. TV TEL. £120 ($198) double. AE, DC, MC, V. Rates include Scottish breakfast. Free parking.

One of the most famous footbridges in Scotland, the Brig o' Doon (immortalized by Robert Burns) lies a few steps from this hotel, on the river's east bank. This new hotel, with its 2 acres of gardens, is obviously the choice place to stay in the area. For several decades, the Burns Monument Hotel stood here, but in 1997 it was torn down and reconstructed from the ground up, and more fetchingly named. Everything, from the plumbing to the stylish bedrooms, is state of the art. So famous are the gardens here that much of the hotel's income derives from the many wedding receptions booked on its premises. The hotel lies 2 miles south of Alloway, a quarter of a mile from the hamlet of Doonfoot, beside B7024. You should reserve early, especially in summer.

MAYBOLE & CULZEAN

Some 12 miles south–southwest of Ayr and 4 miles west of Maybole on A719 is
✪ **Culzean Castle** (☎ **01655/760274**). Built by the famous Scottish architect Robert Adam at the end of the 18th century, this clifftop creation is a fine example of his castellated style. Essentially a dwelling place, Culzean (pronounced "Cul-*lane*") replaced an earlier Scots tower house as the family seat of the powerful Kennedy clan. In 1945 the castle and grounds were given to the National Trust for Scotland. The castle overlooks the Firth of Clyde, with a view to the south of Ailsa Craig, a 1,100-foot-high rounded rock 10 miles offshore, a nesting ground and sanctuary

for seabirds. It's well worth a visit and is of special interest to Americans because of General Eisenhower's connection—in 1946 the National Guest Flat was given to the general for his lifetime in gratitude for his services as supreme commander of Allied Forces in World War II. An exhibition of Eisenhower memorabilia including his North African campaign desk is sponsored by Scottish Heritage U.S.A., Inc. Culzean stands near the famous golf courses of Turnberry and Troon, a fact that particularly pleased the golf-loving Eisenhower. The tour also includes the celebrated round drawing room, delicately painted ceilings, and Adam's outstanding oval staircase.

The castle is open May to September, daily from 10am to 6pm; in April and October, Monday through Friday from noon to 5pm and Saturday and Sunday, including Easter, from 10:30am to 5:30pm. Last admission is half an hour before closing. The charge is £6 ($9.90) for adults, £4 ($6.60) for children. Admission includes entrance to the park described immediately below.

Part of the land surrounding the castle includes **Culzean Country Park** (☎ 01655/760269), which in 1969 became the first such park in Scotland. The 565-acre grounds include a walled garden, an aviary, a swan pond, a camellia house, and an orangery, as well as a deer park, miles of woodland paths, and beaches. It has gained an international reputation for its Visitor Centre (Adam's home farm) and related visitor and educational services. Up to 200,000 people visit the country park annually. The park is open daily from 9am to dusk. Admission is £3.40 ($5.60) for adults and £2 ($3.30) for children, unless you purchased the combined ticket described above.

You can reach Culzean Castle from Ayr. Maidens Bus (no. 60) from the Sandgate Bus Station in Ayr runs to Culzean six times per day; a one-day round-trip ticket costs £2.80 ($4.60) for adults and £1.90 ($3.15) for children.

TURNBERRY

On the Firth of Clyde, the little town of Turnberry, south of the castle, was originally part of the Culzean Estate owned by the marquess of Ailsa. It began to flourish early in this century, when the Glasgow and South Western Railway developed golfing facilities, railway service, a recognized golfing center, and a first-class hotel. From the original two 13-hole **golf courses,** the complex has developed into the two 18-hole courses, Ailsa and Arran, known worldwide. The Ailsa, one of the most exacting courses yet devised, has been the scene of numerous championship tournaments and PGA events. Call ☎ 01655/331000 for information.

Just to the east of Turnberry, you might want to take a short drive to see **Souter Johnnie's Cottage**, Main Road, in Kirkoswald (☎ 01655/760603), 4 miles west of Maybole on A77. This was the 18th-century home of the village cobbler, John Davidson (Souter Johnnie), who, with his friend, Douglas Graham of Shanter Farm, was immortalized by Burns in "Tam o' Shanter." The cottage contains Burnsiana and contemporary cobblers' tools. In the churchyard are the graves of Tam o' Shanter and Souter Johnnie. The cottage is open Good Friday through September daily from 11:30am to 5pm; October, Saturday and Sunday from 11:30am to 5pm. Admission is £180 ($2.95) for adults and £1.20 ($2) for children.

A final sight is **Carleton Castle,** along A77 some 14 miles south of Culzean Castle, 6 miles along the coast from the little seaside town of Girvan. In its heyday it was a watchtower, built to guard the coastline against invaders. A famous ballad grew out of a legend surrounding this castle. It was said to be the headquarters of a baron who married eight times. When this Bluebeard got tired of a wife, he pushed her over the cliff and found himself another spouse. However, he proved no match for his eighth wife, May Cullean. "The Ballad of May Colvin" relates how she is supposed to have tricked and outlived him.

ACCOMMODATION & DINING

✪ **Turnberry Hotel, Golf Courses and Spa.** Maidens Rd., Turnberry, Ayrshire KA26 9LT. ☎ **01655/331000.** Fax 01655/331706. 132 rms, 10 suites. TV TEL. £255–£285 ($420.75–$470.25) double; from £315 ($519.75) suite. AE, DC, MC, V. Rates include Scottish breakfast. Free parking.

Turnberry, 1 hour south of Glasgow on A77, is a remarkable Edwardian property that has undergone one of the most complete glamorizations of any hotel in Scotland. The owners spent millions of dollars on the infrastructure and decor without diminishing the opulent aura of 1908, when the hotel was built. From afar one can see the hotel's white facade, its red-tile roof, and its dozens of gables. In World War II it served as a military hospital, but today it's once again one of the grand hotels of Britain. The public rooms contain Waterford crystal chandeliers, Ionic columns, molded ceilings, and well-polished oak paneling. Each suite and bedroom is furnished in elegant turn-of-the-century style, with a marble-sheathed bath; rooms open onto views of the surrounding lawns, forests, and in some cases, the Scottish coastline.

Dining/Entertainment: The hotel's three eating areas have differing degrees of formality. Most elegant is the Turnberry Restaurant, serving traditional Scottish and French food. Fixed-price dinners cost £43.50 ($71.75) for five courses. The Bay at Turnberry is part of the resort's spa facilities and serves light food; the Clubhouse is headquarters for the golf facilities, built in 1993.

Facilities: Gym equipment, tennis, and Country Club and Spa with leisure center, Turkish bath, sauna, steam rooms, and squash courts.

PRESTWICK

Prestwick is the oldest recorded baronial burgh in Scotland, but most visitors know it for Prestwick Airport. The airport, 2 miles north of Ayr, 32 miles southwest of Glasgow, and 78 miles southwest of Edinburgh, used to be a big international airport, but today it's used mainly for charter flights.

Prestwick goes back to at least A.D. 983. The Mercat Cross stands outside what used to be the Registry Office and marks the center of the oldest part of Prestwick. Behind St. Ninian's Episcopal Church is **Bruce's Well.** The water from the well is reputed to have cured Robert the Bruce of leprosy.

Prestwick is a popular holiday town and is one of Scotland's most attractive resorts, with its sandy coastlines and golf courses. Prestwick opens onto views of Ayr Bay and the Isle of Arran.

Trains from the Central Station in Glasgow leave hourly from Prestwick; call ☎ 0345/484950 in Glasgow for more information. Buses from the Buchanan Street Station in Glasgow leave hourly for Prestwick; call ☎ 0990/808080 for schedules. From Glasgow, motorists take A77 southwest. The tourist information office is at nearby Ayr (see above).

ACCOMMODATION & DINING

St. Nicholas Hotel. 41 Ayr Rd., Prestwick, Ayrshire KA9 1SY. ☎ 01292/479568. Fax 01292/475793. 18 rms (15 with shower). TV TEL. £45 ($74.25) double without shower, £54 ($89.10) double with shower. AE, DC, MC, V. Rates include Scottish breakfast. Free parking.

This three-story stone Edwardian hostelry, on the main road between Prestwick Airport and the train station, is about a 5-minute walk from tennis courts, a swimming pool, and indoor bowling. The hotel has full central heating and double-glazed windows. Standardized bedrooms have tea/coffeemakers. Rooms in back opening onto the park are quieter; those in front open onto the main road with its noisy traffic. Good food and service prevail in the dining room, where lunch, high tea, and dinner are available. William Murdock, the congenial host, goes out of his way to make guests feel at home.

TROON

This holiday resort, 7 miles north of Ayr, 31 miles southwest of Glasgow, and 77 miles southwest of Edinburgh, looks out across the Firth of Clyde to the Isle of Arran. It offers several golf links, including the **"Old Troon" course.** In summer, visitors find plenty of room on its 2 miles of sandy beaches that stretch along both sides of its harbor; the broad sands and shallow waters make it a safe haven. From here you can take steamer trips to Arran and the Kyles of Bute.

Troon is a 20th-century town, its earlier history having gone unrecorded. It takes its name from the curiously shaped promontory that juts out into the Clyde estuary on which the old town and the harbor stand. The promontory was called Trwyn, the Cymric word for nose, and later this became Trone and then Troon. A massive statue of *Britannia* stands on the seafront as a memorial to the dead of the two world wars.

Trains from Glasgow's Central Station arrive at the Troon station several times daily (trip time: 40 min.). Call ☎ **0345/484950** for 24-hour information about departures. Trains also connect Ayr with Troon, a 10-minute ride. From the Ayr bus station, you can reach Troon and other parts of the area by bus. Call ☎ **0990/ 808080** for more details. From Prestwick, motorists head north along B749. A summer-only **tourist information office** is in the Municipal Buildings, South Beach (☎ **01292/317696**).

ACCOMMODATION

Piersland House Hotel. 15 Craigend Rd., Troon, Ayrshire KA10 6HD. ☎ **01292/314747.** Fax 01292/315613. 15 rms, 13 cottage suites. TV TEL. £110–£140 ($181.50–$231) double; £115 ($189.75) suite. AE, DC, MC, V. Rates include Scottish breakfast. Free parking.

Located beside B749, a 3-minute drive south of the town center, this three-story country Victorian was built a century ago by Sir Alexander Walker of the Johnnie Walker whisky family. The importation of 17,000 tons of topsoil transformed its marshy surface into the lush 4-acre garden that visitors see today. The highest prices are for a superior twin, a four-poster double, or for a cottage suite with a bedroom, sitting room, and private bath adjacent to the hotel. The bedrooms have traditional Scottish country-house styling and such amenities as hair dryers and radios. Full room service is available upon request.

Frankly, this establishment is better known as a social center than as a hotel. At lunchtime and in the evening, pub lovers around Troon flock to the Red Bull for a drink or buffet lunch near one of the intricately carved fireplaces. On sunny days the staff sets up tables at the edge of the formal garden, turning it into an outdoor version of a neighborhood pub. The hotel's food is among the best in the area. A fixed-price dinner costs £15.50 to £19.95 ($25.60 to $32.90) and might include such dishes as locally caught scallops and chicken in a white-wine sauce. The hotel and its public rooms are popular as a place to celebrate large birthday parties and wedding receptions for residents of the surrounding region.

DINING

Highgrove House. Old Loans Rd., Troon, Ayrshire KA10 7HL. ☎ **01292/312511.** Reservations recommended. Main courses £6–£12 ($9.90–$19.80) at lunch, £12–£14 ($19.80–$23.10) at dinner. AE, MC, V. Daily noon–2:20pm and 7–9:30pm. Drive 2 miles north of Troon on A78. TRADITIONAL SCOTTISH.

This white-painted, red-roofed brick building is small, charming, and isolated on a hillside known for its scenic view over the sea and the Isle of Arran. Most of its business derives from its restaurant, where a red-and-green color scheme (installed in 1995) complements a big-windowed view and tables that—despite the place's isolation—are filled and cleared with a surprisingly rapid turnover. Menu items include several varieties of steamed salmon, accompanied by a changing array of sauces and such garnishes as crayfish or shrimp, medaillons of Angus beef with rondelles de pâté, and peppercorn sauce; and medaillons of Scottish venison with rowanberry sauce.

Upstairs are nine simply decorated but comfortable bedrooms, which, with breakfast included, rent for £85 ($140.25) double. Each contains TV and telephone.

Marine Highland Hotel. 8 Crosbie Rd. ☎ **01292/314444.** Reservations required. Fairways Restaurant: main courses £15.50 ($25.60); fixed-price 3-course lunch £15 ($24.75); fixed-price 4-course dinner £21.50 ($35.50). Rizzio's Restaurant: main courses £8–£11 ($13.20–$18.15); pizza and pasta buffet £5 ($8.25). AE, DC, MC, V. Fairways: daily noon–2pm and 7–10pm. Rizzio's: daily noon–2:30pm and 5:30–10pm. SCOTTISH/INTERNATIONAL.

The landmark 1890s hotel that houses these two restaurants stands on the Ayrshire coastline overlooking the Royal Troon Golf Course. Either can satisfy your hunger pangs with some degree of style. Rizzio's is a cozy dark red and wood-paneled Italian eatery and is the less formal of the two.

The more formal restaurant, Fairways, provides a proper and somewhat reserved setting for panoramic views of the Isle of Arran. Here you can enjoy traditional Scottish and French cuisine. Try "pillows" of smoked Scottish salmon, followed by rosettes of filet of Scottish beef in peppercorn sauce, or turbot with langoustines or shrimp.

Argyll & the Isles 8

For those who want to sample a bygone era, the old county of Argyll off the coastline of western Scotland is a rewarding journey. The boundaries of Argyll have shifted and changed over the years—part of it was once an independent kingdom known as Dalriada. In Gaelic, Argyll is known as *Earraghaidheal,* "coastland of the Gael." Argyll takes up a lot of the deeply dissected western Highlands, its rivers flowing into the Atlantic. Summers along the coast are usually cool and damp, and winters are relatively mild but wet, with little snow.

The major center for the Argyll district is Oban, meaning "small bay." It's a center of Gaelic culture and a great port for the Western Isles: the gateway to Mull, largest of the Inner Hebrides; to the island of Iona, the cradle of Scottish Christianity; and to Staffa, where Fingal's Cave inspired Mendelssohn to write the *Hebrides Overture* (for these islands, see chapter 12). The ferries to the offshore islands run only twice a day until summer; then there are cruises to Iona from early June to late September. For information about island ferry services to Mull, Iona, and the Outer Hebrides, get in touch with **MacBrayne Steamers** at their office in Oban (☎ **01631/ 562285**). They sail to 23 islands, with fares ranging from £49 ($80.85) for a car and four passengers to Mull, to £122 ($201.30) for a car plus £32.90 ($54.30) per passenger for travel to Barra.

A number of colorful sites are near the port town, including Port Appin and Inveraray, where visitors can soak up the atmosphere of the district away from the major towns.

After leaving Fort William (see chapter 11), our trail around the entire length of the Scottish mainland picks up again after crossing the Ballachulish Bridge. If you've already seen Glencoe (reached along A82), you can hug the coastal road (A828), which will eventually take you into Oban.

Before you begin your exploration of the Hebridean Islands coming up, there are several island destinations off the Argyll coast meriting your time. The long peninsula of Kintyre separates the islands of the Firth of Clyde, including Arran, from the islands of the Inner Hebrides, notably Mull, Islay, and Jura. (For information on Mull, see chapter 12.)

From the Isle of Islay to the Mull of Kintyre, the climate is mild. The land is rich and lush, especially on Arran, giving way on Islay to peat deposits that lend flavor to the making of such fine malt whiskies as Lagavulin, Bruichladdick, and Laproaig. There's a diversity of scenic beauty: hills and glens, fast-rushing streams, and little roads that eventually lead to coastal villages that display their B&B signs in summer.

Yachters are drawn to the sheltered harbors of the Argyll coast. This is active, sports-oriented country, offering golfing, walking, sea angling, and fishing. The best golf is at Machrie and Machrihanish.

The unspoiled and remote island of Jura is easily reached from Islay. And the best news for last: These islands, as well as Kintyre, Scotland's longest peninsula, are among the most economical places to visit in the British Isles.

A DRIVING TOUR OF THE ARGYLL PENINSULA

The ideal way to tour the Argyll Peninsula is by car. Take A82 northwest from Glasgow to the western Highlands. Motorists can also drive to the Kintyre Peninsula (A816 from Oban, heading south). Destinations around Kintyre can be reached by one of the Caledonian MacBrayne ferries.

Day 1   From the Scottish mainland at Ardrossan, southwest of Glasgow, head west on a car ferry to Brodick, capital of the Isle of Arran. Either overnight here or pick one of the adjoining villages (see below). See the island's major attraction, Brodick Castle. The ferry arrives in less than an hour. From Brodick you can head south along A841, which goes around the entire island, passing all the attractions of major interest, before bringing you back to Brodick.

Day 2   Leave Brodick the next morning and head to the ferry departure terminal at Lochranza. Here you can cross the Kilbrannan Sound by car ferry from the north of Arran, landing at Claonaig on the Kintyre Peninsula. Take B842 south to the capital of Campbeltown for the night. After checking into a hotel there, follow B842 south to the fabled Mull of Kintyre at the southern tip for an afternoon's exploration.

Day 3   In the morning, drive northwest along A83 to Tayinloan where a 20-minute car ferry crosses the Sound of Gigha to the Isle of Gigha. Since there are so few roads here, you may want to leave your car parked and explore the island by bicycle (rentals available near where the ferry docks). After spending most of the day exploring this ancient island and its famous gardens, return to Kintyre for the night and drive north along the western coast (A83) to the fishing port of Tarbert for an overnight stopover.

Day 4   From Kennacraig on the Kintyre Peninsula, take a $2^1/_2$-hour trip across the bay to Port Ellen on the Isle of Islay (summer only). To see the island of Islay take A846 north to Brigend and then northeast to Port Askaig. You can find accommodations here or at several other places on the island (see below).

Day 5   Take the short ferry crossing at Port Askaig and spend the day exploring the island of Jura. You can overnight there in its one hotel or else return to Islay.

Day 6   From Islay, return to the peninsula of Kintyre and go along A83 north toward Inveraray. You can explore the western coast of Loch Fyne before arriving at Inveraray, where you can view its castle.

Day 7   Head northeast from Inveraray along A819 for an overnight stay at Dalmally. Use this day to explore both the eastern and western shores of scenic Loch Awe.

Day 8   Take A85 west to Oban and arrive before lunch—plenty of time to view its numerous attractions, including some of the highlights in the environs, especially the Crinan Canal and the old capital of Dunadd.

Argyll Forest Park

Argyll Forest Park, in the southern Highlands, stretches almost to Loch Fyne and is made up of Benmore, Ardgartan, and Glenbranter. The park covers an area of 60,000 acres and contains some of the most panoramic scenery in Scotland. The park takes in a wide variety of habitats, from lush forests and waterside to bleaker grassy moorlands and mountains. The Clyde sea lochs cut deep into the forested areas of the park, somewhat in the way ford "fingers" cut into the Norwegian coastline, and in the northern part are the Arrochar Alps (so called), where Ben Arthur reaches a height of 2,891 feet.

The park attracts those interested in natural history and wildlife as well as rock climbers, hikers, and hill walkers. The park offers many recreational activities and there are dozens of forest walks for trail blazers with all degrees of skill. Trails that lead through forests to the loftier peaks are strenuous and meant for skilled hikers. Others are easier, including paths from the Younger Botanic Garden by Loch Eck leading to Puck's Glen.

There's abundant wildlife in the sea lochs: shark, sea otters, and gray seals, among other inhabitants such as sea scorpions, crabs, shrimp, sea lemons, sea anemones, and sea slugs. Boats and canoes can be rented. One of the park's biggest thrills is to explore the underwater caves of Loch Long.

In the early spring and summer the park trails are at their most beautiful—woodland birds create choruses of song, and the forest is filled with violets, wood anemones, primroses, and bluebells. Sometimes the wildflowers are so thick they're like carpets. In the rainy climate of the southern Highlands, ferns and mosses also grow abundantly.

To reach the park, take A83 to B828 heading for Loch Goll, or follow A815 to Loch Eck and Loch Long. Both Arrochar and Tarbet, stops on the Glasgow–Fort William rail line, are on the periphery of the park's northeast frontier.

The best place for lodging is Dunoon, to the south, on the Cowal Peninsula, which forms an easy gateway to the park. Dunoon has been a holiday resort since 1790, created for the "merchant princes" of Glasgow. Recreational facilities abound here, including an indoor swimming pool, tennis courts, and an 18-hole golf course. To pick up information about the park and a trail map, go to the **Dunoon Tourist Center** at 7 Alexandra Park (☎ **01369/703785**).

1 Isle of Arran

Brodick: 74 miles W of Edinburgh, 29 miles W of Glasgow

At the mouth of the Firth of Clyde, this island is often described as "Scotland in miniature" because of its wild and varied scenery—the glens, moors, lochs, sandy bays, and rocky coasts that have made the country famous. Once on Arran, buses will take you to various villages, each with its own character. A coast road, 60 miles long, runs around the length of the island.

Arran has some splendid mountain scenery, notably the conical peak of **Goatfell** in the north, reaching a height of 2,866 feet, called "the mountain of the winds." Arran is also filled with beautiful glens, especially **Glen Sannox** in the northeast and **Glen Rosa,** directly north of Brodick. The island is only 25 miles long, 10 miles wide, and can be seen in 1 day.

Students of geology flock to Arran to study igneous rocks of the Tertiary. Cairns and standing stones at Tormore intrigue archaeologists as well.

ESSENTIALS
GETTING THERE

BY TRAIN   High-speed electric trains operate from Glasgow Central direct to Ardrossan Harbour, taking 1 hour (for 24-hour rail inquiries, call ☎ **0345/484950**). At Ardrossan you must cross by ferry to Arran (see below), arriving in Brodick on the east coast.

BY CAR   From Glasgow, head southwest along A737 until you reach the port of Ardrossan, where you can board a car ferry.

BY FERRY   Ferries making the 30-minute crossing operate from Ardrossan to Brodick, Arran's major town, on the eastern shore. In summer a small ferry runs between Lochranza in the north of Arran across to Claonaig in Argyll, providing a gateway to the Highlands and a visit to Kintyre. There are six boats daily, and the fare is £45 ($74.25) for a vehicle, plus £6.45 ($10.65) per passenger. For information about ferry departures (which change seasonally), check with Caledonian MacBrayne (call ☎ **01475/650100** at the ferry terminal in Gourock).

VISITOR INFORMATION

The **Arran Tourist Information Office** is at The Pier, Brodick (☎ **01770/302140**).

EXPLORING THE AREA

After the ferry docks at Brodick, you may want to head for Arran's major sight, ✪ **Brodick Castle** (☎ **01770/302202**), 1¹/₂ miles north of the Brodick pierhead. The historic home of the dukes of Hamilton, the castle dates from the 13th century and contains superb silver, antiques, portraits, and objets d'art. Some castle or other has stood on this site since about the 5th century, when the Dalriad Irish, a Celtic tribe, came here and founded their kingdom. The castle is the property of the National Trust for Scotland. It is open March through October daily from 11:30am to 4:30pm. The award-winning gardens and the Country Park are open daily from 11:30am to sunset. Admission to both the castle and gardens is £4.50 ($7.45) for adults or £3 ($4.95) for seniors and children.

South from Brodick lies the village and holiday resort of **Lamlash,** opening onto Lamlash Bay. From here a ferry takes visitors over to Holy Island with its 1,000-foot peak. A disciple of St. Columba founded a church on this island.

In the north, **Lochranza** is a village with a unique appeal. It opens onto a bay of pebbles and sand, and in the background lie the ruins of a castle that reputedly was the hunting seat of Robert the Bruce.

SHOPPING   Divided into three businesses, the **Duchess Court Shops,** Home Farm, Brodick (☎ **01770/302831**), is made up of the Home Farm Kitchen, selling locally produced chutneys, jams, and marmalades; the Nature Shop, which deals in books, jewelry, wood carvings, puzzles, T-shirts, and other assorted goods; and Something Special, which sells natural grooming products. They're open daily from 10am to 5pm. Located 6 miles north of Brodick in Corrie, **Corriecraft & Antiques,** Hotel Square (☎ **01770/810661**), sells small Arran antiques and pottery. It's open daily from 10am to 12:45pm and 2 to 5:30pm. In Lamlash, **Patterson Arran Ltd.,** The Old Mill (☎ **01770/600606**), offers chutneys, mustards, preserves, and other locally produced condiments. It's open daily from 10am to 5pm. The **Old Byre Showroom,** Auchencar Farm (☎ **01770/840227**), located 5 miles north of

The Kintyre Peninsula & Isle of Arran

Blackwaterfoot, along the coastal road in Machrie, sells sheepskin, leather, and tweeds, but its biggest draw is the large selection of locally produced hand- and machine-knitted wool sweaters. It's open daily from 10am to 5pm.

WHERE TO STAY & DINE
IN BRODICK

○ **Auchrannie Country House Hotel.** Auchrannie Rd., Brodick, Isle of Arran KA27 8BZ. ☎ **01770/302234.** Fax 01770/302812. 28 rms. TV TEL. £150 ($247.50) double. Rates include half board. MC, V.

Acclaimed as the finest dining or accommodation choice on the island, this period mansion was once the house of the dowager duchess of Hamilton. In its pristine glory, it stands in 6 acres of landscaped gardens and woods about a mile from the Brodick ferry terminal. A hotel of charm and character, it also features the best re-sort facilities on the island. The people who restored this Victorian period piece did so with taste and imagination. The rooms in the extended new wing are the most comfortable, but each accommodation is furnished with taste, employing select fabrics and decorative accessories.

Dining/Entertainment: Guests enjoy drinks in the cocktail bar or sun lounge be-fore heading for the Garden Restaurant, offering a table d'hôte menu, the finest on Arran. The best of fresh local produce is used. The chef's greatest skill is in the prepa-ration of West Coast seafood. A "Taste of Scotland" is evident in many of the dishes. Outside guests should reserve a table; meals begin at £23 ($37.95). You can also enjoy the Brambles Bistro, offering a wide range of snacks and tasty food throughout the day and evening.

Services: Room service, baby-sitting, laundry.

Facilities: Indoor pool, turbo spa, Turkish bath, sauna, solarium, snooker room, beauty salon.

○ **Kilmichael Country House Hotel.** Isle of Arran KA27 8BY. ☎ **01770/302219.** Fax 01770/302068. 7 rms, 2 suites. TV. £79.90–£119.90 ($131.85–$197.85) double; £123.90 ($204.45) suite. V. Rates include Scottish breakfast.

The most scenically located house on the island, the Kilmichael is an "oasis of tran-quillity," in a favorite phrase. Along with the Auchrannie Country House, it has set new standards of catering on Arran. Standing on its own extensive grounds, it's said to be the oldest house on the island, perhaps in former days a stamping ground for Robert the Bruce. One room is supposedly haunted. The bathrooms are beautifully appointed, as are the well-furnished bedrooms. A combination of the tasteful new and the antique are used throughout. There's an aura of gentility, as reflected by the log fires and the fresh flowers from the garden. Most important, the staff is helpful, courteous, and welcoming.

The food is also worthy, using local Scottish produce whenever possible. Inter-national dishes are featured, and fine wines and an attention to detail go into both the à la carte dishes, ranging from £11 to £16.50 ($18.15 to $27.20), and the chef's special five-course dinner, costing £28.50 ($47.05) per person.

IN LAMLASH

Carraig Mhor. Lamlash. ☎ **01770/600453.** Reservations recommended. £17.50 ($28.90) 2-course fixed-price menu, £20.50 ($33.80) 3-course fixed-price menu. MC, V. Mon–Sat 7–9pm. Closed 2 weeks in Jan and first 2 weeks in Feb. Take the Whiting bus from Brodick. CONTINENTAL.

Carraig Mhor, in a pebbledash 1700s cottage, serves imaginatively prepared and beau-tifully presented dinners. This modernized cottage, to which you are welcomed by

Austrian-born Peter Albrich and his British wife, Penny, stands in the center of the village overlooking the water. The chef, who has had worldwide experience, makes extensive use of local produce—in particular, seafood and game. All bread and ice creams, among other offerings, are made on the premises. In the evening an extensive à la carte menu is available. Meals include a choice of eight starters, five fish dishes, six meat dishes, and seven desserts. The menu changes seasonally, and there are separate dining rooms for smokers and nonsmokers.

Glenisle Hotel. Shore Rd., Lamlash, Isle of Arran KA27 8LS. ☎ **01770/600559.** Fax 01770/600966. 13 rms. TV TEL. £67 ($110.55) double, including Scottish breakfast; £92 ($151.80) double, including half board. MC, V. Take the Whiting bus from Brodick.

Glenisle is said to be one of the oldest buildings in the village, but no one knows its age or even the century of its construction. Across the road from the waterfront, in the heart of the village, the well-kept gardens of this white-sided country B&B, with a view across the bay to the Holy Isle, have flower beds and tall old trees. A reception lounge, a water-view dining room, and a lounge where drinks are available are brightly and cheerfully decorated. Each of the relatively simple bedrooms has flowered curtains, a radio, electric blankets, tea- and coffeemakers, and room call. A fixed-price three-course dinner costs £14.50 ($23.90).

In Whiting Bay

Grange House Hotel. Whiting Bay, Isle of Arran KA27 8QH. ☎ and fax **01770/700263.** 9 rms (7 with tub or shower). TV. £60 ($99) double without bath, £70 ($115.50) double with bath. MC, V. Rates include Scottish breakfast.

Only 100 yards from the sea, opening onto views across the Firth of Clyde, this country-house hotel is operated by Janet and Clive Hughes. Both take a personal interest in their guests (Janet's the chef), and both have an extensive background in catering. A gabled stone house, standing on landscaped grounds, the Grange House offers tastefully furnished traditional bedrooms. Each unit is different, although Victoriana predominates. Some of the rooms can be arranged to accommodate a family. Eight open onto views of Holy Isle and the Ayrshire coastline. One downstairs bedroom is suitable for persons with disabilities, and the hotel also has a sauna and a spa bath. Served between 7 and 8pm, dinner is a three-course affair costing £16 ($26.40) per person.

Royal Hotel. Whiting Bay, Isle of Arran KA27 8PZ. ☎ and fax **01770/700286.** 5 rms, 1 suite. TV TEL. £48 ($79.20) double or suite. No credit cards. Rates include Scottish breakfast. Closed Nov–Mar. Take the Whiting bus from Brodick.

This pleasingly proportioned granite house, whose upper stories have been sheathed in coats of white stucco, was built in 1895 as one of the first hotels on Arran. True to its original function as a temperance hotel, it still serves no alcohol, although dinner guests can bring bottles of their own wine or beer into the dining room. A three-course dinner, served daily at 7pm only, costs £12 ($19.80). Guests enjoy a vista over the bay and its tidal flats from some of the bedrooms. Although all the rooms are priced the same, one contains a four-poster bed and lots of chintz, whereas another has a small sitting room adjacent to its sleeping area. The hotel is in the center of the village beside the coastal road.

In Kildonan

Kildonana Hotel. Kildonan, Isle of Arran, KA27 8SE. ☎ **01770/820207.** Fax 01770/820320. 22 rms (6 with bath). £48 ($79.20) double without bath, £56 ($92.40) double with bath. No credit cards. Rates include Scottish breakfast.

Originally built as an inn in 1760, with a newer section added in 1928, this hotel rises a few steps from the best beach on the island. Designed in Scottish farmhouse style, it has a slate roof, white-painted stone walls, and ample views of seabirds and gray seals basking on the rocks of Pladda Island opposite the hotel. The hotel is owned by Maurice Deighton, his wife Audrey, and their sons and daughters-in-law, any of whom you're likely to find cooking, tending one of the two bars, or maintaining the bedrooms. Beneath six large chandeliers, the spacious dining room presents three-course dinners for £10 to £18 ($16.50 to $29.70). A specialty is crab or lobster salad, made from freshly netted shellfish caught by one of the Deighton sons, who works as a fisherman. A crowd of locals is likely to compete in a friendly fashion over the dartboard and billiards tables in the establishment's pub. The staff can arrange such diversions as putting, boating, fishing, table tennis, waterskiing, and scuba diving.

IN LAGG

Lagg Hotel. Lagg, near Kilmory, Isle of Arran KA27 8PH. ☎ **01770/870255.** Fax 01770/ 870250. 15 rms. £84 ($138.60) double, including Scottish breakfast; £112 ($184.80) double, including half board. AE, MC, V. Closed late Oct to mid-Mar.

Set beside A841, half a mile south of Kilmory and within half a mile of the sea, in a sheltered hollow where some kind of inn has stood since 1791, this pleasantly embellished inn is popular on the island for its dining facilities. Ronald Moore and his family maintain the gardens that stretch beside the rocky stream that adjoins the 16-acre property. If the weather is sunny, you might enjoy tea on the lawn under the shade of the palm trees, which seem to thrive in this mild microclimate. In cooler weather, visitors are likely to be greeted by a log fire blazing in one of the cozy cocktail lounges. The bedrooms are artfully decorated with flowering fabrics and solidly traditional furniture.

Nonresidents are welcome to dine here, although it's wise to phone in advance. Four-course meals are served for £19.95 ($32.90) nightly between 7 and 9pm. Most residents dine in the hotel dining room on the half-board plan. On Friday and Saturday nights, this becomes a carvery. An à la carte restaurant, the Wishing Well, is on the premises. Here meals ranging from £6 to £10 ($9.90 to $16.50) are served nightly from 7 to 10pm.

IN BLACKWATERFOOT

Kinloch Hotel. Blackwaterfoot, Isle of Arran KA27 8ET. ☎ **01770/860444.** Fax 01770/ 860447. 44 rms, 7 suites. TV TEL. £90 ($148.50) double; £110 ($181.50) suite. AE, DC, MC, V. Rates include half board (Scottish breakfast and dinner). Take the Blackwaterfoot bus from Brodick.

This hotel, made from two joined Victorian buildings, appears deceptively small from the road. It's actually the largest building in the hamlet of Blackwaterfoot, set behind a cream-colored stone facade with a contemporary wing jutting out along the coast. The bedrooms are modestly comfortable and conservative, each with a radio, intercom, and teamaking facilities. Most of the double rooms have sea views, whereas singles tend to look out over the gardens in back. On the premises are a sauna, a heated indoor swimming pool, and a large dining room.

ARRAN AFTER DARK

Regulars gather in Brodick's pubs to talk, argue, and drink. The **Brodick Bar,** in the center (but without a street address; ☎ **01770/302-1690**), is an old wooden pub that's open Monday through Saturday from 11am to midnight. Real Scottish ales range from £1.80 to £2.10 ($2.95 to $3.45), and seafood bar meals are served daily from noon to 2:30pm and 5:30 to 10pm. **Duncan's Bar** (no phone and no street address), featuring wood and leather chairs and walls hung with old photographs and riding gear, keeps the same hours and serves real cask ales and lagers starting at £1.75 ($2.90). Meals, available daily from noon to 2pm and 5:30 to 8pm, always include a roast and seafood items.

2 The Kintyre Peninsula

The longest peninsula in Scotland, Kintyre is more than 60 miles in length, with scenery galore, sleepy villages, and miles of sandy beaches. It's one of the most unspoiled areas of Scotland, owing perhaps to its isolation. Kintyre was ancient Dalriada, the first kingdom of the Scots.

If you drive all the way to the tip of Kintyre, you'll be only 12 miles from Ireland. Kintyre is joined to the mainland of Scotland by a narrow neck of land near the old port of Tarbert. The largest town on the peninsula is the port of Campbeltown, on the southeastern coast.

GETTING THERE

BY PLANE   Loganair (☎ 0141/889-1111 in Glasgow for flight information) also makes two scheduled flights a day from the Glasgow Airport to Campbeltown, the chief town of Kintyre.

BY BUS   From Glasgow, you can take buses to the peninsula (schedules vary seasonally). Inquire at the **Western S.M.T. Co. Ltd.,** Travel Centre of Scottish Transport Group, Buchanan Street Bus Station, Glasgow (☎ 0141/226-4826).

BY CAR   Kintyre is virtually an island unto itself. The most efficient way to travel is by private car if you want to explore the peninsula in any depth. From Glasgow, take A82 up to the Loch Lomond side and cut across to Arrochar and go over the "Rest and Be Thankful" route to Inveraray (A83). Then cut down along Loch Fyne to Lochgilphead and continue on A83 south to Tarbert (see below), which can be your gateway to Kintyre. You can take A83 along the western coast or cut east at the junction of B8001 and follow it across the peninsula to B842, which you can take south to Carradale (see below). If your final target is Campbeltown, you can reach it by either the western shore (much faster and a better road) or the eastern shore.

TARBERT

A sheltered harbor protects this fishing port and yachting center, on a narrow neck of land at the northern tip of the Kintyre Peninsula. It's between West Loch Tarbert and the head of herring-filled Loch Fyne, and has been called "the world's prettiest fishing port."

Tarbert means "drawboat" in Norse. It referred to a place where Vikings dragged their boats across land on rollers from one sea to another. In 1093 King Malcolm of Scotland and King Magnus Barelegs of Norway agreed that the Western Isles were to belong to Norway and the mainland to Scotland. An island was defined as anything a Viking ship could sail around. King Magnus proclaimed Kintyre an island by having his dragon ship dragged across the mile of dry land from West Loch Tarbert on the Atlantic to East Loch Tarbert on Loch Fyne. After the Vikings gave way, Kintyre came under the control of the MacDonald lordship of the Isles.

SEEING THE SIGHTS

The ancient castle at Tarbert dates from the 13th century and was later extended by Robert the Bruce. The castle ruins, **Bruce Castle,** are found on a hillock above the village on the south side of the bay. The oldest part still standing is a keep dating from the 13th century.

One of the major attractions of the peninsula is the remains of **Skipness Castle and Chapel,** at Skipness along B8001, 10 miles south of Tarbert, opening onto Loch Fyne. The hamlet was once an old Norse village. The ruins of the ancient chapel and 13th-century castle look out onto the Sounds of Kilbrannan and Bute. In its heyday it could control shipping along Loch Fyne. A five-story tower remains.

WHERE TO STAY

Stonefield Castle Hotel. Tarbert, Argyll PA29 6YJ. ☎ **01880/820836.** Fax 01880/820929. 31 rms, 2 minisuites. TV TEL. £118–£138 ($194.70–$227.70) double; £158 ($260.70) minisuite. AE, DC, MC, V. Rates include half board.

Occupying a commanding position, Stonefield Castle Hotel is a well-appointed hotel on 66 acres of wooded grounds and luxurious gardens, 2 miles outside Tarbert. The castle, with its turrets and steeply pitched roof, was built in the 19th century by the Campbells. The laird collected the rarest plants found in every corner of the British Empire, and the gardens today are believed to be one of the world's best repositories for more than 20 species of tree-size Himalayan rhododendrons, which in April offer a riot of color. Meals utilize produce from the hotel's garden. In the kitchen the staff does its own baking. Dinner starts at £22.50 ($37.15). The hotel has many facilities, including a drawing room overlooking the loch, a cocktail bar, library, outdoor swimming pool, sauna, even a yacht anchorage. Book well in advance, as Stonefield has a large repeat clientele.

West Loch Hotel. Tarbert, Argyll PA29 6YF. ☎ **01880/820283.** Fax 01880/820930. 7 rms. TV. £55 ($90.75) double. MC, V. Rates include Scottish breakfast. Closed Dec–Jan and first 2 weeks of Feb.

In a rustic setting beside A83, a mile southwest of town in low-lying flatlands midway between the forest and the loch, this stone inn was built during the 1700s as a staging post for coaches and for farmers driving their cattle to market. Painted white with black trim, it contains two bars and a handful of open fireplaces and wood-burning stoves. The bedrooms are modestly furnished, often with views of the estuary and a sense of coziness.

The hotel contains a pub and a restaurant that specializes in local seafood and game, using only the best of local ingredients. The bar, open daily from 11am to midnight, serves food from noon to 2pm and 6 to 9pm; the restaurant offers food daily from 6 to 9pm.

WHERE TO DINE

Anchorage Restaurant. Harbour St., Quayside. ☎ **01880/820881.** Reservations recommended. Main courses £7.95–£13.95 ($13.10–$23). MC, V. Daily 7–10pm. Closed Jan. SCOTTISH/SEAFOOD.

The Anchorage retains an unpretentious and natural emphasis despite its many culinary awards. Housed in a stone harborfront building that was once a customs house, it's run by Russell and Natalie Burns. Their daily menu includes such seafood dishes as king scallops sautéed with lemon-lime butter or a brochette of monkfish served with saffron rice. A selection of French and American wines is available to accompany your fish.

CARRADALE

On the lusher eastern coast of Kintyre 14 miles north of Campbeltown, Carradale is a small town opening onto the shores of Kilbrannan Sound. People come here to walk and relax; they can also go pony trekking or windsurfing, or picnic in several scenic spots that have log tables and benches. **Carradale Beach** is equipped with facilities for water sports and you can swim if you don't mind the chilly waters. The fishing fleet is anchored in the harbor and herring boats set out from here each night.

Those interested in historic sites can seek out the ruins of **Saddell Abbey** along B842, 9 miles northwest of Campbeltown. This Cistercian abbey was built in the 12th century by one of the lords of the Isles. The walls of the original building remain and there are several sculptured grave slabs.

SHOPPING   Wallis Hunter Designs, The Steading (☎ 01583/431683), sells handcrafted gold and silver jewelry inspired by Celtic patterns and the designs of Charles Rennie Mackintosh. Hours are Monday through Friday from 8:30am to 5:30pm.

WHERE TO STAY & DINE

Carradale Hotel. Carradale, Argyll PA28 6RY. ☎ and fax **01583/431223.** 17 rms. TV. £68 ($112.20) double, including Scottish breakfast; £98 ($161.70) double. MC, V. Rates include half board.

Built around 1800, the Carradale was the first hotel to open on the eastern side of the peninsula. Set in a garden in the center of this hamlet opposite the War Memorial, the hotel offers a comfortable high-ceilinged dining room, a lounge bar serving pub meals, and squash courts. The guest rooms are simple but pleasantly furnished. Fresh local produce, often from the hotel's own garden, is used in the kitchen. Bar meals, ranging from £5 to £6 ($8.25 to $9.90), are available from 12:30 to 2:30pm and from 6 to 8pm, whereas the restaurant serves a set-price menu for £16.50 ($27.20) nightly between 7 and 9pm.

CAMPBELTOWN

This is a fishing port and a resort at the southern tip of the Kintyre Peninsula, 176 miles northwest of Edinburgh and 135 miles northwest of Glasgow. Popularly known as the "wee toon," Campbeltown has long been linked with fishing. The town has a shingle beach. The **tourist information office** is at MacKinnon House, The Pier (☎ 01586/552056).

EXPLORING THE AREA

Davaar Island, in Campbeltown Loch, is accessible at low tide by those willing to cross the Dhorlin, a half-mile run of shingle-paved causeway; boat trips are also possible. Once on the island, you can visit a crucifixion cave painting, the work of Archibald MacKinnon, a local resident, painted in 1887. It takes about an hour and a half to walk around this tidal island, with its natural rock gardens.

On the quayside in the heart of town is the **Campbeltown Cross,** which dates from the 14th century. This Celtic cross is the finest piece of carving from the Middle Ages left in Kintyre.

SHOPPING   Oystercatcher Crafts & Gallery, with locations at 10 Hall St. (☎ 01586/553070) and 2–4 Main St. (☎ 01586/551255), sells Campbeltown pottery, wood carvings, and paintings by local artists. It's open Monday through Saturday from 10am to 5pm. If you'd like to take a scenic drive and go on a shopping expedition at the same time, head for **Ronachan Silks,** Ronachan Farmhouse at Clachan (☎ **01880/740242**), lying 25 miles north of Campbeltown on Route 83. Here in this unusual location you can purchase some high-fashion clothing and accessories, including kimonos, caftans, women's scarves, men's neckties, waistcoats, wall hangings, and cushions. It is open from Easter until the middle of October daily from 10am to 6pm.

WHERE TO STAY & DINE

Argyll Arms Hotel. Main St., Campbeltown, Argyll PA28 6AB. ☎ **01586/553431.** Fax 01586/553594. 30 rms (12 with bath). TV TEL. £50 ($82.50) double without bath, £60 ($99) double with bath. AE, DC, MC, V. Rates include Scottish breakfast.

This imposing stone building was once owned by the duke of Argyll, who maintained a suite on the second floor even after he sold it as a hotel. It still has an aura of Victorian opulence in its public rooms, although the bedrooms are modernized and fairly modest.

The Farmers Bar is a convivial cubbyhole near the entrance. A second bar is called Wee Toon. Both are open daily from 11am to midnight. The hotel's restaurant serves lunch and dinner daily, with a three-course shopper's lunch going for £4.95 ($8.15). À la carte dinners specialize in fish fresh from the quay and other local produce. Inexpensive main courses range from £3.60 to £5 ($5.95 to $8.25).

CAMPBELTOWN AFTER DARK

Pubs, not surprisingly, are the nightlife here, including two that host live music. Although they have no street addresses, they are easy to find as both are in the center of the village. **The Feathers** (☎ **01586/554604**), with its stone walls, wooden floors, and hanging lamps, hosts free bands playing a range of musical styles on Thursday night. It is open daily from 11am to 1am. **The Commercial** (☎ **01586/553703**) has live music on Thursday through Saturday nights. Again, styles vary and there is never a cover charge. A specialty here is "oatmeal lager." It's open Monday through Saturday from 11am to 1am and Sunday from 12:30pm to 1am. Quieter evenings can be found at the **Burnside Bar** (☎ **01586/552306**), open daily from 11am to 11:30pm. Conversation and local single-malts are the preferred distractions at the old wooden pub "that's always been here."

A SIDE TRIP TO SOUTHEND & THE MULL OF KINTYRE

Some 10 miles south of Campbeltown, the village of **Southend** stands across from the Mull of Kintyre. Three buses a day run Monday through Saturday from Campbeltown to Southend. It has sandy beaches, a golf course, and views across the sea to the Island of Sanda and to Ireland. Legend has it that footprints on a rock near the ruin of an old chapel mark the spot where St. Columba first set foot on Scottish soil. Other historians suggest that the footprints mark the spot where ancient kings were crowned.

Visitors can also go to **Dunaverty Rock,** called "Blood Rock" by the locals, once a MacDonald stronghold, known as Dunaverty Castle. It was the scene in 1647 of a great massacre, where some 300 citizens lost their lives.

About 11 miles from Campbeltown is the **Mull of Kintyre.** From Southend you can take a narrow road until you reach the "gap," from where you can walk down to the lighthouse. This is one of the wildest and most remote parts of the peninsula, and it's this desolation that appeals to visitors. The Mull of Kintyre is only 13 miles from Ireland. When local resident Paul McCartney made it the subject of a song, hundreds of fans flocked to the area.

3 Isle of Gigha

3 miles W of Kintyre's western coast

One of the southern Hebrides, the 6-mile-long Isle of Gigha is often called "sacred" and "legendary." Little changed over the centuries, it's the innermost island of the Hebrides, lying 3 miles off the Kintyre Peninsula's west coast.

ESSENTIALS
GETTING THERE

BY FERRY   Take a ferry to Gigha from Tayinloan, which lies halfway up the west coast of Kintyre. Sailings are daily and take about 20 minutes, depositing you at Ardminish, the main hamlet on Gigha. The round-trip fare is £16 ($26.40) for an automobile plus £4.15 ($6.85) per passenger. For ferry schedules and information, phone ☎ **01880/730252** in Kennacraig.

VISITOR INFORMATION

There is no local tourist office. Ask at Campbeltown on the Kintyre Peninsula (see above). Since most likely you'll arrive without a car, and since there's no local bus service, you can either walk or call McSporran's Taxi at ☎ **01583/505251.**

SEEING THE SIGHTS

Gigha is visited mainly by those wishing to explore its famous gardens, arguably the finest in Scotland. The ✪ **Achamore House Gardens,** a mile from the ferry dock at Ardminish, contain roses, hydrangeas, rhododendrons, camellias, and azaleas, among other flowering plants. They're open year-round, daily from dawn to dusk; admission is £2 ($3.30). Occupying a 50-acre site, they were the creation of the late Sir James Horlick, who was considered one of the great gardeners of the world. The house is not open to the public. For information about the gardens, call the Gigha Hotel (see below).

The island has a rich Viking past, and Cairns and ruins still remain. The Vikings stored their loot here after plundering the west coast of Scotland. **Creag Bhan,** the highest hill, rises more than 330 feet. From the top you can look out onto the islands of Islay and Jura as well as Kintyre; on a clear day you can also see Ireland. The **Ogham Stone** is one of only two standing stones in the Hebrides that bears an Ogham inscription, a form of script used in the Scottish kingdom of Dalriada. High on a ridge overlooking the village of Ardminish are the ruins of the **Church of Kilchattan,** dating back to the 13th century.

WHERE TO STAY & DINE

✪ **Gigha Hotel.** Ardminish, Isle of Gigha, Argyll PA41 7AD. ☎ and fax **015835/05254.** 13 rms (11 with bath). £102 ($168.30) double without bath, £110 ($181.50) double with bath. MC, V. Rates include half board.

This white-painted stone hotel was built in the 1700s as a farmhouse. It stands in a lonely and windswept position, devoid of vegetation except for low shrubs and lichens, a 5-minute walk from the island's only ferryboat landing. It contains the island's only pub, one of its two restaurants, and its only overnight accommodations except for some cottages. The polite staff rents small but cozy bedrooms and serves fixed-price four-course dinners every night between 7 and 9pm. Nonresidents of the hotel often arrive for dinner. Dinners are £20 ($33); bar lunches cost around £6.50 ($10.75).

4 Isle of Islay

16 miles W of the Kintyre Peninsula, ³/4 mile SW of Jura

Islay (pronounced "eye-lay") is the southernmost island of the Inner Hebrides, sepa-rated only by a narrow sound from Jura. At its maximum, Islay is only 20 miles wide and 25 miles long. Called "the Queen of the Hebrides," it's a peaceful and unspoiled island of moors, salmon-filled lochs, sandy bays, and wild rocky cliffs—an island of great beauty.

ESSENTIALS
GETTING THERE

BY FERRY MacBrayne steamers provide daily service to Islay—you leave West Tarbert on the Kintyre Peninsula, arriving in Port Askaig on Islay in about 2 hours. There is also service to Port Ellen. For information about ferry departures, check with Caledonian MacBrayne (call ☎ **01475/650100** at the ferry terminal in Gourock).

VISITOR INFORMATION

The **tourist information office** is at Bowmore, The Square (☎ **01496/810254**).

EXPLORING THE ISLAND

Near **Port Charlotte** are the graves of the U.S. seamen and army troops who lost their lives in 1918 when their carriers, the *Tuscania* and the *Otranto*, were torpedoed off the shores of Islay. There's a memorial tower on the Mull of Oa, 8 miles from Port Ellen.

The island's capital is **Bowmore,** on the coast across from Port Askaig. Here you can see a fascinating Round Church—no corners for the devil to hide in. But the most important town is **Port Ellen** on the south coast, a holiday and golfing resort and Islay's principal port. The 18-hole Machrie golf course is 3 miles from Port Ellen.

The ancient seat of the lords of the Isles, the ruins of two castles, and several Celtic crosses can be seen. The ancient **Kildalton Crosses** are in the Kildalton churchyard, about 7¹/2 miles northeast of Port Ellen. They're two of the finest Celtic crosses in Scotland. The ruins of the 14th-century fortress, **Dunyvaig Castle,** are just south of Kildalton.

In the southwestern part of Islay in Port Charlotte, the **Museum of Islay Life** (☎ **01496/850358**) has a wide collection of island artifacts, ranging from unre-corded times to the present day. The museum is open Monday through Saturday from 10am to 5pm, from Easter to October. Admission is £1.60 ($2.65) for adults, £1.10 ($1.80) for seniors, and 85p ($1.40) for children. The Portnahaven bus from Bowmore stops here.

Loch Gruinart cuts into the northern part of Islay. As the winter home for wild geese, it has attracted bird-watchers for decades. In 1984 the 3,000 acres of moors and farmland around the loch were turned into the Loch Gruinart Nature Reserve.

TOURING THE DISTILLERIES

The island is noted for its distilleries producing single-malt Highland whiskies by the antiquated pot-still method. Of these, **Laphroaig Distillery,** 1¹/2 miles along the road from Ardbeg to Port Ellen (☎ **01496/302418**), offers a guided tour in the morn-ing and another in the afternoon. Admission is free and includes a sample dram. Call first for an appointment. **Lagavoulin,** Port Ellen (☎ **01496/302250**), offers tours Monday through Friday at 10:30am and 2:30pm. Admission is £2 ($3.30) per person, or £3 ($4.95) for admission and a £3 ($4.95) voucher off the price of a bottle of whisky. A sample is included in the tour. A distillery gift shop is open Monday through Friday from 9am to noon and 1 to 4pm. The **Bowmore Distillery,** School Street, Bowmore (☎ 01496/810441), conducts tours Monday through Friday at 10:30am and 2 and 3pm. In summer, there are Saturday tours during the same times. The admission is £2 ($3.30), which includes a voucher worth £2 ($3.30) off the price of a bottle. Samples are included in the tour. Purchases can be made without taking the tour by stopping at the on-premises gift shop, open Monday through Friday from 9am to 4:30pm and Saturday from 10am to noon. Port Askaig is home to two distilleries, **Bunnahabhain** (☎ 01496/840646), which offers tours at no charge by appointment and runs a gift shop on Monday through Friday from 8am to 5pm, and **Coal Ila** (☎ 01496/840207), which has no tours from October to Easter, but thereafter has four tours (two morning, two afternoon) a day on Monday, Tuesday, Thursday, and Friday and two morning tours on Wednesday. Admission is £2 ($3.30). Its gift shop is open for visitors at the end of each tour.

SHOPPING

At Bridgend, you can visit the **Islay Woolen Mill** (☎ 01496/810563), which has been in business for more than a century. It makes a wide range of country tweeds and accessories. It made all of the tweeds used in Mel Gibson's film, *Braveheart.* The mill shop is open Monday through Saturday from 10am to 5pm. They sell a range of items made with the custom-designed Braveheart tweeds, as well as tasteful Shetland wool ties, mufflers, Jacob mufflers and ties, flat caps, travel rugs, and scarves, among many other items. Another good place to find souvenirs is at the **Port Ellen Pottery,** at Port Ellen (☎ 01496/302345), which sells brightly colored goblets, jugs, mugs, and other functional wares. It's open daily from 10am to 5pm. It is important to note that the Pottery does not handle shipping on larger purchases.

WHERE TO STAY & DINE

Bridgend Hotel. Bridgend, Isle of Islay, Argyll PA44 7PF. ☎ 01496/810212. Fax 01496/810960. 10 rms. TV TEL. £80 ($132) double. MC, V. Rates include Scottish breakfast.

Victorian spires cap the slate-covered roofs and roses creep up the stone and stucco walls. This hotel forms part of a complex that includes a roadside barn and one of the most beautiful flower and vegetable gardens on Islay. This is one of the oldest hotels on Islay, with somber charm and country pleasures. Guests enjoy drinks beside open fireplaces in the Victorian cocktail lounge and the rustic pub, where locals gather after a day in the surrounding fields. Many nonresidents opt for a dinner, priced at £20 ($33), in the hotel's high-ceilinged dining room. The bedrooms are comfortably and conservatively furnished, but not exceptional in any way.

Port Askaig Hotel. Hwy. A846 at the ferry crossing to Jura, Port Askaig, Isle of Islay, Argyll PA46 7RD. ☎ 01496/840245. Fax 01496/840295. 8 rms (4 with bath). TV. £60 ($99) double without bath, £72 ($118.80) double with bath. No credit cards. Rates include Scottish breakfast.

This is a genuine old island inn, dating from the 18th century but built on the site of an even older inn. It stands on the Sound of Islay overlooking the pier and offers island hospitality and Scottish fare. The hotel is a favorite of anglers on Islay, and the bar at the inn is popular with local fisherfolk. The restaurant serves a fixed-price dinner £15.75 ($26) daily from 7:30 to 9pm. All its functionally furnished bedrooms have radios and hot-beverage facilities, as well as central heating.

Port Charlotte Hotel. Main St., Port Charlotte. ☎ 01496/850360. Fax 01496/850361. 10 rms. TV TEL. £74 ($122.10) double. MC, V. Rates include Scottish breakfast.

After standing derelict for many years, this hotel, which was built in 1829 as three cottages, has been refurbished and open for business. It immediately won a four-crown rating from the Scottish Tourist Board. All the bedrooms are beautifully appointed, often with antiques, although baths are modern, with both a tub and a shower. Rooms have color TV, direct-dial phones, and tea- and coffeemaking facilities. The hotel is located next to the small sandy beaches of Port Charlotte with views over Loch Indaal. Features include a large conservatory, a comfortable lounge, and a public bar. The hotel is also the best place to dine in the area, with main courses ranging from £11 to £16 ($18.15 to $26.40). Typical dishes include sirloin of Islay steak, freshly caught Islay lobster, and grilled fillet of Scottish turbot. For starters, try the Loch Fyne smoked salmon.

ISLAY AFTER DARK

After work, employees of the distilleries gather at the Harbour Inn, Main Street in Bowmore (☎ 01496/810330), an old pub with stone walls, a fireplace, and wooden floors and furnishings. It's open Monday through Saturday from 11am to 1am, and serves McEwan's beers on tap and a wide selection of single-malts. Meals, mainly of the local seafood, are served from noon to 2pm and 7 to 9pm.

5 Isle of Jura

Three-quarters of a mile E of Islay

This is the fourth-largest island in the Inner Hebrides, 27 miles long and varying from 2 to 8 miles in breadth. It takes its name from the Norse *jura,* meaning "deer island." The red deer on Jura outnumber the people by about 20 to 1. At 4 feet high, the deer are the largest wild animals roaming Scotland. The hearty islanders number only about 250 brave souls, and most of them live along the east coast. The west coast is virtually uninhabited. Jura is relatively little known or explored. Its mountains, soaring cliffs, snug coves, and moors make it an inviting place to be—and it's not at all crowded. The island has actually suffered a drastic loss of population.

George Orwell lived on Jura in the bitter postwar winters of 1946 and 1947. Even though a sick man, he was working on his masterpiece *1984,* a satire on modern politics, which was published in 1949. He almost lost his life when he and his adopted son ventured too close to the whirlpool in the Gulf of Corryvreckan. They were saved by local fishermen and he went on to finish his masterwork, only to die in London of tuberculosis in 1950.

ESSENTIALS

GETTING THERE

BY FERRY   From Kennacraig (West Loch, Tarbert) you can go to Port Askaig on Islay (see above), where you'll have to take a second ferry to Feolin on Jura. For information on departures, call **Western Ferries** at ☎ 01496/840681. Car space must be booked in advance. The cost for a vehicle is £9.20 ($15.20), plus 80p ($1.30) per passenger.

VISITOR INFORMATION

See Isle of Islay (above) for tourist information.

EXPLORING THE ISLAND

The capital, **Craighouse,** is hardly more than a hamlet. From Islay, you can take a 5-minute ferry ride to Jura from Port Askaig, docking at the Feolin Ferry berth.

The island's landscape is dominated by the **Paps of Jura** that reach a peak of 2,571 feet at Beinn-an-Oir. An arm of the sea, **Loch Tarbert** nearly divides the island, cutting into it for nearly 6 miles.

The square tower of **Claig Castle,** now in ruins, was the stronghold of the MacDonalds until they were subdued by the Campbells in the 17th century. The **Jura Distillery,** at Craighouse (☎ **01496/820240**), is closed in July and August but can be toured any other month for free. A free sample is given away at the end of the tour, which can only be booked by calling ahead for an appointment.

The managers of the island's only hotel conduct special tours by Land Rover to such island curiosities as the Corryvreckan whirlpool. Inquire at the hotel; the cost is £10 ($16.50) per person.

WHERE TO STAY & DINE

Jura. Craighouse, Isle of Jura, Argyll PA60 7XU. ☎ **01496/820243.** Fax 01496/820249. 17 rms (11 with bath); 1 suite. £58 ($95.70) double without bath, £69 ($113.85) double with bath; £88 ($145.20) suite for 2. AE, DC, MC, V. Rates include Scottish breakfast. Closed 2 weeks at Dec–Jan.

The only hotel on the island, the Jura has loyal guests who return year after year. It's a sprawling, gray-walled building near the center of the hamlet (Craighouse lies east of Feolin along the coast). Sections of the building date from the 1600s, but what you see today was built in 1956. Kenya-born Fiona Walton and her husband, Steve, are the managing directors. The dining room's specialty is Jura-bred venison. A fixed-price dinner, served daily between 7:30 and 9pm, goes for £16.50 ($27.20). The hotel bar, open from 7pm to 1am daily, serves bar meals ranging from £2 to £10.75 ($3.30 to $17.75).

6 Inveraray

99 miles NW of Edinburgh, 57 miles NW of Glasgow, 38 miles SE of Oban

This small resort and royal burgh occupies a splendid setting on the upper shores of Loch Fyne. It's particularly attractive when you approach from the east on A83. Across a little inlet, you can see the town lying peacefully on a bit of land fronting on the loch.

ESSENTIALS
GETTING THERE

BY TRAIN The nearest rail station is at Dumbarton, 45 miles to the southeast, where bus connections can be made to Inveraray. For rail schedules and information, call ☎ **0345/484950.**

BY BUS The National Express operates buses out of Glasgow, heading for Dumbarton, before continuing to Inveraray. Transit time is 1³/4 hours. From Monday through Saturday, four buses make this run (only two on Sunday). A one-way fare is £5.50 ($9.05) a day, with a round-trip ticket going for £9.50 ($15.65). For bus schedules and more information, call ☎ **0990/808080.**

BY CAR From Oban, head east along A85 until you reach the junction with A819, at which point you continue south.

VISITOR INFORMATION

The **tourist information office** is on Front Street (☎ **01499/302063**).

SEEING THE SIGHTS

At one end of the main street of the town is a Celtic burial cross from Iona. The parish church is divided by a wall that enables services to be held simultaneously in Gaelic and English.

✪ **Inveraray Castle.** Three-quarter mile NE of Inveraray on Loch Fyne. ☎ **01499/302203.**
Admission £4.50 ($7.45) adults, £3.50 ($5.75) seniors, £2.50 ($4.15) children, £12 ($19.80)
family ticket. Apr–June and Sept to mid-Oct, Sat–Thurs 10am–1pm and 2–5:45pm; July–Aug,
Mon–Sat 10am–5:30pm, Sun 1–5:45pm.

The hereditary seat of the dukes of Argyll, Inveraray Castle has been headquarters
of the Clan Campbell since the early 15th century. The castle is among the earliest
examples of gothic revival in Britain, and offers a fine collection of pictures
and 18th-century French furniture, old English and continental porcelain, and an
Armoury Hall, which alone contains 1,300 pieces.

On the grounds of Inveraray Castle is a Combined Operations Museum, the only
one of its kind in the United Kingdom. It displays the role that No. 1 Combined
Training Centre played at Inveraray in World War II. On exhibit are scale models,
newspaper reports of the time, campaign maps, photographs, wartime posters and
cartoons, training scenes, and other mementos. There's a castle shop for souvenirs and
a tearoom where homemade cakes and scones are served.

SIGHTS NEARBY

About 5 miles south on A83 is the **Auchindran Township Open Air Museum**
(☎ **01499/500235**), just outside the hamlet of Furnace. This is an original West
Highland common tenancy township, a unique antique survivor of the long-gone
townships once common in the Highlands. More than 20 structures remain, most
of them restored to illustrate the lifestyle of Highlanders in bygone days. It's open
only April through September, daily from 10am to 5pm. Admission is £3 ($4.95) for
adults, £1.50 ($2.45) for children; a family ticket is £8 ($13.20). There is a Visitor
Centre with displays, a shop, and other facilities.

If you have a car, you can explore this scenic part of Scotland from Cairndow,
which nestles between a hill and Loch Fyne. Head east along A83 until you reach the
junction with A815, at which point you proceed south along the western shore of
Loch Fyne until you come to the famous inn at Creggans (see below), lying directly
to the north of **Strachur.** Five miles south from the Creggans Inn (see below) along
the loch will take you to the old **Castle Lachlan** at Strathiachian, the 13th-century
castle of the MacLachlan clan. Now in romantic ruins, it was besieged by the English
in 1745. The MacLachlans were fervent Jacobites and played a major role in the
uprising.

The **Crarae Glen Gardens** (☎ **0154/688-6614**) are 8 miles southwest of
Inveraray along the A83, near the hamlet of Minard. Lying along Loch Fyne, these
are among Scotland's most beautiful gardens, some 50 acres of rich plantings along
with waterfalls and panoramic vistas of the loch. The gardens are at their best in
blooming season. April through September the gardens are open daily from 10am
to 4:30pm. Admission is £2.50 ($4.15) for adults, £1.50 ($2.45) for children; a family
ticket costs £7 ($11.55). October through March the gardens are open the same
hours; payment is by the honor system—drop your money into the box at the entrance.

WHERE TO STAY & DINE

Great Inn. Front St., Inveraray, Argyll PA32 8XB. ☎ **01499/302466.** Fax 01499/302389.
24 rms (19 with bath). TV TEL. £70 ($115.50) double without bath, £83 ($136.95) double with
bath. AE, DC, MC, V. Rates include Scottish breakfast.

This three-story building, with its view of Loch Fyne and Loch Shira, was first constructed in 1755. Dubbed with several different names during its long and varied
life, after a modernization in 1990 it readopted its original and oldest name, the

The Argyll Peninsula

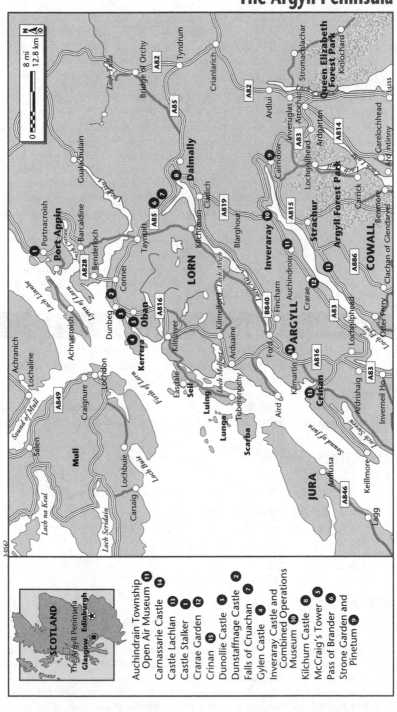

Auchindrain Township
Open Air Museum **11**
Carnassarie Castle **14**
Castle Lachlan **13**
Castle Stalker **1**
Crarae Garden **12**
Crinan **15**
Dunollie Castle **3**
Dunstaffnage Castle **2**
Falls of Cruachan **7**
Gylen Castle **4**
Inveraray Castle and
Combined Operations
Museum **10**
Kilchurn Castle **8**
McCraig's Tower **5**
Pass of Brander **6**
Strone Garden and
Pinetum **9**

Great Inn. There's also a public bar, a residents-only cocktail lounge, and a dignified restaurant where three-course evening meals, with a wide choice of food items, cost £17.50 ($28.90). The bedrooms are comfortable and include decors that range from flowered chintz to modern rooms with no-nonsense functionality.

WHERE TO STAY & DINE

✪ **Creggans Inn.** Strachur, Argyll PA27 8BX. ☎ **01369/860279.** Fax 01369/860637. 20 rms. TV TEL. £90 ($148.50) double. AE, DC, MC, V. Rates include Scottish breakfast.

This famous inn commemorates the spot where Mary Queen of Scots is said to have disembarked from her ship in 1563 on her way through the Highlands. Painted white with green trim, and flanked with gardens, the inn rises across A815 from the sea, exuding a sense of its very long history. The inn is owned by Sir Charles MacLean and his mother, Lady MacLean, who is well known as the author of several best-selling cookbooks, most of which are for sale at the inn. The bedrooms are elegant and understated. Guests may use the upstairs sitting room and the garden-style lounge.

The in-house restaurant has a charcoal grill, which produces succulent versions of Aberdeen Angus steaks and lamb kebabs. You can also enjoy fresh seafood, venison, and the MacLeans' own version of smoked salmon. An in-house bar features pub lunches beside an open fire. Lunch is served daily from 12:30 to 2:30pm, and dinner is daily from 6 to 9pm. Reservations are a must.

7 Dalmally & Loch Awe

99 miles NW of Edinburgh, 24 miles E of Oban, 68 miles NW of Glasgow

Only a mile wide in most places and 22 miles long, Loch Awe acted as a natural moat protecting the Campbells of Inveraray from their enemies to the north. Along its banks and on its islands are many reminders of its fortified past.

In this area the Forestry Commission has vast forests, and a modern road makes it possible to travel around Loch Awe so that more than ever it's a popular angling center.

ESSENTIALS

GETTING THERE

BY TRAIN   Proceed to Oban (see below), then take a connecting bus.

BY BUS   Scottish CityLink, 1 Queens Park Place in Oban (call ☎ 01631/562856 for schedule information), has service to Glasgow with stopovers at Loch Awe.

BY CAR   From Oban, head east along A85.

VISITOR INFORMATION

Consult the tourist office in Oban (see below).

EXPLORING THE AREA

To the east of the top of Loch Awe, Dalmally is small, but because of its strategic position it has witnessed a lot of Scottish history. Its 18th-century church is built in an octagonal shape. The ruins of **Kilchurn Castle** are at the northern tip of Loch Awe, west of Dalmally. A stronghold of the Campbells of Glen Orchy in 1440, it can be viewed from the outside only.

Among other reminders of the days when the Campbells of Inveraray held supreme power in the Loch Awe region, there's a ruined **castle** at Fincharn, at the southern end of the loch, and another on the island of Fraoch Eilean. The Isle of Inishail has an ancient chapel and burial ground. The bulk of **Ben Cruachan,** rising to 3,689 feet, dominates Loch Awe at its northern end and attracts climbers. On the ben is the world's second-largest hydroelectric power station, which pumps water from Loch Awe to a reservoir high up on the mountain.

Below the mountain are the **Falls of Cruachan** and the wild **Pass of Brander,** where Robert the Bruce routed the Clan MacDougall in 1308. The Pass of Brander was the scene of many a fierce battle in bygone times, and something of that bloody past seems to brood over the narrow defile. Through it the waters of the Awe flow on their way to Loch Etive. This winding sea loch is 19 miles long, stretching from Dun Dunstaffnage Bay at Oban to Glen Etive, reaching into the Moor of Rannoch at the foot of the 3,000-foot **Buachaille Etive** (the Shepherd of Etive), into which Glencoe also reaches.

WHERE TO STAY & DINE

✪ **Ardanaiseig.** Kilchrenan by Taynuilt, Argyll PA35 1HE. ☎ **800/548-7790** in the U.S., 800/463-7595 in Canada, or 01866/833333. Fax 01866/833222. 14 rms. TV TEL. £108–£173 ($178.20–$285.45) double. AE, DC, MC, V. Closed Jan to mid-Feb. Take A85 to Taynuilt; then get onto a secondary road, B845, to Kilchrenan and follow the signs to Ardanaiseig.

Although this manorial seat was erected in 1834 by one of the Campbell family patriarchs, it is designed along 18th-century styles. Its builder also planted some of the rarest trees in the British islands, many of them exotic conifers. Today clusters of fruit trees in a walled garden, along with rhododendrons and azaleas (a joy in May and June), add to the arboreal interest of this elegant gray stone house. The house stands between Loch Awe and the peaks of Cruachan, with a golf course within a 40-minute drive. Fishing vessels can be rented. Until recently a private home, the hotel has formal sitting rooms graced with big chintzy chairs, fresh flowers, and polished tables. Upstairs, each of the individually decorated, traditionally furnished bedrooms is well heated. The price of a room depends on its size, ranging from small to a master bedroom with a loch view. No children under 8 are accepted. The owners have employed an excellent chef, who makes use of fresh produce, game, and meats with skill and flair. Views of the loch can be seen from the dining room, which serves sandwiches and soup only for lunch, available daily from 12:30 to 2pm, and a traditional four-course dinner at night between 7:30 and 9pm, costing £26.50 ($43.70).

8 Oban

85 miles NW of Glasgow, 50 miles SW of Fort William

One of Scotland's leading coastal resorts, the bustling port town of Oban is set in a sheltered bay that's almost landlocked by the island of Kerrera. A busy fishing port in the 18th century, Oban is now heavily dependent on tourism for its economic base.

ESSENTIALS

GETTING THERE

BY TRAIN   From Glasgow, the West Highland lines run directly to Oban with departures from Glasgow's Queen Street Station (call ☎ 0345/484950 for 24-hour information about tickets and schedules). Three trains per day—only two on Sunday—make the 3-hour run to Oban, a one-way fare costing £16.40 ($27.05).

BY BUS   Frequent coaches depart from Buchanan Station in Glasgow, taking about the same time as the train, although a one-way fare is only £9.80 ($16.15). Call

Scottish CityLink at ☎ 0141/332-7133 in Glasgow for more information or ☎ 0163/562856 in Oban.

BY CAR   From Glasgow, head northwest along A82 until you reach Tyndrum, then go west along A85 until you come to Oban.

VISITOR INFORMATION

The **tourist information office** is in the Boswell House on Argyll Square (☎ 01631/ 563122).

SPECIAL EVENTS

In August the **Oban Highland Games** are held, with massed pipe bands marching through the streets. Ask at the tourist office for information. The **Oban Pipe Band** regularly parades on the main street throughout the summer.

EXPLORING THE AREA

From **Pulpit Hill** in Oban there's a fine view across the Firth of Lorn and the Sound of Mull. Overlooking the town is an unfinished replica of the Colosseum of Rome, **McCaig's Tower,** built by a banker, John Stuart McCaig, in 1897–1900 as a memorial to his family and to create a local work opportunity during an employment slump. Its walls are 2 feet thick and 37 to 40 feet high. The courtyard within is landscaped and the tower is floodlit at night. Outsiders have been heard to refer to the tower as "McCaig's Folly," but Obanites are proud of the structure and deplore this term.

Near the little granite Cathedral of the Isles, 1 mile north of the end of the bay, is the ruin of the 13th-century **Dunollie Castle,** seat of the lords of Lorn, who once owned a third of Scotland.

On the island of Kerrera stands **Gylen Castle,** home of the MacDougalls, dating back to 1587.

You can visit ✪ **Dunstaffnage Castle** (☎ 01631/562465), 3¹/₂ miles to the north, believed to have been the royal seat of the Dalriadic monarchy in the 8th century. It was probably the site of the Scots court until Kenneth MacAlpin's unification of Scotland and the transfer of the seat of government to Scone in the 10th century. The present castle was built about 1263. The castle is open April through September, daily from 9am to 8pm; March, October, and November, daily from 9am to 6:30pm. It is closed at other times. Admission is £1.50 ($2.45) for adults, £1 ($1.65) for seniors, and 75p ($1.25) for children. You can take a bus from the Oban rail station to Dunbeg, but it's still a 1¹/₂-mile walk to the castle.

SHOPPING   Cathness Glass Oban, Railway Pier (☎ 01631/563386), is the best place for shopping, although you'll find plenty of gift and souvenir shops throughout the town. At this center, locally produced glass items range from functional dinner- and glassware to purely artistic curios. This firm has one of the most prestigious reputations in Scotland among glassmakers. The factory shop is open Monday through Saturday from 9am to 8:30pm in summer (closes at 5:30pm in winter).

WHERE TO STAY
EXPENSIVE

Manor House. Gallanach Rd., Oban, Argyll PA34 4LS. ☎ **01631/562087.** Fax 01631/ 563053. 11 rms. TV TEL. £82–£120 ($135.30–$198) double. MC, V. Rates include Scottish breakfast, £20 ($33) extra for half board. From the south side of Oban, follow the signs for the car ferry, but continue past the ferry entrance for about half a mile.

On the outskirts of Oban, this 1780 stone house was once the home of the duke of Argyll. The hotel opens onto panoramic views of Oban Bay. Many antiques grace the public rooms. The bedrooms are filled with tasteful reproductions, and coordinated curtains and bedcovers create a pleasing effect, often in sun-splashed golds and yellows.

The hotel restaurant is one of the most satisfying in the area, and reason enough for a visit even if you're not a guest. Covered with elegant cream linen, the tables are lit by candles. The menu emphasizes seafood, although there's also a fixed-price menu nightly for £23.95 ($39.50) per person. Vegetarian dishes are also offered. It's family friendly, and children's portions are available. Men should wear a jacket and tie.

MODERATE

Alexandra. Corran Esplanade, Oban, Argyll PA34 5AA. ☎ **01631/562381.** Fax 01631/564497. 77 rms, 2 suites. TV TEL. £69–£93 ($113.85–$153.45) double; £126–£140 ($207.90–$231) suite. AE, DC, MC, V. Rates include Scottish breakfast. Closed Jan.

Alexandra, built in the late 1860s, is a stone hotel with gables and turreted towers, plus a Regency front veranda, enjoying a sunny perch on the promenade a mile from the train station. From its public room you can look out onto Oban Bay, and two sun lounges overlook the seafront. The bedrooms are modestly furnished but pleasing. The restaurant, serving good food, also opens onto the panorama. Around-the-clock room service is available. In 1994 a leisure center opened with a large indoor swimming pool, steam room, gym, and solarium. The hotel owns a motor cruiser, *Ocean Ranger,* and trips for hotel guests can be arranged.

Caledonian Hotel. Station Square, Oban, Argyll PA34 5RT. ☎ **01631/563133.** Fax 01631/562998. 70 rms. TV TEL. £84 ($138.60) double. AE, DC, MC, V. Rates include Scottish breakfast.

Caledonian Hotel, a favorite of coach tours, makes good on its promise of giving you a "taste of the Highlands." A fine example of Scottish 19th-century architecture, it occupies a landmark position, with a good view opening onto the harbor and Oban Bay looking toward the Mull of Kintyre. This convenient location puts you close to the rail, bus, and ferry terminals from which you can book passage to the Isles. The bedrooms have up-to-date amenities and beverage-making equipment. The front rooms are the most desirable. Good reasonably priced Scottish fare is served in the dining room.

Columba Hotel. The Esplanade, North Pier, Oban, Argyll PA34 5QD. ☎ **01631/562183.** Fax 01631/564683. 48 rms, 1 suite. TV TEL. £60–£120 ($99–$198) double; £80–£140 ($132–$231) suite. AE, MC, V. Rates include breakfast. Parking £1.50 ($2.45). The Scottish Midland Bus Company's Ganavan bus passes by.

One of the most impressive Victorian buildings in Oban, the Columba was built in 1870 by the same McCaig who constructed the hilltop extravaganza known as McCaig's Tower. The location is among the best in town. A modernized and big-windowed dining room offers views of the port. The guest rooms are unremarkable but well maintained, and each has a teamaker. An à la carte dinner can be ordered in the restaurant, or you can ask for a bar supper in the cocktail bar. Seafood is a specialty. Live folk music is sometimes presented in the informal Poop Deck bar.

INEXPENSIVE

Lancaster. Corran Esplanade, Oban, Argyll PA34 5AD. ☎ and fax **0631/562587.** 27 rms (24 with shower). TV. £54 ($89.10) double with shower. V. Rates include Scottish breakfast.

The Lancaster is distinguished by its attractive pseudo-Tudor facade. Along the seafront on the crescent of the bay, it commands views from its public rooms of the islands of Lismore and Kerrera, and even the more distant peaks of Mull. Open all year, the hotel welcomes you to one of its modestly furnished bedrooms. All doubles have a private shower, and the style is somewhat 1960s. The Lancaster is only one of two hotels in Oban featuring a heated indoor swimming pool, a sauna, a whirlpool, and a solarium. In its dining room, you can order a table d'hôte dinner for £10 ($16.50). It's fully licensed.

WHERE TO DINE

Balmoral Hotel. Craigard Rd., Oban, Argyll PA34 5AQ. ☎ **01631/562731.** Reservations recommended in midsummer. Main courses £6.50–£18.50 ($10.75–$30.55); average bar meal from £6 ($9.90). AE, DC, MC, V. May to mid-Oct, daily noon–2pm and 6–10pm; Apr and mid-Oct to Dec, daily noon–2pm. SCOTTISH/ENGLISH.

Set at the top of a granite staircase whose corkscrew shape is an architectural marvel, this is one of the best-recommended and most popular restaurants in town. Filled with a 19th-century kind of charm, it contains Windsor chairs and reproduction Georgian-style tables crafted from darkly stained wood. Specialties include sliced chateaubriand with mushrooms, Isle of Mull rainbow trout, smoked Tobermory trout, Scottish haggis with cream and whisky, venison casserole, and roast pheasant. Less expensive bar platters are served in the adjacent bar. The hotel stands on the eastern extension of the town's main commercial street (George Street), a 4-minute walk from the center.

The hotel rents 12 bedrooms, with TV and private bath. Including a Scottish breakfast, doubles cost £66 ($108.90).

✪ **Heatherfield House.** Albert Rd., Oban PA34 5EJ. ☎ and fax **01631/562681.** Reservations recommended. Fixed-price menus £16.50–£22 ($27.20–$36.30). MC, V. Daily 12:30–2pm and 7:30–9:30pm. SEAFOOD.

This is the best and most sophisticated restaurant in Oban. It specializes in seafood that's hauled in from Oban's hundreds of fishing boats. Its cuisine includes influences from faraway Malaysia, thanks to the time that the owner and chef, Alasdair Robertson, spent there as the son of the then-British colony's leading architect. Examples include a mousseline of scallops with a ginger-flavored hollandaise; or a sauté of seafood (sole, halibut, scallops, cod, and fish served with a leek-and-ginger sauce). Also offered are fillets of baby turbot on a bed of spinach and crabmeat with a red-wine butter sauce; or minted breast of duck with an apple-flavored purée. Dessert might be a homemade ice cream flavored with whisky, honey, and lemons. The wine list is more comprehensive and more international than you might expect. Only 20 diners can be accommodated at a time, which adds an undeniable intimacy to a meal whose service rituals are choreographed by Alasdair's charming wife, Jane. The setting is a late 19th-century gray stone manse.

Although overnight accommodations don't preoccupy the owners of this place as much as does the restaurant, the hotel maintains a quartet of high-ceilinged bedrooms outfitted in late-Victorian style, with lots of Sanderson chintz. Each has a private bath and TV, and costs £30 ($49.50) per person, double occupancy, for bed and breakfast; £43.50 ($71.75) per person for dinner, bed, and breakfast.

✪ **Knipoch Hotel Restaurant.** Hwy. A816, Kilninver, Knipoch, by Oban, Argyll PA34 4QT. ☎ **01852/316251.** Reservations required. Table d'hôte dinner £29.50 ($48.70) for 3 courses, £39.50 ($65.20) for 5 courses. AE, DC, MC, V. Daily 7:30–9pm. Closed mid-Nov to mid-Feb. Drive 6 miles south of Oban on A816. SCOTTISH.

Oban has a truly fine restaurant, lying on the shores of Loch Feochan. The only trouble is, you have to travel 6 miles south to enjoy it. Jenny and Colin Craig, a mother-son team, offer a choice of three dining rooms and a daily changing menu of five delectable courses. The oldest part of their whitewashed Georgian house dates from 1592. Salmon and halibut are smoked on the premises, and the menu relies heavily on Scottish produce, including fresh fish. Try the cock-a-leekie soup, followed by Sound of Luing scallops. The wine cellar is excellent, especially in its bordeaux.

The hotel also rents 16 well-furnished rooms, charging £70 to £150 ($115.50 to $247.50) for a double, including a Scottish breakfast.

McTavish's Kitchen. 34 George St. ☎ **01631/563064.** Main courses £4.95–£13.95 ($8.15–$23); budget 2-course lunch £3.95 ($6.50); fixed-price 3-course dinners £5.65–£15 ($9.30–$24.75). MC, V. Self-service restaurant: daily 9am–9pm. Licensed restaurant: daily noon–2pm and 6–10:30pm. Bars: daily 11am–1am. SCOTTISH.

Like its cousin in Fort William, this place is dedicated to preserving the local cuisine. Downstairs is a self-service restaurant that serves breakfast, main meals, and teas with shortbread and scones. Upstairs is the Lairds Bar, and McTavish's Bar, where bar meals are available all day, is on the ground floor. The licensed second-floor restaurant has a more ambitious Scottish and continental menu with higher prices, but there are also budget lunches. The fixed-price menu includes an appetizer, a main-course choice that features fresh salmon, and a dessert such as strawberries or raspberries (in season). The à la carte menu offers haggis, Loch Fyne kippers (oak-smoked herring), prime Scottish steaks, smoked salmon, venison, and local mussels.

OBAN AFTER DARK

From mid-May to the end of September there is entertainment at **MacTavish's Kitchen** (see above), with Scottish music and Highland dancing by local artists, nightly from 8:30 to 10:30pm. Admission is £3 ($4.95) for adults, £1.50 ($2.45) for children. Reduced admission for diners is £1.50 ($2.45) for adults, £1 ($1.65) for children. The **Highland Discovery Centre,** George Street (☎ **01631/562444**), screens new-release major motion pictures as well as stages theatrical productions such as the Mole Theatre Company's *Whisky Galore.* The space is divided into a 250-seat auditorium that hosts both cinematic and theatrical productions and a 26-seat studio cinema. Movie prices are £3.50 ($5.75) for adults, £3 ($4.95) for students, and £2.50 ($4.15) for seniors and children. A family ticket is available at the rate of £2.50 ($4.15) per person. Theater tickets cost £8 ($13.20) for adults, £5 ($8.25) for seniors, and £4.50 ($7.45) for students and children. A family ticket is available for £4 ($6.60) per person. Call for cinema and theatrical schedules.

You can while away the evening with the locals at the **Oban Inn,** Stafford Street and the Esplanade (☎ **01631/562484**), a popular pub with exposed beams and a flag-covered ceiling. Here, pints include McEwan's Export, Ale, and 70 Shilling, as well as Gillespie's Stout. The pub is open daily from noon to 1am. Another popular hangout is the pub at the **Lorne Hotel,** 43 Stevenson St. (☎ **01631/566766**), which has a Victorian oval island bar with a marble top and lots of brass trim. Here a selection of more than 20 regional single-malt whiskies starts at £1.85 ($3.05) per dram, whereas beer, including Orkney Pale Ale, starts at £1.95 ($3.20). The bar can get rowdy when soccer matches are shown on the 8-foot television screen. Hours are daily from 11am to 1am.

SIDE TRIPS FROM OBAN
THE ISLANDS

Oban is the gateway to Mull, largest of the Inner Hebrides, and to the island of Iona. See chapter 12 for information about these destinations. To inquire about island ferry services to Mull, Iona, and the Outer Hebrides, get in touch with **MacBrayne Steamers** at their office in Oban (☎ **01631/562285**).

PORT APPIN

Some 24 miles north of Oban lies a scenic lochside district, including Lismore Island. Port Appin is a small village with stone cottages. On an islet near Port Appin, a famous landmark, **Castle Stalker,** was the ancient seat of the Stewarts of Appin, built in the 15th century by Duncan Stewart, son of the first chief of Appin. Dugald, the ninth chief, was forced to sell the estate in 1765, and the castle slowly fell into ruin. It was recently restored and is once again inhabited, but is no longer open to visitors. In *Monty Python and the Holy Grail*, this castle was depicted as "Castle Aaaaaaaaaaa." It lies at Portnacroish (where it's signposted) 10 miles down A828.

WHERE TO STAY & DINE

✪ **Airds Hotel.** Port Appin, Argyll PA38 4DF. ☎ **01631/730236.** Fax 01631/730535. 15 rms, 1 suite. TV TEL. £232 ($382.80) double; £276 ($455.40) suite. MC, V. Rates include half board.

Airds Hotel is an old ferry inn dating from 1700, in one of the most panoramic spots in the historic district of Appin. One of the outstanding hotels of Scotland, it's a Relais & Châteaux, midway between Oban and Fort William. The hotel, over-looking Loch Linnhe and the island of Lismore and the mountains of Morvern, is an ideal center for touring this area. You can take forest walks in many directions, or go pony trekking, sea angling, or trout fishing. Boats can be rented and trips arranged to see the seals and to visit the island of Lismore. The resident proprietors, Eric and Betty Allen, along with their son, Graeme, welcome you to one of their handsomely furnished bedrooms. Everything is immaculately maintained in a tranquil setting.

Dining/Entertainment: It's the food that makes the Airds such an outstanding place to visit. Betty Allen, one of the great cooks of Scotland, has handed over kitchen duties to her son Graeme, who is continuing her tradition of creating fine Scottish cuisine from fresh local produce. Daily menus are likely to include such dishes as cream of red pepper and fennel soup; salad of Loch Linnhe prawns with herb may-onnaise; breast of wood pigeon with foie gras, truffle, chanterelles and a Madeira sauce; or fillet of wild salmon on a bed of honeyed eggplant with asparagus and hollandaise sauce. Delectable desserts include chocolate ice cream gâteau with crème anglaise and a plum coulis or poached pear shortcake with a caramel-and-lime sauce. A meal here will cost £35 ($57.75). Reservations for dinner, served only at 8pm, are absolutely necessary.

Services: All-day room service for tea and coffee only, baby-sitting, laundry.
Facilities: Garden.

Pierhouse. Port Appin, Argyll PA38 4DF. ☎ **01631/730400.** Fax 01631/730521. 11 rms. TV TEL. £75–£79 ($123.75–$130.35) double. MC, V. Rates include Scottish breakfast.

Although the restaurant associated with this hotel was established by two genera-tions of the McLeod family in 1988, its overnight accommodations are among the newest in Argyll. In 1993 a two-story wing was added containing simple but comfortable bedrooms, many with views over the water. The complex lies in the hamlet's center, adjacent to the pier where ferryboats depart every 2 hours for Lismore Island.

The white-sided restaurant was originally built as a fisher's cottage more than 200 years ago. Its location at the edge of the pier allows much of its seafood to remain alive in underwater cages until just before cooking, ensuring some of the freshest and purest seafood anywhere. Several venison dishes are available as well. Menu items include several different versions of giant prawns, pan-fried scallops served with lemon butter or a cream-cheese-and-wine sauce, and delectable versions of whatever local fishers managed to bring in that day. Main courses cost from £9 to £17 ($14.85 to $28.05). The restaurant is open every day for lunch (noon to 3pm) and dinner (6:30 to 9:30pm). Reservations are recommended.

9

Fife & the Central Highlands

North of Forth from Edinburgh, the County of Fife still likes to call itself a "kingdom." Its name, even today, suggests the romantic episodes and pageantry during the reign of the early Stuart kings. Some 14 of Scotland's 66 royal burghs lay within this shire. Many of the former royal palaces and castles, either restored or in colorful ruins, can be visited today.

Legendary **Loch Lomond** is the largest and most beautiful of the Scottish lakes and famed for its "bonnie banks" of the song. At Balloch in the south, the lake is a Lowland loch of gentle hills and islands. But as it moves north, the loch changes to a narrow lake of Highland character, with moody cloud formations and rugged steep hillsides.

The **Trossachs** is the collective name given to that wild Highland area east and northeast of Loch Lomond. Here and along Loch Lomond you find Scotland's finest scenery in moor, mountain, and loch. The area is famed in history and romance ever since Sir Walter Scott's vivid descriptive passages in *The Lady of the Lake* and *Rob Roy*.

Many sections of the area lie on the doorsteps of Glasgow and Edinburgh; either can be your gateway if you're arriving by air to explore Fife and the central Highlands. Dunfermline and St. Andrews are easily reached by rail from Edinburgh. St. Andrews also has good bus connections with Edinburgh. By car, the main motorway is M9, the express highway that starts on the western outskirts of Edinburgh and is linked to M80 from Glasgow. The M9 motorway passes close to Stirling. M90, reached by crossing the Forth Road Bridge, will take you north into the Fife region.

Stirling is the major rail center for the region, with stops at such places as Dunblane, and much of Loch Lomond has rail connections. Towns and some villages have bus service, but connections are too limited or infrequent for the hurried visitor. For bus connections, Stirling is the central point.

However, much of the Trossachs needs to be explored by car, and your best bet for discovering the hidden villages and scenic lochside roads of the region or the fishing villages of East Neuk is to rent a car and drive.

The Kingdom Of Fife

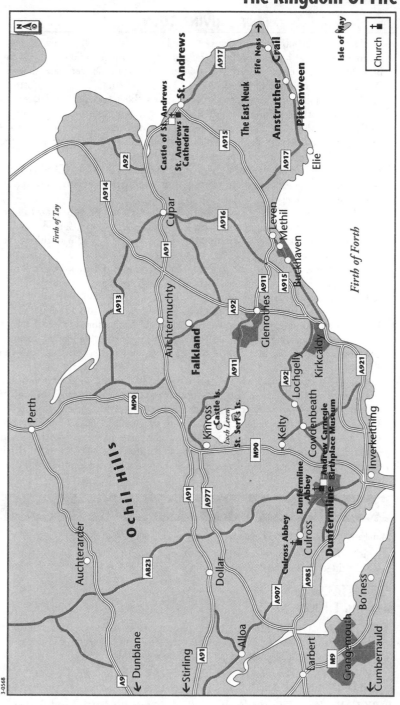

Church

Isle of May

N

A917
Fife Ness
Crail
Anstruther
Pittenweem
The East Neuk
A917
Elie
St. Andrews
Castle of St. Andrews
St. Andrews Cathedral
A915
A92
A914
A916
Cupar
Leven
Methil
Buckhaven
A911
A915
A911
Firth of Forth
Firth of Tay
A913
A92
Glenrothes
Auchtermuchty
Falkland
A911
Kirkcaldy
A921
Lochgelly
A92
M90
Perth
Kinross
Castle Is.
St. Serf's Is.
Loch Leven
Kelty
Cowdenbeath
Andrew Carnegie Birthplace Museum
Inverkeithing
Ochil Hills
A91
A977
M90
Dunfermline Abbey
Dunfermline
Culross Abbey
Culross
A985
Bo'ness
Auchterarder
Dollar
A823
A907
Grangemouth
Cumbernauld
Alloa
Larbert
M9
← Dunblane
← Stirling
A91
A9

3-0568

263

A DRIVING TOUR

Day 1   Leave Edinburgh (see chapter 6) and travel east on A90, following the directions to the Forth Road Bridge. After crossing the bridge, follow the road signs into Dunfermline, 14 miles northwest of Edinburgh, to visit Dunfermline Abbey and Palace and to see the Andrew Carnegie Birthplace Museum. Take A907 northwest to Culross, 6 miles to the west, to explore Culross Abbey and Culross Palace. After lunch, head northeast along the coastal road, beginning southeast of Dunfermline (A92). Follow this route all the way to Elie, going via Kirkcaldy and Buckhaven. At Elie you can explore the villages called the East Neuk. Visit Pittenweem, Anstruther, and Crail. Anstruther or Elie is best for overnighting.

Day 2   Continue along the coast, following A917 until you reach St. Andrews, capital of golf. It deserves at least an overnight stopover; serious golfers, however, will want to stay a lot longer.

Day 3   From St. Andrews, take A9 southwest until you see the turnoff for Falkland, to the northwest. Make this detour to explore Falkland Palace and Garden. Continue northwest from Falkland until you reach the junction of A91 heading southwest into Stirling for the night.

Day 4   After exploring Stirling in the morning and having lunch there, follow A9 north to Dunblane to see its fabled cathedral. From Dunblane, cut west along A820 to Doune to visit its castle, motor museum, and Blair Drummond Safari and Leisure Park (see below). Spend the night in Doune.

Day 5   From Doune, head northwest on A84 to Callander for the night. Callander is surrounded by some of the finest scenery in the central Highlands, including Leny Park, Leny Falls, Bracklinn, Loch Lubnaig, and even Loch Voil, known to Rob Roy.

Day 6   In the morning, leave Callander along A821 on the northern rim of Loch Venachar, which will take you into the Trossachs. After driving through the Trossachs, head south to Aberfoyle for the night.

Day 7   From Aberfoyle you can head south on A81 and then west along A811 (which becomes B837). This will take you to the eastern shores of Loch Lomond, the largest loch in Scotland. You can spend an entire day, or a lot more, driving around this loch. There are many villages where overnight accommodations can be found.

1 Dunfermline

14 miles NW of Edinburgh, 39 miles NE of Glasgow, 52 miles SW of Dundee

This ancient town was once the capital of Scotland. It's easily reached by the Forth Road Bridge, which was opened by Elizabeth II in 1964.

ESSENTIALS
GETTING THERE

BY TRAIN   Dunfermline is a stop along the main rail route from London via Edinburgh to Dundee, which means that it has frequent connections to the Scottish capital. For rail schedules and fares, call ☎ **045/484950.**

BY BUS   From its station at St. Andrews Square in Edinburgh, Scottish CityLink (call ☎ **0990/505050** for information) operates frequent service to Dunfermline.

BY CAR   From Edinburgh, take A90 west, cross the Forth Road Bridge, and follow the signs north to the center of Dunfermline.

VISITOR INFORMATION

A summer-only **tourist information booth** is found at 13–15 Maygate (☎ **01383/720999**).

SEEING THE SIGHTS

✪ **Dunfermline Abbey and Palace.** St. Margaret's Dr. ☎ **01383/739026.** Admission £1.50 ($2.45) adults, £1 ($1.65) seniors, 75p ($1.25) children. Apr–Sept, Mon–Sat 9:30am–6pm, Sun noon–5:30pm; Oct–Mar, Mon–Wed and Fri–Sat 9:30am–4pm, Thurs 9:30am–noon, Sun 2–4pm.

The abbey is on the site of two earlier structures, a Celtic church and an 11th-century house of worship dedicated to the Holy Trinity, under the auspices of Queen Margaret (later St. Margaret). Culdee Church, dating from the 5th and 6th centuries, was rebuilt in 1072. Traces of both buildings are visible beneath gratings in the floor of the old nave. In 1150 the church was replaced with a large abbey, the nave of which remains, an example of Norman architecture. Later, St. Margaret's shrine, the northwest baptismal porch, the spire on the northwest tower, and the flying buttresses were added. While Dunfermline was the capital of Scotland, 22 royal personages were buried in the abbey. However, the only visible memorial or burial places known are those of Queen Margaret and King Robert the Bruce, whose tomb lies beneath the pulpit.

The once-royal palace of Dunfermline stands adjacent to the abbey. The palace witnessed the birth of Charles I and James I. The last king to reside here was Charles II, in 1651. But today only the southwest wall remains of this once-gargantuan edifice.

Andrew Carnegie Birthplace Museum. Moodie St. ☎ **01383/724302.** Admission £1.50 ($2.45) adults, 75p ($1.25) senior citizens, free for age 15 and under. Apr, May, and Sept, Mon–Sat 11am–5pm, Sun 2–5pm; June–Aug, Mon–Sat 10am–5pm; Nov–Mar, daily 2–4pm.

Andrew Carnegie, the American industrialist and philanthropist, was born in 1835 at a site about 200 yards down the hill from the abbey. The museum lies at the corner of Moodie Street and Priory Lane and comprises the 18th-century weaver's cottage in which he was born and a memorial hall provided by his wife. Displays tell the story of the weaver's son from Dunfermline who immigrated to America to become one of the richest men in the world.

From the fortune he made in steel, Carnegie gave away more than $400 million before his death in 1919. Dunfermline, his birthplace, received the first of the 2,811 free libraries he provided throughout Britain and the United States. It also received public baths and Pittencrieff Park and Glen, so rich in history and natural charm. A statue in the park honors the hometown boy who once worked as a bobbin boy in a cotton factory.

WHERE TO STAY

King Malcolm Thistle Hotel. Queensferry Rd., Dunfermline, Fife KY11 5DS. ☎ **01383/722611.** Fax 01383/730865. 48 rms. TV TEL. £94 ($155.10) double. Children 13 and under stay free in parents' room. AE, DC, MC, V. Bus: 72.

The best choice for either a meal or a bed is this modern pastel-colored and fairly stylish hotel. It sits on a roundabout a mile south of Dunfermline on A823. Named after the medieval king of Fife (and later of Scotland), Malcolm Canmore, it was built in 1972 but thoroughly revamped in 1989. Each of its well-furnished although rather standardized bedrooms contains a color satellite TV with video, trouser press, and hair dryer. On the premises is Richmond's, an elegant, glass-sided bar and restaurant in an appealing design. A Scottish/continental cuisine is served from 6:30 to 10pm daily.

A three-course fixed-price dinner runs £16.50 ($27.20). The Canmore Vaults Bar is accessible via a separate entrance.

WHERE TO DINE

New Victoria. 2 Bruce St. ☎ **01383/724175.** Main courses £3.55–£6.95 ($5.85–$11.45); Scottish "high tea" £5.50–£10.95 ($9.05–$18.05). AE, MC, V. Mon–Thurs 9am–7pm, Fri–Sat 9am–9pm, Sun 10am–7pm. SCOTTISH.

To reach Dunfermline's oldest eating house, established in 1923, you must walk up two flights of stairs. Off High Street, in a pedestrian zone in the center overlooking the abbey, the cozy dining room serves good old-fashioned cookery based on healthy ingredients. There's also plenty of it. You might begin with a robust soup, then follow with steak-and-kidney pie, grilled fish, roast beef, or any of an array of grilled Aberdeen Angus steaks. It's a good choice if you're in the neighborhood seeking a high tea.

SIDE TRIPS FROM DUNFERMLINE

CULROSS

The old royal burgh of Culross, 6 miles west of Dunfermline, has been renovated by the Scottish National Trust, and is one of the most beautiful in the country. As you walk its cobblestone streets, admiring its whitewashed houses with their crow-stepped gables and red pantiled roofs, you'll feel as if you're taking a stroll back into the 17th century.

Set in tranquil walled gardens in the center of the village, **Culross Palace** (☎ **01383/880359**) was built between 1597 and 1611 for George Bruce, a prosperous merchant. It contains a most beautiful series of paintings on its wooden walls and ceilings that portray moral scenes with passages in Latin and Scottish, illustrating principles such as "Honor your parents" and "The spoken word cannot be retracted." Restoration by the National Trust from 1991 to 1994 involved replacing all the wooden paneling that had rotted with Russian pine, taking care to match the salvaged panels. During the restoration, archaeologists uncovered the remains of a foundation of a long-forgotten building on the east end of the courtyard and the original doorway—there are plans to restore it for use as the public entrance. Open Easter through September, daily from 11am to 5pm; in October, Saturday and Sunday from 11am to 5pm; November to Easter, by appointment only. Admission is £4 ($6.60) for adults, £2.70 ($4.45) for senior citizens and children.

The other important attraction is **Culross Abbey,** a Cistercian monastery whose founding father was Malcolm, earl of Fife, in 1217. Parts of the nave are still intact, and the choir serves as the Culross parish church. There's also a central tower. The Kingdom of Fife abbey is open from Easter Saturday to the last Saturday in August, on Saturday and Sunday from 10am to 4pm; at other times, it can be visited by prior arrangement with the Rev. David Whyte, the Abbey Manse, Culross, Fife.

LOCH LEVEN

The loch, 12 miles north of Dunfermline, has seven islands. On St. Serf's, the largest of the islands, are the ruins of the **Priory of Loch Leven,** originally built on the site of one of the oldest Culdee establishments in Scotland.

In Kinross, 25 miles north of Edinburgh, take the ferry over to Castle Island, the only means of access to the ruins of **Loch Leven Castle** (☎ **01378/040483**) on Castle Island. "Those never got luck who came to Loch Leven"—this saying sums up the history of this Douglas fortress. The castle dates from the late 14th century, and among its ill-fated prisoners none was more notable than Mary Queen of Scots.

Inside its forbidding walls she signed her abdication on July 24, 1567. However, she effected her escape from Loch Leven on May 2, 1568. Thomas Percy, seventh earl of Northumberland, supported her cause. For his efforts, he, too, was imprisoned and was lodged in the castle for 3 years until he was handed over to the English, who beheaded him at York. The castle is open April through October daily from 9:30am to 6pm; closed off-season. Admission is £2.80 ($4.60) for adults, £1.80 ($2.95) for seniors, and £1 ($1.65) for children. The admission charge for the castle includes the cost of a round-trip by ferry from Kinross to Castle Island.

Where to Stay & Dine

Nivingston House. Hwy. 9097, Cleish Hills by B996, Cleish, Perthshire and Kinross KY13 7LS. ☎ **01577/850216.** Fax 01577/850238. 16 rms, 1 suite. TV TEL. £99.50 ($164.15) double; £135 ($222.75) suite. AE, MC, V. Rates include Scottish breakfast. Children 12 and under stay free in parents' room. Closed Jan 1–14.

Nivingston House, a converted stone farmhouse with parts dating from 1725, is on B9097, 2 miles from exit 5 of the M90 motorway halfway between Edinburgh and Perth, south of Kinross near Cleish. It's set on 12 acres of gardens, and offers modernized rooms and serves some of the finest food in Tayside.

Most visitors come here for the kitchen. Guests rarely have the same meal here twice, as you depend on the inspiration of the chef. But that's hardly a problem. Fresh local produce is used, such as fish, Scottish lamb and beef; fresh charcoal-grilled sardines are offered. Typical dishes include medaillons of venison pan-fried with a red currant, paprika, and marsala sauce; rainbow trout sautéed with almonds, capers, and prawns; and Scottish sirloin steak "Hare and Hounds," with a red-wine and dijon-mustard sauce, glazed with brown sugar. The desserts are luscious; you make your selection from a trolley wheeled to your table. Meals cost £15.50 ($25.60) for lunch and £25 ($41.25) for dinner. Service is daily from noon to 2pm and 7 to 9pm. Always reserve a table.

2 East Neuk

Within a half-hour drive south of St. Andrews (see below) are some of the most scenic and unspoiled fishing villages of eastern Scotland. The villages cannot be reached by rail; the nearest stations are Ladybank, Cupar, and Leuchars, on the main London–Edinburgh–Dundee–Aberdeen rail line serving northeast Fife. Buses from St. Andrews connect the villages.

PITTENWEEM

If you're here in the morning, try to get caught up in the action at the **fish auction** held under a large shed Monday through Saturday. The actual time depends on the tides. Afterward, you can go for a walk through the village and admire the sturdy stone homes, some of which have been preserved by Scotland's National Trust.

ANSTRUTHER

Once an important herring fishing port, Anstruther is now a summer resort, 46 miles northeast of Edinburgh, 34 miles east of Dunfermline, and 23 miles south of Dundee. The **Scottish Fisheries Museum,** St. Ayles, Harbourhead (☎ **01333/310628**), is down by the harbor. Here you can follow the fisherfolk through every aspect of the fishing industry—from the days of sail to modern times. See the old herring drifter *The Reaper,* berthed in the harbor. The museum is open April through October, Monday through Saturday from 10am to 5:30pm and Sunday from 11am to 5pm. From November through March, it is open Monday through Saturday from

10am to 4:30pm and Sunday from 2 to 4:30pm. Admission is £3.40 ($5.60) for adults, £2.30 ($3.80) for seniors and children, and £9.50 ($15.65) for a family ticket. Take bus no. 95.

From the museum, you can walk to the tiny hamlet of **Cellardyke,** adjoining Anstruther. It has many charming stone houses and its own ancient harbor, where in the year that Victoria took the throne (1837) 140 vessels used to put out to sea.

Across the harbor, you can visit a floating exhibit in the old **North Carr lightship.** Entrance is free.

The **Isle of May,** a nature reserve in the Firth of Forth, is accessible by boat from Anstruther. It's a bird observatory and a field station, and contains the ruins of a 12th-century chapel as well as an early 19th-century lighthouse.

WHERE TO STAY

Craw's Nest Hotel. Bankwell Rd., Anstruther, Fife KY10 3DA. ☎ **01333/310691.** Fax 01333/312216. 50 rms. TV TEL. £94 ($155.10) double. AE, DC, MC, V. Rates include Scottish breakfast. Bus: 95.

Originally a Scottish manse, the Craw's Nest Hotel was converted into a popular hotel, with views over the Firth of Forth and May Island. Many extensions were added to the original building under the direction of the owner, Mrs. Edward Clarke, and her son-in-law, Ian Birrell. The black-and-white step-gabled building stands behind a high stone wall. The bedrooms are handsomely equipped and appointed. The public areas, including a lounge bar as well as a bustling public bar, are simply decorated and cozy. The food is good and the wine is priced reasonably in the hotel's dining room. Meals are served daily from 12:30 to 2pm and 7 to 8:30pm. A three-course lunch runs £11.75 ($19.40) and a three-course dinner is £19.75 ($32.60). The bar is open daily from 11am to midnight.

Smuggler's Inn. High St., East Anstruther, Fife KY10 3DQ. ☎ **01333/310506.** Fax 01333/312706. 9 rms. TV TEL. £62 ($102.30) double. AE, DC, MC, V. Rates include Scottish breakfast. Bus: 95.

This warmly inviting inn located in the heart of town evokes memories of smuggling days. An inn has stood on this spot since 1300. In Queen Anne's day it was a well-known tavern. The ceilings are low, the floors uneven, and of course the stairways winding. The guest bedrooms are decorated and comfortably furnished. The hotel's restaurant serves dinner only, daily from 7 to 9:30pm, when a regional cuisine is featured, a three-course table d'hôte going for £17.50 ($28.90). Bar lunches are available for about £5 ($8.25).

WHERE TO DINE

The Cellar. 24 East Green, Anstruther. ☎ **01333/310378.** Reservations recommended. Table d'hôte menu £28.50 ($47.05). AE, MC, V. Wed–Sun 12:30–2pm; daily 7–9:30pm. Bus: 95. SEAFOOD.

Some visitors consider this well-managed seafood restaurant the best eatery in town. It's within the solid stone walls of a cellar whose age is positively dated from 1875 (but probably actually dating from the 16th century). The place is illuminated by candlelight—in winter by twin fireplaces at opposite ends of the room. The cuisine derives from very fresh fish hauled in from nearby waters and is cooked with light-textured sauces. Examples include grilled suprême of halibut dredged in bread crumbs and citrus juices, served with hollandaise sauce; a mixture of turbot with Western Isles scallops served in a chardonnay-cream sauce; monkfish with herb-and-garlic sauce; and a limited array of meat dishes. The staff is youthful.

Haven. 1 Shore Rd., Cellardyke, Anstruther. ☎ **01333/310574.** Reservations recommended. Main courses £6.20–£11.50 ($10.25–$18.95); high tea £5.95–£7 ($9.80–$11.55). AE, V. Daily noon–9:30pm (depending on business, the street-level restaurant, but not the upstairs bar, might close several hours earlier during midwinter). Bus: 95; a James Anderson & Co. bus runs every hour from St. Andrews, 8 miles south, to the door of the restaurant. SCOTTISH.

This unpretentious establishment right on the harborfront serves simple and wholesome food: breaded and pan-fried prawns, fillets of halibut, Angus steaks, local crabmeat salad, and homemade soups and stews. The stone structure was originally two separate 300-year-old fisher's cottages, connected when the restaurant was established. The upper floor contains one of the town's most popular bars, where the same menu is served. The street level, more formal and sedate, is the site of high teas and evening meals.

ANSTRUTHER AFTER DARK

✪ **Dreel Tavern,** 16 High St. (☎ **01333/310727**), was a 16th-century coaching inn, now an old wood-and-stone pub where locals gather to unwind in the evening. Caledonian 80 Shilling and Orkney Dark Island are available on hand pump, along with two "guest beers" that change weekly. The pub is open daily from 11am to midnight.

ELIE

With its step-gabled houses and little harbor, this is many visitors' favorite village along the coast. Lying only a 25-minute ride from Edinburgh, Elie and its close neighbor, Earlsferry, overlook a crescent of golden sand beach, with more swimming possibilities to be found among sheltered coves. The name Elie is believed to be derived from the "ailie," or island, of Ardross, which now forms part of the harbor and is joined to the mainland by a road. A large stone building, a former granary, at the harbor is a reminder of the days when Elie was a busy trading port.

Earlsferry, to the west, got its name from an ancient ferry crossing, which Macduff, the thane of Fife, is supposed to have used in his escape from Macbeth.

East of the harbor stands a stone structure known as the **Lady's Tower,** used by Lady Janet Anstruther, a noted 18th-century beauty, as a bathing cabana. Another member of the Anstruther family, Sir John, added the interesting **bell tower** to the parish church that stands in the center of the village.

Beyond the lighthouse, on a point of land to the east of the harbor, lies **Ruby Bay,** so named because garnets can be found here. Farther along the coast is **Fossil Bay,** where a variety of fossils can be found.

WHERE TO STAY

The Elms. 14 Park Place, Elie, Fife KY9 1DH. ☎ and fax **01333/330404.** 7 rms. £40 ($66) double. No credit cards. Rates include half board.

Run by Cameron and Pat Mann, this 1880 building is set on the wide main street behind a conservative stone facade, with a crescent-shaped rose garden in front. The comfortably furnished rooms are centrally heated and contain washbasins, hair dryers, and tea/coffeemakers. Home cooking is a specialty of the house, and dishes include Scottish lamb, Pittenweem haddock, haggis, and Arbroath kippers. The house is licensed, and a simple dinner is available to nonresidents. There's a large conservatory in the walled flower garden behind the house for guests' use.

Rockview Guest House. The Toft, Elie, Fife KY9 IDT. ☎ **01333/330246.** Fax 01333/330864. 6 rms. £50 ($82.50) double. MC, V.

Next door to the Ship Inn, Rockview overlooks fine sandy beaches around Elie Bay. Rooms are functional but well appointed. A twin-bedded room has a bunk bed for younger children to share with their parents. Family run, the guesthouse can accommodate about a dozen people at one time. Of course, food and drink are available at the Ship Inn.

WHERE TO DINE

✪ **Bouquet Garni.** 51 High St. ☎ **01333/330374.** Reservations required in summer, recommended in winter. Main courses £5.90–£10.90 ($9.75–$18) at lunch, £13.90–£16.90 ($22.95–$27.90) at dinner. AE, MC, V. Mon–Sat noon–2pm and 7–9:30pm, Sun noon–2pm. Closed the second half of Jan and the second week of Nov. FRENCH/SCOTTISH.

In a white-painted stone house on the main street, this restaurant is charming enough to justify a culinary excursion from St. Andrews. Run by owner-chef Andrew Keracher and his wife, Norah (who will greet you in the dining room), the establishment bases its reputation on French recipes, prepared with fresh, all-Scottish ingredients.

Your order will be taken in a small apéritif bar before you're ushered into dining rooms, filled with cream linen and fresh flowers. Dishes on the seasonal menu include lobster and scallops set in a light pastry case with a saffron-flavored brandy sauce and breast of wild pigeon with wild mushrooms and Madeira sauce. Dessert might be a brandy basket with chocolate ganache and seasonal fruits.

✪ **Ship Inn.** The Toft. ☎ **01333/330246.** Main courses £5.60–£13 ($9.25–$21.45). AE, DC, MC, V. Mon–Sat 11am–midnight, Sun 12:30–11pm. SCOTTISH.

Even if you're not stopping over in Elie, we suggest that you drop in at the Ship on the Toft (from the center, follow the signs marked HARBOUR) and enjoy a pint of lager or real ale, or whisky from a large selection. The building occupied by this pub with a nautical atmosphere dates from 1778, and a bar has been in business here since 1830. In summer you can sit outside and look over the water; in colder months a fireplace burns brightly. On weekends in July and August a barbecue operates outside. The set menu with daily specials features such items as pheasant, Angus beefsteaks, and venison, and an abundance of fresh seafood.

CRAIL

The pearl of the East Neuk of Fife, Crail is an artists' colony, and many painters live in cottages around its little harbor. Natural bathing facilities lie at Roome Bay, and many **beaches** are nearby. The **Balcomie Golf Course** is one of the oldest in the world and is still in good condition. Crail is 50 miles northeast of Edinburgh, 23 miles south of Dundee, and 9 miles south of St. Andrews.

WHERE TO STAY & DINE

Croma Hotel. 33–35 Nethergate, Crail, Fife KY10 3TU. ☎ **01333/450239.** 11 rms. TV TEL. £50 ($82.50) double. No credit cards. Rates include Scottish breakfast. Closed Dec–Jan.

This guesthouse one block off High Street near the harbor features the fully licensed Chart Room bar, open 6pm to midnight. The dining room has Windsor chairs set in front of the bay window. Many of the artists who live in this little fishing village come here for drinks and dinner, the only meal served. A three-course evening meal goes for £10 ($16.50). You can also have a bar meal in the Chart Room. The bedrooms are centrally heated, comfortably but very simply furnished, and well maintained.

3 St. Andrews

14 miles SE of Dundee, 51 miles NE of Edinburgh

The medieval royal burgh of St. Andrews was once filled with monasteries and ancient houses that did not survive the pillages of Henry VIII; regrettably, only a few ruins rising in ghostly dignity remain. Most of the town as you'll see it today was built of local stone during the 18th, 19th, and early 20th centuries.

The historic sea town in northeast Fife is also known as the seat wherein the rules of **golf** in Britain and the world are codified and arbitrated. Golf was played for the first time in the 1400s, probably on the site of St. Andrews's Old Course, and enjoyed by Mary Queen of Scots here in 1567. All six of St. Andrews's golf courses are fully owned by the municipality and are open to the public on a more-or-less democratic basis—ballots are polled 1 day in advance. This balloting system might be circumvented for players who reserve with the appropriate starters several days or weeks in advance. To play the hallowed Old Course, a current handicap certificate and/or letter of introduction from a bona-fide golf club must be presented.

The town's misty and verdant golf courses are the very symbol of St. Andrews, and a mecca for golfers around the world. They include the famous Old Course, the New Course (opened in 1896), the Jubilee Course (opened in 1897 in honor of Queen Victoria), the Eden (opened in 1914), the Balgove (a 9-hole course designed for children's golf training, in 1972), and the newest and most far-flung of all, the 18-hole Strathtyrum, which opened in 1993. Encircled by all of them is the world's most prestigious golf club, the **Royal and Ancient Golf Club** (☎ 01334/472112), which was founded in St. Andrews in 1754 and remains more or less rigidly closed as a private-membership men's club. The Royal and Ancient traditionally opens its doors to the public only on St. Andrew's Day to view its legendary trophy room. This usually, but not always, falls around November 30.

Facilities for golfers in St. Andrews are legion. Beside the 18th hole of the Old Course, within premises owned and operated by the Rusacks Hotel, there are links rooms with lockers, showers, and changing facilities, as well as meals and a bar. Virtually every hotel in town maintains some kind of facility to assist golfers in their explorations of the region's golf options.

ESSENTIALS
GETTING THERE

BY TRAIN   BritRail stops 8 miles away at the town of Leuchars (rhymes with euchres) on its London–Edinburgh–Dundee–Aberdeen run to the northeast. About 15 trains per day make the trip. Trip time from Edinburgh to Leuchars is about an hour. A one-way fare is £7.40 ($12.20). For information and schedules, call ☎ 0345/484950.

BY BUS   Once at Leuchars (see above), you can take a bus the rest of the way to St. Andrews. Bus no. 94 or 95 departs about every 30 minutes. Fife Scottish bus no. X24 travels from Glasgow to Glenrothes daily, and from there, bus X59 runs to St. Andrews. Buses operate daily from 7am to midnight, the trip taking between 2$^{1}/_{2}$ and 3 hours. Buses arrive at the St. Andrews Bus Station, Station Road, just off City Road (call ☎ 01334/474238 for schedules).

BY CAR   From Edinburgh, head northwest along A90 and cross the Forth Road Bridge north. Take A921 to the junction with A915 and continue northeast until you reach St. Andrews.

VISITOR INFORMATION

The **tourist information office** is on Market Street (☎ 01334/472021).

SEEING THE SIGHTS

Founded in 1411, the **University of St. Andrews** is the oldest in Scotland and the third oldest in Britain and has been called the "Oxbridge" of Scotland. At term time you can see the students in their characteristic red gowns. The university grounds stretch west of the St. Andrews Castle between North Street and the Scores.

The university's most interesting buildings include the tower and church of St. Salvator's College and the courtyard of St. Mary's College, dating from 1538. An ancient thorn tree, said to have been planted by Mary Queen of Scots, stands near the college's chapel. St. Leonard's College church is also from medieval days. In 1645 the Scottish Parliament met in what was once the University Library and is now a students' reading room. A modern University Library, containing many rare and ancient volumes, was opened in 1976.

Holy Trinity Church. Opposite St. Mary's College, off South St. ☎ **01334/474494.** Free admission, but call in advance to make sure someone is in attendance. Apr–Sept, daily 10am–noon and 2–4pm.

Called the "Town Kirk," this restored medieval church once stood on the grounds of the now-ruined cathedral (see below). The church was moved to its present site in 1410 and considerably altered after the Reformation of 1560. Restored in the early 20th century, the church has much fine stained glass and carvings.

St. Andrews Cathedral and Priory. Off Pends Rd. ☎ **01334/472563.** Admission £1.50 ($2.45) adults, £1 ($1.65) senior citizens, 75p ($1.25) children. Apr–Sept, Mon–Sat 9:30am–6pm, Sun 2–6pm; Oct–Mar, Mon–Sat 9:30am–4pm, Sun 2–4pm.

In the area of the Celtic settlement of St. Mary of the Rock, by the sea at the east end of town, is the semiruin of St. Andrews Cathedral and Priory. It was founded in 1160 and begun in the Romanesque style; however, the cathedral's construction suffered many setbacks. By the time of its consecration in 1318 in the presence of King Robert the Bruce, it had a gothic overlay. At the time the largest church in Scotland, the cathedral established St. Andrews as the ecclesiastical capital of the country. Today the ruins can only suggest its former beauty and importance. There's a collection of early Christian and medieval monuments, as well as artifacts discovered on the cathedral site.

Castle of St. Andrews. The Scores (northwest of the cathedral). ☎ **01334/477196.** Admission £2.30 ($3.80) adults, £1.50 ($2.45) senior citizens, £1 ($1.65) children. Apr–Sept, daily 9:30am–6:30pm; Oct–Mar, Mon–Sat 9:30am–4:30pm, Sun 2–4:30pm.

Also of interest is the ruined 13th-century castle, with its bottle dungeon and secret passages. Founded in the early part of the 13th century, it was reconstructed several times. Eerily posed at the edge of the sea, this was once a bishop's palace and, later, a prison for reformers. The bottle dungeon is carved 24 feet down into the rock. Both prisoners and food were dropped through this dungeon. There is said to be no nastier dungeon in all of Scotland than this one, the despair of any prisoner held here. A notable feature of the castle is its mine and "countermine." Disguised as masons, the reformers broke into the castle and murdered Cardinal Beaton in 1546. The mine was a tunnel dug by besieging forces in the 16th century. The countermine was a tunnel dug by castle defenders to meet and wage battle below ground. You stumble down the narrow countermine to the place where besieged and besiegers met in an underground clash.

○ **Secret Bunker.** Underground Nuclear Command Centre, Crown Buildings (near St. Andrews), Fife. ☎ **01333/310301.** Admission £5.95 ($9.80) adults, £5.35 ($8.85) ages 5–16; free for age 4 and under. Apr–Oct, daily 10am–5pm. Closed Nov–Mar. From St. Andrews follow the signs to Anstruther, driving south for 7 ¹/₂ miles. At that point signs show the way to the bunker.

This amazing labyrinth, built 100 feet below ground and encased in 15 feet of reinforced concrete, is where central government and military commanders would have run the country if the U.K. had been attacked and nuclear war had broken out. Built in great secrecy, it has a guardhouse entrance designed to look like a traditional Scottish farmhouse.

This bunker was called Scotland's best-kept secret for 40 years of cold war. You can visit the BBC studio where emergency broadcasts to Scotland would have been made or the switchboard room set up to handle 2,800 outside lines. Built to withstand aerial attack, the bunker could allow 300 people to live, work, and sleep in safety while coordinating war efforts, including aboveground retaliation. The bunker also contains two cinemas showing authentic cold war films, an audiovisual theater, a cafe, and a gift shop.

You can wander at will through the underground labyrinth, although there are 30-minute guided tours departing daily at 11am, 1pm, and 3pm. The bunker was built in 1951 and decommissioned in 1993. For some amazing reason, the chapel here has been the site of several local weddings since decommissioning.

SHOPPING

Specializing in Scottish art, **St. Andrews Fine Arts,** 84A Market St. (☎ **01334/ 474080**), also sells prints, drawings, and watercolors. Paintings for sale were all produced within the national boundaries of Scotland sometime between 1800 and the present. **Graeme Renton,** 72 South St. (☎ **01334/476334**), is one of the leading dealers of oriental carpets in Scotland, whether you're seeking antique rugs or reasonably priced reproductions. Rugs range from handmade to machine made and come in many different sizes, prices, and styles. Carpets from many different periods and locations are sold. At **Church Square Ceramics & Workshop,** Church Square (☎ **01334/477744**), an array of decorative stoneware and enameled jewelry—most of it produced locally—is for sale. A selection of ceramics is also sold here. **Bankers,** 80 Market St. (☎ **01334/473919**), is a typical tourist shop, hawking T-shirts, regional pottery, and other souvenirs, along with a wide range of cards and stationery.

WHERE TO STAY

Today you can fare much better than Samuel Johnson and James Boswell, who stopped off here for a meal of "rissered haddocks and mut chops."

EXPENSIVE

○ **Rufflets Country House Hotel.** Strathkinnes Low Rd., St. Andrews, Fife KY16 9TX. ☎ **01334/472594.** Fax 01334/478703. 25 rms. TV TEL. £150–£170 ($247.50–$280.50) double. AE, DC, MC, V. Rates include Scottish breakfast. Take B939 1¹/₂ miles from St. Andrews.

The garden-and-golf crowd prefers this cozy 1924 country-house retreat, set in a 10-acre garden. Each bedroom is equipped with a radio, hot-beverage facilities, and alarm clock, and all are well furnished in a warm, homelike way, some with canopied or four-poster beds. The furnishings are often Queen Anne in style. The most modern bedrooms are in the newer wing, although traditionalists request space in the handsome main building, and those in-the-know reserve well in advance, as Rufflets is very popular with the British.

Even if you aren't staying here, you may want to reserve a table at the garden-style Rufflets Hotel Restaurant, which overlooks an award-winning garden. Excellent fresh ingredients are used in the continental and Scottish dishes, and everything we've sampled here has been accurately cooked. The service, too, is polite and efficient. Dinner is the only meal served, a three-course affair costing £28 ($46.20) between 7 and 9pm daily. From 12:30 to 2pm daily, bar lunches, ranging from £6 to £12 ($9.90 to $19.80), are available.

Rusacks. Pilmour Links, St. Andrews, Fife KY16 9JQ. ☎ **800/225-5843** in the U.S., or 01334/474321. Fax 01334/477896. 48 rms, 2 suites. TV TEL. £137–£145 ($226.05–$239.25) double; £275 ($453.75) suite. AE, DC, MC, V.

A grand Victorian pile, the Rusacks sits at the edge of the famous 18th hole of Pilmour Links of the Old Course. The four-story Rusacks was originally built in 1887 by Josef Rusack, a German from Silesia who recognized the potential of St. Andrews as a golf capital. He placed advertisements for his hotel on the front pages of British newspapers, which at the time was considered revolutionary. The hotel's stone walls are capped with neoclassical gables and slate roofs. Inside, chintz picks up the tones from the bouquets of flowers sent in fresh twice a week. Between the panels and Ionic columns of the public rooms, racks of lendable books re-create the atmosphere of a private country-house library. Fireplaces and armchairs add to the allure. Upstairs, the bedrooms, all with private bath, contain some carved antiques, modern conveniences, and spacious charm, although nothing to equal the St. Andrews Old Course Hotel (see below).

The nightlife in the hotel partially explains why the crew and actors of *Chariots of Fire* stayed here during filming. The Golf Club in the basement, overlooking the links, has golf-related photos, trompe-l'oeil racks of books, Chesterfield sofas, and vested waiters. It's open from 6am to 5pm, and light meals and snacks are served. The hotel's Regency-style restaurant, The Master's, offers daily specials along with local game, meat, and fish, accompanied by a wine list from a well-stocked cellar. Open daily from 7 to 9:30pm, it offers a two-course dinner for £26.95 ($44.45), a three-course meal for £28.95 ($47.75).

Services: 24-hour room service, laundry.

Facilities: Sauna, solarium.

St. Andrews Golf Hotel. 40 The Scores, St. Andrews, Fife KY16 9AS. ☎ **01334/472611.** Fax 01334/472188. 22 rms. TV TEL. £130 ($214.50) double. AE, DC, MC, V. Rates include Scottish breakfast.

A combination of greenery, sea mists, and tradition makes this three-story late-Victorian property extremely popular with golfers, despite the fact that many of them confuse it at first glance with the larger and more prestigious St. Andrews Old Course Hotel (see below). Set about 200 yards from the first tee-off of the famous golf course, it was originally built as a private home, and later expanded and transformed into a hotel run by Brian and Maureen Hughes. Comfortable but unstylish bedrooms have radios and such thoughtful extras as coffeemakers, hair dryers, and toiletries. The rooms in the front get not only the view but also the noise. Bar lunches are served Monday through Saturday, and table d'hôte dinners are presented nightly in an oak-paneled restaurant with a fireplace and upholstered seating. A table d'hôte lunch goes for £15 ($24.75), a set dinner for £27.50 ($45.40). Informal meals are served in a basement bistro. Tennis courts are nearby.

✪ **St. Andrews Old Course Hotel.** Old Station Rd., St. Andrews, Fife KY16 9SP. ☎ **01334/474371.** Fax 01334/477668. 125 rms, 17 suites. MINIBAR TV TEL. £235–£270 ($387.75–$445.50) double; from £350 ($577.50) suite. AE, DC, MC, V. Rates include Scottish breakfast. Children 11 and under stay free in parents' room.

Many dedicated golfers prefer the five-story St. Andrews Old Course Hotel, close to A91 on the outskirts of town, where it overlooks the 17th fairway, the "Road Hole" of the Old Course. Fortified by finnan haddie and porridge, a real old-fashioned Scottish breakfast, you can face that diabolical stretch of greenery where the Scots have been whacking away since early in the 15th century and nearly all the world's golfing greats have played.

The hotel is not ancient—far from it. It's very contemporary, and its balconies afford top-view seats at all tournaments. However, don't let the name of the hotel mislead you. It's not related to the famous links of the same name, and access to the links is just as difficult here as it is elsewhere. Some £16 million has been spent to transform the hostelry into one of world-class standard. The facade was altered to keep it in line with the more traditional buildings of St. Andrews, and the bedrooms and suites were remodeled and refurbished, with traditional wooden furniture and marble bathrooms.

Dining/Entertainment: Well-prepared international cuisine is available in the Road Hole Grill, where a three-course table d'hôte costs £36.50 ($60.20). In summer light meals and afternoon tea are served in a plant-filled room known as the Conservatory. The Jigger Inn serves real ale and wholesome food in a traditional pub atmosphere.

Services: 24-hour room service, laundry, baby-sitting.

Facilities: The hotel offers an array of facilities, including health spa, whirlpool, massage room, steam rooms, beauty/therapy salons, pool, changing and locker rooms, and pro shop.

MODERATE

Inn at Lathones. By Largoward, St. Andrews, Fife KY9 1JE. ☎ **01334/840494.** Fax 01334/840694. 14 rms. TV TEL. £76–£95 ($125.40–$156.75) double. MC, V. Rates include Scottish breakfast. Take A915, 5 miles southwest of the center of St. Andrews.

Originally a coaching inn, this 200-year-old manor has been thoughtfully restored and given a comfortable aura. It provides a reasonable alternative for golfers who can't afford the grand tariffs of the grand golf hotels. All its bedrooms—often decorated with pastels—are furnished to a good standard, with individually controlled central heating, coffeemaking equipment, and hair dryers. The two that rent for £95 ($156.75) have log-burning stoves and Jacuzzis.

The public rooms reflect Scottish tradition, with open fires and beamed ceilings. The old-world Stable Bar contains some original artifacts from the coaching inn, and the Manor Bar places its armchairs around an open fire. A new French chef, Marc Guiburt, has introduced such dishes as pan-fried duck magret with fresh pesto, monkfish with a lemon-and-caper sauce, and pan-fried salmon in a tomato basil sauce. Options on the daily menu include à la carte main courses, ranging from £9 to £16 ($14.85 to $26.40), as well as fixed-price menus going for £7 ($11.55) for two courses, £11 ($18.15) for three courses, and £18.95 ($31.25) for a five-course "tasting menu."

Russell Hotel. 26 The Scores, St. Andrews, Fife KY16 9AS. ☎ **01334/473447.** Fax 01334/478279. 10 rms. TV TEL. £82–£88 ($135.30–$145.20) double. MC, V. Rates include Scottish breakfast. Closed Dec 24–Jan 14.

The Russell has an ideal location, overlooking St. Andrews Bay, just a 2-minute walk from the first tee of the Old Course. Once a 19th-century private home, it's well maintained and run by Gordon and Fiona de Vries. The hotel offers fully equipped although rather standard bedrooms with tea/coffeemakers. There's a cozy Victorian pub that serves bar meals and drinks to a loyal local clientele, plus a routine restaurant offering two-course fixed-price dinners for £15 ($24.75), or three courses at £18.50 ($30.55). Service is daily from 7 to 9:30pm.

INEXPENSIVE

Number Ten. 10 Hope St., St. Andrews, Fife KY16 9HJ. ☎ **01334/474601.** Fax 01334/474601. 10 rms. £52 ($85.80) double; £65 ($107.25) family room. DC, MC, V. Rates include Scottish breakfast. Children 11 and under stay in parents' room for half price.

Housed in a classic Georgian building directly south of the Royal and Ancient Golf Club, only a 3-minute walk from the first tee of the Old Course, this guesthouse is centrally heated and has a lounge with a color TV. All the modestly furnished rooms have facilities for making hot beverages. Breakfast is the only meal served. The hosts will arrange tee-off times and minigolf packages for guests.

WHERE TO DINE

Grange Inn. Grange Rd., at Grange. ☎ **01334/472670.** Reservations recommended. Main courses £12.75–£15.70 ($21.05–$25.90). AE, DC, MC, V. Daily 12:30–2pm and 6:30–9:30pm. Drive about 1¹/₂ miles from St. Andrews on B959. SCOTTISH/SEAFOOD.

If you're seeking less formality, a favorite eating spot, well established for many years, is the Grange Inn on B959. In this country cottage with its garden, an old-fashioned hospitality prevails. It offers a good choice of dishes made from fresh produce. Local beef and lamb always appear on the menu, as do fish and shellfish from the fishing villages of East Neuk. Fruits and herbs come from Cupar. Typical of the dishes served are a filet of beef with pork sauce complemented by wild mushrooms, or chicken suprême stuffed with a julienne of vegetables and coated with almonds, then served on a pool of lemon sauce. A classic opener and an old favorite at the inn is a stew of mussels and onions.

NEARBY PLACES TO STAY & DINE

✪ **Ostlers Close.** 25 Bonnygate, Cupar. ☎ **01334/655574.** Reservations recommended. Main courses £9–£10 ($14.85–$16.50) at lunch; £15–£18 ($24.75–$29.70) at dinner. AE, MC, V. Tues–Sat 12:15–2pm and 7–9:30pm. Closed: June 1–15. BRITISH/INTERNATIONAL. From St. Andrews go along A91 for 7 miles to the southwest until you reach the village of Cupar.

Sophisticated and intensely concerned with the quality of its cuisine, this charming restaurant occupies a 17th-century building that functioned in the early 20th century as a temperance hotel that expressly forbade alcohol. Today, from a position in the heart of the hamlet of Cupar, it contains a kitchen within what used to function as the hotel's stables, with a severely elegant set of dining rooms within the hotel's former public areas. Amanda Graham, co-owner and supervisor of the dining room, is the person you're most likely to meet here, along with a staff that serves the cuisine of her husband, Jimmy Graham.

Menu items are based on seasonal Scottish produce and are likely to include roasted saddle of roe venison served with mushroom sauce; pan-fried scallops with fresh asparagus and butter sauce; a very fresh medley of seafood that tastes best when accompanied by a champagne-flavored butter sauce; and filet of Scottish lamb stuffed with skirlie, an old-fashioned but flavorful combination of bacon-flavored oatmeal and herbs. Whenever it's available, opt for the confit of duckling with salted pork and lentils. The establishment's name, incidentally, harkens back to stagecoach days, when its setting was the site of stable boys (ostlers) who lived on either side of the close (alleyway) in back of the hotel.

Peat Inn. Cupar, Fife KY15 5LH. ☎ **01334/840206.** Fax 01334/840530. 8 suites. TV TEL. £135 ($222.75) suite for 2. AE, DC, MC, V. Rates include Scottish breakfast. Closed 2 weeks in Jan and 2 weeks in Nov. From St. Andrews, drive 7 miles southwest along A915, then branch onto B940.

The Peat Inn is in an old inn/post office built in 1760, where David Wilson prepares exceptional cuisine. The inn offers accommodation in beautifully furnished suites.

The restaurant is run by David and his wife, Patricia, who have a reputation for serving high-quality meals in comfortable surroundings. The ingredients are almost all locally grown—even the pigeons (a specialty) come from a St. Andrews farm. Pigeon is offered in a pastry case with wild mushrooms, or you can order the plump breasts in an Armagnac-and-juniper sauce. A meal of signature dishes is likely to begin with julienne of pigeon breast on a bed of sliced pork. According to David, it's a "deliberate clash of Oriental and French traditions, garnished with Scottish produce." For a main course, try the roast monkfish and lobster with asparagus and wild mushrooms. The dessert specialty is a trio of caramel-flavored sweets, including crème caramel, caramel-flavored ice cream, and a caramelized apple pastry, all drizzled with caramel sauce. A set four-course lunch goes for £18.95 ($31.25), with a four-course table d'hôte dinner costing £38.80 ($64). À la carte meals, offered only at dinner, range from £15 to £23 ($24.75 to $37.95) for main courses. Hours are Tuesday through Saturday from 12:30 to 1:30pm and 7 to 10pm.

ST. ANDREWS AFTER DARK

The cultural center of St. Andrews is the **Byre Theatre,** Abbey Street (☎ 01334/476288), which features drama presentations ranging from the works of Shakespeare to musical comedies. Currently being rebuilt from the foundation up, it is expected to be up and running by the summer of 1999. Productions are currently being staged in a variety of venues throughout the town. Pick up a weekly version of *What's on in St Andrews* to find out what is featured, as well as when and where the production is being staged. The tourist office is helpful in providing this type of information.

If you're in town during July and August, you can get a taste of traditional Scottish music and dancing at the **St. Andrews Golf Hotel,** 40 The Scores (☎ 01334/472611), which holds a Scottish ceilidh every Wednesday from 8:30 to 11pm. Admission is £4.75 ($7.85) for adults and £2.75 ($4.55) for children.

Victoria, 1A St. Mary's Place (☎ 01334/476964), is the place to catch a live band in St. Andrews. This student-filled pub features folk, rock, and blues acts on weekend nights. John Smith's, Beamish Stout, McEwan's Lager, 78 Shilling, and 80 Shilling are available on tap. Normally, all pints are £1.75 ($2.90), but if you arrive at happy hour, held nightly from 8 to 9pm, a pint goes for only £1 ($1.65). The bar is open Saturday through Wednesday from 11am to midnight, staying open an hour later on Thursday and Friday.

A pub since 1904, the **Central Bar,** at the corner of Market and College Street (☎ 01334/478296), is an antiquated room that offers more than pints and pub talk on Thursday night. That's when live rock and blues bands start playing at 8:30pm. There's no cover and the best brews here are Old Peculiar, Theaksgton's XB, and McEwan's Lager. The bar is open daily from 11am to 11:45pm. **Chariots,** The Scores (☎ 01334/472451), in the Scores Hotel, attracts mainly a local crowd, ranging in ages from 30 to 60, who gather here in the evening for conversation over a pint. Despite a strong regional tradition of beer brewing, two outsiders, Guinness and Carlsberg, are featured on tap. The pub is open daily from noon to 11:30pm.

4 Falkland

21 miles N of Edinburgh

This royal burgh of cobblestone streets and crooked houses lies at the northern base of the hill of East Lomond. Its notable sight is Falkland Palace and Gardens, now owned by the National Trust of Scotland.

ESSENTIALS
GETTING THERE

BY TRAIN   From Edinburgh, take the train to Markinch, the closest rail link to Falkland. Call ☎ **0345/484950** for information and schedules. Go the rest of the way by bus.

BY BUS   From Markinch, bus no. 36 connects with arriving trains and runs to Falkland.

BY CAR   Take A90 northwest of Edinburgh across the Forth Road Bridge, then continue northeast along A921, which leads into A92. At the junction with A912, head northwest to Falkland.

VISITOR INFORMATION

The nearest **tourist office** is at Kirkcaldy (☎ **01592/267775**), 13 miles south of Falkland.

SEEING THE SIGHTS

✪ **Falkland Palace and Garden.** High St. ☎ **01337/857397.** Admission £4.50 ($7.45) adults, £3 ($4.95) seniors, students, and children. Admission to garden only: £2.30 ($3.80) adults, £1.50 ($2.45) seniors, students, and children. Apr–Oct, Mon–Sat 11am–5:30pm, Sun 1:30–5:30pm. Closed Nov–Mar.

Since the 14th century Falkland has been connected with Scottish kings. Originally a castle stood on the site of today's palace, but it was replaced in the 16th century. Falkland then became a favorite seat of the Scottish court. James V died here. Mary Queen of Scots used to come to Falkland for "hunting and hawking." It was also here that Francis Stuart, fifth earl of Bothwell, tried to seize his young cousin, James VI, son of Mary Queen of Scots. The gardens have been laid out to the original royal plans. Falkland also boasts the oldest royal tennis court in the United Kingdom.

WHERE TO STAY

Covenanter Hotel. The Square, Falkland, Fife KY15 7BU. ☎ **01337/857224.** Fax 01337/857163. 3 rms, 2 apts. TV TEL. £48 ($79.20) double or apt. AE, DC, MC, V. Rates include Scottish breakfast.

Since the early 18th century this has been a popular inn. With modest modernization, it offers a good standard of accommodation. The hotel is built of local stone, with high chimneys, wooden shutters, and a Georgian entry, and is on a small square opposite the church and palace. The dining room is strictly "old style" and for the before-dinner drinks there's an intimate pub, the Covenanter Cocktail Bar. The dining room serves meals from noon to 2pm and 6 to 9pm daily, with a three-course fixed-price menu running £12 ($19.80). There is also a bistro that serves meals during the same hours in the price range of £3.90 to £10.45 ($6.45 to $17.25). Selections include beef-and-ale pie, grilled trout, various steaks, and vegetarian dishes.

WHERE TO DINE

Kind Kyttock's Kitchen. Cross Wynd. ☎ **01337/857477.** Main courses £1.90–£5.45 ($3.15–$9). AE, MC, V. Tues–Sun 10:30am–5:30pm. Closed Dec 24–Jan 5. SCOTTISH.

Located near the palace, this is also an art gallery that displays local crafts and paintings. A specialty is homemade oat cakes with cheese. The bread is also homemade, very fresh tasting. For a tea, we suggest pancakes with fruit and fresh cream. Even better, however, are the tarts with fresh cream. The salads are also good. A cup of scotch broth, served with a slice of whole-meal bread, is a favorite.

5 Stirling

37 miles NW of Edinburgh, 28 miles NE of Glasgow

Stirling is dominated by its impressive castle, perched on a 250-foot basalt rock formed by the River Forth and the River Clyde and the relatively small parcel of land between them. The ancient town of Stirling, on the main east–west route across Scotland, grew up around the castle. It lies in the heart of an area so turbulent in Scottish history that it was called "the cockpit of Scotland." A memorable battle fought here was the Battle of Bannockburn in 1314, when Robert I (the Bruce) defeated the army of Edward II of England and gained Scotland its independence.

Stirling is the central crossroads of Scotland, giving easy access by rail and road to all its major towns and cities. If you use it as a base, you'll be only a short distance from many attractions, including Loch Lomond, the Trossachs, and the Highlands.

The town center boasts several shopping facilities, including the Thistle Centre indoor shopping plaza.

ESSENTIALS
GETTING THERE

BY TRAIN Frequent trains run between Glasgow and Stirling and between Edinburgh and Stirling. A 1-day round-trip ticket from Edinburgh costs £6.60 to £8.40 ($10.90 to $13.85), and from Glasgow, £5.80 to £7.30 ($9.55 to $12.05). For schedules, call National Express Inquiries at ☎ **0345/484950.**

BY BUS Frequent buses run to Stirling from Glasgow. A 1-day round-trip ticket from Glasgow costs £3.90 ($6.45). Check with Scottish CityLink (☎ **0990/808080**) for information.

BY CAR From Glasgow, head northeast along A80 to M80, at which point continue north. From Edinburgh, head northwest along M9.

VISITOR INFORMATION

The **tourist information office** is at 41 Dumbarton Rd. (☎ **01786/475019**).

SEEING THE SIGHTS

The **Church of the Holy Rude** on St. John Street (☎ **01786/475275**) is said to be the only church in the country still in use that has witnessed a coronation. The date was 1567 when the 13-month-old James VI was crowned, the son of Mary Queen of Scots who was to become James I of England. John Knox preached the sermon. The church itself dates from the early 15th century. It's open May to September only, daily from 10am to 5pm.

Stirling Castle. Upper Castle Hill. ☎ **01786/450000.** Admission £4 ($6.60) adults, £2.50 ($4.15) seniors, £1.20 ($2) children. Apr–Sept, daily 9:30am–6pm; Oct–Mar, daily 9:30am–5pm.

On the right bank of the Forth, Stirling Castle dates from the Middle Ages, when its location on a dividing line between the Lowlands and the Highlands made it the key to the Highlands. There are traces of earlier (7th-century) royal habitation of the Stirling area. Later the castle became an important seat of two kings, James IV and James V, both of whom added to the structure, the latter following classic Renaissance style, then relatively unknown in Britain. Here Mary Queen of Scots lived as an infant monarch for the first 4 years of her life. After its final defeat in 1746, Bonnie Prince Charlie's army stopped here. Later the castle became an army barracks and headquarters of the Argyll and Sutherland Highlanders, one of Britain's most celebrated regiments. An audiovisual presentation explains what you're about to see.

Museum of the Argyll and Sutherland Highlanders. In Stirling Castle, Upper Castle Hill. ☎ **01786/475165.** Free admission. Daily 10am–5pm.

At the castle you can visit this regional museum, which presents an excellent exhibition of colors, pipe banners, and regimental silver, along with medals (some of which go back to the Battle of Waterloo) won by Scottish soldiers for valor.

A DAY TRIP TO BANNOCKBURN

An interesting excursion can be taken to Bannockburn, a name that looms large in Scottish history. It was here that Robert the Bruce, his army of 6,000 outnumbered three to one, defeated the forces of Edward II in 1314. Before nightfall on that day, Robert the Bruce had won back the throne of Scotland. The battlefield lies off M80, 2 miles south of Stirling.

At the **Bannockburn Heritage Centre,** Glasgow Road (☎ **01786/812664**), an audiovisual presentation tells the story of these events. The queen herself came here in 1964 to unveil an equestrian statue of the Scottish hero. An exhibition, *The Kingdom of the Scots,* traces the history of Scotland from William Wallace to the Union of Crowns. The site is open all year, but the Heritage Centre and shop are open only from April through October, daily from 10am to 5:30pm, and in March, November, and December, daily from 11am to 3pm. The last audiovisual showing is at 5:30pm. Admission is £2.30 ($3.80) for adults, £1.50 ($2.45) for seniors and children, £6.10 ($10.05) for a family ticket.

From the **Borestone,** where Robert the Bruce commanded his forces, you can see Stirling Castle and the Forth Valley. The location is off M80/M9 at Junction 9.

SHOPPING

McCutcheon's, 30 Spittal St., Old Town (☎ **01786/461771**), is a book dealer specializing in antiquarian books. The dealer claims to "have everything under the sun." Although that's a bit of an exaggeration, the range of books here is startlingly vast, dating from 1473 to 1997. The best woolen gift goods in town are found at **R.R. Henderson,** 6–8 Friar St. (☎ **01786/473681**), a Highland outfitter selling not only woolen goods such as sweaters and scarves but kilts and made-to-order tartans. At the **Cornerstone Gallery,** Mar Place (☎ **01786/474440**), high-quality gifts from Scotland and throughout the U.K. can be found. Tartan items, heraldic crests, chess sets, Scottish pewter, and local jewelry and scarves are among the well-made items found.

Some of the best shopping is not in Stirling itself but in the outlying area, as exemplified by **Barbara Davidson's Pottery Studio,** Muirhall Farm, at Larbert (☎ **01324/554430**), lying 9 miles south of Stirling. Take the A9 to Larbert and at the roundabout follow A18 west until you see the sign. The farm and shop are about half a mile along this road on the right. At this 18th-century farmstead, Barbara Davidson operates a studio and workshop. She is one of Scotland's best-known potters and a large selection of her functional wares is exhibited and sold here.

Located east of Stirling, a trio of towns form the "Mill Trail Country": Alva, Alloa, and Tillicoultry. Many quality textile mills have factory outlets here, offering bargain prices on cotton, woolens, and even cashmere goods. Among the best is **Callant of Scotland Ltd.,** Devonpark Mills, Devonside, Tillicoultry (☎ **01259/752353**), offering discounted classics in clothing for men and women in cashmere, lambswool, and cotton. The store features a viewing window, allowing shoppers to watch production in the mill. For an even greater selection of cashmere fashions, head for

Stirling, Loch Lomond & the Trossachs

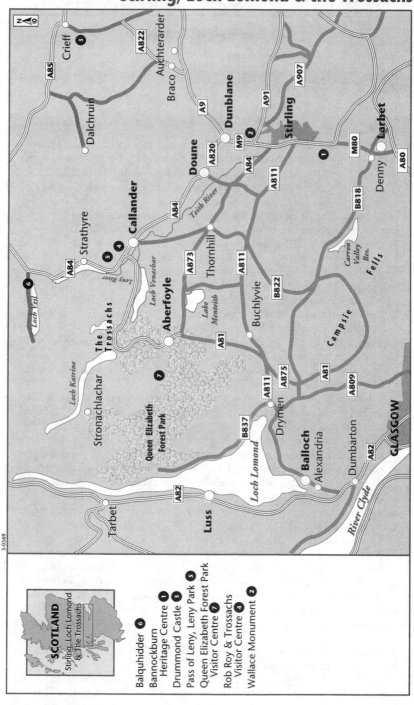

Balquhidder **6**

Bannockburn
Heritage Centre **1**

Drummond Castle **3**

Pass of Leny, Leny Park **5**

Queen Elizabeth Forest Park
Visitor Centre **7**

Rob Roy & Trossachs
Visitor Centre **4**

Wallace Monument **2**

3-0569

The True Story of *Braveheart*

Sir Robert the Bruce at Bannockburn
Beat the English in every wheel and turn,
And made them fly in great dismay
From off the field without delay. . . .

—William McGonagall, "The Battle of Bannockburn"

Robert the Bruce (1274–1329) was the first of three kings of Scotland named Robert. Although neither Mel Gibson nor Liam Neeson selected this daring man as the title subject for a movie, they might well have done so—Robert the Bruce led a life filled with all the excitement and thrills of a 1930s Errol Flynn adventure flick.

In 1292 Edward I of England gave the Scottish crown to John de Balliol, known as "the vassal king," demanding that Scotland pay homage to the English throne. But instead, the Scots formed what was to become known as the Auld Alliance with France in October 1295. Edward viewed this as a declaration of war, and "The Hammer of Scotland" stormed into Scotland, devastating the countryside and capturing and taking home the Stone of Destiny from Scone, coronation stone of Scottish kings.

William Wallace (1274–1305) defeated the English at the 1297 Battle of Stirling Bridge and was made "Guardian of the Realm." Edward, in turn, defeated Wallace at the Battle of Falkirk the following year. Outlawed for his activities, Wallace hid for 7 years until his capture, at which time he was paraded through the streets of London and was hanged and drawn and quartered, with his entrails burned before his eyes as he died. This horrific English method of execution reputedly was devised by Edward especially for William Wallace.

Robert the Bruce replaced Wallace as "Guardian of Scotland." In March 1306 Bruce had himself crowned king of Scotland. Edward rushed north and defeated the forces of Bruce at Methven and at Dalry. Like Wallace, Bruce became an outlaw, forced into hiding, probably on the island of Rathlin, off the Irish coast. There he was said to have learned patience, courage, and hope by watching a spider persevere in spinning a web, swinging from one rafter to another on a fragile thread.

In 1307 he returned to Scotland, where he captured Perth in 1313 and Edinburgh in 1314. At Bannockburn—also in 1314—he defeated the forces of Edward's son, Edward II. The pope excommunicated Bruce, and his sovereignty was not recognized by the royal houses of Europe.

Upon Edward III's coronation in 1327, the Scots launched a raid into England. The following year Edward was almost captured when he led a retaliatory army into Scotland. But in 1328 a peace treaty was signed, acknowledging the independence of Scotland. David, the 4-year-old son of Bruce, was "married" to Joan, the 7-year-old sister of Edward III. The Bruce ruled Scotland wisely until his death at Cardross Castle on the Clyde.

Lochleven Shop, Lochleven Mills, Kinroos (☎ 01577/863528), which offers selections from manufacturers including Henry White.

The best selection of sweaters is available in many designs at **Inverallen Handknitters Ltd.,** Alva Industrial Estate, Alva (☎ 01259/762292). The handknitted traditional sweaters here are particularly appealing. A good selection of clothing for children and infants supplements the selections for men and women at

Glen Alva Ltd., Hallpark, Whine Road, Alloa (☎ **01259/723024**). If you become inspired to try and knit your own creation, head to **Patons & Baldwins,** Kilcraigo Mill, Alloa (☎ **01259/723431**), which manufactures quality hand-knitting and craft yarns.

For more complete details, including any directional information, seasonal closings, or whatever, call or visit the **Mill Trail Visitor Centre,** West Stirling Street at Alva (☎ **01259/769696**), which not only provides information about the above shops in the area but many others as well.

WHERE TO STAY

Golden Lion Hotel. 8–10 King St., Stirling, Stirlingshire FK8 2ND. ☎ **01786/475351.** Fax 01786/472755. 71 rms. TV TEL. £87 ($143.55) double. AE, DC, MC, V. Rates include Scottish breakfast.

About a block downhill from Holyrood Church, one of the oldest and largest hotels in town is the beneficiary of a recent refurbishment that improved and modernized most of the bedrooms. Originally built in 1786 as a three-story coaching inn, its sandstone shell was greatly enlarged with the addition of modern wings in 1962. The hotel contains a pleasant and popular cocktail bar and a restaurant, where a three-course table d'hôte is available for £12.50 ($20.65) daily from 11am to 11pm. Its bedrooms are simple, easy-on-the-eye accommodations, with teamaking facilities and radios.

✪ **Park Lodge Hotel.** 32 Park Terrace, Stirling, Stirlingshire FK8 2JS. ☎ **01786/474862.** Fax 01786/449748. 9 rms. TV TEL. £80–£110 ($132–$181.50) double. MC, V. Rates include Scottish breakfast. Bus: 51 or 52.

This hotel is in a 19th-century Italianate mansion, across the street from a city park in a residential neighborhood uphill from the center of town. Built of stone blocks and slates, it has a Doric portico, a Georgian-era core dating from 1825, and century-old climbing roses and wisteria, along with Tudor-style chimney pots. The hotel qualifies as the most stylish in town. Anne and Georges Marquetty house guests in nine upstairs bedrooms, and suggest that they dine at one of the elegant tables of their restaurant, The Heritage (see "Where to Dine," below). Each bedroom contains antique furnishings (Room 6 has a four-poster bed). You might enjoy tea in a walled garden behind the hotel, with its garden room, widely spaced iron benches, and terra-cotta statues. On the other side of tall casement windows are a pair of French-inspired salons with marble fireplaces, elaborate draperies, and cabriole-legged armchairs.

Stirling Highland Hotel. Spittal St., Stirling, Stirlingshire FK8 1DU. ☎ **01786/475444.** Fax 01786/462929. 76 rms. TV TEL. £123 ($202.95) double; £173 ($285.45) suite. AE, DC, MC, V. Rates include Scottish breakfast.

Stirling's newest hotel in the center of town has also become its most important. This stylish hotel was installed, after major renovations, in what was once the Old High School, a Victorian building to which everyone in town has an emotional link. Respect for the historic atmosphere was maintained and many of the original architectural features were kept. Florals, tartans, and solid wood furnishings dominate both the public rooms and the bedrooms. The bedrooms, fairly routine, are in a three-story annex. From its position close to Stirling Castle, the hotel enjoys views over the town and surrounding region.

Dining/Entertainment: Small but charming, the cocktail bar is usually active in the evening, and most guests dine at their hotel rather than face the uncertain cuisine of the town itself. Scottish cuisine is featured in Scholars Restaurant, while

Rizzio's Restaurant serves the cuisine of Italy. A meal in either place costs £18.95 ($31.25).

Services: Room service, baby-sitting, laundry.

Facilities: Indoor pool, steam room, squash courts, gymnasium, snooker room, Jacuzzi, solarium.

Terraces Hotel. 4 Melville Terrace, Stirling, Stirlingshire FK8 2ND. ☎ **01786/472268.** Fax 01786/450314. 18 rms. TV TEL. £72 ($118.80) double. AE, DC, MC, V. Rates include Scottish breakfast.

Originally built as a fine Georgian-inspired house of buff-colored sandstone, this hotel stands on a raised terrace in a quiet residential neighborhood, a 5-minute walk south of the center near the town's largest shopping center. One of the best values in town, it's owned by the Danish–British partnership of Lars and Julie Christiansen. The half-paneled cocktail bar and velvet-upholstered restaurant provide a popular setting for local parties and wedding receptions. Melville's Restaurant, serving daily from noon to 2:30pm and 6:30 to 9pm, offers both a Scottish and a continental menu, everything from beef Stroganoff to wiener schnitzel, from tagliatelle napolitana to chicken Kiev. Main dishes range from £7.95 to £11.50 ($13.10 to $18.95). Each of the bedrooms is furnished in a country-house motif of flowered curtains and solidly traditional furniture.

WHERE TO DINE

✪ **The Heritage.** 16 Allan Park, Stirling, Stirlingshire FK8 2QC. ☎ **01786/473660.** Fax 01786/451291. Reservations recommended. Main courses £8.45–£12.45 ($13.95–$32.10). Fixed-price 2-course lunch £8.50 ($14); 3-course dinner £12.50–£29 ($20.65–$47.85). MC, V. Daily noon–2pm and 6:30–9:30pm. Closed Sun in winter. INTERNATIONAL/SCOTTISH.

Culinary sophistication and beautiful decor rank it as one of the most sought-after restaurants in the entire district. Near the center of town, a 5-minute walk east of the railway station, it's located on a quiet residential street. You enter a gentleman's parlor, richly outfitted with somber walls and enviable antiques, to have a drink before descending to the low-ceilinged basement restaurant. Amid a French-inspired decor, you'll taste some of the best cuisine in town, prepared with finesse by Georges Marquetty. In his youth he worked as an executive chef in Paris, and later spent 12 years in Cincinnati with his British wife, Anne (where he was voted one of the leading chefs of America). His specialties include scallops, scampi, and prawns in Pernod sauce, filet of wild venison with port and black-currant sauce, scallops with smoked ham in lemon sauce, and foie gras with truffles.

Upstairs, nine handsomely furnished bedrooms, each with private bathroom, TV, and telephone, rent at £80 ($132) for a double, with breakfast included.

Riverway Restaurant. Kildean, outside Stirling. ☎ **01786/475734.** Main courses £4.15–£10 ($6.85–$16.50); high tea £5.35–£7.95 ($8.85–$13.10). V. Daily 10am–noon (coffee and scones), noon–3pm, and 3–6:30pm (high tea). Closed Mon in summer and Mon–Tues Nov–Easter. SCOTTISH.

This fully licensed restaurant has a local reputation for good food at moderate tariffs. Half a mile from the center of Stirling, just off M8 beside Junction 10, it has panoramic views of Stirling Castle, the Wallace Monument, and the Ochil Hills. The Riverway offers well-prepared food, such as honeyed lamb cutlets, deep-fried haddock, and grilled sirloin steaks. At lunchtime you can order a real Scottish menu, including haggis, neeps, and tatties. The high-tea menu has such rib-sticking fare as fried liver, bacon, and onions. Wine of the house is sold by the glass or the bottle.

STIRLING AFTER DARK

Located on the campus of Stirling University, **Macrobert Arts Centre** (☎ 01786/461081) offers plays, music, films, and art exhibitions. The 497-seat main theater often presents dramas and symphony concerts, whereas the 140-seat studio theater is used mainly for film screenings. Cinema tickets cost £3.50 ($5.75) for adults and £2.50 ($4.15) for children, and theater tickets generally run from £7 to £8 ($11.55 to $13.20). Admission to most concerts ranges from £10 to £12 ($16.50 to $19.80). Call for current listings.

All that Jazz, 9 Upper Craigs (☎ 01786/451130), is a lively bar popular with students. Music is usually provided via the stereo, but bands also appear here infrequently. The bar serves a good range of single-malts and pints of Kronenberg, Beamish Red, and McEwans. The adjoining restaurant serves an "Odd Couple" mixture of Cajun and traditional Scottish fare, including the dreaded haggis, between 5 and 10pm every evening. The same menu is available throughout the day in the bar, which is open Sunday through Thursday from 11am to midnight and Friday and Saturday from 11am to 1am.

O'Neill's, 11 Maxwell Place (☎ 01786/446357), is a traditional Irish pub popular with Scottish students. Irish and Scottish folk bands play twice weekly, but there are no set nights for entertainment. To find out who or what's playing, check the flyers posted in the pub. There's never a cover charge. The bar is open Monday through Thursday from 11am to midnight, Friday and Saturday from 11am to 1am, and Sunday from 12:30pm to midnight.

Barnton Bar/Bistro, 3 Barnton St. (☎ 01786/461698), is an art nouveau–style bar with marble-topped tables and high ceilings edged with ornate cornices. It's the center of gay life in Stirling, but draws a mixed crowd of students, professionals, and old-timers as well. The Wednesday Quiz Night, where drinkers compete in general-knowledge trivia, is quite popular. Every other Sunday a rock or pop band plays. There's no cover, and the bar is open Monday through Thursday from 10:30am to midnight, Friday and Saturday from 11am to 1am, and Sunday from noon to midnight.

6 Dunblane

7 miles N of Stirling, 42 miles NW of Edinburgh, 29 miles SW of Perth, 33 miles NE of Glasgow

A small cathedral city on the banks of the Allan Water, Dunblane takes its name from the Celtic Church of St. Blane, which once stood on the site now occupied by the fine 13th-century gothic cathedral.

Sports enthusiasts are attracted to the area because of its golfing, fishing, and hunting.

ESSENTIALS
GETTING THERE

BY TRAIN Trains run between Glasgow and Dunblane with a stopover at Stirling, with a one-way fare costing £4.30 ($7.10). Rail connections are also possible through Edinburgh via Stirling for £4.90 ($8.10) for a one-way fare. For 24-hour information, call ☎ 0345/484950.

BY BUS Buses travel from the Goosecroft Bus Station in Stirling to Dunblane, costing £1.45 ($2.40) each way. Call ☎ 01786/446474 in Stirling for schedule information, or contact Bluebird Buses at ☎ 01324/613777.

BY CAR From Stirling (see above), continue north along M9 to Dunblane.

VISITOR INFORMATION

A year-round **tourist information office** is on Stirling Road (☎ **01786/824428**).

SEEING THE SIGHTS

An excellent example of 13th-century gothic ecclesiastic architecture, ✪ **Dunblane Cathedral,** Cathedral Close (☎ **01786/823388**), was spared the ravages of attackers who destroyed other Scottish worship centers. Altered in the 15th century and restored several times in the 19th and 20th centuries, the cathedral may have suffered most from neglect subsequent to the Reformation. A Jesse Tree window is in the west end of the building, and of interest are stalls, misericords, a pulpit with carved figures of early ecclesiastical figures, and other striking features, including the wooden barrel-vaulted roof with colorful armorials. A Celtic stone from about A.D. 900 can be seen in the north aisle.

A 1687 structure on the grounds of the old manse shelters the personal library of Bishop Robert Leighton, an outstanding 17th-century churchman, which contains a great deal of material on the effects of the troubled times in Scotland. The **Cathedral Museum** (☎ **01786/823440**) on the square is in the Dean's House and contains articles and papers pertaining to both the cathedral and town. Admission is free. It's open late May to September only, Monday through Saturday from 10am to 12:30pm and 2:30 to 4:30pm. The story of Dunblane and its ancient cathedral is displayed in the 1624 house, and you can also visit an enclosed garden with a very old (restored) well.

WHERE TO STAY & DINE

✪ **Cromlix House.** Kinbuck, Dunblane, Perthshire FK15 9JT. ☎ **01786/822125.** Fax 01786/825450. 6 rms, 8 suites. TV TEL. £135–£205 ($222.75–$338.25) double; £170–£265 ($280.50–$437.25) suite. AE, DC, MC, V. Closed Jan. Take A9 to B8033; the hotel is 3¹/₄ miles north of Dunblane just beyond the village of Kinbuck.

Cromlix House is a three-story country-house hotel. The manor, built in 1880 as the seat of a family that has owned the surrounding acreage for the past 500 years, was transformed into an elegant hotel in 1982 on a 3,000-acre estate. The owners still live on the estate and derive part of their income from organizing hunting and fishing expeditions in the surrounding moors and forests and on the River Allan. Croquet mallets, wellies, and fishing rods in the entrance evoke the atmosphere.

Fishing in three private lakes and hunting are available as well as tennis, and guests can walk through the surrounding forests and farmland. The manor has an elegant drawing room with big bow windows, and antiques are among the furnishings of both public rooms and bedrooms. Bouquets of fresh flowers and open fires in cool weather add to the comfort of the place. The bedrooms (including eight suites with sitting rooms) are carpeted and often have Queen Anne furnishings. In addition to a second-floor library, guests are invited to the chapel and gun room.

Lunch is served to residents and nonresidents, daily from 12:30 to 1:30pm at £18 to £25 ($29.70 to $41.25) for table d'hôte, and dinner is served nightly from 7 to 8:30pm for £36.50 ($60.20) per person for five courses.

7 Doune

41 miles NW of Edinburgh, 35 miles N of Glasgow, 8 miles NW of Stirling

This small market town with its 15th-century castle is a good center for exploring the Trossachs. The rivers Teith and Ardoch flow through Doune.

ESSENTIALS
GETTING THERE

BY TRAIN   Stirling (see above) is the closest rail link to Doune.

BY BUS   Buses from the Stirling bus station on Goosecroft run throughout the day to Doune. Call ☎ **0990/808080** for more information.

BY CAR   From Dunblane (see above), continue west along A820.

VISITOR INFORMATION

The nearest **tourist information office** is at Dunblane (see above).

SEEING THE SIGHTS

Doune Castle. Hwy. A820, 4 miles west of Dunblane. ☎ **01786/841742.** Admission £1.50 ($2.45) adults, £1 ($1.65) senior citizens, 50p (85¢) children, free for children 4 and under. Apr–Sept, daily 9:30am–6pm; Oct–Mar, Mon–Wed 9:30am–4pm, Sat 10am–4pm, Sun 2–4pm.

This castle, once a royal palace, stands on the banks of the River Teith. Now owned by the earl of Moray, it was restored in 1883, making it one of the best preserved of Scotland's medieval castles.

Doune Motor Museum. Carse of Cambus (on A84). ☎ **01786/841203.** Admission £3 ($4.95) adults, £2.50 ($4.15) senior citizens and children. Apr–Oct, daily 10am–5pm. Closed Nov–Mar.

After visiting the castle, guests can drive 1¹/₂ miles to this motor museum that contains about 40 vintage motor cars, including the second-oldest Rolls-Royce in the world. This is the finest collection of classic and vintage cars in Scotland. Various motoring events are announced throughout the summer.

Blair Drummond Safari and Leisure Park. Blair Drummond. ☎ **01786/841456.** Admission £7.50 ($12.40) adults, £4.50 ($7.45) senior citizens and ages 3–14, free for age 2 and under. Apr 3–Oct 4, daily 10am–5:30pm. Take exit 10 off M9 onto A84 near Stirling.

South of Doune is the Blair Drummond Safari and Leisure Park. You meet the typical cast of animal-safari characters here, and the park also offers a jungle cruise, a giant Astroglide, and an amusement arcade, as well as a pet farm and a performing sea lions show. A safari bus is available for visitors without vehicles, costing 50p (85¢) extra per person.

You can have refreshments at the Watering Hole Bar or in the Ranch Kitchen (☎ **01786/841430**), or use one of the picnic areas.

WHERE TO STAY & DINE

Woodside Hotel. Stirling Rd., Doune, Perthshire FK16 6AB. ☎ **01786/841237.** Fax 01786/841123. 12 rms. TV TEL. £50 ($82.50) double. MC, V. Rates include Scottish breakfast.

Woodside stands on A84, the main Stirling–Oban road. In the heart of Perthshire, it was originally a coaching inn and dates back to the 18th century. Its bedrooms are comfortably but routinely furnished. The lounge bar has an open fire and offers a selection of more than 100 malt whiskies. You can enjoy traditional dishes on the bar luncheon menu, such as soused herring, homemade pâté, salads, and grilled Aberdeen Angus steaks. The dining room overlooks the garden, and specialties include venison, salmon, and lobster (in season). Dinner costs £16 ($26.40). On Sunday, dinner is served only to residents.

8 Callander

16 miles NW of Stirling, 43 miles N of Glasgow, 52 miles NW of Edinburgh, 42 miles W of Perth

In Gaelic, the Trossachs means the "bristled country," an allusion to its luxuriant vegetation. The thickly wooded valley contains three lochs—Venachar, Achray, and Katrine. In the summer the steamer on Loch Katrine offers a fine view of the splendid wooded scenery.

For many, the small burgh of Callander makes the best base for exploring the Trossachs and Loch Katrine, Loch Achray, and Loch Venachar. For years, motorists—and before them, passengers traveling by bumpy coach—stopped here to rest up on the once-difficult journey between Edinburgh and Oban.

Callander stands at the entrance to the Pass of Leny in the shadow of the Callander Crags. The Rivers Teith and Leny meet to the west of the town.

ESSENTIALS
GETTING THERE

BY TRAIN   Stirling (see above) is the nearest rail link.

BY BUS   Once at Stirling, continue the rest of the way to Callander on a Midland Bluebird bus from the Stirling bus station on Goosecroft Road. Contact the bus station at ☎ **01786/446474,** or Bluebird Buses at **01324/613777.** A one-way fare is £2.70 ($4.45).

BY CAR   From Stirling, head north along M9, cutting northwest at the junction of A84 to Callander, bypassing Doune.

VISITOR INFORMATION

The **Rob Roy & Trossachs Visitor Centre** is at Ancaster Square (☎ **01877/ 330342).** The center will give you a map that pinpoints all the sights.

EXPLORING THE AREA

In the scenic Leny Hills to the west of Callander beyond the Pass of Leny lie **Leny Park** and **Leny Falls.** At one time all the lands in Leny Park were part of the Leny estate, home of the Buchanan clan for more than 1,000 years. In the wild Leny Glen, a naturalist's paradise, deer can be seen grazing. Leny Falls is an impressive sight, near the confluence of the River Leny and the River Teith.

Four miles beyond the Pass of Leny lies **Loch Lubnaig** ("crooked lake"), divided into two reaches by a rock and considered fine fishing waters. Nearby is **Little Leny,** the ancestral burial ground of the Buchanans.

More falls are found at **Bracklinn,** 1¹/₂ miles northeast of Callander. In a gorge above the town, Bracklinn is one of the most scenic of the local beauty spots. Other places of interest include the Roman Camp, the Caledonian Fort, and the foundations of St. Bride's Chapel.

One of the most interesting sites around Callander is **Balquhidder Church,** 13 miles to the northwest off A84. This is the burial place of Rob Roy MacGregor. The church also has the St. Angus Stone from the 8th century, a 17th-century bell, and some Gaelic Bibles.

SHOPPING

A good selection of woolens is at **Callander Woollen Mill,** 12–18 Main St. (☎ **01877/330273),** an outlet for a wide selection of scarves, skirts, jackets, kilts, trousers, and knitwear. At **Mounter Pottery,** 4 Ancaster Square Lane (☎ **01877/**

331052), artist James Mounter sells his functional stoneware at his studio shop. He's the best in the area. Another outlet for woolen goods, **Trossachs Woollen Mill** (☎ 01877/330178), lies outside of town in the hamlet of Kilmahog, 1 mile north of Callander on A84. This mill shop features woolens, tartans, and woven rugs.

WHERE TO STAY

Arran Lodge. Leny Rd., Callander, Perthshire FK17 8AJ. ☎ **01877/330976.** 4 rms. TV. £70–£75 ($115.50–$123.75) double with Scottish breakfast, £92 ($151.80) double with half board. No credit cards. Closed Nov 5–Mar 15.

Arran Lodge stands on the waters of the Leny as they flow downstream to join the River Teith. The 150-year-old bungalow has been restored and now offers four handsomely furnished bedrooms. Our favorite is the Venacher, often called the honeymoon suite, a large low-ceilinged room with a king-size four-poster and a cedar-clad shower room. There are no room phones.

In the elegant lounge are an open fire, custom-made furnishings, and a view south to the gardens and river. No smoking is permitted, and the Victorian dining room with antiques is reserved only for residents of the hotel. Meals are cooked by the owners, Robert and Pasqua Moore, who serve dinner nightly at 7:30pm. A typical dinner menu might begin with duck-and-orange pâté, followed by fillet of Trossachs trout, concluding with dessert.

Highland House Hotel. S. Church St. (just off A84, near Ancaster Square), Callander, Perthshire FK17 8BN. ☎ **01877/330269.** 9 rms (7 with tub or shower). TV TEL. £39.50 ($65.20) double without bath, £47 ($77.55) double with bath. AE, MC, V. Rates include Scottish breakfast. Half board £38.50 ($63.55) per person.

This Georgian-style stone building, full of charm and character, stands on a quiet tree-lined street a few yards from the River Teith and a short walk to the Rob Roy Visitor Centre. All bedrooms have radio alarms and hot beverage facilities, and most have private baths. The hotel is owned and managed by David and Dee Shirley, winners of the 1992 Antartex award for the best hotel or guesthouse in the region. Scottish-style meals are served nightly from 7 to 8pm in the dining room, or in simpler versions in the bar. Game casserole, with choice pieces of game in a rich red wine and port gravy, is a house specialty. The lounge offers 20 to 25 brands of malt whiskies, some of them relatively obscure.

Lubnaig Hotel. Leny Fues, Callander, Perthshire FK17 8AS. ☎ and fax **01877/330376.** 10 rms. TV. £33 ($54.45) per person. MC, V. Rates include Scottish breakfast. Closed Nov–Mar. Proceed on Callander's Main St. to the western outskirts and turn right into Leny Fues, 25 yards past the Poppies Hotel.

An old-fashioned hostelry with plenty of character, the hotel occupies a Victorian stone structure from 1864 with many gables and bay windows in its own acre of garden. The modestly furnished bedchambers, doubles only, have hot-beverage facilities and central heating. Four-course dinners, ranging from £12 to £19 ($19.80 to $31.35), are prepared fresh daily using only the best of Scottish produce. Salmon, sea trout, grouse, pheasant, venison, and Scottish beef all appear on the menu. A fully stocked bar with a wide selection of malt whiskies and wines is available. Guests can enjoy salmon and trout fishing, canoeing, and pony trekking near the River Lemy and the River Teith.

✪ **Roman Camp.** Main St., Callander, Perthside FK17 8BG. ☎ **01877/330003.** Fax 01877/331533. 14 rms, 3 suites. TV TEL. £109–£139 ($179.85–$229.35) double; from £159 ($262.35) suite. Rates include Scottish breakfast. AE, DC, MC, V. As you approach Callander on A84, the entrance to the hotel is signposted between 2 cottages on Callander's Main St.

The leading hotel in town, once a 17th-century hunting lodge with pink walls and small gray-roofed towers, was built on the site of a Roman camp. The modern-day traveler drives up a 200-yard driveway, with shaggy Highland cattle and sheep grazing on either side. The River Teith runs through the 20-acre estate. In summer, flower beds are in bloom. Inside you're welcomed to a country house furnished in a gracious manner. Seven of the units are on the ground floor and one is adapted for use by guests with disabilities. All have hair dryers, radios, and hot-beverage facilities. Some rooms are furnished with bedhead crowns, gilt-framed mirrors, and stenciled furnishings, whereas others are contemporary with blond-wood pieces. The dining room was converted in the 1930s from the old kitchen. The ceiling design is based on Scottish painted ceilings of the 16th and 17th centuries, a feature of houses around the time the Roman Camp hunting lodge was built. The meals—Scottish country-house fare—are available at lunch, served daily from 12:30 to 2pm, with set menus costing £14 to £18 ($23.10 to $29.70), and at dinner, daily from 7 to 8:30pm, a five-course menu going for £34 ($56.10). There's a small but cozy cocktail bar. The library, with its ornate plasterwork and richly grained paneling, is an elegant holdover from yesteryear. The hotel remains open throughout the year.

A SIDE TRIP TO LOCH VOIL

This was an area known to Rob Roy MacGregor, who died in 1734 but lives on in legend as the Robin Hood of Scotland. If you visit Rob Roy's grave at Balquhidder, you may find this remote part of Scotland so enchanting that you'll want to continue to drive west and explore the Braes o' Balquhidder and the banks of Loch Voil.

Stronvar Country House Hotel. Balquhidder, Lochearnhead, Perthshire FK19 8PB. ☎ **01877/384688.** Fax 01877/384230. 4 rms. TV. £59 ($97.35) double. MC, V. Rates include Scottish breakfast. Closed Nov–Feb. At a point 28 miles north of Stirling along A84, turn at the signpost to Balquhidder; then continue 2 miles down the glen and into the village, where signs point the way to Stronvar House.

Originally built in 1850 as the region's manorial seat, this hotel rises imperially in beige sandstone on the shores of Loch Voil. It's set in 2^1/$_2$ acres of garden, surrounded with hundreds of acres of wilderness. Rooms can accommodate a maximum of 10 guests; they are done up in different tartan motifs, with the name of the relevant clan on the door. All are furnished with antiques and four-poster beds, and have teamaking equipment and trouser presses, among other amenities. There are several fireplaces and a "trust bar" where guests help themselves. Dinner, available only to guests, is served nightly from 7:30pm, costing £17.50 ($28.90) per person. Speak up if you're craving something in particular, as requested dishes are prepared whenever possible, sometimes with as little as an hour's notice. A tea shop serves snacks daily from 10:30am to 5pm.

WHERE TO DINE

Dalgair Hotel. 113–115 Main St., Callander, Perthshire FK17 8BQ. ☎ **01877/330283.** Fax 01877/331114. Reservations recommended in the restaurant, not necessary in the bar. Main courses £8.25–£13 ($13.60–$21.45) in the restaurant, £3.95–£10 ($6.25–$15.80) in the bar. AE, DC, MC, V. Restaurant: daily 7:30–9pm. Bar: food service daily noon–9pm. SCOTTISH.

This place is best known for its food and its wine cellar. The hotel building was once a 19th-century private home and later became a shop. Today its bar is lined with gray bricks, rustic accessories, and flickering candles. Food items are "not the kind of thing you can get at home," in the words of the chef. They include halibut and Dover or lemon sole, steaks, and game stews. Australian, German, and Austrian wine, sold by the glass, gives the place the aura of a wine bar. More formal meals are served after dark in the restaurant. Menu items might include sliced pork on a bed of cucumber noodles with oregano and ginger sauce, fillet of chicken in champagne-butter sauce, and different preparations of salmon and Angus steaks.

The hotel's eight bedrooms contain private bathrooms, TVs, and telephones, and—with Scottish breakfast included—cost £45 to £54 ($74.25 to $89.10) for a double.

Lade Inn. Trossachs Rd. at Kilmahog, Callander, Perthshire FK17 8HD. ☎ **01877/330152.** Main courses £6–£15 ($9.90–$24.75). MC, V. Mon–Sat noon–2:30pm and 5:30–9pm, Sun 12:30–3:30pm and 5:30–9pm. Closed Mon–Tues Jan–Feb. Lies 1 mile north of Callander on A84. INTERNATIONAL.

Surrounded by fields, within earshot of the Leny River and a short walk to two old woolen mills, this establishment was originally built as a teahouse. Converted after World War II to a pub and restaurant with overnight accommodations, it attracts residents from the surrounding farmlands as well as visitors from afar. You'll enjoy Highland scenery in views that incorporate Ben Ledi, one of the region's most prominent peaks and a favorite of visiting hill climbers. Many visitors come here to sample the inn's wide range of cask-conditioned ales and cider, but if you're hungry, new owners Angelia and Paul Roebuck prepare meals of such Scottish standards as rack of lamb, pigeon, venison, steaks, salmon, and trout.

The inn also offers two well-furnished bedrooms, each with private bath, costing £29.50 ($48.70) per person nightly, including a full Scottish breakfast.

CALLANDER AFTER DARK

Even if you're in Callander for a night or two, visitors quickly adopt their own "local." Two favorites include the **Brigend Hotel Pub,** Bridge Street (☎ **01877/3301030**), an old watering hole that has been done up in matching dusky red wood paneling and carpet. Tennant brews are available on tap. On Saturday night there is always some form of entertainment, perhaps karaoke. Hours are Sunday through Thursday from 12:30pm to midnight, and Friday and Saturday from 12:30pm to 1am. Another old-fashioned bar that's a local favorite is **Crown Hotel Pub,** Main Street (☎ **01877/330040**), that sometimes features live folk music. Otherwise it's a mellow old place for a pint of lager, served daily from noon to midnight.

9 Aberfoyle

56 miles NW of Edinburgh, 27 miles N of Glasgow

Looking like an alpine village in the heart of Rob Roy country, this small holiday resort near Loch Ard is the gateway to the Trossachs. Shops offer gift items related to the Highlands.

ESSENTIALS
GETTING THERE

BY TRAIN   The nearest rail link is Stirling (see above).

BY BUS   Connections are meager. A postal bus leaves from Callander (see above).

BY CAR   This is by far the best means of reaching Aberfoyle. From Stirling (see above), take A84 west until you reach the junction of A873 and continue west to Aberfoyle.

VISITOR INFORMATION

Open April to October, the Trossachs Discovery Centre is on Main Street (☎ 01877/382352).

EXPLORING THE AREA

About 4 miles to the east of Aberfoyle along A81, **Inchmahome Priory** stands on an island in Lake Menteith. From the Port of Menteith, you can sail to the island if the weather's right. Once here, you'll find the ruins of a 13th-century Augustinian house where Mary Queen of Scots was sent as a baby in 1547. The ferry costs £3 ($4.95) for adults, £1.50 ($2.45) for children—if it's running (everything depends on the weather). For information, call ☎ **01877/385294.**

A nature lover's delight, the ✪ **Queen Elizabeth Forest Park** lies between the eastern shore of Loch Lomond and the Trossachs. Some 45,000 acres of moor, woodland, and mountain have been set aside as a preserve for walking and exploring. Stop at **Queen Elizabeth Park Visitor Centre** for maps and information. The center is installed in the David Marshall Lodge, off A821, 1 mile north of Aberfoyle. It's open mid-March to mid-September, daily from 10am to 6pm. Admission is free. From the lodge you'll enjoy views of Ben Lomond, the Menteith Hills, and the Campsie Fells. **Dukes Pass** (A821), north from Aberfoyle, climbs through Achray Forest, past the Queen Elizabeth Forest Park Visitor Centre (see above), where you can stop for snacks and a panoramic view of the Forth Valley. Information on numerous walks, cycling routes, the Achray scenic forest drive, picnic sites, parking areas, and many other activities is available at the center. The road runs to the Trossachs—the "bristly country"—between Lochs Achray and Katrine.

Loch Katrine, where Rob Roy MacGregor was born, owes its fame to Sir Walter Scott's poem *The Lady of the Lake.* The loch is the principal reservoir of the city of Glasgow. A small steamer, the *S.S. Sir Walter Scott,* plies the waters of the loch, which has submerged the romantic poet's Silver Strand. Sailings are from early May to late September, Sunday through Friday at 11am, between Trossachs Pier and Stronachlachar, at a round-trip fare of £3.70 ($6.10) for adults and £2.30 ($3.80) for children and senior citizens, or £10 ($16.50) for a family pass. Complete information about sailing schedules is available from the **Strathclyde Water Department,** Lower Clyde Division, 419 Balmore Rd., Glasgow, Lanarkshire G22 6NU (☎ **0141/ 355-5333**). Light refreshments are available at Trossachs Pier.

SHOPPING

The **Scottish Wool Centre,** Main Street (☎ **01877/382850**), sells a big selection of knitwear and woolens from surrounding mills, including jackets, hats, rugs, sweaters, and cashmere items. It also houses an amphitheater that holds a textile display area, along with live specimens of different breeds of Scottish sheep (but no clones yet). Spinning and weaving demonstrations are also presented, and baby lambs fill a children's petting zoo. Admission to the shop is free, but the exhibition costs £2.50 ($4.15) for adults and £1.50 ($2.45) for children. The whole complex is open daily from 10am to 6pm.

WHERE TO STAY

Covenanter's Inn Hotel. Duchray Rd., Aberfoyle, Perthshire FK8 3XD. ☎ **01877/382347.** Fax 01877/382785. 53 rms. TV. £86–£100 ($141.90–$165) double. AE, DC, MC, V. Rates include half board (breakfast and dinner).

Set on 6 acres overlooking the headwaters of the River Forth, about half a mile southwest of Aberfoyle, this hotel was originally built as the family home of a local landowner in the early 1800s. Gracefully enlarged during the 1960s and 1980s, its name comes from the famous convention held here in 1949, when a group of Scots church and political leaders issued a then-famous and much publicized "Second Covenant" promoting the separation of Scotland from England. They took their name from the Covenanters who had signed the New Covenant, opposing English policy in the 17th century. On Christmas Eve of 1952 the hotel again became famous (or notorious) after the theft from Westminster Abbey of the Stone of Scone. Following nationwide appeals from Buckingham Palace, the Stone was recovered after having spent a night, it's claimed, in the Covenanter's Inn Hotel. (A controversy continues as to the authenticity of the recovered artifact.) Conjecture and speculation about the event still go on, sometimes heatedly, in the in-house bar.

The bar serves drinks from a wide selection of single-malt whiskies, as well as bar meals, ranging from £2.85 to £7.85 ($4.70 to $12.95). There's also a more formal restaurant serving table d'hôte dinners for £16 ($26.40). The bedrooms are dignified and comfortable, evoking something you might find in a Scottish country house.

WHERE TO DINE

✪ Braeval Restaurant. Callander Rd. (A81). ☎ **01877/382711.** Reservations required. Fixed-price 4-course menu £21.50 ($35.50) at Sun lunch, £30 ($49.50) at dinner. MC, V. Wed–Sat 7–9:30pm, Thurs–Sun 12:30–1:30pm. Closed 1 week in Feb, 1 week in June, and 2 weeks in Oct (dates vary). Drive 1 mile east of Aberfoyle on A81 (Callander Rd.). SCOTTISH.

For dining, the Braeval is the obvious choice. Overlooking a golf course, this top-notch restaurant is housed in a former stone mill. Owners Fiona and Nick Nairn (he's the chef) kept an antique waterwheel to remind diners of the building's former function. Mr. Nairn's repertoire embraces both traditional and modern British dishes on a changing fixed-price menu based on the availability of fresh produce. You might begin with a spiced parsnip and apple soup, followed by game terrine with pear chutney. For main dishes, sample such delights as seared bass bream with salad Niçoise or a lasagna of chicken livers flavored with lemon and thyme. Fillet of salmon with a mussel-and-basil butter sauce is also served. The desserts are innovative, as exemplified by caramel mousse brûlée with caramel parfait or crème brûlée with rhubarb.

WHERE TO STAY & DINE NEARBY

Loch Achray Hotel. The Trossachs, Perthshire FK17 3HZ. ☎ **01877/376229.** Fax 01877/ 376278. 81 rms. £60 ($99) double. Rates include Scottish breakfast. MC, V. Closed Jan.

This sprawling and very visible white-sided hotel stands 9 miles east of Callander on A821, a short walk from Loch Achray, in an isolated estate of 45 acres between Callander and Aberfoyle. Although parts of its foundation date from Jacobean times, the bulk of what you'll see today was built around the turn of the century as a resort for people interested in the flora and fauna of the Highlands. From the hotel, you can step directly into the Achray Forest, part of the vast Queen Elizabeth National Park, which abounds in wildlife, especially roe deer. Many of the building's original architectural details have been removed during its various modernizations. The bedrooms are simple contemporary affairs, each with a tea kettle, functional furniture, and views over the forest. The dining room serves traditional cuisine daily from 6:30 to 8:30pm, at a cost of £12.50 ($20.65) per person. The hotel bar features live traditional music every night, sometimes presenting a full-scale ceilidh. The hotel is usually heavily booked with visiting tour groups, who overnight here between bus excursions through the Highlands. Frankly, it's not a great hotel, but it's the best in the area, and the setting is so incomparable you'll forgive a lot.

10 Along Loch Lomond

The largest of Scotland's lochs, **✪ Loch Lomond** was the center of the ancient district of Lennox, in the possession of the branch of the Stewart (Stuart) family to which Lord Darnley (second husband of Mary Queen of Scots) belonged. The ruins of Lennox Castle are on Inchmurrin, one of the 30 islands of the loch—one with ecclesiastical ruins, one noted for its yew trees planted by King Robert the Bruce to ensure a suitable supply of wood for the bows of his archers. The loch is fed by at least 10 rivers from west, east, and north and is about 24 miles long; it stretches 5 miles at its widest point. On the eastern side is Ben Lomond, which rises to a height of 3,192 feet.

The song "Loch Lomond" is supposed to have been composed by one of Bonnie Prince Charlie's captured followers on the eve of his execution in Carlisle Jail. The "low road" of the song is the path through the underworld that his spirit will follow to his native land after death, more quickly than his friends can travel to Scotland by the ordinary high road.

The easiest way to see the famous loch is not by car but by the *Silver Marlin,* a 62-foot-long (by 17-foot-wide), 125-passenger cruiser, which began its life hauling river traffic on the Thames. On board are two decks, big windows for viewing the scenery, and an amply stocked bar loaded with Scottish malt whisky. Owned by **Sweeney's Cruises Ltd.,** the ship is based at Sweeney's Shipyard, 26 Balloch Rd., Balloch, Dunbartonshire G83 8LQ (☎ **01389/752376**). Cruises last for about an hour and in summer depart every hour on the half hour from 10:30am to 7:30pm. Departures in other months are based on demand. Cruises sail from Balloch to a wooded island, Inchmurrin, year-round home to five families, several vacation chalets, and a summer-only nudist colony. Although the ship docks at the island for only a moment or two before returning to Balloch, passengers can get off to explore and board again on one of the ship's subsequent returns. Per-person round-trip fares are £4.50 ($7.45).

BALLOCH

At the southern end of Loch Lomond, Balloch is the most touristy of the towns and villages around the lake. The town grew up on the River Leven, where the water leaves Loch Lomond and flows south to the Clyde. Today Balloch is visited chiefly by those wanting to take boat trips on Loch Lomond, which sail in season from Balloch Pier.

EXPLORING THE AREA

Set on 200 acres, **Balloch Castle Country Park** is on the "bonnie, bonnie banks of Loch Lomond," three-quarters of a mile north of Balloch Station. The present Balloch Castle (☎ **01389/758216**), replacing one that dated from 1238, was constructed in 1808 for John Buchanan of Ardoch in the "castle-gothic" style. It has a visitor center that explains the history of the property. The site has a walled garden, and the trees and shrubs, especially the rhododendrons and azaleas, reach the zenith of their beauty in late May and early June. You can also visit a "Fairy Glen." The location is about three-quarters of a mile from the center of Balloch, and it's open all year, daily from 8am to dusk, with no admission charge.

Dumbarton District's Countryside Ranger Service is based at Balloch Castle and conducts **guided walks** at various locations around Loch Lomond throughout the summer.

WHERE TO STAY & DINE

Balloch Hotel. Balloch Rd., Balloch, Dunbartonshire G83 8LQ. ☎ **01389/752579.** Fax 01389/755604. 14 rms. TV. £63 ($103.95) double. AE, DC, MC, V. Rates include Scottish breakfast. Closed Jan 1 and Dec 25.

Called the "grande dame" hotel of Balloch, this was the first to be erected in the town. It welcomed the Empress Eugénie, wife of Napoléon III, in 1860 when she toured Scotland (she slept in the Inchmoan Room). It stands beside the river, in the center of the hamlet, offering basic, functionally furnished, and well-maintained rooms.

✪ **Cameron House Hotel & Country Estate.** Balloch, Loch Lomond, Dunbartonshire G83 8QZ. ☎ **01389/755565.** Fax 01389/759522. 93 rms, 5 suites. TV TEL. £170–£185 ($280.50–$305.25) double; from £275 ($453.75) suite. AE, DC, MC, V. Rates include Scottish breakfast.

Set beside A86, this is the finest accommodation and dining choice along Loch Lomond. The turreted mansion, its lawns sweeping down to the banks of the lake, has been skillfully converted to receive guests. With its superb facilities (see below), it qualifies as a country club and luxury hotel. The bedrooms have been beautifully decorated, most often in pastel colors, with excellent reproductions of antique furniture, giving it a traditional aura throughout.

Dining/Entertainment: The hotel contains the award-winning Georgian Room, offering a French and Scottish "Auld Alliance" cuisine against a lavish Victorian backdrop. Nonresidents are welcome, but reservations are essential. An à la carte lunch, served daily between 12:30 and 2:30pm, costs £18.50 ($30.55), and a fixed-price dinner, nightly from 7:30 to 9:45pm, goes for £37.50 ($61.90). No lunch is offered on Saturday and Sunday. The menu changes to reflect the seasons, but you might try such dishes as a terrine of rabbit and hare encased in leeks, followed by medaillons of lamb flavored with fresh herbs and served with a Madeira sauce. A more informal brasserie, opening onto the garden, serves a Sunday buffet lunch for £17.50 ($28.90). If neither of these appeal to you, you might try Breakers, an eatery based on the classic American diner. The hotel also has a cocktail bar.

Services: Room service, laundry, baby-sitting.

Facilities: Swimming pools, gymnasium, squash court, sauna, solarium, steam room, Jacuzzi, badminton.

LUSS

This village, 9 miles north of Ballock on Route A82 on the western side of Loch Lomond, is the traditional home of the Colquhouns. Among its stone cottages, on the water's edge, is a branch of the Highland Arts Studios of Seil. Cruises on the loch and boat rentals may be arranged at a nearby jetty.

If your travels in Scotland inspire you to put on a kilt and blow your own set of bagpipes, stop by **Thistle Bagpipe Works,** in the center of Luss. Here, you can not only order custom-made bagpipes, but you can also purchase a clan kilt to go with the instrument.

WHERE TO STAY AND DINE

Colquhoun Arms Hotel. Hwy. A82, Luss, Alexandria, Dunbartonshire G83 8NY. ☎ **01436/860282.** Fax 01436/860309. 24 rms (21 with bath). TV. £55 ($90.75) double. AE, DC, MC, V. Rates include Scottish breakfast.

Colquhoun Arms Hotel is a pale-yellow and white former coaching inn, located on A82 going north, close to the road under a canopy of large trees near the edge of a lake. The modernized interior is filled with light-grained paneling, plaid carpeting, an attractively lit dining room, and a lounge bar. The bedrooms are traditionally furnished, although nothing to rate a rave. Each double has a private bath, although a few singles don't. Lunches and dinners from the same menu are served both in the bar (where people smoke) and the restaurant (where they cannot). Meals range from £3 to £9 ($4.95 to $14.85).

INVERBEG

This hamlet on the western shore of Loch Lomond stands in a beautiful spot, about 3 miles north of Luss. (It can be reached in about 40 minutes from Glasgow.) The hamlet is known for its old-time ferry inn (see below), the second-oldest youth hostel in Scotland, and several art galleries. A small fleet of Loch Lomond cruisers can usually be seen in the harbor of Inverbeg Bay, and a ferry to Rowardennan and Ben Lomond plies the route three times a day in summer.

WHERE TO STAY & DINE

Inverbeg Inn. Hwy. A82, Luss, Loch Lomond, Dunbartonshire G83 8PD. ☎ **01436/860678.** Fax 01436/860686. 18 rms, 2 suites. TV TEL. £90–£98 ($148.50–$161.70) double; £110 ($181.50) suite. AE, DC, MC, V. Rates include Scottish breakfast.

The site of this inn, 28 miles north of Glasgow and a 5-minute drive north of Luss, has always been important as the ferryboat landing servicing the western end of Loch Lomond. The first thing a cold-weather visitor might see is a blazing fireplace heating the reception room near the entrance. About half the routinely furnished bedrooms look out over a garden in the rear. The establishment serves savory pub lunches as well as more formal restaurant meals throughout the year. The same food is offered in both bar and restaurant, including breaded prawns, halibut, and T-bone steaks. The noticeable difference is in the portions and prices. Bar meals, available daily from noon to 3pm and 6 to 9pm, cost from £3.95 to £13.50 ($6.50 to $22.30), whereas in the restaurant from 7 to 9pm nightly a set-price dinner of generous portions is featured for £21.50 ($35.50).

TARBET

On the western shores of Loch Lomond, Tarbet is not to be confused with the larger center of Tarbert, headquarters of the Loch Fyne herring industry. Loch Lomond's Tarbet is merely a village and summer-holiday base with limited accommodations. In the distance you can see the majesty of Ben Lomond. Boats can be launched from the pier, and Tarbet is one of the stops on the route of the steamship *Countess Fiona*.

WHERE TO STAY & DINE

Tarbet Hotel. Tarbet, Arrochar, Dunbartonshire G83 7DE. ☎ **01301/702228.** Fax 01301/702673. 80 rms. TV. £84 ($138.60) double. AE, DC, MC, V. Rates include half board. Closed Jan 8–Feb 15.

A famous and historic hotel, the Tarbet stands where a simple inn existed more than 400 years ago, at the junction of A82 and A83. A coaching inn was erected on the original foundation in 1760, and a baronial facade and mock-fortification crenellations were added during the Victorian era. The guest rooms are functional, simply furnished, and clean. A cozy cocktail lounge looks past a row of very old yew trees onto the lake. Open to residents only, the dining room serves good meals of local produce. There's a simple bistro-style snack bar, the Buttery, open daily from 9am to 8pm, serving light meals for £4 to £10 ($6.60 to $16.50).

Tayside & Grampian 10

The two history-rich sections of Tayside and Grampian offer a vast array of sightseeing, even though they're relatively small. Tayside, for example, is about 85 miles, east to west, and some 60 miles south to north.

The two regions share the North Sea coast between the Firth of Tay in the south and the Firth of Moray farther north. The so-called Highland Line separating the Lowlands in the south from the Highlands in the north crosses both regions. The Grampians, the highest mountain range in Scotland, are to the west of this line.

Carved out of the old counties of Perth and Angus, **Tayside** is named for its major river, the 119-mile-long Tay. The region is easy to explore. Its tributaries and dozens of lochs and Highland streams are some of the best salmon and trout waters in Europe. One of the loveliest regions of Scotland, Tayside is filled with heather-clad Highland hills, long blue lochs under tree-clad banks, and miles and miles of walking trails. Perth and Dundee are among the six leading cities of Scotland. Tayside provided the backdrop for many novels by Sir Walter Scott, including *The Fair Maid of Perth, Waverley,* and *The Abbot.* Its golf courses are world famous, ranging from the trio of 18-hole courses at Gleneagles to the open championships links at Carnoustie.

The **Grampian region** has Aberdeen, Scotland's third-largest city, and Braemar, site of the most famous of the Highland gatherings. The queen herself comes here for holidays, to stay at Balmoral Castle, her private residence, a tradition dating back to the days of Queen Victoria and her consort, Prince Albert. The very word *Balmoral* seems to evoke images of tartans and bagpipes. As you journey on the scenic roads of Scotland's northeast, you'll pass heather-covered moorland and peaty lochs, wood glens and salmon-filled rivers, granite-stone villages and ancient castles, and fishing harbors as well as North Sea beach resorts.

A DRIVING TOUR

Day 1   From Edinburgh, head west on A90 until you reach the signs for the Forth Road Bridge. After crossing the bridge, take the M90 motorway all the way to Perth, 44 miles north of Edinburgh. You'll have time to see some of the sights, such as the Fair Maid's House, before lunch. After lunch, take an excursion to Scone Palace, 2 miles northeast on the River Tay. Spend the night in Perth.

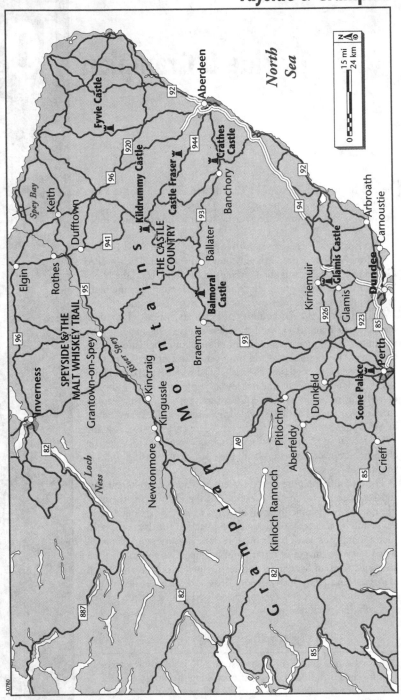

Day 2 From Perth, head west along A85 to Crieff, a distance of 18 miles. Crieff lies on the edge of the Perthshire Highlands. While here, you can visit the Glenturret Distillery and Drummond Castle at Grimsthorpe. Stay overnight in Crieff.

Day 3 From Crieff, head north on A822 to Dunkeld, where you can visit its cathedral and Scottish Horse Museum. Then take A9 northwest to Pitlochry for the night.

Day 4 While still based in Pitlochry, explore some of the major sights in its environs, including the Pass of Killiecrankie, Queen's View, and Blair Castle.

Day 5 Leave Pitlochry in the morning by a different route, A924, which swings northeast and takes you through Glen Brerachan before heading southeast again along A924 and A93 into Rattray. Get on A926 east to Kirriemuir, birthplace of Sir James M. Barrie, author of *Peter Pan*. After lunch here, head south on A928 to Glamis Castle, fabled in *Macbeth*. For lodgings, you can cut south along A928 and A929 to Dundee for an overnight.

Day 6 The following morning, it's a 67-mile drive north to Aberdeen, the "Granite City" of the northeast. The most scenic route into Aberdeen is the coastal road (A92), going via Arbroath, Montrose, and Stonehaven before reaching Aberdeen for the night. Explore some of its attractions in the afternoon and spend the night here.

Day 7 Leave Aberdeen in the morning, stopping first at Banchory with a goal of making Ballater your overnight stopover. Follow A93 west. Ballater lies 41 miles west of Aberdeen and is a center for viewing Balmoral Castle, home of the queen, 8 miles west of Ballater.

Day 8 In the morning, continue on A93 west to Braemar to visit Braemar Castle. Have lunch there. Return to Ballater and take A939 northwest to Grantown-on-Spey, a holiday resort that makes a good center for exploring Speyside, the valley of the second-largest river in Scotland.

Day 9 The following morning leave Grantown-on-Spey and head east along A95 until you come to the junction of B9008. Go south to the Glenlivet Reception Centre, which will mark your beginning of the Whisky Trail. After Glenlivet you can get on B9009 for a short visit to Dufftown before cutting northwest along A941 via the Glen of Rothes toward Elgin for the night. Consider a stopover in the Speyside town of Rothes with its five distilleries. Stay overnight in the ancient royal burgh of Elgin.

1 Perth

44 miles N of Edinburgh, 22 miles SW of Dundee, 64 miles NE of Glasgow

From its majestic position on the Tay, the ancient city of Perth was the capital of Scotland until the middle of the 15th century. Here the Highlands meet the Lowlands.

ESSENTIALS
GETTING THERE
BY TRAIN **ScotRail** provides service between Edinburgh and Perth, with continuing service to Dundee. Trip time to Perth is 1¹/₂ hours. Phone ☎ **0345/484950** in Edinburgh for 24-hour information.

BY BUS Edinburgh and Perth are connected by frequent bus service. A one-way fare costs £4.40 ($7.25). You can even go from London's Victoria Station by bus to

Perth, but the trip takes 12 long hours. A one-way fare costs £22 ($36.30). For bus information and schedules, check with **National Express** at ☎ **0990/808080** or **CityLink** at ☎ **0990/505050.**

BY CAR   To reach Perth from Edinburgh, head northwest along A90 and go across the Forth Road Bridge, continuing north along M90.

VISITOR INFORMATION

The **tourist information center** is at 45 High St. (☎ **01738/638353**).

SEEING THE SIGHTS

The main sightseeing attraction of the "fair city" is the **Kirk of St. John the Baptist,** St. John Street (☎ **01738/626159**); it's believed that the original foundation is from Pictish times. The present choir dates from 1440 and the nave from 1490. In 1559 John Knox preached his famous sermon here, attacking idolatry, which caused a turbulent wave of iconoclasm to sweep across the land. In its wake, religious artifacts, stained glass, and organs were destroyed all over Scotland. The church was restored as a World War I memorial in the mid-1920s and has a fine collection of 20th-century stained-glass windows.

Branklyn Garden. 116 Dundee Rd. (A85), in Branklyn. ☎ **01738/625535.** Admission £2.30 ($3.80) adults, £1.50 ($2.45) children, students, and seniors; £6.10 ($10.05) family ticket. Sept–Apr, daily 9:30am–sunset; May–Aug, daily 9:30am–6:30pm.

Branklyn Garden has been called the finest 2 acres of private garden in Scotland. The garden has been bequeathed to the National Trust for Scotland. It has a superb collection of rhododendrons, alpines, and herbaceous and peat-garden plants from all over the world.

SHOPPING

Cairncross Ltd, 18 St. John's St. (☎ **01738/624367**), sells jewelry, both custom-made and from other manufacturers, in gold and silver. Their specialty, though, is Scottish pearls, which they can mount to your liking if you don't see what you want on the showroom floor. They also offer crystal, clocks, and some antique jewelry. **Timothy Hardie,** 25 St. John's St. (☎ **01738/633127**), deals in antique jewelry and has a large selection of Victorian pieces, including numerous three-stone rings. They also sell antique silver tea service sets. **Whispers of the Past,** 15 George St. (☎ **01738/635472**), offers an odd mixture of items. Here you'll find jewelry, both new and antique, ranging from costume baubles to quality gold and silver pieces, and also china, pine furniture from Scotland and the Eastern Bloc, silk flowers, and linens.

C & C Proudfoot, 104 South St. (☎ **01738/635483**), is an eclectic shop, whose merchandise includes leather jackets, hand-knitted Arran sweaters, Barbour waxed-cotton jackets, sheepskin jackets and rugs, and wool rugs, as well as a range of handbags, briefcases, scarves, and gloves.

Watson of Perth, 163–167 High St. (☎ **01738/639861**), has been in business since 1900. It specializes in bone china produced by a number of manufacturers, including Royal Doulton and Wedgwood. They also offer cut crystal from Edinburgh, Stuart, Waterford, and other companies. Shipping is a standard part of the business, so shop clerks aren't perturbed when you ask them to pack and ship purchases.

Caithness Glass, Inveralmond, on Route A9 (☎ **01738/637373**), is a glass factory located on the edge of Perth. Follow A9, going through the roundabout marked A9 north to Inverness—the well-marked factory is in the industrial complex a short way past the roundabout. Its sales outlet sells paperweights, glass vases, and bowls produced at an adjoining site, balanced with a range of Royal Doulton items. While here, shoppers are welcome to watch the glassblowers at work Monday through Friday from 9am to 4:30pm.

The **Perthshire Shop,** Lower City Mills, Mill Street (☎ **01738/627958**), is an outlet selling jams, mustards, and oatmeal along with items produced in the neighboring mills. There are wooden bowls, spirtles (wooden stirrers often used in making porridge), and Perthshire tartan scarves and ties. They also stock a large selection of cookbooks.

WHERE TO STAY

✪ **Dupplin Castle.** Near Aberdalgie, Perth, Perthshire PH2 0PY. ☎ **01738/623224.** Fax 01738/444140. 6 rms. TEL. £55 ($90.75) per person. MC, V. Rates include Scottish breakfast. From Perth, follow the main highway to Glasgow, turning left onto B9112 toward Aberdalgie and Forteviot.

This modern, stucco-sheathed, severely dignified mansion with sandstone mullions was built in 1968 by well-known architect Schomber Scott to replace the last of three castles, erected in the 1200s, the 1500s, and in 1837. The last of these was visited by Queen Victoria in 1842, then demolished when it became derelict. One of the former owners was the earl of Kinnouill, 17th-century heir to a Barbadian sugar plantation who—in a style befitting a gothic novel—gambled away the family's fortune.

Surrounded by 30 acres of forest and spectacular gardens (some specimens are 250 years old), the site is one of the most beautiful near Perth. Rooms are rented in a spirit of elegance and good manners. The on-site managers are Derek and Angela Straker, who serve dinner to residents only in the style of a casually elegant and distinguished country house. Meals must be booked 24 hours in advance and cost £28 ($46.20). Views from many of the bedrooms overlook the valley of the River Earn. On the grounds is the site of one of the most tragic battles in Scottish history, the Battle of Dupplin in August 1332, where the piled bodies of the slain Scots were said to measure a spear's length in depth.

Hunting Tower. Crieff Rd., Perth, Perthshire PH1 3JT. ☎ **01738/583771.** Fax 01738/583777. 15 rms, 9 lodge suites, 3 cottage suites. MINIBAR TV TEL. £85 ($140.25) double; £125 ($206.25) lodge suite; £90 ($148.50) cottage suite. AE, DC, MC, V. Rates include Scottish breakfast. Drive 3^1/2 miles west on A85.

This late-Victorian country house, about a 10-minute drive from the city center, is set in 3^1/2 acres of well-manicured gardens. It has a mock Tudor facade. Taste and concern went into the public rooms with their fine wood paneling. The bedrooms are also distinguished. They range from rather large to smaller and more compact. Such amenities as hair dryers, radios, minibars, and trouser presses are included; seven have spa baths. The cottage suites, located to the right of the hotel, are in a renovated bungalow. Decorated to match the rooms in the main hotel, each has twin beds, a sitting room, and private bath. More spacious lodge suites, in Scandinavian-style cabins, can sleep up to four. Each has a small kitchen, sitting room, bedroom, and private bath.

Dining/Entertainment: The fine cuisine, both Scottish and continental, is reason enough to stay here. In the elegant restaurant, table d'hôte dinners are served daily from 7 to 9:30pm. A two-course meal costs £15.25 ($25.15), three courses £18.75 ($30.95), and four courses £19.75 ($32.60). The more informal Conservatory serves dinner nightly from 6 to 9:30pm, with main courses on an à la carte menu ranging from £3 to £9 ($4.95 to $14.85).

Services: Room service, baby-sitting.

✪ **Parklands Hotel & Restaurant.** 2 St. Leonard's Bank, Perth, Perthshire PH2 8EB.
☎ **01738/622451.** Fax 01738/622046. 14 rms. TV TEL. Mon–Thurs £99.50–£115 ($164.15–$189.75) double, Fri–Sun £80–£90 ($132–$148.50) double. AE, DC, MC, V. Rates include Scottish breakfast. Free parking.

Luxuriously overhauled, this hotel near the rail station opened in 1991 and immediately became the most fashionable hotel in Perth. Allen Deeson set out to create a country-house hotel in the middle of the city—and succeeded admirably. The beautifully decorated bedrooms, filled with wood paneling and corniches, overlook the South Inch Park. All the rooms are spacious and contain teamakers and hair dryers.

Dining/Entertainment: Breakfast begins with such classic Scottish dishes as Loch Fyne kippers, deviled kidneys, smoked kedgeree, and smoked salmon. For dinner you can enjoy such specialties as sautéed chicken livers with a ginger dressing, and marinated scallops or oysters in citrus juices flavored with dill and garlic. Sweets include an iced honey-and-whisky mousse on a coriander sauce. There is a table d'hôte menu served in the restaurant at dinner, priced at £24.95 ($41.15) for three courses or £27.50 ($45.40) for four courses. A set lunch is also served here, costing £15.50 ($25.60). On site is an informal bistro where platters range from £6.95 to £15 ($11.45 to $24.75) at both lunch and dinner.

Services: Room service (from early morning until late in the evening), babysitting, laundry.

Facilities: Victorian conservatory.

WHERE TO DINE

✪ **Let's Eat.** 77–79 Kinnoull St. ☎ **01738/621464.** Reservations recommended. Main courses £6.50–£11 ($10.75–$18.15) at lunch, £8–£13 ($13.20–$21.45) at dinner. AE, MC, V. Tues–Sat noon–2pm and 6:30–9:45pm. BRITISH/MEDITERRANEAN.

Hailed for some of the most creative cuisine in Perth is this restaurant in a former theater. Within a sprawling terra-cotta–colored setting with green napery and lots of plants, you can enjoy a roster of seasonal venison and game, and lots of extremely fresh fish. An apéritif can be enjoyed before the meal while relaxing on one of the sofas near a blazing fireplace. Menu items include such airy and light fare as a gratin of goat's cheese studded with roasted peppers and served with rocket salad, new potatoes, and chutney; filet of roasted venison with port wine sauce (and in some cases with juniperberries and herbs); marinated tuna on a bed of couscous; a selection of terrines that vary from day to day; and grilled brochettes of monkfish with king prawns, rice, and salad. Also look for handmade black puddings served with "smash" (mashed potatoes), apple sauce, and onion gravy; risotto studded with wild mushrooms; and chicken breasts in ginger-and-lime sauce. Dessert might be any of several "puddings"—including an apple strudel—that are headlined on the menu as "glorious" and that usually live up to their billing.

Littlejohn's. 24 St. John's St. ☎ **01738/639999.** Main courses £3.95–£12.85 ($6.50–$21.20). AE, DC, MC, V. Daily 10am–11pm. INTERNATIONAL.

On one of Perth's busiest commercial streets behind a century-old wood facade, this large dining room has old-fashioned wood paneling, antique signs, and lots of Scottish charm. Despite the traditional setting, the food is eclectic—pizzas, pastas, Mexican tortillas, burgers, steaks, and an occasional lobster dish. A wide range of sandwiches and vegetarian fare is also offered. There's not much pretentiousness here—instead, you're likely to joke with whichever staff member pours you a beer and slams down your tortillas. Its name, incidentally, is the same as its founder, Simon Littlejohn.

Number Thirty Three. 33 George St. ☎ **01738/633771.** Reservations required. Main courses £10.65–£14.90 ($17.55–$24.60). MC, V. Tues–Sat 12:30–2:30pm and 6:30–9:30pm. Closed last week of Jan and first 2 weeks of Feb. SEAFOOD.

Acclaimed as one of the finest dining choices in Perth, this restaurant is the creation of Gavin Billinghurt, who employs a thoughtful, considerate staff. Many patrons come here just to enjoy the treats from the oyster bar. In the art deco dining room beyond, you can sample such dishes as moules marinières, served in a pyramid (which keeps the shellfish at the bottom hot until the last morsel is consumed). You might begin with a terrine made from prawns and crabmeat, then order medaillons of monkfish with pasta and water chestnuts as a main course. When Mary's seafood soup was once removed from the menu, it "nearly caused a local riot" until it was restored. One dish that might be a first for you is grilled sparlings, which are big spratlike fish caught in the Tay estuary. Baked rock turbot is another specialty, but you can also order meat dishes. Since the restaurant is small, with only seven tables, reservations are vital.

PERTH AFTER DARK

The Victorian **Perth Repertory Theatre,** 185 High St. (☎ **01738/621031**), hosts performances of plays and musicals between mid-August and May. From the end of May to early June, it's also a venue for some of the events of the Perth Festival of Arts. Performance nights vary, but shows start at 7:30pm, and the box office is open Monday through Saturday from 10am to 7:30pm. Tickets range in price from £6.50 to £14 ($10.75 to $23.10).

Perth City Hall, King Edward St. (☎ **01738/624055**), is a year-round venue for musical performances and dances; many local organizations—including the Freemasons, churches, and various amateur societies—book events here year after year. Entertainment is usually along the lines of a classical concert or a Highland ball, and ticket prices are at the discretion of the organization that sponsors the event. *Note:* City Hall will be closed from January to April of 1998 for renovations.

SIDE TRIPS FROM PERTH

SCONE

Old Scone, 2 miles from Perth on the River Tay, was the ancient capital of the Picts. On a lump of sandstone, the "Stone of Destiny," the early Scottish monarchs were enthroned, and for 400 years the British sovereigns were crowned on the stone, now in Edinburgh.

The seat of the earls of Mansfield and birthplace of David Douglas of fir-tree fame, ✪ **Scone Palace,** along A93 (☎ **01738/552300**), was largely rebuilt in 1802, incorporating the old palace of 1580. Inside is an impressive collection of French furniture, china, ivories, and 16th-century needlework, including bed hangings executed by Mary Queen of Scots. A fine collection of rare conifers is found on the grounds in the Pinetum. Rhododendrons and azaleas grow profusely in the gardens and woodlands around the palace. To reach the palace, head 2 miles northeast of Perth on A93. The site is open from Good Friday to mid-October only, daily from 9:30am to 5pm. Admission is £5 ($8.25) for adults, £2.80 ($4.60) for children, including entrance to both house and grounds. Admission to the grounds only is £2.50 ($4.15) for adults and £1.40 ($2.30) for children.

Where to Stay & Dine

✪ **Murrayshall.** New Scone, Perthshire PH2 7PH. ☎ **01738/551171.** Fax 01738/552595. 24 rms, 2 suites. TV TEL. £120 ($198) double; £150 ($247.50) suite. AE, DC, MC, V. Rates include Scottish breakfast. Take A94, 1¹/₂ miles east of New Scone.

The Murrayshall is an elegant country-house hotel and restaurant set in 300 acres of parkland. It was completely refurbished in 1987 and reopened as one of the show-pieces of Perthshire. The Victorian mansion offers its own 18-hole, par-73 golf course, interspersed with trees, water hazards, and white-sand bunkers. The hotel is traditionally styled in both its public rooms and its bedrooms. The size of the rooms varies, as does the decoration.

Dinner runs to £18.30 ($30.20) for three courses, and it's a worthy choice—in fact, the finest dining in the area. The Old Master's restaurant takes its name from reproductions of paintings that hang on its walls. The menu reflects Scottish flavor with French inspiration. Main courses might include fillet of Shetland Isles farmed salmon, sirloin of Scottish beef, or deep-fried fillet of North Sea haddock. Dinner is served in the candlelit restaurant daily from 7 to 9:30pm. Nonresidents are welcome, but must reserve.

GLENEAGLES

This famous **golfing center and sports complex** is on a moor between Strath Earn and Strath Allan. The center gets its name from the Gaelic Gleann-an-Eaglias, mean-ing "glen of the church." St. Mungo's Chapel, higher up the glen, has monuments of the Haldane family.

Gleneagles has several 18-hole golf courses connected with the hotel: the King's Course, the longest one, and the Queen's Course, next in length, are among the best in Scotland, and the sports complex is one of the best equipped in Europe.

Gleneagles provides a good—but far from inexpensive—base from which to explore the major attractions of central Scotland. It's in the ancient royal burgh of Auchterarder, many centuries old and strategically placed on the road that led from the royal residence at Scone to Stirling Castle. Today it's on A9, about halfway between Perth and Stirling, a short distance from the village of Auchterarder. It lies 55 miles from Edinburgh and 45 miles from Glasgow. The year-round **tourist information center** is at 90 High St., Aucherarder (☎ **01764/663450**).

Where to Stay & Dine

✪ **Auchterarder House.** Auchterarder, Perthshire PH3 1DZ. ☎ **01764/663646.** Fax 01764/662939. 9 rms, 3 suites. TV TEL. £225 ($371.25) double; £160–£180 ($264–$297) suite. AE, DC, MC, V. Rates include Scottish breakfast.

Auchterarder House lies 1 mile from Gleneagles and 1 1/2 miles from Auchterarder, sitting in its own grounds off B8062 between Auchterarder and Crieff. A fine example of 1830s architecture and construction in the Scots Jacobean style, the mansion house has been completely restored and the interior refurbished to a high standard of luxury by its present owners, the St. Christopher Wren Group. The house, which welcomes a lot of corporate clients, has elegant public rooms and comfortable bedrooms, all with amenities calculated to please a discerning clientele. Suites cost less than doubles because doubles are bigger and have better views. The three most desirable rooms are located in the main house; others are behind the main hotel or in a turreted wing. Afternoon tea is served in the glass conservatory with its marble fountain. The hand-some bar was originally designed as the building's chapel. Lunch and dinner are offered in the Victorian dining room or in the library. You can choose from a French or a British menu. Dinner will cost £32.50 ($53.65), the price including canapés, coffee, and petits fours.

Free courtesy-car service is offered from the Gleneagles station, and the staff will help arrange tours of the area as well as sports activities, including golf. You may be content, however, just to browse around the 20 acres of grounds, where a fine col-lection of rare shrubs, trees, and rhododendrons is nurtured.

✪ **Gleneagles Hotel.** Auchterarder, Perthshire PH3 1NF. ☎ **01764/662231.** Fax 01764/662134. 234 rms, 18 suites. MINIBAR TV TEL. £260–£365 ($429–$602) double; from £395 ($651.75) suite. AE, DC, MC, V. Rates include Scottish breakfast. Take A9, 1 1/2 miles southwest of Auchterarder.

Gleneagles Hotel stands in its own 830-acre estate. Built in isolated grandeur in 1924, it was for many years after its establishment the only five-star hotel in Scotland, a position it maintained until the early 1990s. It's sought after for its golf courses (see "Facilities," below). The service and decor are considered among the finest in the country. Each of the luxurious bedrooms has satellite TV. The rooms contain elegant furnishings, and offer views of hills and glens of the surrounding countryside.

Dining/Entertainment: Guests can dine in the Strathearn, paying £41 ($67.65) for a table d'hôte dinner. The emphasis is on regional dishes, and live music is played in the evening. The restaurant is open daily from 7:30 to 10pm. The chef uses fresh Scottish produce, cooked in a light style while still incorporating traditional flair and imagination. Service is impeccable. You can also have pasta and salads at the Gallery Brasserie, and there's a cocktail bar.

Services: 24-hour room service, laundry/valet, baby-sitting.

Facilities: The hotel's country club, enclosed in a glass dome to provide a year-round tropical climate, offers members and hotel guests use of a swimming pool, whirlpool, Turkish bath, saunas, plunge pool, and children's pool. If you're really hardy, you can use the Canadian hot tubs outdoors. The spa includes rooms for treatments, beauty, and massages. There are also squash courts, a gym, snooker tables, tennis courts, croquet lawns, and a bowling green, not to mention fishing on the River Tay. In addition, there are the Gleneagles Jackie Stewart Shooting School and the Gleneagles Equestrian Centre. For the coddling of golfers, the Dormy House (old name for a clubhouse) beside the 18th greens of the King's and Queen's courses has a restaurant and bar, showers, and changing rooms.

The hotel maintains legendary golf courses sought after by golfers throughout the summer and winter. (Diehards have been known to brush away piles of light snow to improve their golfing skills even in January.) The course is open only to residents of Gleneagles, who pay £70 ($115.50) per person to play the course's famous 18 holes.

2 Crieff

18 miles W of Perth, 60 miles NW of Edinburgh, 50 miles NE of Glasgow

At the edge of the Perthshire Highlands, with good fishing and golf, Crieff makes a pleasant stopover. This small burgh was the seat of the court of the earls of Strathearn until 1747. The gallows in its marketplace was once used to execute Highland cattle rustlers.

You can take a "day trail" into **Strathearn,** the valley of the River Earn, the very center of Scotland. Highland mountains meet gentle Lowland slopes, and moorland mingles with rich green pastures. North of Crieff, the road to Aberfeldy passes through the narrow pass of the **Sma' Glen,** a famous beauty spot, with hills rising on either side to 2,000 feet.

ESSENTIALS
GETTING THERE

BY TRAIN There is no direct service. The nearest rail stations are at Gleneagles, 9 miles away, and at Perth, 18 miles away (see above). Call ☎ **0345/484950** for information and schedules.

BY BUS   Once you arrive in Perth, you'll find regular connecting bus service hourly during the day. The bus service from Gleneagles is too poor to recommend.

BY CAR   From Perth, continue west along A85.

VISITOR INFORMATION

The year-round **tourist information office** is in the Town Hall on High Street (☎ 01764/652578).

EXPLORING THE AREA

Glenturret Distillery. Hwy. A85, Glenturret. ☎ **01764/656565.** Guided tours £2.90 ($4.80) adults, £2.40 ($3.95) seniors and ages 12–17, free for age 11 and under. Mar–Dec, Mon–Sat 9:30am–6pm, Sun noon–6pm; Jan, Mon–Fri 11:30am–4:30pm; Feb, Mon–Sat 11:30am–4pm, Sun noon–4pm. Closed Jan 1–2 and Dec 25–26. Take A85 toward Comrie; 3/4 of a mile from Crieff, turn right at the crossroads; the distillery is 1/4-mile up the road.

Scotland's oldest distillery, Glenturret was established in 1775 on the banks of the River Turret. Visitors can see the milling of malt, mashing, fermentation, distillation, and cask filling, followed by a free "wee dram" dispensed at the end of the tour. Guided tours leave every 10 minutes and take about 25 minutes. The Glenturret Heritage Centre incorporates a 100-seat audiovisual theater and an Exhibition Display Museum. The presentation lasts about 20 minutes. The distillery shop has the full range of the Glenturret Pure Single Highland Malt scotch whisky and the Glenturret malt liqueur, together with an extensive range of souvenirs. At the Smugglers Restaurant and Whisky Tasting Bar, you can taste older Glenturret whiskies, such as 10-year-old, high-proof, 12- and 15-year-old, and the Glenturret malt liqueur.

Crieff Visitors Centre. A822, directly south of Crieff. ☎ **01764/654014.** Daily 9am–6pm (closing hours are earlier in winter but vary).

This is a complex that not only has a restaurant and dispenses information for visitors, but is also the site of a paperweight manufacturer. A small pottery factory and an inexpensive restaurant are also on site. During the week you can tour the factory, seeing various paperweights being made. The factory also produces hand-painted pottery, often with Thistle designs, and millefiori glass. All of these items are for sale, of course.

Drummond Castle Gardens. Grimsthorpe, Crieff. ☎ **01764/681257.** Admission £3 ($4.95) adults, £2 ($3.30) seniors, £1.50 ($2.45) children. May–Sept, daily 2–6pm. Closed Oct–Apr. Take A822, 3 miles south of Crieff.

The gardens of Drummond Castle, first laid out in the early 17th century by John Drummond, second earl of Perth, are said to be among the finest formal gardens in Europe. A panoramic view can be obtained from the upper terrace, overlooking an example of an early Victorian parterre in the form of St. Andrew's Cross. The multifaceted sundial by John Mylne, master mason to Charles I, has been the centerpiece since 1630. Guests are able to visit the castle gardens only, not the castle itself.

SHOPPING   Stuart Crystal, Muthill Rd. (☎ **01764/654004**), is a factory outlet that sells a full line of Stuart crystal. Six days a week, a cutter sets up in the shop and demonstrates his craft. During demonstrations, one-of-a-kind patterns are cut, and these pieces, available for sale, are very popular as souvenirs. The shop also sells crystal by Wedgwood and Waterford, as well as a line of hand-crafted Ortak jewelry, featuring intricate Celtic patterns, Dunoon glazed stoneware mugs, Heritage bronze figurines, and Scottish shortbread. Within the shop is a smaller shop that offers a wide range of Scottish woolens.

WHERE TO STAY & DINE

Murraypark Hotel. Connaught Terrace, Crieff, Perthshire PH7 3DJ. ☎ **01764/653731.** Fax 01764/655311. 19 rms, 1 suite. TV TEL. £75 ($123.75) double or suite. Rates include Scottish breakfast. AE, DC, MC, V. Approaching from Perth, take the first right after the golf club; the hotel will be on your left.

Originally built by a sea captain late in the 19th century as a refuge from his trips abroad, this stone-fronted house lies in a residential neighborhood about a 10-minute walk from Crieff's center. In 1993 a new wing was opened, enlarging the public rooms and the number of simply furnished guest accommodations. You can drink in the bar before dinner. Recipes are based on Scottish, French, and international inspirations. Main courses on an à la carte menu range from £7 to £10 ($11.55 to $16.50), and service is nightly from 7:30 to 9:30pm. A typical meal might include a choice of appetizers such as steamed mussels in white wine or main courses along the lines of grilled halibut steak in an orange-and-tarragon butter or sautéed strips of beef in a dijon mustard-and-onion sauce. A large dessert-laden oak table allows guests to choose from several selections.

3 Aberfeldy

76 miles NW of Edinburgh, 73 miles NE of Glasgow, 32 miles NW of Perth

The "Birks o' Aberfeldy" are among the beauty spots made famous by Robert Burns. Once a Pictish center, this small town makes a fine base for touring Perthshire's glens and lochs. Loch Tay lies 6 miles to the west; Glen Lyon, 15 miles west; and Kinloch Rannoch, 18 miles northwest. The bridge spanning the Tay was built in 1733 by General Wade.

ESSENTIALS
GETTING THERE

BY TRAIN   There is no direct service into Aberfeldy. You can take a train to either Perth (see above) or Pitlochry (see below), then continue the rest of the way by bus. Call ☎ **0345/484950** for schedules.

BY BUS   Connecting buses at either Perth or Pitlochry make the final journey to Aberfeldy. The one-way fare from Perth is £3.40 ($5.60), or else £2.30 ($3.80) from Pitlochry. The private bus line, **Stagecoach** (☎ **01738/629339**), handles much of the bus travel to the small towns and villages in the area.

BY CAR   Aberfeldy lies about a 1³/₄-hour drive from Edinburgh and about 2 hours from Glasgow. Take M9 from Stirling, then A9 to Perth, and continue on A9 to Ballinluig, then A827 to Aberfeldy. Or take the scenic route—M9 from Stirling, then A9, turning off at Greenloaning onto A822 to Crieff; continue on A822 to Gilmerton; then after going through Amulree, take A826 to Aberfeldy.

VISITOR INFORMATION

A **tourist information office** is at The Square (☎ **01887/820276**).

EXPLORING THE AREA

On the opposite bank of the Tay, west of the center, lies the **Clan Menzies' Museum** (☎ **01887/820982**), a formerly fortified tower and house from the 1500s. Now devoted to regional exhibits of the area, including clan relics, it is open April until mid-October only, Monday through Saturday from 10:30am to 5pm and Sunday from 2 to 5pm. Admission is £2.50 ($4.15).

If you'd like to go boating on Loch Tay, head for the **Loch Tay Boating Centre,** Carlin and Brett, Pier Road at Kenmore (☎ 01887/830291), renting canoes and cabin cruisers from April through October.

Aberfeldy is also a good base for exploring **Glen Lyon,** one of the most beautiful in the central part of the country, with forests, prehistoric sites, and a raging river. Follow the A827 to Fearnan, then head north to Fortingall (signposted) if you'd like to see the most attractive part of the glen.

SHOPPING   The town's shops have good buys in tweeds and tartans, plus other items of Highland dress. The **Highland Gift Shop,** Bridgend (☎ 01887/820257), sells only products of Scotland, ranging from Ortak silver jewelry, hand-knitted sweaters for the whole family, crystal, Scottish books, shortbread and sweets, to "anything that can be covered in tartan," including soft children's toys and men's and women's clothing. **P & J Haggart,** 42 Dunkeld St. (☎ 01887/820306), is a manufacturer of tweeds who turns out an array of men's and women's clothing items, all for sale here. Much of what you'll find is outdoor wear aimed at the sportsperson. At **Gemini,** 21 Dunkeld St. (☎ 01887/820625), you'll find regional ceramic ornaments and pottery, cards, and gift items.

WHERE TO STAY & DINE

✪ **Farleyer House Hotel.** Hwy. B846, Aberfeldy, Perthshire PH15 2JE. ☎ 01887/820332. Fax 01887/829430. 19 rms. TV TEL. £150 ($247.50) double; £170 ($280.50) suite. AE, DC, MC, V. Rates include Scottish breakfast. Take B846, 2 miles west of Aberfeldy.

A tranquil oasis, this Scottish hotel of character stands on 30 acres of grounds in the Tay Valley. It's a former dower house of the Menzies clan, and Castle Menzies, their 16th-century mansion, can be seen in the distance. The public rooms are immaculate and beautifully furnished, and the bedrooms are well maintained and comfortable. Each has a radio, TV, VCR, and hair dryer.

Dining/Entertainment: The formal dining room, open only for dinner, offers a fixed-price menu of five courses that is changed daily for £29.50 ($48.70). A typical menu might begin with a salad of wood pigeon and langoustine, followed by Tay salmon or seared loin of Perthshire lamb with an Aberfeldy malt sauce, finishing with a red port wine sabayon with melon. This is followed by coffee and truffles. There's also an à la carte menu with specialties, including, on occasion, roast fillet of Highland venison. Less formal is the on-site Scottish Bistro, serving lunch daily from noon to 2:30pm and dinner from 6 to 10pm.

Services: Room service, laundry/valet, baby-sitting.

Facilities: Reception desk will arrange for golf, fishing, sailing, waterskiing, windsurfing, and clay shooting, as well as tennis and swimming.

4 Dunkeld

58 miles N of Edinburgh, 14 miles N of Perth, 98 miles SW of Aberdeen

A cathedral town, Dunkeld lies in a thickly wooded valley of the Tay River at the edge of the Perthshire Highlands. Once a major ecclesiastical center, it's one of the seats of ancient Scottish history and was an important center of the Celtic church.

ESSENTIALS
GETTING THERE

BY TRAIN   Trains from Perth arrive every 2 hours at unmanned Dunkeld Station, which is actually in the neighboring town of Birnam. For information and schedules, call ☎ 0345/484950.

BY BUS Pitlochry-bound buses leaving from Perth make a stopover in Dunkeld, letting you off at the Dunkeld Car Park. Contact **Stagecoach** at ☎ **01738/629339** for information and schedules.

BY CAR From Perth, continue north on the Pitlochry road (A9) until you reach Dunkeld.

VISITOR INFORMATION

A **tourist information office** is at The Cross (☎ **01350/727688**).

EXPLORING THE AREA

Founded in A.D. 815, the **Cathedral of Dunkeld** was converted from a church to a cathedral in 1127 by David I. It stands on Cathedral Street in a scenic setting along the River Tay. The 14th and 15th centuries witnessed subsequent additions. The cathedral was first restored in 1815, and traces of the 12th-century structure clearly remain today. It can be visited May through September, daily from 9:30am to 7pm; October to April, daily from 9:30am to 4pm. Admission is free.

The National Trust for Scotland has restored many of the old houses and shops around the marketplace and cathedral that had fallen into decay. The trust owns 20 houses on High Street and Cathedral Street as well. Many of these houses were constructed in the closing years of the 17th century after the rebuilding of the town following the Battle of Dunkeld. The Trust runs the **Ell Shop,** The Cross (☎ **01350/727460**), open from Easter weekend to May and September to December 22, Monday through Saturday from 10am to 5:30pm; June to August, Monday through Saturday from 10am to 5:30pm and Sunday from 1:30 to 5:30pm.

The **Scottish Horse Museum,** The Cross (no phone), has exhibits tracing the history of the Scottish Horse Yeomanry, in uniforms, trophies, maps, photographs, and regimental records. From the time of the raising of the cavalry force in Scotland and South Africa in 1900 to its amalgamation with the Fife & Forfar Yeomanry in 1956, the Scottish Horse Mounted Yeomanry Regiment was the only such fighting body besides the Lovat Scouts. The museum is open from Easter to the end of October only, Saturday through Wednesday from 9:30am to 5:30pm. Admission is 50p (85¢) for adults, free for children.

Shakespeare fans may want to seek out the oak and sycamore in front of the destroyed Birnam House, a mile to the south. This was believed to be a remnant of the **Birnam Wood**—in Shakespeare's drama, Macbeth, you may recall, could be defeated only when "Birnam Wood came to Dunsinane."

The Hermitage, lying off A9 about 2 miles west of Dunkeld, was called a "folly" when it was constructed in 1758. Today it makes for one of the most scenic woodland walks in the area. The folly was built above the wooded gorge of the River Braan and restored in 1984. An unmanned site, it's always accessible and free to the public.

SHOPPING **Dunkeld Antiques,** Tay Terrace (☎ **01350/728832**), is a shop with serious collectors in mind. It carries an extensive range of 18th- and 19th-century pieces, with emphasis on dining furniture, decorative boxes and clocks, Japanese ceramics, shooting and fishing memorabilia, and out-of-print books.

Highland Horn & Deerskin Centre, City Hall, High Street (☎ **01350/ 727569**), as its name implies, sells moccasins, shoes, hats, and waistcoats made of deerskin, along with items carved from antlers, such as whistles and cutlery with stag handles. A range of waxed jackets and other outdoor wear is available as well.

WHERE TO STAY & DINE

✪**Kinnaird.** Kinnaird, Kinnaird Estate, Dunkeld, Perthshire PH8 0LB. ☎ **01796/482440.** Fax 01796/482289. 8 rms, 1 suite. TV TEL. £235–£295 ($387.75–$486.75) double; £315 ($519.75) suite. AE, MC, V. Rates include Scottish breakfast. No children under 12 accepted. Traveling north on A9 after passing Dunkeld on your right, turn left onto B898 (signposted Balnaguard and Dalguise); follow this road for 4^1/2 miles and the main gate of Kinnaird will be on your right.

Opened in 1990, Kinnaird, set on a 9,000-acre private estate, is a small hotel of great warmth, charm, and comfort. All the beautifully furnished bedrooms have king-size beds, private baths, and views. Some rooms overlook the valley of the River Tay, and others open onto gardens and woodlands. Built originally in 1770 as a hunting lodge for the duke of Atholl, the house was purchased in 1927 by the Ward family. Today its present owner, American-born Constance Cluett Ward, has restored the house to its previous grandeur.

Dining/Entertainment: Kinnaird House Restaurant brings a high-caliber cuisine to the area. The chef cooks in the modern, postnouvelle British and continental style, depending on fresh ingredients, with changing menus based on the season. John Weber has prepared meals for some of the golden palates of Europe, notably at Cliveden House, former seat of Lady Astor. Lobster, Scottish salmon, and the best of local beef, pork, and poultry go into his kitchen and turn up like delicate artwork on the plate. Lunch is priced at £19.50 ($32.15) for two courses and £24 ($39.60) for three courses. A fixed-price four-course dinner goes for £39.50 ($65.20) per person.

Services: Room service, laundry/valet, baby-sitting.

Facilities: Sporting facilities on the estate include salmon and trout fishing, roe stalking, and shooting for pheasant, grouse, and duck. All equipment is provided, including ghillies, gamekeepers, and kennels for gun dogs.

✪**Stakis Dunkeld House Resort Hotel.** Dunkeld, Perthshire PH8 0HX. ☎ **01350/727771.** Fax 01350/728924. 83 rms, 3 suites. MINIBAR TV TEL. £130 ($214.50) double; £180–£200 ($297–$330) suite. AE, DC, MC, V. Rates include Scottish breakfast. Drive about a mile north-west of Dunkeld on the road leading to Pitlochry (signposted).

Built in 1903 as the private home for the duke and duchess of Atholl, this property was acquired and much enlarged by the Stakis chain. Today it offers the quiet dignity of life in a Scottish country house. It's ranked as one of the leading leisure and sports hotels in the area. On the banks of the Tay, the surrounding grounds— 280 acres in all—are planted with trees and flowering bushes, making a parklike setting. The house is beautifully kept, and the accommodations come in a wide range of styles, space, and furnishings. The hotel, extensively restored and expanded, now offers first-class bedrooms.

Dining/Entertainment: Its restaurant is one of the finest in the area, paying homage to its "Taste of Scotland" dishes, but also serving an international cuisine as well. Fixed-price dinners go for £30 ($49.50).

Services: Room service, laundry/valet, baby-sitting.

Facilities: Guests can fish for trout and salmon right on the grounds. Facilities include all-weather tennis courts and an indoor swimming pool. Archery is also popular.

5 Pitlochry

71 miles NW of Edinburgh, 27 miles NW of Perth, 15 miles N of Dunkeld

This charming and popular holiday resort center is a touring headquarters for the Valley of the Tummel. It is also home to the renown **Pitlochry Festival Theatre,** Scotland's "theater in the hills" (see below).

Pitlochry doesn't just entertain tourists, although it would appear that way in summer—it also produces scotch whisky. It's a good overnight stop between Edinburgh and Inverness, 85 miles to the north.

ESSENTIALS
GETTING THERE
BY TRAIN Five trains per day (☎ **0345/484950**) arrive from Edinburgh and an additional three per day arrive from Glasgow (trip time from each: 2 hours). A one-way fare is £7.40 ($12.20) from either city.

BY BUS Buses to Pitlochry arrive hourly from Perth (see above). The one-way fare is £3.25 ($5.35). Contact **Stagecoach** at ☎ **01738/629339** for information and schedules.

BY CAR From Perth, continue northwest along A9.

VISITOR INFORMATION
The **tourist information office** is at 22 Atholl Rd. (☎ **01796/472215**).

EXPLORING THE AREA
Pitlochry Dam was created because a power station was needed, but in effect the engineers created a new loch. The famous "salmon ladder" here was built to help the struggling salmon upstream. An underwater portion of the ladder—a salmon observation chamber—has been enclosed in glass to give fascinated sightseers a look. An exhibition (☎ **01796/473152**) is open here from Easter to the last Sunday in October only, daily from 10am to 5:30pm, costing £1.80 ($2.95) for adults, £1 ($1.65) for seniors, and 80p ($1.30) for children.

DISTILLERY TOURS
You can begin your whisky trail by touring the two distilleries in the area.

Bell's Blairathol. Perth Rd., ¹/₂ mile south of town. ☎ **01796/472234.**

In 1997 Bell's celebrated 200 years as a popular whisky distillery. You can take a distillery tour (in summer, there's a tour every half hour; in winter, call and check). The £3 ($4.95) fee charged to adults for the tour is redeemable as a voucher off the price of any single-malt purchased in the Visitor Centre, where you'll find Bell's single-malt, Bell's blend, and single-malts by other regional distilleries.

Edradour Distillery. On the A924, Pitlochry. ☎ **01796/472095.**

Take the A924 east toward Braemar to find this distillery located 2 miles outside of town. The Visitor Centre offers distillery tours every 20 minutes throughout the day, and the gift shop sells Edradour single-malt, as well as various blends that contain the whisky.

SHOPPING Featuring tweeds and tartans, **McNaughton's,** Station Road ☎ **01796/472722**), offers a full range of Highland wear, including the inevitable kilts. There are departments devoted to both men and ladies, and there is also a fabric center, where a wide variety of Scottish fabrics can be purchased by the meter. The shop also carries a good selection of hand-knitted sweaters.

WHERE TO STAY
East Haugh House (see "Where to Dine," below) also rents rooms.

Balrobin. Higher Oakfield, Pitlochry, Perthshire PH16 5HT. ☎ **01796/472901.** Fax 01796/474200. 16 rms. TV. £54 ($89.10) double. MC, V. Rates include Scottish breakfast. Closed Nov–Feb.

A Scottish country house run by the Hohman family since 1980, this traditional hotel opens onto views of the Perthshire hills and the Tummel Valley. The home was originally a 19th-century private holiday cottage, used by the owners for fishing or shooting holidays. Today a two-star hotel, it offers bedrooms that are furnished in simple provincial styling with such amenities as hair dryers. Added to the "auld hoose" were a west and east wing in keeping with the stone construction. A four-course dinner is served daily from a changing menu. There's a residents-only bar and a country lounge.

Green Park Hotel. Clunie Bridge Rd., Pitlochry, Perthside PH16 5JY. ☎ **01796/473248.** Fax 01796/473520. 37 rms. TV TEL. £92 ($151.80). MC, V. Rates include half board.

Green Park Hotel lies about half a mile from the center, at the northwest end of Pitlochry. Against a backdrop of woodland, the white-painted mansion with its carved eaves enjoys a scenic position; its lawn reaches to the shores of Loch Faskally. The hotel is supervised by Anne and Graham Brown. Visitors who reserve well in advance get one of the half dozen or so rooms in the garden wing, all of which enjoy a view of the loch. Some rooms have recently been refurbished. Guests order drinks in a lounge overlooking the water. The dining room is popular during festival season. Dinner is served until 8:30pm, and many traditional Scottish dishes are featured on the £16 ($26.40) set menu.

Pine Trees Hotel. Strathview Terrace, Pitlochry, Perthshire PH16 5QR. ☎ **01796/472121.** Fax 01796/472460. 20 rms. TV TEL. £98 ($161.70) double. MC, V. Rates include Scottish breakfast. Turn right up Larchwood Rd., below the golf course on the north side of Pitlochry.

The country-house Pine Trees Hotel was built in 1892 on 14 acres of private grounds. It's only about a 15-minute walk to the town center and 5 minutes to the golf course, home of the Highland Open Championships. Well appointed and family run, the Pine Trees has spacious public rooms, an atmosphere of warmth and relaxation, and a reputation for good food and wine. Bar lunches and full luncheon and dinner menus are offered, with fresh and smoked salmon always on the menu. Trout and salmon fishing can usually be arranged. The bedrooms are in either the main house or a 1970s annex designed to blend into the period of the central structure. They're constantly being renovated and are furnished with traditional pieces. Housekeeping is good here.

WHERE TO DINE

East Haugh House. Old Perth Rd., East Haugh, Pitlochry, Perthshire PH16 5JS. ☎ **01796/473121.** Fax 01796/472473. Reservations recommended. Table d'hôte dinner £26.95 ($44.45); bar platters £1.75–£16 ($2.90–$26.40). MC, V. Restaurant: daily 7–10:30pm. Bar: daily noon–2:30pm and 6–10:30pm. Closed 2 weeks in Feb. Drive a mile south of Pitlochry on A9 toward Inverness; it's across the road from the Tummell River. MODERN BRITISH.

Although it contains eight comfortably furnished bedrooms, this establishment is best known for its well-prepared cuisine. In a Teutonic-looking granite house originally commissioned in the 1600s by the duke of Atholl for one of his tenant farmers, it offers a menu that relies exclusively on fresh Scottish ingredients and that changes every 2 days. Meals in the cozy bar area might include mixed grills, Scottish lamb, steaks, and haggis. The cuisine in the more elegant restaurant is more adventurous, featuring such dishes as zucchini flowers stuffed with a duxelle of wild mushrooms, grilled and marinated Scottish goat cheese with a mixed leaf and pine-nut salad, terrine of local pigeon with orange salad and mange tout (a kind of bean), and many different variations of salmon. Dessert might include a dark-chocolate torte with crème fraîche, or a hot thin apple flan with caramel sauce. Scottish-born

Neil McGown and his English wife, Lesley, are the hardworking and gracious owners.

The bedrooms are outfitted like rooms in a Scottish country mansion, with conservative dignity, private bathrooms, telephones, and TVs. Depending on the season, with Scottish breakfast included, doubles range from £78 to £110 ($128.70 to $181.50).

PITLOCHRY AFTER DARK

The town is famous for its **Pitlochry Festival Theatre** (☎ **01796/472680** for information). Founded in 1951, the festival theater draws people from all over the world to its repertory of plays (which change daily), its Sunday concerts, and varying art exhibitions, presented from April 30 to October 9. Performances in the evening begin at 8pm, and on Wednesday and Saturday there's a matinee at 2pm. The theater complex opened in 1981 on the banks of the River Tummel near the dam and fish ladder, with a parking area, a restaurant serving coffee, lunch, and dinner, and other facilities for visitors. Tickets for plays and concerts cost £14 to £16 ($23.10 to $26.40). For details by mail, address correspondence to the Pitlochry Festival Theatre, Pitlochry PH16 5DR.

If it's a pub you're seeking, head for the **Killiecrankie Hotel,** signposted from A9 north of Pitlochry (☎ **01796/473220**). It's the best in the area. In a country hotel set on peaceful grounds, it serves 20 malt whiskies, as well as some of the most reasonably priced food in the area. Try the deep-fried fresh haddock in beer batter or one of the daily specialties. Upholstered chairs, wildlife paintings, and plants and flowers make for an inviting atmosphere. Hours are daily from 11am to 2:30pm and 5:30 to 11pm.

6 Dundee

63 miles N of Edinburgh, 67 SW of Aberdeen, 83 miles NE of Glasgow

This royal burgh and old seaport is now an industrial city on the north shore of the Firth of Tay. When steamers took over the whaling industry from sailing vessels, Dundee took the lead as home port for the ships from the 1860s until World War I. Long known for its jute and flax operations, Dundee today is linked with the production of the rich Dundee fruitcakes and Dundee marmalades and jams. This was also the home of the man who invented stick-on postage stamps, James Chalmers.

Spanning the Firth of Tay is the **Tay Railway Bridge,** opened in 1888. Constructed over the tidal estuary, the bridge is some 2 miles long, one of the longest in Europe. There's also a road bridge 1¹/₄ miles long, with four traffic lanes and a walkway in the center.

ESSENTIALS

GETTING THERE

BY TRAIN ScotRail offers frequent service between Perth, Dundee, and Aberdeen. A one-way fare from Perth to Dundee is £4.20 ($6.95); from Aberdeen, £15.90 ($26.25). For information and schedules, call ☎ **0345/484950.**

BY BUS National Express buses offer frequent bus service from Edinburgh and Glasgow. A one-way fare from Glasgow costs £6.60 ($10.90); from Edinburgh, £5.80 ($9.55). For schedules and information, phone ☎ **0990/080080.**

BY CAR From Edinburgh, take M90 north to Perth, then cut northeast along A85.

VISITOR INFORMATION

The year-round **tourist information office** is at 4 City Square (☎ **01382/434664**).

SEEING THE SIGHTS

For a panoramic view of Dundee, the Tay bridges across to Fife, and mountains to the north, go to **Dundee Law,** a 572-foot hill a mile north of the city. The hill is an ancient volcanic plug.

HMS *Unicorn*. Victoria Dock. ☎ **01382/200893.** Admission £3 ($4.95) adults, £2 ($3.30) seniors and children, £8 ($13.20) family ticket. Jan–Mar 25, Mon–Fri 10am–4pm; Mar 26– Oct 31, daily 10am–5pm. Closed Nov–Dec.

This 46-gun ship of war commissioned in 1824 by the Royal Navy, now the oldest British-built ship afloat, has been restored and visitors can explore all four decks: the quarterdeck with 32-pound carronades, the gundeck with its battery of 18-pound cannons and the captain's quarters, the berth deck with officers' cabins and crew's hammocks, and the orlop deck and hold. Various displays portraying life in the sailing navy and the history of the *Unicorn* make this a rewarding visit.

RRS *Discovery*. Discovery Quay, Discovery Point. ☎ **01372/201245.** Free admission. Apr– Oct, Mon–Sat 10am–5pm, Sun 11am–5pm; Nov–Mar, Mon–Sat 10am–4pm, Sun 11am–4pm.

This weather-beaten vessel was used by Captain Robert Scott on polar explorations. An exhibition details Scott's first two expeditions to the Antarctic, and on-board exhibits re-create the rugged life aboard.

Broughty Castle. Castle Green, Broughty Ferry. ☎ **01382/776121.** Free admission. July– Sept, Mon 11am–5pm, Tues–Thurs 10am–1pm and 2–5pm, Sun 2–5pm; Oct–June, Mon 11am– 5pm, Tues–Thurs 10am–1pm and 2–5pm. Bus: 7, 9, 11, or 24.

This 15th-century estuary fort lies about 4 miles east of the city center on the seafront, at Broughty Ferry, a little fishing hamlet and once the terminus for ferries crossing the Firth of Tay until the bridges were built. Besieged by the English in the 16th century and attacked by Cromwell's army under General Monk in the 17th, it was eventually restored as part of Britain's coastal defenses in 1861. Its gun battery was dismantled in 1956, and it's now a museum with displays on local history, arms and armor, seashore life, and Dundee's whaling story. The observation area at the top of the castle provides fine views of the Tay estuary and northeast Fife. Regrettably, it is not open during the peak visiting days of Friday and Saturday.

WHERE TO STAY

Invercarse Hotel. 371 Perth Rd., Dundee, Angus DD2 1PG. ☎ **01382/669231.** Fax 01382/ 644112. 31 rms, 1 suite. TV TEL. £80 ($132) double; £90 ($148.50) suite. AE, MC, V. Rates include Scottish breakfast.

In landscaped gardens overlooking the River Tay, this privately owned hotel lies 3 miles west of the heart of Dundee. Many prefer it for its fresh air, tranquil location, and Victorian country-house aura. The guest rooms open onto views across the Tay to the hills of the Kingdom of Fife. A frequent venue for conferences and local banquets, the hotel with its large parking area is also suitable as a center for exploring the nearby region, not just Dundee. Most rooms are singles. Accommodations come in a variety of sizes, but all are well maintained and furnished, often with pieces crafted from light-grained wood. Guests enjoy drinks in the bar, furnished in red leather. Dinner, featuring a continental or Scottish cuisine, is served nightly from 7 to 9:30pm, a three-course table d'hôte costing £14.95 ($24.65), although you can also order à la carte.

Stakis Earl Grey Hotel. Earl Grey Place, Dundee, Angus DD1 4DE. ☎ **01382/229271.** Fax 01382/200072. 102 rms, 2 suites. TV TEL. £118–£121 ($194.70–$199.65) double; £170–£175 ($280.50–$288.75) suite. AE, DC, MC, V. Free parking. Bus: 1A, 1B, or 20.

Along the waterfront, this chain hotel helped rejuvenate the once-seedy waterfront of Dundee. Built in a severe modern style, it takes its name from a famous English tea, which most often accompanies Dundee marmalade and Dundee fruitcakes, the city's two most famous products. Some of the well-furnished bedrooms overlook the Firth, the river, or the Tay Bridge. It's an easy walk from the hotel to the *Unicorn,* a wooden frigate, now a museum, or to Captain Scott's R.R.S. *Discovery.*

Dining/Entertainment: Guests can dine at Juliana's Table Restaurant, featuring buffet-style meals along with table d'hôte lunches and dinners. Another dining choice, although not one to rate a rave, is Epicures, featuring an à la carte menu.

Services: Room service, baby-sitting, laundry/valet.

Facilities: Heated indoor swimming pool, exercise equipment, sauna, whirlpool.

WHERE TO DINE

Jahangir Tandoori. 1 Sessions St. (at the corner of Hawk Hill). ☎ **01382/202022.** Reservations recommended. Main courses £6.50–£15 ($10.75–$24.75). AE, MC, V. Daily 5pm–midnight. INDIAN.

Built around an indoor fish pond in a dining room draped with the soft folds of an embroidered tent, this is the best Indian restaurant in Dundee and one of the most exotic in the region. Meals are prepared with fresh ingredients and cover the gamut of recipes from both north and south India. Food is sometimes slow-cooked in clay pots (tandoori) and is seasoned to the degree of spiciness you prefer. Both meat and meatless dishes are available, and the staff is polite and discreet.

DUNDEE AFTER DARK

Your best venue is the **Dundee Rep Theatre,** Tay Square (☎ **01382/223530**), which is likely to stage any and everything from Peter Pan to a jazz festival, from plays to Scottish ballet, even flamenco. Tickets can be booked Monday through Saturday from 10am to 7:30pm (until 6pm on performance days). Tickets depend on the event, of course, but are in the general range of £3.75 to £10.50 ($6.20 to $17.35). The theater is sometimes a venue for opera. On site is the **Het Theatercafé** (☎ **01382/206699**), open Monday through Thursday from 11am to 7:30pm, Friday from 11am to 10pm, Saturday from 10am to 10pm; closed Sunday. Main courses range from £5 to £8 ($8.25 to $13.20).

SIDE TRIPS FROM DUNDEE

GLAMIS

The little village of Glamis (pronounced without the "i") grew up around ✪ **Glamis Castle,** Estate Office, Glamis (☎ **01307/840393**). After Balmoral Castle, visitors to Scotland most want to see Glamis Castle for its architecture and its link with the crown. For six centuries it has been connected to members of the British royal family. Queen Elizabeth, the Queen Mother, was brought up here; and Princess Margaret was born here, becoming the first royal princess born in Scotland in three centuries. The present owner, the queen's great-nephew, is the 18th earl of Strathmore and Kinghorne and the direct descendant of the first earl. The castle contains Duncan's Hall, supposedly the setting for the banquet given by Shakespeare's *Macbeth,* Thane of Glamis, when the ghost of one of his victims appeared.

The present Glamis Castle dates from the early 15th century, but there are records of a hunting lodge having been in existence in the 11th century—Malcolm II was

In Search of Peter Pan

The little town of **Kirriemuir** is reached by heading north of Glamis Castle for 4 miles or by traveling 16 miles north of Dundee via A929 and A928. Kirriemuir receives thousands of visitors yearly who come to pay their respects to Sir James M. Barrie (1860–1937), author of *Peter Pan*. Kirriemuir itself was disguised in fiction as the "Thrums" of his tales.

The little town of red sandstone houses and narrow, crooked streets—the heart of Scotland's raspberry country—saw the birth of Barrie in 1860. His father was employed as a hand-loom weaver of linen. **Barrie's birthplace** still stands at 9 Brechin Rd. (☎ 01575/572646), now a property of the National Trust for Scotland. The small house contains manuscripts and mementos of the writer. A little wash house outside the four-room cottage was used by Barrie as his first makeshift theater. The house is open May to September, Monday through Saturday from 11am to 5:30pm and Sunday from 1:30 to 5:30pm; in October, Saturday from 11:30am to 5:30pm and Sunday from 1:30 to 5:30pm. Admission is £1.80 ($2.95) for adults, £1.20 ($2) for seniors, students, and children, and £4.80 ($7.90) for a family ticket.

Though he spent most of his working life in London, Barrie is buried in Kirriemuir Cemetery. To reach **Barrie's grave,** turn left off Brechin Road and follow the cemetery road upward. The path is clearly marked, taking you to the grave pavilion. A Camera Obscura in the **Barrie Pavilion** on Kirriemuir Hill gives views over Strathmore to Dundee and north to the Highlands.

Barrie first became known for his sometimes-cynical tales of Kirriemuir, disguised as Thrums, in such works as *Auld Licht Idylls* (1888) and *A Window in Thrums* (1889).

Barrie turned to the theater and in time became known for bringing supernatural and sentimental ideas to the stage. It's said that talking to a group of children while walking his dog gave him the idea for the stories about Peter Pan, which were first presented to the public in 1904. It wasn't until 1957 that *When Wendy Grew Up: An Afterthought* was published.

He went on to write more dramas, including *Alice Sit-by-the-Fire* (1905), *What Every Woman Knows* (1908), *The Will* (1913), and *Mary Rose* (1920), the latter a very popular play in its day. But who remembers these works today except a Barrie scholar? On the other hand, Peter Pan has become a legendary figure, known by almost every child in the Western world through films, plays, and, of course, the original book, *Peter Pan.*

---

carried there mortally wounded in 1034 after having been attacked by his enemies while hunting in a nearby forest.

Glamis Castle has been in the possession of the Lyon family since 1372, when it was given to Sir John Lyon by Robert II. Four years later Sir John married the king's daughter, Princess Joanna. The castle was altered in the 17th century and restored and enlarged in the 18th and 19th centuries. It contains some fine plaster ceilings, furniture, and paintings.

The castle is open to the public, with access to the Royal Apartments and many other rooms, and also to the fine gardens, from the end of March until the end of October only, daily from 10:30am to 5:30pm. Admission to the castle and gardens is £5.20 ($8.60) for adults, £2.70 ($4.45) for children. If you wish to visit the grounds only, the charge is £2.40 ($3.95) for adults, £1.20 ($2) for children. Buses run between Dundee and Glamis.

Where to Stay

✪ **Castleton House.** Eassie by Glamis, Forfar, Angus DD8 1SJ. ☎ **01307/840340.** Fax 01307/840506. 6 rms. TV TEL. £120 ($198) double. Children stay free in parents' room. Rates include Scottish breakfast. AE, MC, V. Drive 3 miles west of Glamis on A94.

This Victorian hotel has been restored with love and care by its owners, Maureen and William Little. In cool weather (often the case around here), you're greeted by welcoming coal fires in both the bar and public lounge, and a youthful staff that's the most considerate we've encountered in the area. Bedrooms of various sizes are furnished with reproduction antiques. Guests can have meals in the high-ceilinged dining room or the plant-filled conservatory. The chef features a set luncheon and a fixed-price dinner. The menu changes daily but is based on the freshest produce in any given season. Dishes usually include tender Angus steak and grilled or roasted Highland lamb. Fresh fish, such as North Sea monkfish, regularly appears on the menu.

Where to Dine

Strathomore Arms. Glamis. ☎ **01307/840248.** Reservations recommended. Main courses £4.95–£15 ($8.15–$24.75). MC, V. Daily noon–2pm and 6:30–9pm. CONTINENTAL/SCOTTISH.

Try this place near the castle for one of the best lunches in the area. You might begin with a freshly made soup of the day or cheddar-filled mushrooms wrapped in bacon and grilled. Another appetizer is warm breast of pigeon on a bed of tossed salad leaves. Grilled lamb cutlets are regularly featured, as is poached sole with prawns and mushrooms in a light curry sauce. You might also try filet of Angus beef in a whisky sauce.

CARNOUSTIE

Carnoustie is the home of the famous ✪ **Carnoustie Golf Links,** Links Parade (☎ **01241/853789;** fax 01241/852720). In 1999, the British Open is scheduled to be held on the Championship Course, adding an undeniable luster to this world-renowned course. Carnoustie also boasts the Burnside Course and the relatively new Buddon Links Course, which opened in the 1970s. (See chapter 4, section 1, for more information.) To reach Carnoustie from Dundee, go east 10 miles along A92, or take the coastal road, A930, which is signposted.

Where to Dine

11 Park Avenue. 11 Park Ave. ☎ **01241/853336.** Reservations recommended. Main courses £10–£15 ($16.60–$24.75). AE, DC, MC, V. Apr–Sept Tues–Sat noon–2pm and 7–10pm; Feb–Dec Tues–Sat 7–10pm. Closed Jan. SCOTTISH.

A few steps from High Street, this restaurant is the most prestigious in town. Its dignified gold-and-burgundy premises are a showcase for the cuisine of Stephen Collinson. Menu items, made with the freshest ingredients available, reflect Scottish tradition. Depending on the season, the chef might tempt you with Scottish mussels served in a white wine sauce or fillet of lamb with fresh basil and tomato-flavored port wine sauce. For dessert nothing is better than the caramelized lemon tart, or the selection of Scottish cheeses.

7 Aberdeen

130 miles NE of Edinburgh, 67 miles N of Dundee

Bordered by fine sandy beaches (delightful if you're a polar bear), Scotland's third city is often called the "Granite City," since its buildings are constructed largely of pink or gray granite, hewn from the Rubislaw quarries.

The harbor in this seaport is one of the largest fishing ports in the country, and is filled with kipper and deep-sea trawlers. The city lies on the banks of the salmon- and trout-filled Don and Dee rivers. Spanning the Don is **Brig o' Balgownie,** a steep gothic arch, begun in 1285.

Aberdeen is the capital of the oil workers of six North Sea oilfields. Their numbers have dwindled in recent years, however.

ESSENTIALS
GETTING THERE

BY PLANE   Aberdeen is served by a number of carriers, including British Airways and Air Ecosse. If you're flying directly from North America to Scotland, there's an air link from Glasgow to Aberdeen. For flight information, phone the Aberdeen Airport at ☎ **01224/722331.** The airport is about 6 miles away from the heart of town and is connected to it by a bus service.

BY TRAIN   Aberdeen has direct rail links to the major cities of Britain. SuperSaver fares, available by avoiding travel on Friday and Saturday, make the price difference between a one-way fare and a round-trip ticket negligible. Eighteen trains per day arrive from Edinburgh; a regular one-way ticket costs £31 ($51.15). Some 15 trains per day arrive from Glasgow, costing £34 ($56.10) one-way or £38 ($62.70) round- trip. Some 4 trains per day arrive from London as well, with a one-way fare of £75 ($123.75) and a round-trip fare of only £76 ($125.40). For rail information and schedules, call ☎ **0345/484950.**

BY BUS   Coach is the least expensive way to get here. Several bus companies have express routes serving Aberdeen, and many offer special round-trip fares to passen- gers avoiding travel on a Friday or Saturday. Frequent buses arrive from both Glasgow, costing £17 ($28.05) round-trip, and Edinburgh, going for £16.50 ($27.20) round-trip. There are also frequent arrivals from Inverness, a round-trip costing only £10 ($16.50). For bus information and schedules in Aberdeen, call ☎ **01224/212266.**

BY CAR   It's also easy to drive to the northeast. From the south, drive via Edinburgh over the Forth and Tay Road bridges, and take the coastal road. From the north and west, approach the area from the much improved A9, which links Perth, Inverness, and Wick.

VISITOR INFORMATION

The **Aberdeen Tourist Information Centre** is in St. Nicholas House, Broad Street, Aberdeen, Aberdeenshire AB9 1DE (☎ **01224/632727**).

SEEING THE SIGHTS

In old Aberdeen is **Aberdeen University,** a fusion of two separate colleges. King's College, dating from 1483, is the oldest school of medicine in Great Britain; Marischal College was founded in 1593.

The **Cathedral of St. Machar,** Chanonry (☎ **01224/485988**), was founded in 1131, although the present structure dates from the 15th century. Its splendid heraldic ceiling contains three rows of shields. The magnificent modern stained-glass windows are the work of Douglas Strachan. The cathedral is open daily from 9am to 5pm. Only buses 6 and 25 go right by the cathedral.

Cruickshank Botanic Garden, University of Aberdeen on St. Machar Drive (☎ **01224/272449**), displays alpines, shrubs, and many herbaceous plants, along with rock and water gardens. It's open all year, Monday through Friday from 9am

Aberdeen

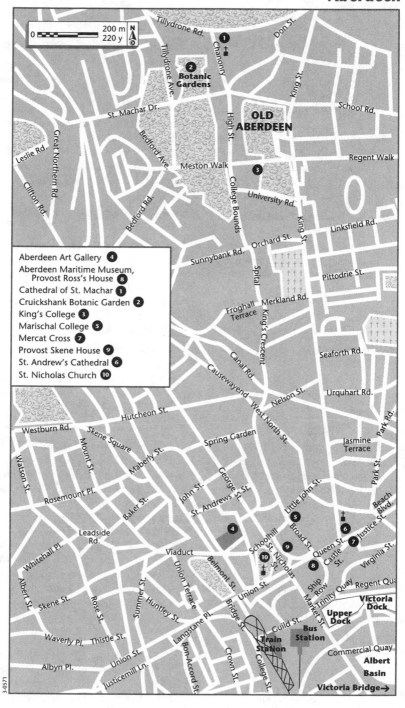

3-0571

to 4:30pm; in summer, it's also open Saturday and Sunday from 2 to 5pm. Take bus no. 20.

The **Fish Market** on Market Street near Palmerston Road is well worth a visit; it's the liveliest in Britain.

✪ **Aberdeen Art Gallery.** Schoolhill. ☎ **01224/646333.** Free admission. Mon–Sat 10am–5pm, Sun 2–5pm. Bus: 20.

Built in 1884 in a neoclassical design by A. Marshall MacKenzie, this building houses one of the most important art collections in Great Britain. It contains 18th-century portraits by Raeburn, Hogarth, Ramsay, and Reynolds, and acclaimed 20th-century artworks by Paul Nash, Ben Nicholson, and Francis Bacon. The exhibits also include excellent impressionist works by Monet, Pissarro, Sisley, and Bonnard. There's a collection of Scottish domestic silver and examples of other decorative arts. Special exhibitions and events are frequently offered.

Aberdeen Maritime Museum. Shiprow. ☎ **01224/337700.** Free admission. Mon–Sat 10am–5pm, Sun 11am–5pm. Bus: 20.

One of Scotland's finest visitor attractions, the new Aberdeen Maritime Museum tells the story of the city's long and fascinating relationship with the sea. The story is told through a unique collection of ship models, paintings, artifacts, computer interaction, and exhibitions. A major display on the offshore oil industry features a model of the Murchison oil platform. The complex is on four floors, incorporating the 1593 Provost Ross House linked by a modern glass structure to the granite Trinity Church building. Windows open onto panoramic views of the harbor.

Provost Skene House. 5 Guestrow. ☎ **01224/641086.** Free admission. Mon–Sat 10am–5pm. Bus: 20.

Provost Skene House is named for a rich merchant who was Lord Provost of Aberdeen during 1676–85. Off Broad Street, it's a museum with period rooms and artifacts of domestic life. Provost Skene's kitchen has been converted into a cafe.

A SIGHT NEARBY

Dunnottar Castle (☎ **01569/762173**) is 2 miles south of Stonehaven off A92. The best way to reach it is by a dramatic 30-minute walk from Stonehaven along the cliffs. The well-preserved ruins are on a rocky promontory towering 160 feet above the surging sea. "Dunnottar speaks with an audible voice," says an old proverb; "every cave has a record, every turret a tongue." The ruins include a great square tower and a chapel constructed in 1392. William Wallace stormed it in 1297 but failed to take it. More recently it was the setting for Zeffirelli's 1991 film of *Hamlet,* with Mel Gibson. You can reach Stonehaven from Aberdeen by taking a Bluebird Northern or Scottish CityLink bus. Departures are every 30 minutes during the day; the trip takes 30 minutes. The castle is open Easter through October, Monday through Saturday from 9am to 6pm, Sunday from 2 to 5pm. November to Easter, hours are Monday through Friday from 9am to 3:30pm. Admission is £3 ($4.95) for adults and £1 ($1.65) for children.

SHOPPING

The main shopping districts center around specialty shops on **Chapel** and **Thistle streets,** and well-known chains on **George** and **Union streets.** Of interest to collectors, **Colin Wood,** 23 Rose St. (☎ **01224/643019**), stocks furniture, wall clocks, and grandfather clocks from the 17th to the early 20th century. Their specialty, however, is maps, ranging from the Elizabethan through the Victorian eras, including a good selection of Jacobean maps. The shop also sells 17th- to early 20th-century prints of northern Scotland. You may also want to browse through the eclectic mix of small "bric-a-brac" antiques available at **Elizabeth Watt's Studio,** 69 Thistle St. (☎ **01224/647232**), where items include glass, brass, china, silver, and small furniture pieces. It's actually best known for its china and glass restoration studio, located in the back of the shop.

To trace Scottish ancestry, go to the **Aberdeen Family History Shop,** 164 King St. (☎ **01224/646323**), where membership to the Aberdeen and North East Family History Society will cost you $20 cash U.S. currency, or $25 U.S. currency if you pay by check. Once you join, you can go through a vast range of publications kept on hand to help members trace their family histories.

Quality men's suits and overcoats are available at the mill shop of the **Crombie Woolen Mill,** Grandholm Mills (☎ **01224/483201**). A multitude of gifts can be found at **Nova,** 20 Chapel St. (☎ **01224/641270**), which stocks china, silver jewelry, rugs, clothing, children's toys, cards, and gift paper. For a large selection of yarns marketed by the Westminster Trading Co., head to **Harlequin,** 65 Thistle St. (☎ **01224/635716**), which also stocks a small number of cross-stitch and tapestry kits.

WHERE TO STAY

Because of increasing numbers of tourists and business visitors to the "Granite City," Europe's offshore oil capital, hotels are likely to be heavily booked any time of year. If you haven't booked ahead, it's best to go to the **Aberdeen Tourist Information Centre,** in St. Nicholas House on Broad Street (☎ **01224/632727**). There's a wide range of accommodations, whether you prefer to stay in a family-run B&B, a guesthouse, or a hotel, and the center's staff can usually find just the right kind of lodging.

EXPENSIVE

✪ **Ardoe House.** S. Deeside Rd., Blairs, Aberdeen, Aberdeenshire AB1 5YP. ☎ **01224/867355.** Fax 01224/861283. 68 rms, 3 suites. TV TEL. £155 ($255.75) double; £210 ($346.50) suite. Children 11 and under stay free in parents' room. AE, DC, MC, V. Free parking. Drive 5 miles southwest of the center on B9077.

Known for its tranquil, scenic setting at the end of a winding drive, this Scottish baronial house stands on large grounds on the south bank of the River Dee. Imbued with charm and character, its architecture is graced with soaring turrets. Constructed back in 1878 of silver granite, it still retains much of its original Aberdeen design, including its carved oak paneling. Guests can opt for the traditional rooms in the old house or else be sheltered in a large extension with more modern units.

Dining/Entertainment: Guests relax in the drawing room and cocktail bar before going in to dinner. Naturally, salmon freshly caught in the Dee is the chef's specialty. Dinner, served only in the Garden Room, is offered nightly from 6:30 to 9:45pm, with main courses beginning at £12.95 ($21.35). Bar meals, served the same hours, range from £8.20 to £10.50 ($13.55 to $17.35).

Services: Room service, laundry, baby-sitting.

Facilities: Garden, pétanque.

Caledonian Thistle Hotel. 10–14 Union Terrace (off Union St.), Aberdeen, Aberdeenshire AB10 1WE. ☎ **01224/640233.** Fax 01224/641627. 71 rms, 6 suites. MINIBAR TV TEL. £80–£140 ($132–$231) double; £110–£185 ($181.50–$305.25) suite. Children 11 and under stay free in parents' room. AE, DC, MC, V. Free parking. Bus: 16 or 17.

The five-story Caledonian Thistle Hotel sits in a grandly detailed, stone-fronted Victorian building in the center of Aberdeen. Recent restorations have added a veneer of Georgian-era gloss to one of the most elegant series of public rooms in town. The amenity-filled rooms with double-glazed windows are at the top of a 19th-century stairwell, with Corinthian columns and a freestanding atrium. Some bathrooms have showers only, and the front rooms can be noisy. There is also elevator service. The hotel offers Elronds (see "Where to Dine," below), plus a more formal dining area, the Restaurant on the Terrace, that serves dinner nightly. Lunch is served Monday through Friday only. Parking is in a walled-in lot on a street paralleling the hotel.

✪ **Marcliffe at Pitfodels.** N. Deeside Rd., Aberdeen, Aberdeenshire AB1 9YA. ☎ 01224/ 861000. Fax 01224/868860. 42 rms. MINIBAR TV TEL. £135–£175 ($222.75–$288.75) double. AE, DC, MC, V.

On the western edge of the city, lying about a mile off A92 at the Aberdeen ring road and less than half an hour from the airport, this deluxe hotel is clearly the best in Aberdeen today, far superior to the Caledonian Thistle and the Ardoe House. The newly built, traditionally styled three-story manor house was constructed around a courtyard. It stands on 6 acres of landscaped grounds. The oriental rugs, placed on stone floors, and the tartan sofas set the decor note in the public rooms; a scattering of antiques add a grace note. The rather spacious bedrooms are furnished in Chippendale and reproduction pieces, with armchairs and desks, plus a host of extras (even fresh milk in the minibar).

Dining/Entertainment: A conservatory restaurant offers such regional dishes as Highland lamb and freshly caught Scottish salmon. There's also a more expensive restaurant favored by corporate clients in Aberdeen when entertaining out-of-town business guests. In the library lounge, guests can choose from more than 100 scotch whiskies, and in the morning at breakfast they can sample Aberdeen rowies, a local specialty like a croissant that's been flattened.

Services: 24-hour room service, laundry.

Facilities: Garden. The lack of health-club facilities is cited as the major drawback to an otherwise top-notch hostelry.

Stakis Aberdeen Hotel. 161 Springfield Rd., Aberdeen, Aberdeenshire AB9 2QH. ☎ 01224/ 313377. Fax 01224/312028. 110 rms, 2 suites. TV TEL. £115 ($189.75) double; £135 ($222.75) suite. AE, DC, MC, V. Bus: 11.

A 10-minute drive west of the center of Aberdeen off A93, this comfortable hotel built in the 1960s and renovated in 1991 has a sweeping white facade of traditional design. The windows of its 112 good-size contemporary bedrooms look over landscaped grounds. Rooms have tile-lined baths and many other extras. Some rooms have balconies with lake views; half the rooms are for nonsmokers. The leather-covered chairs of the paneled main bar offer a cozy conversation spot. You can dine in the elegant Season's Restaurant or in Rocco's Ristorante, the bistro-style Italian restaurant. The hotel invites guests to take advantage of the Leisure Club, with swimming pool, whirlpool, gym, sauna, jogging machine, sunbeds, two all-weather tennis courts, and sports training.

MODERATE

Mannofield Hotel. 447 Great Western Rd., Aberdeen, Aberdeenshire AB10 6NL. ☎ 01224/ 315888. Fax 01224/208971. 9 rms. TV TEL. £40–£69 ($66–$113.85) double. AE, MC, V. Rates include Scottish breakfast. Bus: 17, 18, or 19.

Built of silver-toned Aberdeen granite as an opulent private house around 1880, this hotel looks like a Victorian architectural fantasy, with step-shaped gables, turrets, spires, and protruding bay windows. Inside, a mahogany-and-teakwood staircase sweeps upstairs. The bedrooms, modernized into a no-nonsense monochromatic design in 1990, contain teamaking facilities. The hotel, a favorite of visiting businesspeople from other parts of Britain, contains a well-used cocktail bar and a restaurant.

The hotel stands 1 mile west of the city center with good transportation links. Bruce and Dorothy Cryle are joint owners, offering a warm Scottish welcome to visitors.

INEXPENSIVE

✪ **Jays Guest House.** 422 King St., Aberdeen, Aberdeenshire AB24 3BR. ☎ **01224/638295.** 10 rms. TV. £46–£60 ($75.90–$99) double. No credit cards. Rates include Scottish breakfast. Bus: 1, 2, 3, 4, or 7.

This is one of the nicer guesthouses in Aberdeen, mainly because of the high standards of the owner, Mrs. Alice Jennings. It's near the university and the Offshore Survival Centre. Everything runs smoothly, and the rooms are bright and airy, each newly renovated. All the attractively furnished accommodations have hot-beverage facilities and central heating.

NEARBY PLACES TO STAY

✪ **Kildrummy Castle Hotel.** Kildrummy by Alford, Aberdeenshire AB33 8RA. ☎ **019755/ 71288.** Fax 019755/71345. 16 rms. TV TEL. £130–£150 ($214.50–$247.50) double. Rates include Scottish breakfast. AE, MC, V. Closed Jan.

Kildrummy Castle Hotel, about 1 1/2 miles south of the village of Kildrummy on A97, overlooks the ruined castle of Kildrummy, 35 miles west of Aberdeen. This 19th-century gray stone mansion, set in acres of landscaped gardens, has well-equipped bedrooms, with hair dryers and tea- and coffeemakers. The public rooms have oak-paneled walls and ceilings, mullioned windows, and cushioned window seats. The drawing room and bar open onto a flagstone terrace from which you can see the gardens of the castle. Traditional Scottish food is served in the handsome dining room, including Cullen skink (smoked haddock soup), fillet of sole stuffed with smoked Scottish salmon, and Aberdeen Angus steaks. Lunch, served daily from 12:30 to 1:45pm, includes an à la carte menu and a four-course table d'hôte for £14.95 ($24.65). Dinner is from 7 to 9pm, costing £28 ($46.20) for a four-course meal.

✪ **Muchalls Castle.** Muchalls by Stonehaven, Kincardineshire AB3 2RS. ☎ **01569/731170.** Fax 01569/731480. 7 rms. TV. £110–£140 ($181.50–$231) double. Rates include Scottish breakfast. No credit cards. From the main Aberdeen–Dundee road (A90), turn off at Bridge of Muchalls (signposted Netherley), 3 miles north of Stonehaven; from Netherley Rd., go for 1 mile up the hill and turn right at the top.

Built in 1619, this is an unaltered example of a 17th-century Scottish laird's house. The house stands in 5 acres of grounds overlooking the North Sea. Its plaster ceilings are from 1624, and its Great Hall has an ornamented fireplace with a royal coat-of-arms. Lived in for four centuries without interruption, this is a rare historic place and it provides an unusual way to visit northeast Scotland.

The bedrooms are traditional and some have four-poster beds. All accommodations have private baths, except one that has private (but not *en suite*) facilities. The Turret Room is a favorite, named in honor of its matched pair of towers and its large bed canopied in jade silk. The original laird's bedroom has a gold-and-crimson canopy over the bed, reputedly slept under by James II. The ground-floor bedrooms are in a series of vaulted storerooms. The original 17th-century vaulted kitchen is now the main dining room. A four-course dinner, including Scottish and continental cuisine, is served every evening by candlelight.

✪ **Pittodrie House Hotel.** Chapel of Garioch Rd., Pitcaple, Aberdeenshire AB5 9HS. ☎ **01467/681444.** Fax 01467/681648. 27 rms. TV TEL. £140 ($231) double. AE, DC, MC, V. Rates include Scottish breakfast.

Pittodrie House Hotel was originally one of the castles in the area. Dating from 1490, it was burned down and rebuilt in 1675 as a family home, and that changed into a country-house hotel when Royal Deeside came into prominence through Queen Victoria's adoption of Balmoral as her holiday retreat. The public rooms have antiques, oil paintings, and open fires. The elegant restaurant serves venison, grouse, partridge, pheasant, or woodcock, depending on the season, and fresh fish. Dinners are served daily from 7:30 to 8:45pm (last orders), a five-course table d'hôte costing £29 ($47.85). Bar lunches are served Monday through Saturday from 12:30 to 1:30pm. The hotel is 21 miles northwest of Aberdeen, 1³/₄ miles southwest of Pitcaple near Inverurie.

✪ **Thainstone House Hotel & Country Club.** Inverurie, Aberdeenshire, AB51 9NT. ☎ **01467/621643.** Fax 01467/625084. 48 rms. TV TEL. £84–£112 ($138.60–$184.80) double. AE, DC, MC, V. Rates include Scottish breakfast.

One of the most elegant country hotels in northeast Scotland, set on 40 acres of ground 14 miles northwest of Aberdeen, the Thainstone House Hotel can be both a retreat and a center for exploring this history-rich part of Scotland, including the Malt Whisky Trail. A four-star luxury hotel, this establishment is housed in a Palladian-style mansion whose adornments give it the air of a country club. Entrance is through a grand portal up an elegant stairway. The estate has dim origins in the Dark Ages, and a property that stood here in the 1700s was torched by the Jacobites. James Wilson, the owner, not only escaped the fire but fled to America where he was later to sign the Declaration of Independence. Today's mansion was designed by Archibald Simpson, the famed architect of many of Aberdeen's public buildings. The high ceilings, columns, neoclassical plaster reliefs, and cornices evoke Simpson's trip to Italy. A new section has been added to the original house that skillfully blends the old with the new. The rooms are elegantly furnished and contain many amenities including direct-dial phone, TV, radio, beverage-making equipment, hair dryer, and trouser press. Several rooms have original four-poster beds.

Dining/Entertainment: In the Georgian ambience of Simpson's Restaurant, an award-winning chef turns out a continental and a "Taste of Scotland" menu with a light, inventive touch. Dining is more informal in Cammie's Grill, where local game is served along with Aberdeen Angus beef, seafood from the coast, and fresh salmon and trout from the Rivers Spey and Don.

Services: Room service, laundry, baby-sitting.

Facilities: Country Club Jacuzzi and steam room, fully equipped "trimnasium," snooker room, swimming pool designed in the style of an ancient Roman bath.

WHERE TO DINE

Atlantis. In the Melecca Hotel, 349 Great Western Rd. ☎ **01224/591403.** Reservations recommended. Main courses £10–£26 ($16.50–$42.90). AE, DC, MC, V. Mon–Fri noon–2pm and 7–10pm, Sat 7–10pm. Bus: 23. SEAFOOD.

Atlantis is one of the best seafood restaurants in Aberdeen. You can enjoy several preparations of lobster, fish chowder, and an array of sole, scampi, and halibut. Some meat dishes are offered, and the fresh vegetables, salads, and desserts will complete your meal.

Elrond's Cafe Bar and Restaurant. In the Caledonian Thistle Hotel, 10–14 Union Terrace. ☎ **01224/640233.** Main courses £6–£9 ($9.50–$14.20); pot of tea with a pastry £2 ($3.30). AE, DC, MC, V. Restaurant: Mon–Sat noon–2pm and 5:30–11:45pm, Sun 5:30–11pm. Cafe bar: Mon–Sat 10am–midnight, Sun 10am–11pm. Bus: 16 or 17. INTERNATIONAL.

White marble floors, a long oak-capped bar, evening candlelight, and a garden-inspired decor create the ambience here. No one will mind if you show up just for a drink, a pot of tea, a midday salad or snack, or a full-blown feast. Specialties include burgers, steaks, pastas, fresh fish, lemon chicken suprême, chicken Kiev, and vegetarian dishes. This is not the world's greatest food, but it's a popular venue nevertheless. Although it's in one of Aberdeen's well-known hotels, it has a separate entrance.

Ferryhill House. Bon Accord St., Aberdeen, Aberdeenshire AB1 5NL. ☎ **01224/590867.** Fax 01224/586947. Reservations recommended Sat–Sun. Main courses £6–£12 ($9.90–$19.80). AE, DC, MC, V. Bus: 22. INTERNATIONAL.

In its own park and garden on the city's southern outskirts, half a mile from the center, Ferryhill House was built 250 years ago by the region's most successful brick maker and quarry master. It has Georgian detailing and an interior whose rich panels and ceiling beams have accumulated many decades of patina. It has one of the region's largest collections of single-malt whiskies—more than 140 brands. There's a fireplace for chilly afternoons and an outdoor beer garden for midsummer. Food items include shrimp or vegetable tempura, steak jambalaya, ploughman's platters, fried fillet of haddock or plaice, pastas, and chili.

The establishment also rents nine modestly furnished bedrooms, all with bath, TV, and phone. The double rate is £75 ($123.75) Sunday through Thursday and £55 ($90.75) Friday and Saturday. A Scottish breakfast is included.

Gerard's. 50 Chapel St. ☎ **01224/639500.** Reservations recommended. Lunch main courses £8.50–£13 ($14–$21.45); business lunch £8.50 ($14) 2 courses, £10.55 ($17.40) 3 courses; dinner main courses £9–£17.95 ($14.85–$29.60), fixed-price dinner £16.95 ($27.95); cafe main courses £6–£9 ($9.90–$14.85). AE, DC, MC, V. Restaurant: daily noon–2:30pm and 6–10:45pm. Cafe: daily 10am–midnight; meals, noon–2:30pm and 5:30–10:30pm. FRENCH/INTERNATIONAL.

Restaurateur Gerard Flecher's popular eatery is inspired by the cuisine of France, but often makes a nod to other regions as well. The restaurant is split into the more formal main dining room and the relaxed Café Colmar, which has a separate entrance at the rear of the building. In Gerard's, expect such dishes as pan-fried maigrette of duck and Cumberland sausage with a five-bean fricassee served on a cabernet sauvignon jus, or medaillons of Aberdeen Angus filet on a potato crostini with oyster mushrooms, Provençal salsa, and stuffed tomato served on an *au poivre* sauce. In the cafe, dishes include the likes of roasted Mediterranean vegetables with lemongrass and a spicy Thai sauce served in a pastry case on a bed of rice pilaf, or breast of chicken filled with creamed lemon cheese in a leek cream sauce. The bar stocks a wide range of single-malts and ports, along with French wines unavailable anywhere else in the region.

✪ **Silver Darling.** Pocra Quay, Footdee. ☎ **01224/576229.** Reservations recommended. Main courses £15.50–£17.50 ($25.60–$28.90); lunch £4.95–£9.50 ($8.15–$15.65). AE, DC, MC, V. Mon–Fri noon–2pm and 7–9:30pm, Sat 7–9:30pm. Closed Dec 23–Jan 8. Bus: 14 or 15. FRENCH/SEAFOOD.

The Silver Darling (a local nickname for herring) is a definite asset to the dining picture in Aberdeen. Occupying a former Customs House at the mouth of the harbor, it spins a culinary fantasy around the freshest catch of the day. You might begin with a savory fish soup, almost Mediterranean in flavor, then go on to one of the barbecued fish dishes. Salmon is the invariable favorite of the more discriminating diners.

ABERDEEN AFTER DARK

This is the regional spot for nightlife, whether you're in the mood for fine arts performances or pop music. Tickets to events at most venues are available by calling the **Aberdeen Box Office** (☎ 01224/641122).

THE PERFORMING ARTS

The **Aberdeen Arts Centre,** King Street (☎ 01224/635208), has a 350-seat theater that is rented to professional and amateur groups hosting everything from poetry readings and plays to musical concerts in various styles. Ticket prices and performance times vary; call for information. Also on the premises is a 60-seat video projection theater that screens world cinema offerings, with tickets costing £3.50 ($5.75) for adults, and £2.50 ($4.15) for seniors and children. A large gallery room holds monthlong exhibitions of visual art in many different styles and mediums. A cafe/bar, offering light meals and drinks, is open during performance times.

Near Tarves, about 20 miles from Aberdeen, you'll find **Haddo House,** which hosts operas, ballets, and plays from Easter to October. An early 20th-century hall built of pitch pine, Haddo House is based on the Canadian town halls that Lord Aberdeen saw in his travels abroad. The hall was built for the people of the surrounding area on Aberdeen family land and the present Lady Aberdeen still lives in a house on this property. Follow B9005, 18 miles north to Tarves, then follow the National Trust and Haddo House signs 2 miles east to arrive here. Ticket prices range from £5 to £12 ($8.25 to $19.80). A stylish cafe offers light meals, tea, and other beverages daily, Easter to October, from 11am to 6pm.

The 19th-century **Music Hall,** Union Street (☎ 01224/632080), is an ornately guilded 1,282-seat theater that stages concerts by the Scottish National Orchestra, the Scottish Chamber Orchestra, visiting international orchestras, and pop bands, as well as hosting ceilidhs, crafts fairs, and book sales. Tickets for year-round musical performances average £7.50 to £8.50 ($12.40 to $14). The **Aberdeen International Youth Festival** is held annually in this hall in August, and features youth orchestras, choirs, and dance and theater ensembles. Daytime and evening performances are held, and tickets range from £1 to £20 ($1.65–$33). Contact the Music Hall or the Aberdeen Box Office for more information.

The only theater in the world built entirely of granite, **His Majesty's Theatre,** Rosemount Viaduct (☎ 01224/637788), was designed by Frank Matcham in 1906. The interior is late Victorian, and the 1,445-seat theater stages operas, dance performances, dramas, classical concerts, musicals, and comedy shows year-round. Tickets range from £5.50 to £34.50 ($9.05 to $56.95).

VARIETY & LIVE MUSIC

A mixed venue is the **Lemon Tree,** 5 W. North St. (☎ 01224/642230). Its 150-seat theater stages dance recitals, theatrical productions, and stand-up comedy, with tickets generally priced between £2.50 and £3.50 ($4.15 and $5.75). On Saturday, there is often a matinee at 2 or 3pm, and evening performances are at 7pm. Downstairs, the 500-seat cafe-theater hosts folk, rock, blues, jazz, and comedy acts, with shows starting between 8 and 10pm. On Wednesday night the Folk Club is on stage, and other nights have varied offerings, except Monday and Tuesday, when it's closed. On Sunday afternoon there is free live jazz, making this a popular place for a light brunch. Ticket prices for evening shows vary from £2 to £10 ($3.30 to $16.50).

Live jazz can be heard at no charge every Saturday night at the **Masada Continental Lounge,** Rosemount Viaduct (☎ 01224/641587). This old traditional bar is open nightly and serves Tennant's Lager, McEwan's Export, Blackthorn Cider, Guinness, and Murphy's on tap.

DANCE CLUBS

The dance scene is important in Aberdeen. **DeNiro's,** 120 Union St. (☎ **01224/ 640641**), has dancing to house music from 10pm until 2am on Friday, Saturday, and Sunday only. The cover charge on Friday is £6 ($9.90), on Saturday £8 ($13.20), and on Sunday only £2 ($3.30). Named after the inn where it's housed, **Hotel Metro,** 17 Market St. (☎ **01224/583275**), offers dancing 7 nights a week from 10pm until 2am. Tuesday night the club features dancing to a live country-and-western band, with disco on the other nights. The cover charge on Monday is £1 ($1.65) before 11pm and £2 ($3.30) after; on Tuesday £2.50 ($4.15) all night; on Wednesday night men pay £2 ($3.30) and women enter free; on Thursday and Sunday everyone pays £2 ($3.30) all night, and on Friday and Saturday the cover is £2 ($3.30) before 11pm and £3 ($4.95) after.

The ever-popular **Ministry,** 16 Dee St. (☎ **01224/211661**), is a sophisticated dance club that features different theme nights throughout the week. On Monday, Moist is a popular student night. Friday's Rapture is when guest deejays from England and America take over the sound system—New York's hottest deejay of the moment, or perhaps a celebrity such as Boy George. Saturday Club Ministry packs the dancers in; Wednesday is unnamed; Sunday features Wicked, a night of dancing to hard-rock music. Cover charges range from £1 to £12 ($1.65–$19.80) throughout the week, depending on who the deejay is and what's happening.

PUBS

✪ **Prince of Wales,** 7 St. Nicholas Lane (☎ **01224/640597**), in the heart of the shopping district, is the best place in the old city center to go for a pint. Furnished with pews in screened booths, it boasts Aberdeen's longest bar counter. At lunch it's bustling with regulars who devour chicken in cider sauce or Guinness pie. On tap are such beers as Buchan Gold and Courage Directors. Orkney Dark Island is also sold here. Open 11am to midnight on Monday through Saturday and 12:30pm to midnight on Sunday.

A SIDE TRIP FROM ABERDEEN

✪ **Archeolink.** Oyne, near Insch. ☎ **01464/851500.** Adults £3.90 ($6.45), seniors and ages 5–16 £2.35 ($3.90), family ticket £10 ($16.50). Mar–Oct, daily 9:30am–5pm; Nov–Feb, Mon–Fri 11am–4pm, Sat–Sun 10am–4pm. From Aberdeen, drive 23 miles NW along the A96, following signs to Inverness. Then turn north onto B9002, driving another 1 1/2 miles, following signs to Archeolink and the hamlet of Oyne.

Although there are more than 4,000 prehistoric sites scattered throughout Aberdeenshire, this museum—inaugurated in 1997—is the most historically accurate, the most imaginative, and the most ecologically sensitive. Opened in 1997 and funded by the European Regional Development Fund (ERDF), this museum occupies 40 "big sky" acres whose centerpiece, Berryhill, contains a ruined Iron Age fortress.

Here, lavish landscaping encourages visits by both able-bodied hill climbers and—thanks to a series of ramps—visitors with wheelchairs. The overwhelming preoccupation involves a celebration of the epic cultural changes that have swept over northeastern Scotland throughout the previous 70 centuries. The museum's centerpiece is a massive concrete dome, most of which lies beneath several feet of earth and grass. Your tour begins with a 20-minute film that segues from views over the surrounding landscapes to equivalent landscapes of 7,000 years ago. Dioramas and illustrations, many of them computerized, provide explanations and insights into the region's stone circles and dolmens, as well as a gruesome re-creation of Iron Age battles and sometimes frenzied hunting scenes. Especially intriguing is a gallery devoted to myths and legends. A narration of ancient tales often speaks to the heart of an audience's collective unconscious. Sometimes pagan and early Christian images are mixed within the same tale. One subdivision of the site, Archeoquest, provides computer-generated, personalized information on other prehistoric sites within Aberdeenshire, with directions and access information printed on takeaway maps.

SIDE TRIPS IN CASTLE COUNTRY

Aberdeen is the center of "castle country"—40 inhabited castles lie within a 40-mile radius.

Castle Fraser. Sauchen, near Kemnay. ☎ **01330/833463.** Admission £4.20 ($6.95) adults, £2.80 ($4.60) children, free for age 4 and under. Easter weekend and Oct, Sat–Sun 2–5pm; May–June, daily 1:30–5pm; July–Aug, daily 11am–5:30pm; Sept, daily 1:30–5:30pm. Closed Nov–Mar. Head 3 miles south of Kemnay, 16 miles west of Aberdeen, off A944.

One of the most impressive of the fortresslike castles of Mar, Castle Fraser stands in a 25-acre parkland and woodsy setting. The sixth laird, Michael Fraser, began the structure in 1575, and his son finished it in 1636. Its Great Hall is spectacular and you can wander around the grounds, which include an 18th-century walled garden.

Kildrummy Castle. Hwy. A97, Kildrummy. ☎ **019755/71331.** Admission £1.50 ($2.45) adults, £1 ($1.65) seniors, 75p ($1.25) children. Easter–Sept, Mon–Sat 9:30am–6pm, Sun 2–6pm; Oct–Nov, Mon–Sat 9:30am–4pm, Sun 2–4pm. Closed Dec–Easter. Take A97, 35 miles west of Aberdeen; it's signposted off A97, 10 miles west of Alford.

The ruins of the ancient seat of the earls of Mar, this is the most extensive example of a 13th-century castle in Scotland. You can see the four round towers, the hall, and the chapel from the original structure. The great gatehouse and other remains date from the 16th century. The castle played a major role in Scottish history up to 1715, when it was dismantled.

✪ **Fyvie Castle.** Turriff, on the Aberdeen–Banff road. ☎ **01651/891266.** Admission £4 ($6.60) adults, £2.70 ($4.45) seniors and children. Apr–June and Sept, daily 1:30–5:30pm; July–Aug, daily 11am–5:30pm; Oct Sat–Sun 1:30–5:30pm. Closed Nov–Mar. Lies in the hamlet of Fyvie, 8 miles southeast of Turiff and 7 miles northwest of Old Meldrum. Fyvie lies beside the A947, 23 miles NW of Aberdeen.

The National Trust for Scotland opened this castle to the public in 1986. The oldest part of the castle, dating from the 13th century, has been called the grandest existing example of Scottish baronial architecture. There are five towers, named after Fyvie's five families—the Prestons, Melddrums, Setons, Gordons, and Leiths—who lived here over five centuries. Originally built in a royal hunting forest, Fyvie means "deer hill" in Gaelic. The interior, created by the first Lord Leith of Fyvie, a steel magnate, reflects the opulence of the Edwardian era. His collections contain arms and armor, 16th-century tapestries, and important artworks by Raeburn, Gainsborough, and Romney. The castle is rich in ghosts, curses, and legends.

8 Banchory

118 miles NE of Edinburgh, 17 miles W of Aberdeen, 55 miles NE of Dundee

In lower Deeside, this pleasant resort is rich in woodland and river scenery. From this base, you can take excursions to two of the most popular castles in the Grampian region, Crathes and Craigievar.

ESSENTIALS
GETTING THERE

BY TRAIN   Go to Aberdeen (see below), then take a connecting bus the rest of the way. For information and schedules, call ☎ **0345/484950.**

BY BUS   A Bluebird bus runs between the bus station on Guild Street in Aberdeen and Braemar, going via Banchory. The one-way fare is £3 ($4.95). For more information, call ☎ **01224/212266** in Aberdeen.

BY CAR   From Aberdeen, head west along A93; or from Braemar, head east along A93.

VISITOR INFORMATION

A year-round **tourist information office** is on Bridge Street (☎ **01330/822000**). It is open only from March through October.

SEEING THE SIGHTS

✪ **Crathes Castle and Gardens.** Banchory. ☎ **01330/844525.** Admission £4.50 ($7.45) adults, £3 ($4.95) children and senior citizens; £12.80 ($21.10) family ticket. Grounds and park: daily 10:30am–sunset. Castle: visitor center, shop, restaurant, and adventure area, Good Friday–Oct, daily 11am–5:30pm; closed Nov–Good Friday.

This castle 2 miles east of Banchory has royal historical associations dating from 1323, when the lands of Leys were granted to the Burnett family by King Robert the Bruce. The Horn of Leys, said to have been given by the Bruce to symbolize the gift, is in the Great Hall. The castle's features include remarkable late 16th-century painted ceilings. The garden is a composite of eight separate gardens that give a display all year. The great yew hedges date from 1702. The grounds are ideal for nature study, and there are five trails, including a long-distance layout with ranger service. The complex includes a licensed restaurant, a visitor center with permanent exhibitions, a souvenir shop, a wayfaring course, picnic areas, and a parking lot.

✪ **Craigievar Castle.** Hwy. A980, 6 miles south of Alford. ☎ **013398/83635.** Admission £5.50 ($9.05) adults, £3.70 ($6.10) seniors and children. Castle: May–Sept, daily 1:30–4:45pm; closed Oct–Apr. Grounds: year-round, daily 9:30am–sunset.

Structurally unchanged since its completion in 1626, Craigievar Castle is an exceptional tower house where Scottish baronial architecture reached its pinnacle of achievement. It has contemporary plaster ceilings in nearly all its rooms. The castle had been continuously lived in by the descendants of the builder, William Forbes, until it came under the care of the National Trust for Scotland in 1963. The family collection of furnishings is complete.

Some 4 miles from the castle, near Lumphanan, is **Macbeth's Cairn,** where the historical Macbeth is supposed to have fought his last battle.

WHERE TO STAY & DINE

Banchory Lodge. Dee St., Banchory, Kincardineshire AB31 3HS. ☎ **01330/822625.** Fax 01330/825019. 22 rms. TV TEL. £110–£130 ($181.50–$214.50) double. AE, DC, MC, V. Rates include half board.

Banchory Lodge is an 18th-century country house with much Georgian charm. It's on the banks of the Dee, where the Dee joins the Water of the Feugh. Guests are accommodated in well-furnished bedrooms, some of which overlook the river; others are in a deluxe annex added in 1994. In the dining room, furnishings and decor are in period style. Specialties include fresh Dee salmon and Aberdeen Angus roast beef. Guests can fish from the lawn or in one of the hotel's boats by arrangement.

✪ **Raemoir House.** Hwy. A980, Banchory, Kincardineshire AB31 4ED. ☎ **01330/824884.** Fax 01330/822171. 28 rms, 4 suites. TV TEL. £85–£95 ($140.25–$156.75) double; from £125 ($206.25) suite. AE, DC, MC, V. Rates include Scottish breakfast. Turn off A93 at the eastern end of Banchory onto A980 (Raemoir Rd.); the hotel entrance is at the junction 2 miles down the road.

Raemoir House is an 18th-century manor standing on 3,500 acres of grounds with such sporting attractions as shooting, fishing, and riding. It lies 2½ miles north of Banchory on A980. A journey into nostalgia, the hotel has a ballroom, fine tapestries, and log fires burning in the colder months. The rooms are handsomely decorated and most of them are quite large. Some superior rooms have paneled walls hung with tapestries.

What is so lovely about Scotland is its curious mixture—in this case, an 18th-century manor house with its own helipad. The hotel is run just like a private house. The adjoining 16th-century Ha' House was once used by Mary Queen of Scots.

Dining/Entertainment: Meals are served in an attractive Georgian dining room and feature a standard repertoire of familiar dishes, rather well done. Service is informal and prompt. Bar lunches are offered Monday through Saturday for £6 to £12 ($9.90 to $19.80). A fixed-price dinner in the evening costs £25.50 ($42.05) and you can also order à la carte.

Services: Room service (7am to 11pm), laundry, baby-sitting.

Facilities: Helipad, garden, solarium, sauna; there's an all-weather tennis court and a nine-hole pitch-and-putt course on the grounds.

Tor-Na-Coille. Inchmarlo Rd., Banchory, Kincardieshire AB31 4AB. ☎ **01330/822242.** Fax 01330/824012. 22 rms. TV TEL. £95 ($156.75) double. Children 11 and under stay free in parents' room. AE, DC, MC, V. Rates include Scottish breakfast. Closed Dec 25–27.

Tor-Na-Coille is an 1873 country-house hotel—really a Victorian ivy-clad mansion—standing on its own wooded grounds of about 6 acres. The public rooms are suitably spacious and comfortable, and the whisky always tastes good in the modern bar. If you're on your way to see Balmoral Castle or to attend the Highland Gathering at Braemar, you can relax here and enjoy the gracious hospitality, as did Charlie Chaplin and his family, who once used the place as a retreat. The bedrooms, many of which are quite large and restful, have radios and coffeemakers. The hotel is interesting architecturally and the room assigned to you may have a lot of character.

Dining/Entertainment: Lunches are light meals in the bar, including smoked venison sausage blended with rum and red wine. At night your meal is accompanied by music from an accordion player, as is Sunday brunch. This place might be your chance to try real Scottish salmon (the salmon leap at the Falls of Feugh nearby). Dinner is likely to feature the chef's special pheasant. The hotel has a high reputation for its food. Dinner costs £23.50 ($38.80).

Services: 24-hour room service, baby-sitting, laundry.

Facilities: Deeside Indoor Sporting Club, with two indoor bowling alleys and four snooker tables, plus two squash courts outdoors.

9 Ballater

111 miles N of Edinburgh, 41 miles W of Aberdeen, 67 miles NE of Perth, 70 miles SE of Inverness

On the Dee River, with the Grampian mountains in the background, Ballater is a holiday resort center. The town still centers around its Station Square, where the royal family used to be photographed as they arrived to spend holidays. The railway is now closed. From Ballater you can drive west to view the scenery of Glen Muick and Lochnagar, where you'll see herds of deer.

ESSENTIALS
GETTING THERE

BY TRAIN Go to Aberdeen (see below) and continue the rest of the way by connecting bus. For information and schedules, call ☎ **0345/484950.**

BY BUS Regular buses run daily from Aberdeen west to Ballater. The bus station in Aberdeen is on Guild Street (call ☎ **01224/212266** for information about schedules), beside the train station. Bus no. 201 from Braemar runs to Ballater. A one-way fare is £3 ($4.95).

BY CAR From Aberdeen, head west along A93. From Braemar, go east along A93 to reach Ballater.

VISITOR INFORMATION

The summer-only **tourist information office** is at Station Square (☎ **013397/ 55306**).

SEEING BALMORAL

✪ **Balmoral Castle.** 7 miles west off A93, Balmoral, Ballater. ☎ **013397/42334.** Admission £3.50 ($5.75) adults, £2.50 ($4.15) senior citizens, £1 ($1.65) ages 5–16, free for age 4 and under. Apr 10–May 30, Mon–Sat 10am–5pm; June 1–Aug 2, daily 10am–5pm. Closed Aug 3–Apr 9. Crathie bus from Aberdeen to the Crathie station; Balmoral Castle is signposted from there (¹/₄-mile walk).

"This dear paradise" is how Queen Victoria described Balmoral Castle, rebuilt in the Scottish baronial style by her beloved Albert. Today Balmoral is still a private residence of the British sovereign. Albert, Victoria's prince consort, leased the property in 1848 and bought it in 1852. As the original castle of the Farquharsons proved too small, the present edifice was built, completed in 1855. Its principal feature is a 100-foot tower.

Balmoral is 8 miles from Banchory. Of the actual castle, only the ballroom is open to the public; it houses an exhibition of pictures, porcelain, and works of art. On the grounds are many memorials to the royal family. In addition to the gardens there are country walks, pony trekking (a 1-hour ride costs £15/$24.75), souvenir shops, and a refreshment room.

SHOPPING

Countrywear, 15 and 35 Bridge Streets ☎ **013397/55453**), offers country clothing, guns, ammunition, fishing tackle, and other outdoor-related items. At no. 35, a range of women's clothing, including handknits, woolens, and tartans, is sold. **Goodbrand Knitwear,** 1 Braemar Rd. (☎ **013397/55947**), mainly sells Scottish machine-made knitwear, with a few hand-knitted pieces thrown in. Clothing for children, men, and women is available in Shetland wool and lambswool.

McEwan Gallery, on A939, 1 mile west of Ballater (☎ **013397/55429**), has been selling Scottish paintings, ranging from 17th-century works to contemporary pieces, for 25 years. They also have a large section of antiquarian books, mainly Scottish and clan histories, as well as books on golf.

Dee Valley Confectioners, Station Square (☎ **013397/55499**), manufactures all its own sweets. Among the delectables sold are "hard boilings" (hard sugar candies), macaroon bars, toffee, and shortbread.

WHERE TO STAY

Craigendarroch Hotel and Country Club. Braemar Rd., Ballater, Aberdeenshire AB35 5XA. ☎ **013397/55858.** Fax 013397/55447. 39 rms, 5 suites. TV TEL. £138 ($227.70) double;

£208 ($343.20) suite. AE, DC, MC, V. Rates include half board in the Club House Bistro; £10 ($16.50) per person supplement for half board in The Oaks. Take A93 a few minutes' drive outside Ballater heading toward Braemar.

The hotel, built in the Scottish baronial style, is set amid old trees on a 28-acre estate. The 20th-century comfort has been added, but the owners have tried to maintain a 19th-century aura. The public rooms include a regal oak staircase and a large sitting room. The fair-size bedrooms open onto views of the village of Ballater and the River Dee. Guest rooms are furnished in individual styles, and all have radios, hair dryers, trouser presses, private baths (with showers), and small refrigerators (not minibars). The public facilities are luxurious, especially the study with oak paneling, a log fire, and book-lined shelves.

Dining/Entertainment: The elegant dining choice is The Oaks (see below), but you can dine less expensively in the Club House Bistro.

Services: 24-hour room service, laundry/dry cleaning, baby-sitting.

Facilities: The Leisure Club includes a spa pool, two swimming pools, a sauna, and a solarium, along with various games and a beauty salon. Tennis courts are outside, and there's a dry ski slope.

✪ **Monaltrie Hotel.** 5 Bridge Square, Ballater, Aberdeenshire AB35 5QJ. ☎ **013397/55417.** Fax 013397/55180. 25 rms. TV TEL. £50–£70 ($82.50–$115.50) double. Rates include Scottish breakfast. AE, DC, MC, V.

This hotel, built in 1835 of Aberdeen granite, was the first hotel in the region. It accommodated the clients of a now-defunct spa, which used to be at the opposite end of the Royal Bridge. Today the hotel bustles with a contemporary clientele who come for the live music in its pub and for the savory food served in its two restaurants. The more unusual of the two is a Thai restaurant, which serves dinner only Thursday through Tuesday from 7 to 10pm. Maintained by the Thai-born Laddawan Anderson, it offers a four-course fixed-price Thai meal for £16.95 ($27.95). Each of the bedrooms contains an unobtrusive monochromatic decor and comfortable beds. The hotel is a 4-minute walk east of the center of town.

WHERE TO DINE

Green Inn. 9 Victoria Rd., Ballater, Aberdeenshire AB35 5QQ. ☎ **013397/55701.** Reservations required. Fixed-price menu £21 ($34.65) for 2 courses, £23.50 ($38.80) for 3 courses; fixed-price Sun lunch £9.25 ($15.25) for 2 courses, £12.25 ($20.20) for 3 courses. MC, V. Mon–Sat 7–9:30pm, Sun 12:30–1:45pm and 7–9pm. Closed the first week in Jan and 2 weeks in Oct. SCOTTISH.

In the heart of town, this pink-granite inn was a temperance hotel when it was built in 1840. That condition has now been rectified. It is one of the finest dining rooms in town, especially for traditional Scottish dishes. The chef places his emphasis on local produce, including home-grown vegetables when available. In season, loin of venison is served with a bramble sauce, and you can always count on fresh salmon and the best of Angus beef.

Three very simply furnished double bedrooms are rented here, all with private bath (with shower) and TV. The half-board rate is £49.50 ($81.70) per person.

✪ **The Oaks Restaurant.** In the Craigendarroch Hotel and Country Club, Braemar Rd. ☎ **013397/55858.** Reservations strongly recommended. Fixed-price 4-course dinner £25 ($41.25); fixed-price Sun lunch £12.75 ($21.05). AE, DC, MC, V. Mon–Sat 7–10:30pm, Sun 12:30–2:30pm and 7–10:30pm. Take A93, 1 mile west of Ballater. BRITISH.

The most glamorous restaurant in the region, The Oaks (Craigendarroch means "Hill of the Oaks" in Gaelic) is in the century-old mansion that was originally built by the "marmalade kings" of Britain, the Keiller family. (Keiller marmalade is still a household word throughout the U.K.) This is the most upscale of the restaurants in a resort complex that includes hotel rooms, time-share villas, and access to a nearby golf course. The daily menu includes such appetizers as a warm salad of queen scallops with bacon, mixed greens, potato, and a grapeseed oil dressing or venison and duck terrine flavored with orange and brandy and served with a warm black conch vinaigrette. Main courses are more straightforward, including such selections as roast rack of lamb, breast of Grampian chicken, loin of venison, or filet of Aberdeen Angus beef.

BALLATER AFTER DARK

The **Coach House Hotel Pub,** 1 Netherley Place (☎ 013397/55462), is an old pub that has been refurbished as a contemporary bar. Locals gather here during the evening. Every other Sunday, there's karaoke. But the real draw is conversation and on-tap selections of Guinness, Tennant's Lager, 70 Shilling, and 80 Shilling. **Monaltrie Hotel Pub,** 5 Bridge Square (☎ 013397/55417), and its host hotel have been around for 200 years, and the ambience here is very old world, with a beamed ceiling and lots of hardwood. On Friday night there's a band, usually country-and-western, and a cover charge. On tap, you'll be able to choose from Guinness, Theakston 80 Shilling, or McEwan's Lager.

10 Braemar

85 miles N of Edinburgh, 58 miles W of Aberdeen, 51 miles N of Perth

In the heart of some of Grampian's most beautiful scenery, Braemar is known for its castle. It's also a good center for exploring the area that includes Balmoral Castle (see "Ballater," above) and is home to the most famous of the Highland gatherings (see below). This Highland village is set against a massive backdrop of hills, covered with heather in summer, where Clunie Water joins the River Dee. The massive **Cairn Toul** towers over Braemar, reaching a height of 4,241 feet.

ESSENTIALS
GETTING THERE

BY TRAIN   Take the train to Aberdeen (see below), then continue the rest of the way by bus. For information and schedules, call ☎ 0345/484950.

BY BUS   Regular buses run daily from Aberdeen west to Braemar. The one-way fare is £5 ($8.25). The bus station in Aberdeen is on Guild Street (call ☎ 01224/212266 for information about schedules), beside the train station.

BY CAR   Two excellent routes extend from the south, M6 and A1. Head for Perth and follow the Braemar signs from M90.

VISITOR INFORMATION

The year-round **Braemar Tourist Office** is in The Mews, Mar Road (☎ 013397/41600).

SPECIAL EVENTS

The spectacular ✪ **Royal Highland Gathering** takes place annually in the Princess Royal and Duke of Fife Memorial Park, in late August or early September. The queen herself often attends the Gathering. These ancient games are thought to have originated with King Malcolm Canmore. That chieftain ruled much of Scotland at the time of the Norman conquest of England, and he selected his hardiest warriors from all the clans for a "keen and fair contest."

For more information, call the tourist office (see "Visitor Information," above; also see "Highland Games & Gatherings," in chapter 2). Braemar is overrun with visitors during the Gathering—anyone thinking of attending would be wise to reserve accommodations anywhere within a 20-mile radius of Braemar not later than early April.

EXPLORING THE AREA

If you're a royal family watcher, you might be able to spot members of the family, even the queen, at **Crathie Church,** 9 miles east of Braemar on A93 (☎ 013397/422208). They attend Sunday services here when they're in residence. Services are at 11:30am; otherwise the church is open to view April to October only, Monday through Saturday from 9:30am to 5:30pm and Sunday from 2 to 5:30pm.

Nature lovers may want to drive to the **Linn of Dee,** 6 miles west of Braemar, a narrow chasm on the River Dee, which is a local beauty spot. Other beauty spots include Glen Muick, Loch Muick, and Lochnagar. An unmanned **Glenmuick Wildlife Trust Visitor Centre,** reached by a minor road, is located in Glen Muick, off the South Deeside road. You can pick up leaflets here, but for more information contact the Memorial Ranger Service at ☎ 013397/55059. An access road joins B976 at a point 16 miles east of Braemar. The tourist office (see above) will give you a map pinpointing these beauty spots.

✪ **Braemar Castle.** On the Aberdeen–Ballater–Perth road (A93). ☎ 013397/41219. Admission £2.50 ($4.15) adults, £2 ($3.30) seniors and students, £1 ($1.65) ages 5–15; free for age 4 and under. Mon after Easter to Oct 15, Sat–Thurs 10am–6pm. Closed Oct 16 to Easter. Take A93 ¹/₂ mile northeast of Braemar.

This romantic 17th-century castle is a fully furnished private residence of architectural grace, scenic charm, and historical interest. It's the seat of Capt. A. A. C. Farquharson of Invercauld. Opening onto the Dee River, it was built in 1628 by the earl of Mar. John Farquharson of Inveraray, the "Black Colonel," attacked and burned it in 1689. The castle has barrel-vaulted ceilings and an underground prison and is known for its remarkable star-shaped defensive curtain wall. There's a gift shop and a free parking area.

SHOPPING

Capercaille, 3 Invercauld Rd. (☎ 013397/41249), has quality crafts, mostly of Scottish manufacture. Pottery, carved wood, jewelry, and handmade children's toys are representative of the crafts found here, alongside a wide selection of women's hand-knitted and velvet clothing items. At **Lamont Sporran,** 8 Invercauld Rd. (☎ 013397/41404), you can find complete Highland outfits, including sporran (the small leather or fur pouch used in place of pockets when wearing a kilt), kilts, belt, jacket, stockings, and brogues. **McLeans of Braemar,** 10–12 Invercauld Rd. ☎ 013397/41629), carries a wide range of regional products, from knickknacks to clothing. Among the items are stag-horn and cow-horn crafts, jewelry, china, paperweights, Scottish woolens, tartans, and tartan accessories, and men's and women's country clothing.

WHERE TO STAY & DINE

Braemar Lodge Hotel. 6 Glenshee Rd., Braemar, Aberdeenshire AB35 5YQ. ☎ and fax 013397/41627. 7 rms. TV. £50–£72 ($82.50–$118.80) double. MC, V. Rates include Scottish breakfast. Closed Nov. Bus: 201.

This hotel, popular with skiers at the nearby Glenshee slopes, was originally built in 1870 as a hunting lodge. Set on 2 acres of grounds at the head of Glen Clunie, half a mile from the center of Braemar, it contains a bar, lounge, and reading room for guests. The bedrooms have a strikingly modern decor. Dinner, served in the restaurant from 7pm, includes regional dishes on the à la carte menu. Lunch is not served. The food is excellent. The chef's specialties include venison with red wine, bacon, mushroom, and onion sauce; steaks served in a creamy pepper sauce; and sautéed fillet of trout with hollandaise sauce. Guests should reserve in advance if they want to dine at the hotel so that menus can be planned. The hotel is on the road to the Glenshee ski slopes, near the cottage where Robert Louis Stevenson wrote *Treasure Island.*

Invercauld Arms Thistle Hotel. Braemar, Aberdeenshire AB35 5YR. ☎ **013397/41605.** Fax 013397/41428. 68 rms. £139 ($229.35) double. AE, DC, MC, V. Rates include Scottish breakfast. Bus: 201.

This hotel is an old granite building whose original part dates back to the 18th century. In cool weather there's a roaring log fire on the hearth. You can go hill walking and see deer, golden eagles, and other wildlife. Fishing and, in winter, skiing are other pursuits in the nearby area. The bedrooms are comfortably furnished but rather uninspired.

In the pub close by, you'll meet the "ghillies" and "stalkers" and then return to the Scottish and international fare with fresh Dee salmon, Aberdeen Angus beef, venison, and grouse. A dinner averages £24 ($39.60) per person.

BRAEMAR AFTER DARK

Fife Arms Pub, Mar Road, in the Fife Arms Hotel (☎ **013397/41644**), has free live music, usually Scottish dance bands, on 2 weeknights and live rock bands every Saturday night. On tap you'll find McEwan's Lager and 80 Shilling, Theakston's Best Bitter, and Foster's Lager. The pub is open Monday through Thursday from 11am to 2:30pm and 5 to 11pm, Friday from 11am to 2:30pm and 5pm to midnight, Saturday from 11am to midnight, and Sunday from noon to 11pm. Although the **Invercauld Arms Pub,** in the Invercauld Arms Thistle Hotel (☎ **013397/41605**), has retained its wooden beamed ceiling, it has been modernized into a typical bar. It's a popular gathering spot for the locals and about once a month during the weekend there's a live rock band as entertainment. On tap you'll find Guinness Export, Carlsberg Export, Blackthorn Cider, Carlsberg's Lager, and McEwan's Lager and 80 Shilling. It's open daily from 5pm until midnight.

11 Speyside

The valley of the second-largest river in Scotland, the Spey, lies north and south of Aviemore. It's a land of great natural beauty. A journey north through Speyside will take you toward the Malt Whisky Trail. The Spey is born in the Highlands above Loch Laggan, 40 miles south of Inverness. Little more than a creek at its inception, it gains in force, fed by the many "burns" that drain water from the surrounding hills. It's one of Scotland's great rivers for salmon fishing, and it runs between the towering Cairngorms on the east and the Monadhliath mountains on the west. Its major center is Grantown-on-Spey.

NEWTONMORE

This Highland resort in Speyside is a good center for the Grampian and Monadhliath mountains, and it offers excellent fishing, golf, pony trekking, and hill walking. A track from the village climbs past the Calder River to Loch Dubh and the massive **Carn Ban** (3,087 ft.), where eagles fly. **Castle Cluny,** ancient seat of the MacPherson chiefs, is 6 miles west of Newtonmore.

Newtonmore lies 113 miles northwest of Edinburgh and 43 miles south of Inverness.

SEEING THE SIGHTS

Clan Macpherson House & Museum. Main St. ☎ **01540/673332.** Free admission, but donations accepted. May–Sept, Mon–Sat 10am–5:30pm, Sun 2:30–5:30pm. Closed Oct–Apr. The Edinburgh–Inverness bus stops nearby.

Most motorists zip through on the way to Aviemore, but sightseers may want to stop off and visit this museum at the south end of the village. Displayed are clan relics and memorials, including the Black Chanter and Green Banner as well as a "charmed sword," and the broken fiddle of the freebooter, James MacPherson, a Scottish Robin Hood. Relics associated with Bonnie Prince Charlie are also here. An annual clan rally is held in August.

WHERE TO STAY & DINE

Pines Hotel. Station Rd., Newtonmore, Inverness-shire PH20 1AR. ☎ **01540/673271.** 6 rms. TV. £78 ($128.70) double. No credit cards. Rates include dinner and breakfast. Closed Nov–Mar.

Built in 1903 of somber-looking granite, this house sits on a hill overlooking the Spey Valley and lies a quarter-mile west of the hamlet's center. Your hosts are John and Fran Raw, émigrés from Liverpool, who maintain a half-dozen cozy bedrooms, each with flowered wallpaper and an ambience where "you can put your feet up and relax." This you can do whenever you're not tramping through the wooded garden or the surrounding pine forests, or brewing a cuppa on your bedroom's teamaking facilities. Almost everyone here opts for half board, because of the wholesome, straightforward British cuisine made from ultrafresh ingredients. Examples include roast lamb with mint sauce, poached salmon steak in white-wine sauce, venison casserole with red wine and onions, and two dessert specialties such as sherry trifle or lemon meringue pie. Regrettably, the dining room is usually closed to nonresidents.

KINGUSSIE

Your next stop along the Spey might be at the little summer holiday resort and winter ski center of Kingussie (it's pronounced "King-*you*-see"), just off A9, the so-called capital of Badenoch, a district known as "the drowned land" because the Spey can flood the valley when the snows of a severe winter melt in the spring.

Kingussie practically adjoins Newtonmore (see above), for it lies directly northeast along A86. The location is 117 miles northwest of Edinburgh, 41 miles south of Inverness, and 11 miles southwest of Aviemore.

A summer-only **tourist information center** is on King Street (☎ **01540/ 661297**).

SEEING THE SIGHTS

Highland Folk Museum. Duke St. ☎ **01540/661307.** Admission £3.50 ($5.75) adults, £2.50 ($4.15) children and senior citizens, £7 ($11.55) family ticket. Apr–Oct, Mon–Sat 10am–6pm, Sun 2–6pm. Closed Nov–Mar.

This is the first folk museum established in Scotland (1934) and its collections are based on the life of the Highlanders. You'll see domestic, agricultural, and industrial items. Open-air exhibits are a turf kailyard (kitchen garden), a Lewis Island "black house," and old vehicles and carts. Traditional events such as spinning, music-making, and handcraft fairs are held throughout the summer.

West Grampian & Speyside

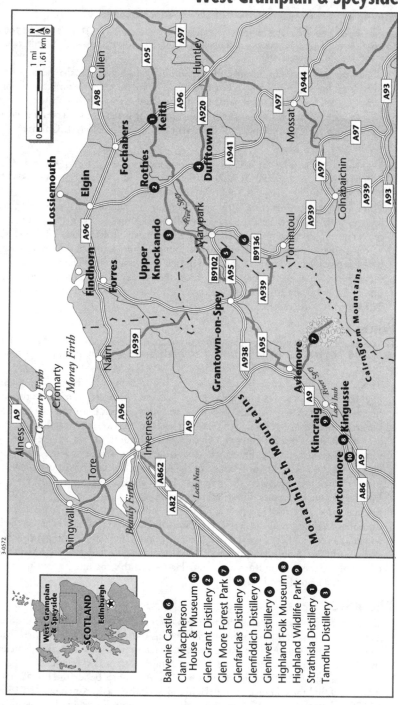

Balvenie Castle **6**
Clan Macpherson
    House & Museum **2**
Glen Grant Distillery **2**
Glen More Forest Park **7**
Glenfarclas Distillery **5**
Glenfiddich Distillery **4**
Glenlivet Distillery **6**
Highland Folk Museum **8**
Highland Wildlife Park **9**
Strathisla Distillery **1**
Tamdhu Distillery **3**

WHERE TO STAY

Homewood Lodge. Newtonmore Rd., Kingussie, Inverness-shire PH21 1HD. ☎ **01540/ 661507.** 4 rms. £40 ($66) double. Half board £27.50 ($45.40) per person. No credit cards. Rates include Scottish breakfast.

One of the best B&Bs in the area, this small Highland house offers large, comfortable rooms for either two travelers or families. The rooms are pleasantly but simply furnished. Set on a half acre of garden and woodland, the house has a sitting room with an open fire and a TV. Good traditional local fare is served in the evening when reservations are a must, and summer barbecues are also offered. Children are welcome.

Osprey Hotel. Ruthven Rd. (at High St.), Kingussie, Inverness-shire PH21 1EN. ☎ and fax **01540/661510.** 8 rms. £85–£98 ($138.60–$161.70) double. AE, DC, MC, V. Rates include half board. Closed Nov 1–14.

This 1895 Victorian structure, 300 yards from the rail station, is a convenient place to stay, with comfortable although very plain bedrooms, all with private baths, central heating, electric blankets, electric fires, and heated towel racks. The hotel has a licensed bar, residents' lounge, and TV lounge. Baby-sitting and baby-listening service is provided, and laundry and ironing facilities are available. The place is known for its pure, fresh, 100% homemade food. Prime Scottish meats are served; in summer, salmon and trout from local rivers are offered either fresh or peat-smoked. The wine list is extensive.

WHERE TO DINE

✪ **The Cross.** Tweed Mill Brae, off the Ardbroilach road, Kingussie, Inverness-shire PH21 1TC. ☎ **01540/661166.** Fax 01540/661080. Reservations recommended. Fixed-price 5-course dinner £35 ($57.75). Mar–Nov, Wed–Mon 7–9pm. Closed Dec–Feb. SCOTTISH.

This chic restaurant comes as a surprise: In an out-of-the-way setting in a remote Highland village, it serves superlative meals that involve theater as much as they do fine food. The restaurant stands on 4 acres, with the Gynack Burn running through the grounds. The main building of the complex is an old tweed mill, and the restaurant has an open-beam ceiling and French doors leading onto a terrace over the water's edge where alfresco dinners are served, depending on the weather. Specialties depend on the availability of produce in the local markets and might include venison Francatelli, wild pigeon with grapes, or Highland lamb with sorrel. A selection from more than 300 wines rounds out any menu.

Nine rooms are rented in a new building, which has been designed in the old style. Each room is different in size and style—for example, two rooms have canopied beds, and another has a balcony overlooking the mill pond. Doubles, including half board, go for £190 ($313.50). Personal service and attention to detail go into the running of this place, operated by Ruth and Tony Hadley; Ruth's cooking has put it on the gastronomic map of Scotland.

KINCRAIG

Kincraig enjoys a scenic spot at the northern end of Loch Insh, overlooking the Spey Valley to the west and the Cairngorm mountains to the east. From Kingussie, continue northeast along A9 (the route north to Aviemore) to reach Kincraig. Kincraig lies 37 miles south of Inverness and 119 miles northwest of Edinburgh.

About a mile from Kincraig, 6 miles south of Aviemore, beside the B9152 highway, you'll find the entrance to the **Highland Wildlife Park,** Kincraig (☎ **01540/ 651280**). Established in 1972 on 260 acres that are administered by the Royal Zoological Society of Scotland (the folk who operate the Edinburgh Zoo), it incorporates a bowl-shaped depression ringed with mountains, and terrain that includes peat bogs, birch and pine forests, and tundra. Some of the animals you'll see here are exceedingly rare outside the boundaries of the park and include herds of European bison, who enjoy rolling around in the peat bogs in the park's center, as well as red deer, shaggy Highland cattle, wild horses, red foxes, gray wolves, lynx, pine martens (a form of tree weasel), and bears.

Among the protected birds are golden eagles and several species of grouse, including the capercaillie, a large European grouse that's a native of Scotland's pine forests. Roads within the park are designed as "drive throughs" that allow maximum exposure to the terrain thanks to many winding turns. Of the park's 260 acres, 60 are reserved only for trekkers and hill climbers. The park is open every day throughout the year at 10am. Between April and October, the last entrance is at 4pm, except during July and August, when the last entrance is at 5pm. Between November and March, the last entrance is at 2pm. All people and vehicles are expected to vacate the park within 2 hours of the day's last admission. Walkers pay £6 ($9.90) each; occupants of cars pay £6 ($9.90) if there's one person in the car, £12 ($19.80) if there are two people in the car, and between £4 and £5.50 ($6.60 and $9.05) per person if the car contains between 3 and 6 people.

The park contains a visitor center with a somewhat lackluster gift shop, a cafe, and an exhibition center. Ample parking and picnic sites are available.

Adjacent to the park, beside Hwy. B9152, are a handful of satellite industries, one of the more amusing of which is **Working Sheepdogs,** Leault, Kincaig (☎ **01540/ 651310**). Here, Neil Ross and his family keep eight sheepdogs who corral sheep and perform tricks. There's also a herd of ducks who meander and quack their way through labyrinths. Depending on business, there are between two and four shows every day between May and October. Each lasts an hour and is charming despite an undeniable hoakiness. Visitors pay £3.50 ($5.75) per person.

GRANTOWN-ON-SPEY

This holiday resort, with its gray granite buildings, is 34 miles southeast of Inverness in a wooded valley that commands views of the Cairngorm mountains. It's a key center of winter sports in Scotland. Fishers are also attracted to the salmon fishing in this setting. Grantown, one of Scotland's many 18th-century planned towns, was founded on a heather-covered moor in 1765 by Sir James Grant of Grant and became the seat of that ancient family. Grantown became famous in the 19th century as a Highland tourist center, enticing visitors with its planned concept, the beauty of surrounding pine forests, the Spey River, and the mountains around it.

From a base here, you can explore the valleys of the Don and Dee, the Cairngorms, and Culloden Moor, scene of the historic battle in 1746.

A year-round **tourist information office** is on High Street (☎ **01479/872773**).

SHOPPING   Speyside Heather Centre, Skye of Curr (☎ **01479/851359**), is a shop that sells nearly 300 varieties of heather and also runs a full greenhouse operation. In the gift shop, you'll find small Scottish crafts and gifts, including heather crafts. The stylish **The Kist,** 74 High St. (☎ **01479/873043**), offers regional souvenir items such as Orkney silverware, Border Fine Arts figurines, limited edition paintings and prints, jewelry, recycled glassware, cards, and Edinburgh, Waterford, and Stuart crystal.

WHERE TO STAY

Garth Hotel. The Square, Castle Rd., Grantown-on-Spey, Morayshire PH26 3HN. ☎ **01479/ 872836.** Fax 01479/872116. 18 rms. TV TEL. £60–£80 ($99–$132) double. Half board £64 ($105.60) per person. AE, MC, V.

The elegant, comfortable Garth was built as a private house in the 17th century standing on 4 acres of grounds beside the town square. Guests enjoy the use of a spacious upstairs lounge, whose thick walls, high ceilings, wood-burning stove, and vine-covered veranda make it the perfect place for morning coffee or afternoon tea. This attractive hotel features handsomely furnished bedrooms, with all amenities. In the dining room, "Taste of Scotland" dishes are featured, with emphasis on fresh local produce, including seafood, salmon, venison, game, and beef.

✪ **Tulchan Lodge.** Advie, Grantown-on-Spey, Morayshire PH26 3PW. ☎ **01807/510200.** Fax 01807/510234. 12 rms. TEL. £350–£500 ($577.50–$825) double. No credit cards. Rates include full board. Closed Feb–Mar. Drive 9 miles northeast of Grantown on B9102.

Tulchan Lodge, built in 1906 to serve as the 23,000-acre Tulchan Estate's fishing and shooting lodge, is a place for both sports-oriented visitors and travelers who want to experience a place designed with the elegance required by Edward VII, who came here for the sports. The lodge has panoramic views of the Spey Valley. Each bedroom is different in size and furnishings, and all have private baths. Tulchan Lodge is open from April to January.

Dining/Entertainment: In the two elegant dining rooms, Scottish and international dishes are served, with particular attention to Scottish beef, lamb, game, and fresh local seafood. The vegetables are grown in the lodge's garden. Only full-board residents are accepted.

Services: Room service (8am–9pm), dry cleaning/laundry service, nightly turn-down, baby-sitting, secretarial/business services.

Facilities: Tennis court, nature trails; golf course nearby.

WHERE TO DINE

Craggan Mill. Hwy. A95, ³/₄ mile south of Grantown-on-Spey. ☎ **01479/872288.** Reservations recommended. Main courses £6.95–£12.50 ($11.45–$20.65). MC, V. June–Sept, daily noon–2pm and 6–10pm; Oct–May, Tues–Sun 7–10pm. BRITISH/ITALIAN.

This licensed restaurant and lounge bar, a 10-minute walk south of the town center, is housed in a restored ruined granite mill whose waterwheel is still visible. The owners offer British or Italian cuisine at attractive prices. Therefore your appetizer might be smoked trout in deference to Scotland, or ravioli, inspired by sunny Italy. For a main course, the selection might be breast of chicken with cream or chicken cacciatore, followed by a dessert of either rum-raisin ice cream or peach Melba. You've probably had better versions of all the dishes offered here, but what you get isn't bad. A good selection of Italian wines is also offered.

12 West Grampian

Much of the region covered in this section is in the Moray district, on the southern shore of the Moray Firth, a great inlet cutting into the northeastern coast of Scotland. The district stretches in a triangular shape south from the coast to the wild heart of the Cairngorm Mountains near Aviemore. It's a land steeped in history, as its many castles, battle sites, and ancient monuments testify. It's also very sports oriented, attracting not only fishers but also golfers.

The major tourist attraction is the **Malt Whisky Trail,** running through the glens of Speyside. Here distilleries, many of which can be visited, are known for their production of *uisge beatha* or "water of life." Whisky (note the spelling without the e) is its more familiar name.

Half the malt distilleries in the country lie along the River Spey and its tributaries. Here, peat smoke and Highland water are used to turn out single-malt (unblended) whisky. The Malt Whisky Trail is 70 miles long. There are five malt distilleries in the area: Glenlivet, Glenfiddich, Glenfarclas, Strathisla, and Tamdhu. Allow about an hour each to visit them.

If you're traveling north on the A9 road from Perth and Pitlochry, your first stop might be at Dalwhinnie, which has the highest whisky distillery in the world at 1,888 feet. It's not in the Spey Valley but is at the northeastern end of Loch Ericht, with views of lochs and forests.

GLENLIVET & GLENFARCLAS

To reach your first distillery on the designated Malt Whisky Trail, you leave Grantown-on-Spey and head east along A95 until you come to the junction with B9008. Go south along this route and you can't miss it. The location of **The Glenlivet Reception Centre** (☎ 01542/783220) is 10 miles north of the nearest town, Tomintoul. Near the River Livet, a Spey tributary, this distillery is one of the most famous in Scotland, and it's open to visitors from mid-March until the end of May, in October from Monday to Saturday 10am to 4pm, and Sunday from 11:30am to 4pm. June through September, hours are Monday to Saturday 10am to 5pm and Sunday 11:30am to 5pm. The £2.50 ($4.15) admission fee includes a £2 ($3.30) voucher off the purchase of a bottle of whisky.

Back on A95, you can visit the **Glenfarclas Distillery** at Ballindalloch (☎ 01807/ 500245), one of the few malt-whisky distilleries that's still independent of the giants. Founded in 1836, Glenfarclas is managed by the fifth generation of the Grant family. It's open all year, Monday through Friday from 9am to 5pm, and June through September, also on Saturday from 10am to 4pm and Sunday from 12:30 to 4:30pm. The admission fee of £2.50 ($4.15) can be applied as a discount voucher on a whisky purchase. There's a small craft shop, and each visitor is offered a dram of Glenfarclas Malt Whisky.

WHERE TO STAY & DINE

Minmore House Hotel. Glenlivet, near Ballindalloch, Banffshire AB37 9DB. ☎ **01807/ 590378.** 10 rms. TEL. £130 ($214.50) double, including breakfast, afternoon tea, and 5-course dinner. MC, V. Closed mid-Oct to May 1.

Standing on 7 acres of private grounds adjacent to the Glenlivet Distillery, this house was built around 1850 by George Smith, the founder of the distillery. For many decades it was a private home. Public rooms, including the drawing room, are elegantly furnished, opening onto views of the Ladder Hills and an outdoor swimming pool. The well-furnished bedrooms have tea/coffeemakers, and drinks can be enjoyed in the oak-paneled lounge bar, which has an open log fire on chilly nights. The Scottish food is excellent, served in a Regency-style dining room with mahogany tables and matching chairs.

DUFFTOWN

James Duff, the fourth earl of Fife, founded this town in 1817. The four main streets of town converge at the battlemented **clock tower,** which is also the tourist information center. A center of the whisky-distilling industry, Dufftown is surrounded by seven malt distilleries. The family-owned **Glenfiddich Distillery** is on A941, half a mile north of Dufftown (☎ 01340/820373). It's open Monday through Friday from 9:30am to 4:30pm, and from Easter to mid-October it's also open on Saturday from 9:30am to 4:30pm and on Sunday from noon to 4:30pm. Guides in kilts show visitors around the plant and explain the process of distilling. A film of the history of distilling is also shown. At the end of the tour you're given a dram of malt whisky.

The tour is free. There's a souvenir shop. The first whisky was produced on Christmas Day back in 1887.

Other sights include **Balvenie Castle** (☎ 0131/668-8600) along A941, the ruins of a moated stronghold from the 14th century that lie on the south side of the Glenfiddich Distillery. During her northern campaign against the earl of Huntly, Mary Queen of Scots spent 2 nights here. From 1459 to the 17th century, the earls of Atholl retained Balvenie. It's open April through September, Monday through Saturday from 9:30am to 7pm and Sunday from 2 to 6pm; closed off-season. Admission is £1.20 ($2) for adults, 60p ($1) for children.

The **Mortlach Parish Church** in Dufftown is one of the oldest places of Christian worship in the country. It's reputed to have been founded in 566 by St. Moluag. A Pictish cross stands in the graveyard. The present church was reconstructed in 1931 and incorporates portions of an older building.

WHERE TO DINE

✪ **Taste of Speyside.** 10 Balvenie St. ☎ 01340/820860. Reservations recommended in the evening. Main courses £8–£12.80 ($13.20–$21.10); Speyside platter £8.20 ($13.55) at lunch, £9.50 ($15.65) at dinner. AE, MC, V. Daily 11am–5:30pm and 6–9pm. Closed Nov–Feb. SCOTTISH.

True to its name, this restaurant in the town center, just off the main square, avidly promotes a Speyside cuisine as well as Speyside malt whiskies, and in the bar you can buy the product of each of Speyside's 46 distilleries. A platter including a slice of smoked salmon, smoked venison, smoked trout, pâté flavored with malt whisky, locally made cheese (cow or goat), salads, and homemade oat cakes is offered at noon and at night. Nourishing soup is made fresh daily and is served with homemade bread. There's also a choice of meat pies, including venison with red wine and herbs or rabbit. For dessert, try Scotch Mist, which contains fresh cream, malt whisky, and crumbled meringue.

KEITH

Keith, 11 miles northwest of Huntly, grew up because of its strategic location, where the main road and rail routes between Inverness and Aberdeen cross the River Isla. It has an ancient history, but owes its present look to the "town planning" of the late 18th and early 19th centuries. Today it's a major stopover along the Malt Whisky Trail.

The oldest continuously operating distillery in the Scottish Highlands, the **Strathisla Distillery,** on Seafield Avenue, in Keith (☎ 01542/783044), was established in 1786 and now operates as a proudly individualistic producer of single-malts under the supervision of the Grants & Glenlivit Group, a division of Seagrams. Hours are February to mid-March, Monday through Friday from 9:30am to 4pm; mid-March to November 30, Monday through Saturday from 9:30am to 4pm, Sunday from 12:30 to 4pm; closed December and January. Admission is £4 ($6.60) for adults, free for ages 8 to 18, children 7 and under not admitted. The admission fee includes a £2 voucher redeemable in the distillery shop. Be warned that tours of this distillery are self-guided.

WHERE TO STAY & DINE

Royal Hotel. Church Rd., Keith, Banffshire AB5 5BQ. ☎ 01542/882528. Fax 01542/886101. 16 rms (3 with bath). £38 ($62.70) double without bath; £45 ($74.25) double with bath. AE, MC, V. Rates include Scottish breakfast.

In addition to being a cozy and comfortable hotel, this stone establishment a quarter-mile north of town beside A96, serves as the village pub and social center. Built beside the road in 1883, it has probably welcomed the grandparents and parents of virtually every longtime resident of Keith. A handful of the more expensive bedrooms contain TV sets and teamaking facilities. On the premises is a restaurant; inexpensive platters are served as bar snacks in the lounge.

ROTHES

A Speyside town with five distilleries, Rothes is just to the south of the Glen of Rothes, 49 miles east of Inverness and 62 miles northwest of Aberdeen. Founded in 1766, the town lies between Ben Aigan and Conerock Hill. A little settlement, the basis of the town today, grew up around **Rothes Castle,** ancient stronghold of the Leslie family, who lived here until 1622. Only a single massive wall of the castle remains.

The region's best-organized distillery—at least for the purposes of conducting tours—is the **Glen Grant Distillery** (☎ **01542/783318**). Established in 1840 by a hardworking hard-drinking pair of brothers, James and John Grant, and now administered by the Chivas & Glenlivet Group (a division of Seagrams), it's located a half-mile north of Rothes, beside the Elgin–Perth (A941) highway, and is clearly signposted from the town center. Visits are possible June through September, Monday through Saturday from 10am to 5pm and Sunday from 11:30am to 5pm; mid-March to May 31 and in October, hours are Monday through Saturday from 10am to 4pm and Sunday from 11:30am to 4pm; closed November to mid-March. Admission is £2.50 ($4.15) for adults, free for ages 8 to 18, children 7 and under not allowed. Visits include a whisky tasting and the opportunity to buy the brand's whisky at a discount of £2 ($3.30) per bottle. Although the Grant family's nearby mansion was demolished in the early 1990s, the verdant, circa 1896 gardens once associated with the structure were revitalized and restored recently. The waterfall that functions as the centerpiece of the garden's upper region is worth a visit.

WHERE TO STAY & DINE

Rothes Glen Hotel. Rothes, Morayshire AB38 7AQ. ☎ **01340/831254.** Fax 01340/ 831566. 16 rms. TV TEL. £120–£150 ($198–$247.50) double. AE, MC, V. Rates include Scottish breakfast. Take A941 and drive 3 miles north of Rothes, or 6 miles south of Elgin.

The old turreted house, with many of its original pieces of furniture, stands back from the road and is surrounded by 10 acres of fields with grazing Highland cattle. This historic castlelike building was designed by the architect who built Balmoral. The dining room is paneled in wood, and good wholesome meals are served in true Scottish tradition. A fixed-price four-course dinner costs £32.50 ($53.65).

ELGIN

The center of local government in the Moray district, an ancient royal burgh, this cathedral city lies on the Lossie River, 38 miles east of Inverness and 68 miles northwest of Aberdeen. The city's medieval plan has been retained, with "wynds" and "pends" connecting the main artery with other streets. The castle, as was customary in medieval town layouts, stood at one end of the main thoroughfare, with the cathedral at the other. Nothing remains of the castle.

Samuel Johnson and James Boswell came this way on their Highland tour and reported a "vile dinner" at the Red Lion Inn in 1773.

Lady Hill stands on High Street, opposite the post office. This is the hilltop location of what was once the royal castle of Elgin. Edward I of England stayed here in 1296 during the Wars of Independence. Only a fragment of the mighty castle now remains.

Birnie Kirk, at Birnie, 3 miles south of Elgin and west of A941 to Rothes, was for a time the seat of a bishopric. It dates from about 1140 when it was constructed on the site of a much earlier church founded by St. Brendan. One of the few Norman churches in Scotland still in regular use, it's open daily from 10am to 4pm.

On King Street is the ✪ **Cathedral of Moray** (☎ 01343/547171). Now in ruins, it was once called the "lantern of the north." The cathedral was founded in 1224 but was destroyed in 1390 by the "wolf of Badenoch," the natural son of Robert II. After its destruction, the citizens of Elgin rebuilt their beloved cathedral and turned it into one of the most attractive and graceful buildings in Scotland; the architect's plan was that of a Jerusalem cross. However, when the central tower collapsed in 1711, the cathedral was allowed to fall into decay. Best preserved is the 15th-century chapter house. The cathedral stands beside the river in the town center, off North College Street near A96. Admission is £1.50 ($2.45) for adults, £1 ($1.65) for seniors, 75p ($1.25) for children. It's open April to September, Monday through Saturday from 9:30am to 6:30pm and Sunday from 2 to 6:30pm; October to March, Monday through Saturday from 9:30am to 4:30pm and Sunday from 2 to 4:30pm.

SHOPPING   Gordon and MacPhail, South Street ☎ 01343/545111), has been in business more than 100 years and offers a large selection of international wines, along with rare single-malt whiskies dating back to 1936. **Johnstons of Elgin,** Newmill (☎ 01343/554099), is a factory shop that sells cashmeres, tweeds, camel hair, and Arran knits. Hourly tours of the factory are offered on weekdays, and there's an on-premises coffee shop that provides light snacks and beverages.

WHERE TO STAY

Eight Acres Hotel. Sheriffmill, Elgin, Morayshire IV30 3UN. ☎ 01343/543077. Fax 01343/540001. 55 rms, 1 suite. TV TEL. £68 ($112.20) double; £80 ($132) suite. AE, DC, MC, V. Rates include Scottish breakfast.

This hotel was built in the 1970s in a motel-inspired format about a mile west of the center of Elgin, beside the main A96 road leading to Inverness. The guest rooms, though streamlined and functionally furnished, are warm and clean. There's a no-nonsense restaurant and bar on the premises, as well as a swimming pool, gym, and squash courts.

Mansion House Hotel. The Haugh, Elgin, Morayshire IV10 1AW. ☎ 01343/548811. Fax 01343/547916. 23 rms. MINIBAR TV TEL. £120–£150 ($198–$247.50) double. AE, DC, MC, V. Rates include Scottish breakfast. Follow A96 onto Alexandra Rd. to the turnoff onto Haugh Rd.

Mansion House Hotel is an elegantly appointed hotel, with the baronial proportions of the original design intact. It lies at the edge of the River Lossie, about a quarter-mile from the center of Elgin. Each bedroom contains a radio alarm clock and hot-beverage equipment; most have four-poster beds. Public rooms include a bistro, a lounge bar, and a dining room. The hotel has a country club with a swimming pool, Jacuzzi, sauna, Turkish bath, and gym.

WHERE TO DINE

Abbey Court Restaurant. 15 Greyfriars St. ☎ 01343/542849. Reservations recommended. Main courses £5.25–£15.65 ($8.65–$25.80). AE, DC, MC, V. Mon–Sat noon–2pm and 6:30–9:45pm. SCOTTISH/ITALIAN.

Abbey Court, in the center of town behind the County Building, is an excellent restaurant decorated with stone- and earth-colored quarry tile, along with an artificial pergola, a separate bistro corner, and a more formal dining area in the rear with lots of plants. The fresh pasta is homemade, and fresh fish is delivered daily. Game is also a feature. The cooking is straightforward and unpretentious. The owner is a local wine importer who stocks more than 150 varieties.

ELGIN AFTER DARK

Linked historically to the Stewart clan as far back as 1715, **Thunderton House Pub,** Thunderton Place (☎ **01343/548767**), is best known as the place where Bonnie Prince Charlie stayed for 10 days in 1746 on his way to Culloden. It is reported that his ghost still haunts the room in which he slept. Nowadays, the old pub, with a wood-and-brass bar, is a gathering place for locals who amuse themselves with karaoke on Thursday and Sunday nights. Occasionally, a band is booked as well. The bar keeps Tennant's beers on tap, along with the local brewery Tomintoul's real ale.

  Flanagan's, 4 Shepherd's Close (☎ **01343/549737**), is a small dark bar with brick walls and old floorboards, a traditional Irish pub that draws a crowd for Irish and folk bands on the weekend. On tap, you can choose from Kilkenny, Guinness, Murphy's, Calder's, Carlsberg Lager, and three guest cask ales. **Cottarhouse,** Thornhill Road (☎ **01343/547903**), is composed of two ancient cottars' (farm workers') cottages and has retained the original wood floors, stone fireplaces, and stone walls. Every Saturday there's live traditional music that you can enjoy while drinking "the best pint of Guinness in Scotland." Also available are McEwan's 70 Shilling and 80 Shilling. The friendly bartender especially invites Americans to stop by "so you can discover what beer is really like."

FINDHORN

As you travel westward from Elgin to Forres, a turn to the right and then to the left will bring you to Findhorn, a tiny village that used to be a busy commercial fishing port. Findhorn lies at the end of B9011, and a local bus from Forres stops here.

  These days, the unique tidal bay at the mouth of the River Findhorn makes the village an ideal center for yacht racing, sailing, and windsurfing. Across the bay from Findhorn is the Culbin Sands, under which lies a buried village.

  Just before Findhorn Village, you'll see the home of the **Findhorn Foundation,** The Park, Forres IV36 0TZ (☎ **01309/690311**), an international educational community founded in 1962 and based on spiritual principles and organic farming. It owns and runs the **Findhorn Bay Caravan Park** (☎ **01309/690203**); and the macrobiotically conscious **Phoenix Shop** (☎ **01309/690110**), where you can purchase health foods, books, and craft items. Tours of the complex are offered every afternoon, between April and September, at 2pm. Don't expect architectural grandeur—the complex is small-scale and unpretentious, and includes goodly numbers of aluminum-sided buildings and trailers. But the organization's strong emphasis on interdenominational spiritual healing has attracted aficionados from around the world and a fame much larger than its simple setting would suggest. If you're interested in living within the Findhorn community for a while, working and studying, write to the address above or call ☎ **01309/673655.**

WHERE TO STAY & DINE

Crown & Anchor Inn. Findhorn, Morayshire IV36 0YF. ☎ **01309/690243.** Fax 01309/690201. 6 rms. TV. £44 ($72.60) double. MC, V. Rates include Scottish breakfast.

  The Crown & Anchor dates from 1739 when it was constructed of stone to cater to travelers making the run between Edinburgh and Inverness. On the seafront near the pier, bar snacks and meals are served daily. Locals drop in to enjoy the real ales and malt whiskies served in the bar. The rooms are simply and modestly furnished but clean.

11

The West Highlands

The romantic glens and rugged mountainous landscapes of the West Highlands suggest a timeless antiquity. You can see deer grazing only yards from the highway in remote parts, and you can stop by a secluded loch for a picnic or to fish for trout and salmon. The region's beauty has been praised by such authorities as Robert Burns, Dr. Johnson, and Daniel Defoe. The shadow of Macbeth still stalks the land (locals will tell you that this 11th-century king was much maligned by Shakespeare). The area's most famous resident, however, is said to live in mysterious Loch Ness. First sighted by St. Columba in the 6th century, "Nessie" has evaded searchers ever since.

Centuries of invasions, rebellions, and clan feuds are distant memories now. The Highlands are not as remote as they once were, when many Londoners seriously believed that the men of the Highlands had tails.

Fort William is a major center for the West Highlands, surrounded by wildly beautiful Lochaber, called "the land of bens, glens, and heroes." Dominating the area is Ben Nevis, Britain's highest mountain. This district is the western end of what is known as Glen Mor—the Great Glen, geologically a fissure that divides the northwest of Scotland from the southeast and contains Loch Lochy, Loch Oich, and Loch Ness. The Caledonian Canal, opened in 1847, linked these lochs, the River Ness, and Moray Firth. It provided sailing boats a safe alternative to the stormy route around the north of Scotland. Larger steamships made the canal out of date commercially, but fishing boats and pleasure steamers still use it. Good roads run the length of the Great Glen, partly following the line of General Wade's military road. From Fort William you can take steamer trips to Staffa and Iona (see chapter 12).

Aviemore and the villages and towns of the Spey Valley offer many activities for the visitor. In the Spey Valley you're at the doorway to the "Malt Whisky Trail" (see section 11 in chapter 10). Aviemore is the winter sports capital of Britain, and Aviemore Centre offers a multitude of outdoor pursuits: golfing, angling, skiing, and ice-skating.

Inverness and legendary **Loch Ness** are the most popular attractions of the West Highlands and consequently are overcrowded in

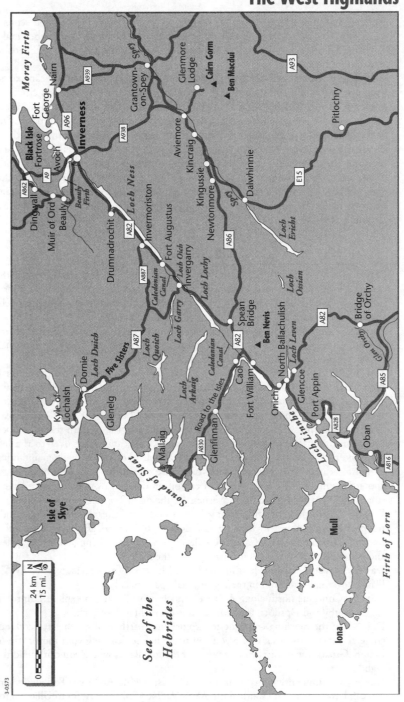

The West Highlands

3-0573

summer, but they're surrounded by villages and towns that also make good centers, especially if you're driving. If you're dependent on public transportation, make Inverness your base, as it has good rail and bus connections to the rest of Scotland and also to England.

Finally, if you've caught Highland fever, and if you have the time, you can extend your stay in the region by visiting the far north, where the mainland of Scotland comes to an end. This section of the Highlands, **Sutherland** and **Caithness,** is not for everyone. It's the loneliest part of Scotland. But for some, that's part of its undeniable charm. Crumbling watchtowers no longer stand guard over anything except the sheep-cropped wilderness. Moss-green glens give way to inland lochs and sea fords. In summer the deep-blue lochs and towering cliffs, as well as the gentle glens, are to be enjoyed in the sun. Many relics of Scotland's turbulent past dot the landscape. Castles are left in ruins. Today potteries and craft centers encourage visitors; crafts include silversmithing, stone polishing, glassmaking, and most definitely weaving.

A DRIVING TOUR

Day 1　Using Fort William as your gateway to the West Highlands, spend the morning exploring the town, then drive to Glencoe after lunch. Lying on the shores of Loch Leven, the glen was the scene of the famous massacre where the Campbells killed the MacDonalds. Return to Fort William for the night.

Day 2　Take A830 west to Mallaig, 47 miles northwest of Fort William, one of the most scenic drives in all of Scotland. You can either spend the night in this small fishing village or return to Fort William for the night.

Day 3　Head for Aviemore by following A82 (later A86) northeast, passing through Newtonmore and Kingussie; either would make a good luncheon stopover. In the afternoon view the attractions of this summer/winter resort and spend the night here.

Day 4　From Aviemore, retrace your trail along A86 back to the junction at Spean Bridge. Here join A82 north, which will take you along the western shores of Loch Lochy and then Loch Oich. At Fort Augustus you can switch over to the left bank and take A82 along the western shores of fabled Loch Ness while maintaining a monster watch. At Urquhart Castle you'll have one of the best views of the loch, and at Drumnadrochit you can see an exhibition devoted to the sea beast. After a stopover, A82 will take you into Inverness for the night.

Day 5　Spend the morning viewing Inverness. In the afternoon visit the seaside resort of Nairn, reached by heading east along A96. You can also explore the most romantic castle in Scotland, Cawdor Castle, of *Macbeth* fame, lying between Inverness and Nairn on B9090. Return to Inverness for the night.

Day 6　Devote a day to exploring the Black Isle, west of Inverness, reached by A9. Plan an overnight stopover in the region, perhaps at Beauly.

Day 7　Continue north along A9 to Dornoch, where you can explore Dunrobin Castle nearby and Dornoch Cathedral. Stay overnight at Dornoch.

Day 8　In the morning continue to explore the coastline of northwest Scotland, going all the way to Wick where you can pause before finishing your motor trip to John o' Groats, the most northerly point of the mainland, where you can spend the night.

Day 9　Continue driving west around the coast, taking A836 via Tongue (where you can have lunch). Dip south along A838, A894, A837, and A835 to Ullapool for 2 nights. On the second day, while based in Ullapool you can take in as many of the scenic excursions in the environs as time will allow.

Climbing Britain's Tallest Mountain

In the Central Highlands, **Ben Nevis** at 4,406 feet is the tallest mountain in Britain. Although laughable when compared to the towering mountains of the Alps, Ben Nevis can still pose a formidable challenge to climbers. The pony track to the top is often filled with walkers, but nevertheless it's a difficult 8-hour jaunt that requires participants to be physically fit. The unpredictable Scottish weather adds to the challenge. The mean monthly temperature of Ben Nevis falls below freezing; snow has been reported at all times of the year, even during the hottest months of July and August. Howling winds are frequent.

Mountain trekkers go for the view—the challenge is always there, but the view is not guaranteed because of weather conditions. On a clear day, you can see the Irish foothills some 120 miles away, the Hebridean Isle of Rhum 92 miles away, and of course, the Glencoe peaks—Ben Lawers, Torridon, and the Cairngorms. If you don't want to climb, a cable car takes visitors to a height of 2,300 feet for viewing.

The trail is much rougher but even more beautiful if approached from Glen Nevis, one of the country's most scenic glens. The midpart of this trek has been called "Himalayan" in landscape. Clear rivers and cascading waterfalls add to the drama of the scenery; meadows and moors evoke the landscape of Austria.

Before going, discuss the climb with the tourist office in Fort William. The staff can give you advice as well as maps of the area, and they'll pinpoint the best places to begin the climb. A signpost to the north of Nevis Bridge points to the path up Ben Nevis. Allow 8 1/2 hours for the under-10-mile trip. Take along a windbreaker, sturdy footwear, food, and water.

A word of warning: Sudden weather changes may pose a safety hazard. And that final 1,000 feet is really steep terrain, but having gone this far, few can fail the challenge. Some Brits call Ben Nevis "the top of the world." It really isn't. It just feels that way when you finally reach the pinnacle.

1 Around Loch Linnhe & Loch Leven

To the south of Fort William is one of the most history-rich sections of Scotland, a group of settlements around Loch Linnhe and Loch Leven (not the also-famous Loch Leven near Dunfermline). The best-known hamlet here is Glencoe, site of the famous 1692 massacre when the Campbells slaughtered the MacDonalds. Glencoe is considered the most beautiful glen in Scotland.

Around both lochs are impressive landscapes and moorland, with flora and fauna unique to the western Highlands. Robert Louis Stevenson captured much of the essence of this moorland and wilderness in his novel *Kidnapped.*

ONICH

On the shores of Loch Linnhe, this charming little village lies to the north of Ballachulish Bridge, 9 miles southwest of Fort William. It's a good center if you're taking the western route to Inverness, or going to Skye and Fort William.

WHERE TO STAY & DINE

Creag Dhu (The Lodge on the Loch). Creag Dhu, Onich, Inverness-shire PH33 6RY. ☎ **01855/821237.** Fax 01855/821238. 21 rms (19 with bath). TV TEL. £81–£98 ($133.65–$161.70) double without bath, £131–£148 ($216.15–$244.20) double with bath.

MC, V. Rates include half board. Closed Jan 5 to mid-Mar and mid-Nov to Dec 25. Drive 12 miles south to Fort William on A82.

Originally built in 1860, this house was transformed into a hotel by the Young family. Still a family-run hotel, it lies south of Fort William between Ben Nevis and Glencoe, with expansive lochside and mountain views. The loch views are of prawn-filled Linnhe and Leven. The bedrooms have radios, hair dryers, trouser presses, and tea- and coffeemakers. The kitchen offers traditional Scottish dishes, among other fare. Lunches are bar meals, with platters priced from £3 to £7 ($4.95 to $11.55), and a table d'hôte dinner is offered for £25.50 to £29.50 ($42.05 to $48.70). Boating, sailing, waterskiing, and Aqua-Lung diving are available nearby, along with good sea- and freshwater fishing, pony trekking, riding, golfing, swimming, and tennis. Rates include complimentary use of the pool, sauna, and steam room at the Creag Dhu's sibling hotel, Isles of Glencoe. The hotel has an enthusiastic repeat clientele.

GLENCOE

Near to the spot where Loch Leven joins Loch Linnhe, **Ballachulish Bridge** links the villages of North and South Ballachulish at the entrance to Glencoe. The bridge saves a long drive to the head of the loch if you're coming from the north, but the scenic drive to Kinlochleven lets you come upon the wild and celebrated Glencoe from the east. This is an area of massive splendor, with towering peaks and mysterious glens where you can well imagine the fierce battle among the kilted Highlanders to the skirl of the pipes and the beat of the drums.

Glencoe runs from Rannoch Moor to Loch Leven between majestic mountains, including 3,766-foot **Bidean nam Bian.** Known as the "Glen of Weeping," Glencoe is the place where, on February 11, 1692, the Campbells massacred the MacDonalds—men, women, and children—who had been their hosts for 12 days. Although mass killings were not uncommon in those times, this one shocked even the Highlanders because it was a breach of hospitality. The **Monument to the Massacre of Glencoe** at Carnoch was erected by the chief of the MacDonald clan. After the incident, the crime of "murder under trust" was introduced into Scottish law as an aggravated form of murder that carried the same penalty as treason.

The glen, much of which now belongs to the National Trust for Scotland, is full of legend. A tiny lochan is known as "the pool of blood" because by its side some men are said to have quarreled over a piece of cheese and killed each other.

Glen Orchy, to the south, is well worth a visit too, for the wild river and photogenic mountain scenery. It was the birthplace of the Gaelic bard Duncan Ban MacIntyre, whose masterpiece is the song "In Praise of Ben Doran."

WHERE TO STAY & DINE

✪ **Ballachulish House.** Ballachulish, Argyll PA39 4JX. ☎ **01855/811266.** Fax 01855/811498. 5 rms. £118–£126 ($194.70–$207.90) double. Rates include dinner and breakfast. MC, V. Closed Nov–Mar. Drive west of Ballachulish for 2¹/₂ miles, following the A82 until it intersects with the A828. From here, follow the signs to Ballachulish House.

This elegant country mansion was burned down in the early 1700s because of the associations of its owners with the doomed Stuarts. It was rebuilt in 1764 and retains its lime-washed original stone form, even though it was tastefully expanded in 1997. Your hosts are John and Liz Grey and their son Seumas. The family has spent enormous sums renovating the place since they bought it in 1989, and since then many well-known people, such as Michael Forsyth, secretary of state for Scotland, have enjoyed this cozy environment. Bedrooms are outfitted with flowered wallpaper and a mixture of old and new furniture, and each room has a view of the loch or the forest. Dinner is a highlight here, making use of fresh ingredients and culinary care. Menu items might include prawn cakes with guacamole; spinach and cream cheese crêpes; tomato-mint soup; venison in a green-pepper sauce; poached salmon with watercress sauce; and a daily pudding that might consist of fresh lime tart or apple-flavored sorbet. Nonresidents who phone ahead can sometimes share an evening meal for a set price of £23.50 ($38.80) per person. There's a billiard room and ample opportunities for long walks beside the loch (sometimes one or two of the owners' dogs will join you). Don't confuse this place with either the Ballachulish Hotel or Ballachulish Farm, both of which accept paying overnight guests and have similar names.

Clachaig Inn. Glencoe, Ballachulish, Argyll PA39 4HX. ☎ **01855/811252.** Fax 01855/811679. 19 rms (16 with tub or shower). £58–£66 ($95.70–$108.90) double with bath. MC, V. Rates include Scottish breakfast.

After the bleakness of Glencoe, the trees ringing this place make it seem like an oasis. It's the only hotel in the glen (look for the signs on the highway), on the site where the massacre took place. It's reached by a winding gravel-covered road off the main highway. The Daynes family offers Highland hospitality, good food, and an excellent selection of British ales. They rent some contemporary chalets in the back garden, plus several bedrooms in the main house. Furnishings are basic and simple; some singles are without bath but all doubles have either a shower or tub. Live folk music now brings the place alive every night during the winter season and three to four times a week during the summer season.

Glencoe Hotel. Glencoe, Argyll PA39 4HW. ☎ **01855/811245.** Fax 01855/811687. 15 rms. £48–£72 ($79.20–$118.80) double. AE, DC, MC, V. Rates include Scottish breakfast. Closed 1 week at Christmas.

This white-fronted, slate-roofed building in Glencoe Village is owned by the McConnacher family. The hotel boasts a flowering outdoor patio overlooking the Pap of Glencoe and the islands in Loch Leven. Each room contains teamaking facilities, trouser presses, hair dryers, and simple furnishings. The hotel's restaurant serves plain table d'hôte dinners for £17.25 ($28.45), and the two lively bars serve lunch and dinner platters daily for around £5.50 ($9.05).

King's House Hotel. Glencoe, Argyll PA39 4HZ. ☎ **01855/851259.** Fax 01855/851216. 22 rms (12 with bath). TEL. £46 ($75.90) double without bath, £52 ($85.80) double with bath. MC, V. Guests can arrange to be met at the Bridge of Orchy railway station.

The solid walls of this historic inn were built in the 1600s on a windswept plateau beside A82, 12 miles southeast of Glencoe village, at the strategic point where Glencoe joins the Glen Etive near a jagged mountain, Buachaille Etive Mor. This is one of the oldest licensed inns in Scotland, although modernization has changed its interior. The hotel is a ski center and maintains a ski lift a short walk from its entrance. Warm, modestly furnished bedrooms usually offer sweeping views of majestic scenery. There's a bar where simple meals are served; prices range from £3.50 to £10.50 ($5.75 to $17.35) for platters. The dining room boasts a selection of fine wines and freshly prepared meals. A three-course table d'hôte dinner costs £16.50 ($27.20).

2 Fort William

133 miles NW of Edinburgh, 68 miles S of Inverness, 104 miles N of Glasgow

This town, on the shores of Loch Linnhe, is a good center for exploring the western Highlands. Fort William stands on the site of a fort built by General Monk in 1655 to help crush any rebellion Highlanders might have been plotting. After several reconstructions, it was finally torn down in 1864 to make way for the railroad. During the notorious Highland Clearances, many starving and evicted people were shipped from here to America.

Today Fort William is a bustling town, thriving very well on the summer tourist trade. It's filled with shops, many selling tartans and tweeds, as well as hotels and cafes.

ESSENTIALS
GETTING THERE

BY TRAIN   Fort William is a major stop on the West Highland rail line that begins its run at the Queen Street Station in Glasgow and ends at Mallaig on the west coast of Scotland. There are three trains a day at a one-way cost of £22 ($36.30). For information about schedules, call ☎ **01397/703791** in Fort William.

BY BUS   Four buses run from Glasgow to Fort William per day, taking 3 hours and costing £9.80 ($16.15) for a one-way ticket. Call the Buchanan Bus Station at ☎ **0141/332-7133** in Glasgow for information about departures and tickets.

BY CAR   From Glasgow, head north along A82.

VISITOR INFORMATION

The **tourist information office** is at Cameron Centre, Cameron Square (☎ **01397/ 703781**).

EXPLORING THE AREA

The ruins of **Old Inverlochy Castle,** scene of the famous battle in 1645, can be reached by driving 2 miles north of Fort William on A82. At a point just 1 mile north of Fort William is **Glen Nevis,** one of the most scenic glens in Scotland.

About 14 miles west of Fort William, on A830 toward Mallaig, at Glenfinnan at the head of Loch Shiel, is the **Glenfinnan Monument,** which marks the spot where Bonnie Prince Charlie unfurled his proud red-and-white silk banner on August 19, 1745, in his ill-fated attempt to restore the Stuarts to the British throne. The figure of a kilted Highlander tops the monument. At a visitor center you can learn of the prince's campaign from Glenfinnan to Derby that ended in his defeat at Culloden.

Neptune's Staircase, 3 miles northwest of Fort William off A830 at Banavie, is a series of nine locks that were constructed at the same time as the Caledonian Canal, raising Telford's canal 64 feet.

West Highland Museum. Cameron Sq. ☎ **01397/702169.** Admission £2 ($3.30) adults, £1.50 ($2.45) senior citizens, 50p (85¢) children. July–Aug, Mon–Sat 10am–5pm, Sun 2–5pm; Sept–June, Mon–Sat 10am–5pm.

The collection in this museum sheds light on all aspects of local history, especially the 1745 Jacobite Rising; it also has sections on tartans and folk life. It lies in the center of town next to the tourist office.

SHOPPING   The **Ben Nevis Woolen Mill,** Belford Road (☎ **01397/704244**), in the north end of town, is only a shop, not a functioning woolen mill. Here you'll find a large selection of clothing and accessories: wools, tweeds, and tartans, and some hand-knit Arran sweaters. An on-premises restaurant features regional fare.

The **Granite House,** High Street (☎ **01397/703651**), is a family-run business that's been around for 21 years. The owners call themselves "giftmongers" and see their shop as a mini-department store. There is a large selection of Scottish jewelry, with silver pieces in both traditional and contemporary designs, and numerous watches. Collectibles such as Royal Doulton and Lilliput Lane china and crystal by

Edinburgh, Wedgwood, and Border Fine Arts are found here, and the traditional music department offers more than 1,000 Irish and Scottish music CDs and an array of traditional instruments, including pennywhistles and *bhodrain* (a large drum struck with sticks on both ends). There's a bit of everything—casual clothing, soft toys, numerous gadgets, even furniture.

The **Scottish Crafts & Whisky Centre,** 135–139 High St. (☎ 01397/704406), is another place with a good mix of the best of all things Scottish: regionally produced jewelry, garden fountains, rugs, and clothing. Whisky connoisseurs will find some limited-edition and very rare bottles stocked, including a 1958 Ben Nevis. Handmade chocolates by Ferguson's are also available.

Treasures of the Earth, Main Street, Corpach (☎ 01397/704406), 5 miles west of Fort William along route A830, sells crystals, minerals, and polished stones from around the world. These are available loose or set in jewelry, watches, and clocks.

WHERE TO STAY

There is no shortage of B&B accommodations in Fort William, most with a good view of Loch Linnhe or Ben Nevis. The tourist information office can supply you with a list.

VERY EXPENSIVE

✪ **Inverlochy Castle.** Torlundy, Fort William, Inverness-shire PH33 6SN. ☎ 01397/702177. Fax 01397/702953. 14 rms, 3 suites. TV TEL. £305–£330 ($503.25–$544.50) double; from £400 ($660) suite. AE, MC, V. Rates include Scottish breakfast. Closed early Jan to late Feb. Take A82, 3 miles northeast of town.

Inverlochy Castle, set against the scenic backdrop of Ben Nevis, is another place where Queen Victoria stayed. In her time it was a newly built (1870) Scottish mansion belonging to Baron Abinger. The monarch claimed in her diary, "I never saw a lovelier or more romantic spot." Now a Relais & Châteaux hotel, Inverlochy has recently undergone a major refurbishment. The hotel has retained its charm as well as its large, friendly staff, and remains one of the premier places of Scotland. Luxurious appointments, antiques, artwork, and crystal, plus a profusion of flowers, create a mood of elegance and refinement. The prices reflect this opulence.

Dining/Entertainment: The cuisine is one of the finest in Scotland, with food cooked to order and served on silver platters. Salmon from the Spean, crayfish from Loch Linnhe, and produce from the hotel's own farm garden are part of the fare; partridge and grouse are offered in season. Jackets and ties are required, and no smoking is permitted in the dining room. Outsiders can dine here if there's room, but reservations are mandatory. Meals are served daily from 12:30 to 1:45pm and 7:15 to 9:15pm.

Services: 24-hour room service, concierge, valet parking, baby-sitting, laundry.

Facilities: Garden, tennis, game fishing.

MODERATE

The Moorings Hotel. Banavie, Fort William, Inverness-shire PH33 7LY. ☎ 01397/772797. Fax 01397/772441. 21 rms. TV TEL. £60–£90 ($99–$148.50) double. AE, DC, MC, V. Rates include Scottish breakfast.

One of the most modern and up-to-date hotels in the region, the Moorings was designed in a traditional style in the mid-1970s, with bay and dormer windows and a painted black-and-white facade. The hotel is 3 miles north of Fort William in the hamlet of Banavie, beside B8004 and the Caledonian Canal, and provides easy access to the many lakes and forests of the surrounding region.

The interior is richly paneled in the Jacobean style. The bedrooms, most of which have undergone recent redecoration, are attractive and modern. Bar lunches and suppers are served in the cellar in the Mariner Wine Bar, offering 40 kinds of wine from around the world. More formal meals are served in the Moorings Restaurant, where an even greater selection of wine (more than 200 vintages) accompanies such dishes as smoked venison, Scottish oysters, homemade terrines, cullen skink (the traditional smoked-haddock soup of Scotland), wild salmon in a lemon-butter sauce, and halibut in a wild-mushroom sauce.

INEXPENSIVE

Alexandra. The Parade, Fort William, Inverness-shire PH33 6AZ. ☎ **01397/702241.** Fax 01397/705554. 98 rms. TV TEL. £64–£104 ($105.60–$171.60) double. AE, DC, MC, V. Rates include Scottish breakfast.

Directly across from the rail terminal, the Alexandra is a familiar sight, a hotel with tall gables and formidable granite walls so common in this part of the Highlands. It has been completely modernized, offering pleasant rooms with tea- and coffeemakers. Service and housekeeping standards are good. The chef makes excellent use of fresh fish and the wine cellar is amply endowed. The vegetables are simply cooked with enjoyable results.

Croit Anna Hotel. Druimarbin, Fort William, Inverness-shire PH33 6RR. ☎ **01397/702268.** Fax 01397/704099. 95 rms (80 with bath). TV. £36–£44 ($59.40–$72.60) double without bath, £72–£88 ($118.80–$145.20) double with bath. MC, V. Rates include Scottish breakfast. Closed Nov–Mar. Take A82 2$^1/_2$ miles south of town.

Overlooking Loch Linnhe, the hotel has fine views of the Ardgour Hills, and is owned and managed by the same family who built it on a traditional Highland croft that has been in their possession for more than 250 years. All rooms have tea- and coffeemakers. In the hotel dining room, a four-course à la carte meal costs £17 ($28.05). Hotel facilities include a games room, panoramic lounge, gift shop, lounge bar, and guest launderette. It's open from April to October, and entertainment is provided on most evenings in season.

WHERE TO DINE

Crannog Seafood Restaurant. Town Pier. ☎ **01397/705589.** Reservations recommended. Main courses £10–£14 ($16.50–$23.10); lunch £6–£9 ($9.50–$14.20). MC, V. Daily noon–2:30pm and 6–9:30pm. Closed Jan 1–2 and Dec 25–26. SEAFOOD.

In a converted ticket office and bait store in a quayside setting overlooking Loche Linnhe, this restaurant serves seafood so fresh that locals claim "it fairly leaps at you." Much of the fish comes from the owner's own fishing vessels, or from their own smokehouse that turns out smoked salmon, mussels, and trout. Bouillabaisse is a chef's specialty, as are Loch Linnhe prawns and langoustines. A vegetarian dish of the day is invariably featured. Look also for the daily specials listed on the chalkboard.

FORT WILLIAM AFTER DARK

Ben Nevis Pub, 103–109 High St. (☎ **01397/702295**), offers free entertainment by rock, blues, jazz, and folk bands on Thursday and Friday nights. On tap you'll find McEwan's, Foster's, and Kronenberg lagers, McEwan's 70 Shilling, and Guinness and Gillespie's stouts. **McTavish's Kitchen,** High Street (☎ **01397/702406**), presents a Scottish show, featuring tartan-clad dancers, bagpipes, and other traditional instruments every night from May through September at 8:30pm. You can see the show with or without dinner. A three-course "Taste of Scotland" meal costs £14.95 ($24.65). On tap is Tennant's Special and Lager, available for £2.10 ($3.45) per pint. Admission to the show is £1.50 ($2.45) for adults and £1 ($1.65) for children if you're eating; the show only is £3 ($4.95) for adults and £1.50 ($2.45) for children. The **Grog & Gruel,** 66 High St. (☎ 01397/705078), serves up such regional cask-conditioned ales as Arrol's 80 Shilling. There's an occasional live band, ranging from rock and pop to folk and Scottish music.

3 Mallaig

179 miles NW of Edinburgh, 47 miles NW of Fort William, 96 miles NW of Oban

This small fishing village is a good touring center for the western Highlands and the islands. Steamers call here for the Kyle of Lochalsh, the Isle of Skye, the Outer Hebrides, and the sea lochs of the northwest coast. At the tip of a peninsula, Mallaig is surrounded by moody lochs and hills. The distance between Morat and Mallaig is just 3 miles.

ESSENTIALS
GETTING THERE

BY TRAIN   Trains from Fort William to Mallaig take you along one of the most panoramic routes in Scotland, well worth experiencing even if you don't want to go to Mallaig. Four trains per day make the run Monday through Saturday; service drops to two trains on Sunday. A one-way ticket costs £7 ($11.55). Call ☎ 01397/703791 for departure times.

BY BUS   Two buses per day run to Mallaig from Fort William; a one-way ticket is £4.50 ($7.45). Call ☎ 01599/534328 for information about departure times and trip length.

BY CAR   From Fort William, take A830, the scenic road, west to Mallaig.

VISITOR INFORMATION

A summer-only **tourist information office** (☎ 01687/462170) is in the center of Mallaig; look for the signs.

WHERE TO STAY & DINE

Marine Hotel. 10 Station Rd., Mallaig, Inverness-shire PH41 4PY. ☎ **01687/462217.** Fax 01687/462821. 19 rms. TV. £52–£64 ($85.80–$105.60) double. MC, V. Rates include Scottish breakfast. Half board £39–£50 ($64.35–$82.50) per person.

This family-owned business is located in the vicinity of the train station. All the comfortably furnished but basic rooms are heated and contain beverage-making facilities. Guests gather in the cocktail bar or TV lounge after enjoying a home-cooked meal, usually locally caught seafood. The Marine stays open all year.

4 Invergarry

25 miles NE of Fort William, 158 miles NW of Edinburgh

A Highland center for fishing and deer stalking, Invergarry is noted for its fine scenery. It's a good center for exploring Glen Mor and Loch Ness. At Invergarry the road through the western Highland glens and mountains begins, forming one part of the famous "Road to the Isles" that terminates at Kyle of Lochalsh.

ESSENTIALS
GETTING THERE

BY TRAIN   Go to Fort William (see below) and proceed the rest of the way by a connecting bus.

BY BUS   Highland Omnibuses service the area from Fort William. Since there's no bus station to go to for information in Fort William, the tourist office there will provide a list of schedules and departures.

BY CAR   In Fort William, proceed north on the Inverness road (A82) to Invergarry.

VISITOR INFORMATION

For tourist information, ask at Fort William (see section 2, above).

SEEING THE SIGHTS

Near Invergarry, you can visit the **Well of the Heads,** on the west side of Loch Oich near its southern tip, erected in 1812 by MacDonnell of Glengarry to commemorate the decapitation of seven brothers who had murdered the two sons of a 17th-century chief of Clan Keppoch, a branch of the MacDonnell clan. The seven heads were washed in the well before being presented to the chief of the MacDonnells at Glengarry.

You can also see the ruins of **Invergarry Castle,** the stronghold of the MacDonnells of Glengarry. The site of the castle on Raven's Rock, overlooking Loch Oich in the Great Glen, was a strategic one in the days of clan feuds and Jacobite risings. Because the castle ruins are not safe, you should view them only from the outside.

WHERE TO STAY & DINE

Glengarry Castle Hotel. Invergarry, Inverness-shire PH35 4HW. ☎ **01809/501254.** Fax 01809/501207. 26 rms. TV TEL. £84–£116 ($138.60–$191.40) double. MC, V. Rates include Scottish breakfast.

This is a mansion built between 1866 and 1869 on extensive grounds that contain the ruins of Invergarry Castle. With its gables and chimneys, it's an impressive sight, lying on the River Garry, which runs into Loch Oich. Glengarry makes a pleasant base for a holiday combining fishing, tennis, walking, and rowing. There are two lounges where drinks are served to residents, and the dining room offers good home-cooked but rather basic meals made from local produce. Light lunches are served for around £5.50 ($9.05); a special Sunday lunch costs £10.50 ($17.35) for three courses. Nightly table d'hôte dinners are £21 ($34.65). The rooms are comfortably old-fashioned, like something from the 1950s.

5 Aviemore

129 miles N of Edinburgh, 29 miles SE of Inverness, 85 miles N of Perth

This year-round holiday complex on the Spey was opened in 1966 in the heart of the Highlands, at the foot of the historic rock of **Craigellachie.** This rock was the rallying place for Clan Grant.

ESSENTIALS
GETTING THERE

BY TRAIN   Aviemore, on the main Inverness–Edinburgh rail line, is the major transportation hub of the area. For rail schedules and information in Aviemore, call ☎ **01479/810221.** Some 12 trains a day from Inverness pass through (trip time: 45 min.), at £8.50 ($14) for a one-way ticket. Twelve trains per day also arrive from either Glasgow or Edinburgh. Trip time from each city is 3 hours and a one-way ticket from either departure point is £26.10 ($43.05).

BY BUS   Aviemore is on the main Inverness–Edinburgh bus line with frequent service. The trip from Edinburgh takes about 3 hours (call ☎ **0990/808080** in

Edinburgh for schedules and information). Frequent buses throughout the day also arrive from Inverness (trip time: 40 min.).

BY CAR From Edinburgh, after crossing the Forth Bridge Road, take M90 to Perth, then continue the rest of the way along A9 into Aviemore.

VISITOR INFORMATION

The **tourist information office** is on Grampian Road (☎ **01479/810363**).

EXPLORING THE AREA

In the heart of the resort, the **Aviemore Mountain Resort** (☎ **01479/810624**) is an all-purpose cultural, sports, and entertainment complex. Built nearly a quarter of a century ago, inside a loop road, it contains four hotels and their grounds. The center's activities are suitable for everyone and include ice-skating, a dry ski slope, squash, snooker, discos, putting, go-karting, and much more. Most sports facilities are open daily from 10am to 1pm, 2 to 5pm, and 6 to 9pm. The Speyside Theatre, seating 710, changes its film programs weekly and often is host to live shows and concerts.

In winter, ski runs are available for both beginners and experts (four chairlifts and seven T-bar tows). The ice rink is the second-largest indoor ice rink in Britain, with seven curling lanes and ice-skating on a separate 4,000-square-foot pad. At night, younger people are attracted to the many pubs. Also offered are Scottish nights, folk singing, country dancing, or supper dances. In summer, sailing, canoeing, pony trekking, hill walking, and mountain climbing, as well as golf and fishing, are just some of the many activities.

North of Aviemore, the **Strathspey Railway,** Dalfaber Road (☎ **01479/810725**), is billed as providing "a trip into nostalgia." The railway follows the valley of the River Spey between Boat of Garten and Aviemore, a distance of 5 miles. The train is drawn by a coal-burning steam locomotive. The newest locomotive used was made some 35 years ago, the oldest being of 1899 vintage. The railway takes you through scenes unchanged in a century—the trip is meant to re-create the total experience of travel on a Scottish steam railway that once carried wealthy Victorians toward their hunting lodges in "North Britain." The round-trip takes about an hour. The rail station at Boat of Garten, where you can board the train, has also been restored.

Round-trip passage costs £6 ($9.90) in first class, £4.60 ($7.60) in second class. Schedules change frequently, but from July to the end of August trains make five round-trip journeys daily. In spring and fall, the trains run only on Wednesday, Thursday, and Sunday, making four round-trip journeys each day. There is no regular service during the winter; however, special trips are made during the Christmas season during which Santa Claus makes an appearance. To complete the experience, you can wine and dine aboard on Wednesday in July and August, when a single-seating casual lunch is served. The cost for the fare and meal is £15 ($24.75). Reservations must be made for the meals. The dining car is a replica of a Pullman parlor car, the Amethyst. For reservations and hours of departure, call ☎ **01479/831692.**

OUTDOOR PURSUITS You can journey to the sky on the **Cairngorm Chair Lift** (☎ **01479/861261**), whose lowest section lies 10 miles east of Aviemore. A round-trip passage on this, the longest chairlift in Scotland, costs £5 ($8.25) for adults and £3 ($4.95) for children 17 and under. During the summer months, the lift runs daily from 9:30am to 5:30pm. In winter, hours are daily from 9am to 4pm; the uppermost reaches are closed during periods of high winds. The highest section is 4,084 feet above sea level. In summer, on a clear day you can see Ben Nevis in the west, and the vista of Strathspey from here is spectacular, from Loch Morlich set in the Rothiemurchus Forest to the Spey Valley.

Skiers are attracted to the area anytime after October, when snow can be expected. Ski equipment and clothing can be rented at the Day Lodge at the main Cairngorm parking area. Weather patterns can change quickly in the Cairngorm massif. Call the number above for a report on the latest weather conditions. To reach the area, take A951, branching off from A9 at Aviemore, then head for the parking area at the Day Lodge.

SHOPPING   Cairngorm Whisky Centre, on the ski road, 1 mile east of Aviemore (☎ 01479/810574), stocks 500 single-malt whiskies at any given time. With that many options, you may want to step into their tasting room, where £3 ($4.95) entitles you to sample four whiskies. The shop, open Monday through Saturday from 9:30am to 5:30pm, and Sunday from 12:30 to 5pm, shortens its hours from November through February, opening Monday through Saturday from 10am to 5pm and Sunday from 12:30 to 4pm.

WHERE TO STAY

Best Western Aviemore Highlands Hotel. Aviemore Mountain Resort, Aviemore, Inverness-shire PH22 1PJ. ☎ 800/528-1234 or 01479/810771. Fax 01479/811473. 103 rms. TV TEL. £88 ($145.20) double. AE, DC, MC, V. Rates include Scottish breakfast.

This resort hotel caters to winter and summer sports enthusiasts. Its beige-brick, two-story exterior rambles in a labyrinthine progression of wings, staircases, and long hallways, which funnel into public rooms illuminated with big windows overlooking the countryside. In summer, doors open to reveal flagstone outdoor terraces ringed with viburnum and juniper. You can drink in the Illicit Still Bar, which has an antique whisky still and copper-top tables. The main restaurant is capped with a soaring ceiling, trussed with beams. Dinner is served in the formal restaurant. The bedrooms are well furnished and some family rooms are available. Room service is provided throughout the day and evening.

Stakis Coylumbridge Resort Hotel. Rothiemurchus, Aviemore, Inverness-shire PH22 1QN. ☎ 01479/810661. Fax 01479/811309. 175 rms, 4 suites. TV TEL. £120 ($198) double; £132 ($218) family room; £142 ($234) suite. AE, DC, MC, V. Rates include Scottish breakfast.

On 65 acres of tree-studded grounds facing the slopes of the Cairngorms, this hotel has extensive sports and leisure facilities. Bedrooms are well appointed, each with in-house films, hot-beverage equipment, fresh fruit, and a daily newspaper. Meals are served in either Walker's Restaurant or the Grant Room. In the hotel are two heated swimming pools, a sauna, whirlpool, steam bath, gym, hairdressing salon, gift shop, and games room. House entertainment is a regular feature during the evening, particularly on weekends. In winter, downhill and cross-country skiing equipment and training are available. There's a sports hall for children.

WHERE TO DINE

The Bar/The Restaurant. In the Dalfaber Golf and Country Club. ☎ 01479/811244. Reservations required in the restaurant. Main courses £5.50–£12 ($9.05–$19.80); table d'hôte meals £7–£16 ($11.55–$26.40); Sun lunch £8.50 ($14); bar platters £3–£5.50 ($4.95–$9.05). MC, V. Restaurant: Mon–Sat 6–9:30pm, Sun noon–7:30pm. Bar: daily 11am–11pm. SCOTTISH.

Although the golf course, the health club, and the leisure facilities of this country club are open only to members, visitors are welcome in the cozy and well-managed bar and restaurant, about a mile north of the center of Aviemore. It's outfitted in tartan carpets and upholstery, with heavy brocade curtains and views from big windows over the surrounding conifers and tundra. In the bar, where live entertainment is featured nightly, the fare includes venison cutlets or filets, sandwiches, homemade steak pies, and any of a variety of malt whiskies. The restaurant serves seafood, such as skewered tiger prawns soaked with butter, as well as grilled Angus steaks and main-course salads. There is also a limited number of vegetarian dishes. Several nights per week, the restaurant hosts theme nights with entertainment. A table d'hôte menu is served as performers sing and dance.

AVIEMORE AFTER DARK

Crofters, off Grampian Road at the Aviemore Mountain Resort (☎ **01479/810624**), has dancing with no cover charge nightly from 10pm until 1am, with guest deejays bringing in their own music and setting the mood. The bar opens at 10:30am and serves Tennant's Lager and Guinness on tap. Located a mere 2-minute walk from the center of Aviemore, the private drive leading here is well marked from Grampian Road.

6 Along Loch Ness

Sir Peter Scott's *Nessitera rhombopteryx* continues to elude her pursuers. "Nessie," as she's more familiarly known, has captured the imagination of the world, drawing thousands of visitors yearly to Loch Ness. The Loch Ness monster has been described as the world's greatest mystery. Half a century ago A82 was built alongside the banks of the loch's western shores. Since that time many more sightings have been claimed.

All types of high-tech underwater contraptions have gone in after the Loch Ness monster, but no one can find her in spite of the photographs that have appeared. Dr. Robert Rines and his associates at the Academy of Applied Science in Massachusetts maintain an all-year watch with sonar-triggered cameras and strobe lights suspended from a raft in Urquhart Bay.

Some people in Inverness aren't very keen on collaring the monster, and you can't blame them. An old prophecy predicts a violent end for Inverness if the monster is ever captured.

The loch is 24 miles long, a mile wide, and some 755 feet deep. If you'd like to stay along the loch and monster-watch instead of seeking lodgings at Inverness, you can do so at the centers mentioned below. Even if the monster doesn't put in an appearance, you can enjoy the scenery. In summer, from both Fort Augustus and Inverness you can take boat cruises across Loch Ness.

Motorists should take A82 between Fort Augustus and Inverness running along Loch Ness. Buses from either Fort Augustus or Inverness also traverse A82, taking you to Drumnadrochit.

DRUMNADROCHIT

This bucolic hamlet lies about a mile from Loch Ness at the entrance to Glen Urquhart. It's the nearest village to the part of the loch in which sightings of the monster have been reported most frequently.

SEEING THE SIGHTS

Official Loch Ness Monster Exhibition. Drumnadrochit. ☎ **01456/450573**. Admission £4.50 ($7.45) adults, £3.50 ($5.75) students, £2.50 ($4.15) senior citizens and ages 7–16, free for age 7 and under; £11.50 ($18.95) family ticket. Mar–June and Sept–Oct, daily 9:30am–5:30pm; July–Aug, daily 9am–7:30pm; Nov–Feb, daily 10am–3pm.

This official exhibition is Drumnadrochit's big attraction, featuring a scale replica of Nessie. It opened in 1980 and has been packing 'em in ever since. You can follow the

Spotting Nessie

She's affectionately known as "Nessie," although her more formal name is *Nessitera rhombopteryx,* and she has the unflattering designation of "Loch Ness Monster." Is she the beast that never was, or the world's most famous living animal? You decide. Real or imagined, she's the virtual mascot of Scotland, and even if she doesn't exist, she's one of the major tourist attractions of the country. Who can drive along the dark waters of Loch Ness without staring at the murky depths and expecting a head to appear above the water's surface at any minute?

Nessie is hardly young. Her lineage is ancient. An appearance in A.D. 565 was recorded by that respected 7th-century biographer, St. Adamnan, who is not known as a spinner of tall tales. The claim is that St. Columba was en route along Loch Ness to convert Brude, king of the Picts, to Christianity. The saint ordered a monk to swim across the loch and retrieve a boat. However, in midswim Nessie attacked. The monk's life was saved only when Columba confronted the sea beast with a sign of the cross and a shouted invocation.

Columba's calming effect on Nessie must have lasted over the centuries, because no attacks have been reported since. Of course, there was that "accident" in the 1500s when a chronicle reported that "A terrible beast issuing out of the water early one morning about midsummer knocked down trees and killed three men with its tail." Again, in 1961, 30 hotel guests reported seeing two humps that rose out of the water just before their craft exploded and sank. Bertram Mill has offered £20,000 to have the monster delivered alive to his circus.

Since Scotland is the land not only of Nessie but whisky, it might be assumed that some of these sightings were hallucinations brought on by the consumption of far too many wee drams. However, sightings have come from people of impeccable credentials who were stone sober. Nessie seems to like to show herself to monks, perhaps a tradition dating from St. Columba. Several monks at the Fort Augustus Abbey claim to have seen her. A monk who is an organist at Westminster Cathedral reported a sighting in 1973.

Belief in Nessie's existence is so strong that midget yellow submarines and all types of high-tech underwater contraptions have been used in an attempt to track her down. Many photographs exist—most of them faked—usually from the site of the ruins of Urquhart Castle on the loch's shore. Other photographs exist that have not been so easily explained.

If Nessie does exist, exactly who is she? A sole survivor from prehistoric times? A gigantic sea snake? It has even been suggested that she's a "cosmic wanderer through time." Whatever, chances are you won't see her on your visit, but you can see a fantasy replica of the sea beast at the Loch Ness Monster Exhibition at Drumnadrochit.

story from A.D. 565 to the present in photographs, audio, and video, as well as climbing aboard the sonar research vessel *John Murray.* The Exhibition Centre is the most visited place in the Highlands of Scotland, with more than 200,000 visitors annually.

✪ **Urquhart Castle.** Loch Ness along A82. ☎ 01456/450551. Admission £3.20 ($5.30) adults, £2.20 ($3.65) senior citizens, £1 ($1.65) children. Apr–June, daily 9:30am–5:45pm; July–Sept, daily 9:30am–3:45pm.

This ruined castle, one of Scotland's largest, is 1¹/₂ miles southeast of Drumnadrochit on a promontory overlooking Loch Ness. The chief of Clan Grant owned the castle in 1509, and most of the existing building dates from that period. In 1692 the castle was blown up by the Grants to prevent it from becoming a Jacobite stronghold. It's here at Urquhart Castle that sightings of the Loch Ness monster are most often reported.

WHERE TO STAY & DINE

Loch Ness Inn. Lewiston, near Drumnadrochit, Inverness-shire IV3 6UN. ☎ **01456/450225.** Fax 01456/450429. 9 rms. £60 ($99) double. MC, V. Rates include Scottish breakfast.

Built in the mid-1700s as a brewery, this white-painted building was connected a century ago to an adjacent farmer's cottage. The result was an L-shaped building whose wings today embrace a garden, where it's said that a 19th-century ghost makes occasional appearances, feeding her ghostly chickens. It's owned by Donald Skinner. There's a thriving pub, the Bonnie Prince Charlie Tavern, where meals costing £5 to £12 ($8.25 to $19.80) are served. The restaurant features an à la carte menu, offering steaks, local game, and seafood. Meals start at £10 ($16.50) per person. Bedrooms are well maintained and comfortably furnished. The Loch Ness Inn is near the center of the hamlet beside A82.

✪ **Polmaily House Hotel.** Drumnadrochit, Inverness-shire IV3 6XT. ☎ **01456/450343.** Fax 01456/450813. 11 rms. £72–£124 ($118.80–$204.60) double. MC, V. Rates include Scottish breakfast. Drive 2 miles west of Drumnadrochit on A831.

In 1994 John and Sonia Whittington-Davis, third-generation hoteliers, purchased this Edwardian inn that graciously re-creates the pleasures of manorial country-house living. The house, on an 18-acre estate featuring mixed gardens and woodland, is believed to have been built in 1776. Spacious and elegant bedrooms tastefully filled with antiques have high ceilings, leaded-glass windows, and flowered wallpaper. The hotel has a tennis court and a croquet lawn as well as a heated indoor swimming pool, a sauna, and a gym.

The restaurant attracts locals as well as hotel residents. The most exquisite dishes are prepared using the best of fresh local ingredients, such as Aberdeen beef and fresh salmon. A daily changing table d'hôte dinner costs £20 ($33) for four courses.

INVERMORISTON

If you stop at this hamlet 168 miles northwest of Edinburgh and 29 miles south of Inverness, you'll be in one of the beauty spots along Loch Ness. **Glenmoriston** is one of the loveliest glens in the Highlands. You can take walks along the riverbanks, with views of Loch Ness. The location is at the junction of the Loch Ness Highway (A82) and the road to the Isle of Skye (A887).

WHERE TO STAY & DINE

Glenmoriston Arms Hotel. Invermoriston, Inverness-shire IV3 6YA. ☎ **01320/351206.** Fax 01320/351308. 8 rms. TV TEL £90 ($148.50) double. MC, V. Rates include Scottish breakfast.

This has been a roadside inn for 2 centuries. It's a lot like a woodsy, intimate hunting lodge, with antique weapons, old trophies, well-polished paneling, and more than 160 varieties of single-malt whisky. The bedrooms are clean and modest. A nightly table d'hôte menu is served, costing £23 ($37.95) per person. You'll find the hotel at the junction of A82 and A887.

FORT AUGUSTUS

This Highland touring center stands at the head (the southernmost end) of Loch Ness. The town took its name from a fort named for a duke of Cumberland, built after 1715. The present Benedictine abbey stands on its site. The location is 36 miles south of Inverness along A82 and 166 miles northwest of Edinburgh.

Bisecting the actual village of Fort Augustus is the **Caledonian Canal,** and the locks are a popular attraction when boats are passing through. Running across the loftiest sections of Scotland, the canal was constructed between 1803 and 1822. Almost in a straight line, it makes its way from Inverness in the north to Corpach in the vicinity of Fort William. The canal is 60 miles long: 22 man-made miles and the rest natural lochs. In summer you can take several pleasure craft along this canal, leaving from Fort Augustus.

WHERE TO STAY & DINE

Inchnacardoch Lodge. Hwy. A82, Fort Augustus, Inverness-shire PH32 4BL. ☎ **01320/ 366258.** 14 rms. TV TEL. £60–£78 ($99–$128.70) double. AE, DC, MC, V. Rates include Scottish breakfast. Closed Nov–Feb. Drive ¹/₂ mile north of Fort Augustus on A82.

The Inchnacardoch Lodge is a family-run no-smoking hotel in a panoramic setting overlooking Loch Ness. Once a country residence of the chief of the Fraser clan, Lord Lovat, the hotel offers comfortable bedrooms with private baths and tea- and coffeemaking facilities. The common areas of the lodge have recently been refurbished, but the traditional ambience remains. You can relax in the lounge bar while watching the waters for the mysterious monster; a wee dram of malt too much and you may just find her. If you can tear yourself away from the view of the water, the hotel restaurant serves a three-course table d'hôte dinner for £17.50 ($28.90). The entire lodge is designated a no-smoking zone.

Lovat Arms. Hwy. A82, Fort Augustus, Inverness-shire PH32 4DU. ☎ **01320/366206.** Fax 01320/366677. 21 rms. TV TEL. £62–£72 ($102.30–$118.80) double. MC, V. Rates include Scottish breakfast.

Built between 1840 and 1860, with wings added in the 1890s and 1990s, it was reputedly owned long ago by Lord Lovat, scion of one of the oldest Norman lineages of Scotland, the Fraser family. The stucco-covered house with sandstone window and door frames is well known in the region for its convivial pub, where tasty meals are served at lunch and dinner. Also on the premises is a spacious lounge bar where good food is available at reasonable prices at lunch and in the evening, and a dining room where a table d'hôte menu features Scottish fish and meat. A four-course dinner costs £19.50 ($32.15), whereas lunches consisting of bar platters are priced from £3.95 to £4.50 ($6.50 to $7.45). Each of the comfortable, rather functional bedrooms is carpeted and very clean. On cold days a fire burns in an area reserved for residents. The Lovat Arms stands beside one of the two major roads through the Highlands and is an ideal base from which to explore Loch Ness.

7 Inverness

156 miles NW of Edinburgh, 134 miles NW of Dundee, 134 miles W of Aberdeen

The capital of the Highlands, Inverness is a royal burgh and seaport lying at the north end of Great Glen on both sides of the Ness River. It's considered the best base for touring the north.

ESSENTIALS
GETTING THERE

BY PLANE   Domestic flights from various parts of Britain arrive at the Inverness Airport. Flight time from London's Heathrow to the Inverness/Dalcross Airport is 75 minutes. Call ☎ 01463/232471 in Inverness for flight information.

BY TRAIN   Some five to seven trains per day arrive from Glasgow and Edinburgh (on Sunday, two or three trains). A one-way fare from either city is £25.50 ($42.05). Trains pull into Station Square, off Academy Street in Inverness (☎ 0345/484950 for schedules and information).

BY BUS   Scottish CityLink coaches provide service for the area (☎ 0990/505050 for schedule information). Frequent service through the day is possible from either Edinburgh or Glasgow, at a one-way fare of £11.60 or £10.60 ($19.15 or $17.50), respectively.

BY CAR   From Edinburgh, take M9 north to Perth, then follow along the Great North Road (A9) until you reach Inverness.

VISITOR INFORMATION

The information office of the **Highlands of Scotland Tourist Board** is at Castle Wynd (☎ 01463/234353).

GETTING AROUND

For transportation facilities and information about the surrounding area, the **bus station** is at Farraline Park, off Academy Street (☎ 01463/233371), and the **railway station** is on Academy Street (☎ 0345/484950). **Taxis** are found off Academy Street by the Station Square. Call **Tartan Taxis** (☎ 01463/233033) or **Highland Taxis** (☎ 01463/220222) for service. If you'd like to park your car and tour the center of Inverness, there's a multistory parking lot on Rose Street, charging reasonable rates.

TOURS & CRUISES   If you're interested in bus tours of the Highlands and cruises on Loch Ness, go to **Inverness Traction,** 6 Burnett Rd. (☎ 01463/239292). In summer, there are also cruises along the Caledonian Canal from Inverness into Loch Ness.

FAST FACTS

In an emergency, dial ☎ **999** to summon police, an ambulance, or firefighters. For exchanging currency and other banking affairs, you can go to the **Bank of Scotland,** 9 High St. (☎ 01463/663266), open Monday, Tuesday, Thursday, and Friday from 9am to 5pm, and Wednesday from 10am to 5pm. The **head post office** is at Queensgate (☎ 01463/243574), open Monday through Friday from 9am to 5:30pm and Saturday from 9am to 6:30pm.

SPECIAL EVENTS

At the **Highland Games** in July, with their sporting competitions and festive balls, the season in Inverness reaches its social peak. For more information and exact dates, consult the tourist office (see "Visitor Information," above).

SEEING THE SIGHTS

Inverness is one of the oldest inhabited localities in Scotland. On **Craig Phadrig** are the remains of a vitrified fort, believed to date from the 4th century B.C. One of the most important prehistoric monuments in the north, the **Stones of Clava** are about 6 miles east of Inverness on the road to Nairn. These cairns and standing stones are from the Bronze Age.

The old castle of Inverness stood to the east of the present Castlehill, and the site still retains the name "Auld Castlehill." David I built the first stone castle in Inverness around 1141. The **Clock Tower** is all that remains of a fort erected by Cromwell's army between 1652 and 1657. The 16th-century **Abertarff House,** on Church Street, is now the headquarters of An Comunn Gaidhealach, the Highland association that preserves the Gaelic language and culture.

Opposite the town hall is the **Old Mercat Cross,** with its Stone of the Tubs, an Inverness landmark, said to be the stone on which women rested their washtubs as they ascended from the river. Known as "Clachnacudainn," the lozenge-shaped stone was the spot where local early kings were crowned.

St. Andrews Cathedral, on Ardross Street, is open to visitors daily from 8:30am to 6pm, and this northernmost diocese of the Scottish Episcopal church boasts a fine example of Victorian architecture. The icons given to Bishop Eden by the tsar of Russia should be viewed. For information, get in touch with the Provost, 15 Ardross St. (☎ 01463/233535).

West of the river rises the wooded hill of **Tomnahurich,** known as "the hill of the fairies." It's now a cemetery, and from here the views are panoramic. In the Ness are wooded islands, linked to Inverness by suspension bridges and turned into parks.

Inverness Museum and Art Gallery. Castle Wynd, off Bridge St. ☎ **01463/237114.** Free admission. Mon–Sat 9am–5pm.

This museum in the town center is a top attraction. It has displays representing the social and natural history, archaeology, art, and culture of the Scottish Highlands, with special emphasis on the Inverness district. There's an important collection of Highland silver, with a reconstructed silversmith's workshop; displays on the "Life of the Clans"; a reconstruction of a local taxidermist's workshop; a reconstructed Inverness kitchen of the 1920s; and an art gallery. There's also a permanent exhibition on the story of the Inverness district, from local geology and archaeology to the present. Other facilities are a souvenir shop, a coffee shop, and an information service.

NEARBY SIGHTS

From Inverness, you can visit **Culloden Battlefield,** Culloden Moor, 6 miles to the southeast, where Bonnie Prince Charlie and the Jacobite army were finally crushed on April 16, 1746. Leanach Cottage, around which the battle took place, still stands and was inhabited until 1912. A path leads from the visitor center through the Field of the English, where 52 men of the duke of Cumberland's forces who died during the battle are said to be buried. Features of interest include the Graves of the Clans, communal burial places with simple stones bearing individual clan names; the great memorial cairn, erected in 1881; the Well of the Dead; and the huge Cumberland Stone, from which the victorious "Butcher" Cumberland is said to have reviewed the scene. The battle lasted only 40 minutes; the prince's army lost some 1,200 men out of 5,000, and the king's army 300 out of 9,000.

A **visitor center** (☎ 01463/790607) is open November and December, daily from 10am to 4pm, and February to October, daily from 9am to 6pm. The center is closed during January. Admission of £2.90 ($4.80) for adults and £2 ($3.30) for senior citizens and children includes a visit to an audiovisual presentation of the background and history of the famous battle.

Fort George (☎ 01667/462777), on Moray Firth by the village of Ardersier, was called "the most considerable fortress and best situated in Great Britain" in 1748 by Lt. Col. James Wolfe, who went on to fame as Wolfe of Québec. Built after the Battle of Culloden, the fort was occupied by the Hanoverian army of George II and is still an active army barracks. The rampart, almost a mile around, encloses some 42 acres. Dr. Samuel Johnson and James Boswell visited here in 1773 on their Highland trek. The fort contains the **Queen's Own Highlanders Regimental Museum,** with regimental exhibits from 1778 to today, representing a number of Highland regiments as well as its namesake. The public can visit some parts of the fort as well as the museum April to September, daily from 9:30am to 5:45pm; October to March, Monday through Saturday from 9:30am to 4:30pm and Sunday from 2 to 4:30pm. Admission to the fort is £2.80 ($4.60) for adults, £1.80 ($2.95) for senior citizens, and £1 ($1.65) for ages 5 to 15; free for age 4 and under. Once inside, you can visit the museum for free. Fort George is 11 miles northeast of Inverness.

SHOPPING

A family-owned shrine to Scottish kilt-making is **Duncan Chisholm & Sons,** 47–53 Castle St. (☎ **01463/234599**). The tartans of at least 50 of Scotland's largest clans are available in the form of kilts and kilt jackets for men and women. If your heart is set on something more esoteric, the staff can acquire whatever fabric your ancestors would have worn to make up your garment. There's a workshop on the premises, which can be visited, and also a section devoted to Scottish gifts (neckties, scarves, yard goods, kilt pins in thistle patterns) and memorabilia. If you don't find what you're hankering for, take a short walk down the street to Chisholm's most important competitor, **Hector Russel, Kiltmaker,** 4–9 Huntly St. (☎ **01463/222781**), where an equivalent collection of garments is available.

The town's most visible jewelry store, with an unusual collection of bangles and bracelets inspired by the decorative traditions of Celtic Scotland, is **D&H Norval,** 88 Church St. (☎ **01463/232739**). Two additional shops that specialize in local crafts and jewelry inspired by medieval Ireland's *Book of Kells* are the **Celtic Craft Centre,** 15 Inglis St. (☎ **01463/713123**), and its newer and larger annex, **Celtic Spirit,** 14 Church St. (☎ **01463/714796**), where the focus is on New Age books and an unusual collection of wind chimes.

If you want to record your experiences in the Highlands on film, or if you need a new set of eyeglasses, head for the town's best photography and optical shop, **Lizar's,** 14 Inglis St. (☎ **01463/224464**).

A final note: In the 1990s, a shopping mall based on the North American model opened on the eastern perimeter of town. If you're looking for housewares or more mainstream clothing or sporting goods, head for **Eastgate Shopping Complex,** on Eastgate, where at least 50 merchants have shops.

WHERE TO STAY
VERY EXPENSIVE

✪ **Culloden House.** Culloden, Inverness, Inverness-shire IV1 2NZ. ☎ **01463/790461.** Fax 01463/792181. 28 rms, 10 suites. TV TEL. £190 ($313.50) double; £230 ($379.50) suite. AE, DC, MC, V. Rates include Scottish breakfast. Drive 3 miles east of Inverness on A96.

Culloden House is a Georgian mansion with a much-photographed Adam facade. It includes part of the Renaissance castle in which Bonnie Prince Charlie slept the night before Culloden, the last great battle on British soil. Superbly isolated, with extensive gardens and parkland, it's perfect for a relaxed Highland holiday. At the iron gates to the broad front lawn, a piper in full Highland garb plays at sundown, the skirl of the bagpipe accompanied by the barking of house dogs. The prince of Wales and the crown prince of Japan have stayed here, perfectly at home among the exquisite furnishings and handsome plaster friezes. Public rooms are spacious, and beautifully painted and furnished. The cozy bedrooms have sylvan views and history-laden atmosphere. The hotel maintains traditional ideas of personal service.

Dining/Entertainment: In the elegant Adam Dining Room, chef Michael Simpson presents beautifully prepared traditional Scottish cuisine. Fresh produce and in-season game are used, along with high-quality, locally raised cattle. Lunch, served daily from 12:30 to 2:30pm, is à la carte. Dinner consists of a selection of various appetizers and main dishes; diners can choose to have a three- to five-course meal. Evening service begins at 7pm, with last orders taken at 9pm.

Services: 24-hour room service, laundry.

Facilities: Tennis, sauna, solarium.

EXPENSIVE

Bunchrew House Hotel and Restaurant. Bunchrew, Inverness, Inverness-shire IV3 6TA. ☎ **01463/234917.** Fax 01463/710620. 11 suites. MINIBAR TV TEL. £110–£140 ($181.50–$231) suite for 2. AE, MC, V. Rates include Scottish breakfast. Drive 3 miles west of Inverness on A862.

This fine Scottish mansion on the shores of Beauly Firth is the ancestral home of both the Fraser and the McKenzie clans. The house, built by Simon Fraser, eighth Lord Lovat, dates to 1621. Set in 15 acres of landscaped gardens, the house has been restored as a country-house hotel. Guests get a glimpse of a bygone era when they relax in the paneled drawing room with roaring log fires in winter. Bedrooms are individually designed and decorated. The Lovat Suite has a fully canopied four-poster bed, and the Wyvis Suite boasts a half-tester bed.

Dining/Entertainment: You can dine in the candlelit restaurant on prime Scottish beef, fresh lobster and crayfish, local game and venison, and fresh vegetables. Lunch is served daily from noon to 2pm. Dinner is offered from 7 to 9pm.

Services: Room service, laundry, baby-sitting.

Facilities: Free salmon fishing on the estate.

✪ **Dunain Park Hotel.** Dunain Park, Inverness, Inverness-shire IV3 6JN. ☎ **01463/230512.** Fax 01463/224532. 6 rms, 8 suites and cottages. TV TEL. £140–£150 ($231–$247.50) double; from £158 ($260.70) suite or cottage. AE, DC, MC, V. Rates include Scottish breakfast. Drive 2^1/2 miles southwest of Inverness on A82.

Dunain Park Hotel stands in 6 acres of garden and woods, between Loch Ness and Inverness. This 18th-century house was opened as a hotel in 1974 and is furnished with fine antiques, china, and clocks, allowing it to retain its atmosphere of a private country house. Although Dunain Park has won its fame mainly as a restaurant, it does offer bedrooms with a host of thoughtful details and pretty, soft furnishings.

Dining/Entertainment: The breakfast served here is exceptional, but it's at dinner that the chef really delivers. See "Where to Dine," below.

Services: Room service, laundry.

Facilities: Indoor heated swimming pool and sauna.

Kingsmills Hotel. Culcabock Rd., Inverness, Inverness-shire IV2 3LP. ☎ **01463/237166.** Fax 01463/225208. 79 rms, 6 suites. TV TEL. £145 ($239.25) double; £175 ($288.75) suite. AE, DC, MC, V. Rates include Scottish breakfast. Children 13 and under stay free in parents' room. Take Kingsmill Rd. 1 mile east of the center of Inverness.

Once a private mansion, this hotel is an 18th-century country house of much charm set in 4 acres of woodland garden adjacent to an 18-hole golf course. The owner maintains a country-house atmosphere with an informal and hospitable Highland staff. The furnishings throughout the hotel are of a high quality, and all the bedrooms are attractively furnished. A dozen rooms are reserved for nonsmokers.

Dining/Entertainment: Dinner is offered nightly from 7 to 9pm. The fish dishes are exceptional. Bar lunches and snack meals offer a wide choice, including Scottish fare. A notice in the lobby tells you that Robert Burns dined here in 1787, and the "Charles" who signed the guest register in 1982 was (you guessed it) the prince of Wales. His sister, Princess Anne, has also stayed here.

Services: 24-hour room service, laundry/valet, baby-sitting.

Facilities: Indoor pool and health spa (with a sauna, steam room, spa bath, fitness room, and sunbed), hairdressing salon, children's playground, three-hole minigolf course.

MODERATE

Glen Mhor Hotel. 9–12 Ness Bank, Inverness, Inverness-shire IV2 4SG. ☎ **01463/234308.** Fax 01463/713170. 29 rms. TV TEL. £59–£94 ($97.35–$155.10) double. AE, DC, MC, V. Rates include Scottish breakfast.

This hotel looks out onto the River Ness. A house of gables and bay windows, Glen Mhor is a hospitable, family-run hotel with an endearing charm. The owners provide many thoughtful touches, such as a log fire blazing in the entrance lounge. From many of the individually styled bedrooms you have views of the river, castle, and cathedral. Some rooms are suitable for families, and children under 11 sharing a room with two adults are accommodated free. Amenities in the rooms include trouser presses, hair dryers, and baby-listening service. Ten of the hotel's bedrooms are in an annex called "The Cottage." These fully modernized rooms are small by American standards, but comfortable and well equipped. Two of the ground-floor rooms are suitable for disabled individuals.

In the Riverview Restaurant overlooking the river and specializing in Scottish dishes, you can enjoy such fine food as salmon caught in the river outside, shellfish, lamb, game, and beef. The wine list is one of the best in the country. In addition to the cozy cocktail lounge, there's a European Bistro bar called Nico's, open at lunch and in the evening. It's a popular nightspot, serving traditional Scottish meals and Italian pastas. Members of the royal family have eaten at the hotel. Nicky Tams is called a "stable bar," serving a wide range of beer and ale.

Station Hotel. 16–18 Academy St., Inverness, Inverness-shire IV1 1LG. ☎ **01463/231926.** 67 rms (53 with bath). TV TEL. £80 ($132) double without bath, £99 ($163.35) double with bath. AE, DC, MC, V. Rates include Scottish breakfast.

Built in 1854, the Station Hotel, adjacent to the railway station, offers a high standard of first-class service, comfortable accommodations, and well-prepared food. The occupants of those baronial Highland mansions like to stop here when they're in Inverness on shopping or social expeditions. Grandly Victorian, the bedrooms are tastefully decorated and welcoming. The dining room is one of the finest in Inverness, serving good-quality Scottish dishes, plus some excellently cooked continental favorites. Lunch is served in the bar/lounge. High tea is offered in the restaurant (light food daily from 5:30 to 9:15pm, scampi and fillets of fish). A three-course table d'hôte dinner is served in the dining room from 7 to 9:15pm; the price is £15.95 ($26.30). An à la carte menu is also offered.

INEXPENSIVE

Ballifeary House Hotel. 10 Ballifeary Rd., Inverness, Inverness-shire IV3 5PJ. ☎ **01463/ 235572.** Fax 01463/717583. 5 rms. £68 ($112.20) double. MC, V. Rates include Scottish breakfast. Closed mid-Oct to Easter.

This well-maintained 1876 Victorian stone villa, with a pleasant garden, is one of the better B&Bs in the area. Mr. and Mrs. Luscombe, the owners, offer their guests individual attention. Bedroom facilities include hair dryers, clock radios, and beverage-making equipment. An optional set-menu dinner is offered nightly at 7pm. For £17.50 ($28.90) the Luscombes will provide a home-cooked sampling of traditional Scottish fare. The hotel is a no-smoking establishment. In addition, the hotel does not offer family rooms and therefore discourages families with small children.

Ivybank. 28 Old Edinburgh Rd., Inverness, Inverness-shire IV2 3HJ. ☎ **01463/232796.** 5 rms (3 with bath). £38–£40 ($62.70–$66) double without bath, £50 ($82.50) double with bath. No credit cards. Rates include Scottish breakfast.

Ivybank, off Castle Road about a 10-minute walk north of the town center, was built in 1836 and retains its original fireplaces and an oak-paneled and beamed hall with a rosewood staircase. It has a walled and landscaped garden and comfortably furnished bedrooms, each with hot and cold running water, central heating, and beverage-making equipment. Mrs. Catherine Cameron is the gracious hostess, making guests feel at ease and welcome. There's ample parking within the walled garden, and although no meals other than breakfast are served, the staff offers advice and directions to many of the city's restaurants.

Trafford Bank. 96 Fairfield Rd., Inverness, Inverness-shire IV3 5LL. ☎ **01463/241414.** 5 rms. TV. £50 ($82.50) double. AE, DC, MC, V. Rates include breakfast. Bus: 19.

In a residential neighborhood about a half-mile west of Inverness's center, this dignified sandstone house was originally built in 1873 as the manse for the Episcopal bishop of the Inverness cathedral. In 1994, when the bishop retired in a huff because of the ordination of women into the Episcopal church, the manse became available and was purchased by Peter and Caroline McKenzie. Today, it functions as a B&B, with five comfortable, severely dignified bedrooms and a social life that revolves around copious Scottish breakfasts. The McKenzies work hard to make your stay pleasant and have built up a loyal North American and British following. Evening meals can be arranged, with advance notification, for £15 ($24.75) per person.

Whinpark Hotel. 17 Ardross St., Inverness, Inverness-shire IV3 5NS. ☎ and fax **01463/232549.** 10 rms. TV. £40–£50 ($66–$82.50) double. MC, V. Rates include Scottish breakfast.

This B&B is housed in a 19th-century, stone-fronted building on the southern periphery of town, close to the edge of the River Ness. Mike Sutherland purchased these accommodations in 1994 and renovated the bedrooms as well as the public rooms. Each bedroom is individually decorated, containing a hair dryer, shower, and tea/coffeemaking facilities.

WHERE TO DINE

Café 1. 75 Castle St. ☎ **01463/716363.** Reservations recommended. Main courses £7–£9.25 ($11.55–$15.25). Fixed-price lunches £6.95–£8.95 ($11.45–$14.75). AE, DC, MC, V. Mon–Sat noon–2:30pm and 6–10pm. INTERNATIONAL.

One of the most consistently pleasant restaurants in town is in a century-old, stone-fronted building in the heart of Inverness, on a street dotted with lots of shops. Inside, you'll find varnished paneling, wooden tables, verdant potted plants, and a soothing New Age atmosphere. Portions are generous, redolent with herbs, and include a velvety version of chicken liver pâté with chutney, salmon, crab, and thyme sausages served with a spicy tomato-flavored vinaigrette sauce; and breast of chicken with roasted herbs, buttered pasta, and game sausages. Vegetarians appreciate the availability of a vegetarian tart studded with caramelized onions and zucchini, served with stewed tomatoes and onions. Dessert might be a succulent version of dark chocolate tart with white chocolate shavings. Beginning at 10:30am, and throughout the afternoon, the place functions as a cafe.

Dickens International Restaurant. 77–79 Church St. ☎ **01463/713111.** Reservations required on weekends. Main courses £6.50–£25 ($10.75–$41.25). AE, DC, MC, V. Daily noon–2pm and 5:30–11pm. INTERNATIONAL.

The decor of this establishment has been revamped and updated with Charles Rennie Mackintosh–style furniture and lowered ceilings by its owner, George Kong. It's on a downtown street next to the oldest house in Inverness, Aberton House, between Bank Street and Academy Street. A wide selection of European, Chinese, and international dishes is offered, including seafood and vegetarian dishes. On the menu are Dickens's own steak, Peking duck, fresh local salmon, and chateaubriand. The widest choice of side dishes in Inverness is found here, including fried rice, bean sprouts, and cauliflower with cheese.

✪ **Dunain Park Restaurant.** In the Dunain Park Hotel, Dunain Park. ☎ **01463/230512.** Reservations recommended. Fixed-price dinner £32.50 ($53.65). AE, DC, MC, V. Daily 7–9pm. SCOTTISH.

Ann Nicoll presides over the kitchen here, offering Scottish fare with French flair, prepared with fresh local ingredients. A game terrine of chicken and guinea fowl is layered with venison and pigeon. Meats are wrapped in bacon and served with a delicious onion confit. Other dishes that may appear on the ever-changing menu are casserole of hare and pigeon with roasted shallots and wild mushrooms and Shetland salmon baked in sea salt, served with a white port, lime, and ginger sauce. The restaurant also specializes in steaks from Aberdeen Angus–accredited herds. To end the meal, try one of the desserts served from a buffet: crème brûlée, chocolate roulade, or marshmallow pudding.

✪ **Restaurant No 1.** 1 Greig St. ☎ **01463/716363.** Reservations required. Main courses £6–£9.50 ($9.90–$15.65). MC, V. Mon–Sat 12:30–2:30pm and 6:30–10:15pm. Closed Mon Oct–Mar. SCOTTISH/FRENCH.

The center of Inverness was somewhat of a gastronomic wasteland until the late '90s, when Restaurant No 1 brightened the picture. Owners Avril and Fergus Euart have hired a talented chef, Charles Lockley, who is waking up the sleepy taste buds of the town center. Opening onto the River Ness, the restaurant has a full view of the kitchen behind glass. Lockley takes the finest of regional produce and gives it French flair and innovation. The menu is wisely limited to about four choices per category, from appetizers to desserts. Seasonal adjustments to the menu are made to take advantage of the best of the market. Try the bisque of lobster, followed by grilled filet steak with a red wine and blue cheese sauce. For dessert the most Scottish item is likely to be ice cream made with honey and oatmeal. Wines are reasonable in price and often are available in half bottles.

Restaurant Riviera. In the Glenmoriston Hotel, 20 Ness Bank. ☎ **01463/223777.** Main courses £12.45–£16.50 ($20.55–$27.20). Daily 12:30–2:30pm and 6:30–9:30pm. BRITISH/INTERNATIONAL.

Upper tier, well staffed, and conscious of its role as a prestigious place for local family celebrations, this restaurant occupies the ground floor of a turn-of-the-century stone-sided hotel that rises from the riverbank near the center of Inverness. At least five chefs labor away in the kitchen. Meals here are part of an entire evening's entertainment; don't come expecting rapid or snappy service. But if you have a lot of time to devote to the rite of dinner and want a setting that's ever-so-polite and just a bit staid, the choice might be appropriate. Menu items include involtini of smoked salmon stuffed with seafood mousseline, presented with saffron- and dill-flavored dressing; slices of warm breast of duckling scented with heather-flavored honey and dressed with walnut oil; filet of veal stuffed with smoked ham and Italian cheese, flambéed in cognac and served with wild mushrooms and tarragon; and medallions of lamb wrapped in Parma ham on a bed of dauphinois potatoes with a green peppercorn sauce.

Riva. 4–6 Ness Walk. ☎ **01463/237377.** Reservations required. Main courses £4.95–£10.85 ($8.15–$17.90). AE, MC, V. Restaurant: Mon–Sat noon–2pm and 6–9:30pm (last order), Sun 5–9:30pm. Cafe: Mon–Sat 9am–9:30pm, except during above-mentioned meal hours. ITALIAN/INTERNATIONAL.

One of Inverness's newest restaurants occupies a site on the opposite *riva* (riverbank) from the rest of the town. Deliberately unpretentious, it maintains only 17 tables in a small-scale environment where many of the staff members are related to each other. At least a dozen kinds of pastas might be either starters or a main course. Main courses include sweet-and-sour salmon with spinach tagliatelle and red-onion/chile dressing; monkfish in red pepper sauce; and chicken with Parma ham, spinach noodles, and Chianti sauce. Between mealtimes, the place functions as a simple coffeehouse, selling sandwiches for £2.95 ($4.85) each.

INVERNESS AFTER DARK

Despite its prominence as capital of the Highlands, Inverness is a sprawling small town without much nightlife. You can spend an evening in the town's pubs sampling single-malt whiskies or beers on tap. Though the pubs in town may not have the authentic charm of the isolated pubs in more rural areas, you'll still find a lot of Highlander flavor. Try the pub in the **Loch Ness House Hotel,** Glenurquhart Road (☎ **01463/231248**), on the western periphery of town; **Gellions Pub,** on Bridge Street (☎ **01463/233648**); **Gunsmith's Pub,** 30 Union St. (☎ **01463/710519**); and its nearby neighbor **MacCallums,** 40 Union St. (☎ **01463/234805**). If you want to go dancing with a younger crowd geared to punk rock and heavy metal, head for either of the town's discos: **Blue,** on Rose Street (☎ **01463/222712**), or **Mfr G's,** 9–21 Castle St. (☎ **01463/233322**).

SIDE TRIPS FROM INVERNESS

Muir of Ord and Beauly, just at the edge of the Black Isle Peninsula, make good stopovers or touring centers for exploring the region.

MUIR OF ORD

This small town, 10 miles west of Inverness, makes a good touring center for a history-rich part of Scotland. If you stay at the hotel recommended below, you can take day trips in many directions. Sportspersons are attracted to the region's good fishing, roe and red deer stalking, golfing, and shooting.

Where to Stay & Dine

✪ **Dower House.** Highfield, Muir of Ord, Ross-shire IV6 7XN. ☎ **01463/870090.** Fax 01463/870090. 4 rms, 1 suite, 1 cottage. TV TEL. £120 ($198) double; £130 ($214.50) suite or cottage. MC, V. Rates include Scottish breakfast. Drive 1 mile north of A862.

This charming guesthouse is a perfect base for exploring the area. The main house has four double rooms and one suite, all of which are decorated in the fine tradition of a Scottish country house. A small three-bedroom guest cottage is also available and is perfect for families. Be sure to make reservations for the Dower House well in advance; the comfortable atmosphere is very much in demand.

Even if you don't stay here, call for a dinner reservation. The fixed-price menu is served nightly at 7:30pm and costs £30 ($49.50) per person. After an apéritif in the inviting lounge, guests proceed to the dining room for a four-course table d'hôte menu. Robyn Aitchison is an inspired chef who prepares modern British cuisine using produce grown on the grounds of the hotel. The menu changes daily but always includes rich after-dinner coffee, which is a perfect end to the meal.

BEAULY

A local bus company, Inverness Traction, has bus service to Beauly from Inverness, buses arriving during the day at the rate of one per hour. The French monks who settled here in the 13th century named it literally "beautiful place"—and it still is. You'll see the **Highland Craftpoint** on your left as you come from Inverness. In summer, there is an interesting exhibition of Scottish handcrafts. Beauly is 12 miles west of Inverness on A862.

Dating from 1230, the **Beauly Priory** (☎ 01463/782309) is the only remaining one of three priories constructed for the Valliscaulian order, an austere body drawing its main components from the Cistercians and the Carthusians. Some notable windows and window arcading can still be seen in the ruins. Hugh Fraser of Lovat erected the Chapel of the Holy Cross on the nave's north side in the early 15th century. You can tour the priory at any time; if it's locked, ask for a key from the Priory Hotel across the way.

On the south bank of the River Beauly southwest of the town is **Beaufort Castle,** a 19th-century baronial mansion that's the seat of the Frasers of Lovat, whose ancestor was Simon, Lord Lovat, a Jacobite agent, known as the "Lovat of the Forty-five." The original seat of the Lovats was Castle Dounie, built about 1400, but it was destroyed by "Butcher" Cumberland after his victory at Culloden.

SHOPPING   If you're interested in tweeds, don't miss **Campbell's of Beauly,** Highland Tweed House (☎ 01463/782239), operated by the same family since 1858. An excellent selection of fine tweeds and tartans is offered, and you can have your material tailored if you wish. Blankets, travel rugs, tweed hats (deer stalkers and fishing hats), and kilts are sold here, as well as sweaters in cashmere and lambswool. Shetland knits can be found here also. The establishment is open from 9am to 1pm and 2 to 5:30pm Monday through Saturday (closing at 1pm on Thursday). It's on the main street at the south end of the village square, next to the Royal Bank of Scotland.

Where to Stay & Dine

Priory Hotel. The Square, Beauly, Inverness-shire IV4 7BX. ☎ **01463/782309.** Fax 01463/782513. 27 rms. TV TEL. £73 ($120.45) double. AE, DC, MC, V. Rates include Scottish breakfast.

Priory Hotel is directly on the historic main square of town, a short walk from the ruins of the priory. The hotel has recently expanded into an adjacent building, adding four rooms to its comfortable, well-furnished offerings. All rooms are equipped with tea- and coffeemaking facilities and ironing boards. The highlight of your stay is likely to be the choice of food available in the bars and restaurant. A frequently changing à la carte dinner menu features a variety of fish and local game as well as a good selection of steaks. Meals usually cost from £20 to £25 ($33 to $41.25). Bar meals are similar dishes served in smaller portions; the cost is around £12 ($19.80). In addition, high tea is served daily.

8 Nairn

172 miles N of Edinburgh, 91 miles NW of Aberdeen, 16 miles E of Inverness

A favorite family seaside resort on the sheltered Moray Firth, Nairn (from the Gaelic for "Water of Alders") is a royal burgh at the mouth of the Nairn River. Its fishing harbor was constructed in 1820 and golf has been played here since 1672—as it still is today.

Nairn has been a popular seaside resort since 1855, when the Inverness–Nairn rail line was completed. It was also the center of a thriving fishing settlement, and its old Fishertown provides an insight into those past times.

A large uncrowded beach draws a horde of vacationers in summer. Anglers also find that the area is a good spot to practice their sport. Nairn is great walking country, and the tourist office will give you a map and details about the various possibilities, including hikes along the banks of the River Nairn.

ESSENTIALS
GETTING THERE
BY TRAIN   Nairn can be reached by train from the south, with a change at either Aberdeen or Inverness. The service between Inverness and Nairn is frequent; this is the most popular route for visitors. For information, check with the Inverness train station at Station Square (☎ **0345/484950**).

BY BUS   From Inverness, Inverness Traction runs daily buses to Nairn. Call ☎ **0990/808080** for schedules.

BY CAR   From Inverness, take A96 east to Nairn.

VISITOR INFORMATION
The summer-only **tourist information office** is at 62 King St. (☎ **01667/452753**).

EXPLORING THE AREA
To the south of Nairn, you encounter 600 years of Highland history at ✪ **Cawdor Castle,** Cawdor (☎ **01667/404615**), between Inverness and Nairn on B9090 off A96. Since the early 14th century it has been the home of the thanes of Cawdor. Although the castle was constructed 2 centuries after his time, it has nevertheless been romantically linked to Shakespeare's *Macbeth*. The castle has all the architectural ingredients you might associate with the Middle Ages: a drawbridge, an ancient tower (this one built around a tree), and fortified walls. Its severity is softened by the handsome gardens, flowers, trees, and rolling lawns. The castle is open to the public from May 1 to the second Sunday in October only, daily from 10am to 5pm. Admission is £5.20 ($8.60) for adults, £4.20 ($6.95) for senior citizens, and £2.80 ($4.60) for children 5 to 15. Children under 5 are admitted free.

The castle has extensive nature trails, a nine-hole golf course, putting green, snack bar, picnic area, shops, and a licensed restaurant that serves hot meals, teas, coffees, and fresh baked goods all day.

SHOPPING
Brodie Country, A96, 3 miles east of Nairn in Brodie (☎ **01309/641555**), is a family-owned shopping complex, with shops that carry a variety of merchandise. Of greatest interest are the regionally produced knitwear, gift items, and foodstuff; the latter includes smoked meats, jams, mustards, and other condiments. Also on the premises is a fully licensed restaurant that serves Scottish cuisine from 11am to 5pm, with main courses averaging about £5 ($8.25).

Nairn Antiques, St. Ninian Place (☎ **01667/453303**), carries a broad range of antiques and a section of upmarket crafts and reproductions. Of particular interest are the collections of Scottish pottery, silver, and fine porcelains, but there's also furniture and bric-a-brac from around the world. This is the only shop in the entire north country to stock high-quality Lalique crystal from France.

A Taste of Moray, Nairn–Inverness Road, 6 miles north of Nairn (☎ **01667/462340**), is all about the pleasures of preparing and consuming Scottish cuisine, with products ranging from quality cookware to regional domestic stoneware. The food hall offers an array of Scottish condiments and smoked meats, and if shopping here makes you hungry, you can step into the adjacent restaurant, which serves seafood dishes and steaks, with main courses averaging £10 ($16.50). Food service is daily from 10am to 9pm.

WHERE TO STAY

Clifton House. 1–3 Viewfield St., Nairn, Nairnshire IV12 4HW. ☎ **01667/453119.** Fax 01667/452836. 12 rms. £91–£106 ($150.15–$174.90) double. AE, DC, MC, V. Rates include Scottish breakfast. Turn east of the town roundabout on A96.

Clifton House reflects the dynamic personality of J. Gordon Macintyre, owner of this honey-colored sandstone, vine-covered Victorian mansion. Clifton House has been "home" to the present owner for the last 61 years. Fully licensed, it stands on the seafront, 3 minutes from the beach and equidistant to both golf links. Mr. Macintyre has spent a great deal of time and care in decorating, refurbishing, and preserving the house. Most of the furniture is antique; the collection of paintings, prints, etchings, engravings, and drawings is unusual and extensive. Each of the bedrooms is pleasantly appointed; telephones and TVs are purposely not part of the amenities—instead Mr. Macintyre organizes a series of concerts, chamber operas, plays, and recitals to entertain his guests. The hotel is a licensed theater, and performances are presented September through April.

Dining/Entertainment: The Clifton has the most extensive wine list in the north of Scotland and also serves the best food in Nairn, using only basic fresh raw ingredients. The kitchen is very traditional, utilizing the best of local Highland produce, cooked with classic techniques. For instance, game pie, double-stuffed chicken, lamb in mustard, mallard duck, wild salmon, brill, turbot, and sole are among the offerings. Dinner hours are 7 to 9:30pm daily. Lunch is from 12:30 to 1pm. Reservations are necessary. Breakfast is very old-fashioned Scottish (no packaged cereals); juice is squeezed while you wait; homemade oat cakes and marmalade and local honey are served from 8am until lunchtime.

Services: Room service, laundry, baby-sitting.

Facilities: Garden.

Greenlawns Private Hotel. 13 Seafield St., Nairn, Nairnshire IV12 4HG. ☎ **01667/452738.** Fax 01667/452738. 8 rms (7 with bath). TV. £25–£30 ($41.25–$49.50) double without bath, £40–£50 ($66–$82.50) double with bath. MC, V. Rates include Scottish breakfast. Turn down Albert St. from A96.

This Victorian house within easy reach of the beaches and golf courses is a pleasant base for touring the Loch Ness region. The new owners, David and Sheila Southwell, have completely refurbished the house while retaining its traditional charm. All bedrooms are equipped with tea- and coffeemaking facilities, as well as electric blankets. Two rooms have been upgraded to demisuites with small sitting areas. In addition to personal service to ensure that their guests have a pleasant stay, Mrs. Southwell, a certified genealogist, offers help to those who are interested in exploring their Scottish family ties.

WHERE TO DINE

The Longhouse. 8 Harbour St. ☎ **01667/455532.** Reservations recommended. Main courses £3.25–£5.95 ($5.35–$9.80) at lunch, £5.95–£9.95 ($9.80–$16.40) at dinner; high tea £5.95 ($9.80). AE, MC, V. Daily lunch 11am–4pm; high tea 4–6pm; dinner 6–10pm. Closed Mon in Oct–Mar and 1 week in Oct. SCOTTISH.

Established in 1997, the domain of the Rennie family focuses on traditional Scottish cuisine. In a cream-colored stone house in the center of town, the restaurant is named after the turn-of-the-century building's long and narrow design. Cozy and candlelit, it seats only 33 diners at a time. Menu items are less ambitious at lunchtime, when platters are likely to include lasagna, fried fillets of fresh fish, and roasted pork with wine sauce. High tea, which includes a platter of food, tea, and homemade pastries, is favored by local residents inclined to retire early.

At dinner the cuisine shines. Its tradition is strongly Scottish; expect sauces laced with whisky and such dishes as black pudding with whisky-mustard sauce; rack of lamb with wine-rosemary sauce and mint-infused poached pears; mussels in white wine, onion, and dill sauce; and fillet of salmon with a white wine, lemon, and prawn sauce. A particularly popular dish here is "Highland Olives," thin-sliced strips of fried flank steak wrapped around a filling of haggis. Desserts usually include a slice of shortbread served with fresh cream and fresh raspberries. The restaurant is licensed only for alcohol served with a meal.

NAIRN AFTER DARK

The comfortable **Claymore House Hotel Bar,** Seabank Road (☎ **01667/453731**), features free live jazz every Monday night at 8:30pm. Other nights, locals gather to drink and talk in a room with a padded bench running all the way around the wall, sofas, and several tables with chairs. During cold weather, an open fireplace takes the chill out of the air, as does the bar's selection of malt whiskies. On tap you'll find the ever-present Guinness alongside guest pumps that feature a real ale, two lagers, and a dark beer. **Clifton House,** 1–3 Viewfield St. (☎ **01667/453119**), offers classical concerts by solo artists and small ensembles about once every 3 weeks from September through April. They also stage two plays a year, in November and February or March, with an admission of £10 to £12 ($16.50 to $19.80). An optional Scottish buffet dinner is available for an additional £16 ($26.40) per person. The old **Millford Hotel Pub,** Mill Road (☎ **01667/453941**), features live music every Saturday night for free, mainly middle-of-the-road country, pop, blues, or folk bands. Once a month, on Sunday, there's a country-and-western night with dancing. On tap you can choose from Tartan Special, McEwan's 60 Shilling, Raeburn's, or Murphy's Stout, and pints start at £1.60 ($2.65).

9 The Black Isle

Cromarty: 23 miles NW of Inverness (via Kessock Bridge)

This is, in our opinion, one of the most enchanting peninsulas of Scotland, a land rich in history, beauty, and mystery. Part of Ross and Cromarty County, it lies north of Inverness. A car tour would be about 37 miles, allowing plenty of time for stopovers along the way. It's a 20-minute drive or bus ride west from Inverness.

There's much confusion about the name of the peninsula, since it's neither black nor an island. In summer the land is green and fertile, and tropical plants flourish. It has forests, fields of broom and whin, and scattered coastal villages.

No one seems to agree on how it got its name. What is known is that the "isle" has been inhabited for 7,000 years, as 60-odd prehistoric sites testify. Pictish kings, whose thrones passed down through the female line, once ruled this land. Then the Vikings held sway, and the evidence of many Gallows Hills testify that their justice was harsh.

The Far North

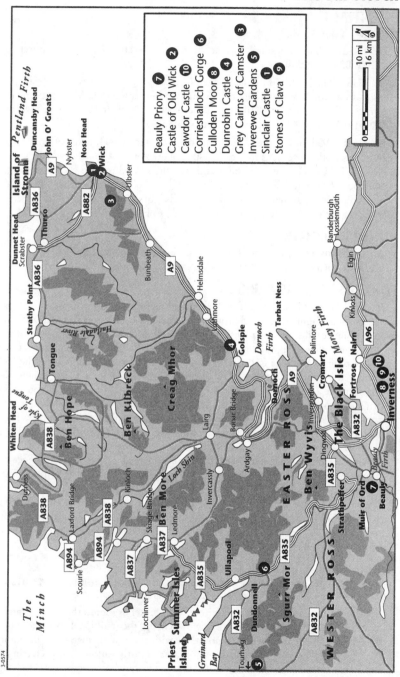

Beauly Priory 7
Castle of Old Wick 2
Cawdor Castle 10
Corrieshalloch Gorge 6
Culloden Moor 8
Dunrobin Castle 4
Grey Cairns of Camster 3
Inverewe Gardens 5
Sinclair Castle 1
Stones of Clava 9

10 mi
16 km

3-0574

ESSENTIALS

GETTING THERE

BY TRAIN   The nearest railway is at Inverness (see section 7); for bus connections, call ☎ **0345/484950.**

BY BUS   The Highland Bus and Coach Company from Inverness services the peninsula (nos. 26, 26A, and 126), making stops at North Kessock, Munlochy, Avoch, Fortrose, Rosemarkie, and Cromarty. Buses depart from Farraline Park in Inverness (☎ **01463/233371** for information and schedules).

BY CAR   Making Fortrose your first stopover (see below), take A9 north from Inverness (follow the signs toward Wick). Follow A9 for 4 miles until you see the Kessock Bridge. Go over the bridge and take the second road to the right, toward Munlocky (Fortrose is 8 miles from this turnoff). Follow A832 through the village of Munlochy and at the junction take the road right, signposted Fortrose. Continue straight on through Avoch (pronounced "och") to Fortrose.

VISITOR INFORMATION

Ask at the **Inverness Tourist Office** (see section 7, above) for information on Black Isle, since the peninsula is often included on a day tour from that city.

FORTROSE & ROSEMARKIE

If you're touring the area, your first goal might be **Fortrose.** Along the way you'll pass a celebrated wishing well or **"clootie well,"** which is festooned with rags. Dedicated to St. Boniface, the well has a long tradition, dating back to pagan times. It's said that anyone removing a rag will inherit the misfortunes of the person who placed it there.

The ruins of **Fortrose Cathedral** stand in the sleepy village. Founded in the 13th century, the cathedral was dedicated to St. Peter and St. Boniface. Fine detailing dating from the 14th century can still be seen throughout the structure. If you notice that the stones scattered about don't seem to be enough to fill in the gaps, it's because Cromwell's men removed many of them to help build a fort in Inverness. There is no formal tour of the ruins; visitors are invited to wander through self-guided at any time.

Fortrose adjoins **Rosemarkie,** up the road. The site has been inhabited since the Bronze Age. A center of Pictish culture, it saw the arrival of the first Christian missionaries. It's reported that St. Moluag founded a monastery here in the 6th century. Rosemarkie became a royal burgh in 1216. The twin hamlets share a golf course today, and they're the site of the Chanonry Sailing Club, whose annual regatta brings entries from all over Scotland. Right beyond Rosemarkie is the mysterious **Fairy Glen,** signposted at the end of the village.

WHERE TO STAY & DINE

Royal Hotel. At the corner of Union St. and High St., Fortrose, Ross-shire IV10 8SU. ☎ **01381/ 620236.** 14 rms. £80 ($132) double. MC, V. Rates include half board.

Built in 1865 as a coaching lodging, the Royal Hotel overlooks the ancient monument of Fortrose Cathedral. Under new ownership, the traditional Victorian house has recently undergone extensive renovations with guest room upgrades. The proprietor, Graham Law, has left the common areas mostly untouched, preferring to retain the mix of modern and traditional decor. The hotel has two bars and a lounge where pub meals are served. There is also a restaurant where an à la carte menu is featured; dishes are traditional Scottish fare and tend to include a variety of local produce.

CROMARTY

Cromarty stands at the tip of the peninsula where the North and South Sutors guard the entrance to the Cromarty Firth, the second-deepest inland waterway estuary in Europe, always considered of strategic importance to the Royal Navy. Once a flourishing port and a former royal burgh, the town gave the world a famous son: Hugh Miller. Born here in 1802, Miller was a stonemason as a young man. But in time he became a recognized expert in the field of geology, as well as a powerful man of letters in Scotland. His thatched cottage was built in 1698. **Hugh Miller's Cottage,** on Church Street (☎ **01381/600245**), is on view to the public today, containing many of his personal belongings and collections of geological specimens. It's open only from May 1 to September 30, daily from 10am to 5:30pm. Admission is £1.80 ($2.95) for adults and £1.20 ($2) for students and senior citizens. A family ticket, good for two adults and up to six children, is £4.80 ($7.90).

WHERE TO STAY & DINE

Royal Hotel. Marine Terrace, Cromarty, Ross-shire IV11 8YN. ☎ **01381/600217.** 10 rms. TV. £55 ($90.75) double. AE, MC, V. Rates include Scottish breakfast. Bus: 26, 26A, or 126 from Inverness.

The only hotel in town, it sits on an embankment near one of the deepest estuaries in Europe. Around 1940 the British navy combined a series of waterfront buildings into living quarters for sailors. Today the hotel is a cozy enclave with wood-burning stoves and open fireplaces. There's a comfortable lounge bar, a public bar, and a dining room that spills onto a glassed-in extension opening onto the harbor. The dining room features an à la carte menu; specialties include steaks and stroganoff. You can also enjoy a good bar menu, with a tempting list of burgers, crêpes, and salads; light meals begin at around £5 ($8.25).

10 Sutherland

It's been called the "gem of Scotland." It's got more sheep than people (20 to 1) and is the least-written-about area of Scotland, but its devotees (and not just the local residents) maintain that it's the most beautiful county in Scotland. Adding to the scenic sweep of haunting beauty are lochs and rivers, heather-covered moors and mountains—in all, 2,000 square miles of territory. The duke of Sutherland used to own most of it.

It's a country of quiet pleasures. It offers few amusements in the conventional sense except sporting activities such as golf and fishing. It's an ancient unspoiled landscape that has witnessed a turbulent history.

To the northwest of Inverness, Sutherland has three coastlines—on the north and west, the Atlantic; on the east, the North Sea. Most villages have populations of only 100 or so hearty souls. Sutherland was the scene of the notorious Highland Clearances when many of its residents were driven out from their ancestral crofts. Many made their way to the New World where they went on to prosperity. The sheep, known as the "white plague," took over after their departure. This dislocation of the people of Sutherland in the 19th century has been termed an "orgy of ruthless social engineering." In many a deserted glen you can still see traces of former crofting villages.

DORNOCH

The ancient cathedral city of Dornoch, 63 miles northwest of Inverness and 219 miles northwest of Edinburgh, is Sutherland's major town and the most interesting stopover in the area. The major sightseeing attraction nearby is **Dunrobin Castle** (see Golspie, below).

A **tourist information office** is found at The Square (☎ 01862/810400). From the Inverness bus station at Farraline Park, off Academy Street (call ☎ 01463/233371 for schedule information), three different local companies run daily buses to Dornoch: Stagecoach, Caledonian Express, and Scottish CityLink.

EXPLORING THE AREA

Village-like Dornoch has long been known for its golf club on the sheltered shores of Dornoch Firth, the northernmost first-class course in the world. The turf of the **Royal Dornoch Golf Club,** Golf Road (☎ 01862/810219), has been called "sacred" by aficionados. Golf was first played there in 1616. The cathedral town also attracts visitors to its beaches in summer.

Dornoch Cathedral, Castle Street, was built in the 13th century and partially destroyed by fire in 1570. It has had many restorations, including one in 1924, but its fine 13th-century stonework can still be seen. The cathedral is famous for its modern stained-glass windows—three are in memory of Andrew Carnegie, the American "steel king." The cathedral is open daily from 9am to dusk.

SHOPPING   The **Dornoch Craft Centre,** Town Jail, Castlestreet (☎ 01862/810555), in the center of town opposite the cathedral, occupies what was the town jail in 1844. You can wander through the selection of Scottish crafts, jewelry, and pottery, then visit the Textile Hall and browse through the range of knitwear, tartans, mohair goods, and tweeds. On the top floor is a small coffee shop selling sandwiches and drinks. From Easter to October, the center is open Monday through Saturday from 9am to 5pm; the rest of the year, Monday through Saturday from 10am to 4pm. In July and August, Dornoch Craft Center also opens on Sunday from noon to 4pm.

WHERE TO STAY & DINE

✪ **Carnegie Club at Skibo Castle.** Skibo Castle, Dornoch, Sutherland IV25 3RQ. ☎ 01862/894600. Fax 01862/894601. 30 rms. TV TEL. £425 ($701.25) double for members, £550 ($907.50) double for nonmembers. AE, DC, MC, V. Rates include meals, drinks, and sporting activities (including greens fees at the resort's golf course). Membership costs £2,000 ($3,160) per year per family. The club will send a car to Dornoch or anywhere in Inverness to meet new arrivals.

Skibo Castle is as massive a baronial house as you're likely to find in Scotland, an Edwardian pile created from a unique combination of Scottish heritage and one of the most potent fortunes of the New World's Industrial Revolution. Steel magnate Andrew Carnegie, who emigrated from Scotland's woolen mills to America in the mid-19th century, yearned for a return to the land of his birth after he acquired his fortune. When the Scottish castle of his dreams (Cluny, seat of the McPherson clan) was not available for sale at any price, Carnegie and his wife settled on the historic but dilapidated Skibo Castle, 5 miles east of Dornoch. After they bought it (for the relatively reasonable price of £85,000) in 1898, Carnegie and his second wife, Louise, massively enlarged the place, pouring £2 million into its refurbishment. There they welcomed a stream of distinguished visitors, including Edward VII, during the months every year they spent in Scotland in their final years. Descendants of Carnegie remained on site until 1983.

In 1990, Peter de Savary, the force behind posh semiprivate clubs in London and Antigua, acquired the property and its 7,000 acres, installed an 18-hole golf course designed by Donald Steel that follows the approximate layout of one used by Andrew

Carnegie himself, and created a resort that is a combination of golfing mecca and semiprivate club. About half the accommodations are within the baronial walls of Carnegie's mansion; others are scattered in the lodges and cottages where the staff of gardeners, ghillies, and caretakers once lived.

Meals are consumed in the style of an Edwardian house party at a long, baronial table. Evenings of Scottish dance are featured every Saturday night; other nights, there are dinner performances of Scottish flute, Celtic harp, or piano. Sports opportunities (part of the price) include trap and skeet shooting, falconry, trout and salmon fishing, and golf (on the resort's Championship Links course or at the nearby Royal Dornoch Course).

Dornoch Castle Hotel. Castle St., Dornoch, Sutherland IV25 3SD. ☎ **01862/810216.** Fax 01862/810981. 19 rms. TV TEL. £70–£87 ($115.50–$143.55) double. AE, MC, V. Rates include Scottish breakfast.

This unusual hotel, close to the Royal Dornoch Golf Course, is in the massive walls of what was once the residence of the bishops of Caithness. It was built of local stone in the center of town in the late 15th or early 16th century. Today its winding stairs, labyrinthine corridors, and impenetrable cellars have been converted into a well-directed hotel and restaurant. Its rooms are a bit dowdy, but it has one of the most notable facades in the area. Six rooms are in the original building; the rest are in an extension that overlooks the garden. A fixed-price four-course meal is served nightly in the stone-walled dining room for £21 ($35.65) per person. Menu specialties include leg of Sutherland lamb with onion marmalade, and Highland Estate venison with blackcurrants. Reservations are suggested.

Fourpenny Cottage. Embo Rd., Dornoch, Sutherland IV25 3HR. ☎ and fax **0162/810727.** 6 rms. TV. £25 ($41.25) per person double. MC, V. Rates include Scottish breakfast. Closed Dec–Mar. From Dornoch center, drive 3 miles south on the Embo/Golspie road.

This pleasant white-sided cottage, 1 1/2 miles north of the famous Royal Dornoch course, is a favorite of golfers, many of them repeat visitors. Rooms are divided between the main house, a reconstruction and enlargement of an antique crofter's cottage, and a modern brick-sided annex. Sheila Board and her family prepare hearty breakfasts and maintain the cozy, flower-patterned bedrooms. The ambience is informal, very akin to that in a private home. According to legend, this was the last parcel of land sold for four pence in Scottish history—hence its name.

GOLSPIE

Today a family resort with a golf course, Golspie was once part of the vast holdings of the earls and dukes of Sutherland. The town, lying on A9, looks out across the water to the Dornoch Firth. A crescent of sandy beach is an attraction to visitors. Golspie lies 228 miles northwest of Edinburgh and 72 miles northwest of Inverness.

SEEING THE SIGHTS

Golspie is visited chiefly because of a towering attraction half a mile northeast on A9, ✪ **Dunrobin Castle** (☎ **01408/633177**), home of the earls and dukes of Sutherland. It's the most northerly of the great houses of Scotland and also the biggest in the northern Highlands, and dates in part from the early 13th century. Formal gardens are laid out in the manner of Versailles. On the grounds is a museum overlooking the gardens, containing many relics from the Sutherland family; trophies and regimental colors of the 93rd Sutherland Highlanders are on view. Some of the castle's 180 rooms are open to the public—the ornately furnished dining room, a billiard room–cum–family museum, and the room and gilded four-poster bed where

Queen Victoria slept when she visited in 1872. The countess of Sutherland has apartments here, but many rooms are empty.

The castle is open April, May, and October, Monday through Saturday from 10:30am to 4:30pm and Sunday from 1 to 4:30pm. From June to September, it's open Monday through Saturday from 10:30am to 5:30pm and Sunday from 12:30 to 5:30pm. Last entrance is 30 minutes before closing. Admission is £5 ($8.25) for adults, £3.50 ($5.75) for senior citizens and children 5 to 16, and £15 ($24.75) for a family ticket (two adults and two children).

WHERE TO STAY & DINE

Golf Links Hotel. Church St., Golspie, Sutherland KW10 6TT. ☎ **01408/633408.** Fax 01408/634184. 9 rms. TV. £50 ($82.50) double. £150 ($247.50) per week for self-service apartments. V. Rates include Scottish breakfast.

Constructed in the early 1900s, this stone structure was originally built as the rectory for the local minister and was converted to a hotel in 1955. Much of the establishment's clientele is made up of golfers drawn to the nearby Golspie, Royal Dornoch, and Brora courses. Rooms in the main building are well furnished and have tea- and coffeemaking facilities. The self-service units, rented by the week, are in an annex; all have kitchens and two to four bedrooms. A first-class chef prepares Scottish and Continental cuisine served in a dining room opening onto a view of Ben Bhraggie. A nightly fixed-price dinner is offered; the price is £20 ($33) for four courses. The contemporary lounge bar looks through big plate-glass windows onto Dornoch Firth. Bar lunches are served daily around noon, for £4 ($6.60) and up. There is also a hairdressing salon on the hotel grounds.

TONGUE

Heading north along A836, you cross high moors and brooding peaks to Tongue, 257 miles northwest of Edinburgh and 101 miles northwest of Inverness. For the nature lover there is much to see, from the mighty cliffs of **Clo Mor,** near Cape Wrath (known for its large colonies of puffins), to waterfalls such as **Eas-Coul-Aulin** (the highest in Britain) and the **Falls of Shin,** where you can see salmon leap. Masses of land suddenly rise from a barren landscape, including **Ben Loyal,** known as the "queen of Scottish mountains."

West of Tongue on a promontory stand the ruins of **Castle Varrich,** said to have been built by the Vikings. Possibly dating from the 14th century, this castle was the Mackay stronghold. Mackays from North America visit Tongue annually, seeking lore about their ancestral roots.

Tongue House, from 1678, was a home base for the chief of the Mackays, but it now belongs to the estate of the duke of Sutherland. On the shores of the Kyle of Tongue, it has a walled garden and is open to the public only one Sunday in August.

WHERE TO STAY & DINE

Ben Loyal Hotel. Main St., Tongue, Sutherland, IV27 4XE. ☎ **01847/611216.** Fax 01847/611212. 12 rms (9 with bath). TV. £56 ($92.40) double without bath, £76 ($125.40) double with bath. MC, V. Rates include Scottish breakfast.

This is a good choice, with everything under the careful attention of Mel and Pauline Cook. The rooms are a bit plain but are comfortably furnished in the traditional style. Several "superior" rooms have four-poster beds and views over the castle ruins and loch. All accommodations are equipped with hot- and cold-water basins, electric blankets, and tea- and coffeemaking facilities. A five-course table d'hôte menu is served nightly for £22.50 ($37.15). Meals are home-cooked and feature locally reared beef and produce grown on the grounds of the hotel. A fine wine list and an assortment of malt whisky choices complement the cuisine. The Ben Loyal Hotel structures incorporate 19th-century stables, a former post office, a shop, and a village bakery.

Tongue Hotel. Tongue, Sutherland IV27 4XD. ☎ **01847/611206.** Fax 01847/611345. 17 rms. TV TEL. £56–£76 ($92.40–$125.40) double. MC, V. Rates include Scottish breakfast.

Ever since Queen Victoria's day, the best place to stay in town has been the Tongue Hotel, a mile north of the village center, beside the road leading to Durness. Built of gray stone in the baronial style, it opens onto the Kyle of Tongue and still possesses much of its initial character and many of its antiques. It was constructed around 1850 as a hunting lodge for the duke of Sutherland. To identify its builder, an **S** is carved into the stonework high above one of the doorways. Both the bedrooms and the public rooms are decorated in the Victorian style, with flowered curtains and well-upholstered furniture. The establishment is known for the quality of its food. A hearty three-course dinner, which usually includes a choice of game or fresh fish caught in the region, costs £18 ($29.70) and up on the table d'hôte menu. Accessible through a separate entrance is a paneled and popular pub with its own open fireplace and impressive collection of whiskies. There's also a more sedate cocktail lounge. In the bar and lounge, you can enjoy pub meals starting at about £5 ($8.25). Offerings often include mussels, oysters, and garlic-sautéed mushrooms, as well as more substantial meals.

11 Caithness

It doesn't look like the Highlands at all, but Caithness is the northernmost county of mainland Scotland. The landscape here is gentle and rolling.

Caithness is ancient. In fact, within its 700 square miles you'll find signs of the Stone Age—the enigmatic Grey Cairns of Camster date from 4,000 B.C. The county is filled with cairns, mysterious stone rows and circles, and standing stones. The Vikings once occupied this place with its rock stacks, old harbors, craggy cliffs, and quiet coves, and many place names are in Old Norse. It has churches from the Middle Ages, as well as towering castles on cliff tops. The Queen Mother's home, Castle of Mey, dating from 1570, lies between John o' Groats and Thurso.

Rich in bird and animal life, Caithness is unspoiled country. Fishing draws people to the area: The wild brown trout are found in some 100 lochs, along with salmon in the Thurso and the Wick rivers.

Most people head for Caithness with John o' Groats as their final destination. John o' Groats, with its many souvenir shops, is popularly called the extreme northern tip of the British mainland. Actually, Dunnet Head is farther north by a few miles.

Scrabster, a ferry harbor, is the main car-and-passenger service that operates all year to the Orkney Islands. There are day trips in summer.

WICK

This famous old herring port on the eastern coastline of Caithness is a popular stopover for those heading north to explore what is often called the John o' Groats Peninsula. Wick has some claim as a holiday resort as well. Robert Louis Stevenson spent part of his boyhood in Wick when his father worked here on an engineering project. Today a sleepy nostalgia hangs over the town.

Wick lies 287 miles northwest of Edinburgh and 126 miles northwest of Inverness. There is daily bus and rail service from Inverness, from which train connections are possible via Edinburgh, Glasgow, or Stirling.

SEEING THE SIGHTS

At **Caithness Glass,** Airport Industrial Estates (☎ **01955/602286**), you can watch the glass-blowing and tour the factory Monday through Friday from 9am to 5pm. The shop and restaurant are open Monday through Friday from 9am to 5pm and Saturday from 9am to 1pm (until 5pm on Saturday in June to September).

The **Wick Heritage Centre,** 20 Bank Row (☎ **01955/605393**), has many exhibitions pertaining to the herring-fishing industry in Wick in days of yore. You can also see farm implements from Caithness. It's open May to October, Monday through Saturday from 10am to 5pm; last admission is 3:45pm. Admission is £2 ($3.30) for adults and 50p (85¢) for ages 5 to 16; free for age 4 and under.

The most important site in the area are the two megalithic **Grey Cairns of Camster,** 6 miles north of Lybster on the Watten Road off A9. The ruins of the **Castle of Old Wick** are also worth exploring. The location is off A9, 1 1/2 miles south of Wick. Once known as Castle Olipant, the ruined structure dates back to the 14th century. You may also want to seek out **castles Sinclair** and **Girnigoe,** 3 miles north of Wick (follow the airport road in the direction of the Noss Head Lighthouse). These adjacent castles were built on the edge of a cliff overlooking the Bay of Sinclair. At one time they were the stronghold of the Sinclairs, the earls of Caithness. The older structure, Girnigoe, dates from the latter 1400s; Sinclair was constructed in the early years of the 17th century. By 1679 both castles had been deserted and allowed to fall into ruins.

WHERE TO STAY & DINE

Breadalbane House Hotel. 20 Breadalbane Crescent, Wick, Caithness KW1 5AQ. ☎ **01955/603911.** Fax 01955/603911. 10 rms (8 with bath). TV. £47 ($77.55) double with bath. AE, MC, V. Rates include Scottish breakfast.

This 1891 building on the southern outskirts of town, a 5-minute walk from the center, was once the home of a local furniture maker who is thought to have built the interior woodwork, including the door and window frames and the staircase. It's now an unpretentious guesthouse with uncomplicated, traditionally furnished rooms. Two singles have no private bath. Guests can dine in the restaurant or in the cozy bar. Food offerings vary from curries and steaks to a traditional roast dinner served on weekends.

Greenvoe. 8 George St., Wick, Caithness, KW1 4DE. ☎ **01955/603942.** 3 rms (none with bath). £30 ($49.50) double. No credit cards. Rates include Scottish breakfast. Closed 2 weeks at Christmas.

Your hosts are Dorothy and Jimmy Johnston, whose circa-1983 home occupies a 1 1/2-acre garden near the heart of town. Panoramas from the windows encompass lots of greenery and views over the estuary known as the Wick River. Bedrooms are color coordinated, functional, unpretentious, and comfortable. A generous Scottish breakfast, as well as an 8:30pm light snack consisting of sandwiches and tea, is included in the rate.

JOHN O' GROATS

John o' Groats is the northern equivalent of Land's End at the tip of the Cornish peninsula in England. The southern tip of England is 878 miles south of John o' Groats. Visitors are fond of having their pictures taken at the "Last House," standing at the end of A9. From John o' Groats there are views north to the Orkney Islands and the Pentland Firth. John o' Groats lies 17 miles north of Wick.

John o' Groats is named after a Dutch ferryman, Jan de Groot. His tombstone can still be seen at Cabisbay Church. The town abounds in souvenir shops, some selling

Groatie buckies or small Arctic cowrie shells once used as decoration by the first settlers in Caithness. Interesting walks can be taken along the coast to Duncansby Head and to the great Stacks.

In the summer months there is a daily passenger-only ferry service to Orkney. Bus tours of the island are included. The Orkney Islands are just a 45-minute sail from John o' Groats across the Pentland Firth.

WHERE TO STAY & DINE

Seaview Hotel. John o' Groats, Caithness KW1 4YR. ☎ **01955/611220.** 9 rms (5 with bath). £32 ($52.80) double without bath, £36–£42 ($59.40–$69.30) double with bath. No credit cards. Rates include Scottish breakfast.

One of the most northerly hostelries on the British mainland, the Seaview is a family-run hotel whose severe and streamlined sides rise abruptly from a flat and windswept landscape beside the town's only highway near the hamlet's center. Built in the 1950s and enlarged in 1991, it's covered with a roughly textured white stucco that locals refer to as "pebble dash." Each accommodation is a fair size and rather austerely furnished, with tea- and coffeemakers and electric blankets. There's a pub on the premises, where bar lunches and dinners draw an appreciative clientele. Main courses in the formal restaurant range from £6 to £8 ($9.90 to $13.20).

JOHN O' GROATS AFTER DARK

Located in an old converted country school, the **Lythe Arts Centre** (☎ **01955/ 641270**) stages performances of innovative and experimental works by small-scale touring companies. The program is year-round and includes drama, dance, jazz, folk, world, and new music. There is also a permanent collection of art related to northern Scotland, and in July and August, touring exhibitions of contemporary art, photography, and some crafts. Exhibitions are open daily from 10am to 6pm; admission is £1.50 ($2.45) for adults, 75p ($1.25) for children, and free for students. Performances usually start at 7:30pm. Advanced booking is necessary for all shows, so call first for scheduling and ticket information. Tickets cost £8 ($13.20) for adults, £5 ($8.25) for senior citizens, and £3 ($4.95) for students and children. Coffee, tea, and light snacks are available on performance evenings. The arts center is signposted, 4 miles off the A9/A99 between Wick and John o' Groats.

THURSO

Motorists pass through this northern port when they are heading for Scrabster, where year-round ferries leave for the Orkney Islands. In Thurso you can visit the ruins of **St. Peter's Church,** near the harbor in the old restored district.

There's a **golf course** nearby. To the west are the **cliffs** of Holborn Head and Dunnet Head, which boasts a lighthouse. A nuclear energy establishment was installed to the west at Dounreay. The town lies 133 miles northwest of Inverness and 21 miles northwest of Wick.

WHERE TO STAY & DINE

Pentland Hotel. Princes St., Thurso, Caithness KW14 7AA. ☎ **01847/893202.** Fax 01847/ 892761. 48 rms. TV TEL. £54 ($89.10) double. MC, V. Rates include Scottish breakfast. Street parking available.

This is a relatively modern hotel with cream-colored walls, bay and dormer windows, and a revolving glass door giving access to a streamlined lobby. It occupies most of a full city block a short walk from the center of the village. Recently under new ownership, the hotel should be undergoing refurbishments sometime within the life of this edition. Guest rooms are clean, comfortable, and functional, nothing more. Fully licensed, the hotel contains its own bar as well as a dining room. Food is served nightly until 8:30pm and features fresh fish, local lamb, and Scottish beef.

ULLAPOOL

Ullapool is an interesting village, the largest in Wester Ross, lying 59 miles northwest of Inverness. It was built by the British Fishery Society in 1788 as a port for herring fishers and is still a busy harbor. The original town plan has not been changed, and many of the buildings look much as they did at the time of their construction, although mellower and more weather-beaten. Ullapool has long been an embarkation point for travelers crossing the Minch, a section of the North Atlantic separating Scotland from the Outer Hebrides.

A short drive south to Gairloch takes you into the heart of Wester Ross, with its scenery, mountains, and Atlantic seascape.

WHERE TO STAY & DINE

✪ **Altanaharrie Inn.** Loch Broom, Ullapool, Ross-shire IV26 2SS. ☎ **01854/633230.** 8 rms. £155–£185 ($255.75–$305.25) per person. MC, V. Rates include half board. Closed Nov–Easter. Transportation is by private ferry.

This is one of those places you feel you shouldn't tell anyone about, for fear they won't have room for you when you get here. The Altanaharrie was once a 17th-century drover's inn on the banks of Loch Broom. There is no access by road, so guests are brought over the loch by a private launch, the *Mother Goose*. Once you've landed, you're greeted with a warm log fire in a lounge and a dram before dinner. The cooking is among the best in northwest Scotland, using locally caught seafood. Shellfish is kept in creels in the loch until ready for consumption. There's no choice on the five-course menu, but guests are asked their likes and dislikes or allergies beforehand. The bedrooms are simple, clean, and tasteful, housed either in the main building or in small cottages on the grounds. There are no TVs, no room phones, nothing to distract. At night the generator is switched off, and candles and torches provide needed illumination. In the morning, it's a delight to find a breakfast that might include homemade jams, buttery croissants, and perhaps even venison sausages.

Dromnan House. Garve Rd., Ullapool, Ross-shire IV26 2SX. ☎ and fax **01854/612333.** 7 rms. TV. £38–£44 ($62.70–$72.60) double. MC, V. Rates include breakfast.

Mrs. MacDonald is your hostess at this well-conceived guesthouse, which occupies a third-acre plot on the southern outskirts of town within a 10-minute walk from the center. Originally built of white-painted stone in the 1970s and later enlarged, it was named after a nearby rise (Dromnan Hill) where one of the MacDonald family's ancestors was born and reared. The establishment is very clean, well maintained, and bedrooms are described by the kindly owner as being decorated in a combination of Marks & Spencer department store goods and "Shand-Kydd" coordinated wallpapers and fabrics designed by the mother of the late Princess of Wales.

Royal Hotel. Garve Rd., Ullapool, Ross-shire IV26 2SY. ☎ **01854/612181.** Fax 01854/612951. 50 rms. TV TEL. £52–£138 ($85.80–$227.70) double. MC, V. Rates include Scottish breakfast. Closed Nov to mid-Mar.

The Royal Hotel sits on a knoll on the "Inverness side" of town, overlooking the harborfront. Graced with curved walls and large sheets of glass, it was rebuilt in 1961 from an older building, with an added east wing. It offers well-furnished bedrooms, 21 of which have balconies opening onto views over Loch Broom. Live entertainment in season is offered. If someone wants to show up for a fixed-price dinner, a table d'hôte in the dining room costs only £12 ($19.80). Later, guests sit around a log fire in the well-appointed lounge.

SIDE TRIPS FROM ULLAPOOL

There are a number of day trips that can be made from Ullapool, including a trip to the **Corrieshalloch Gorge,** 12 miles southeast of town, a national nature reserve along A835 at Braemore. From this point, the Falls of Measach plunge 150 feet into a mile-long wooded gorge.

Another interesting excursion is to the **Inverewe Gardens** (☎ 01445/781200). Osgood MacKenzie created these gardens a century and a quarter ago, when he planted species from many countries. An exotic mixture of plants from the South Pacific, the Himalayas, and South America allows the gardens to have color year-round. The gardens can be reached along A832, 6 miles northeast of Gairloch. They're open Monday through Saturday from 9:30am to sunset and Sunday from noon to sunset. Admission is £4.50 ($7.45) for adults, £3 ($4.95) for senior citizens and children, and £12 ($19.80) for a family ticket (two adults and up to six children).

From either Ullapool or Achiltibuie, it's possible to take excursions in season to the ✪ **Summer Isles,** a beautiful group of almost uninhabited islands off the coast. The islands get their name because sheep are transported here in summer for grazing. The largest is Tanera More. The islands are a mecca for bird watchers. Information about how to reach the islands is available from the summer-only **tourist information office** on Argyle Street (☎ 01854/612135). Boat schedules can vary, depending on weather conditions.

It is now possible to stay on Summer Isles in an idyllic hotel, but don't even consider a visit here unless you're looking for isolated natural splendor and a setting in a fishing hamlet where there's almost nothing to do other than enjoy the land- and seascapes around you. Access to the village and its only hotel involves negotiating a 15-mile single-track road through a mostly treeless, heather-covered landscape.

What you'll find is a century-old, stone-sided, white-painted hotel, appropriately called the **Summer Isles Hotel,** Achiltibuie by Ullapool, Ross-shire IV 26 2YG (☎ 01854/622284; fax 01854/622251). It rents 11 rooms, all with bath, for £72 to £150 ($118.80 to $247.50) for a double including half board (MC, V). The hotel is open only from Easter through October, and its only neighbors are a cluster of crofters and fishers' cottages. Originally built as a fishing lodge and converted later into this rustically appealing place, it contains a sophisticated restaurant, a cozy cocktail lounge and pub, and bedrooms in two distinct settings: Four are within the main building and seven are in modern annexes that might remind you of veranda-fronted log cabins in Sweden. Guests congregate within the TV lounge or either of the drinking areas. Expect glamorous dinners, priced at £34.50 ($56.95) for five courses, and less formal lunches that consist of bistro-style platters served in the bar. Activities include beach walking, boat trips on the nearby sea, fishing, and bird watching.

12 The Hebridean Islands

Once the Hebridean islands were visited only by geologists, bird watchers, and the occasional fisher or mountain climber. Today the chain of islands just off the Scottish mainland that makes up the Inner Hebrides is becoming more and more accessible to the general visitor.

What about the Outer Hebrides? One of the lesser-known parts of Western Europe, these are a splintered sweep of windswept islands that stretch for some 130 miles, from the Butt of Lewis in the north all the way to Barra Head at the southernmost tip. With rugged cliffs, clean beaches, archaeological treasures, and tiny bays, the Outer Hebrides are just beginning to awaken to their touristic possibilities.

From Gourock, the ferry terminal near Glasgow, **Caledonian MacBrayne** (☎ **01475/650100** for information, ☎ 0990/650000 for reservations), sails to 23 Scottish islands in the Firth of Clyde and the Western Isles, including Skye and Mull, as well as the Outer Hebrides. The company also offers inclusive tours that are ideal for visiting places well away from the beaten track. The information office at Gourock is most helpful and will assist you in planning a trip if you wish to plot your own journey.

If you're driving from the mainland, you can take the "Road to the Isles," heading for the Kyle of Lochalsh if your destination is Skye. For Mull and Iona, Oban is your port. These islands are part of the Inner Hebrides and enjoy fairly good connections with the mainland. The more remote Outer Hebrides are also linked by car ferries from such mainland ports as Ullapool (call ☎ **01851/702361** for schedules). The main islands to visit here are Lewis and Harris. Glasgow has air service to the airport at Stornoway on Lewis (call ☎ **0345/222111** in Glasgow for more information).

A DRIVING TOUR

Day 1   From Oban (see chapter 8), sail to the Isle of Mull for a day of exploration. Chances are you'll land at Craignure. Before the day ends, you'll have time to explore Torosay Castle and Gardens, 1 1/2 miles south of Craignure on A849. If time remains, consider a visit to Duart Castle, on A849 on the eastern point of Mull.

Day 2   While still based in Mull, continue that morning along A849 through the village of Bunessan. Going on, you reach

Fionnphort, where there's ferry service to the island of Iona. After exploring Iona Abbey, and if time permits, pay a visit by boat to Fingal's Cave, 6 miles north of Iona (see below). Return to your hotel on Mull for the night.

Day 3   From Craignure-on-Mull, take the 45-minute crossing back to Oban. From Oban, get on A828 northeast to Fort William, then head west along A830 to Mallaig, where frequent ferries depart for the Isle of Skye. Sail to Skye and spend the remaining day (too little, really) exploring the island.

Day 4   Return to the mainland. From Uig on the northwestern tip of Skye, take a ferry to the Isle of Harris, arriving at Tarbert. From Tarbert, you can take A859, the single and only road going north. This will deliver you to Stornoway where you can spend the night. Stornoway is the capital of the Isle of Lewis, which is the largest and most northerly of the archipelago in the Outer Hebrides.

1 Kyle of Lochalsh

204 miles NW of Edinburgh, 82 miles SW of Inverness, 125 miles N of Oban

This popular center is the gateway to the island of Skye (now reached by toll bridge; see below). You can drive the length of Skye in a day, returning to the mainland by night if you want to.

ESSENTIALS
GETTING THERE
BY TRAIN   Four trains per day (two on Sunday) arrive from Inverness daily, taking about 2¹/₂ hours. Call ☎ **0345/484950** for schedules and information.

BY BUS   Both Scottish CityLink and Skye-Ways coaches arrive daily from Glasgow at the Kyle of Lochalsh (trip time: 5 hours). Skye-Ways also operates three buses a day from Inverness (trip time: 2 hours). Call ☎ **0990/808080** for more information.

BY CAR   From Fort William, head north along A82 to Invergarry, where you cut west onto A87 to the Kyle of Lochalsh.

VISITOR INFORMATION
A summer-only **tourist information center** is at the Kyle of Lochalsh Car Park (☎ **01599/534276**).

A NEARBY ATTRACTION
Eilean Donan Castle. Dornie. ☎ **01599/555202.** Admission £3 ($4.95) adults, £2 ($3.30) senior citizens, students, and children; £7 ($11.55) family ticket (2 adults and up to 3 children). Apr–Oct, daily 10am–5:30pm. Closed Nov–Mar. Drive 8 miles east of the Kyle of Lochalsh on A87.

This romantic and photogenic castle was built in 1214 as a defense against the Danes. In ruins for 200 years, it was restored by Colonel MacRae of Clan MacRae in 1932 and is now a clan war memorial and museum, containing Jacobite relics, mostly with clan connections. There's a shop that sells kilts, woolens, and souvenirs.

WHERE TO STAY & DINE
Lodgings are limited, just barely adequate to meet the demand for rooms.

Kyle Hotel. Main St., Kyle of Lochalsh, Ross-shire IV40 8AB. ☎ **01599/534204.** Fax 01599/534932. 31 rms. TV TEL. £60–£70 ($99–$115.50) double. AE, MC, V. Rates include Scottish breakfast.

This modernized stone hotel in the center of town, a 5-minute walk from the train station, is your best all-around bet in the moderate category. The bedrooms are furnished in a functional modern style, with shaver outlets, hair dryers, and teamakers. The hotel serves reasonably priced dinners in the lounge nightly from 6 to 9pm.

Lochalsh Hotel. Ferry Rd., Kyle of Lochalsh, Ross-shire IV40 8AF. ☎ **01599/534202.** Fax 01599/534881. 38 rms. TV TEL. £85–£120 ($140.25–$198) double. AE, DC, MC, V. Rates include Scottish breakfast.

There's no way a visitor can talk about the Kyle of Lochalsh without mentioning this landmark hotel. It was built as a luxury oasis when the British Railway finally extended its tracks in this direction. Today, in memory of the period when it was the headquarters of a Royal Navy mining operation in World War II, a large (defused) mine sits near the flagpole on the seaside lawn. Its crafted small-paned windows with hardwood and brass fittings will remind you of those on an oceangoing yacht. The bedrooms have been stylishly overhauled. Evening meals begin at around £20 ($33) and include the best of Scottish cuisine and ingredients. The ground-floor bar stocks a variety of malt whiskies, and the dining room has a panoramic view. On a hillside above the hotel, the Ferry Boat Inn, run by the hotel, is one of the most popular pubs in the area, attracting locals as well as visitors.

THE INNER HEBRIDES

If you travel here, you'll be following in the footsteps of Samuel Johnson and his faithful Boswell. The chain of Inner Hebridean islands lies just off the west coast of the Scottish mainland. The Isle of Skye is the largest. Mull has wild scenery and golf courses, and just off its shores is the important site of Iona, the isle that played a major part not only in the spread of Christianity in Britain but in the preservation of the culture and learning of the ancient world when it was being forgotten all over Europe. Adventurous travelers will also seek out Coll and Tyree as well as the Isle of Colonsay and Rhum (also Rum), Eigg, or the tiny island of Raasay, off the Isle of Skye.

2 Isle of Skye

83 miles W of Inverness, 176 miles NW of Edinburgh, 146 miles NW of Glasgow

Located off the northwest coast of Scotland, the mystical Isle of Skye, largest of the Inner Hebrides, is 48 miles long and varies between 3 and 25 miles wide. It's separated from the mainland by the Sound of Sleat (pronounced "Slate"). At Kyleakin, on the eastern end, the channel is only a quarter of a mile wide.

Dominating the land of summer seas, streams, woodland glens, mountain passes, cliffs, and waterfalls are the Cuillin Hills, a range of jagged black mountains that are a mecca for rock climbers. The Peninsula of Sleat, the island's southernmost arm, is known as the "Garden of Skye." There are many stories as to the origin of the name *Skye.* Some believe it's from the Norse *ski,* meaning a cloud, whereas others say it's from the Gaelic word for "winged." There are Norse names on the island, however, as the Norsemen held sway for 4 centuries before 1263. Overlooking the Kyle is the ruined Castle Moal, once the home of a Norwegian princess.

On the island you can explore castle ruins, duns, and brochs, and enjoy a Highland welcome. For the Scots, the island will forever evoke images of Flora MacDonald, who conducted the disguised Bonnie Prince Charlie to Skye after the Culloden defeat.

The Hebrides

Atlantic Ocean

THE OUTER HEBRIDES

THE INNER HEBRIDES

Butt of Lewis
Port of Ness
Arnol
Barvas
Gallan Head
Breasclete
Miavaig
North Tolsta
Tolsta Head
Garynahine
Stornoway
Brenish
Achmore
Tiumpan Head
Lewis
Balallan
Eye Peninsula
Hushinish
Lemreway *Kebock Head*
Toe Head Sacrista
Harris Tarbert
Cluer
Sound of Shiant
Rodel
Newtonferry
Renish Point
North Uist
Bayhead
Lochmaddy
Kilmaluag
Carinish
Trumpan
Uig
Benbecula
Creagorry
Ardivachar Point
Colbust
South Uist
Dunvegan
Skeabost
Brochel
Daliburgh
Portree
Raasay
Clachan
Kilbride Lochboisdale
Bracdale
Sconser
Barra Eriskay
Drynoch
Sligachan
Vatersay Castlebay
Isle of Skye
Kyle of Lochalsh
Dornie
Broadford
Kyleakin
Sea of the Hebrides
Canna
Elgol
Armadale
Glenelg
Rhum (Rum)
Kinloch Castle
Ardvasar
Mallaig
Eigg
Muck
Arinagour **Coll**
Tyree
Scarinish
Tobermory
Fort William
Dervaig
Salen
Staffa
Mull
Port Appin
Iona
Craignure
Fionnphort
Bunessan
Firth of Lorn
Oban

0 — 50 km / 31.25 mi
N

SCOTLAND
The Hebridean Islands
Glasgow

Aros Castle Ruins **5**
Dungaith Castle **4**
Dunvegan Castle **2**
Eilean Donan Castle **1**
Knock Castle **3**
Moy Castle **6**
Standing Stones of Callanish **8**
Steinacleit Cairn & Stone Circle **9**
Torosay Castle & Gardens **7**

3-0575

Crafts on Skye

Edinbane Pottery (☎ **01470/582234**) celebrated its 25th anniversary in 1997. The three artists working in this studio produce wood-fired stoneware and salt-glazed pottery, and they are capable of producing almost anything you might request and can fill custom orders in a wide range of finishes. The pottery is on A850, 8 miles east of Dunvegan.

Artist Tom Mackenzie's etchings, prints, aquatints, and greeting cards are all inspired by the scenery and day-to-day life of the island. You can find his work at **Skye Original Prints at Portree,** 1 Wentworth St. (☎ **01478/612544**).

Since 1974 Stewart John Wilson has been designing and producing silver and gold jewelry, ceramic tiles, cheese boards, platters, and clocks here, all featuring intricate Celtic patterns. His work can be seen at **Skye Silver** (☎ **01470/511263**). The selection of tiles is especially vast, and Stewart's wife Elizabeth, who tends the shop, is friendly and knowledgeable. Skye Silver is in the Old School, on the Glendale Road (B884), 7 miles west of Dunvegan.

Craft Encounters, in the Post Office building in Broadford (☎ **01471/822754**), showcases many of Skye's talented artists. Here, you'll find pewter jewelry, stained-glass "light catchers," salt-dough bric-a-brac, folk and landscape paintings, silk scarves, tartan silk ties and potpourri bags, rubber stamps, and handmade jumpers. Celtic patterns show up on glassware, tableware, linens, and pieces of marquetry. The island's local musical talent is represented in a selection of traditional Scottish island music CDs.

Skye Batik in Armadale (☎ **01471/844396**) has been voted the best crafts shop in Scotland for 2 years running. Skye Batik sells wall hangings and cotton, tweed, wool, and linen clothing handprinted with Celtic designs from the 6th to the 8th centuries A.D. The shop is located 220 yards from the ferry landing at Armadale, along the only road leading inland.

In **Harlequin Knitwear** (☎ **01471/833321**), local knitter Chryssy Gibbs designs men's and women's machine-knit Shetland wool sweaters. Her work is bright and colorful. Despite the fact that she does all of the knitting and runs the shop singlehandedly, there are numerous sweaters to choose from. She's next to the Duisdale Hotel on Sleat.

If you want a tweed jacket, go to **Ragamuffin** on the pier in Armadale (☎ **01471/844217**). The shop features jackets made of tweeds designed on the premises, and has quality Scottish, Irish, and British hand-knits for the whole family as well as accessories such as hats, gloves, and scarves.

ESSENTIALS
GETTING THERE
BY CAR   From the Kyle of Lochalsh, head west along the newly constructed toll bridge over the strait to Kyleakin, paying £5.40 ($8.90) to cross one-way.

VISITOR INFORMATION
There's a **tourist information center** at Bayfield House in Portree (☎ **01478/612137**).

KYLEAKIN
The ferry from the Kyle of Lochalsh docks at this tiny waterfront village. There are a few quiet, well-kept places to stay.

WHERE TO STAY

Dunringell Hotel. Kyleakin, Isle of Skye, Inverness-shire IV41 8PR. ☎ **01599/534180.** Fax 01599/534460. 18 rms (10 with bath). £34–£36 ($56.10–$59.40) double without bath, £54–£60 ($89.10–$99) double with bath. MC, V. Rates include Scottish breakfast. MC, V.

Rhododendrons, azaleas, and other flowering shrubs on this hotel's 4$^1/_2$ acres provide a riot of color from March to July. The Dunringell is a spacious structure, built in 1912. Both smoking and no-smoking lounges are maintained for guests. Many of the modestly furnished bedrooms open onto scenic views; all have tea- and coffee-making facilities. For those who wish to participate, the proprietors, Mr. and Mrs. MacPherson, hold a short worship service in one of the lounges each evening.

White Heather Hotel. Kyleakin, Isle of Skye, Inverness-shire IV41 8PL. ☎ **01599/534577.** Fax 01599/534427. 20 rms (7 with tub or shower). £36–£38 ($59.40–$62.70) double without bath, £45–£47 ($74.25–$77.55) double with bath. MC, V. Rates include Scottish breakfast. Closed Dec–Feb.

This hotel, which consists of three connected buildings, provides basic accommodations with up-to-date amenities. The bedrooms are simple but clean and are all equipped with tea- and coffeemaking facilities. A fixed-price menu is presented nightly in the dining room; several selections are offered for each course. The hearty meal costs £14 ($23.10) per person. The hotel's lounge, which is licensed only to serve guests, has a pleasant view of the Castle Moil. White Heather is convenient to both the ferryboat dock and the bus terminals.

SLIGACHAN

This village sits at the head of a sea loch in a setting of scenic beauty with views of the Cuillin Hills (pronounced "Coolin"). It's one of the best bases for exploring Skye because of its central location. Visitors enjoy sea-trout fishing with an occasional salmon caught on the Sligachan River. It's also possible to rent a boat from the hotel below to explore the Storr Lochs, 15 miles from Sligachan and known for their good brown-trout fishing from May until September.

WHERE TO STAY & DINE

Sligachan Hotel. Sligachan, Isle of Skye, Inverness-shire IV47 8SW. ☎ **01478/650204.** Fax 01478/650207. 22 rms. TV. £40–£80 ($66–$132) double. MC, V. Rates include Scottish breakfast.

The Sligachan Hotel nestles at the foot of the Cuillins on the main road between Portree and Kyleakin, and is an ideal touring center from which to explore Skye. This family-run hotel is one of Skye's oldest coaching inns, built sometime in the 19th century. Accommodations are old and outdated, so be duly warned, but the food is good. The restaurant serves a nightly table d'hôte meal that features freshly caught seafood, as well as at least one vegetarian selection. Guests can choose to have two courses for £14.95 ($24.65) or three courses for £17.95 ($29.60). The bar also serves simple meals, along with a fine selection of malt whiskies, in front of an open fireplace.

PORTREE

Skye's capital, Portree, is the port for steamers making trips around the island and linking Skye with the 15-mile-long island of Raasay. Sligachan, 9 miles south, and Glenbrittle, 7 miles farther southwest, are centers for climbing the Cuillin Hills.

WHERE TO STAY & DINE

✪ **Cuillin Hills Hotel.** Portree, Isle of Skye IV51 9LU. ☎ **01478/612003.** Fax 01478/613092. 25 rms. TV TEL. £84–£156 ($138.60–$257.40) double. AE, DC, MC, V. Rates include dinner, bed, and breakfast.

Set within a half-mile north of Portree's center, this stone-sided, white-painted manor was built in the 1820s as a hunting lodge for members of the MacDonald clan. Today, it functions as a comfortable and very Scottish bed-and-breakfast hotel that appeals to the walkers and bird watchers who spend large portions of their day rambling over the surrounding heath and heather. Views from all of the bedrooms encompass the unspoiled Cuillin Hills, Portree's harbor, and/or the sea, and each is outfitted with reproductions of old-timey furniture and some kind of flowered wallpaper. Many clients here opt for half board, so there's a lot of emphasis placed on evening meals, which are served from 6:30 to 9pm. These are available to nonresidents who phone in advance for £24 ($39.60) per person. Menu items change virtually every night but might include a Highland terrine of game on a pool of wild rowan and juniperberry jelly; sliced smoked breast of duck served on an herb crêpe with sweet raspberries; roasted grouse with bacon and mushrooms; suprême of chicken on a bed of leeks with tarragon-flavored cream sauce; and a particularly succulent version of oven-roasted whole sea bass with oil, garlic, fresh herbs, and lemon. For dessert, you can never go wrong with the strawberries sautéed in butter, cognac, peppercorns, and cream, served in puff pastry. Lunches, incidentally, are much less formal, consisting of sandwiches and platters served in the bar, and priced at £2.50 to £13 ($4.15 to $21.45).

Rosedale Hotel. Beaumont Crescent, Portree, Isle of Skye, Inverness-shire IV51 9DF. ☎ **01478/613131.** Fax 01478/612531. 23 rms. TV TEL. £70–£90 ($115.50–$148.50) double. MC, V. Rates include Scottish breakfast. Closed Oct to mid-May.

In one of the more secluded parts of Portree, on the harbor 100 yards from the village square, Rosedale opens directly onto the sea. It was created from a row of dwellings dating from the reign of William IV. The rooms in this warm and welcoming place are decorated in modern style and have radios and other amenities. The food is standard Scottish fare with the requisite seafood of all island hotels. A five-course table d'hôte menu is served nightly for £25 ($41.25).

Royal Hotel. Bank St., Portree, Isle of Skye, Inverness-shire IV51 9BU. ☎ **01478/612525.** Fax 01478/613198. 25 rms. TV TEL. £60–£90 ($99–$148.50) double. MC, V. Rates include Scottish breakfast.

The Royal Hotel stands on a hill facing the water and is said to have extended hospitality to Bonnie Prince Charlie during his flight in 1746. In less dramatic circumstances, you can book one of its comfortable bedrooms; the preferred ones open onto the sea. All the accommodations have tea/coffeemakers and central heating. A la carte meals and bar snacks are offered; a dinner in the restaurant averages £17 ($28.05).

UIG

This village is on Trotternish, the largest Skye peninsula. The ferry port for Harris and Uist in the Outer Hebrides, it's 15 miles north of Portree and 49 miles from the Kyle of Lochalsh. **Monkstadt House,** 1¹/₂ miles north, is where Flora MacDonald brought Prince Charles after their escape flight from Benbecula. In **Kilmuir churchyard,** 5 miles north, Flora was buried, wrapped in a sheet used by the prince. Her grave is marked by a Celtic cross.

WHERE TO STAY

Ferry Inn. Uig, Isle of Skye, Inverness-shire IV51 9XP. ☎ **01470/542242.** 6 rms. TV. £50–£54 ($82.50–$89.10) double. MC, V. Rates include Scottish breakfast.

The hotel's popular pub is this place's main focus. John and Betty Campbell maintain the building, which was first a bank and later the post office. Today there are a

The Young Pretender

He was called "Bonnie Prince Charlie," and he blazed across the pages of British history in his gallant but ill-fated attempt to regain the British crown for the Catholic Jacobite dynasty. Born in 1720 in exile in Rome, Charles Edward Stuart had a direct claim to the throne of Britain, but had lost the succession to the German Protestant House of Hanover.

On July 23, 1745, when the prince landed on the Isle of Eriskay from France, islanders advised the 25-year-old pretender to return home. Within 2 days he crossed to the mainland at Loch nan Uamh in Arisaig to rally support, and on August 19 he raised his royal standard at Glenfinnan. Many clans rallied to his call, and backed by 1,200 troops he marched south, gathering an ever larger army as he went.

Amazingly, he took Edinburgh by stealth on September 17. And on September 21, the prince's army crushingly defeated the English at the Battle of Prestonpans. The prince proclaimed his father as James VIII, king of Scotland, with himself as regent. For a few weeks he held court at the Palace of Holyroodhouse in Edinburgh.

On November 8 he directed his army south, crossing into England and capturing the town of Carlisle. His invading armies took Kendal, Penrith, Lancaster, and Preston. Even Manchester fell, as the Scots were joined by English Jacobites. By December they were only 120 miles from London. There was panic in the streets of the English capital, and King George planned an escape to Hanover.

Charles wanted to press forward, but his military advisers warned him to turn back. Slowly they retreated to Scotland and settled down for the winter in Inverness. In the meantime, the duke of Cumberland's army was moving up to challenge the prince's forces. Charles decided to confront them on the desolate Moor of Culloden, an ill-fated choice. On the morning of April 16, 1746, backed by anti-Jacobite Scots, the English army crushed the Scottish forces and earned for its general the name of "Butcher" Cumberland. The Battle of Culloden ended in notorious atrocities, including the burning alive of injured prisoners and the killing of women and children.

The prince began 5 long months of wandering across the Highlands and islands. He had a £30,000 price tag on his head—unbelievable wealth in those days—but no one turned him in. Finally, in the words of the song, he went "over the sea to Skye" disguised as the servant girl of Flora MacDonald, the Highland heroine.

On September 20, 1746, Bonnie Prince Charlie returned to France secretly on the vessel *L'Heureux*. There he drifted and drank, eventually ending in Rome, where he died, all but forgotten by the world. A piper played "Lochaber No More" outside the window of his death chamber.

His brother assumed the Jacobite mantle, and—believe it or not—there is still a claimant to the throne today. His name is Prince Michael Stuart. He lives in exile in Paris, but stays abreast of events in Scotland and even has plans of what he will do "when I'm restored to the throne, as I inevitably will be."

handful of cozy bedrooms upstairs. You'll recognize this place in the town center by its roadside design of late-Victorian gables. There's a modern TV lounge on the premises. In summer, à la carte dinners are served in the dining room for £10 to £15 ($16.50 to $24.75). In winter, lunches and dinners are served less expensively in the pub and cost £3 to £5 ($4.95 to $8.25) each.

DUNVEGAN

The village of Dunvegan, northwest of Portree, grew up around ✪ **Dunvegan Castle** (☎ 01470/521206), the principal sight on the Isle of Skye, seat of the chiefs of Clan MacLeod who have lived here for 750 years. The castle, which stands on a rocky promontory, was once accessible only by boat, but now the moat is bridged and the castle is open to the public. It holds many relics, including a "fairy flag," and is reputed to be the oldest inhabited castle in Britain. It's open from mid-March to the end of October, daily from 10am to 5pm; November through February daily 11am to 4pm. Admission to the castle and gardens is £4.80 ($7.90) for adults, £4.20 ($6.95) for senior citizens, and £2.60 ($4.30) for children. Admission to the gardens only is £3.50 ($5.75) for adults and senior citizens and £1.80 ($2.95) for children.

Boats leave the castle jetty at frequent intervals every day from May to the end of September for the **seal colony.** The seals in Loch Dunvegan, both brown and gray varieties, aren't bothered by the approach of people in boats and can be studied at close range. The 25-minute round-trip costs £3.70 ($6.10) for adults and senior citizens and £2.50 ($4.15) for children. There's also a longer cruise that winds through the smaller islands of the area. The trip takes a little under 2 hours and costs £7 ($11.55) for adults and £5 ($8.25) for senior citizens and children.

At **Trumpan,** 9 miles north of Dunvegan, are the remains of a church that was set afire in 1597 by MacDonald raiders while the congregation, all MacLeods, were inside at worship. Only one woman survived. The MacLeods of Dunvegan rushed to the defense and only two MacDonalds escaped death.

WHERE TO STAY

Atholl House Hotel. Dunvegan, Isle of Skye, Inverness-shire IV55 8WA. ☎ **01470/521219.** Fax 01470/521481. 9 rms (8 with bath or shower). TV. £44–£60 ($72.60–$99) double; £60–£76 ($99–$125.40) 4-poster room; £20–£23 ($33–$37.95) per person, family room. AE, MC, V. Rates include Scottish breakfast. Closed Jan–Feb.

This guesthouse stands right in the village of Dunvegan, opposite the post office and near Dunvegan Castle. The well-furnished units contain facilities for making hot beverages; some singles do not have private bath. The guest rooms are well appointed and are equipped with tea- and coffeemaking facilities and hair dryers. Two rooms have four-poster beds along with the best views of the surrounding mountain moorland and Loch Dunvegan. In addition, there is a family room, which accommodates three cots. In the dining room, a chef prepares quality cuisine using an abundance of locally caught seafood. Other dishes feature lamb and venison as well as fresh-grown produce. A three-course table d'hôte menu with coffee costs £18 ($29.70) per person. In the dining room, emphasis is placed on friendly service and well-prepared local produce, including lamb, venison, salmon, and shellfish in season. It has a residents-only license. From the hotel, you have views over mountain moorland and Loch Dunvegan.

WHERE TO DINE

✪ **Three Chimneys Restaurant.** Hwy. B884, Colbost. ☎ **01470/511258.** Reservations required at dinner, recommended at lunch. Main courses £5–£20 ($8.25–$33) at lunch; £25–£30 ($41.25–$49.50) fixed-price dinner. MC, V. Mon–Sat noon–2pm (last order) and 7–9pm (last order). Closed Nov–Feb. Drive 4 miles west of Dunvegan on B884. SCOTTISH.

Winner of several culinary awards, including one in 1990 that dubbed it the best restaurant in Scotland, the Three Chimneys is in a stone crofter's house. Two of the three chimneys funnel smoke from a pair of blazing fireplaces during cold and foggy weather.

The food is prepared by Edinburgh-born Shirley Speare and served by her London-born husband, Edward. Specialties include fresh seafood and shellfish and Highland game dishes. Examples include traditional dishes as well as modern cuisine such as roasted fillet of wild salmon served with warm lime-and-peppercorn vinaigrette, and a trio of Highland game (venison, wild hare, and pigeon) with a rich beet root and blackcurrant sauce. An exceptionally good starter is the wild duck pâté, which is accompanied by wafer-thin grilled potato scones. More than 100 vintages from one of the most complete wine lists on Skye is available to accompany your meal.

SKEABOST BRIDGE

Eastward from Dunvegan, Skeabost Bridge has an island cemetery of great antiquity. The graves of four Crusaders are here.

WHERE TO STAY

✪ **Skeabost House Hotel.** Skeabost Bridge, Isle of Skye, Inverness-shire IV51 9NP. ☎ **01470/532202.** Fax 01470/532454. 26 rms. TV TEL. £61–£100 ($100.65–$165) double. MC, V. Rates include Scottish breakfast. Closed Dec–Mar.

This is one of the most inviting country homes of Skye. It's thoroughly modernized and architecturally interesting with its dormers, chimneys, tower, and gables. Built in 1870 as a private estate, it has been converted into a lochside hotel, standing on grounds studded with flowering bushes. The location is 35 miles west of the Kyle of Lochalsh and 6 miles north of Portree. The hotel owns 8 miles of the bank of the River Snizort, so it attracts many sports people who come to pull trout and salmon from the waters. In addition, guests can play the hotel's par-three golf course. There are two restaurants to choose from: One focuses on an extensive buffet bar that features a variety of cold salads; the Conservatory Restaurant offers three, four, or six-course table d'hôte menus from £22 to £28 ($36.30 to $46.20). Seafood, of course, is a specialty.

SLEAT PENINSULA

A lot of Skye can look melancholy and forlorn, especially in misty weather. For a change of landscape, head for the Peninsula of Sleat, the southeastern section of the island. Because of the lushness of its vegetation, it has long been known as the "Garden of Skye." Shores here are washed by the warmer waters of the Gulf Stream.

SEEING THE SIGHTS

A ruined stronghold of the MacDonalds, **Knock Castle** lies off A851 some 12 miles south of Broadford. It can be visited, admission free, throughout the day.

Another MacDonald stronghold, **Dunsgiath Castle** has some well-preserved ruins open to view. They're found at Tokavaig on an unclassified road (a sign directs you) at a point 20 miles south and southwest of Broadford.

Clan Donald Visitor Centre. Armadale. ☎ **01471/844305.** Admission £3.40 ($5.60) adults, £2.20 ($3.65) senior citizens and ages 5–15, free for age 4 and under. Apr–Oct, daily 9:30am–5:30pm.

At Armadale, you don't have to have MacDonald as your last name to enjoy a visit to Skye's award-winning Clan Donald Visitor Centre, with its historical exhibition "The Headship of the Gael," woodland gardens, restaurant, and gift shop. From Broadford, travel along a winding seaside road to the recently restored and well-kept grounds surrounding the sculptured ruins of Armadale Castle and the rebuilt baronial stables. The multimedia exhibition is in part of the castle and tells of the lost culture of the ancient Gaelic world under the MacDonalds as lords of the Isles.

There's a countryside ranger service with a full summer program of guided walks and talks to introduce you to several miles of trails and the history and workings of the adjacent Highland estate. The licensed restaurant in the stables offers home baking and good local food, from teas and coffees to a full meal.

The drive from the ferryboat at Kyleakin is about 30 minutes, and the center is along A851 (follow the signs) near the Armadale–Mallaig ferry.

WHERE TO STAY & DINE

✪ **Ardvasar Hotel.** Ardvasar, Isle of Skye, Inverness-shire IV45 8RS. ☎ **01471/844223.** 9 rms. TV. £75 ($123.75) double, £80 ($132) family room. MC, V. Rates include Scottish breakfast. Closed Nov.

The oldest part of this 250-year-old coaching inn is a stone-trimmed pub in what was originally a stable. Today virtually every off-duty resident in the area heads here for a mug of lager and perhaps a taste of the cuisine prepared by Bill Fowler, the owner and chef, and his wife, Greta. À la carte evening meals are offered for £14 to £18 ($23.10 to $29.70) and up, and might include flavorful preparations of fresh local fish as well as homemade pâté with tomato vinaigrette, fresh halibut with hollandaise, or Scottish sirloin steak with local prawns and Drambuie. Dessert might consist of a chocolate rum pot with cream. Bar meals at lunch and suppertime average about £10 ($16.50) each.

In 1990 a major renovation added private baths to each of the bedrooms and a "cottage cozy" decor that includes pastel colors, flowered chintz, and pinewood furniture. Guests are free to congregate in their own residents' lounge, which contains separate sections for TV watching and reading, and a fireplace.

Fiordhem. Ord, Sleat, Isle of Skye, Inverness-shire IV44 8RN. ☎ **01471/855226.** 3 rms. £37–£40 ($61.05–$66) per person. Minimum stay 3 nights. No credit cards. Rates include half board. Closed Oct–Easter. Take A852 south along the eastern coast of Skye, but cut west along an unclassified road toward Ord to the west coast of the island.

Some kind of stone-sided house has stood in this spot for hundreds of years. The present version is a rebuilt fisher's cottage, enlarged in 1990, within 20 feet of the edge of Loch Eishort. The guest bedrooms are on the upper floor, with panoramic views of the Cuillin Hills and the islands of Canna and Rhum. It's a place to stop and linger a bit. Fresh fish and seafood, along with lamb and venison, are featured on the menu. The dining room is pleasantly furnished with antiques, and the welcome is warm and hearty. In the sitting room are comfortable armchairs, gleaming copper and brass, and an open fireplace for peat and log fires.

Kinloch Lodge. Isleornsay, Sleat, Isle of Skye, Inverness-shire IV43 8QY. ☎ **01471/833333.** Fax 01471/833277. 10 rms. £100–£180 ($165–$297) double. AE, MC, V. Rates include Scottish breakfast. Closed Dec–Feb.

The white stone walls of this dignified manor house are visible from across the scrub- and pine-covered hillsides bordering the edges of this historic property. When it was built in 1680, it was a hunting lodge for the MacDonald estates. Today, after much rebuilding and expansion, the linden-flanked manor house is the private residence of Lord and Lady MacDonald, who welcome discriminating guests into the confines of their very elegant home. Portraits of the family's 18th-century forebears are a striking feature of the reception rooms, where open fireplaces illuminate the burnished patina of scores of family antiques. Many of the bedrooms have been freshly papered and painted and all have private baths. From the windows of some of the bedrooms, guests sometimes catch glimpses of the sea, which washes up to the edge of the property's sloping gardens.

Every evening guests enjoy drinks in a peach-colored drawing room before one of the well-prepared meals for which Lady MacDonald is famous. The author of 13 cookbooks, she applies her imaginative recipes to ingredients shot, trapped, netted, or grown on the Isle of Skye. A five-course fixed-price dinner costs £35 ($57.75) per person.

3 Rhum (Rum)

9 miles SW of the Isle of Skye

This enticingly named island is only about 8 miles wide and 8 miles long. There are those who will tell you not to go: "If you like a barren desert where it rains all the time, you'll love Rhum," a skipper in Mallaig recently told us. It's stark all right. And very wet. In fact, with more than 90 inches of rainfall recorded annually, it's said to be the "wettest" island of the Inner Hebrides.

Since the mid-1950s Rhum has been owned by the Edinburgh-based Nature Conservancy Council, an ecological conservation group. Conservation is of paramount importance, and attempts are being made to bring back the sea eagle, which used to inhabit the island in Queen Victoria's day.

On this storm-tossed outpost in summer, mountain climbers meet challenging peaks and anglers go for its good trout fishing. Bird-lovers seek out the Manx shearwaters that live on the island in great numbers. Red deer and ponies, along with the wildflowers of summer, add color to an otherwise bleak landscape.

ESSENTIALS

Note: Before traveling to Rhum, visitors must get permission from **Martin Curry,** who is in charge of tourist count for the island, at the Scottish Natural Heritage Nature Reserve (☎ **01687/4620226**). No one is allowed to stay overnight without prior bookings.

GETTING THERE

BY FERRY   A passenger ferry from Mallaig, on the western coast of Scotland, leaves about four times a week. No cars are allowed on the island. For information, contact **Caledonian MacBrayne** (☎ **01687/462403** in Mallaig). Sailings are from May to September only, on Monday through Thursday at 11am, Friday at 6am, and Saturday at 5am and 12:30pm. A round-trip costs £17.25 ($28.45) for adults, £8.60 ($14.20) for children. *Murdo Grant* (☎ **01687/450224**) sails to Rhum on Tuesday, Thursday, Saturday, and Sunday at 11am. A round-trip ticket is £17 ($28.05) for adults, £6 ($9.90) for ages 12 to 16, and £3 ($4.95) for those under age 12. Schedules can vary, so it's best to call for confirmations. It takes about 3 hours to reach Rhum from one of these ports.

WHERE TO STAY & DINE

Kinloch Castle. Kinloch, Isle of Rhum, Inverness-shire PH43 4RR. ☎ and fax **01687/462037.** 3 rms (none with bath), 30 hostel beds. Rooms: £45 ($74.25) double. Hostel: £10 ($16.50) per person, in rooms with 2 to 5 beds each. No credit cards.

Quite astonishingly in such a forbidding place, you come upon a hotel that has been called "Britain's most intact example of an Edwardian Country House." It's on the seafront in the center of Rhum's biggest hamlet, Kinloch, and its very inaccessibility may have kept this mansion of imposing stature and grandeur unchanged over the years. It was completed in 1901 for Sir George Boullough, a wealthy Lancashire textile magnate, and decorated under the direction of his wife, Lady Monica (both are buried in the family mausoleum on the island's west coast). The castle still contains their ballroom, with its gold curtains and upholstery, a massive inglenook Adam-style fireplace, and the monumental paintings and stuffed animals that were *de rigueur* in such mansions when Kinloch Castle was in its heyday.

The former servants' quarters are now a simple and functional hostel. The more elegant and much more private rooms are furnished with heavy four-poster oak beds and share spacious bathroom facilities. Because the residents spend their days trekking around the island, all lunches are packed picnics, priced at £3.50 ($5.75) per person. The bistro-style restaurant serves breakfast and hearty evening meals for reasonable prices.

4 Eigg & Muck

Eigg: 4 miles SE of Rhum; Muck: 7 miles SW of Eigg

The tiny islands of Eigg and Muck lie in the Sea of the Hebrides, which separates the Inner from the Outer Hebrides.

ESSENTIALS
GETTING THERE

BY FERRY **Caledonian MacBrayne** ferries (☎ **01687/462403** in Mallaig) go from Mallaig to Eigg. Sailings are on Monday, Tuesday, and Thursday at 10:30am, on Friday at 6am, and on Saturday at 5am and 12:30pm. The round-trip ticket costs £17.25 ($28.45) for adults and £8.60 ($14.20) for children. From Airsaig, another ferry line, **Murdo Grant** (call ☎ **01687/450678** for schedule information), sails to Muck on Monday, Wednesday, and Friday (but departure days and times can vary, so always call first). Sailings to Eigg are Friday through Wednesday. Most departures are at either 11 or 11:30am (subject to change, based on weather conditions). The round-trip fare for either excursion is £13 ($21.45) for adults, £6 ($9.90) for ages 12 to 16, and £3 ($4.95) for those under 12.

VISITOR INFORMATION

For details about a possible holiday on the island of Eigg, phone the estate office at ☎ **01687/482413** at Eigg, or ☎ **01651/842367** on mainland Scotland.

EIGG

Eigg, about 4¹/₂ miles by 3 miles in size, lies some 12 miles out in the Atlantic. The island is owned by the Isle of Eigg Heritage Trust, consisting of about 63 island residents and the Highland Council and Scottish Wildlife Trust. The farmers, shepherds, fishers, and guesthouse keepers who live there raised $2.4 million through a worldwide public appeal over the Internet to buy their island.

Visitors can see the **Sgurr of Eigg,** a tall column of lava, said to be the biggest such pitchstone mass in the United Kingdom. Climbers on its north side try to attain its impressive height of 1,300 feet. It's said that the last of the pterodactyls roosted there. The bones of this towering bat-winged and beaked flying dinosaur were discovered in the 7th century, or so it is reported, by St. Donnan, a Christian missionary.

After your arrival at **Galmisdale,** the principal hamlet and pier, you can take an antique omnibus to Cleadale. Once here, you walk across moors to **Camas Sgiotaig,** with its well-known beach of the Singing Sands (its black-and-white quartz grains are decidedly off-key).

MUCK

Lying 7 miles to the southwest of Eigg, Muck has such an unappetizing name that visitors may turn away. However, the name of this little 2¹/₂-square-mile island was originally a Gaelic word, *muic,* meaning the "island of the sow." Naturalists come here to look for everything from rare butterflies to otters. The large colonies of nesting seabirds in May and June should be viewed.

Muck is actually a farm. There are hardly more than two dozen people on Muck and all are concerned with the running of the farm. Visitors are welcome. The entire island is owned by two brothers: the Laird of Muck, Lawrence MacEwan, and his younger brother, Ewen MacEwan. There are no vehicles on the island except for bicycles and tractors.

WHERE TO STAY & DINE

Port Mhor House. Port Mhor, Isle of Muck, Inverness-shire PH42 4RP. ☎ **01687/462365.** 8 rms (none with bath). £64 ($105.60) double. No credit cards. Rates include half board and parking. Closed Sept 15–May 15.

This solidly weatherproof hotel with its varnished planks of Scots pine was personally built by Ewen MacEwan. Its construction required 5 years (1975–80) and most of its building materials were barged in from the mainland. Almost everyone checks in here on the half-board plan. For visitors to the island, a fixed-price evening meal is offered for £14 ($23.10). Vegetarian dishes are available upon request. Residents can get a drink in the cocktail lounge, and during cold weather a log fire is blazing. The kitchen uses produce from the island's farm for plain and wholesome fare well suited to the brisk climate. The bedrooms are functional, clean, and comfortable, with lots of pinewood trim. The hostelry is only a few steps from the island's only ferry-boat landing.

5 Coll & Tyree

90 miles NW of Glasgow, 48 miles W of Fort William

If you like your scenery stark and tranquil, try Coll and Tyree, tiny islands that attract visitors seeking remoteness. Coll and Tyree are very much sibling islands, exposed to the open Atlantic. The outermost of the Inner Hebrides, they're said to have the highest sunshine records in Britain. On Tyree (also spelled Tiree), the shell-sand machair (sand dunes) increase the arable area, differentiating it from the other inner isles.

Trees are rare on either island, but that doesn't mean that they're bleak. Both are rich in flora, with some 500 species, along with bird life. It's estimated that some 150 bird species are found here, including Arctic skuas and razorbills. Both common and gray seals have breeding colonies on the islands.

If that sun does come out in midsummer, you'll find silver beaches. Boat rentals and sea angling can be arranged on both Coll and Tyree. Many visitors bicycle around the island and there are a few cars for rent. Tyree has the least expensive method of transport: A mail bus serves most of the island.

Both islands have accommodations, but there are no officially designated campsites. Campers must ask a local farmer for permission, and it's usually granted.

ESSENTIALS
GETTING THERE
BY PLANE British Airways (☎ **01345/222111** in Glasgow for flight information) flies directly to Tyree from Glasgow, with about six scheduled flights weekly (none on Sunday).

BY FERRY & CAR The car ferry sails from Oban to Mull and then, if conditions are right, goes on to Coll and Tyree, although sometimes gales may force cancellation of the trip. You can be stranded on an island for a while, waiting for the next departure. Details and bookings, essential for cars, are available from **Caledonian MacBrayne** (☎ 01631/562285 at the ferry terminal at Oban).

COLL

Lying in the seemingly timeless world of the Celtic west, the little island of Coll, with a population of some 130 hearty souls, is rich in history, even prehistory. Distances from one place to another are small on Coll, since the island averages about 3 miles in breadth; at its longest point, it stretches for some 13 miles.

SEEING THE SIGHTS

Coll has a restored castle, **Breacachadh,** a stronghold of the Macleans in the 15th century. This is a private residence but also a center for Project Trust, which prepares young people for voluntary service overseas. On some occasions it's open to the public.

The so-called **New Castle,** built for Hector Maclean in 1750, provided shelter for Samuel Johnson and James Boswell when they were stranded on the island for 10 days because of storms at sea. The castle was altered considerably in the 19th century and embellished with pepper-pot turrets and parapets.

In the western part of the island at Totronald are two standing stones called **Na Sgeulachan** ("the teller of tales"). The stones predate the Druids and are thought to have been the site of a temple. It's also been suggested that they may have been an astronomical laboratory, recording the movements of the sun and moon.

The highest point on Coll is **Ben Hogh** (340 feet), which can be climbed for a panoramic view. The boulder on the hill, supported by smaller stones, is believed to have been left that way from the Ice Age.

On the road to Sorisdale, at **Killunaig,** stand the ruins of a church from the late Middle Ages and a burial ground. Going on to **Sorisdale,** you'll see the ruins of houses occupied by crofters earlier in this century. Hundreds of families once lived here. Some were chased away in the wake of the potato famine and many were forced out in Land Clearance programs. Enduring great hardships at sea, including disease, they went to Canada, Australia, the United States, and New Zealand.

WHERE TO STAY & DINE

Isle of Coll Hotel. Arinagour, Isle of Coll, Argyll PA78 6SZ. ☎ **01879/230334.** Fax 01879/ 230317. 6 rms (3 with bath). TV. £50 ($82.50) double without bath, £60 ($99) double with bath. AE, DC, MC, V. Rates include Scottish breakfast.

It enjoys the dubious honor of being immediately rejected by Samuel Johnson and James Boswell as an inappropriate place to spend the night during their 18th-century tour of Scotland. They eventually succeeded in securing lodgings with the laird of Coll instead. Today the establishment's rooms are far more comfortable, with electric blankets, teamaking facilities, and simple but functional furniture. A good dinner will cost £21 ($34.65) in the dining room. The hotel contains the town's only pub, so you're likely to meet the locals over a pint of ale and a platter of bar food. The hotel sits on a hilltop at the end of the Arinagour estuary about a 10-minute walk north of town, beside B8071. Its facilities include a sauna, solarium, and games room.

TYREE (TIREE)

A fertile island, one of the richest in the Hebrides, flat Tyree earned the Gaelic nickname "the land below the wave tops." Tyree has a population of some 800 residents, mostly in farming communities, who enjoy its gentle landscape, sandy beaches, and rolling hills. At Vaul is a nine-hole golf course open to visitors.

SEEING THE SIGHTS

As you travel about the island, you'll see many Hebridean **crofters' houses** with thatched roofs constructed in the early 1800s. In 1886 the duke of Argyll caused a scandal when he sent in marines and police to clear the crofters off the land. Many were sent destitute to Canada. But today crofters once again occupy the land.

Most of the population is centered around **Scarinish,** with its little stone harbor where lobster boats put in. Fishing isn't what it used to be; the appearance of fast and dangerous squalls and storms are said to scatter the fishing fleet as far as the shores of North America.

Bird watchers are drawn to the shores of **Loch Bhasapoll,** a favorite gathering place of wild geese and ducks. Another sightseeing target for bird watchers is a cave on the coast at **Kenavara,** where many seabirds can be observed. The Reef was an important air base for the Royal Air Force in World War II and is still in use.

Ancient duns and forts are scattered around Tyree. The best of these is a broch at **Vaul Bay,** which has walls more than 12 feet thick. It's 30 feet in diameter. At **Balephetrish,** on the northern rim of the island, stands a huge granite boulder. Locals call it the "Ringing Stone," because when struck it gives off a metallic sound. In the western part of the island, at Kilkenneth, are the ruins of the **Chapel of St. Kenneth,** a comrade of St. Columba.

WHERE TO STAY & DINE

Tiree Lodge Hotel. Kirkatol, Isle of Tiree, Argyll PA77 6TW. ☎ **01879/220368.** Fax 01879/220884. 11 rms (7 with bath). TV. £42 ($69.30) double without bath, £47 ($77.55) double with bath. MC, V. Rates include Scottish breakfast.

Originally built as a simple island hunting lodge around 1790 for the duke of Argyll, it was greatly enlarged in the 1970s with a modern addition, and the interior was brought severely up-to-date. Today, a mile east of the island's only ferryboat landing, its big plate-glass windows offer views of emerald-green fields and the beach. The hotel, run by Kenneth and Irene Hutchinson, contains one of the island's two pubs (the other is almost 3 miles away). Because of the crowd of locals and visitors who keep the place packed, renovations have expanded both the bar and restaurant. Meals are served in both places; bar meals begin at about £8 ($13.20), while an average à la carte meal in the dining room costs £14 ($23.10). The bedrooms are clean and comfortable and have tea- and coffeemaking facilities.

6 Mull

121 miles NW of Edinburgh, 90 miles NW of Glasgow

The third-largest island in the Hebrides, Mull is rich in legend and folklore, a land of ghosts, monsters, and the wee folk. The island is wild and mountainous, characterized by sea lochs and sandy bars. Be sure to bring a raincoat to Mull: It's known as one of the wettest islands in the Hebrides, a fact that upset Dr. Johnson, who visited here in 1773. Actually, Dr. Johnson was a latecomer to Mull, which has an ancient history. It was known to the classical Greeks, and its prehistoric past is recalled in forts, duns, and stone circles.

Many visitors consider Mull more beautiful than Skye, a controversy we don't choose to get involved in, since the islands are different and each has many attractions. Mull has varied scenery with many waterfalls. The wild countryside of Mull was the scene of many of David Balfour's adventures in *Kidnapped* by Robert Louis Stevenson. Its highest peak is **Ben More** at 3,169 feet, but it also has many flat areas. It's rich in wildlife, including roe deer, golden eagles, polecats, seabirds, and feral goats. Mull is additionally enticing as a launching pad to the famed islands of Iona and Staffa.

Guarding the bay (you'll see it as you cross on the ferry) is **Duart Castle,** restored just before World War I. It was once the seat of the fiery Macleans, who shed much blood in and around the castle during their battles with the lords of the Isles. In the bay—somewhere—lies the *Florencia,* a Spanish galleon that went down laden with treasure. Many attempts have been made to find it and bring it up, but so far all have failed.

To the southeast, near Salen, are the ruins of **Aros Castle,** once a stronghold of the MacDonalds, lords of the Isles. Its ruins date from the 14th century, and it was last occupied in the 17th century. On the far south coast at Lochbuie, **Moy Castle** has a water-filled dungeon.

If you're driving along any of the single-track roads of Mull, remember to take your time and let the sheep and cattle have the right-of-way. Also, a car coming downhill toward you has preference, so seek a spot to pull off.

There are two nine-hole **golf courses** on the island. The Western Isles Golf Course at Tobermory, the island's capital, dates from the 1930s and is said to have possibly the best views of any course in the world. A newer course, flat and tight, opened in 1980 at Craignure. Sea **fishing** and river fishing are also popular on Mull, where anglers seek salmon and three kinds of trout in the fast-flowing rivers and hill lochs of the island: rainbow, sea, and brown. Some sports lovers take to the sea in pursuit of sharks and monster skate. Stalking, hiking, and hill walking are other common activities.

At the end of the day, you might enjoy a dram of malt whisky from the **Tobermory Malt Whisky Distillery** (☎ 01688/302647), which has had a troubled history but is now back in business. Visitors are welcome to visit the distillery in Tobermory, established in 1823. Tours are from 10:15am to 4:15pm daily and cost £2.50 ($4.15) for adults, £1 ($1.65) for senior citizens. There is no charge for age 17 and under. Be sure to call to arrange a tour in advance, as the distillery seems to shut down operations from time to time.

ESSENTIALS
GETTING THERE

BY FERRY & CAR   It's a 45-minute car-ferry trip from Oban to Craignure on Mull. For times of departure, contact **Caledonian MacBrayne** (☎ 01631/562285 at the ferry terminal at Oban). It's a roll-on/roll-off operation for your car. From Oban, there are about five or six sailings per day at a cost of £5.40 ($8.90) for adults and £2.70 ($4.45) for children.

GETTING AROUND

BY BUS   Take the ferry to get here (see above), then use a local bus service, **Essbee Coach Hire,** to go around the island (☎ 01631/566999 for more information). Coaches connect with the ferry at least three times per day and will take you to Fionnphort or Tobermory for £3.50 ($5.75) or £6.50 ($10.75) round-trip. Fares for children are half price. Another option is to purchase a tour ticket, which combines the cost of the ferry with a guided bus tour to Fionnphort and Iona. The tour begins when you board the 10am ferry from Oban and ends at approximately 5:40pm, once again at Oban. The cost is £15 ($24.75).

VISITOR INFORMATION

The **tourist information center** is on Main Street in Tobermory (☎ 01688/302182).

SPECIAL EVENTS

The **Mull Highland Games** are held annually in July, filled with all the traditional events such as bagpipes, caber tossing, and dancing. The **Tour of Mull Rally** is held in early October of every year. Ask at the tourist office for exact dates.

CRAIGNURE

Even passengers who arrive on Mull with a car might want to take an excursion on the **Mull Railway,** Old Pier Station, Craignure (☎ **01680/812494**), the only passenger railway in the Hebrides. It was inaugurated in 1983, and its puffing engine and narrow-gauge tracks give the impression of a frontier-style excursion into the past. The tracks begin at the Old Pier in Craignure, running 1 1/2 miles to Torosay Castle and its famous gardens. Some of the engines are powered by steam, others by diesel. The view is one of unspoiled mountains, glens, and seaside; otters, eagles, and deer can sometimes be seen in the course of the 20-minute journey. The trains operate between late April and mid-October only. The most frequent service is between June and mid-September, when daily trips begin around 11am. One-way fares are £2 ($3.30) for adults, £1.30 for children. A special round-trip ticket is available for families with two parents and two children at £7.50 ($12.40). For more information, call the Mull & West Highland Railway Company in Craignure (☎ **01680/300389**).

A good way to see the sights of Mull is to book a ticket for "The Mull Experience," a tour offered by **Caledonian MacBrayne** (☎ **01680/812421**). The tour begins in Oban, where participants board a ferry for Craignure. Once in Craignure, you catch the train to Torosay Castle where you'll spend a few hours exploring the Victorian structure and its gardens. The next stop is the castle of Duart, the 13th-century home of the chief of Clan Maclean. You then return to Oban by ferry. The tour is offered May to September, Sunday through Thursday, three times daily, and twice on Friday. The cost is £16 ($26.40) for adults and £8 ($13.20) for children.

SEEING THE SIGHTS

✪ **Torosay Castle and Gardens.** Craignure. ☎ **01680/812421.** Admission to castle and gardens: £4.50 ($7.45) adults, £3.50 ($5.75) senior citizens and students, £1.50 ($2.45) ages 6–16, free for age 5 and under. Admission to gardens and tearoom only: £3.50 ($5.75) adults, £2.75 ($4.55) senior citizens and students, £1 ($1.65) children. Easter to mid-Oct, daily 10:30am–5:30pm.

This Victorian mansion, 1 1/2 miles south of Craignure on A849, was constructed in the mid-19th century by David Bryce, a famous Scottish architect. In his early years Winston Churchill was a frequent visitor there. It's set in gardens designed at the turn of the century and attributed to Sir Robert Lorimer. One writer said that a visit here is like returning to the "Edwardian age of leisure"—and so it is. To the surprise of hundreds of visitors, the armchairs are labeled "Please sit down" instead of "Please keep off." This is very much a family place, the only privately occupied castle and garden open daily to the public in the western Highlands. The family portraits are by such famous artists as Sargent. Its numerous exhibits intrigue its visitors, including evidence for the existence of the Loch Ness monster. You can wander through 12 acres of Italian-style terraced gardens, a water garden with shrubs that grow in the Gulf Stream climate, and a Japanese garden with life-size figures by Antonio Bonazza. You can enjoy extensive views of the Appin coastline from Ben Nevis to Ben Cruachen.

Duart Castle. Off A849, on the eastern point of Mull. ☎ **01680/812309.** Admission £3.50 ($5.75) adults, £3 ($4.95) senior citizens and students, £1.75 ($2.90) ages 5–16, free for age 4 and under. May to mid-Oct, daily 10:30am to 6pm.

Both Torosay Castle and Duart Castle can ideally be visited on the same day. Located 3 miles west of Torosay, this castle dates from the 13th century and was the home of the Maclean clan. An imposing and majestic structure, it was sacked in 1791 by the dukes of Argyll in retaliation for the Macleans' support of the Stuarts in 1715 and 1745. It was allowed to fall into ruins. However, Sir Fitzroy Maclean, the 26th chief of the clan and grandfather of the present occupant, began a restoration in 1911 when he was 76, spending a considerable fortune. It had been his ambition since he was a boy to see his ancestral home restored (he lived until he was 102). Visitors can wander about, taking in such rooms as the Banqueting Hall, which is in the keep, the great tower that's the heart of the castle.

WHERE TO STAY & DINE

Isle of Mull. Craignure, Isle of Mull, Argyll PA65 6BB. ☎ **01680/812351.** Fax 01680/812462. 87 rms. TV TEL. £60–£92 ($99–$151.80) double. V. Rates include Scottish breakfast. Closed mid-Oct to mid-Mar.

The Isle of Mull stands near the ferry and the meeting point of the Sound of Mull and Loch Linnhe. From the picture windows of its public rooms you'll have panoramic vistas of mountains and the island of Lismore. The bedrooms are handsomely furnished and come with tea/coffeemakers. The chef serves both British and continental food in the attractive dining room, which faces both sea and hills. A three-course fixed-price dinner begins at £18 ($29.70). Other facilities include a cocktail bar and a residents' lounge.

CRAIGNURE AFTER DARK

Don't let the name fool you. **Ceilidh Place,** opposite the ferry terminal, Craignure (☎ **01680/812471**), is mainly a place to catch live rock bands and other pop music. Once a month there actually is a ceilidh held here, but no matter what the entertainment is, there's no cover charge. On tap you'll find Guinness, along with the lagers of Tennant's and McEwan's. Locals, however, tend to favor the malt whiskies, of which there are more than 100 varieties.

SALEN

Near Salen are the ruins of **Aros Castle,** once a stronghold of the lords of the Isles, the MacDonalds. It dates from the 14th century and it was last occupied in the 17th century.

WHERE TO STAY

Glenforsa Hotel. By Salen, Aros, Isle of Mull, Argyll PA72 6JN. ☎ **01680/300377.** Fax 01680/300535. 16 rms. £77.50 ($127.90) double. AE, MC, V. Rates include Scottish breakfast.

This 1968 Norwegian pine log construction, in secluded grounds by the Sound of Mull and the River Forsa 11 miles southeast of Tobermory, is known in late summer for its seafront and salmon. The rooms are well appointed and spacious. The bar serves an array of tempting pub food, with venison, trout, and salmon offered in season for guests and nonresidents alike. The dining room serves much the same fare, with meals starting at about £17.50 ($28.90). The hotel has an adjacent grass airstrip, at which Dakotas and other private and charter planes can land from dawn to dusk. A parking area is alongside.

TOBERMORY

The **Mull Museum** (☎ **01688/302208**) has local exhibitions relating to the island, displayed in an old bakery building on Main Street, open Easter to mid-October only,

Monday through Friday from 10:30am to 4:30pm and Saturday from 10:30am to 1:30pm, charging £1 ($1.65) for adults and 10p (15¢) for children.

The **Western Isle Golf Course** dates from the 1930s and is said to have possibly the best views of any golf course in the world.

SHOPPING

Isle of Mull Silver, Main Street (☎ **01688/302345**), stocks jewelry made by a number of Scottish designers. This shop, open since 1975, also produces some of the silver and gold pieces available here. Among the unique items made on the premises are traditional Scottish silver *quaich* (drinking vessels) and christening spoons.

The 4-year-old **Mull Pottery,** Main Street (☎ **01688/302057**), is the domain of potter Pete Walker, who produces tableware, ovenware, and lamps in sea-shore, seagull, and turquoise patterns. Among the more unusual of his items is a large crock designed for bread storage. The shop also stocks the wares of other Scottish potters.

Sgriob Ruadh Dairy/Isle of Mull Cheese, Glengorm Road (☎ **01688/302235**), a family-run farm, one-half mile outside Tobermory, has been producing cheeses for more than 20 years. You're welcome to watch the cheese-making process and check out the farm. The shop itself is an attractive glass house where you'll find Isle of Mull cheese, a softer washed-curd cheese, and flavored variations of both. The flavor of the cheese is unique for much the same reason Scottish malt whiskies are unique—the naturally occurring qualities of the water and the natural grazing, supplemented with a feed made of grains used in producing malt whiskies, which feed the cattle. There's a simple country restaurant on the premises, where good, inexpensive home-cooked meals are available from 10am to 4pm. Among the most popular items: any of a rotation of hearty soups served with as much freshly baked bread as you care to eat—a meal in itself for £1.60 ($2.65). You can also get an Isle of Mull cheese board with a salad and as much bread as you want for £3.50 ($5.75).

Tackle & Books, Main Street (☎ **01688/302336**), as the name suggests, carries fishing gear, bait, and an impressive array of reading materials. The shop sells "anything in print about Mull" and works by local authors. There's also a decent selection of contemporary fiction and publications about Scottish history, regional folklore, all things Celtic, and natural history, including books on bird watching and whale watching on the island.

WHERE TO STAY

The capital of Mull, Tobermory (or Tobar Mhoire, "well of Mary," in Gaelic) is the town best equipped with accommodations.

Tobermory Hotel. 53 Main St., Tobermory, Isle of Mull, Argyll PA75 6NT. ☎ **01688/302091.** Fax 01688/302254. 17 rms. £68–£90 ($112.20–$148.50) double. MC, V. Rates include Scottish breakfast. Parking available on nearby streets.

On the upper end of the town's main street, a minute's walk from the center, this hotel has a sense of privacy and intimacy. It has recently undergone major renovations, with the guest rooms getting special attention; all have been upgraded and have private bathrooms. Thirteen of the rooms have views of the fishing boats bobbing at anchor in the harbor just off the road; the remaining four have views of the steep and tree-dotted cliff that rises abruptly behind the hotel. The hotel's dining room features a nightly table d'hôte menu with four courses costing £21.50 ($35.50). The menu includes a wide selection of seafood as well as whatever game may be in season at the time of your stay.

Western Isles Hotel. Tobermory, Isle of Mull, Argyll PA75 6PR. ☎ **01688/302012.** Fax 01688/302297. 25 rms. TV TEL. £74–£170 ($122.10–$280.50) double. MC, V. Rates include Scottish breakfast. Closed Jan.

In a scenic location above the harbor, Western Isles is a large gray stone country inn on a bluff. It was constructed by the Sandeman sherry company in the late 1880s as a hunting and fishing lodge for their top-level staff and customers. The current owners welcome guests to rooms decorated in a mixture of styles that are homelike and spotless, equipped with electric heaters and tea- and coffeemaking facilities. The hotel has a conservatory bar as well as two restaurants. The main dining room serves table d'hôte meals for £24.50 ($40.40), whereas the other restaurant features à la carte Oriental food. Meals cost around £17 ($28.05).

WHERE TO DINE

Gannet's Restaurant. 25 Main St. ☎ **01688/302203.** Main courses £3–£9.50 ($4.95–$15.65). MC, V. Easter–Oct, daily 10am–10pm; Nov–Easter, daily 10am–3:30pm.

This place enjoys a quayside setting in one of the stone-fronted 200-year-old buildings along Main Street. It's one of the best independent restaurants here. You get fresh seafood, much of it caught locally, along with salads, roast venison, tender and juicy steaks, and some fine vegetable dishes, finished off by creamy desserts. During the day you might stop in for sandwiches and fresh coffee.

TOBERMORY AFTER DARK

Macgochan's Pub, Ledag (☎ **01688/302350**), is an old traditional pub that has free Scottish music almost every night from 8pm to 1am. On tap you can choose from beers that include Guinness and McEwan's or Tennant's 60 Shilling. Upstairs, an updated loft houses pool tables and a jukebox. Although recently updated, the **Mishnish Hotel,** Main Street (☎ **01688/302009**), is faux traditional pub style, which fits the Scottish music featured here nightly just fine. Real ales on tap include Younger's #3, whereas lagers include McEwan's 70 and 80 Shilling. In pleasant weather you can step into the beer garden for a breath of fresh air.

DERVAIG

The most charming village of Mull, Dervaig or "The Little Grove" lies an 8-mile drive west from Tobermory. A Maclean built the town in the closing year of the 18th century.

SEEING THE SIGHTS

From Dervaig, you can cruise to the lonely **Treshnish Isles,** a sanctuary for seabirds and seals. These islands form a group unto themselves, including Fladda (is flatter) and Lunga (is longer), along with the well-named Dutchman's Cap, or Bac Mor.

Just outside Dervaig is the Mull Little Theater, founded in 1966, which seats 43 viewers. According to the *Guinness Book of World Records*, this makes it the smallest professional theater in Great Britain. See below for details.

Old Byre Heritage Centre. Dervaig. ☎ **01688/400229.** Admission £2 ($3.30) adults, £1.50 ($2.45) senior citizens and students, £1 ($1.65) ages 5–12, free for age 4 and under. Easter–Oct, daily 10:30am–6:30pm. Take the twice-daily bus from Tobermory.

This center houses one of the most charming museums you could hope to find. The main exhibit features 25 scale models, painstakingly researched and made by a local historian, that show the history of Mull from the first settlers to the Highland clearances. The models are also featured in a film that is shown hourly and on the half hour (last show at 5:30pm). A fully licensed tearoom serves light meals from 10:30am to 6pm.

WHERE TO STAY & DINE

Druimnacroish Country House. Dervaig, Isle of Mull, Argyll PA75 6QW. ☎ **01688/400274.** Fax 01688/400311. 3 self-catering apartments. TV TEL. £55 ($90.75) 1 bedroom, £72 ($118.80) 2 bedrooms. Minimum stay of 2 nights. MC, V.

Wendy and Donald Maclean have recently converted their small hotel into spacious apartments that are perfectly suited for travelers who want a "home" while touring the islands. Each unit is handsomely furnished and well appointed with such amenities as a dishwasher and washer and dryer. Unfortunately, Wendy, who is a superb cook, no longer prepares meals for guests. Instead she devotes her time to the property's lush 3-acre garden. You can prepare your own meals in your apartment (the Macleans provide basic breakfast staples such as bacon, eggs, and biscuits as part of the room rate) or dine in one of several restaurants located within 2 miles.

DERVAIG AFTER DARK

Mull Little Theatre. Tobermory–Dervaig Rd. ☎ **01688/400377.**

Located 8^1/$_2$ miles south of Tobermory, this facility is indeed quite small, with an audience capacity of 43 persons for the dramas and comedies housed inside a stone-built byre (stable) turned theater. Productions are staged from Easter through September, with visiting companies filling the bill early on and the small-but-capable Mull Theater Company staging plays later in the season. On performance nights, the doors open at 8pm, and the curtain goes up 30 minutes later. Adult tickets run £10 ($16.50); senior citizens, students, and children pay £6 ($9.90). Because of the size of the facility, tickets are sold only on a first-come first-served basis, but some performances are actually held in larger venues in Tobermory.

FIONNPHORT

At the western tip of the Ross of Mull, Fionnphort is a tiny port that sees a lot of traffic. This is where the road ends and regular ferry passage is available across the mile-long Sound of Iona to the Isle of Iona, one of the most visited attractions in Scotland (see the next section). Iona is clearly visible from Fionnphort. Less than 2 miles to the south is the tidal island of Erraid, where David Balfour had adventures in Stevenson's *Kidnapped.*

WHERE TO STAY

Achaban House. Fionnphort, Isle of Mull, Argyll PA66 6BL. ☎ **01681/700205.** Fax 01681/700649. 7 rms. £18–£25 ($29.70–$41.25) per person. No credit cards. Rates include Scottish breakfast.

Its almost indestructible walls (3 feet thick in many places) were built in 1820 of pink granite for the supervisor of the local quarry. Shortly thereafter the building was converted into the manse (pastor's residence) for the local church. Today it sits beside the town's only highway, a 10-minute walk (or a 1-minute drive) east of the ferryboat landing servicing Iona, in a windswept, treeless, and isolated position. Thirty feet from the hotel's entrance stands a Druidic dolmen, 10 feet tall, erected by prehistoric inhabitants of Mull several thousand years ago.

Recent refurbishments have upgraded all of the guest rooms. Four double rooms have bathrooms in the rooms; two have private facilities just across the hall. One family room is available and sleeps up to five people. The public rooms include some family antiques. Succulent aromas invite you to sample the cuisine of German-born Camilla Baigent and her husband, Chris. Fixed-price evening meals are offered and might include excellent preparations of poached local salmon wrapped in a sheath of herbs, and such local game dishes as wild hare or venison.

WHERE TO DINE

Keel Row. At the harborfront. ☎ **01681/700458.** Main courses £5.50–£10 ($9.05–$16.50); sandwiches and burgers £1.25–£2.25 ($2.05–$3.70). AE, MC, V. Restaurant: summer only, daily noon–3pm and 6–9pm. Snacks and drinks, year-round, daily 11am–11:30pm. Meals served in the bar during the winter, daily 6–8:30pm.

The undisputed leader in providing food and drink to passengers waiting for a ferryboat to Iona, this efficient and friendly place is in two connected buildings near the pier at the end of A849. Food is served in a box-shaped cedar-sided building with big windows overlooking the waterfront. Drinks are offered in a 19th-century stone cottage whose rustic walls and blazing fireplace add cheer to many a gray day. Meals include fillet of salmon poached in a tangy lemon sauce and grilled venison served with a rich herb sauce. Lighter fare includes sandwiches, steaming pots of tea, and pastries. Andrew MacDonald is your world-traveled host.

7 Iona & Staffa

Iona: ¹/₈ mile W of Mull; Staffa: 6 miles NE of Iona

A remote, low-lying, green, and treeless island with high cliffs and rolling meadows, Iona lies off the southwestern coast of Mull across the Sound of Iona. It's only 1 mile by 3¹/₂ miles in size.

Staffa, with its famous musical cave, is a 75-acre island in the Inner Hebrides, lying to the west of Mull. For transportation to Staffa, see below.

ESSENTIALS

GETTING THERE

BY FERRY Iona is accessible only by passenger ferry from the Island of Mull (cars must remain on Mull). Service is informal, although fairly frequent in summer. The ferry makes the 5-minute crossing approximately every 15 minutes daily from noon to 4pm in the summer months; less frequent crossings are made daily between 8:45 and 11:45am and 4:30 and 6:15pm. The round-trip fare is £2.60 ($4.30). In the off-season, transport depends entirely on the weather, but is usually every 30 minutes daily from 10am to 5pm. Call **Caledonian MacBrayne** in Tobermory (☎ **01688/302017**) for exact times, as schedules are subject to change.

IONA

Someone once said, "When Edinburgh was but a barren rock and Oxford but a swamp, Iona was famous." It has been known as a place of spiritual power and pilgrimage for centuries. It was the site of the first Christian settlement in Scotland and preserved the learning that was nearly lost in the Dark Ages.

The island was owned by the dukes of Argyll from 1695, but the 12th duke was forced to sell it to pay $1 million in real estate taxes. The island was purchased by Sir Hugh Fraser, former owner of Harrods. He secured Iona's future and made it possible for money raised by the National Trust for Scotland to be turned over to the trustees of the restored abbey. The only village on Iona, Baille Mor, sits in the island's most sheltered spot, allowing some trees and garden plots to be cultivated.

The best way to get around Iona is to walk. If that's not for you, you can take horse-drawn carriage tours (for information about these, call ☎ **01681/704230**).

SEEING THE SIGHTS

Iona is known for its **"Graves of the Kings."** A total of 48 Scottish kings, including Macbeth and his supposed victim, Duncan, were buried on Iona, as were four

Irish kings and eight Norwegian kings.

Today the island attracts nearly 1,000 visitors a week in high season. Most of them come to see the ✪ **Abbey of Iona,** part of which dates back to the 13th century. But they also visit relics of the settlement founded here by St. Columba in 563, from which Celtic Christianity spread through Scotland and beyond it to Europe. The abbey has been restored by the Iona Community (see below), which conducts workshops on Christianity, sponsors a youth camp, offers tours of the abbey, and each Wednesday leads a 7-mile hike to the various holy and historic spots on the island.

Despite the many visitors to the abbey, the atmosphere on the island remains very peaceful and spiritual. It's possible to walk off among the sheep and cows that wander freely everywhere to the top of Dun-I, a small mountain, and contemplate the ocean and the landscape as if you were the only person on earth.

One reader, Capt. Robert Haggart of Laguna, California, described his experience this way: "I was enchanted by the place. It really has a mystic atmosphere—one feels something ancient here, something spiritual, sacred, long struggles, and wonderment about the strength of religion."

STAYING AT IONA ABBEY

Some travelers consider a visit to Iona the highlight of their trip to Scotland. Aside from viewing it as an unusual historical and archaeological site, many people come back with a renewed interest in both their faith and the power of religion. The **Iona Community** is an ecumenical religious group that maintains a communal lifestyle in the ancient abbey. They offer full board and accommodation to visitors who want to share in the community's daily life. The only ordained members of the group are its two "wardens," who are members of either the Presbyterian Church of Scotland or the Scottish Episcopal church.

Between March and October, the community leads a series of discussion seminars, each of which lasts a week, stretching from Saturday to Saturday. The cost of a week's full board during one of these seminars is £167 ($275.55) per person. The abbey also opens its doors to guests from late November to mid-December, although there are no seminars offered. The per-week price is the same as in summer. Guests are expected to contribute a small portion of their day—about 30 minutes—to the execution of some kind of household chore. The daily schedule involves a wakeup call at 8am, communal breakfast at 8:20am, a morning religious service, and plenty of unscheduled time for conversation, study, and contemplation. Up to 44 guests can be accommodated at one time in bathless, bunk-bedded twin rooms. In addition to the abbey, there is the Iona Community's center for reconciliation, the **MacLeod Centre,** built for youth, persons with disabilities, and families. It also accommodates up to 50 guests during the summer months only. For further details, phone ☎ **01681/700404.**

For day visitors, the community leads tours through the rebuilt Benedictine abbey, maintains a gift and book shop, and runs a coffee shop. Each is open daily from 10am to 4:30pm.

The **Abbey Shop** (☎ **01681/700404**) is run by the Iona Community and features numerous books of Christian literature, along with locally made pottery and Celtic crosses and jewelry.

WHERE TO STAY & DINE

Most of the islanders live by crofting and fishing. They supplement their income by taking in paying guests in season, usually charging very low or at least fair prices. You can, of course, check into the hotels recommended below, but a stay in a private home may be an altogether rewarding travel adventure. If you don't stay on Iona, you must catch one of the ferries back to Mull.

Argyll Hotel. Isle of Iona, Argyll PA76 6SJ. ☎ **01681/700334.** Fax 01681/700510. 17 rms (15 with bath). £82–£92 ($135.30–$151.80) double with bath. MC, V. Rates include Scottish breakfast. Closed early Oct to Easter.

Housed in a Victorian structure built in 1868, this famous hotel, well run by Mrs. Fiona Menzies, stands 200 yards from the ferry dock, overlooking the Sound of Iona and Mull in the distance. The rooms, including two singles without bath, are attractive. You get good home cooking and baking, and vegetarian meals are available; a nightly fixed-price meal will cost you £18.30 ($30.20) for three courses plus coffee and biscuits. In summer, vegetables are home-grown, and there's a nice selection of wines. The hotel is licensed to serve alcoholic drinks to residents.

St. Columba Hotel. Isle of Iona, Argyll PA76 6SL. ☎ **01681/700304.** 23 rms. £94–£98 ($155.10–$161.70) double. MC, V. Rates include half board. Closed Oct–Easter.

This hotel, built of clapboard and white stone, is just uphill from the village about a quarter of a mile from the jetty, a 2-minute walk from the abbey. Originally built as a manse for Presbyterian clergy in 1847, it was transformed into a hotel in 1868 and continues to attract a stream of pilgrims. A set meal is served nightly at 7pm. Food is hearty and wholesome, and the fish dishes are especially good. Vegetarian meals are available on request. Try to get a room overlooking the sea, but keep in mind that it's virtually impossible to secure an accommodation here in summer without a reservation made well in advance.

In the hotel is the **Old Printing Press Bookshop** (☎ **01681/700304**), which specializes in antiquarian books about and from the west of Scotland, with selections ranging back to the mid-18th century.

STAFFA

The attraction of this island, 6 miles north of Iona, is ✪ **Fingal's Cave,** a lure to visitors for more than 200 years and the inspiration for music, poetry, paintings, and prose. Its Gaelic name, An Uamh Ehinn, means "musical cave." It is the only known such formation in the world that has basalt columns—over the centuries the sea has carved a huge cavern in the basalt, leaving massive hexagonal columns. After a visit, Queen Victoria stated: "The effect is splendid, like a great entrance into a vaulted hall. The sea is immensely deep in the cave. The rocks under water were all colors—pink, blue, and green." The sound of the crashing waves and swirling waters caused Mendelssohn to write the *Fingal's Cave Overture.* Turner painted the cave on canvas, and Keats, Wordsworth, and Tennyson all praised it in their poetry.

The island of Staffa has been uninhabited for more than 170 years. Visitors can still explore the cave, which is strictly protected from development by the National Trust. Entrance to the cave is free, requiring only payment for boat passage from Mull or Iona. Boat trips from Mull or Iona cost £10 ($16.50) for adults and £5 ($8.25) for children. You're taken to Staffa's only pier, which was enlarged and rebuilt in 1992 near a lesser attraction known as Clamshell Cave. Visitors then walk along a basalt path into Fingal's Cave, where a guardrail separates them from the water and waves below. Inside, the noise of the pounding surf is deafening. The boat carries 67 passengers and runs twice daily from Iona and Mull between March and October, departing from Iona at 10am and 2pm, stopping briefly at Fionnphort, on Mull, just across the channel, to pick up additional passengers. Tours last 60 to 75 minutes each, depending on weather conditions. During violent storms no tours are possible, and reservations are important. Rubber-soled shoes and warm clothing are recommended for this excursion.

Phone **Mrs. Carol Kirkpatrick,** whose husband, David, operates the boat, at Tigh-na-Traigh (House by the Shore), Isle of Iona (☎ **01681/700358**), for reservations and departure information.

8 Isle of Colonsay

15 miles S of the Isle of Mull

The most remote of the islands of Argyll, Colonsay, with Oransay its tidal neighbor, shares some of the same characteristics as Iona, Tyree, and Coll. To the west it faces nothing but the open Atlantic—only a lighthouse stands between Colonsay and Canada.

The island encompasses 20 square miles, enjoying an equable climate because of the warming waters of the Gulf Stream. It's more tranquil than Mull or Skye because it doesn't accommodate "day trippers."

ESSENTIALS

GETTING THERE

BY FERRY & CAR   A ferry, operated by **Caledonian MacBrayne** (☎ **01631/562285** in Oban for schedule information), sails between Oban and Colonsay three times a week. The 37-mile crossing takes 2^1/$_2$ hours.

SEEING THE SIGHTS

All parts of the island can be explored along its one-lane roads. Many visitors prefer to rent a bicycle rather than drive. You can rent sailing dinghies and rowboats and sail around the island, following in the grand tradition of the Vikings. The Vikings also held several ship burials on the island. Some of the sites have been excavated, but, regrettably, the ships have decayed.

Wildlife abounds, including golden eagles, falcons, gray seals, otters, and wild goats with elegant horns and long shaggy hair. Prehistoric forts, stone circles, and single standing stones attest to the antiquity of Colonsay, which has been occupied since the Stone Age.

It's estimated that there are some 500 species of flora on the island. The gardens of **Colonsay House** are filled with rare rhododendrons, magnolias, and eucalyptus, even palm trees. Colonsay House, dating from 1722 and seat of the laird, Lord Strathcona, is not open to the public. There is also an 18-hole golf course.

The little island of Oransay was named for Oran, a disciple of St. Columba. It's joined at low tide by the Strand, and visitors can wade across the sands during a 2-hour period. The ancient monastic ruins here date from the 6th century, and tradition has it that they were founded by St. Columba. You can see some tombstones of carved stone. The most notable is the **Great Cross of Prior Colin,** from the early 16th century.

Back at your hotel, if you're lucky you might join in a ceilidh on a summer evening.

WHERE TO STAY & DINE

Isle of Colonsay Hotel. Isle of Colonsay, Argyll PA61 7YP. ☎ **01951/200316.** Fax 01951/200353. 11 rms (8 with bath), 3 cottages. £60–£80 ($99–$132) per person double; £140–£495 ($231–$816.75) cottage per week. AE, DC, MC, V. Room rates include half board.

Dating from the 18th century, this place is the most isolated hotel in Great Britain—it's Colonsay's social center. Above the harbor, 400 yards from the ferryboat landing, it's situated at a point that's within 5 miles of everything on the island. Solidly constructed gables and chimneys rise above surrounding herb and vegetable gardens. Guests who want to get close-up views of the island's abundant flora and fauna can ask to be dropped off by courtesy car to go on rambles.

There are three self-contained cottages, each with a combined living room and kitchen, a veranda, a double bedroom, an upper level with three single beds, and maid service. The cottages are suitable for up to six people. Electricity, which is metered at cost, is not included in the weekly rate.

A meal in the hotel's tongue-and-groove paneled dining room is an event for the local residents, who appreciate the ambience of the cocktail lounge and the public bar. The inn is licensed, serving lunch daily from noon to 1:30pm and dinner at 7:30pm. A meal is likely to include homemade soup, fresh mussels, trout, scallops, and prawns, with vegetables from the garden. Fixed-price dinners cost £23 ($37.95) and up.

THE OUTER HEBRIDES

At first you may feel that you've come to a lunar landscape where there's a sense of infinite time. The character of the Outer Hebrides is quite different from the chain of the Inner Hebrides that we just visited. The string of islands lie some 30 to 40 miles off the northwest coast of Scotland. The main islands to visit are Lewis and Harris (parts of the same island in spite of different names), North Uist, Benbecula, South Uist, and Barra. The archipelago also takes in some minor offshore islands. From the Butt of Lewis in the north to Barra Head in the south, the chain stretches for some 130 miles.

Gaelic is spoken here; its gentle cadence is said to have been the language spoken in the Garden of Eden. Presbyterianism is still very strong (in one B&B house, for example, watching TV on Sunday is forbidden). Before you go, you might read Compton Mackenzie's novel *Whisky Galore.*

The islands today, which knew 2 centuries of Viking invasions, are the retreat of many a disenchanted artist from the mainland. They come here, take over old crofters' cottages, and devote their days to such pursuits as pottery making and weaving.

Bird watchers flock to the islands to see the habitats of the red-necked phalarope, the corncrake, the golden eagle, the Arctic skua, and the grayleg goose along cliffs, in peat bog, and in farmland. Golfers come here to play on these far-northern courses, including one at Stornoway (Lewis) and another at Askernish (South Uist). Anglers also come here to fish for salmon, brown trout, and sea trout among the fishing lochs found throughout the island chain.

Much of the dim past can be seen on these islands, including a version of Stonehenge. A good time to visit is in June and July when adults' and children's choirs compete for honors. You can attend these festivals celebrating Gaelic music and poetry.

Each of the main islands has tourist accommodations, and reservations are important. Most are small family-run guesthouses and hotels, and many are crofters' cottages that take in B&B guests, mainly in summer.

9 Lewis

209 miles NW of Edinburgh, 213 miles NW of Glasgow

The most northerly of the islands of the Outer Hebrides, and also the largest, Lewis is easily reached by ferry from Ullapool (see chapter 11). The island was once known as "Lews," or more poetically, "the island of heather." The sweetness of lamb raised here is said to come from the heather diet. Lewis and Harris form part of the same island, stretching for a combined length of some 95 miles. Lewis is about 60 miles long and from 18 to 28 miles across. Even though the whole world has heard of "Harris tweed," it might as well be called "Lewis tweed," as Stornoway has taken over the industry. There are some 600 weavers on the island, and one of the attractions of this rather bleak port is to visit a mill shop or a weaver's cottage.

With a population of some 5,000 souls, **Stornoway** is the only real town in the Outer Hebrides. On the eastern side of the island, it's a landlocked harbor where you can see gray seals along with fishing boats setting out.

Filled with marshy peat bogs, the landscape is relatively treeless, thanks in part to the Norse raider, Magnus Barelegs. Although the island used to have trees, Barelegs and his tree-burning Viking warriors left much of Lewis as bare as his shanks. Efforts at reforestation have been unsuccessful.

ESSENTIALS
GETTING THERE

BY PLANE An airport, which doubles as an RAF base, lies 3¹/₂ miles from the center of Stornoway. Stornoway receives flights from Glasgow and Inverness every day except Sunday, as well as frequent service from Benbecula. Phone ☎ 0345/222111 in Glasgow to confirm schedules or to make reservations.

BY FERRY & CAR Monday through Saturday, **Caledonian MacBrayne** operates two or three ferries from Ullapool to Stornoway. One-way passage costs £11.40 ($18.80). For reservations and general information, check with Caledonian MacBrayne (☎ 01475/650000 at the ferry terminal in Gourock). Cars can be transported as well. Trip time is 3¹/₂ hours.

VISITOR INFORMATION

The **Western Isles Tourist Board,** which has information about all the Outer Hebrides, is at 26 Cromwell St., Stornoway (☎ 01851/703088).

EXPLORING THE ISLAND

The major attraction is the Neolithic temple of Callanish, called the ✪ **Standing Stones of Callanish.** This unique cruciform setting of megaliths, off A858, 16 miles west of Stornoway, is outranked in prehistoric archaeological splendor only by Stonehenge. From a circle of 13 stones, a road of 19 monoliths leads north. Branching off to the south, east, and west are rows of more stones. A tiny chambered tomb is inside the circle.

In the more immediate vicinity, you can visit the grounds of **Lews Castle** (the old spelling), west of the harbor at Stornoway. The castle itself, built in 1818, is closed to the public. You can, however, wander through the garden at its flowery best in May.

At Arnol, 15 miles northwest of Stornoway, off A858, you can visit the **Lewis Black House** (☎ 01851/710501), a thatched house that has been preserved to show visitors what a typical Hebridean dwelling looked like. It's called a "black house" because it was believed that the smoke from the open peat fires was good for the thatched roof; therefore the Leodhasach (as the islanders are called) built their houses with no chimneys so the smoke could go through the thatch. The house was constructed without mortar. Many of its original furnishings are intact. It's open April to September, Monday through Saturday from 9:30am to 6pm; October to March it closes at 4pm. The house closes from 1 to 2pm for lunch year-round. Admission is £1.50 ($2.45) for adults, £1 ($1.65) for senior citizens, and 75p ($1.25) for children.

For the serious student of history and ancient monuments, the **Steinacleit Cairn and Stone Circle** are the ruined fragments of what was once a rather substantial house built in the mists of prehistory. The house was found beneath huge layers of peat. At the southern end of Loch an Duin, Shader, 12 miles north of Stornoway, it can be visited throughout the day for no fee.

The **Clach an Trushal** at Balanthrushal, Barvas, is the largest single monolith in northern Scotland. It's 19 feet tall and 6 feet wide. Near this same site was the field of the last battle fought between the Macaulays of Uig and the Morrisons of Ness.

Dun Carloway Broch is a broch tower, about 30 feet high, left over from the Iron Age. It stands along A858, 20 miles west and northwest of Stornoway. It can be visited throughout the day for no fee. At Arnish, near Stornoway, is the **Bonnie Prince Charlie Monument.**

At Dun Borranish, near the village of Ardroil, the famous Lewis Chessmen were dug up in 1831 outside Uig Sands. Made of walrus tusks, they now form an outstanding exhibit in the British Museum in London. If you're a chess player, you may want to purchase a reproduction set in Lewis.

Ui Church, at Aignish, off A866, 2 miles east of Stornoway, is now in ruins. Pronounced "eye," it was the burial grounds of the MacLeods of Lewis. You can see their carved tombs. The ruins are on the Eye Peninsula, also known as "The Point." At Ness, toward that northerly outpost, the Butt of Lewis, is **St. Moluag's Church,** a Scottish Episcopal church. You can attend an occasional service here. The chapel, known in Gaelic as Teampull Mhor or "big temple," is from about the 12th century, founded by Olav the Black during the Norse occupation of the island. The original church is said to have been founded in the 6th century by a companion of St. Columba.

SHOPPING   At **Gifts Unlimited,** 9 Bayhead St., Stornoway (☎ 01851/703337), owner Beatrice Schulz stocks pottery, woodcraft, and jewelry from Scotland and beyond. She also sells knitwear, ranging from handknits to designer wear, and a variety of Harris tweeds. There's a good selection of items from which to choose. **Borge Pottery,** on A856, at Borve, 17 miles from Stornoway on the road to Ness (☎ 01851/850345), has been in business for more than 20 years, producing hand-thrown stoneware pieces for kitchen and table use, available in pink, blue, red, green, black, and cream. Its name is spelled with a "g," the Gaelic spelling of Borve.

WHERE TO STAY

Cabarfeidh Hotel. Manor Park, Stornoway, Lewis, Outer Hebrides H51 2EU. ☎ **800/528-1234** in the U.S., or 01851/702604. Fax 01851/705572. 47 rms. TV TEL. £93 ($153.45) double. AE, DC, MC, V. Rates include Scottish breakfast.

About a mile north of Stornoway, midway between the hamlets of Laxdale and Newmarket, the Cabarfeidh, one of the best hotels on Lewis, shelters guests from the chilly winds behind unadorned white walls designed as a contemporary arrangement of cubes. It was completely renovated in 1990. A member of the Best Western chain, it's one of the most luxurious places in the Outer Hebrides. It was built by a Mackenzie, who named it after the battle cry of his fighting clan, "stag antlers," and the decor includes a collection of just that. There's a convivial bar shaped like a Viking longship. Bedrooms have radios, trouser presses, and hair dryers along with other amenities. The dining room offers the best of local produce, fresh fish (especially trout and salmon), local beef and lamb, and scallops. You can enjoy a three-course table d'hôte menu that changes nightly for £17.95 ($29.60) or choose your own combination of courses from the à la carte menu.

Caledonian Hotel. 4–6 S. Beach St., Stornoway, Lewis, Outer Hebrides H51 2XI. ☎ **01851/ 702411.** Fax 01851/702610. 10 rms. TV TEL. £60 ($99) double. AE, MC, V. Rates include Scottish breakfast.

Today the hotel has an uncomplicated modern design, but it displays yellowing photographs of its original, stone-fronted manifestation, lost in a fire in the 1970s. It prides itself on its yearlong reasonable rates. Each of the simple but comfortable bedrooms contains tea- and coffeemaking facilities, a trouser press, and a hair dryer. Dining is in a restaurant with a panoramic view of Stornoway Harbour; the average dinner costs around £14 ($23.10). The hotel also contains two bars that serve sandwiches and snacks from noon to 2pm and 5 to 9pm daily.

Seaforth Hotel. 9 James St., Stornoway, Lewis, Outer Hebrides HS1 2QN. ☎ **01851/ 702740.** Fax 01851/703900. 70 rms. TV. £79 ($130.35) double. Rates include Scottish breakfast. AE, MC, V.

A 5-minute walk from the town center, the Seaforth is one of the most modern hotels in the Outer Hebrides. Guest rooms are well equipped; all contain tea- and coffeemaking facilities and some have trouser presses and hair dryers. The public rooms have several full-size snooker tables, as well as a bar/lounge. The hotel's restaurant offers a very reasonably priced nightly table d'hôte menu—three courses cost £9.95 ($16.40). The fare is rather plain but is hearty and filling.

WHERE TO DINE

Park Guest House. 30 James St., Stornoway, Lewis, Outer Hebrides H51 2QN. ☎ **01851/ 702485.** Reservations required. Main courses £14–£26 ($23.10–$42.90); fixed-price 3-course dinner (served only 5:30–6:30pm) £13.75 ($22.70). MC, V. Tues–Sat 5:30–9pm. Closed Oct.

In a century-old stone house about a 10-minute walk north of the ferryboat terminal, this is one of the best dining rooms in town, a favorite of local residents. Owned and operated by island-born Roddy and Catherine Afrin, it contains a dignified fireplace in the style of Charles Rennie Mackintosh and a country-house decor designed by Catherine, a graduate of the Glasgow School of Art. Menu items feature seasonal game and choices from the bounties of the nearby seas. They might include, depending on availability, grilled lobster served thermidor style with brandy sauce; oysters served either raw or au gratin; pan-fried scallops in lemon butter and herbs; and fillet of turbot grilled with herb butter. The establishment is fully licensed and is at its most elegant and appealing between 7 and 9pm.

The Afrins also offer seven simple rooms. Rates range from £40 ($66) per night for a double to £56 ($92.40) per night for a family room that sleeps up to six. Rates include breakfast.

STORNOWAY AFTER DARK

Just about any of the pubs lining the waterfront in this town have live music on the weekend, usually of Celtic or Scottish derivation. There's generally no cover charge, so for the price of a pint the sounds of the region are available for your listening pleasure.

An Lanntair Gallery, Town Hall, South Beach Street (☎ **01851/703307**), produces and stages musical and theatrical events with a strong emphasis on Gaelic culture. Besides Gaelic music, the center has jazz, folk, and traditional music concerts. Classic and contemporary drama and comedy and children's shows are part of the year-round repertoire. Shows start at 8pm, and tickets are £3 to £10 ($4.95 to $16.50) for adults, and around £3 ($4.95) for seniors, students, and children. Depending on the show, productions take place in either the gallery space, which seats 55, or the town hall, which holds 350.

A private club, **British Legion,** South Beach Street (☎ **01851/702452**), has some nights open to the public. On other nights, a word to the doorman that you're visiting the island will get you signed in as a guest. On Friday and Saturday nights, traditional Scottish music is played, beginning at 9pm. The friendly bartender adds, "We've got beers on tap, but why would that matter when we've got plenty of whiskies?" There's no cover charge.

Clachan Bar, South Beach Street (☎ **01851/703653**), is split into a public bar and a lounge bar. It's a typical barroom, with none of the quaintness of a traditional pub, but locals and visitors alike come on Friday and Saturday nights for live bands, which play in both rooms. On Friday there's music from 10:30pm to 1am, and on Saturday it runs from 9 to 11pm. A range of Tennant's beers is available on tap. Another updated bar that features live music is **Lewis Bar,** South Beach Street (☎ **01851/704567**). On Saturday night the stage here might hold anything from a rock band to a traditional Scottish group. The free music starts at 9pm, and there's a selection of Tennant products on tap.

10　Harris

218 miles NW of Glasgow, 56 miles NW of Mallaig, 246 miles NW of Edinburgh, 34 miles S of Stornoway

Harris, south of Lewis, has a different geography. North Harris is full of mountains, dominated by the **Clisham,** which at 2,600 feet is the highest peak in the Outer Hebrides. Harris may not have as many ancient relics as Lewis, but most visitors agree that the mountains, beaches, and scenic vistas make up for that lack. Explorers can seek out the beaches in the west, either for swimming or camping, or go to the bays in the east that are ideal for fishing and sailing.

The local people, some 3,000 in all, are called Hearach, and they, too, are different from the people of Lewis, even speaking with a different accent. If you've arrived in Lewis, you can drive to Harris, as the two islands are connected by a small single-lane road, going from pass to pass. As you go along the rugged terrain, you might see a fell walker. Occasionally you'll meet another car. If you do, "passing places" have been provided. In any case, you should drive slowly, because sheep might suddenly scamper in front of your wheels. The distance from Stornoway, the capital of Lewis, to Tarbert, the capital of Harris, is 34 miles.

Many visitors, however, prefer to take the ferryboat from the little port of Uig on the Isle of Skye that heads for Harris daily except Sunday. Even in the busiest season Harris is not overrun with visitors. From Harris you can also make connections to Lochmaddy on North Uist (see below).

Harris has long been known for its hand-weaving and tweed. Though that industry has now passed to Stornoway, it's still possible to buy Harris tweed jackets in

Harris. In summer you'll see them displayed on the walls of corrugated iron sheds along the road. You get very good prices here.

The main village of Harris is **Tarbert,** a one-street town. The island is bisected by two long sea lochs that meet at Tarbert, which is surrounded by rocky hills. Whatever you need in the way of supplies, you should pick up here—otherwise you'll be out of luck. If you're touring by private car, also fill up with "petrol" (gas) at Tarbert. Ask at the information center about the bus tours that are conducted in summer around Harris, and for an adventure take the car ferry that runs regularly across the sound to the little fishing community of **Scalpay,** an offshore island.

ESSENTIALS
GETTING THERE

BY FERRY   You can take a ferry to Tarbert, capital of Harris, from Uig on the Isle of Skye, Monday through Saturday. There are one or two ferries per day, and a one-way ticket costs £7.60 ($12.55). Contact **Caledonian MacBrayne (☎ 01859/502244** in Tarbert) for schedules and more information.

BY BUS   Buses run from Stornoway to Tarbert daily. Phone ☎ **01859/2441** for schedules. At least four buses per day make the run Monday through Saturday.

BY CAR   From Stornoway on Lewis in the north, drive south along A859 to reach Tarbert.

VISITOR INFORMATION

A summer-only **tourist information center** operates from the port at Tarbert (☎ **01859/502011**).

EXPLORING THE ISLAND

Because of the lack of roads, you can't make a circular tour of Harris. However, using Tarbert as your base, you can set out northwest along the coastline of **West Loch Tarbert,** with the Forest of Harris to your north. Or you can go south from Tarbert, hugging the western coastal road along the Sound of Taransay, with Rodel as your final destination.

Taking the northwesterly route first, you come to an **Old Whaling Station** at Bunavoneadar. Norwegians set up a whaling station here in the early 20th century, but because of dwindling profits it was abandoned in 1930. Slipways and a chimney can still be seen. Continuing north along B887, you'll arrive at the **Amhuinnsuidhe Estate,** a Scottish baronial castle constructed by the earl of Dunmore in 1868. Sir James Barrie stayed here while working on *Mary Rose.* The river to the left has one of the most beautiful salmon leaps in Scotland.

The road beyond the castle continues to **Hushinish Point.** In addition to machair, the area in springtime becomes a bed of wildflowers. At Hushinish you can see the little offshore island of Scarp, which was once inhabited. Returning to Tarbert, you can take A859 south.

Some of the South Harris coastline will remind you of Norway, with its sea lochs and "ford fingers." The main road to Rodel is mostly two lanes and well surfaced; however, if you take the east-coast road, you'll find it not only single lane but tortuous and winding.

Along the way you'll pass the **Clach Mhicleoid,** or standing stone. The locals call it MacLeod's Stone. This monolith, placed above the Nisabost Sands, stands as a lonely sentinel at night, a silent witness to what it has seen over the centuries.

From here you can look out across the Sound of Taransay to the **Island of Taransay,** which was named after St. Tarran. The island has several ancient sites, including the remains of St. Tarran's Chapel. Like Scarp, it was once populated, but now its grazing fields have been turned over to sheep. Continuing on the coastal road along the wild Atlantic—actually the Sound of Taransay—you'll see another ancient stone, the **Scarista Standing Stone.** But before reaching it you'll pass **Borve Lodge,** the former home of Lord Leverhulme, the soap tycoon.

The road south passes the little promontory of Toe Head jutting into the Atlantic. An ancient chapel, **Rudh'an Teampull,** stands about three-quarters of a mile west of Northton, reached by a sand track. Many prehistoric sites were uncovered and excavated on the tiny machair-studded peninsula of Toe Head. Bone tools and Neolithic pottery were found, the earliest recorded habitations of the Western Isles.

The next hamlet is **Leverburgh,** named after Lord Leverhulme, the soap magnate. He's credited with trying to bring the people of the area into the 20th century, but his efforts to rejuvenate the economy largely failed. From here you can take a small passenger ferry to North Uist and Berneray. You can also visit the **An Clachan Centre** at Leverburgh, where you can purchase many items of local craftware.

Finally, you drive east to **Rodel,** where ✪ **St. Clement's Church** stands high in the village. Overlooking Loch Rodel, this church is one of the most important monuments in the Western Isles. Cruciform in plan, it has a western tower, a nave, and two cross aisles. Some of the masonry work in freestone is similar to that used at Iona Abbey. The church is believed to have been built around the closing years of the 15th century or the very early years of the 16th century. There are three tombs inside, including one that's among the finest in the islands. The tomb contains part of the MacLeod coat-of-arms.

In the Sound of Harris, separating Harris from North Uist, lie the islands of **Ensay, Killegray,** and **Pabbay.** Once they were populated, but now they have been turned over to grazing sheep.

WHERE TO STAY & DINE
IN TARBERT

✪ **Ardvourlie Castle.** Highway A859, Tarbert, Harris, Outer Hebrides HS3 3AB. 4 rms. £160 ($264) double. No credit cards. Rates include dinner and breakfast. Closed Oct–Mar. Drive 10 miles north of Tarbert, or 27 miles south of Stornaway, along the highway that interconnects them, A859.

In 1860, the Earl of Dunmore commissioned the construction of a substantial-looking hunting lodge. In the early 1980s, after the building lay empty for at least 40 years, experienced London-born chef Derek Martin acquired the crumbling stone-sided structure, chased out the cobwebs and the sheep that were foraging inside, and expanded the number of bathrooms inside from a single cold-water tap to the quintet of mahogany-sheathed facilities you'll see today.

Fifteen years of backbreaking work—including the planting of 7,000 trees that are finally taking on recognizable forms, gave the place and the 13 isolated acres that surrounded it a dramatic new lease on grandeur. You'll find yourself in a tasteful, elegant-looking house filled with English and Scottish antiques and 'nary a hint that a decorator ever fussed too much with the predictably coordinated fabrics. Bedrooms overlook the Loch of Seaforth or an evocatively desolate tundra that leads up to the highest mountain on Harris. There's a cocktail lounge, interesting libraries full of books, well-stoked fireplaces, lots of dignified comforts, and a dining room presided over by Pamela Martin, Derek's sister, who serves splendid food concocted from ultrafresh ingredients. Examples include honey-marinated duck that's crisp enough to have rendered up most of its fattiness, served with an orange-flavored Drambuie sauce and garlic potatoes; prawns with orange segments and a celery/Tabasco sauce; halibut in a mushroom sauce; and desserts that might include either a "Tipsy Laird" (trifle with Drambuie and sherry), or baked apples with sultanas and a hot whisky sauce.

Harris Hotel. Tarbert, Harris, Outer Hebrides HS3 3DL. ☎ **01859/502154.** Fax 01859/502281. 24 rms (16 with bath). TV. £59 ($97.35) double without bath, £65.60 ($108.25) double with bath. MC, V. Rates include Scottish breakfast.

This Queen Anne–style hotel has been a local landmark since it first accepted customers in 1904. Today it's one of the most popular places in the Outer Hebrides. Each room has hot and cold running water, lots of old-fashioned comfort, and modern amenities. Some family rooms are available, many looking out over the garden, one of the largest in Harris. Dinner is offered for £14.55 to £15.75 ($24 to $26), and the food is good and plentiful. The pub here is the social center of town for locals, including the "ghillies" who show guests who come for fishing holidays how it's done. You can order pub grub throughout the day and evening.

In Scarista

✪ **Scarista House.** Scarista, Harris, Outer Hebrides HS3 3HX. ☎ **01859/550238.** Fax 01859/550277. 5 rms, 2 apts. TEL. £100–£114 ($165–$188.10) double; £235–£450 ($387.75–$742.50) apartment. MC, V. Room rates include Scottish breakfast. Closed mid-Sept to mid-May.

This is a lovely hotel on A859, about 15 miles southwest of Tarbert on the west coast of Harris. It was constructed long ago as a Georgian vicarage. Each handsomely decorated bedroom is centrally heated. Scarista house has two self-catering apartments; one accommodates two people whereas the other is suitable for families with up to six members. A few of the summer guests enjoy an occasional bracing dip in the 55° water of nearby Scarista Beach. Others prefer to read in the well-stocked library.

Here you get the best breakfast in the Outer Hebrides: freshly squeezed orange juice and a compote of fresh and dried fruits, along with organic oatmeal porridge with cream and kippers from Lewis—and that's only the beginning. These dishes are followed by Stornoway black pudding, bacon, sausage, and fresh eggs, plus fresh herring rolled in oatmeal. There's also homemade whole-wheat bread and a variety of other baked items. If you plan to burn off this morning feast, a packed lunch will be provided. Most guests return in the evening for a drink near the fireplace of the hotel's beautifully appointed drawing room before a five-course dinner. A full dinner featuring locally caught shellfish and heather-fed lamb, among other ingredients, begins at £29 ($47.85). Meals are served at 8:15pm.

11 North & South Uist

90–100 miles NW of Glasgow

Standing stones and chambered cairns, ruins and fortresses, tell of a history-rich past on these two old islands, connected by the smaller island of Benbecula.

ESSENTIALS
Getting There

BY PLANE   British Airways flies daily except Sunday between Benbecula Airport (the nearest connection for North Uist) and Glasgow. Phone ☎ **0141/887-1111** at the Glasgow Airport for flight information.

BY CAR   North Uist is linked to Benbecula and South Uist by causeways and bridges, so you can travel to or from either of these islands by car along A867, which becomes A865.

BY FERRY   For information about car-ferry services, consult **Caledonian MacBrayne** (☎ **01876/500337** in Lochmaddy). Monday through Saturday, one ferry per day runs from Oban to Lochboisdale on South Uist. A one-way passenger ticket is £16.45 ($27.15). Some of these ferries stop at Castlebay on Barra. Other ferries run from Uig on the Isle of Skye to Lochmaddy on Monday through Saturday one or two times per day. The most popular connection, this ferry trip takes anywhere from 2 to 4 hours and a one-way ticket costs £7.60 ($12.55).

Lochboisdale is the site of the ferry terminal, which provides a link between South Uist and the mainland at Oban, taking 5 1/2 hours. Call ☎ **01631/562285** in Oban for more details.

Visitor Information

Consult with the Western Isles Tourist Board in Stornoway (see section 9 on Lewis, above). There's also a **tourist information center** in the center of Lochmaddy (☎ **01876/500321**), open Monday through Friday from 9am to 5pm and Saturday from 9am to 1pm and 2 to 5pm. The staff here can arrange accommodations if you have arrived without a reservation. The office is also open from 8 to 9pm when a ferry comes in during that time.

At Lochboisdale the **tourist information center** is found at the pier (☎ **01878/700286**), open Easter to October only, Monday through Saturday from 9am to 5pm. It's also open for late ferry arrivals, usually 10 to 11pm on Monday through Thursday and Friday and Saturday from 8 to 9pm. Accommodations can be arranged through this office.

NORTH UIST

A real bogland, where hardy crofters try to wrestle a living from both a turbulent sea and disappointing ground, North Uist is one of the least-frequented islands in the Outer Hebrides. That's a pity, because it's so beautiful. Its antiquity is reflected in its brochs, duns, wheelhouses, and stark monoliths, all left by the island's prehistoric dwellers.

The population of North Uist is about 2,000, and the island is about 12 1/2 miles wide by 35 miles at its longest point. North Uist is served by a circular road, most often the single-lane variety with passing places, and there are several feeder routes branching east and west. Road surfaces are usually good.

The main village is **Lochmaddy,** on the eastern shoreline. Whatever you need, you're likely to find it here (if it's available on North Uist at all), from a post office to a petrol station. Lochmaddy is the site of the ferry terminal. In addition to the ferries from Oban and Uig, a small private ferry runs from Newton Ferry, north of Lochmaddy, to Leverburgh on Harris. This is not a car ferry, but allows small motorcycles or bicycles. A small vehicular ferry will also take you to the island of Berneray. In keeping with the strict religious tradition of these islands, the ferry doesn't operate on Sunday, and neither, seemingly, does anything else.

Exploring the Island

For such a small island, the scenery of North Uist is extremely varied. The eastern shores have an untamed beauty. The coastline is dotted with lochs filled with trout, and everything is set against a backdrop of darkened, rolling, heather-clad hills. Nights come on fast in winter; sunsets linger in summer. The western side of North Uist is a land of rich meadows filled with wildflowers. Here you find long white beaches, where Atlantic rollers attract the hardier surfers.

Heading northwest from Lochmaddy for 2¹/₂ miles you come to **Blashaval,** where you'll find the **Three Standing Stones of the False Men.** Local tradition has it that this trio of stones, known in Gaelic as Na Fir Bhreige, actually were men, wife deserters from Skye turned into stone by a witch.

Continuing along the road for 4 miles, you approach an island on the west side of **Loch an Duin** where access is possible on foot only at periods of low tide. Caution should be exercised. **Dun Torcuill** is a fine example of a broch that provided defense for the villagers against raiders.

Turning north on B893, you come to **Newton Ferry** (see above). A 15-minute crossing will take you to the little offshore island of **Berneray,** which has some ancient sites, including the Borve Standing Stone. There's a privately run hostel here. The 140 or so people who live on the island are mainly engaged in crofting and fishing, and may regard *you* as a sightseeing attraction.

After you return to Newton Ferry, head south on the same road. A left-hand fork takes you to **Trumisgarry** to see the ruins of an old chapel where an early Christian settlement was founded. **St. Columba's Well** (Tobar Chaluim Chille, in Gaelic) is named after the saint.

Returning to the main road, head west toward Sollas. On both sides of the road are cairns and standing stones, many from 2000 B.C.—some hard to reach, including those on uninhabited islands. Pass through **Hosta,** site of the Highland Games, heading for the **Balranaid Nature Reserve,** 3 miles northwest of Bayhead. At a reception cottage at **Goulat,** near Hougharty, you can learn more about the birds inhabiting the Outer Hebrides. You can walk through the reserve at any time at no charge, but guided tours are given at 2pm on Tuesday and Friday. The cost is £2.50 ($4.15) for adults and £1 ($1.65) for children.

Back on the main road again, you'll pass through **Bayhead** heading to the southeast. Again, the area is filled with an astonishing number of ancient monuments; many more have disappeared since the 1920s, reclaimed by the Atlantic. At the junction, take A867 back toward Lochmaddy. You'll see a sign pointing to Barpa Langass. On the slopes of **Ben Langass** is a chambered cairn thought to be at least 3,000 years old, one of the best preserved on the island. Some historians believe a warrior chieftain was buried here, but others suggest it was a communal burial ground. Bones and pottery fragments removed from excavations here were sent to the National Museum in Edinburgh.

Returning to the main road again, retrace your trail and head south for Carinish, a hamlet known for the **Carinish Stone Circle** and the **Barpa Carinish,** the site of the major attraction on the island, **Trinity Temple** (Teampull na Trionad, in Gaelic), lying off A865 some 8 miles southwest of Lochmaddy. Admission is free and it's open at all times. The monastery is said to have been founded in the 13th century by Beathag, the first prioress of Iona, daughter of Somerland, an Irish mercenary and the founding father of the MacDonalds. In the Middle Ages, on this site was a great college that the Franciscan scholar, Duns Scotus (1265–1308), was said to have attended. He later became one of the most influential medieval philosophers and theologians.

Nearby is **Teampull Clann A'Phlocair,** the chapel of the MacVicars. You can see a number of ancient "cup and ring" markings. The site of a clan battle is also nearby. Appropriately called the "Field of Blood," it's where the MacLeods of Harris and the MacDonalds of Uist met in 1601.

You can continue southeast to the island of **Grimsay,** connected by a causeway and known for its lobster ponds. You'll also find the remains of Michael's Chapel and the ruins of Dun Bay Grimsay, an ancient fortification.

WHERE TO STAY & DINE

Langass Lodge. Locheport, North Uist, Outer Hebrides HS6 5HA. ☎ **01876/580285.** 6 rms. £56 ($92.40) double. TV TEL. MC, V. Rates include Scottish breakfast. Closed Feb.

Its spaciousness and comfort comes as a welcome surprise after the miles of wind-swept, barren countryside you traverse before you reach it. Its multiple chimneys and mint-green-colored facade are softened by the nearby presence of half a dozen sycamore trees, cited by the staff as among the few trees on all of North Uist. Originally built as a hunting lodge in 1876, the hotel has been comfortably modernized and today accepts a clientele of hunters, fishers, and nature lovers from Britain, Europe, and North America. The bedrooms were completely refurbished in 1996 and 1997. Solid furnishings, pleasant decor, and additions such as TVs, telephones, and tea- and coffeemakers make the accommodations homey and inviting. In addition, the rooms open onto views of the nearby loch. The hotel offers guests a three-course evening meal in the dining room for £18 ($29.70). Meals are also served in the bar, where main courses start at £5 ($8.25).

Lochmaddy Hotel. Lochmaddy, North Uist, Outer Hebrides HS6 5AA. ☎ **01876/500331.** Fax 01876/500210. 15 rms. TV TEL. £60–£75 ($99–$123.75) double. AE, MC, V. Rates include Scottish breakfast.

You can't miss the peaked gables of this white-walled hotel a few steps from the ferry terminal. Visitors who come to fish for the area's brown trout, sea trout, and salmon often stay here (anyone who wants to weigh his or her catch of the day is welcome to use the hotel's set of scales). This is one of the few outlets on the island where you can buy fishing permits; prices vary from £6 to £40 ($9.90 to $66) a day, according to what kind of fish you're seeking and the season. There's an accommodating pub, a cocktail bar, and a dining room, serving a table d'hôte dinner for £15 ($24.75). At dinner you are likely to be offered fresh local produce, lobster, king prawns, venison, or salmon, and bar meals are served both at lunch and in the evening. The bar also offers about the best collection of single-malt whiskies in the Outer Hebrides. The bedrooms are uncluttered and tasteful, having benefitted from a renovation in 1997.

SOUTH UIST

A rich treasure trove of antiquity can be found on South Uist. A number of ecclesiastical remains are scattered along its shores, and Clan Ranald, which ruled the island, left many ruins and fortresses known as "duns." Ornithologists and anglers are attracted here. Part bogland, the island is 20 miles long and 6 miles wide at its broadest point. A main road, A865, bisects the island, with feeder roads, single-track lanes with passing places, branching off east and west. Some of the most interesting sights, all ruins, lie off these little roads.

EXPLORING THE ISLAND

The biggest village in South Uist is **Lochboisdale,** at the head of a deep-sea loch in the southeastern part of the island. It was settled in the 19th century by crofters who had been forced off their land in the notorious Land Clearances of those troubled years. However, the ruins of a small medieval castle can also be seen at the head of the loch on the island of Calvay, one of the many places where Bonnie Prince Charlie hid out.

Leaving Lochboisdale, A865 goes west for 3 miles to Daliburgh, from where you can pick up the B888 south to Pollachar on the southern shore, a distance of 6 miles—the hamlet is named for the **Pollachar Standing Stone.** Continue east along a minor road for 2¹/₂ miles to the Ludag jetty, where a private ferry goes to Eriskay and to Barra. Then head north again in the direction of Daliburgh to visit the contemporary **Church of Our Lady of Sorrows,** at Garrynamonie, a short drive north of Pollachar. Consecrated in 1964, it has a mosaic of "Our Lady," and can be visited daily at any time.

The next stop is at the **Klipheder Wheelhouse,** 2 miles west of A865, the meager ruins of a circular building from A.D. 200. Back on the main road again, you come to Askernish, site of a nine-hole **golf course.** At Mingarry are the remains of a big chambered cairn.

Three miles north from Daliburgh, at Airidh Mhuilinn, is a **Flora MacDonald memorial.** West of A865, about 200 yards up a little farm track half a mile north of Milton, a cairn on top of a little hill marks the spot where this woman, so revered in legend, was born in 1722. Staying on the minor roads, you'll see the dramatic machair-fringed shoreline and pass through the hamlets of Bornish, Ormiclete, and Stoneybridge. At Ormiclete are the ruins of **Ormiclete Castle,** constructed by the Clan Ranald chieftains in the early 18th century.

Rejoin the main road at Howbeg. The part of the island directly north of Howbeg is rich in archaeological remains. Ruins of several medieval chapels are all that's left of a major South Uist ecclesiastical center. An ancient graveyard nearby was the burial ground of the Clan Ranald chieftains.

Farther north, A865 passes the **Loch Druidibeg National Nature Reserve,** the most significant breeding ground for the native grayleg goose in the country. Attracting the dedicated bird-watcher, it's a setting of machair and brackish lochs. At Drimsdale lie the ruins of a big dun, a fortification in a loch where the villagers retreated when under attack. It continued as a stronghold for the Clan Ranald until the early 1500s.

The road continues past the Royal Artillery Rocket Range (heed those warning signs). On the flank of Reuval Hill, called "the mountain of miracles," stands **Our Lady of the Isles,** a 30-foot statue of the Virgin and Child. Erected in 1957, the statue was the creation of artist Hew Lorimer, and Catholic contributions from around the world financed the project. It's the largest religious statue in Britain.

Loch Bee, inhabited by mute swans, nearly bisects the northern part of South Uist.

SHOPPING   You'll find **Hebridean Jewelry,** Garrieganichy, Lochdar (☎ **01870/ 610288**), signposted on the north end of the Iochdar Road. The shop produces silver and gold pendants and brooches featuring Celtic patterns. The artists here can create custom pieces upon request.

WHERE TO STAY & DINE

Borrodale Hotel. Daliburgh, South Uist, Outer Hebrides HS8 5SS. ☎ **01878/700446.** Fax 01878/700611. 14 rms (12 with bath). TV. £60 ($99) double without bath, £70 ($115.50) double with bath. V. Rates include Scottish breakfast.

Set near the center of the island, 2¹/₂ miles west of Loch Boisdale along A865, this hotel stands in a landscape of freshwater lakes, heather, and gorse. A row of gables runs across the building's second floor, and the interior contains a cocktail bar, a pub, and a restaurant where table d'hôte lunches cost £9 ($14.85) and table d'hôte dinners go for £16.50 ($27.20). The hotel underwent extensive renovations in 1997, which updated the guest rooms and common rooms of the building. The owners will assist in arranging fishing and golf expeditions.

Lochboisdale Hotel. Lochboisdale, South Uist, Outer Hebrides HS8 5TH. ☎ **01878/700332.** Fax 01878/700367. 18 rms (17 with bath). £70–£80 ($115.50–$132) double with bath. MC, V. Rates include Scottish breakfast.

This hotel is the quintessential fisher's refuge. Solidly built of local stone in 1892, it's in the center of town a half-minute walk from the ferryboat terminal. It proudly displays tile-covered tables and scales near its entrance for weighing and preparing the daily catch of its residents. The hotel estimates that 75% of its international clientele come to fish in local waters. Trophies and memorabilia decorate the half-paneled walls of the cocktail lounge and restaurant. Both have blazing fireplaces and a feeling of conviviality. A three-course à la carte dinner costs £17.50 ($28.90). The hotel's public bar is the only one within 4 miles and is frequented by local residents. The bedrooms are outfitted in English country-house style, with chintz curtains and solidly comfortable furniture. One single does not have a bathroom in the room, but does have access to private facilities nearby.

12 Barra

118 miles NW of Edinburgh, 88 miles NW of Glasgow

Called "the garden of the Hebrides," Barra lies at the southern end of the Outer Hebrides. Locals claim that it has some 1,000 varieties of wildflowers. The island is one of the most beautiful in the Hebridean chain, with heather-clad meadows, beaches, sandy grasslands, peaks, rocky bays, and lofty headlands. Since the days of the conquering Vikings it has been associated with the Clan MacNeil.

A circular road of 10 miles will take you around Barra, which is about 4 by 8 miles in size. **Cockle Strand,** the airport, is a long and wide beach of white sand, the only runway in Britain washed twice daily by sea tides.

Most of the 200 inhabitants of Barra are centered at **Castlebay,** its capital, a 19th-century herring port and the best place to stock up on supplies. In the background of the port is **Ben Heaval,** at 1,250 feet the highest mountain on Barra.

ESSENTIALS
GETTING THERE

BY PLANE At the northern end of Barra is Cockle Strand, the airport. Loganair, the Scottish airline, flies here from Glasgow, or from Benbecula on Lewis. Phone ☎ **0345/222111** in Glasgow for flight information.

BY FERRY From the mainland at Oban, Barra can be reached by **Caledonian MacBrayne** car ferry, which docks at Castlebay. Subject to weather conditions, departures from Oban are on Monday, Wednesday, Thursday, and Saturday, with a return on Tuesday, Thursday, Friday, and Sunday. Sailing time is 5 hours, and a one-way ticket costs £16.45 ($27.15). Call ☎ **01631/562285** in Oban for sailing information.

From South Uist you can also take a car ferry from Lochboisdale to Castlebay. A privately operated 12-passenger ferry will take you from Eoligarry, north of the Cockle Strand airport, to Ludag on South Uist. It operates only Monday through Saturday (☎ **01878/700216** for schedules).

VISITOR INFORMATION

Castlebay Tourist Information Centre (☎ **01871/810336**) is found near the pier where the ferryboat docks. It's open Easter to mid-October, Monday through Friday from 9am to 5pm and Saturday from 9am to 5pm. The staff here will help you locate a room should you arrive on Barra without a reservation.

EXPLORING THE ISLAND

The most important sightseeing attraction of Barra is in the bay. **Kismul Castle** (☎ **01871/810336**) was built for strategic purposes on a small islet, the longtime stronghold of the notorious MacNeils of Barra, a clan known for piracy and lawlessness. Their 35th chief, Ruari the Turbulent, was even so bold as to seize a ship of a subject of Elizabeth I. When the direct male line died out in 1863, leadership of the clan reverted to the Canadian branch.

The oldest part of the castle is a tower dating from 1120. An accidental fire swept through the 15th- and 16th-century part of the structure in 1795. In 1938 the 45th chieftain of the clan, the late Robert Lister MacNeil of Barra, an architect, began restoration work on his ancestral home. After many interruptions, including World War II, the job was completed in 1970. The castle may be visited May to September only, on Monday, Wednesday, and Saturday afternoons. A boatman will take you over and back at 2pm. Entrance is £5 ($8.25), including the boat ride.

To drive around the island, head west from Castlebay until you reach Kinloch. On the left is **Loch St. Clair,** reached by a tiny track road. In the loch on an islet stand the ruins of St. Clair Castle, called MacLeod's Fort. In the vicinity you can also see St. Columba's Well, named for the saint.

Continuing north to Borve, you'll see the **Borve Standing Stones** on your left. At Borve, the north fork leads to a chambered cairn and the hamlet of **Craigston,** which has a church dedicated to St. Brendan, the Irish navigator who many cite as the discoverer of America. In the area are two interesting ruins: **Dun Bharpa,** a collection of stones encircled by standing stones, and **Tigh Talamhanta,** a ruined wheelhouse.

Continue north to Allasdale. **Dun Cuier** is one of the few excavated Hebridean Iron Age forts, better preserved than most. Opposite Allasdale is **Seal Bay,** a beauty spot where the seals do as much inspection of you as you do of them.

At **Northbay** at Loch an Duin, the remains of an old dun protrude from the water. Continue north to Eoligarry, site of a small ferry terminal taking passengers to Ludag on South Uist. Eoligarry's proud possession is **St. Barr's Church,** named after St. Findbarr of Cork (A.D. 550–623), who is said to have converted the islanders to Christianity after finding many of them practicing cannibalism when he arrived. The original 12th-century chapel was restored by Fr. Callum MacNeil. The Celtic stones in the churchyard are called "Crusader stones." This was the old burial ground of the MacNeil chieftains. Novelist Compton MacKenzie is buried here. Near Eoligarry, on the summit of a small hill, is **Dun Scurrival,** another ruined fort, this one measuring 39 by 52 feet.

WHERE TO STAY & DINE

Castlebay Hotel. Castlebay, Barra, Outer Hebrides HS9 5XD. ☎ **01871/810223.** Fax 01871/810455. 13 rms. TV. £60 ($99) double. MC, V. Rates include Scottish breakfast. Closed Dec 22–Jan 5.

Originally built around 1890, its gables overlook the bay and the ferryboat terminal where most of the island's visitors disembark. Its cocktail bar has a quiet corner reserved for dining. Meals start at about £8 ($13.20). Adjacent to the hotel, and under the same management, is the Castlebay Bar, the island's most popular gathering place (its open fireplace is particularly welcome on a cold night). The bedrooms are simply but comfortably furnished and are equipped with tea- and coffeemaking facilities.

Isle of Barra Hotel. Tangusdale, Castlebay, Barra, Outer Hebrides HS9 5XW. ☎ **01871/810383.** Fax 01871/810385. 30 rms. TV. £80 ($132) double. MC, V. Rates include Scottish breakfast. Closed Oct 18–Mar 20.

The low-slung rooflines of this seashore hotel are part of a design by an architect who won an award in the late 1970s for his work. For the Outer Hebrides, it's a luxury selection. It was erected as a project of the Highlands and Islands Development Board, which adorned its brick walls with nautical paraphernalia and contemporary tapestries. It commands a view of the tranquil less-populated western shore of the island.

Its pub, the most westerly in Scotland, is widely touted as "the last dram before America." From the dining room and many of the well-furnished bedrooms you can see everything that's coming and going at sea. At the suggestion of their Scottish nanny, the shah of Iran used this hotel as a safe haven for his children when a revolution was knocking at his door. The shah and his retinue are long gone, but the hotel remains a favorite with the yachting crowd. Some of the best food on Barra is served here. A set dinner costs £15.50 ($25.60) for three courses and £17.95 ($29.60) for four courses.

The Orkney & Shetland Islands 13

Northern outposts of civilization, the Orkney and Shetland archipelagos consist of about 200 islands, about 40 of which are inhabited. "Go to Shetland for scenery, Orkney for antiquities"—or so the saying goes. That doesn't mean that Orkney doesn't have scenery too. It does, in abundance.

These far-flung and scattered islands are rich in a great Viking heritage. Ceded to Scotland by Norway as part of the dowry of Princess Margaret in 1472 when she married James III, the islands were part of the great Norse earldoms. They were a gathering place for Norse fleets, and celebrated in the *Orkneyinga Saga,* which detailed the exploits of the Viking warriors.

Before the Vikings, however, tribes of Stone Age people occupied both Shetland and Orkney. The Picts came later, and ruins of their round forts can still be seen dotting the coastlines. The island chains are not part of the Highlands, and totally differ from both the Inner and Outer Hebrides. Clans, Gaelic, and kilts were unfamiliar to the Orcadians and the Shetlanders—until the Scots arrived. At first these merchants and newcomer landlords were bitterly resented. Even today the islanders are fiercely independent. They speak of themselves as Orcadians and Shetlanders instead of as Scots. Not only are Orkney and Shetland different from the Highlands, they're different from each other, as you'll soon see.

Change, as was inevitable, has come to Orkney and Shetland by the way of oil and modern conveniences. But tradition is still strong. It has a lot to do with climate and with ancestry.

GETTING TO ORKNEY & SHETLAND P&O Ferries (☎ **01856/850655**) provides service between Scrabster (near Thurso) on Scotland's north coast to the Orkneys. Trips are made two to three times per day every day but Sunday in the summer, each taking 2 hours. In winter, service drops to one trip per day. While P&O accommodates both vehicles and individuals on foot, a **ferry from John o' Groats** accepts passengers only. Ferries operate from Easter to September two to four times daily. The trip takes approximately 45 minutes (☎ **01955/611353** for information). **British Airways** (☎ **0345/222111**) flies into the Orkneys, as it does to Sumburgh, 26 miles south of Lerwick, the most important center on the Shetland Islands. P&O Ferries provides overnight ferry service once daily, Monday through Friday between Aberdeen in northeast Scotland and Lerwick.

DRIVING TOURS

ORKNEY

Day 1 Arrive by plane in Kirkwall, the capital, and spend the day wandering about the town for your first "taste of the Orkneys."

Day 2 In your rented car, take A965 west to Maes Howe, from about 2700 B.C., a huge burial chamber. Continue along A965 to Skara Brae, reached via B9056 and signposted. Last occupied in 2700 B.C., this ruined Neolithic village site, 19 miles northwest of Kirkwall, was discovered in 1850. Follow the signs south along A965 to the Ring of Brogar, a stone circle of some 36 stones dating from 1560 B.C. Continue south to Stromness, where you can visit the Pier Arts Centre and the Stromness Museum. Stay overnight in Stromness.

Day 3 In the morning cut across to Maes Howe again, following the signs to the Unstan Chambered Tomb, which lies about midway between Stromness and Kirkwall, some 3^1/$_2$ miles from each. This burial mound dates from 2500 B.C. After an exploration, follow the signs back to Kirkwall where you should check into a hotel for the night. However, in the afternoon continue south along A961 to the ruins of the Orphir church, Scotland's only medieval church from the 12th century. It lies 8 miles southwest of Kirkwall and is open at all times. The road continues south to South Ronaldsay, where you can see an Italian chapel in the hamlet of St. Mary's. Italian prisoners in 1943—detained here by the British—created a chapel of concrete and scrap metal. Follow A961 south for 10 miles to see the Orkney Wireless Museum at St. Margaret's Hope, 11 miles south of Kirkwall. It's a museum of wartime communications. Return to Kirkwall for the night.

SHETLAND

Day 1 Arrive in Lerwick, capital of the Shetland Islands, and walk around for minor exploring. You'll spend a good part of the day just reaching the island from the mainland of Britain.

Day 2 Take A970 south and follow the signs to the Shetland Croft House Museum. Then continue south to Sumburgh (also along A970). Here you can view the centuries-old Jarlshof, with prehistoric remains. Retrace your route to Skelberry, making a left turn onto Route B9122, for a look at St. Ninian's Isle, actually a spit of land where archaeologists discovered the St. Ninian treasure, a collection of 28 silver objects from the 8th century. Get back on A970, which will take you back to Lerwick for the night.

Day 3 In the morning, take B9075 to Kergord, with its forest, unusual in these climes. Rejoin A970 by heading left off B9075 at Laxo. Drive through Voe to Brae, home of the Busta House Hotel, the oldest continuously operated hotel in the Shetlands. Try to schedule a luncheon stopover here. Return to A970 and drive northeast, turning left at the junction with B9078. Here you can view the forlorn but dramatic cliffs of Esha Ness. Return to Lerwick for the night, but if time remains, visit Scalloway, on the western coast, signposted from Lerwick, a distance of 6 miles. Scalloway was once the capital of Shetland.

1 The Orkney Islands

6 miles N of John o' Groats (mainland Scotland) across Pentland Firth, 280 miles N of Edinburgh

To visit the Orkney Islands is to look at 1,000 years of history. Orkney is an archipelago of islands extending for about 50 miles north and northeast. Covering a land area of 376 square miles, they lie some 6 miles north of the Scottish mainland. The terrain has a lot of rich and fertile farmland, but also some dramatic scenery: Britain's highest perpendicular cliffs rise to 1,140 feet.

The population of the entire chain is less than 20,000, spread sparsely across about 29 inhabited islands. The people are somewhat suspicious of strangers, and if you meet an Orcadian in a local pub you'll have to break the ice.

The climate is far milder than the location would suggest because of the warming currents of the Gulf Stream. There are few extremes in temperature. May to July you get some astonishing sunsets, with the midsummer sun over the horizon for 18 1/4 hours a day. The Orcadians call their midsummer sky "Grimlins" from the old Norse word *grimla,* which means to twinkle or glimmer. There's enough light for golfers to play at midnight.

Who comes here other than golfers? Archaeologists, artists, walkers, climbers, and bird watchers are likely to share your breakfast table. Orkney is a virtual archaeological garden. Some 100 of the 500 known brochs—often called the "castles of the Picts"—are found here. Built by Orkney chiefs, these brochs were fortified structures where islanders could find refuge from invaders. Wells inside the structures provided water. The *Orkneyinga Saga,* written in the 9th or 10th century, is the record of the pomp and heraldry of Orkney's "golden age."

Divers are often drawn here by the remains of the warships of the German Imperial Navy that were scuttled here on June 21, 1919, on orders of Rear Admiral Ludwig von Reuter. Most of the vessels have been salvaged, but there are still plenty lying down there in the deep.

Anglers come in droves. Unlike in other parts of Scotland, fishing is free in Orkney, because of old Norse law and ancient Udal tradition. The wild brown trout is said to be the best in Britain. The season runs from mid-March until the first week in October.

A large percentage of the world's gray seal population visits Orkney to breed and molt. The islanders call the seal a "selkie." Wildfowl migrate from Iceland and northern Europe in winter, including the goldeneye, the red-throated diver, known locally as the "rain goose," and the short-eared owl or "cattieface," as well as such breeding seabirds as kittiwakes, puffins (called "tammie-honies" locally), and guillemots. The resident bird of prey on the island is the hen harrier. Some 300 species have been identified in the islands.

Orkney is also known for its flora, including the Scottish primrose, which is no more than 2 inches in height and is believed to have survived the Ice Age by growing in small ice-free areas. The amethyst, with a pale-yellow eye, is found only in Orkney and parts of northern Scotland.

Accommodations are few in the Orkneys; the greatest number are found in Kirkwall and Stromness, both on the same island, which is called "the Mainland." Stromness is in the west, Kirkwall in the east.

ESSENTIALS
GETTING THERE

BY PLANE   British Airways offers service to Kirkwall Airport on Mainland Orkney every day except Sunday. British Airways flies from Glasgow, Inverness, and Aberdeen, with connections from London and Birmingham; ☎ **0345/222111** for schedule information.

BY CAR   If you're driving over, head for Scrabster, near Thurso, in the northern province of Caithness. Here, P&O's *St. Ola* operates a roll-on/roll-off ferry service with 2-hour sailings to Stromness on Mainland Orkney. The ferry sails two or three times a day in summer. A round-trip fare with car is £70 ($115.50). For more information, check with **P&O Ferries** (☎ **01856/850655** in Stromness).

BY FERRY   If you aren't driving, it's faster and cheaper to go from "end-of-the-line" John o' Groats to Burwick. The daily ferries operate only from May through September, with ferries leaving four times per day. Round-trip fares are from £21 to £29 ($34.65 to $47.85) per person depending on departure time. **John o' Groats Ferries Ltd.** can be reached at ☎ **01955/611353. P&O Ferries** (☎ **01856/ 850655**) schedules departures from Scabster at noon daily with additional ones on Monday and Friday at 5:35pm and on Saturday at 5:45pm. A passenger round-trip fare is £29 ($47.85) per person.

GETTING AROUND

BY PLANE   Island-hopping is common in the north of Scotland. Loganair operates scheduled flights from Kirkwall Airport on Mainland to the isles of Sanday, Stronsay, Westray, Eday, North Ronaldsay, and Papa Westray. For information and reservations call **British Airways** at ☎ **0345/222111.**

BY FERRY   The **Orkney Islands Shipping Co.** operates scheduled ferry service from Kirkwall to Orkney's north and south islands: Eday, Papa Westray, Sanday, Stronsay, Westray, North Ronaldsay, and Shapinsay. From Houton there's service to the south isles: Flotta, Graemsay, and Hoy at Longhope and Lyness; and from Tingwall to Rousay, Egilsay, and Wyre. Contact the shipping line in Kirkwall at ☎ **01856/872044.**

There's also a private ferry service to take you to Hoy, departing from Stromness. The tourist office will have the latest details on departures.

BY CAR   The Churchill barriers, erected to impede enemy shipping in World War II, have been turned into a road link between the islands of Mainland and South Ronaldsay.

VISITOR INFORMATION

If you want to know what's taking place at the time of your visit, you'll have to consult *The Orcadian,* a weekly published since 1854.

There are **tourist information centers** at both Kirkwall, on 6 Broad St. (☎ **01856/ 872856**), and at Stromness (☎ **01856/850716**), the two principal "towns" of Orkney. In winter the office in Stromness stays open for only 2 hours a day to meet the ferry coming from Scrabster on the mainland (the information booth is in the ferry terminal building).

SPECIAL EVENTS

The **Orkney Traditional Folk Festival** attracts musicians from Scandinavia to Stromness during the last week of May each year. For information call the Stromness tourist office or write to the Festival Office at P.O. Box 4, Stromness, Orkney KW16 3AA.

TOURS

Bus tours operate March through October, visiting the major sights. One reliable operator is **"Go Orkney,"** South Cannigall, St. Ola (☎ **01856/874260** for detailed information). Sinclair Dunnett's luxury coach takes in such attractions as prehistoric monuments and seals. The tours are popular, and it's wise to book seats in advance. Tours range from £7 to £23 ($11.55 to $37.95).

Orkney

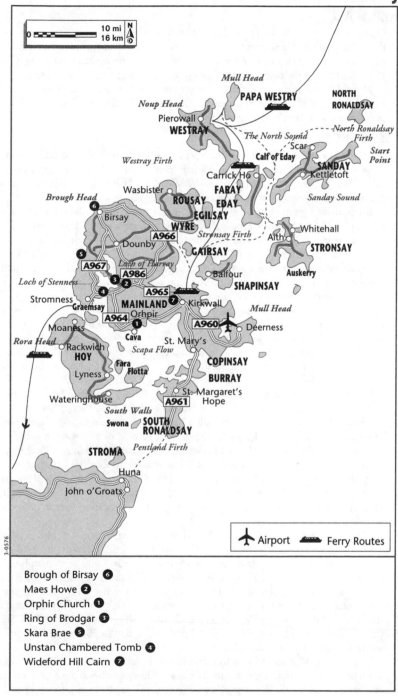

Legend:
- 0 — 10 mi / 16 km (scale bar), N

Airport ✈

Ferry Routes 🚢

Brough of Birsay ⑥
Maes Howe ②
Orphir Church ①
Ring of Brodgar ③
Skara Brae ⑤
Unstan Chambered Tomb ④
Wideford Hill Cairn ⑦

Map labels:

Mull Head
PAPA WESTRY
NORTH RONALDSAY
Noup Head
Pierowall
WESTRAY
The North Sound
North Ronaldsay Firth
Scar
Calf of Eday
SANDAY
Start Point
Westray Firth
Carrick Ho
FARAY
Kettletoft
Wasbister
ROUSAY
EDAY
Sanday Sound
Brough Head
EGILSAY
Birsay
WYRE
Whitehall
Dounby
A966
Stronsay Firth
Aith
STRONSAY
Loch of Harray
GAIRSAY
A967
A986
Balfour
Auskerry
Loch of Stenness
Stromness
A965
SHAPINSAY
Graemsay
MAINLAND
Kirkwall
Mull Head
Orphir
A964
A960
Deerness
Cava
St. Mary's
Moaness
Rora Head
Rackwich
Scapa Flow
COPINSAY
HOY
Fara
BURRAY
Flotta
St. Margaret's Hope
Lyness
Wateringhouse
A961
South Walls
Swona
SOUTH RONALDSAY
STROMA
Pentland Firth
Huna
John o'Groats

3-0576

KIRKWALL

On the bay of Firth, Kirkwall, established by Norse invaders, has been the capital of the Orkney Islands for at least 900 years. It used to be called Kirkjuvagr or "church bay," after a church built around 1040 honoring the memory of King Olaf Harraldsson, later the patron saint of Norway. That church no longer stands.

The old Norse streets of Kirkwall are very narrow to protect the buildings from galelike winds. But don't get the idea they're pedestrian walkways. That myth is dispelled when a car comes roaring down the street.

SEEING THE SIGHTS

For the best view of Kirkwall and the North Isles, head up **Wideford Hill,** about 2 miles west of town. Here you'll enjoy a panoramic sweep. On the western slope of this hill, 2^1/$_2$ miles west of Kirkwall, is the **Wideford Hill Cairn,** a trio of concentric walls built around a passage and a megalithic chamber.

Kirkwall was granted a royal charter from James III in 1486. "The Pride of Orkney" is ✪ **St. Magnus Cathedral,** Broad Street, burial place of the martyred St. Magnus, patron saint of the island chain. The cathedral was founded to honor him in 1137 by Jarl Rognvald, his nephew. The remains of both the saint and Jarl Rognvald were interred between the two large East Choir piers. It's a "Norman" building, constructed of gray and pinkish rose sandstone. Work went on over centuries and additions were made in the transitional and very early gothic styles. It's still in regular use as a church and can be visited April through September, Monday through Saturday from 9am to 6pm and Sunday from 2 to 6pm. From October through March it is open Monday through Saturday from 9am to 1pm and 2 to 5pm.

Across from the cathedral are the ruins of a 12th-century **Bishop's Palace,** Broad Street, with a round tower dating from the 16th century. King Haakon came here to die in 1263, following the Battle of Largs and his attempt to invade Scotland. The palace was originally constructed for William the Old, a bishop who died in 1168.

An easy walk will take you to the impressive ruins of **Earl Patrick's Palace,** on Watergate. Built in 1607, it has been called "the most mature and accomplished piece of Renaissance architecture left in Scotland." Earl Patrick Stewart was the son of the illegitimate brother of Mary Queen of Scots. The palace figured in the novel by Sir Walter Scott *The Pirate.* Both the Bishop's Palace and Earl Patrick's Palace are open April through September, Monday through Saturday from 9am to 6pm and Sunday from 2 to 6pm. A ticket price of £1.50 ($2.45) for adults, £1 ($1.65) for senior citizens and students, and 75p ($1.25) for ages 5 to 16 covers admission to both palaces; free for age 4 and under.

Nearby is **Tankerness House,** on Broad Street, dating from 1574. This is an example of a merchant laird's mansion, with crow-stepped gables, courtyard, and gardens. A museum here depicts life in Orkney over the past 5,000 years. Exhibitions range from the bones of the earliest prehistoric inhabitants to Neolithic pottery to farming and domestic utensils. You'll see, among other items, a Pictish stone symbol, bronze jewelry, and temporary exhibitions as well. It's open all year, Monday through Saturday from 10:30am to 12:30pm and 1:30 to 5pm; May through September, also on Sunday from 2 to 5pm. Admission is £2 ($3.30) for adults, free for senior citizens, students, and children.

The **Orkney Wireless Museum,** Kiln Corner, Junction Road, Kirkwall, is a museum of wartime communications used at Scapa Flow, which was a major naval anchorage in both World War I and World War II. Today this sea area, enclosed by Mainland and several other islands, has developed as a pipeline landfall and tanker terminal for North Sea oil. You can also see a large collection of early domestic radios. Admission is £2 ($3.30) for adults, £1 ($1.65) for children. Open April through September, Monday through Saturday from 10am to 4pm, Sunday from 2:30 to 4:30pm.

In the environs, you can visit the **Grain Earth Houses** at Hatson, near Kirkwall. This is an Iron Age souterrain (underground cellar), with stairs leading down to the below-ground chamber. Another Iron Age souterrain, **Rennibister Earth House,** is about 4¹/₂ miles west and northwest of Kirkwall. This excavation also has an underground chamber that has supporting roof pillars.

Shopping

You may not think of the Orkney Islands as a place to shop, but there are many interesting purchases, especially of jewelry, to be made here.

The Longship, 11 Broad St. (☎ **01856/873251**), is the retail outlet of Ola Gorie, for Orkney jewelry in Kirkwall. Now in its third decade, this family business has a wide range of high-quality jewelry, including some inspired by stone carvings found at archaeological digs, others by the rich flora and fauna of the islands. A collection based on designs by Charles Rennie Mackintosh has proved popular. The Longship also offers a variety of gifts, including fashion and furnishing accessories by Orkney-based Tait & Style.

Ortak Jewelry, 10 Albert St. (☎ **01856/873536**), is the main street shop of the famous jewelry studio that produces a wide range of silver and gold pieces featuring Celtic, traditional Arcadian, Victorian, and art nouveau designs. The shop also sells items such as pottery, barometers, and crystal made by other local artists. The **Ortak Factory Shop,** Hatston Industrial Estate (☎ **01856/872224**), is adjacent to the Ortak factory, and it's the only shop that carries the complete Ortak line. A visitor center on the premises features videos about jewelry making, and factory tours are offered free between 9am and 5pm Monday through Friday. In winter, the shop and visitor center closes for lunch from 1 to 2pm.

Judith Glue, 25 Broad St. (☎ **01856/874225**), produces and sells hand- and machine-made knitwear for the entire family. The artisans tend to favor old-fashioned island patterns, handed down over the generations. Also available in the shop are wares of other local artists, and you'll find an interesting selection of handmade pottery, jewelry, greeting cards, soaps, and island music CDs available.

Nearby, about 1¹/₂ miles from Kirkwall, **Robert Towers' Workshop,** Rosegarth House, St. Ola (☎ **01856/873521**), displays the Orkney pine or walnut chair, a famous design, with or without the hood and/or drawer.

Joker Jewelry, East School, Holm (☎ **01856/781336**), located 7 miles south of Kirkwall on the Kirkwall–South Ronaldsay Road, is a studio shop that sells the output of six local potters who produce ceramic giftware, including clocks, wind chimes, jigsaw puzzles, indoor fountains, and candleholders. Guests are welcome to watch the artists at work, and custom pieces can be made upon request.

WHERE TO STAY

Ayre Hotel. Ayre Rd., Kirkwall, Orkney KW15 1QX. ☎ **01856/873001.** Fax 01856/876289. 33 rms. TV TEL. £80–£98 ($132–$161.70) double. AE, MC, V. Rates include Scottish breakfast.

Set midway between the town's copper-spired church and the harborfront, a 2-minute walk from the town center, this white-sided hotel consists of a stone core from 1792 and a sprawling rather uninspired modern addition added during the 1970s. When it was first built, it was a social center for the town, hosting dances and bridge parties. Today guests congregate in the establishment's popular bar. Bar lunches and dinners begin at £4 ($6.60) each. In the resataurant, à la carte meals average about £19 ($31.35) for three courses. The guest rooms here are functionally modern and well appointed, having benefitted from complete refurbishments in 1996.

Leckmelm. Annfield, Crescent, Kirkwall, Orkney KW15 1NS. ☎ **01856/873917.** 3 rms (none with bath). TV TEL. £34 ($56.10) double. No credit cards. Rates include Scottish breakfast.

This comfortable guesthouse is located about 10 minutes away from the harbor by foot—be warned, the walk is all uphill. The elevated location of the house, however, provides guests with a splendid view of the North Isles. Mrs. Margaret A. Scott, the owner, has a fairly extensive collection of books on Orkney and local ornithological interests that she is happy to share with her guests. The rooms are well kept and are equipped with tea- and coffeemaking facilities and hair dryers. Mrs. Scott will also help guests with laundry if her time allows. The atmosphere here is homey and welcoming.

Royal Hotel. Victoria St., Kirkwall, Orkney KW15 1DN. ☎ **01856/873477.** Fax 01856/ 872767. 32 rms (16 with bath). TV. £35–£45 ($57.75–$74.25) double without bath, £55–£65 ($90.75–$107.25) double with bath. MC, V. Rates include Scottish breakfast.

Recently acquired by new owners, this hotel should be fully refurbished for the 1998 summer season. Although rooms have been and will continue to be fully modernized (with amenities such as tea- and coffeemakers and hair dryers), the overall style of the hotel is traditional. The Royal Hotel has a restaurant where a table d'hôte menu is served nightly for around £15 ($24.75). There's also an extensive à la carte selection. In addition to the restaurant, the hotel runs two well-stocked bars, the Public Bar and the Lounge Bar.

West End Hotel. 14 Main St., Kirkwall, Orkney KW15 1BU. ☎ **01856/872368.** Fax 01856/ 876181. 16 rms. TV TEL. £55 ($90.75) double. AE, MC, V. Rates include Scottish breakfast.

This three-story hotel just outside the town center was originally built in 1837 by a retired sea captain who had made his fortune running contraband goods between Britain and the Baltics. Today, Jimmy and Isabelle Curry own and operate the establishment, offering their guests a warm welcome and comfortable rooms. The hotel has been refurbished in the last few years and is fresh and inviting despite its long history. Guest rooms are equipped with tea- and coffeemaking facilities, and hair dryers and ironing equipment are provided on request. Meals, served in a small restaurant or the hotel's bar, are from an à la carte menu; a filling three-course dinner costs £10 ($16.50). The hotel is fully licensed, attracting both locals and visitors.

WHERE TO DINE

Foveran Hotel. St. Ola, Kirkwall, Orkney KW15 1SF. ☎ **01856/872389.** Fax 01856/876430. Reservations recommended. Main courses £11.50–£13.50 ($18.95–$22.30). MC, V. Mon–Sat 7–9pm, Sun (residents only) 7–9pm. SCOTTISH.

Located 2 miles west of Kirkwall, overlooking the Scapa Flow, where the German Imperial Fleet was sunk in 1919, the Foveran looks like a modern hotel of Scandinavian design. Fully licensed, its restaurant offers the best cuisine in the area and emphasizes "Taste of Scotland" menus. The catch of the day might turn out to be lobster, grilled salmon, deep-fried squid, giant crab claws (known locally as "partan toes"), or brown trout. Vegetarian meals are also offered, as well as succulent portions of Orkney Island beef, lamb, and farm-made cheeses.

The hotel also rents eight pleasant bedrooms; seven are double with private baths. The price for B&B is £70 ($115.50) double.

EXPLORING MAINLAND FROM KIRKWALL TO STROMNESS

Heading south from Kirkwall along the southern coastal road toward Stromness, we come first to the hamlet of Orphir. **Orphir Church,** along A964, is 6 miles southwest of Kirkwall. The ruins here are of the country's only circular medieval church. It was constructed in the first part of the 1100s and dedicated to St. Nicholas. In the vicinity is the site of Earl's Bu, a great banqueting hall of the earls of Orkney.

At Orphir, you can see vast tracts of land set aside for bird watching. If you're an angler, the fishing is free on Kirbister Loch. Ferries leave the Houton Terminal for Hoy and Flotta five or six times a day.

In the area is the **Cuween Hill Cairn,** along A965, half a mile south of Finstown and 6 miles west and northwest of Kirkwall. The owner of a nearby farmhouse has the key that will open a door to reveal a low mound over a megalithic passage tomb, probably dating from the third millennium B.C. Ancient men's bones, along with those of their oxen and dogs, were excavated here.

Bypassing Stromness for the moment, you can continue with a circular tour of the island. In the vicinity of Stromness, lying off A965, is **Maes Howe,** 10 miles west of Kirkwall. Dating from 2700 B.C., this is a superb achievement of prehistoric architecture, constructed from single slabs more than 18 feet long and some 4 feet wide. There's a passageway that the sun shines through only at the winter solstice. It also contains the world's largest collection of Viking rune inscriptions, the work of marauding Norsemen who broke into the chambered cairn in search of buried treasure.

The ✪ **Ring of Brodgar,** between Lochand Stenness and Loch of Harray, is found 5 miles to the northwest of Stromness. A circle of some 36 stones is surrounded by a deep ditch carved out of solid bedrock. The best stone circle in Scotland, it has been dated to 1560 B.C. While it has been suggested that it was a lunar observatory, like Stonehenge, its exact purpose remains a mystery. In the vicinity, the **Stenness Standing Stones** are a quartet of four upright stones, all that's left from a stone circle from 3000 B.C.

The ✪ **Unstan Chambered Tomb,** 2 miles northeast of Stromness along A965, 10 miles west of Kirkwall, is a big (115 feet in diameter) burial mound dating from 2500 B.C. For its type, it's unsurpassed in Western Europe. There's a chambered tomb more than 6 feet high. It's open throughout the day; admission is free. For information, call ☎ **01856/872856.** Unstan Ware is the name given to pottery discovered in the tomb.

Last occupied about 2500 B.C., ✪ **Skara Brae,** 7¹/₂ miles north of Stromness, was a collection of Neolithic village houses joined by covered passages. It was believed to have sheltered farmers and herders. The housing colony remained buried in the sands for 4,500 years, until a storm in 1850 revealed the ruins. You can see the remains of six houses and a workshop. Once there were 10 dwellings. The walls were made from flagstone rock and the roofs were skins laid on wooden or whalebone rafters. A fireplace was in the center; beds were placed against the side walls. The bed "linen" was bracken or heather, and the "quilts" were animal skins. This prehistoric village is the best preserved of its type in Europe. It's open April through September, Monday through Saturday from 9:30am to 6pm and Sunday from 11:30am to 6pm; October through March, Monday through Saturday from 9:30am to 4pm and Sunday from 2 to 4pm. Admission is £2.80 ($4.60) for adults, £1.80 ($2.95) for senior citizens, and £1 ($1.65) for children.

The **Brough of Birsay,** at Birsay, at the northern end of Mainland about 11 miles north of Stromness, is the ruin of a Norse settlement and Romanesque church on an islet that can be reached only at low tide. You can see a replica of a Pictish sculptured stone (the original was removed to a museum for safekeeping). The site is open daily year-round and admission is free. Nearby are the ruins of the **Earls' Palace** at Birsay, a mansion constructed in the 16th century for the earls of Orkney.

Click Mill, off B9057, 2 miles northeast of Dounby, is the only still-functioning example of an old horizontal water mill on the island.

WHERE TO DINE AT ORPHIR

Scorrabrae Inn. Orphir. ☎ **01856/811262.** Reservations recommended. Main courses £4–£9 ($6.60–$14.85). No credit cards. May–Aug, Mon–Sat noon–2pm and 6–10pm, Sun 12:30–10pm; Sept–Apr, daily 6–10pm, Sat–Sun noon–2pm. Bar open year-round until at least 11:30pm nightly. BRITISH.

In an extension attached to a 19th-century grocer's shop, this simple but convenient restaurant also contains the town's only pub. The bar features whiskies that are locally distilled in Orkney, as well as beers. The à la carte menu offers a wide variety of dishes, including several fish and chicken dishes, lasagna, salads, and vegetarian meals.

STROMNESS

Set against a hill, Brinkie's Brae, on the west coast of Mainland, Stromness was once known as *Hamnavoe* or "haven bay" in Old Norse. With its sheltered anchorage, it's the main port of Orkney. Its stone-flagged main street is said to "uncoil like a sailor's rope." It's really about three-quarters of a mile of narrow street and not much else. The ferryboat *St. Ola* comes in here from the mainland, having left from Scrabster. Fishing boats find shelter here from storms in the North Atlantic.

With its waterfront gables, nousts (slipways), and jetties, Stromness strikes many visitors as more interesting than Kirkwall. In the old days you could see whaling ships in port, along with vessels belonging to the Hudson's Bay Company. Some young men of Orkney left with them to man lonely fur stations in the far outposts of Canada. For many transatlantic vessels, Stromness was the last port of call before the New World. At Login's Well, many ships were outfitted for Arctic expeditions.

SEEING THE SIGHTS

A small but well-planned bookshop, **Stromness Books and Prints,** 1 Graham Place (☎ **01856/850565**), specializes in books about Orkney and has in-stock copies of the *Orkneyinga Saga.* Open Monday through Saturday from 10am to 6pm and during ferry arrival times in the evening.

The **Pier Arts Centre,** Victoria Street (☎ **01856/850209**), has dazzled Orcadians with its "St. Ives school" of art, including works displayed by Barbara Hepworth and Ben Nicholson. Admission is free, and it's open Tuesday through Saturday from 10:30am to 5pm; closed 12:30 to 1:30pm in winter.

At **Stromness Museum,** 52 Alfred St. (☎ **01856/850025**), you can see a collection of artifacts relating to the history of Orkney, especially a gallery devoted to maritime subjects, such as the Hudson's Bay Company and the story of the sinking of the German Imperial Fleet. Founded in 1837, the year Victoria became queen, the museum has been much changed and altered over the years. There's a natural history section, with excellent collections of local birds and their eggs, fossils, shells, butterflies, and moths. Admission is £1.50 ($2.45)for adults, 35p (60¢) for age 13 and under, £3.50 ($5.75)for a family ticket; open May through September, daily from 10am to 5pm; October through April, Monday through Saturday from 10:30am to 12:30pm and 1:30 to 5pm.

WHERE TO STAY & DINE

Ferry Inn. John St., Stromness, Orkney KW16 3AA. ☎ **01856/850280.** Fax 01856/851332. 17 rms (13 with bath, 3 with shower only). TV. £34 ($56.10) double without bath, £40 ($66) double with shower only, £50 ($82.50) double with bath. AE. MC, V. Metered daytime parking available.

As its name implies, this three-story hotel is close to the ferryboat. It has been modernized and central heating added. The bedrooms are simple and a bit utilitarian, but adequate. All have tea- and coffeemakers and some are equipped with trouser presses. Meals are served from either a pub menu or an à la carte selection; main courses start at about £5.50 ($9.05). From noon to 2pm and 5:30 to 10pm daily, you can enjoy typical Scottish fare such as haggis, smoked salmon, and steak pie. To finish, try a cloutie dumpling with cream.

Stromness Hotel. Victoria St., Stromness, Orkney KW16 3AA. ☎ **01856/850298.** Fax 01856/850610. 40 rms. TV TEL. £66 ($108.90) double. MC, V. Rates include Scottish breakfast.

This is the most important hotel in the Orkneys' second-most-important community, located about 100 yards from the ferry terminal in the town center. The Orkneys' largest hotel, it sits behind an elaborately Victorian facade of symmetrical bay windows and beige sandstone blocks. It was once a bit dowdy, but was extensively renovated in 1996 and 1997. Rooms are outfitted with old-fashioned furniture and have tea- and coffeemaking facilities. Many offer views of the water. There's a cocktail lounge where lunch and dinner are served; meals are simple but hearty. A restaurant serves à la carte meals in the evening only, with three courses costing £17 ($28.05). The menu focuses on seafood and steaks from Orkney.

BURRAY

Burray and South Ronaldsay (see below) are two of the most visited of the southeastern isles, lying within an easy drive of Kirkwall on Mainland. Both are connected to Mainland by the Churchill barriers causeway that links the islands of Glims Holm, Burray, and South Ronaldsay.

WHERE TO STAY & DINE

Watersound Restaurant/Sands Motel. Burray Village, Burray, Orkney KW17 2SS. • ☎ **01856/731298.** Fax 01856/731298. 4 apts. TV. £280 ($462) per week for 1 to 6 occupants. MC.

One of the island's most prominent structures, this three-story, stone-fronted building was originally a fish-processing plant. Today the structure contains a reputable restaurant, the Watersound. The hostelry sits in the center of Burray Village, 8 miles north of the passenger ferry at Burwick, on South Ronaldsay. There are a quartet of self-catering upper-story flats. Each contains three rooms and a kitchenette, and can be rented (most likely in low season) for less than a week if not fully booked.

The Watersound Restaurant contains the island's only pub, open daily from 11am to 11:30pm. Meals are served Monday through Saturday from noon to 1:45pm and 7 to 9:45pm and Sunday from 12:30 to 2pm and 6:30 to 10pm. Main courses may include preparations of local trout as well as other Orkney produce. On Sunday, specials are offered; a favorite is the full roast beef lunch, which includes generous servings of meat and vegetables.

SOUTH RONALDSAY

Also joined by the barrier, the island of South Ronaldsay is unspoiled fertile countryside. **St. Margaret's Hope,** a hamlet, was named after the young Norwegian princess, the "Maid of Norway," who was Edward II's child bride. Had she lived, she was slated to become queen of England, which at the time laid claim to Scotland.

SHOPPING   **The Workshop,** Back Road (☎ 01856/831587), is a craft produc-ers' cooperative in the center of the village of St. Margaret's Hope. It sells a wide range of locally produced crafts, including pottery, jewelry, baskets, rugs, and fine-quality handknits. It's open April through December, Monday through Saturday from 10am to 5:30pm; January through March, Monday through Saturday from 10am to 1pm.

WHERE TO DINE

✪ **Creel Restaurant.** Front Rd., St. Margaret's Hope, Orkney KW17 2SL. ☎ 01856/831311. Reservations recommended. Main courses £10–£16 ($16.50–$26.40). MC, V. Daily 7–9pm. SCOTTISH.

This small, cozy eating place overlooking the bay uses fresh local produce and offers a large selection of local products. It's a Scottish winner of the "Taste of Britain" award. Specialties include Orkney crab soup, followed by filet steak served with an onion-and-chile marmalade. You might also try the pan-fried seafood assortment presented on a thick tomato, basil, and leek stew, or the roasted monkfish tails with sweet pepper dressing. For a change from the traditional clootie dumpling you may have sampled elsewhere, the clootie dumpling parfait is a lighter version of the origi-nal. The strawberry shortcake, made with home-made shortbread, cream, and fresh Orkney strawberries in season, is also a treat.

The restaurant also rents three bedrooms, each with private bath. The charge is £60 ($99) for a double, including a Scottish breakfast.

SHAPINSAY

If you don't have time to inspect many islands, Shapinsay will give you an idea of what one is like. Getting here is fairly easy if you're based on Kirkwall. The **Orkney Ferries Ltd.,** Shore Street (☎ 01856/872044), in Kirkwall, goes there six times a day. The round-trip passage is £13.20 ($21.80) for vehicles, £4.40 ($7.25) for adults, and £2.20 ($3.65) for children.

The island was the seat of the Balfours of Trenabie. John Balfour was a nabob, making his fortune in India before becoming the member of Parliament for Orkney and Shetland in 1790. He launched the Scottish baronial castle, Balfour.

Washington Irving's father was born on Shapinsay. There are several Neolithic sites on the island, but most remain unexcavated. Visitors come here mainly for Shapinsay's secluded beaches, its many walking trails, and its wildlife, including seals, which can be seen often.

WHERE TO STAY & DINE

✪ **Balfour Castle.** Balfour Village, Shapinsay, Orkney KW17 2DY. ☎ 01856/711282. Fax 01856/711283. 6 rms. £82 ($135.30) per person. MC, V. Rates include half board. Discount for age 12 and under.

The region's most important benefactors were the worldwide shipping magnates, the Balfour family. John Balfour began work on this castle, but it was completed by his heir in 1847. In the southwest corner of Shapinsay, it dominates the approach to the island. In the 1950s when the last Balfour died without an heir, the castle and estate were purchased by a former Polish officer, Tadeusz Zawadski, and his Scottish wife, Catherine.

Today the place is run by the widow Catherine, with her family. The castle accepts no more than 12 guests at a time, and the family treats them to conversation and entertainment. The cuisine relies on such tempting ingredients as local wild duck and freshly caught scallops, crabmeat, and lobster. Guests who catch their own dinner will have it cheerfully prepared for them. The estate shelters the only forest in the Orkney Islands, planted in the 19th century by the Balfours, and composed chiefly of sycamores. In its center, a 12-foot stone wall surrounds the kitchen gardens, where greenhouses produce peaches, figs, and grapes. Strawberries, cabbages, and salad greens grow well within the shelter of the wall, providing a constant summertime supply of fresh produce.

The estate is still a working farm, involved with beef cattle, sheep, and grain production. The hosts will take the time to tour the property with guests and will also arrange fishing trips or bird-watching tours, as well as photographic and ornithological trips with guide and boat. Between May and July the birdlife here is unbelievably profuse. Guests may also be taken to the family's privately owned 100-acre uninhabited island where a colony of gray seals and puffins like to say hello to visitors.

ROUSAY

Called the "Egypt of the North," the island of Rousay lies off the northwest coast of Mainland. Almost moon-shaped, and measuring about 6 miles across, it's known for its trout lochs, which draw anglers from all over Europe. Much of the land is heather-covered moors. Part of the island has hills, including **Ward Hill,** which many people walk up for a panoramic sweep of Orcadian seascape. In the northwestern part of the island is **Hellia Spur,** one of the most important seabird colonies in Europe. Here you can see the much-photographed puffin.

But where does the Egypt come in? Rousay has nearly 200 prehistoric monuments, including one of the most significant, the Iron Age ✪ **Midhowe Broch and Tombs,** in the west of the island, excavated in the 1930s. The walled enclosure on a promontory is cut off by a deep rock-cut ditch. The cairn is more than 75 feet long and was split among a dozen stalls or compartments. The graves of some two dozen settlers, along with their cattle, were found inside. One writer called the cairn the "great ship of death." The other major sight, the **Blackhammer Cairn,** lies north of B9064 on the southern coast. This megalithic burial chamber is believed to date from the third millennium B.C. It was separated into about half a dozen different compartments for the dead.

Excavation began in 1978 on a Viking site at **Westness.** The place figured in the *Orkneyinga Saga.* A farmer digging a hole to bury a dead cow came across an old Norse grave site. Three silver brooches, shipped to the National Museum of Antiquities at Edinburgh, were discovered among the ruins. The earliest one dated from the 9th century.

To reach Rousay, you can rely on the service provided by the **Orkney Ferries Ltd.** (☎ 01856/872044), in Kirkwall. The trip is made six times daily; round-trip passage for vehicles is £13.20 ($21.80). For passengers, the ticket costs £4.40 ($7.25) for adults and £2.20 ($3.65) for children.

WHERE TO STAY & DINE

Taversoe Hotel. Frotoft, Rousay, Orkney KW17 2PT. ☎ 01856/821325. 3 rms (1 with bath). £25 ($41.25) per person with Scottish breakfast, £30–£36 ($49.50–$59.40) per person with half board. No credit cards.

On a treeless landscape, this little guesthouse provides shelter from the storm in unpretentious accommodations. Open all year, it offers clean and comfortable bedrooms; two rooms overlook the sea (the occupants share a bathroom), plus a third without a view but with a private bath. The hotel has a dining room that is open for lunch and dinner. Guests and nonresidents alike enjoy what the proprietor calls "peasant meals" prepared with fresh fish and local produce.

EDAY

Called the "Isthmus Isle of the Norsemen," Eday is the center of a hardworking and traditional crofting community. Life is not easy, for most of this north isle is barren, with heather-clad and hilly moorlands that often lead to sheer cliffs or give way to sand dunes with long sweeping beaches. Chambered cairns and standing stones speak of ancient settlements. In the 18th and 19th centuries the island was a major supplier of peat.

Today most of the population derives its income from cattle and dairy farming, although other products include hand-knit sweaters, cheese, and a highly rated beer brewed in individual crofts by local farmers and their families.

People come to this almost-forgotten oasis today for bird watching, beachcombing, and sea angling. Others prefer the peaceful walks to the Red Head cliffs, likely to be filled with guillemots and kittiwakes. The cliffs rise to a height of 200 feet, and on a clear day you can see Fair Isle.

On its eastern coastline, Eday opens onto Eday Sound where John Gow, the pirate, was captured. After a trial in London, he was hanged in 1725; his exploits are detailed in *The Pirate* by Sir Walter Scott. Following his capture, Gow was held prisoner at **Carrick House,** in the northern part of the island. Carrick House was built in 1633 by James Stewart, the second son of Robert Stewart, who had been named earl of Carrick.

Despite the sale of various parcels of land to the island's 130 to 140 inhabitants, most of the island is owned by the laird of Eday, Mrs. Rosemary Hebdon Joy, whose link to the island dates back to around 1900, when her grandfather bought the island from his London club. Interestingly, since then the circumstances that have surrounded the island's inheritance have made it one of the few matriarchal lairdships in Scotland because its ownership has passed from mother to daughter for several generations. Mrs. Joy and her husband, retired from Britain's diplomatic corps, spend their winters in Worcestershire and the warm-weather months on Eday.

Again, because of limited accommodations Eday is most often visited on a day trip. **Loganair** in Kirkwall offers service to Eday one time per week on Wednesday. Call **British Airways** at ☎ **0345/111222** for information and reservations. The **Orkney Ferries Ltd.,** Shore Street (☎ **01856/872044**), in Kirkwall, crosses to Eday about three times daily except Sunday. Vehicles pay £19.80 ($32.65) for round-trip fare, whereas passengers pay £8.80 ($14.50). Children's fares are half price.

WHERE TO STAY & DINE

If you'd like to find lodgings on the island, you can get in touch with the **Eday Tourist Information Centre** (☎ **01857/622248**), which will supply you with details about farmhouses and B&B cottages offering meals. You can also visit the studios of working artists and can travel about by bicycle or car, even boat, and can also rent a pony.

✪ **Skaill Farm.** Skaill, Eday, Orkney KW17 2AA. ☎ and fax **01857/622271.** 2 rms (none with bath). £54 ($89.10) double. No credit cards. Rates include half board.

Operated by a pair of English expatriates fleeing the congestion of the London suburbs, this establishment is the centerpiece for the island's third-largest farm. Set on 800 acres of windswept grazing land, midway along the length of the island near its narrowest point, 5 miles from both Calfsound and Backaland, it's in a stone building whose 18th-century core was constructed on the foundations of the island's medieval skaill. (A skaill is the honorific home of an earl, designed to shelter him during his visits from other parts of his realm.) Part of the farmstead dates from 1850, when it was nearly doubled in size. Michael and Dee Cockram welcome visitors to their home, providing them with well-prepared evening meals and comfortable but simple overnight accommodations. Meals are usually served between 7 and 8pm. Menus might include freshly grown vegetables from the family's garden, lobsters, scallops, lamb, and beef.

WHERE TO DINE

Little Croft House. Isle of Eday, Orkney KW17 2AB. ☎ **01857/622248.** Reservations required with as much advance warning as possible. £15 ($24.75) per person. No credit cards. Time to be arranged when making reservations. SCOTTISH.

One of the most charming possibilities for a meal on Eday is provided by Yorkshire-born Mrs. Emma Popplewell, who, if notified in advance, will prepare table d'hôte lunches and dinners. Meals are often served to a loyal following of "off-island" yacht owners enjoying the nautical challenges of the local waters. The setting is a croft cottage whose 30-inch-thick stone walls were originally built around 1900. Its flower and vegetable garden slopes down to the edge of the sea, source of some of the kelp and seaweed that Mrs. Popplewell uses to flavor her succulent versions of Orkney lamb. Depending on what's available that day, menu items might include grilled halibut with scallops and local dill and fennel, salads made with wild greens gathered from the nearby hills, homemade versions of raspberry bramble sorbet, locally made cheeses and beers, and aromatic crusty bread that's freshly baked every morning.

In one of the croft's outbuildings (a former boathouse), Mrs. Popplewell sells sweaters, accessories, and caftans that are hand-knit on Eday by local women. (In recent years, this merchandise has found an enthusiastic market in such places as Colorado, New Hampshire, and Texas.) Also for sale are paintings and sculpture by island artists, among which are included the watercolors by Mrs. Popplewell's husband, Geoffrey.

The Popplewells rent four comfortably furnished rooms containing TVs; the two doubles offer private baths. Doubles with bath cost £48 ($79.20), including Scottish breakfast.

SANDAY

The name of this island means "sand island," which is appropriate; the long, white beaches have grown as tides have changed over the last century. With few residents or visitors, the stretches of seashore here are often deserted—perfect for solitary walks. Among the North Isles, Sanday is part of the eastern archipelago.

One of the largest of the North Isles, some 16 miles in length, Sanday has one of the most spectacular chambered cairns found in the Orkney Island chain, the ✪ **Quoyness Chambered Tomb,** and it lies on the tidal island of Elsness. The tomb and its principal chamber date from around 2900 B.C., reaching a height of some 13 feet. Access is by key, which is available at the local post office in Lady Village. Other ancient monuments, including Viking burial grounds and broch sites, have been found on Sanday.

Rare migrant birds and terns can be seen at the **Start Point Lighthouse.** The early 19th-century lighthouse is one of the oldest in the country, but since the early 1960s it has been on "automatic pilot." The number of ships wrecked off Sanday's shore is topped only by North Ronaldsay; the wreck of a German destroyer can be seen on the Sand of Langamay.

While on the island you may visit the **Isle of Sanday Knitters,** which has a large selection of high-quality knitwear in both classic and modern design. A display and a sales room are found in the Wool Hall at Lady Village. This cooperative, the largest of its kind in the North Isles, employs more than 100 women.

Accommodations are extremely limited, so arrive with a reservation if you're planning to stay over. **Loganair** flies in from the Kirkwall Airport (☎ **01856/872494**) one or two times a day except on Sunday. Also the **Orkney Ferries Ltd.,** Shore Street (☎ **01856/872044**), in Kirkwall, crosses to the island about two times daily except Sunday. Round-trip fare for passengers is £8.80 ($14.50), £4.40 ($7.25) for children. If you're driving, the cost for vehicles is £19.80 ($32.65).

WHERE TO STAY & DINE

Belsair Hotel. Kettletoft, Sanday, Orkney KW17 2BJ. ☎ **01857/600206.** 6 rms (3 with bath). TV. £38 ($62.70) double without bath, £52 ($85.80) double with bath. No credit cards. Rates include full Scottish breakfast.

Located in the hamlet of Kettletoft, site of about 15 buildings and the most central of the island's four communities, this hotel contains one of the island's two pubs and its only restaurant. The ancestors of its present owners built it of stone and clapboards in 1879. Functionally furnished bedrooms were upgraded and renovated in 1992. Gardens across the road produce many of the vegetables served in the hotel's dining room. Dishes include straightforward but flavorful preparations of fish, beef, and lamb. An à la carte menu is offered in the dining room, as is a nightly table d'hôte menu with four courses costing £7 ($11.55). Bar meals, served from 11am to 10pm daily, will cost from £3 to £8 ($4.95 to $13.20). The owner and manager, Mrs. Joy Foubister, is the island's postmistress, and her husband, Kenneth, is the postman. The establishment lies about 8 miles northeast of Sanday's roll-on/roll-off ferryboat pier, which was erected in 1992.

WESTRAY

One of the biggest of the North Isles, Westray is a fertile island with a closely knit community, many of whom are said to have Spanish blood, owing to shipwrecks of the Armada off its stormy shores. The western shoreline is the steepest, rising in parts to some 200 feet, from which panoramic vistas can be enjoyed. Seabirds such as guillemots can be seen around Noup Head, with its red sandstone cliffs. The island is a bird watcher's paradise. Along the lochs are many sandy beaches.

Below the cliffs is the so-called **Gentleman's Cave.** A Balfour of Trenabie is said to have found refuge in this cave, along with his comrades, after the defeat at Culloden in 1746. As winter winds howled outside, they drank to the welfare of the "king over the water," Bonnie Prince Charlie.

At **Pierowall,** the major hamlet, you can see Pierowall Church, a ruin with a chancel and a nave. There are also some finely lettered grave slabs.

The most famous attraction is **Noltland Castle,** a former fortress overlooking Pierowall. A governor of the island, Thomas de Tulloch, had this castle built in 1420. Eventually it was occupied by Gilbert Balfour of Westray, and its present ruins date from around the mid-1500s. It was destroyed in part by a fire in 1746. A kitchen, a stately hall, and a winding staircase can still be seen. Gilbert Balfour had it designed as a fortress, constructed in a "three-stepped" or Z plan, which provided complete all-round visibility against attack. It was never finished. One of John Knox's "men without God," Gilbert Balfour was involved in many intrigues around Mary Queen of Scots—he was perhaps implicated in the murder of Darnley. Eventually he fled to Sweden, but more intrigues there led to his hanging in 1576.

Orkney Ferries Ltd. (☎ **01856/872044** in Kirkwall) sails to Pierowall, Westray, two times daily except Sunday. Bookings are required for cars; the cost is £19.80 ($32.65) round-trip. Passengers for round-trips pay £8.80 ($14.50) for adults and £4.40 ($7.25) for children. **Loganair** flies to Westray one to two times daily except

Sunday throughout the year. Phone ☎ **01856/872494** in Kirkwall for information; for reservations, call **British Airways** at ☎ **0345/222111.**

WHERE TO STAY & DINE

Since accommodations are very limited on the island, always go armed with reservations.

Pierowall Hotel. Pierowall Village, Westray, Orkney KW17 2BZ. ☎ **01857/677208.** Fax 01857/677707. 5 rms (2 with bath). £30 ($49.50) double without bath, £38 ($62.70) double with bath. No credit cards. Rates include Scottish breakfast.

Originally built a century ago as a manse (clergyman's residence) for a nearby Presbyterian church, this cozy hotel is the domain of Mrs. Jean Fergus. It lies 7 1/4 miles north of the roll-on/roll-off ferryboat terminal, adjacent to the old ferryboat terminal (which services the island's fishing boats). The hotel was refurbished in 1997, when ensuite bathrooms were added to two rooms—one double room, one twin. These accommodations also have televisions. The other five rooms have benefitted from new furnishings and carpeting as well as redecorations. The hotel has a pub that offers food and drink to anyone who stops in. The à la carte menu features the requisite fresh fish as well as other local fare. Meals range from £3.50 to £6.50 ($5.75 to $10.75), although most dishes cost around £4 ($6.60).

PAPA WESTRAY

Both the bird watcher and the student of history are drawn to Papa Westray, which was believed to have been settled at least by 3500 B.C. One of the most northerly isles in the Orkney archipelago, it's rich in archaeological sites. In the fertile farmland around Holland, the **Knap of Howar** was discovered, the earliest standing dwelling house in northwestern Europe, dating from before 3000 B.C.

On the eastern shore of Loch Treadwell, visits are possible to **St. Treadwell's Chapel,** which is believed to have marked the arrival of Christianity in the Orkney Islands. The chapel, now in ruins, was dedicated to Triduana, a Celtic saint. When a Pictish king, Nechtan, admired her lovely eyes, she is said to have plucked them out and sent them by messenger to the king—she hoped he would learn that it was foolish to admire physical beauty. After that she went to a nunnery. For many decades the chapel was a place of pilgrimage for those suffering from eye problems.

St. Boniface Church is also a Celtic site. Stone Celtic crosses were found here on a location north of the airfield. Grave slabs were carved of red sandstone. This is believed to have been a Christian Viking burial ground.

A major attraction is **Holland House,** formerly the home of the Traills of Holland. Dating from the 17th century, the house is a fine example of a circular "Horse Engine House," which was driven by 11 horses and a dovecote. At one time the Traills owned most of Papa Westray.

The northern end of the island has been turned into a nature reserve. Along with colonies of guillemots and kittiwakes, **North Hill** is the site of one of the largest breeding colonies of the Arctic tern. Once the great auk flew over this island, but the last male was shot in 1813. If you'd like to see what an auk looked like, you'll find a typical one stuffed in the British Museum in London.

Twice daily flights to Papa Westray from Kikwall on Mainland are offered by **Loganair** (☎ **01856/872494**). You can also call **British Airways** at ☎ **0345/ 222111** for reservations on this airline. **Orkney Ferries Ltd.,** Shore Street (☎ **01856/872044**), in Kirkwall, sails to Papa Westray twice daily Monday through Saturday. Round-trip fares are £19.80 ($32.65) for vehicles, £8.80 ($14.50) for adults, and £4.40 ($7.25) for children.

WHERE TO STAY & DINE

Beltane House. Papa Westray, Orkney KW17 2BU. ☎ **01857/644267.** 4 rms (all with shower only). £46 ($75.90) double. MC, V. Rates include Scottish breakfast.

Built in 1983 about 2 miles from the island's main pier, this all-purpose accommodation was developed by the island's local farm cooperative. A row of stone-sided farmworkers' cottages was renovated to form a complex of shops, a guesthouse (whose prices are quoted above), and a bare-bones youth hostel containing two dormitories (male and female) with bunk beds. June and July are the busiest months, requiring advance reservations. Prices for overnights in the youth hostel are £8 ($13.20) per person for residents age 18 and over; £6.15 ($10.15) per person for those 17 and under. *Warning:* Rates are set by the Scottish Youth Hostel Association and change frequently. There are no meals provided in the hostel, although there is a self-catering kitchen. Residents also sometimes choose to join the guests of the main house for the nightly set-price dinner. A selection of two or three main courses is offered with three other courses for a cost of £14 ($23.10).

ORKNEY AFTER DARK

These sparsely populated islands generate quite a bit of cultural activity, especially in celebrating the music of the region. A number of festivals draw both curious visitors and fans of Scottish and, more specifically, Orkney music. Information, including schedules and ticket prices, for all events and activities is available through the tourist office at Kirkwall (see above). This office publishes the yearly Orkney diary, listing annual events and dates, as well as a monthly events list, filling in the details of performances at these yearly events in addition to information about weekly offerings in the various halls and pubs scattered about the islands.

The festival season kicks off in February with the **Drama Festival,** which hosts traveling stage companies presenting an array of productions in venues spread across the islands. Ticket prices tend to hover around £3 to £4 ($4.95 to $6.60). Early May brings the **Country and Irish Festival,** whereas late May finds the **Orkney Traditional Folk Festival** in full swing. Both feature ceilidhs and concerts of traditional music spread throughout the parish halls of the islands, and tickets to most events are in the £4 to £5 ($6.60 to $8.25) range. June brings a change of pace in the form of the **St. Magnus Festival,** which celebrates classical music and the dramatic arts, as well as music and drama workshops. These productions are spread throughout the various venues as well, and tickets average £6 to £7 ($9.90 to $11.55).

Every Wednesday night, the **Ayre Hotel** (☎ **01856/873001**) in Kirkwall hosts the weekly **Accordian and Fiddle Club,** and on Thursday night locals gather at the Town Hall to enjoy the music of the **Reel and Strathspey Society.** Admission to these events costs about £2 to £3 ($3.30 to $4.95). Parish halls located in the different communities host an erratic schedule of ceilidhs and concerts throughout the year. As suggested above, check with the Kirkwall tourist office for details about events scheduled during your stay.

2 Fair Isle

27 miles S of Lerwick, Shetland Islands

Called the "most isolated inhabited part of Britain," Fair Isle lies on the same latitude as Bergen, Norway. Measuring only about 1 mile by 3¹/₂ miles, it sits in the lonely sea, about midway between Orkney and Shetland, administered by the latter. Relentless seas pound its 20-mile coastline in winter, and powerful westerly winds fling Atlantic spray from one side of the island to the other. It's home to fewer than 100 hearty, rugged, and self-reliant souls.

An important staging point for migrating birds, Fair Isle is even better known for the patterned pullovers produced here. These pullovers came into fashion again in the 1970s, and they greatly aid the island's economy. In the chic boutiques of London, Milan, New York, and Paris, you'll see these intricately patterned garments retailing at high prices. But the homegrown product is sold on Fair Isle at half the price. Fair Isle knitting is even a part of the curriculum at all primary schools, and many jobless men have turned to knitting.

Originally the fame of the sweaters was spread in the 1920s by the then prince of Wales. The pattern is of mysterious origin. Some suggest that it was derived from Celtic sources, others that it came from the island's Viking heritage. A more daring theory maintains that the themes were Moorish, learned from Spanish sailors shipwrecked off Fair Isle from the Armada in 1588.

In 1954 the island was acquired by the National Trust for Scotland. The bird observatory installed here is considered the most remarkable in the country. Since work began in 1948, some 200 different species have been ringed. Fair Isle is an important breeding ground for everything from the puffin to the Arctic skua, from the razorbill to the storm petrel.

ESSENTIALS
GETTING THERE

BY PLANE Loganair operates scheduled service in a seven-seat "Islander" (flight time: 25 min.). From Sumburgh Airport, there's a flight on Saturday only, which links with incoming Loganair flights from both Glasgow and Edinburgh. From Lerwick Airport, flights are twice daily on Monday, Wednesday, and Friday, plus once on Saturday. Call **Loganair** at ☎ **01856/872494** or **British Airways** at ☎ **0345/222111** for more information.

BY BOAT The mailboat *Good Shepherd* sails on Tuesday and Saturday, and alternate Thursdays and Fridays, from Grutness Pier, Sumburgh Head, on Shetland. It's advisable to check sailing times from Grutness by telephoning before 9:30am on the morning of the scheduled departure for Fair Isle, in case of weather delay, which is frequent. Bookings for the trips to Fair Isle can be made through **J. W. Stout,** Skerryholm, Fair Isle (phone ☎ **01595/760222** for schedule information). A one-way fare is £1.60 ($2.65), and the trip takes 2¹/₂ hours.

VISITOR INFORMATION

Ask at Lerwick (see "The Shetland Islands," below). The telephone area code is **01595.**

WHERE TO STAY & DINE

Fair Isle Lodge and Bird Observatory. Fair Isle, Shetland ZE2 9JU. ☎ and fax **01595/ 760258.** 14 rms (none with bath). £70 ($115.50) double; £25 ($41.25) dormitory bed. MC, V. Rates include full board. Closed Nov–Mar.

Even if you're not a bird watcher, you might stay at this low-slung, big-windowed isolated building in the shelter of treeless hillsides, near the sea at the northern end of the island. This establishment was the dream of a well-respected ornithologist, George Waterston, who bought the lodge in 1948 and created the observatory. It's now administered by the Fair Isle Bird Observatory Trust. The establishment is most popular during the spring and autumn bird migrations. It's always wise to reserve well in advance, especially during those seasons. On the premises you'll find an extensive collection of reference books on birds. Sometimes the wardens will take guests on before-breakfast tours of bird traps which, for tagging purposes, are placed in strategic points along the stone dikes surrounding the island.

Adjacent accommodations were constructed to provide housing for visitors. There are 32 beds for rent. It's also possible to stay here in a dormitory room, with four or five, maybe even six beds.

3 The Shetland Islands

60 miles N and NE of the Orkneys

The northernmost part of the British Isles, the archipelago of the Shetland Islands includes some 100 islands that make up 50 square miles of land. Many are merely islets or rocks, but 17 are inhabited. The major island is called **Mainland,** as in Orkney. This island, on which the capital, **Lerwick,** is located, is about 55 miles long and 20 miles wide. It has been turned into what some critics have called "a gargantuan oil terminal." Shetland handles about half of Britain's oil.

The islands have been called that "long string of peat and gneiss that stands precariously where three seas—the Atlantic Ocean, the North Sea, and the Arctic Ocean—meet." Shetland's fordlike "voes" or sheer rock cliffs make the islands beautiful in both seascape and landscape. But it's a stark beauty, wild and rugged, with windswept moors. Because there are few trees, the landscape at first looks barren. But after a while it begins to take on a fascination, especially when you come upon a typical Shetlander, in his sturdy Wellington boots and thick woolen sweater, cutting peat along a bog as his ancestors did before him. Shetlanders are proud, warm, and hospitable, and often eager to share the treasures of their island chain with you. At no point in Shetland are you more than 3 miles from the sea—the coastline stretches for some 3,000 miles.

The major airport is at **Sumburgh,** on the southern tip of the southernmost island of Mainland, on a level with St. Petersburg in Russia. The far-northern outpost is **Muckle Flugga Lighthouse,** an advanced achievement of engineering. Standing poised on near-vertical rock, it's called "the last window on the world" through which Great Britain looks out to the north. It's not as cold here as you might think: The Shetland archipelago benefits from the warming influence of the Gulf Stream, though even in summer the weather tends to be chilly, and Shetland has less than half the annual rainfall recorded in the western Highlands. In summer there's almost continuous daylight. The Shetlanders call it "Simmer Dim." In midwinter there are no more than 5 hours of daylight.

Shetland civilization is old, dating back some 5,000 years. Shetland was inhabited more than 2,000 years before the Romans, who called it "Ultima Thule." Through these islands paraded Neolithic people, followed by the people of the Iron and Bronze Ages, who gave way to the Picts and the Celts. But the most enduring influence of all came from the Vikings, who ruled Shetland until some 500 years ago. The Norse established an influence that was not only to last for centuries but is still evident today in language, culture, and customs.

The Vikings held the islands from A.D. 800 until they were given to Scotland in 1469 as part of the wedding dowry of Princess Margaret of Norway when she married James III. Scotland's takeover of Shetland marked a sad period in the life of the islanders, who found themselves under the sway of often cruel and unreasonable feudal barons. One of the most hated of rulers was Earl Patrick Stewart, who was assigned the dubious task of imposing Scottish customs on a people who had known only Viking law. His son matched him in cruelty, and eventually both earls were executed in Edinburgh for their crimes. Shetlanders still think of themselves as separate from Scots.

The impact of the North Sea oilmen on this traditionally straight-laced community is noticeable, both in overcrowding and other ways. However, away from all the oil activity, life in the Shetland Islands goes on much as it always did, except for the profusion of modern conveniences and imported foodstuff—you'll notice that food on Shetland tastes better when it's from Shetland; for example, try the Reestit mutton, salted and smoked, with a distinctive flavor.

The islands are famous for their ponies and their wool. Shetland ponies roam freely among the hills and common grazing lands in the island chain. Some are shipped south to England where they're popular as children's mounts.

Shetland also has 10% of all the seabirds in the British Isles, and several of the smaller islands or islets have nature reserves. There are 300 recorded species. Seals are protected and welcomed here. You can see them drifting among the waves, sliding down in pursuit of a fish dinner, or lounging about on the rocks and beaches, enjoying a sunny day. You'll recognize most of them as the Atlantic gray seal, with its big angular head. The common seal, with a dog-shaped head, is most often found on the islet of Mousa. If you want to see the otter, you have a better chance in Shetland than anywhere else in Britain.

Fishers find some 200 freshwater lochs in Shetland, and deep-sea angling makes for a memorable sport. Many world fishing records have been set in Shetland. "Ton-up" fish are common.

The island craftspeople are noted for their creativity, reflected in their handcrafts, jewelry, and knitware. In some places you can watch these items being made in the workshops of the artists. Hand-knitted sweaters are still produced in great numbers on the island, and anyone contemplating a visit might want to return with at least one.

It's imperative to have advance reservations if you're considering a trip to Shetland, especially in midsummer when most of the visitors arrive.

ESSENTIALS
GETTING THERE

BY PLANE It's a 2¹/₂-hour flight from London. By air or sea, Aberdeen is the major departure point from Scotland. **British Airways** (for flight information, call ☎ 800/247-9297 in the U.S. or 0345/222111) flies four times per day to Shetland from Aberdeen between 9:30am and 5pm, with reduced service on Saturday and Sunday. The flight takes less than an hour.

BY FERRY Roll-on/roll-off car ferries operate to Shetland from Aberdeen one to two times a week, carrying up to 600 passengers and 240 automobiles. On-board facilities include restaurants, cafeterias, bars, lounges, and gift shops. The trip takes about 14 hours. For more information, get in touch with **P&O Ferries,** Jamieson's Quay (☎ 01224/572615), in Aberdeen.

P&O offers ferry service once a week, departing on Sunday at noon from Stromness, Orkney, heading for Lerwick in the Shetlands. Service is in both summer and winter. For information in Stromness, call ☎ 01856/850655.

GETTING AROUND

If you have a problem with transportation either to or around the islands, you can always check with the tourist office in Lerwick (see below).

BY PLANE **Loganair** (☎ 01595/840246) provides daily and weekly service to the islands of Whalsay, Fetlar, Foula, and Out Skerries. Although flying is a bit more

---

Up Helly Aa!

The farther north one travels in Scotland, the stronger are the undercurrents of pagan myth and pageantry, culminating in the vivid Norse traditions of the Shetlands. Here, on the rocky and moss-covered surface of the 100-or-so islands that comprise the archipelago, the collective unconscious of the locals is sometimes startlingly revealed as something other than Anglo-Saxon or Celtic.

Ask anyone in a local pub, and he or she will tell you that the islands are Scottish only because of the fiscal embarrassment of a long-ago Norwegian king, who sold the Shetlands to the Scottish monarchs in 1469 with the tacit understanding that they would eventually be returned to the Scandinavian fold.

Although for many generations the Shetlanders retained their Norse dialect and allegiance to Viking ways, the switch back to Norway never happened. Perhaps in reaction to their medieval role as bartered chattel between the two northern kingdoms, the Shetlands remained dourly outside Scottish culture, with a populace who referred for many generations to the provincial capital of Lerwick as "the mainland," and not to the mainland of Scotland.

How do the Shetlanders celebrate their Nordic heritage? By brightening up the midwinter darkness with the Up Helly Aa festival, which is held—in fair weather, snow, or storm—every year on the last Tuesday in January. The festival's centerpiece is a meticulously crafted re-creation of a Viking longboat. The people of Lerwick parade by torchlight through the streets in Viking costume, and the highlight of the evening comes when the longboat is set alight and its dragon-head prow is engulfed in flames. Presiding over the ritual is an elected master of ceremonies, the Guizer Jarl (a significant honor bestowed only on a longtime resident male of proven civic worth and integrity).

This ancient ritual celebrates the death of winter and the return of the sun and the earth's rebirth with the coming of spring. The ceremony is based on an ancient Viking death ritual when the body of a dead earl (Jarl) would be set ablaze at sea. An essential part of the ritual is the almost immediate removal of all traces of the burned-out hulk of the longboat after the cremation is over—the morning after the Up Helly Aa ceremony, even the ashes of the celebration have been carted off, and Lerwick resumes its outwardly Christian and Scottish demeanor—until the Viking tradition of the Up Helly Aa is revived again the following year.

---

expensive than taking a ferry, the bonus is that you can go and return on the same day as opposed to spending 2 or possibly 3 days on a rather small island.

BY FERRY Most of the inhabited islands are reached from the Shetland "Mainland," and passenger fares are nominal since they're heavily subsidized by the government. Service is 13 to 16 times a day to the islands of Unst, Yell, Whalsay, Fetlar, and Bressay. Passenger/cargo vessels service the islands of Fair Isle, Foula, the Skerries, and Papa Stour. Scheduled services to the little-visited places only operate once or twice a week, however. Boat trips to the islands of Mousa and Noss can be arranged in summer. Call ☎ **01595/693434** for more information.

BY BUS In summer, buses travel around Mainland to all the major places of interest. Call the leading bus company, **John Leask & Son,** at ☎ **01595/693162,** or pick up a copy of the "Inter-Shetland Transport Timetable," costing 50p (80¢) at the tourist office, and seek assistance here if you're planning to tour by public transport.

The Shetland Islands

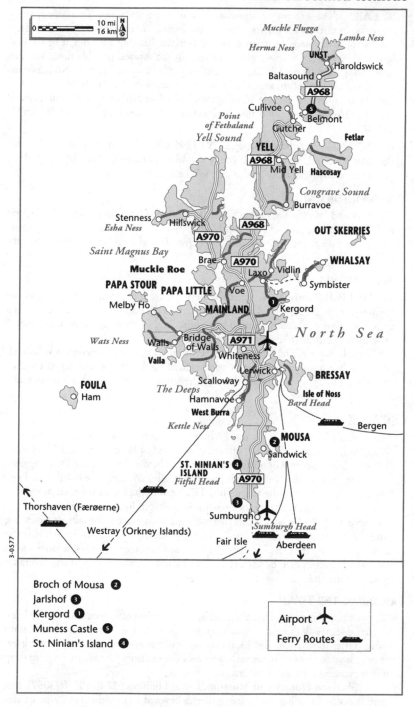

Broch of Mousa ②
Jarlshof ③
Kergord ①
Muness Castle ⑤
St. Ninian's Island ④

Airport ✈
Ferry Routes ⛴

BY CAR It's easier than you think, as there are some 500 miles of passable roads—no traffic jams, no traffic lights. Many of the islands are connected by road bridges, and for those that aren't, car ferries provide service. Renting a car might be the best solution if you want to cover a lot of ground in the shortest possible time. You can either bring a car from mainland Scotland or pick one up in Lerwick. No major international car-rental firm as yet maintains an office in the Shetlands. However, Avis and Europcar have, as their on-island agents, **Bolts Car Hire,** North Road in Lerwick (☎ 01595/692855); a competitor is **Grantsfield Garage,** North Road (☎ 01595/692709).

BY BICYCLE **Grantsfield Garage** (☎ 01595/692709) also rents bikes in Lerwick for a cost of £6 ($9.90) per day. If you're planning on renting a bike for several days, call at least a day in advance so that one will be reserved for you.

VISITOR INFORMATION

The **Shetland Islands Tourism** office is at the Market Cross in Lerwick (☎ 01595/693434). The helpful staff does many things, such as arranging rooms and providing information about ferries, boat trips, car rentals, and local events—they even rent fishing tackle.

SPECIAL EVENTS

Shetland Folk Festival takes place at Lerwick around the end of April and the beginning of May. Young fiddlers on the island take part, and international artists fly in for 4 days of concerts, musical workshops, and informal jam sessions, climaxed by what they call their "Final Foy."

Up Helly Aa, a Viking tradition left over from pagan days, is celebrated at Lerwick with great relish in January. Blazing torches light up the dark winter sky as a replica of a Viking longship is paraded through the streets of Lerwick, then ceremonially burned (see box above).

LERWICK

The capital of Shetland since the 17th century, Lerwick, on the eastern coast of "Mainland," is sheltered by the little offshore island of Bressay. In the 19th century it was the herring capital of northern Europe, and before that, a haven for smugglers. The fishing fleet of the Netherlands put in here after combing the North Sea. Even before Victoria came to the throne in 1837, Lerwick had a bustling, cosmopolitan atmosphere. That's even truer today, with the influx of foreign visitors.

Believe it or not, Lerwick is sometimes the sunniest place in Britain, experiencing some 12 hours of sunshine a day in the early summer. Commercial Street is the town's principal artery, and it's said that beneath the steep and narrow lanes runs a network of passages used by smugglers. Lerwick today is the main port and shopping center of Shetland.

EXPLORING THE TOWN

Your first stop should be at the Shetland Islands Tourism office (see above). The helpful staff does many things, such as arranging for rooms and providing information about ferries, boat trips, and local events. You can even rent fishing tackle here. They're used to unusual requests: Sometimes visitors from Canada or America drop in here wanting their ancestors traced.

The **Shetland Library and Museum,** Lower Hillhead (☎ 01595/695057), has, in addition to a reading room, four galleries devoted to exhibits that cover art and textiles, shipping, archaeological digs, and oil exploration. Admission is free. It's open

Monday, Wednesday, and Friday from 10am to 7pm and Tuesday, Thursday, and Saturday from 10am to 5pm.

Fort Charlotte, built in 1665, is pentagonal in shape, containing high walls with gun slits pointing, naturally, at the sea. Eight years after it was constructed, it was burned by the Dutch. Restoration came in 1781. It's open year-round, daily from 9am to 10pm. Admission is free, and entrance is via Market Street.

Clickhimin Broch, about a quarter of a mile southwest of Lerwick, was fortified at the beginning of the Iron Age. Excavated in the 1950s, the site revealed 1,000 years of history. It was at one time turned into a broch, rising 17 feet and built inside the fort. Admission is free, and it's open daily throughout the year with no set hours.

A 40-foot replica of a Viking longboat, *Dim Riv* (**"Morning Light"**), anchored in the harbor of Lerwick, is available for a tour of the harbor on a summer evening. The boat was constructed by Lerwick craftsmen in 1980 and has been a popular tourist attraction ever since. Ask at the tourist office (see above).

SHOPPING

Shopping is so interesting in Lerwick that it might be termed a sightseeing attraction. Of the many shops, you may want to drop in at **Anderson & Co.,** Shetland Warehouse, Commercial Street (☎ 01595/693714), which sells handmade crofter and designer sweaters as well as other cottage-industry goods.

Selling the wares of the local Judane factory, **Millers,** 116 Commercial St. (☎ 01595/692517), features machine-knit clothing items, including sweaters and capes, and rugs. A variety of solid tones and patterns are available, with Argyle being predominant.

J. G. Rae, 92 Commercial St. (☎ 01595/692517), sells silver and gold jewelry featuring Celtic motifs, and images based on Norse mythology and Shetland tales and legends. Gold- and silversmith Rosalyn Thompson produces the jewelry sold at **Hjaltasteyn,** 161 Commercial St. (☎ 01595/693714), where you'll find a selection of sterling silver and 9-carat-gold items, some of which are set with garnets and amethysts.

Yet another good bet for jewelry is **Shetland Jewelry,** Sound Side, Weisdale (☎ 01595/830275), a studio shop that produces gold and silver pieces featuring Celtic and Norse designs. In business since 1953, the 13 artists here sometimes incorporate local quartz and amethysts in their work. Visitors are welcome to watch the artisans at work, and custom pieces are available upon request.

WHERE TO STAY

Glen Orchy Guest House. 20 Knab Rd., Lerwick, Shetland ZE1 0AX. ☎ 01595/692031. 14 rms. TV. £58 ($95.70) double. No credit cards. Rates include Scottish breakfast.

Set near the top of a brae (gently sloping hill) near a nine-hole golf course that's free to the public, Glen Orchy House is a 4-minute walk from the center of town. The building was originally constructed in 1904 as an Episcopalian nunnery; the most recent modifications to the structure were in 1996 and 1997 when Trevor and Joan Howarth added a new wing and upgraded the existing guest accommodations. In addition to single and double rooms, there are now two family rooms with single beds or bunk beds. All rooms have central heating and air-conditioning, as well as tea- and coffeemaking facilities and satellite television. A table d'hôte menu is provided to those who request it.

Grand Hotel. 149 Commercial St., Lerwick, Shetland ZE1 0AB. ☎ 01595/692826. Fax 01595/694048. 22 rms. TV TEL. £67 ($110.55) double; £95 ($156.75) family room (quad) with bath. AE, DC, MC, V. Rates include Scottish breakfast. Free parking in a nearby public lot.

As its name implies, a grander hotel would be hard to find anywhere in Shetland. With its pointed turrets, weather vanes, crow's-step gables, and solid stone walls, it's one of the most ornate buildings in Lerwick. It lies a block from the waterfront, in the town center. All the bedrooms have hot-beverage facilities, among other necessities. The extensively modernized hotel has two lounge bars, a dining room, and a nightclub (Poser's Disco) that opens its doors 3 nights a week to every night-owl in Lerwick. The Grand Hotel shares its reservations facilities and some of its staff with the Queens Hotel (see below).

Lerwick Hotel. South Rd., Shetland ZE1 0RB. ☎ **01595/692166.** Fax 01595/694419. 35 rms. TV TEL. £79.95 ($131.90) double. AE, MC, V. Rates include Scottish breakfast. Take Scalloway Rd. west from the center for 5 minutes.

This is one of the biggest and most up-to-date hotels in Shetland, sprawling beside a gravel- and kelp-covered beach. Its streamlined bedrooms offer various amenities, including radios and hair dryers. They're simply furnished and about half have views over the water toward the Isle of Bressay. The full-service restaurant features a nightly three-course table d'hôte menu for £21.50 ($35.50). The selection of main dishes is likely to include at least one seafood and one vegetarian choice as well as chicken or wild game. In the summer, dinner-dances that combine hearty meals with traditional Scottish fun are frequently held. As an alternative to dining in the restaurant, bar meals are served at both lunch and dinner.

Queens Hotel. 24 Commercial St., Lerwick, Shetland ZE1 0AB. ☎ **01595/692826.** Fax 01595/694048. 25 rms. TV TEL. £82 ($135.30) double. AE, DC, MC, V. Rates include Scottish breakfast.

Its foundations rise directly from the sea at the harborfront, in the town center, so that on blustery nights fine sprays of saltwater sometimes coat the windowpanes of the lower floors. Originally built of natural stone around 1900, the Queens rivals the nearby Grand Hotel (see above) as the most prestigious hotel in Lerwick. They share the same reservations staff. Inexpensive bar lunches are offered in the cocktail lounge, whereas more formal dinners are served every night in the dining room. The bedrooms are conservatively and comfortably furnished.

Shetland Hotel. Holmsgarth Rd., Lerwick, Shetland ZE1 0PW. ☎ **01595/695515.** Fax 01595/695828. 66 rms, 1 suite. TV TEL. £89 ($146.85) double; £99.50 ($164.15) suite. AE, DC, MC, V. Rates include Scottish breakfast.

Built in 1984, this four-floor brick, stone, and concrete structure with square windows is one of the most modern hotels in Shetland. It's close to the center of town, opposite the ferry terminal, with a good view of the harbor. The guest rooms are well furnished and contain trouser presses, tea- and coffeemakers, and hair dryers. For a fee, the hotel provides laundry service as well. The building also houses a public bar, a cocktail lounge, and two restaurants. Meals are served from an à la carte menu in one restaurant whereas the other features a table d'hôte menu. The four-course meal costs £23.50 ($38.80) and often includes selections such as local fish and vegetarian items.

WHERE TO DINE

Golden Coach. 17 Hillhead. ☎ **01595/693848.** Reservations required Sat–Sun. Main courses £7–£12 ($11.55–$19.80); fixed-price 2-course lunch £7 ($11.55). MC, V. Mon–Fri noon–2pm and 5:30–11pm, Sat–Sun noon–11pm. CHINESE.

The only Chinese restaurant in the Shetlands, this intimate place is softly lit and contemporary in decor. The cuisine is basically Peking, with a wide array of poultry, pork, seafood, duckling, and beef dishes. Try the barbecued Peking duck or deep-fried shredded beef in a hot sweet-and-sour sauce. Malaysian chicken comes in a peanut sauce, or you can order king prawns Peking with garlic sauce.

Oasis Bistro. In the Shetland Hotel, Holmsgarth Rd. ☎ **01595/695515.** Main courses £7–£12 ($11.55–$19.80). AE, DC, MC, V. Daily 11am–9:30pm; hot meals noon–2pm and 5–9:30pm. SCOTTISH.

On the second floor of the four-story Shetland Hotel, this eatery is a good choice for a light snack at odd hours; salads and sandwiches are served all day. The restaurant also offers hot meals at lunch and dinner. Emphasis is on fresh local produce, including fresh fish and vegetarian fare straight from Shetland gardens.

Queens Hotel. 24 Commercial St. ☎ **01595/692826.** Reservations recommended. Main courses £7.95–£19.75 ($13.10–$32.60); fixed-price 3-course dinner £15.75 ($26). AE, DC, MC, V. Daily noon–2pm and 6–9pm. BRITISH.

Located on the lobby level of the previously recommended hotel (see "Where to Stay," above), its pink-and-white premises overlook the sea, the wharves, and the many fishing boats bobbing at anchor. It caters to families, many of whom seem to arrive in groups as part of scheduled reunions. Many residents consider it the best restaurant in Lerwick, a staple on the island's culinary scene. Menu specialties include goujons of haddock with tartar sauce, roast sirloin of beef with Yorkshire pudding, chicken Caribbean with pineapple sauce, braised lamb cutlets, surf and turf, and conservative preparations of fish dishes.

LERWICK AFTER DARK

From May through September, the **Islesburgh Community Centre,** King Harold Street (☎ **01595/692114**), hosts dancing to Shetland fiddle music on Wednesday and Friday nights from 7 to 9:30pm. Admission is £2 ($3.30) for adults and £1 ($1.65) for senior citizens, students, and children. Another outlet for fiddle music, the **Lounge Bar,** Mounthooly St. (☎ **01595/692231**), hosts an informal evening of traditional music on Wednesday night, usually starting sometime between 9 and 10:30pm, and again on Saturday afternoon at 2pm. There's no admission fee to this old traditional pub, which has been under the same management for 40 years. Belhaven and Tennant beers, along with Guinness, are available on tap.

Also see "Shetland After Dark," at the end of this chapter.

SCALLOWAY

On the western coast, 6 miles west of Lerwick, Scalloway was once the capital of Shetland. This town was the base for rescue operations in Norway during the darkest days of World War II. Still an important fishing port, Scalloway has changed because of the oil boom. New businesses have opened, attracting more and more people to the area, which has emerged after a long slumber into a prosperous and lively place in this remote corner of the world.

EXPLORING THE TOWN

The ruins of **Scalloway Castle** (☎ **01595/880243**), commissioned by the dreaded Earl Patrick at the beginning of the 17th century, dominate the town. The castle was allowed to deteriorate after the earl was executed in Edinburgh (no one in Scalloway wanted to perpetuate his memory). The castle was built in the corbel-turreted medieval style. Admission is free and hours are those of the Shetland Woollen Company (see below), from which you must get the key to enter.

The **Shetland Woollen Company** (☎ **01595/880243**) is open to visitors, Monday through Friday from 9am to 5pm. In summer, the facilities are also open Saturday from 9am to 5pm. You can see the processing and finishing of Shetland knitware. Later you can visit the showroom where a selection of garments made locally is sold, along with Icelandic knitwear.

North of Scalloway, and 5 miles northwest of Lerwick in the hamlet of Veensgarth, off A971, is the **Tingwall Agricultural Museum** (☎ 01595/840344). Set in the surroundings of a working farmstead, Mrs. Jeanie Sandison's private collection on Shetland's agricultural and domestic past is unequaled in the islands. All buildings date from the mid-1700s—a granary, stable, bothy, smithy, and dairy. There's a slide room where a 25-minute documentary is shown. The museum is open June through August only, Monday through Saturday from 10am to 1pm and 2 to 5pm. Admission is £1.50 ($2.45) for adults and £1 ($1.65) for senior citizens and children.

Shetland folklore evenings are held at the museum in summer, followed by food and entertainment at the Tingwall Public Hall. Visitors can see something of Shetland history, taste traditional island food, and be entertained by local musicians and storytellers. There are usually two folklore evenings in June, two in July, and two in August. Dates vary, but information and tickets can be picked up at the tourist office in Lerwick.

WEST MAINLAND

It's said that you can see more of Shetland from the **Scord of Weisdale** than from any other vantage point in the archipelago. But West Mainland has many more attractions than panoramic vistas.

SHOPPING NEAR WHITENESS

Shetland's only stone-polishing business operates at **Hjaltasteyn,** Whiteness, 9 miles west of Lerwick. Here gemstones are turned out from raw materials in fetching hand-wrought silver settings. Unfortunately, the workshop is not currently open to visitors. You can, however, visit the showroom at 161 Commercial St. in Lerwick (☎ 01595/696224) to see what's been made. It's open Monday through Thursday from 10am to 3pm and Friday through Saturday from 9:15am to 4:45pm. The shop closes from 1 to 2pm for lunch.

Continuing north, at Weisdale you can watch high-quality jewelry being made at **Shetland Jewelry,** Soundside, Weisdale (☎ 01595/830275), where the artisans base many of their designs on ancient Celtic and Viking patterns. Visitors may go through the workrooms and later stop in for an inspection of the stocks available in the showroom. It is open Monday through Friday from 9am to 1pm and 2 to 5pm.

WHERE TO STAY

Westings Hotel. Wormadale, West Mainland, Shetland ZE2 9LJ. ☎ 01595/840242. Fax 01595/840500. 6 rms. TV, TEL. £62.50 ($103.15) double. MC, V. Rates include Scottish breakfast.

Set just below the summit of one of the region's tallest hills, in an isolated position 9 miles west of Lerwick, this hotel was built by the British army as an observation post during World War II. On clear days it offers views of up to 40 miles from the east to the southwest, and if you climb to the hill's summit you can enjoy simultaneous views of the Atlantic and the North Sea. Modified and improved since its original construction, it has a Scandinavian look, with asymmetrical roofs and low-slung horizontal lines. Each of the half-dozen rooms contains a radio and teamaking facilities. The restaurant serves table d'hôte evening meals, and a pub offers bar meals. The owners will organize pony treks on Shetland ponies or indicate which of the nearby spots to seek out for the best sea fishing or hill walks.

WHERE TO DINE

Norseman's Inn. Voehead, Weisdale Parish. ☎ **01595/830304.** Main courses £4 ($6.60). No credit cards. Pub hours: Mon–Fri 11am–2pm and 5pm–midnight, Sat–Sun 11am–1am. Food: Apr–Sept only, Fri–Sun 5–10pm. SCOTTISH.

This is your basic Scottish pub on the main A970 highway, 12 miles northwest of Lerwick. Built in 1981 at the head of one of the most dramatic estuaries in the Shetlands, it's a popular place for both locals and visitors. On weekends, only in the high season, the pub serves up a variety of hot dishes to accompany the spirits. Shrimp scampi, lasagna, sweet-and-sour chicken, and baked fresh fish are a few house favorites. The atmosphere is rustic, cozy, and inviting.

AROUND WALLS

You can continue your tour of West Mainland by heading west along A971 toward Walls. You come first to **Staneydale Temple,** $2^3/4$ miles outside Walls. This early Bronze Age (perhaps Neolithic) hall once had a timbered roof. It's called a temple because it bears a remarkable resemblance to similar sites on Malta, lending support to the theory that the early settlers of Shetland came from the Mediterranean.

Continuing past several lochs and sea inlets, you come to Walls, a hamlet built on the periphery of two voes. Its natural harbor is sheltered by the offshore islet of Vaila.

Where to Stay & Dine

✪ **Burrastow House.** Walls, West Mainland, Shetland ZE2 9PD. ☎ **01595/809307.** Fax 01595/809213. 6 rms. £160 ($264) double, £80 ($132) per person family room. MC, V. Rates include half board. Closed Oct–Mar.

Set about 3 miles southwest of the hamlet of Walls, a 40-minute drive northwest of Lerwick, this simple but comfortable building was originally constructed in 1759 as a *haa* house (home of the farm manager of a laird's estate). Set amid lands still used in summer for grazing sheep, it lies at the widest section of a windswept peninsula with views of a cluster of rocky and sparsely inhabited islands. The guest bedrooms are well furnished and evoke country-house living. One family suite, consisting of a double room and a twin room connected by a bathroom, is available.

The food is the best on the island. The daily menu in the oak-paneled dining room is likely to include nettle and oatmeal fritters, mussel brose (a stew of mussels thickened with oatmeal), monkfish with anchovy stuffing, lamb, and Scottish beef. Lunch is served daily from 12:30 to 2pm, high tea from 3:30 to 5:30pm, and dinner from 7:30 to 9pm. The proprietors here ask that you call ahead if you want a hot meal, although they will accommodate you with fresh-baked bread, cheese, and homemade soup if you fail to do so. Lunches and high teas cost £4.50 to £9 ($7.45 to $14.85); main courses with salad and bread average about £17 ($28.05). The restaurant is closed Sunday evening and all day Monday to nonresidents of the hotel

PAPA STOUR

The "great island of priests," in the shape of a large starfish, lies off the west coast of Mainland, 25 miles northwest of Lerwick. As its name indicates, it was an early base for monks. Two centuries ago there was a leper colony here on the little offshore islet of Brei Holm.

Legend has it that its profusion of wildflowers had such a strong scent that old fishers could use the perfume—borne far out on the wind—to fix their positions. Papa Stour is very isolated, and once it was feared that the island might be depopulated, but about 26 settlers live here now.

In the darkest days of winter, bad weather can cut it off for days. But if you see it on a sunny day, it's striking. Encircled by pillars of rock and reefs, its sea caves, sculpted by turbulent winds and raging seas, are among the most impressive in Britain. The largest of these is **Kirstan's Hole,** extending some 80 yards.

Boats go to Papa Stour about four times a week from West Burrafirth on Mainland. Call ☎ **01595/810460** for information about these constantly changing details.

Where to Stay & Dine

North-house. North-house, Papa Stour, Shetland ZE2 9PW. ☎ **01595/873238.** 4 rms (1 with bath). £46 ($75.90) double without bath, £50 ($82.50) double with bath. No credit cards. Rates include full board.

Within walking distance of the island's only pier, just outside Housa Voe (the island's only hamlet, with seven buildings), this stone croft is an archaeologically unusual building. The foundations are Viking, and Dutch coins dating from the 1620s have been unearthed here. It's the domain of Andrew and Sabina Holt-Brook, who moved from the mainland of Scotland more than 20 years ago in search of affordable land. Now owners of 30 acres of windswept peninsula (which geologists define as an ancient Devonian fish bed), they offer the only overnight accommodations and/or meals on the island. Guest rooms are comfortable and inviting. The "garden room" has its own entrance. Meals are served to both guests and nonresidents, but for just a meal, call in advance. A set-price dinner costs £24 ($39.60) and may include locally raised beef or lamb or just-caught crab or fish. The working farm also supplies the Holt-Brooks with free-range eggs and fresh vegetables. Lunches are brown-bag affairs to be taken along to eat while you enjoy the island's wild landscapes.

FOULA

This tiny remote island—only 3 miles wide by 5 miles long—with five high peaks is an "Edge of the World" place. Called the "Island West of the Sun," Foula may have been the Romans' legendary Thule. In local dialect, *foula* means "bird island"—and the name fits. Uncountable numbers of birds haunt the isle. Its towering sea cliffs include the second-highest cliff face in Britain, the **Kame,** at 1,220 feet. About 3,000 pairs of the world's great skuas live here. They're known as "bonxie." On the island you'll hear many stories about the rock-climbing prowess of locals who go in search of gulls' eggs.

The island lies 27 miles west of Scalloway on the west coast of Mainland, where the locals are vastly outnumbered by sheep. Until the beginning of the 19th century, Old Norse was the language spoken here. Its 400 people remain very traditional. If you are very lucky you might see them dance the Foula reel, a classic dance in Shetland.

If the weather's right, a weekly mailboat sails to Foula from Walls on Mainland. Even in summer the seas are likely to be turbulent, and in winter Foula has been known to be cut off from the rest of Britain for weeks. The trip takes 2 1/2 hours. Loganair also operates a summer service from Tingwall on Monday, Wednesday, and Friday (trip time: 15 min.).

Where to Stay & Dine

Because of the interest by visitors in recent years, some islanders have taken to doing B&B, offering accommodations that include half board.

Mrs. Marion Taylor. Leraback, Isle of Foula, Shetland ZE2 9PN. ☎ **01595/753226.** 3 rms (shared bath), 1 cottage. £44 ($72.60) double; £20 ($33) per person in cottage for up to 4 occupants. No credit cards. Rates include half board in a double.

This cozy modern and weathertight farmhouse is near the geographical center of the island, within walking distance of everything. Bryan and Marion Taylor emigrated from Edinburgh 14 years ago. Comfortable rooms in the main house have easy access to the large kitchen whose brick hearth is the focal point of the farm. The Taylors' 7 acres is a sheep farm, and they extend their income by knitting and spinning—you can order a custom-made hand-knit sweater.

NORTH MAINLAND

The most rugged scenery Shetland has to offer is in the northern part of the island of Mainland. Some visitors have found the area reminds them of Norway, and we agree. That's especially true in the tiny village of **Voe,** with its little wooden houses.

VIDLIN

Heading north from Voe along A970, you'll reach the eastern junction of B9071, which will take you to Vidlin, where **Lunna Kirk,** one of the oldest churches in the archipelago, is still used by its congregation. Construction began in 1753. The church has a "leper hole," from which the poor victims could listen to the sermon without being seen.

Where to Stay & Dine

Mrs. Barbara Ford. Skeo Green, Lunning, Vidlin, Shetland ZE2 9QB. ☎ **01806/577302.** 1 rm (without bath). £14 ($23.10) per person. No credit cards. Rates include Scottish breakfast.

Mr. and Mrs. Ford rent one family room, consisting of a double bed and a single bed. Both of the Fords are artists, and they allow access to their studio and darkroom to guests who want to use them. Even if you're not an artist, you'll appreciate the relaxed atmosphere here. Evening meals, featuring local produce, are available to both guests and nonresidents for £7 to £9 ($11.55 to $14.85).

BRAE & BUSTA

Heading west back to A970, continue north toward the sightseeing attraction of **Mavis Grind.** The most "touristic" thing to do in North Mainland is to pause at Mavis Grind, take a couple of stones, and throw one to your right into the North Sea and the other to your left into the Atlantic Ocean.

In the vicinity of the hamlets of Brae and Busta, you'll find some of the best food and hotels in Shetland. Oil contractors, helicopter pilots, and shipping executives sent by mainland companies to service the nearby Sullom Voe, site of the largest oil terminal in Europe, often stay in this area.

Where to Stay & Dine

Brae Hotel. Brae, North Mainland, Shetland ZE2 9QJ. ☎ **01806/522456.** Fax 01806/522459. 28 rms. TV TEL. £70 ($115.50) double. AE, DC, MC, V. Rates include Scottish breakfast. Discounts offered for stays of 4 or more days.

Built in 1979, this earth-toned modern building lies in the center of the hamlet, 28 miles north of Lerwick beside the main A970 highway about a mile south of the narrow isthmus that separates North from South Mainland. The interior is appealingly paneled, and the restaurant serves generous portions in fixed-price meals costing £7.50 ($12.40) for three courses. The bedrooms are wallpapered and painted in pastels, and reassuringly warm. On the premises are a bank, a billiard room, and a unisex hairstyling salon.

✪ **Busta House.** Busta, near Brae, North Mainland, Shetland ZE2 9QN. ☎ **01806/522506.** Fax 01806/522588. 20 rms. TV TEL. £88.50 ($146.05) double. AE, DC, MC, V. Rates include Scottish breakfast.

Busta House is the oldest continuously inhabited house in the Shetland Islands. Built in 1580, with ample extensions added in 1714 and 1983, it was the original *busta* (homestead) of the medieval Norwegian rulers of the island. Later inhabited by the island's laird, it once welcomed Elizabeth II at teatime during her tour of the Shetlands on the royal yacht *Brittania*. The estate's long and tormented history includes episodes of multiple drownings, a handful of resident ghosts, and some of the most famous lawsuits in Britain. Some literary enthusiasts claim that the house in all its drama was the inspiration for Dickens's *Bleak House.*

In recent times, the important economic agreement that paved the way for the construction of the massive Sullom Voe oil terminal (the Busta House Agreement) was signed here between the local government and Britain's multinational oil companies.

Painted white, and rising above its own small harbor a short drive from A970, a 10-minute drive south of the hamlet of Sullom, 1¹/₂ miles from Brae, the hotel has crow's-foot gables, stone walls measuring 6 feet thick, and an appearance of a fortified manor house. Peter and Judith Jones, the resident proprietors, maintain the antique allure of both the public rooms and the chintz-filled bedrooms. Each room contains a trouser press, teamaking facilities, and a radio; same-day laundry facilities are available. They prepare a four-course evening meal for £19 ($31.35), and there's a cocktail lounge with an impressive array of malt whiskies as well as a quiet library. The ambience is much like that of a prestigious country-house hotel.

HILLSWICK

If you head north along A970, we suggest you take the secondary road going west to **Esha Ness,** where you'll come upon the most dramatic cliff scenery not only in Shetland but in all of Britain. On the way to this panoramic scenery, 15 miles northwest of Brae, you come to the little fishing hamlet of Hillswick, opening onto the bay in Ura Firth.

Where to Stay & Dine

St. Magnus Bay Hotel. Hillswick, Shetland ZE2 9RW. ☎ **01806/503372.** Fax 01806/503373. 27 rms. TV TEL. £58 ($95.70) double. AE, DC, MC, V. Rates include Scottish breakfast.

In an isolated position at the head of St. Magnus Bay, this hotel building was prefabricated of solid pine in Norway, barged across the North Sea, and assembled as part of Glasgow's Great Exhibition of 1896. In 1900 it was floated to Hillswick and reassembled as one of the terminals for the old North of Scotland Shipping Co. Despite its black-with-white-trim and double-gabled severity, it's one of the most lavish Edwardian buildings in the Shetlands, and has a boisterously popular pub. Bar meals cost, on average, £4 ($6.60). Meal service in the pleasingly old-fashioned dining room is daily from 12:30 to 2pm and 7:30 to 9pm. Specialties include fresh lobster in season, fresh haddock, sea trout, Aberdeen Angus beef, local salmon, a local and distinctively flavored Shetland lamb, and a traditional Scottish version of cullen skink.

SOUTH MAINLAND

This part of Shetland, reached by heading south along A970, is both ancient and modern. On the one hand there's the gleaming **Sumburgh Airport,** which has played a major role in the North Sea oilfields development and services many of the offshore rigs today. On the other hand, you stumble upon the ruins of Jarlshof (see below), which may have been inhabited for some 3,000 years.

EXPLORING THE AREA

As you go down the "long leg" of Shetland, as it's called, heading due south, passing a peaty moorland and fresh meadows, the first attraction is not on Mainland at all but on an offshore island called Mousa, to see the famous ○ **Broch of Mousa,** a Pictish defense tower that guarded the little islet for some 2,000 years. It reached the then-incredible height of some 40 feet and was constructed of local stones, with two circular walls, one within the other. They enclosed a staircase that led to sleeping quarters. It's the best-preserved example of an Iron Age broch in Britain. The hamlet of Sandwick, 7 miles south of Lerwick, is the ferry point for reaching Mousa. There's daily bus service between Lerwick and Sandwick. A local boatman will often take you across to Mousa at a price to be negotiated. It takes about 15 minutes to cross from Mainland. Mousa can be visited April through September only, Monday through Saturday from 9:30am to 6pm and Sunday from 2 to 6pm.

South of Sandwick, you reach the parish of Dunrossness. At Boddam is the **Shetland Croft House Museum** (☎ 01595/695057), east of A970 on an unmarked road 25 miles south of Lerwick. Rural Shetland life comes alive here in this thatched croft house from the mid-1800s. The museum also has some outbuildings and a functioning water mill. It's open year-round, Monday, Wednesday, and Friday from 10am to 7pm and Tuesday, Thursday, and Saturday from 10am to 5pm. There is no admission charge.

Continuing south, you reach the outstanding man-made attraction in Shetland, ○ **Jarlishof,** Sumburgh (☎ 01950/460112), near the Sumburgh Airport. It has been called "the most remarkable archaeological discovery in Britain." A violent storm in 1897 performed the first archaeological dig. Washing away sections of the large mound, it revealed huge stone walls. Excavations that followed turned up an astonishing array of seven distinct civilizations. The earliest was from the Bronze Age, but habitation continued at the site through the 1500s, from wheelhouse people to Vikings, from broch builders to medieval settlers. A manor house was built here in the 16th century by the treacherous earl, Patrick Stewart, but it was sacked in 1609. The site is open April through September only, Monday through Saturday from 9:30am to 6:30pm and Sunday from 2 to 6:30pm. Admission is £2.30 ($3.80) for adults, £1.50 ($2.45) for senior citizens, and £1 ($1.65) for children.

In the vicinity is **Sumburgh Lighthouse,** one of the many Scottish lighthouses constructed by the grandfather of novelist Robert Louis Stevenson. The lighthouse is now fully automated. The property offers a self-catering three-bedroom cottage, costing £343 ($565.95) per week. Built in 1821, it can be visited by the public, but you must phone the Lerwick tourist office (☎ 01595/693434) for an appointment or reservations for the cottage.

On the coast at the tip of Scatness, about a mile southwest of Jarlshof at the end of the Mainland, is the **Ness of Burgi,** which was a defensive Iron Age structure related to a broch.

Heading back north in the direction of Lerwick, you can veer to the west for a trip to **St. Ninian's Island** in the southwestern corner of Shetland. It's reached by going along B9122. The island is approached by what is called a tombolo or bridging sandbar. An early monastery once stood on this island, but it was not uncovered until 1958. Puffins with their orange beaks often favor the islet, which has a pure white sandy beach on each side.

The island became famous in 1958 when a group of students from Aberdeen came upon a rich cache of Celtic artifacts, mainly silverware, including brooches and other valuable pieces. Monks are believed to have hidden the treasure trove, fearing a Viking attack. The St. Ninian treasure is in the National Museum of Antiquities at Edinburgh.

WHERE TO STAY & DINE

Sumburgh Hotel. Sumburgh Head, Virkie Parish, Shetland ZE3 9JN. ☎ **01950/460201.** Fax 01950/460394. 32 rms. TV TEL. £58–£70 ($95.70–$115.50) double. AE, MC, V. Rates include Scottish breakfast.

Its turrets and towers were built in 1857 of local stone for the laird of Virkie, the Victorian descendant of Robert the Bruce. Set on 12 barren acres of land jutting dramatically out to sea, it lies at the southernmost end of the Shetland Islands, at the end of A970. A modern addition completed in the 1960s doubled the size of the establishment, which contains the Voe Room restaurant and two very popular bars. Recent refurbishments to the guest rooms have brightened them up and made them more inviting. A three-course table d'hôte meal is served nightly in the dining room for £14.50 ($23.90).

UNST

The northernmost point of Britain, remote and beautiful Unst is easy to reach. After crossing over to Yell, you can drive along A968 to the little harbor at Gutcher in the northeast of Yell. The **ferry to Unst** crosses from here about every hour. If you want to bring your car over, call for a reservation (☎ **01957/722259**). **Loganair** (☎ **01595/840246**) also flies to Unst on Wednesday.

EXPLORING THE ISLAND

Robert Louis Stevenson stayed here for a time. His father, Alan Stevenson, was designing and building the Muckle Flugga lighthouse on an outermost skerry, which is even farther north than Labrador.

Unst is steeped in folklore and legend. An Old Norse longhouse, believed to date from the 9th century, was excavated at Underhoull. The best beach is at Skaw, set against the backdrop of Saxa Vord, legendary home of the giant Saxi. A drive to the top will reward you with a view of the Burra Firth. Visitors go to Haroldswick to mail their cards and letters in the northernmost post office in the British Isles.

The roll-on/roll-off car ferry from Yell will come into Belmont. Nearby is **Muness Castle,** constructed in 1598 by Laurence Bruce, a relative of the notorious Earl Patrick Stewart who ruled Shetland so harshly. Adam Crawford, who designed Scalloway Castle for the ruling earls on Mainland, also drew up the plans for Muness. Built with rubble and known for its fine architectural detail, the castle was inhabited for less than a century. Normally it's open April through September only, daily from 9:30am to 7pm; if it's closed, ask for the key at Mrs. Peterson's cottage across the way. For information, phone ☎ **01957/755215.**

The ruins of the **Kirk of Lund,** dating from the Middle Ages, can also be seen on Unst. Like Lunna Kirk in Vidlin, it, too, had a "leper hole" through which victims could hear the service.

Unst is home of the **Hermaness Bird Reserve,** one of the most important ornithological sites in Britain. Its 600-foot cliffs are filled with kittiwakes, razorbills, guillemots, and the inevitable puffins.

WHERE TO STAY & DINE

Baltasound Hotel. Baltasound, Unst, Shetland ZE2 9DS. ☎ **01957/711334.** 28 rms (25 with shower). TV TEL. £54 ($89.10) double with or without bath. MC, V. Rates include Scottish breakfast.

Originally built 150 years ago for the family of the local laird, and converted into a hotel in 1939, this granite house sits in lonely isolation on an acre of its own land beside the sea about a quarter-mile from the hamlet of Baltasound. Many of this hotel's clients are bird watchers and geologists. Its guest rooms are in what local residents call a "Scandinavian extension" jutting out to the building's side, sheathed with blackened wood siding. It contains simple and uncluttered bedrooms carefully sealed against the blustering winds. Late in 1992 the hotel was enlarged with a series of motel-like "chalet" rooms, fully attached to the main building and very similar to conventional bedrooms except that their entrances open directly into the great outdoors. There are two bars on the premises, both serving inexpensive dinners nightly from 7 to 8:30pm. The hotel's restaurant offers a four-course fixed-price meal for £18.50 ($30.55).

THE SHETLAND ISLANDS AFTER DARK

Festivals and a festive atmosphere surround the communities of these remote islands, where the slightest excuse will kick off music and revelry. Pubs and community centers regularly schedule music and dancing, and during most weekend nights all you have to do is go in search of a pint of beer to find one of the many live traditional music options.

January finds Lerwick hosting its famous **Fire Festival** on the last Tuesday of the month, where a thousand locals, torches held high, are cheered on as they storm an effigy of a Viking longship and set it aflame. These heroes and their witnesses follow this with 2 straight days of eating, drinking, playing music, and dancing. The celebrations spread out from here, and more remote communities hold their local versions of the event over the next 3 months.

For 4 days in April, the **Shetland Folk Festival** features the best of the local musicians in combination with invited artists from around the world in a celebration of Shetland folk and other musical forms. Concerts, usually incorporating dinner and dancing, are held in local halls throughout the islands, with most events costing about £8 to £9 ($13.20 to $14.85). Often festival entertainers will convene at the various pubs and join local performers in jam sessions celebrating the local musical tradition.

Summer months are marked by artistic and cultural **exchange programs** with Norway, Holland, and, for the first time in 1998, Sweden. Highlights during these events include musical and dramatic performances by the visiting artists. Information about the varying dates, venues, and prices can be obtained by contacting the tourist information center in Lerwick (☎ **01595/693434**). Summer weekends also bring regularly scheduled **local regattas,** where different communities compete in sailing and rowing competitions. Afterward, there are celebratory dinners, music, and dancing in local venues.

Index

FROMMER'S® COMPLETE TRAVEL GUIDES

(Comprehensive guides to destinations around the world, with selections in all price ranges—from deluxe to budget)

Acapulco, Ixtapa & Zihuatenejo
Alaska
Amsterdam
Arizona
Atlanta
Australia
Austria
Bahamas
Barcelona, Madrid & Seville
Belgium, Holland & Luxembourg
Bermuda
Boston
Budapest & the Best of Hungary
California
Canada
Cancún, Cozumel & the Yucatán
Cape Cod, Nantucket & Martha's Vineyard
Caribbean
Caribbean Cruises & Ports of Call
Caribbean Ports of Call
Carolinas & Georgia
Chicago
China
Colorado
Costa Rica
Denver, Boulder & Colorado Springs
England

Europe
Florida
France
Germany
Greece
Hawaii
Hong Kong
Honolulu, Waikiki & Oahu
Ireland
Israel
Italy
Jamaica & Barbados
Japan
Las Vegas
London
Los Angeles
Maryland & Delaware
Maui
Mexico
Miami & the Keys
Montana & Wyoming
Montréal & Québec City
Munich & the Bavarian Alps
Nashville & Memphis
Nepal
New England
New Mexico
New Orleans
New York City
Northern New England
Nova Scotia, New Brunswick & Prince Edward Island
Oregon
Paris

Philadelphia & the Amish Country
Portugal
Prague & the Best of the Czech Republic
Provence & the Riviera
Puerto Rico
Rome
San Antonio & Austin
San Diego
San Francisco
Santa Fe, Taos & Albuquerque
Scandinavia
Scotland
Seattle & Portland
Singapore & Malaysia
South Pacific
Spain
Switzerland
Thailand
Tokyo
Toronto
Tuscany & Umbria
USA
Utah
Vancouver & Victoria
Vienna & the Danube Valley
Virgin Islands
Virginia
Walt Disney World & Orlando
Washington, D.C.
Washington State

FROMMER'S® DOLLAR-A-DAY GUIDES

(The ultimate guides to comfortable low-cost travel)

Australia from $50 a Day
California from $60 a Day
Caribbean from $60 a Day
Costa Rica & Belize from $35 a Day
England from $60 a Day
Europe from $50 a Day
Florida from $50 a Day
Greece from $50 a Day
Hawaii from $60 a Day
India from $40 a Day

Ireland from $50 a Day
Israel from $45 a Day
Italy from $50 a Day
London from $60 a Day
Mexico from $35 a Day
New York from $75 a Day
New Zealand from $50 a Day
Paris from $70 a Day
San Francisco from $60 a Day
Washington, D.C., from $60 a Day

FROMMER'S® PORTABLE GUIDES

(Pocket-size guides for travelers who want everything in a nutshell)

Bahamas
California Wine Country
Charleston & Savannah
Chicago

Dublin
Las Vegas
London
Maine Coast
New Orleans

Puerto Vallarta, Manzanillo
& Guadalajara
San Francisco
Venice
Washington, D.C.

FROMMER'S® AMERICA ON WHEELS

(Everything you need for a successful road trip, including full-color road maps and ratings for every hotel)

California & Nevada
Florida
Great Lake States &
Midwest

Mid-Atlantic
New England & New York
Northwest & Great Plains

South-Central States
& Texas
Southeast
Southwest

FROMMER'S® MEMORABLE WALKS

(Memorable neighborhood strolls through the world's great cities)

Chicago
London

New York
Paris

San Francisco
Spain's Favorite Cities

FROMMER'S® NATIONAL PARK GUIDES

(Everything you need for the perfect park vacation)

Grand Canyon
National Parks of the American West
Yellowstone & Grand Teton

Yosemite & Sequoia/
Kings Canyon
Zion & Bryce Canyon

SPECIAL-INTEREST TITLES

Arthur Frommer's New World of Travel
The Civil War Trust's Official Guide to
the Civil War Discovery Trail
Frommer's Caribbean Hideaways
Frommer's Complete Hostel
Vacation Guide to England,
Scotland & Wales
Frommer's Europe's Greatest
Driving Tours
Frommer's Food Lover's Companion
to France
Frommer's Food Lover's Companion
to Italy
Israel Past & Present
New York City with Kids
New York Times Weekends

Outside Magazine's Adventure Guide
to New England
Outside Magazine's Adventure Guide
to Northern California
Outside Magazine's Adventure Guide
to the Pacific Northwest
Outside Magazine's Adventure Guide
to Southern California & Baja
Outside Magazine's Guide to Family
Vacations
Places Rated Almanac
Retirement Places Rated
Washington, D.C., with Kids
Wonderful Weekends from New York City
Wonderful Weekends from San Francisco
Wonderful Weekends from Los Angeles

THE COMPLETE IDIOT'S TRAVEL GUIDES
(The ultimate user-friendly trip planners)

Cruise Vacations	New York City	San Francisco
Las Vegas	Planning Your Trip	Walt Disney World
New Orleans	to Europe	

THE UNOFFICIAL GUIDES®
(Get the unbiased truth from these candid, value-conscious guides)

Atlanta	The Great Smoky	Mini-Mickey	Walt Disney World
Branson, Missouri	& Blue Ridge	New Orleans	Walt Disney World
Chicago	Mountains	New York City	Companion
Cruises	Las Vegas	San Francisco	Washington, D.C.
Disneyland	Miami & the Keys	Skiing in the West	

FROMMER'S® IRREVERENT GUIDES
(Wickedly honest guides for sophisticated travelers)

Amsterdam	Manhattan	Paris	Santa Fe
Chicago	New Orleans	San Francisco	Walt Disney World
London			Washington, D.C.

FROMMER'S® BY NIGHT GUIDES
(The series for those who know that life begins after dark)

Amsterdam	Los Angeles	Manhattan	Paris
Chicago	Madrid	Miami	Prague
Las Vegas	& Barcelona	New Orleans	San Francisco
London			Washington, D.C.

FROMMER'S® DRIVING TOURS
(Four-color photos and detailed maps outlining spectacular scenic driving routes)

America	Florida	Ireland	Scotland
Britain	France	Italy	Spain
California	Germany	New England	Western Europe

FROMMER'S® BORN TO SHOP
(The ultimate guides for travelers who love to shop)

Caribbean Ports	Great Britain	London	New York
of Call	Hong Kong	Mexico	Paris
France	Italy	New England	

TRAVEL & LEISURE GUIDES
(Sophisticated pocket-size guides for discriminating travelers)

Amsterdam	Hong Kong	New York	San Francisco
Boston	London	Paris	Washington, D.C.

WHEREVER YOU TRAVEL, *H*ELP IS NEVER FAR AWAY.

From planning your trip to

providing travel assistance along

the way, American Express®

Travel Service Offices are

always there to help

you do more.